D1733471

Reins of Liberation

Reins of Liberation

An Entangled History of Mongolian

Independence, Chinese Territoriality,

and Great Power Hegemony, 1911–1950

Xiaoyuan Liu

Woodrow Wilson Center Press
Washington, D.C.

Stanford University Press
Stanford, California

EDITORIAL OFFICES

Woodrow Wilson Center Press
Woodrow Wilson International Center for Scholars
One Woodrow Wilson Plaza
1300 Pennsylvania Avenue, N.W.
Washington, DC 20004-3027
Telephone: 202-691-4010
www.wilsoncenter.org

Order from

Stanford University Press
Chicago Distribution Center
11030 South Langley Avenue
Chicago, Ill. 60628
Telephone: 1-800-621-2736

2 4 6 8 9 7 5 3 1

Library of Congress Cataloging-in-Publication Data

Liu, Xiaoyuan, 1952–

Reins of liberation : an entangled history of Mongolian independence, Chinese territoriality, and
great power hegemony, 1911–1950 / Xiaoyuan Liu.
p. cm.
Includes bibliographical references and index.
ISBN-13: 978-0-8047-5426-8 (cloth : alk. paper)
1. Mongolia—Relations—China.   2. China—Relations—Mongolia.   3. Mongols—China—
History—20th century.   4. Mongolia—Relations—Foreign countries.   I. Title.   II. Title:
Entangled history of Mongolian independence, Chinese territoriality, and great power hegemony,
1911–1950.
DS798.63.C6L58 2006
951′.704—dc22
2006012624

**Woodrow Wilson
Center Press**
Washington, D.C.

The Woodrow Wilson International Center for Scholars, established by Congress in 1968 and headquartered in Washington, D.C., is a living national memorial to President Wilson. The Center's mission is to commemorate the ideals and concerns of Woodrow Wilson by providing a link between the worlds of ideas and policy, while fostering research, study, discussion, and collaboration among a broad spectrum of individuals concerned with policy and scholarship in national and international affairs. Supported by public and private funds, the Center is a nonpartisan institution engaged in the study of national and world affairs. It establishes and maintains a neutral forum for free, open, and informed dialogue. Conclusions or opinions expressed in Center publications and programs are those of the authors and speakers and do not necessarily reflect the views of the Center staff, fellows, trustees, advisory groups, or any individuals or organizations that provide financial support to the Center.

The Center is the publisher of *The Wilson Quarterly* and home of Woodrow Wilson Center Press, *dialogue* radio and television, and the monthly newsletter "Centerpoint." For more information about the Center's activities and publications, please visit us on the web at www.wilsoncenter.org.

For My Friends in Duud Nuur, Ujumuchin

Contents

Maps

Acknowledgments

The research and writing of this book stretched over nearly a decade. Progress was made only because of many people's and organizations' assistance. To trace back the gradual completion of the project, my gratitude goes first to Chang Su-ya of the Institute of Modern History, Academia Sinica (Taiwan); Chen Zhongxian and Ke Wei of the Archives of the Inner Mongolian Autonomous Region; Chu Chung-sheng and Chang Hung-ming of the Academia Historica (Taiwan); Martin Heijdra of the Gest Library of Princeton University; Lin Tsung-chie of the Historical Council of the Guomindang (Taiwan); Li Yongpu of the Center of Modern and Contemporary Chinese Historical Materials; Nong Weixiong of the Library of Modern History Institute of the Chinese Academy of Social Sciences; Shen Zhengle of the People's Republic of China Central Archives; Uljeyt of the Library and Information Center of the Inner Mongolian Academy of Social Sciences; Wan Renyuan of the Second Historical Archives of China; Zhang Sulin and Hao Weihua of the Archives of the People's Republic of China Ministry of Foreign Affairs; and Liu Luning of Beijing Library for providing valuable guidance and assistance to my research at their organizations. Systemic declassifications of documents and established research procedures at the National Archives of the United States, the Public Record Office of England, the British Library, the Archives of the Harry Truman Library, and the Library of Congress spare the researchers unnecessary suspense and anxieties. I am grateful to these institutions' staffs for their efficient professional services.

The research, writing, and revision of the book received generous support from the Smith Richardson Foundation's Grant for Junior Faculty in International History, Politics, and Security Issues, the Social Science Research Council–MacArthur Foundation Fellowship on Peace and Security in a Changing World, Friends of Princeton University Libraries Fellowship, Harry S. Truman Library Institute Research Grant, and the Center for Excellence in the Arts and Humanities Fellowship of the Iowa State University. Several years ago, Dr. Lu Fangshang, then director of the Institute of Modern History, Academia Sinica, agreed to host my research visit in Taipei. His and his colleagues' hospitality made my stay a very pleasant experience. Similarly, my research in the Second Historical Archives was facilitated by my friends Zhang Xiaoming and Fang Shengli, who persuaded their parents to accommodate this academic nomad in their families in Nanjing. My research brought me to the Washington area more than once. On these occasions, I could always count on the hospitality of Drs. Xiaohong Liu and John Paden. A significant portion of the book was written when I was a visiting scholar at the Fairbank Center for East Asian Research of Harvard University. Professors Ezra Vogel and William Kirby were wonderful hosts. The last phase of the project was supported by a Wilson Center–George Washington University Asian Policy Studies Fellowship. Director Robert Hathaway of the Wilson Center's Asia Program, Director Mike Mochizuki of the Sigur Center for Asian Studies of George Washington University, and the staffs of these programs were most helpful in making my sojourn in the Washington area a success. During my fellowship tenure in Washington, the Department of History of Iowa State University graciously granted me leave time and supported me in various ways.

The ideas in this study have been presented on different occasions. These include seminars organized by the Asia Program of the Woodrow Wilson Center, the Sigur Center for Asian Studies of George Washington University, the Center for Asian Pacific Economic Cooperation of George Mason University, the International Workshop on China's Interaction with the World (co-organized by Harvard University's Asian Center and East Asian Seminar of the Free University Berlin) in Berlin, the Summer Institute of the Yale Center for International and Area Studies, the International Conference on China's Surrounding Region in the Cold War in the Wuyi Mountain of Fujian, and the International Workshop on Mongolia and the Cold War in Ulaanbaatar. I wish to thank Chen Jian, Robert Hathaway, William Kirby, Lin Gang, Mike Mochizuki, Vojtech Mastny, Shen Zhihua, and Ye Wenxin for bringing me to these stimulating venues and for providing valuable comments and suggestions on my project. Professors Okhonoin Batasaikhan, Chang Ch'i-xiong, Shen Zhihua, Chen Li-wen, Wang Jianmin, Zhang Zhuhong, Yang Kuisong, Guo Jianping, and Yu Minling were most gracious in sharing with me findings of their own research and documentary information they collected. Dr. Christopher Atwood introduced me to Andrew Shimunek, who did a superb job translating some Mongolian materials for me. Professors Uradyn Bulag and Steven Levine were most generous in agreeing to read the original and longer version of the work. Their insightful critiques helped me enormously in improving the work. I shall, of course, take full responsibility for all the remaining shortcomings of the book. The book would not have reached its readers without the unfailing, enthusiastic endorsement of Joseph Brinley, the director of the Wilson Center Press, and Yamile Kahn and Muriel Bell, editors at the Wilson Center Press and the Stanford University Press. Alfred Imhoff, the copyeditor, did a wonderful job of improving the text. And, again, in marking one more step on my scholarly journey, the book has materialized under the kind guidance and help in various ways from Professors Lawrence Gelfand, Warren Cohen, and Akira Iriye.

My family endured the inconvenience of traveling, relocating, and rescheduling, and other nuisances caused by this project. They always put up with me and maintained a humorous attitude toward this roving historian. My love and deepest gratitude therefore go to Hongxing, Ying Ying, and Tanya. Erlao and Xiaoxi on the other side of the Pacific know how their involvement in the project is appreciated. My father would have enjoyed seeing the book in print, but I could not complete the project soon enough. Finally, more than three decades ago, the seeds of this project were sown in the grassland around Duud Nuur, a beautiful "singing lake" of East Ujumuchin. The book is dedicated to all my Han and Mongol friends from those years.

Introduction

In China, most people in the first "postliberation" (*jiefanghou*), or post-1949, generation grew up without questioning the alleged epochal superiority of their time over the "preliberation" (*jiefangqian*) era. That is, they did not do the questioning until they themselves were "liberated" en masse by Mao Zedong's "Cultural Revolution." Mao first "liberated" them from the supposedly "bourgeois education system" of the People's Republic of China, and then he sent them to the countryside to receive "reeducation" from the laboring masses. I shared this experience with my contemporaries. In the late 1960s, when making a four-day journey from Beijing to East Ujumuchin Banner of Inner Mongolia, my designated locale for "reeducation," I ran into a horse-cart driver in Baochang, a small town about 150 kilometers north of Zhangjiakou. In a shabby "horse-cart inn" (*dachedian*), my new acquaintance treated me to my first-ever cup of salty, bitter brick tea and told me enthusiastically: "Commander Teng Haiqing finally backed us up!" When the conversation proceeded, I realized that "us" meant the Han, and that Commander Teng of the Inner Mongolian Military District supported "us" against the Inner Mongols, who were allegedly "anti-Han and discriminatory against outsiders" (*fan Han pai wai*). Thus, despite Chairman Mao's intention of having us "face the world and brave the storm of class struggles," my first lesson of "reeducation" was ethnic, not class, oriented.

Only after I arrived in the pastoral land of Ujumuchin did I realize how Mao's "Great Proletarian Cultural Revolution" rampaged throughout Inner Mongolia in a twisted form, *wa su yundong,* a shortened name for the "campaign to dig out and purge the New Inner Mongolian People's Revolutionary Party." Countless alleged underground members of the nonexistent organization were framed and persecuted for conspiring for Inner Mongolia's accession to the Mongolian People's Republic, then labeled "Mongolian revisionists" (*meng xiu*). Later, before leaving Ujumuchin in the mid-1970s, I witnessed a "reversal of the verdict" in the grassland, which "liberated" ordinary herdsmen and their families en masse and cleared them of the alleged crime. The madness of the Mao era in Inner Mongolia, however, has never received as much attention in the Han-dominant country as other atrocities of the "Cultural Revolution."

Clearly, "liberation" was an overused and much abused conception in twentieth-century China. It carried different meanings to different people but was rarely defined by the people themselves. The primary purpose of this book is not to set straight the historical record of the Inner Mongolian People's Revolutionary Party, though the Inner Mongols' struggle for "national liberation" before 1949 constitutes an important part of this inquiry. Rather, my intention is to use the Mongolia question to illustrate a much larger issue of twentieth-century Asian history: how wars, revolutions, and great power rivalries induced and restrained formations of nationhood and territoriality, two basic items on the agendas of many Asian peoples' national struggles in the last century. In connecting national identity with geopolitical domains, a useful definition puts geopolitical visions as "translations of national-identity concepts in geographical terms and symbols."[1] Any nationalist drive is inevitably concerned with a "geobody," substantiated or imaginary.[2] When two nations' interests based on real or imagined geobodies come into conflict, one's willful pursuit of a self-defined national identity becomes the other's apocalyptic omen. A nation's pursuit of the geopolitical realization of its identity can hardly be an isolated enterprise and is bound to provoke others' reactions.

Since the early nineteenth century, a grand historic enterprise in Asia's political life has been unfolding. It is a collective effort to define China's geobody in a modern sense. The effort is "collective," because from the Manchu emperors of the Qing Dynasty to the Communist leaders of the People's Republic of China, no dominant political force in China has been able to proceed with the enterprise without assorted "contributions" from

---

1. Gertjan Dijkink, *National Identity and Geographical Visions: Maps of Pride and Pain* (New York: Routledge, 1996), 14.
2. Thongchai Winichakul's original study, *Siam Mapped: A History of the Geo-Body of a Nation* (Honolulu: University of Hawaii Press, 1994), 17, defines "geo-body" of a nation as a "man-made territorial definition which creates effects—by classifying, communicating, and enforcement—on people, things, and relationships."

external foreign powers and internal ethnopolitical groups. Understandably, the enterprise has been conflict prone. Given the magnitude of the issue, the "Chinese" geopolitical vision cannot avoid overlapping and clashing with those held by non-Han and non-Chinese participants in Asian affairs.

I have argued elsewhere that during the twentieth century, ethnic frontiers and ethnopolitics occupied a singularly important position in China's political life, especially in connection with the Chinese Communist Party's (CCP's) political survival and ascendancy.[3] On its way to build a *communist* state, the CCP was nevertheless confronted with a series of fundamental issues pertinent to China's modern transformation into a *national* state. This book continues the argument in two ways. It focuses on the Mongolia question that ran through Chinese politics about national and geopolitical identity during the first half of the twentieth century, and it expands the investigation to include relevant "local" and "international" affairs.

Between 1911 and 1950, the course of the Mongolia question illustrated the geneses, clashes, and convergence of "Chinese" and "Mongolian" national identities and geopolitical visions in the contexts of civil wars, revolutions, and international conflicts. To examine a vast and immensely complex political landscape, this study has to be multinational and multilevel. This is therefore a history of interethnic, international, and interbloc relations concerning simultaneously Mongolia's struggle for independent nationhood, China's pursuit of modern territoriality, and the great powers' rivalry for hegemony.

This unwieldy approach is adopted out of necessity. The conception of the "Mongolia question" actually conceals a multilateral clash involving China, Mongolia, and several great powers. At its genesis and during its evolution, the Mongolia question necessarily conveyed the Mongols' political aspirations. Meanwhile, on many occasions Chinese political forces and interested foreign countries have used the "Mongolia question" to cover up or equivocate about their own agendas. After all, the question germinated in connection with the Chinese Revolution of 1911, the Russian Revolution of 1917, and a realignment in great power politics connected to World War I. Whereas the Chinese revolutionaries shattered the Qing Empire into pieces, the Bolsheviks soon collected Russia's neighboring areas into a Soviet Empire, both affecting directly the form and degree of Mongolian independence.

---

3. Xiaoyuan Liu, *Frontier Passages: Ethnopolitics and the Rise of Chinese Communism, 1921–1945* (Washington, D.C., and Stanford, Calif.: Woodrow Wilson Center Press and Stanford University Press, 2004).

Later, treated by great powers as either a diplomatic trade-off or a strategic buffer, Mongolia became successively entangled with the Asian-Pacific part of World War II and with the formation of a Cold War status quo in postwar Asia. Obviously, any single-dimensional attempt to study such an intricate subject would easily result in distortion and misunderstanding.

In his latest warning against human-made catastrophes on the Earth, England's astronomer royal, Sir Martin Rees, laments: "Nuclear weapons can be dismantled, but they cannot be uninvented."[4] Social scientists and historians may have reasons to deplore nationalism in the same manner: Nationalism can be "contained" but cannot be "uninvented" either.[5] A plethora of nationalism variants has enormously increased the chance for scientific innovations' being turned into potential or ready means of destruction, and it has been responsible for countless conflicts since the beginning of modernity. Yet, as long as colonialist, imperialist, hegemonic, and exploitative modes of nationalism linger, "national" liberation, independence, equality, and development will continue to serve as powerful ideologies to propel the struggles of disadvantaged peoples.

Modern Chinese and Mongolian "nations" were invented not far apart in the early twentieth century, both taking on a self-protective character in their formative years. But, in the existing hierarchical and often oppressive world order of supposedly "equal" nation-states, the Chinese and Mongolian nations were locked into a head-on conflict from the outset. In its struggle against foreign imperialism, China changed from a traditional empire into a modern national state. The Chinese nation in the making jealously guarded its territorial inheritance from the late Qing Empire and pursued a dream of "grand unity" in attempting to roll back foreign inroads in China dated back to the early nineteenth century. Hence, early on, the Han-centered "Chinese nation" assumed an imperial posture in its relations with the non-Han groups within the late Qing's domain. Throughout the twentieth century, the centralizing tendency and de-imperializing claim of Chinese nationalism constituted a recurring pair of contradictions in China's ethnopolitical and foreign affairs.

To Mongolian nationalists, only a nationhood of their own, vested with

---

4. Martin Rees, *Our Final Hour: A Scientist's Warning: How Terror, Error, and Environmental Disaster Threaten Humankind's Future in This Century—On Earth and Beyond* (New York: BasicBooks, 2003), 2.

5. Michael Hechter, *Containing Nationalism* (Oxford: Oxford University Press, 2000), lists several institutional and legal approaches to "contain" nationalist conflicts.

political power and delimited as a territorial space, could save the Mongolian people from a Chinese-inflicted fate of cultural and ethnic extinction. The disintegration of the Qing Empire in the first decade of the twentieth century both intensified the sinicization process in Mongolia and stimulated the Mongol elites' activities in seeking a way out. These led to Asia's first national secession movement in the twentieth century, one that directly challenged China's territoriality and ethnicity as defined by Chinese nationalists.

The historical clash between the Chinese and the Mongolian national and geopolitical visions has hitherto resulted in two Mongolias: The "autonomous" Inner Mongolia is part of China, whereas the independent Mongolia is a full-fledged member of the international community. Unlike the current division between Taiwan and the People's Republic of China, which has roots in a Chinese civil war, the causes for Mongolia's partition in the twentieth century were basically external to the Mongolian people. During the period under consideration, despite interventions from various ideologies and events, Mongolian nationalism remained a unifying force that straddled the Gobi Desert and embraced both the "outer" and "inner" halves of Mongolia. "Outer" and "Inner" Mongols' political experiences during the first half of the twentieth century were indeed rather different. When the former strove for independence but had to see their nationhood being "settled" again and again by others, the latter launched waves of autonomous movements but could never bring their aspirations to a satisfactory result. During the twentieth century, Mongolian nationalism was forced to operate in two segregated realms, mainly because of conditions beyond the Mongols' control.

Although the Mongolian nation ranked as the weakest among all the forces involved in the Mongolia question, it was nevertheless contained constantly from different directions. The specter of so-called pan-Mongolism was usually alleged as the reason for containment. In reality, during the twentieth century, any "pan-Mongol" tendency of *Mongolian* origins sought mainly to gain internal coherence for an independent Mongolian people but not to expand their external reaches. The effort, however, confronted a geopolitical landscape of East Asia that allocated no room to a unified Mongolian state. The great powers, including China, could not tolerate indigenous "pan-Mongolism." This was not because such an expression actually provoked fear of a revived Mongolian power on the scale of Genghis Khan. Rather, on most occasions the epithet served as the great powers' punching bag: They beat it up either when they needed to flex their muscles against one another or when they wanted to prevent inconvenient Mongolian initiatives from getting in the way of their own agendas.

This is not to suggest that the Mongols were merely passive victims of the great powers' balancing games. Mongolian ethnopolitics did not exist in isolation from those defining political events in twentieth-century Asia. In striving to determine the Mongols' status either as a distinct nation or as one of the ethnic components of the "Chinese nation," Mongolian nationalists tried to take advantage of and took sides in twentieth-century events such as the Chinese and the Russian revolutions, World War II, and the Cold War. Inevitably, they assumed various political identities in addition to being advocates of a Mongolian national state. Their particular ethnic identity and national loyalty could be colored or even overshadowed by ideologies and alliance orientations characterized by adjectives such as progressive or conservative, revolutionary or reactionary, and democratic or communist. Thus, although Mongolian nationalists of different political persuasions shared an ultimate goal of national independence and national unification, their separate searches for a path to attain the goal created opportunities for external forces to manipulate.[6]

Given all the obstacles, Mongolian nationalists achieved remarkable results in defining modern Mongolian identity and political space. As of the mid–twentieth century, the independent Mongolian People's Republic existed as the sole national state that shared with China the heritage of the Qing Empire. Within China, although unable to translate their cultural ethnicity into political nationhood, the Inner Mongols nevertheless managed to achieve an official ethnopolitical standing buttressed by territorial autonomy. They also exerted a country-wide impact in setting a precedent of an ethnic autonomous region for the multiethnic system of the People's Republic of China.

A leitmotif of this study is how macro historic issues such as territoriality, ethnicity, and nationhood are entangled with micro historical phenomena like wars, revolutions, regime changes, great power diplomacy, and ideological confrontation. As the case of Mongolia demonstrates, although the independent Mongolian state benefited from events of the latter category during the first half of the twentieth century, in the long run, the making of

---

6. The most informative discussion of the internal differences of Mongolian revolutionaries in the early twentieth century is Christopher P. Atwood, *Young Mongols and Vigilantes in Inner Mongolia's Interregnum Decades, 1911–1931* (Leiden: Brill, 2002). Uradyn E. Bulag's *The Mongols at China's Edge: History and the Politics of National Unity* (Lanham, Md.: Rowman & Littlefield, 2002) and *Nationalism and Hybridity in Mongolia* (Oxford: Clarendon Press, 1998) are two historical anthropological studies that discuss intelligently and accessibly Inner Mongolian nationalism in the twentieth century.

a modern Mongolian nation suffered from these in leaving more than half the ethnic Mongols as "minority nationalities" in China and the Soviet Union. Mongolia's historical transformation from a dependency of the Qing Empire to a modern nation was thus segmented by twentieth-century politics.

The macro historical perspective, as demonstrated in Ray Huang's and Philip Kuhn's works on Chinese history, is especially useful for our understanding of China's experience in the twentieth century. In following the examples of these scholars' macro examinations of monetary manageability and the constitutional basis for the Chinese state in Chinese history, this study explores another long-range issue: Chinese territoriality.[7] An ancient geopolitical entity transforming from a Confucian empire into a modern national state, China encountered a problem not so much about its right to nationhood as about how a "Chinese" nationhood should be defined. The Mongolia question highlighted China's predicament in ascertaining and asserting its modern territoriality and ethnic composition.

As Charles Maier argues in his seminal essay in *American Historical Review,* the conventional, morality-laden approach to studying the twentieth-century history as a peculiar epoch "obscures one of the most encompassing or fundamental sociopolitical trends of modern world development, namely the emergence, ascendancy, and subsequent crisis of what is best labeled 'territoriality.'" Maier defines "territoriality" as "simply the properties, including power, provided by the control of bordered political space, which until recently at least created the framework for national and often ethnic identity."[8] A new vista is thus opened for viewing modern Chinese history, which has particularly been controversial in moral and value terms.

Although the conception and practices of "extraterritoriality" have featured prominently in both Chinese and Western historical literature on modern China, China's modern "territoriality crisis" has not been systematically studied, except in relation to a fragmentary and misleading notion about "China's lost territories." Conventionally, "lost territories" refer to Chinese territories ceded and "leased" to or simply seized by foreign powers during the nineteenth and the twentieth centuries. These were indeed part of China's "territoriality crisis." Yet the lost-territories conception is misleading because,

---

7. See Ray Huang, *China: A Macro History* (Armonk, N.Y.: M. E. Sharpe, 1990); and Philip A. Kuhn, *Origins of the Modern Chinese State* (Stanford, Calif.: Stanford University Press, 2002).

8. Charles S. Maier, "Consigning the Twentieth Century to History: Alternative Narratives for the Modern Era," *American Historical Review* 105(3): 807–8, 812.

while denoting China's "national humiliations," it obscures a "national lesson" to China: The days for China's sovereigns to unilaterally claim an ambiguous imperial domain were over; China's "national" boundaries must now be defined precisely through international agreements in order to gain the international community's endorsement.

In focusing on Chinese–foreign relations, the lost-territories conception also presents an incomplete picture of China's modern struggle for gaining control of its bordered political space. There have been interethnic conflicts or collaborations over the modern identities and status of the Qing imperial frontiers. These constitute the "domestic" aspect of China's "territoriality crisis." During the twentieth century, the issues of Mongolia, Tibet, Taiwan, and Xinjiang were prominent cases in this category. These, except Taiwan, were never qualified in modern Chinese political discourse as "lost territories." Clearly, whereas the issue of "lost territories" has gradually run out of steam since the end of World War II (Hong Kong's return to China in 1997 and Macao's in 1999 actually marked the end of the issue), China's "territoriality crisis" is far from over because of its troubling "internal" aspect.

Considered from a China-centric perspective, the settlement of the Mongolia question in the twentieth century indicated how China's modern territoriality was achieved through a two-pronged process of internalizing and externalizing the late Qing's peripheral possessions. Mongolia's division as of the midcentury therefore reflected a modified Chinese geopolitical vision dictated by ethnic, domestic political, and international conditions. In the process, the northern reaches of the Chinese nation's political space were demarcated. Until the Mongolian situation was finalized by the Mao–Stalin negotiations in Moscow in 1950, various Chinese, Mongolian, and foreign forces had tried different formulas for fixing Mongolia's position within or without the bordered land of China. The Guomindang (GMD, Nationalist Party) and the CCP, China's two principal centralizing national forces, took separate paths in ascertaining the Chinese–Mongolian relationship. Remarkably, although the two parties' ferocious efforts at mutual destruction consumed the better part of twentieth-century Chinese political history, their approaches to the question of Chinese territoriality were basically convergent in purposes and mutually supplementary in means. This was so even during their final, and "decisive encounter" during the Chinese Civil War of 1945–49.[9]

---

9. Odd Arne Westad, *Decisive Encounters: The Chinese Civil War, 1946–1950* (Stanford, Calif.: Stanford University Press, 2003).

Therefore, before the GMD–CCP civil war turned Chinese history from the page of the Republic of China to that of the People's Republic of China, at a certain point the two forces, despite their apparently divergent ideologies, policies, and mutual animosities, also experienced a definitive convergence over some long-range historic questions facing China. The convergence guaranteed that the GMD and the CCP pages of history belonged to the same book. By identifying these long-range historic questions, territoriality among them, the macro historical approach depoliticizes events and developments of a given historical period and reevaluates their positions in the lengthy stream of history. Observed from such a vantage point, certain historical events or phenomena that rightly occupied so-called defining positions in their own times become just ephemeral conditions for the evolution of those constantly present historic questions.

It is from such a perspective that this study sets the usually marginal Mongolia question at the center, for the question directly reflects the entangled evolution of territoriality and nationhood in twentieth-century East Asia. Meanwhile, the Chinese and the Soviet revolutions, World War II, the Chinese Civil War, and the Cold War, which have been the focal points of previous historiographies on twentieth-century China and East Asian international relations, are treated here as circumstantial variables affecting the direction of the Mongolia question.

This apparently "upside-down" approach makes no contention that the importance of territoriality or any other long-term historic questions should be elevated to slight other vital concerns of a given historical period. This is just to point out that some enduring historic questions can be easily overlooked, and that we recognize their constant presence and evolution only after the nimbus of our immediate concerns disappears or disperses. This point can be most clearly seen in the world's ethnic and national conflicts unleashed by the conclusion of the Cold War era. During the Cold War, the perilous nuclear confrontation and inflated ideological contest between the two superpowers consumed the second half of the twentieth century while smothering many other threads of global and local developments. Ethnic conflicts that have resurfaced in recent years are not "post–Cold War" phenomena at all but signs of a historic question's return with a vengeance. The collapse of the Soviet Union and Yugoslavia impressed upon the world that the bloc politics of the Cold War era had not solved but just painted over some of the most fundamental issues of this nation-state world. There is therefore an urgent need to understand these issues' pre–Cold War origins.

During the initial years of the Cold War, the "domestic" aspect of China's territoriality crisis erupted in the face of the GMD and the CCP. When these parties locked themselves into a civil war for China's "central" power, decentralizing and separatist forces on the "peripheries" such as Inner Mongolia, Tibet, and Xinjiang struggled to enter the rank of the world's nation-states. To a large extent, because of the burgeoning Cold War between the superpowers as well as the Chinese Civil War, these struggles in China's ethnic frontiers were rarely understood in their ethnopolitical significance then and ever since. To redress the problem, this study deliberately marginalizes those conventional "central" issues of the Cold War in order to unveil an ethnopolitical content of the Cold War history pertinent to China. Soviet and American involvements in Mongolian affairs during the early Cold War years are discussed here not to demonstrate how the Mongolia question was important to the Cold War. Rather, my purpose is to show how the superpowers' contest in East Asia and their respective policies served as external conditions to induce a "settlement" of the Mongolia question in China.

The book is arranged in three parts to highlight ethnicity and territoriality in East Asia's eventful twentieth century. Part I includes three chapters tracing the historical evolution of the Mongolia question from the end of the Qing Empire to the end of World War II. Chapter 1 tackles some questions arising from Chinese and Mongolian nationalists' struggles to construct their respective successor states in the wake of the Qing Empire. Chapter 2 considers Soviet Russia's Mongolian entanglement under a world-revolution ideology drifting toward geopolitical calculations. Chapter 3 examines the meaning of the Mongolia question to the Chinese Communist movement in the context of the CCP's changing political fortune and ethnogeographic environments.

Part II highlights the crucial position of the Inner Mongols' struggle for autonomy in the Chinese Civil War of 1945–49. The Inner Mongols' ethnopolitical maneuvering between the GMD and the CCP is covered by chapters 4 and 5. Chapters 6 and 7 separately analyze the two Chinese parties' policies and tactics in coping with the Inner Mongolian situation while fighting each other on political and military fronts. The case of Inner Mongolia is thus used to illustrate how China's partisan, class, and ethnic struggles became intertwined.

The international environments that conditioned postwar development and the settlement of the Mongolia question are discussed in part III. Chapter 8 reconstructs a hitherto overlooked aspect of Washington's China policy during the Chinese Civil War—its hesitant exploration of the Inner Mongolian frontier amid the GMD's political-military catastrophe. Chapter 9 clarifies a two-Mongolias stratagem followed by Moscow in its postwar Asian entanglements. Chapter 10 presents a hypothesis that the Mongolia question was an unstated item on the agenda of the Mao–Stalin negotiations between late 1949 and early 1950, and that its settlement in Moscow sealed a new balance of power in East Asia as well as the People's Republic's territorial reaches in the north. The study ends with chapter 11, an epilogue that summarizes some of the themes discussed in the previous chapters and highlights the relationships between territoriality, power, and legitimacy.

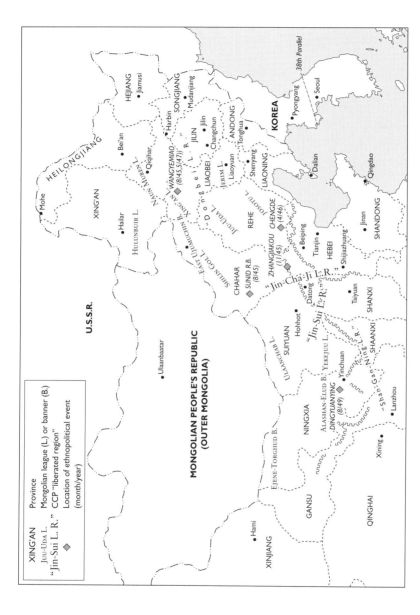

Map 1. The Political Situation on China's Northern Frontiers, 1945–1949

CENTERS OF SOVIET INTRIGUE

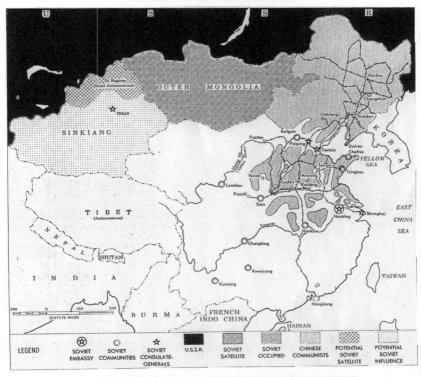

CHINA'S SOVEREIGNTY UNDERGOING SEVERE TESTS

Successful Communist military operations threaten the survival of the Chinese Government as an effective, national, political entity. Continued economic deterioration characterized by an unbalanced budget, spiraling inflation, lack of production, stagnation of commerce, and commodity shortages may culminate in financial collapse. Tribal rebellions in Sinkiang Province threaten China's ability to hold that area, and recognition of Outer Mongolia as an independent state has strengthened the autonomy movement of the Inner Mongolians. The Soviet position on the status of Dairen and Port Arthur has weakened Chinese authority in Manchuria by denying those ports to the government.

Map 2. An American View of the Soviet Threat to China, 1948
Source: Duplicate of Intelligence Division, General Staff, U.S. Army, Department of the Army, "Strategic Intelligence Estimate of China," *Intelligence Review,* Supplement No. 3, August 1948, Truman Papers, PSF / Subject File, box 173.

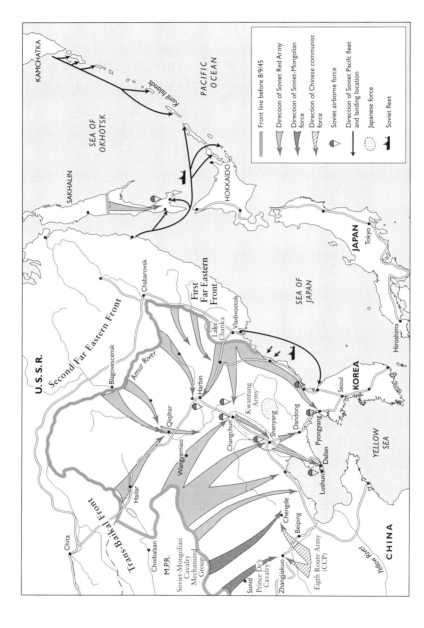

Map 3. The Soviet Entry into the Asian-Pacific War, August 9–September 2, 1945

Reins of Liberation

Part I

Independence and Revolution, 1911–1945

1

China and Mongolia:
From Empire to National States

Since the Peace of Westphalia established the principle of a state's exclusive control within its territory, the "nation-state" has been the principal realm for defining state sovereignty.[1] The twentieth century was especially productive in increasing the number of the world's nation-states. After World War I, a group of new European states was organized on the basis of "national self-determination," which was advocated separately by U.S. president Woodrow Wilson and Russian revolutionary Vladimir Lenin. Then World War II brought about a new wave of nation building in Asia and Africa in conjunction with a process of decolonization. New boundaries were thus created in Asia, as their European precedents served as "emotional and psychological" as well as "political-geographical" divides. Seen from the identity-sensitive perspective of our own time, these modern Asian frontiers erected a "cell wall of the basic unit of national identity."[2]

To this overview, the making of the modern Mongolian frontiers constitutes a prominent exception. First, in its time span, the making of the modern Mongolian state straddled the two world wars, and yet on both occasions the process was sidestepped by the contemporary international trends of "nation building" and "decolonization." Second, the resultant Mongolian boundaries served more as artificial barricades that segregated the Mongols in three different states (China, the Mongolian People's Republic, and the

---

1. Stephen D. Krasner, *Sovereignty: Organized Hypocrisy* (Princeton, N.J.: Princeton University Press, 1999), 20, defines the Westphalian model of state as "based on two principles: territoriality and the exclusion of external actors from domestic authority structures."

2. Malcolm Anderson, *Frontiers: Territory and State Formation in the Modern World* (Cambridge: Polity Press, 1996), 3.

3

Soviet Union) than as natural "cell walls" demarcating national identities. As such, the Mongolia question is a case study that defies any simple theory and definition about "national" and "international" affairs. Like many other historical processes in twentieth-century Asia, the Mongolian case calls for special attention to those subnational and supranational dimensions of events involving modernization, revolutions, and international rivalries.

This historical inquiry begins with the heritage of the Qing Empire contested between two potent twentieth-century revolutions of Asia. The Chinese Republican Revolution of 1911 threw out the Manchu monarchy along with China's imperial system of two millenniums, but later its Nationalist and Communist incarnations, both powered by Chinese nationalism, were poised to inherit the entire imperial domain created during the Qing period. Hence a Han-centric "Chinese nation" was turning itself into the leading core of a multiethnic "national state." In contrast, the Mongolian Independence Revolution of 1911 and its successors attempted a typical ethnonationalist cause of "rendering the boundaries of the nation congruent with those of its governance unit," or creating an independent Mongolian state from the Mongolian constituencies of the Qing Empire.[3] When the competition between the Chinese and the Mongolian revolutions evolved during the first half of the twentieth century, the process also became entangled with a range of intricate and devastating conflicts.

Facets of the Mongolia Question

It is quite common for scholars of Mongolia to define as unfortunate the land's geopolitical position between its two giant neighbors, China and Russia. After the historian Thomas Ewing described Mongolia's position as one "between the hammer and the anvil," Baabar (Bat-Erdene Batbayar), a Mongolian politician-scholar, cited a popular Mongolian lyric in a recent study and likened the pastoral country to a "baby otter caught between the rocks."[4] Yet, in the long history of Inner Asia, Mongolia suffered not only

3. Michael Hechter, *Containing Nationalism* (Oxford: Oxford University Press, 2000), 7.

4. Baabar, *Twentieth Century Mongolia* (Cambridge: White Horse Press, 1999),77; Thomas Ewing, *Between the Hammer and the Anvil? Chinese and Russian Policies in Outer Mongolia, 1911–1921* (Bloomington: Research Institute for Inner Asian Studies of Indiana University, 1980).

from the miseries of a weak people but also from the sadness of a fallen power. In Chinese and Russian historical memories, there was a "time of the Mongol Yoke." During the era of Pax Mongolica, the arrows of Genghis Khan and his descendants reined in all of Eurasia and beyond. After Mongolian rule in China ended in the mid–fourteenth century, it continued in Russia for another century. Afterward, Mongolia's historical fortune was reversed. By the seventeenth century, it had become sandwiched between the expansionist thrusts from the Qing Empire of China and the Tsarist Empire of Russia. This was the beginning of Mongolia's reluctant "buffer" position between Russia in the north and whichever power that came to dominate China in the south.[5]

In the recurring imperial contests for Inner Asia, the Mongolian "buffer" was neither an integral entity nor existed independently for long. During the seventeenth and eighteenth centuries, the Western (or Oriat) Mongols participated in the contests, but most of the time the process was characterized by the Qing and Russian Empires' commandeering different groups of Mongols and using Mongolian regions as their barriers of defense or fulcrum of further expansion.[6] Between the seventeenth and nineteenth centuries, the Manchu rulers of China used a double-layered ("Inner" and "Outer") Mongolian frontier to fend off external intruders as well as to contain the Chinese population within the Qing Empire. In the twentieth century, the masters of the Kremlin deployed Buryat and Khalkha ("Outer") Mongols

5. Rene Grousset's classic *Empire of the Steppes: A History of Central Asia* (New Brunswick, N.J.: Rutgers University Press, 1970) remains an effective, detailed introduction. The Mongolian conquest and rule of China is presented lucidly in Morris Rossabi, *Khubilai Khan: His Life and Times* (Berkeley: University of California Press, 1988). Thomas Barfield's *The Perilous Frontier: Nomadic Empires and China* (Cambridge: Basil Blackwell, 1989) offers an insightful reinterpretation of the interaction between the Chinese and nomadic empires in the steppe. Pamela Kyle Crossley, *A Translucent Mirror: History and Identity in Qing Imperial Ideology* (Berkeley: University of California Press, 1999), is indispensable for understanding the ethnopolitical arrangements of the Qing Empire. For Russia's empire building, John P. LeDonne, *The Russian Empire and the World, 1700–1917: The Geopolitics of Expansion and Containment* (New York: Oxford University Press, 1997); Dominic Lieven, *Empire: The Russian Empire and Its Rivals* (New Haven, Conn.: Yale University Press, 2000); and G. Patrick March, *Eastern Destiny: Russia in Asia and the North Pacific* (Westport, Conn.: Praeger, 1996), are especially useful studies.

6. Peter Perdue, "Military Mobilization in Seventeenth and Eighteenth-Century China, Russia, and Mongolia," *Modern Asian Studies,* 30(4) (1996): 757–93, discusses a three-sided contest for Inner Asia from the mid–seventeenth to the late eighteenth centuries.

as their "political Cossacks" in extending the southern and eastern frontiers of the Russian Empire.[7] It was not by accident that when the rulers of Russia and China demarcated their domains on the Gobi Desert, the resultant borders invariably cut through the Mongolian ethnographic zone.[8]

If in the past Mongolian society lacked internal coherence because of tribal friction, after the seventeenth century, the disunity of Mongolia became "other dominated" and was therefore especially distasteful to Mongol nationalists of the twentieth century. Unsurprisingly, pan-Mongolism was a central theme in any spontaneous Mongolian nationalist movement of the twentieth century. Although Mongol nationalists tended to invoke Genghis Khan as the most glorious symbol for rallying the "Mongolian nation," in practice their idea was a far cry from the grandiose Genghis Empire. They only called for substitution of the Mongols' traditional as well as modern forms of disunity with a coherent national entity.

The first page of modern Mongolia began on a July day in 1911, when princes and the nobility of the four Khalkha aimags (leagues) of Outer Mongolia held a secret meeting.[9] They decided to separate Mongolia from the Qing Empire and make it an independent state. A delegation was dispatched to Russia for assistance. Then, on December 29, an independent Mongolian theocracy was declared in the political center of Outer Mongolia, Urga (a.k.a. Kulun to the Chinese; today's Ulaanbaatar). The religious leader Javzandamba Hutagt was "elevated" by the ruling princes of Outer Mongolia and a number of Inner Mongolian banners as the "Great Khan" of all Mongols

---

7. The Qing Empire's "domestication" of the "Inner" and "Outer" Mongols took place separately in the 1630s and 1690s. Also, by the mid–seventeenth century, the Buryat Mongols of the Lake Baikal region had come under Russian domination. See LeDonne, *Russian Empire,* 10–11, 149, 221, 368, for the Cossacks' role as "pathfinder" of the Russian expansion. Lieven, *Empire,* 229–30, 303–4, discusses how Russian rulers of the tsarist and Soviet eras first manipulated and then sacked the Cossack frontier society.

8. The Treaty of Nurchinsk of 1689 and Treaty of Kiakhta of 1728 started the modern border between the Qing and Russian empires that kept Outer Mongolia on Qing's side. Then, in August 1945, a Sino-Soviet agreement allowed Outer Mongolia's legal separation from China, implying at the same time that Inner Mongolia was part of China.

9. "Aimag" was the term for the traditional tribal divisions among the Khalkha Mongols of Outer Mongolia. During the Qing Dynasty, the Manchu rulers used "banners" as basic administrative units to affix the Mongols to their designated territories and used "leagues" as a midlevel administrative tool. In Outer Mongolia, the four traditional aimags were identical with the four leagues. For more information, see Christopher P. Atwood, *Encyclopedia of Mongolia and the Mongol Empire* (New York: Facts on File, 2004), 5, 30–2, 329.

and was enthroned as the Bogd Khan.[10] The significance of Mongolian secession from the Qing Empire went beyond the issue of Mongolian independence. The act in this remote, landlocked location actually brought out a series of vital questions in modern East Asian history.

First, following the Qing Empire's loss of its external tributary system in the nineteenth century, the event marked the collapse of the Qing's internal polyethnic mechanism. The sequence of events in 1911 can correct a misunderstanding that only *after* the Chinese Revolution of 1911 overthrew the Manchu rule did the Mongols decide to set themselves free in order to avoid submission to a new Chinese overlordship. The reality is that the Mongolian princes took steps toward secession months before Chinese revolutionaries stumbled into their Wuchang uprising in early October. Therefore, the Urga independence of 1911 was not an impulsive reaction to the Chinese revolutionaries' fatal attack on the Qing government but an accumulative effect resulting from a long and complex process of erosion of the Qing system.

The historian Owen Lattimore attributed the erosion to the "Western impact" on China during the nineteenth century. Defining Mongol aristocrats as "complacent allies of the Manchus" during the Qing conquest of China, Lattimore hypothesized how, after the Western "opening" of China in the mid–nineteenth century, "the nominal privileges of the Mongols began to decline in real value as the Manchu dynasty itself declined in real power."[11] This view has been balanced by other scholars' investigation of an internal and older force: Chinese civilization. That is, when the Manchus incorporated China and Inner Asian regions into their empire, they also opened themselves and other Inner Asian frontier peoples to the "assimilative power of Chinese civilization."[12]

According to this thesis, although Manchu rulers' initial intention was to segregate the Chinese population from the Inner Asian borderlands, lawful and illicit Chinese penetrations, in forms of commercial expansion and

10. Thomas E. Ewing, "Ch'ing Policies in Outer Mongolia 1900–1911," *Modern Asian Studies,* 14(1) (1980): 145–57; Urgunge Onon and Derrick Pritchatt, *Asia's First Modern Revolution: Mongolia Proclaims Its Independence in 1911* (Leiden: E. J. Brill, 1989), 6, 13.

11. Owen Lattimore, "Prince, Priest and Herdsman in Mongolia," *Pacific Affairs,* 8(1) (March 1935): 35–47.

12. Joseph Fletcher, "Ch'ing Inner Asia *c.* 1800," in *The Cambridge History of China, Volume 10: Late Ch'ing, 1800–1911, Part I* (Cambridge: Cambridge University Press, 1978), 39.

agricultural migration, never ceased throughout the Qing period. By the early nineteenth century, the Manchu court's policy in the steppes already became favorable to Chinese monetary interests vis-à-vis Mongolian princely privileges. When the Qing court started the so-called New Administration reforms at the beginning of the twentieth century, the sinicization of the Mongolian frontier was already an official policy for countering Russian and Japanese expansion. The nineteenth-century injection of Western influence into China was important only because it expedited the expansion of Chinese power and increased the Manchus' reliance on the Han in managing their empire.[13] In other words, during the three-century Manchu reign of China, the internal balance of the Manchu–Mongolian–Han triarchy shifted from the hard power of a military alliance between the Manchu bannermen and the Mongolian cavalries to the soft power of a political-economic collaboration between the Manchu monarch and Han bureaucrats, gentry, farmers, and merchants.

It is generally agreed that the New Administration reforms after 1905 constituted the Manchu rulers' last-ditch effort to save their empire. The reforms also became the last straw that the Mongol princes refused to bear. In both Inner and Outer Mongolia, these reforms meant a series of new offices of economic, education, and military functions as well as increased agricultural cultivation by Han farmers. Until this point, the Mongol nobility had managed to shift the consequences of pauperization of the Mongolian society to the commoners. But now these new measures implied not only an additional financial burden for them but also possible degradation of their remaining political power. This meant that a Manchu–Mongol vassal agreement dating back to the late seventeenth century was breached by the former. On the surface, the Mongol princes' decision to secede in the summer of 1911 was a rebellion against their Manchu overlords' usurpation of feudal privileges. In reality, the decline of Manchu power must have been so obvious to the Mongols that they finally decided to pull themselves out of the Manchus' "great enterprise" in China that had already turned into a great Chinese march into Inner Asia.[14]

13. C. R. Bawden, "A Joint Petition of Grievances Submitted to the Ministry of Justice of Autonomous Mongolia in 1919," *Bulletin of the School of Oriental and African Studies* 30(3) (1967): 548–50; Fletcher, "Ch'ing Inner Asia," 35–58; Joseph Fletcher, "The Heyday of the Ch'ing Order in Mongolia, Sinkiang and Tibet," in *Cambridge History of China, Volume 10,* 351–60.

14. Uradyn E. Bulag, *Nationalism and Hybridity in Mongolia* (Oxford: Oxford University Press, 1998), 12; Mei-hua Lan, "China's 'New Administration' in Mongolia," in

The second question arising from the Urga independence of 1911 concerns the territoriality of China. Lattimore made the following remark some seven decades ago:

> The so-called Mongol revolution of 1911 was not in reality either a rebellion or a revolution. It was merely an assertion of the historical principle that Mongolia is not part of China. . . . The idea that a Chinese republic could claim to inherit the Manchu overlordship in Mongolia was historically a *non-sequitur.*[15]

Although later, during the Cold War, Lattimore changed the "historical principle" into a "political principle," the gist of his argument that China, Mongolia, and Tibet were separate territories all conquered by the Manchus has been repeatedly reaffirmed by other scholars. In the past decade, several important works have argued that the Qing Empire was an alien's rule in China and that the Manchus, more than the Han, recognized Inner Asia's importance and managed to preserve or renew their own Inner Asian identity vis-à-vis the Han. The Manchus thereby maintained their "ethnic sovereignty" over the huge domain of a polyethnic empire. Whereas the degree or fact of the Manchus' own sinicization, and therefore the "Chineseness" of the Qing Dynasty, has been debated heatedly, some studies have taken the history of the Qing Empire out of China's "national historiography" and reexamined it as part of the world history of imperialism. These arguments about the difference between the Han and the Manchus and about the similarities between Qing imperialism and Western colonialism point to the same conclusion: Historically, the Inner Asian territories of the Qing Empire were not part of China.[16]

Mongolia in the Twentieth Century: Landlocked Cosmopolitan, ed. Stephen Kotkin and Bruce Elleman (Armonk, N.Y.: M. E. Sharpe, 1999), 39–53; Sergei Luzyanin's review of "Belov, E. A., *Russia and Mongolia, 1911–1919,*" *Far Eastern Affairs* (hereafter *FEA*), 1 (2000): 106–9; S. C. M. Paine, *Imperial Rivals: China, Russia, and Their Disputed Frontier* (Armonk: M. E. Sharpe, 1996), 344–45; Baabar, *Twentieth Century Mongolia,* 127–33; Frederic Wakeman Jr., *The Great Enterprise: The Manchu Reconstruction of Imperial Order in Seventeenth-Century China* (Berkeley: University of California Press, 1985).

15. Lattimore, "Prince, Priest and Herdsman in Mongolia," 44.

16. Recent studies of the Manchu identity and imperial practices include Pamela Kyle Crossley, *Orphen Warriors: Three Manchu Generations and the End of the Qing World* (Princeton, N.J.: Princeton University Press, 1990), and Crossley, *A Translucent*

This controversial relationship between time and space resembles a seasonal lake often seen in the Mongolian Plateau—as the stream of historical times flows through, the size of China has either expanded or shrunk. The concern here is not to find a historical foundation for any political argument that supports or disputes China's right to claim an Inner Asian territory but to understand how in history in general and in the Qing period in particular "China" was redefined repeatedly. Obviously, Chinese nationalist historiography, which claims territories such as Mongolia and Tibet as "always" part of China, and Western studies that stress the "never" element in China's Inner Asian territoriality use different coordinates in the chart of time and space. The former basically imposes the Qing domain backward on different historical periods of China, whereas the latter, in insisting that from the beginning to the end the Qing Dynasty was an alien or foreign rule of China, seems to stop "Chinese" imperial history at the end of the Ming Dynasty.[17]

It can easily be seen that the question of what territory should be classified as "part of China" denotes rather different meanings for the premodern and modern phases of Chinese history. After the Qing Dynasty for the first time established a unified empire of China, traditional China, when unified under a series of central dynasties of either Chinese or Inner Asian origins,

---

Mirror: History and Identity in Qing Imperial Ideology (Berkeley: University of California Press, 1999); Mark C. Elliott, *The Manchu Way: The Eight Banners and Ethnic Identity in Late Imperial China* (Stanford, Calif.: Stanford University Press, 2001); Laura Hostetler, *Qing Colonial Enterprise: Ethnography and Cartography in Early Modern China* (Chicago: University of Chicago Press, 2001); and Evelyn Rawski, *The Last Emperors: A Social History of Qing Imperial Institutions* (Berkeley: University of California Press, 1998). For the issues in the scholarly debate on the Manchus' sinicization, see Evelyn Rawski, "Presidential Address: Reenvisioning the Qing—The Significance of the Qing Period in Chinese History," *Journal of Asian Studies* 55(4) (November 1996): 829–50, and Ping-ti Ho, "In Defense of Sinicization: A Rebuttal of Evelyn Rawski's 'Reenvisioning the Qing,'" *Journal of Asian Studies* 57(1) (February 1998): 123–55. For a cluster of comparative studies of Qing imperialism and Western colonialism, see *International Historical Review* 20(2) (June 1998), esp. Peter C. Perdue, "Comparing Empires: Manchu Colonialism," 255–61, and "Boundaries, Maps, and Movement: Chinese, Russian, and Mongolian Empires in Early Modern Central Eurasia," 263–86; Nicola Di Cosmo, "Qing Colonial Administration in Inner Asia," 287–309; Dorothea Heuschert, "Legal Pluralism in the Qing Empire: Manchu Legislation for the Mongols," 310–24; and Michael Adas, "Imperialism and Colonialism in Comparative Perspective," 371–88.

17. Yet, again, Western and Chinese historical literature disagree whether Tibet was part of the Ming Empire. For a standard Chinese perspective of the Ming space, see Tan Qixiang, ed., *Jianming Zhongguo Lishi Dituji* (Simplified Historical Atlas of China) (Beijing: Zhongguo Ditu Chubanshe, 1991), 61–62, 63–64.

incorporated basically two types of territories. The first category included interior districts of different levels administered directly by the imperial bureaucracy. These, in different periods, assumed names such as *xian* (county), *jun* (commandery), *zhou* (prefecture), *fu* (superior prefecture), *dao* (circuit), and *sheng* (province). The second category included peripheral dependencies that were reigned loosely under the imperial hegemony and variously named *duhufu* (protectorate), *jimizhou* (subordinated prefecture), *dudufu* (area commandery), *dusi* (regional military commission), *xuanweisi* (pacification commission), *jiangjunfu* (regional commandery), and *banshi dachen xiaqu* (superintendency).[18] In the traditional East Asian world order centered on Chinese civilization, the ambiguity of "sovereignty" was the rule of interstate relations and loose or indirect reign was the key to imperial success. The vassal–lord relationship between a dependency and the central dynasty could be either ceremonial or substantive, cordial or hostile; the link could be made through bribery, conquest, intermarriage, and oath brotherhood. Most of all, the relationship was unstable, expedient, and reversible.

Therefore, if the question about what was a "part of China" is asked with the full connotation that the modern world order of nation-states entails, territories such as Tibet and Mongolia not only were not part of the "Chinese China" but also were not part of the "Manchu China." The Manchu court began to modernize its imperial administration only after repeated frustration in dealing with Western powers during the nineteenth century. While former tributary states such as Korea, Vietnam, Burma, and Liuqiu (the Ryukyus) fell under foreign colonial rule, peripheral territories that were hitherto administered in various ways were brought under the Qing court's internal sovereignty and changed into provinces. This course of internalization was applied to Xinjiang in 1883, to Taiwan in 1885 before it was lost to Japan ten years later, and to Manchuria in 1907 (the region was then divided into three provinces, Fengtian, Jilin, and Heilongjiang). When the twentieth century began, the only two dependencies yet to be internalized were Tibet and Mongolia. In this context, the Urga revolt in 1911 was propelled by an anxiety that Mongolia would be turned into "part" of the Manchu Empire in the modern sense.

Another aspect of the "part of China" question involves the sinicization

---

18. Gu Jigang and Shi Nianhai, *Zhongguo Jiangyu Yange Shi* (History of China's Changing Territories) (Beijing: Shangwu Yanshuguan, 2000), was first published in 1938 and has remained a useful reference. Also see Tan, *Jianming Zhongguo Lishi Dituji*, for names of administrative districts under different dynasties.

of the Qing Empire. Whereas works by Pamela Crossley, Evelyn Rawski, and Mark Elliott convincingly document how the Manchus, as a ruling minority, managed to maintain their ethnic identity during a three-century immersion in Chinese society, Ping-ti Ho contends that the sinicization of the Manchus and the Manchus' unique way of managing their Inner Asian territories do not have to be put in a dichotomy.[19] There is, however, no disagreement among scholars that biculturalism was the most valuable asset of these partially sinicized Inner Asian ruling elites. Without question, from the beginning to the end the Qing *Dynasty* was Manchu in the sense that from the royal clan (Aisin Gioro) down to ordinary bannermen, the Manchus, despite the degree of their sinicization, remained the ruling core with a distinctive set of ethnopolitical interests.

Yet the "Manchuness" of the Qing *Empire* cannot be determined so easily. A discernible trend throughout the Qing period is that under the Manchu dynasty the Qing Empire became increasingly "Chinese."[20] Aside from imperial ambitions and policymaking at the dynastic level, empire building had to involve military forces, local bureaucrats, and commercial and agrarian colonists in the frontiers. For instance, as pointed out by specialists on the Qing Empire, the "Manchu" pacification of Xinjiang could not have been accomplished without contributions by Han colonists from Gansu and Shaanxi Provinces. Eventually, the Xinjiang garrison included both Manchu banner troops and Han Green Standard soldiers. From the second half of the eighteenth century, the court's management of Mongolian affairs was no longer an exclusive business of the Lifan Yuan (Board of Dependencies) staffed by Manchu and Mongol officials. The undertaking also involved the Grand Council and the Board of Punishments, on which Han officials held positions. Without any intention to impose the Chinese laws upon the Mongols, Qing legal codes of Chinese origin were nevertheless introduced into Mongolia.[21] As pointed out incisively by Joseph Fletcher, "In its long-range historical effect, the expansion of the Ch'ing [Qing] armies into Inner Asia

19. Crossley, *Translucent Mirror;* Elliott, *Manchu Way;* Rawski, *Last Emperors;* Ping-ti Ho, "In Defense of Sinicization," 125.

20. A practice in the field is to use "Chinese" and "Manchu" interchangeably in discussing the Qing administration of the empire and thus also to obscure the empire's ethnic transformation. A recent example is Paine, *Imperial Rivals,* an otherwise informative diplomatic history.

21. Di Cosmo, "Qing Colonial Administration," 292–95, 302–3; Heuschert, "Legal Pluralism in the Qing Empire," 310–16.

in the seventeenth and eighteenth centuries meant the spread of Han Chinese influence, culture, and population."[22]

The Manchus' Inner Asian instinct guarding against the Han indeed continued and resulted in policies to restrict Chinese commercial and agricultural penetration into Inner Asia. As of the nineteenth century, however, when the Qing Empire's outer defense against Western powers crumbled, the Manchus' inner defense against the Han had to be reevaluated. A new insight thus obtained by the Manchus was not just a passive admission that the restrictive policies in the past had been ineffective but also mainly a positive recognition that the mobile commercial and agricultural elements of sedentary Chinese society turned out to be the most effective forces in substantiating the Manchu court's internal and external sovereignty in the vast and largely nomadic land of Inner Asia. Thus, "increasingly, Ch'ing [Qing] interests in Mongolia became Han Chinese interests."[23]

The nineteenth-century encounter between the Qing Empire and Western powers significantly accelerated the process. Internally, Western influence wreaked havoc in the Chinese socioeconomic structure, and externally it forced the Manchu court to adopt the modern-cum-Western mode of international practices. The self-contained Qing Empire began to be transformed into a "national state" while gingerly socializing with the international community. Under the circumstances, the Manchu court voluntarily adopted policies to accelerate the sinicization of the empire. Chinese bureaucratic, commercial, and agricultural expansion in Inner Asian territories constituted the court's principal means of "modernizing" the empire. The irony is that before the Manchus could "Westernize" their empire externally, they had to "sinicize" it internally. The resultant effects on Inner Asian societies were often calamitous. At the turn of the centuries, consequently, what appeared to be the Mongols' "peculiar attitude toward China" was actually not only ethnoculturally against the Han and feudal-politically against the Manchu but also historically against a mode of modernity that the Qing imperial government and, indirectly, Western influence tried to force upon Mongolian society.[24]

Hence a third question—ethnonationalism—in twentieth-century Chinese politics. Mainly because of the Western inroads into China in the nineteenth

22. Fletcher, "Ch'ing Inner Asia," 36.
23. Fletcher, "Heyday of the Ch'ing Order," 352.
24. Victor A. Yakhontoff, "Mongolia: Target or Screen?" *Pacific Affairs* 9(1) (March 1936): 15.

century, the Qing Dynasty did not run its "natural course." Nor did its demise in 1911 start another "dynastic cycle." A different cycle in Chinese history, consisting of Inner Asians' conquest followed by Chinese restoration, did seem to run its course in the Manchu–Han relationship. The reversal of this relationship arrived too fast for the Manchus to complete their scheme of sinicizing the entire empire. Not by accident, Tibet and Outer Mongolia, the two least sinicized territories of the Qing imperial domain, managed to achieve practical separation from China at the end of the Qing Dynasty. Clearly, on the eve of the Chinese Revolution of 1911, the Manchus already lost the Mongols' allegiance in their final fight to save the dynasty. In the meantime, Manchu rulers' long effort of segregating the land of Outer Mongolia from the rest of China preserved a cultural and territorial haven, which, even though eroding rapidly in late Qing, provided the Mongols with a chance to start anew.[25]

The events around 1911 are illuminating in showing how "nation" became a determinant in the political life of China and Mongolia. It has been aptly argued that in Europe "nations" were formed as a consequence of a "triple Western revolution"—economic transformation from feudalism to capitalism, political centralization through military and administrative professionalization, and cultural and educational reformation by way of rationalization and standardization.[26] None of these were preconditions for the formation of either the Chinese or the Mongolian nation. The Chinese nation, like many other Asian nations, took shape through "imitation and rejection" vis-à-vis the Asian extension of European nationalism: colonialism.[27]

There was, however, a unique ethnopolitical twist in the Chinese case, because China's response to the West took place under the polyethnic enterprise of the Qing Empire. The so-called national response of China actually consisted of diverse and even contradictory responses from different ethnic groups. By 1911, both Chinese and Mongol elites harbored anti-Manchu sentiments, yet for different reasons. Whereas the Chinese revolutionaries of 1911 wanted to remove the Qing court because it hindered China's advance to modernity, the Mongol secessionists of 1911 split with their Manchu

25. Fletcher, "Ch'ing Inner Asia," 41, 52; Fletcher, "Heyday of the Ch'ing Order," 352; Di Cosmo, "Qing Colonial Administration," 302–3.

26. Anthony D. Smith, *The Ethnic Origins of Nations* (Oxford: Blackwell Publishers, 1988), 130–34.

27. Harry G. Gelber, *Nations Out of Empires: European Nationalism and the Transformation of Asia* (New York: Palgrave, 2001), 150–51, 213.

overlords to preserve the traditional status quo of Mongolia. To Chinese revolutionaries, "anti-Manchuism" meant restoration of the Han as China's ruling stock, or "core *ethnie*," to preside over the existing polyethnic entity. In contrast, for Mongol aristocrats, because their original compact with the Manchus was beyond salvage and a Chinese option was unacceptable, it was time to stay away from Chinese politics and to stand on their own feet again.[28]

If in European history it was the Third Estate's social agenda that brought the issue of nation to the fore, in modern Asia the question of national survival (revival, in the Mongolian case) was often intertwined with social divides. In 1911, the first battle cry of Mongolian nationalism was let out by traditional ruling elites. As indicated in a petition for help that Mongol secessionists handed to the Russian government in the summer of 1911, their grievances against the "Manchu–Chinese rulers" were more conservative than progressive, and their justification for Mongolian independence was more ethnocultural than national-political. Although the "grievances" did mention commoners' economic sufferings, Urga's proclamation for independence was devoid of any content of social reform. As a matter of fact, Mongol aristocrats and upper-stratum lamas had a significant share of responsibility for pauperizing Mongolian society. To sustain their extravagant lifestyle and meet their tax responsibilities to the Manchu court, they borrowed heavily from unscrupulous Chinese merchants and then shifted the burden to the commoners. The Bogd Khan and the Urga regime's prime minister and foreign minister were among the biggest debtors to Chinese merchants and had a huge financial stake in repudiating the Chinese debts through Mongolian independence.[29]

The social divide had a different effect on the issue of independence in Inner Mongolia. Here the Qing court's imperial sinicization advanced much faster and inflicted much more severe damages on the Mongolian population than in Outer Mongolia. Yet, again, the consequences were shared unevenly by different social strata. There were instances in which Inner Mongolian princes even welcomed Chinese immigration because it meant their access to goods, money, and overlordship over Chinese tenants. Another kind of

---

28. Smith, *Ethnic Origins,* 141; Chang Ch'i-hsiung, *Waimeng Zhuquan Jiaoshe* (Negotiations over Sovereignty in Outer Mongolia) (Taipei: Zhongyang Yanjiuyuan Jindaishi Yanjiusuo, 1995), 38–41.

29. Christopher Kaplonski, "Creating National Identity in Socialist Mongolia," *Central Asian Survey* 17(1) (1998): 37–39; Gerald M. Friters, "The Prelude to Outer Mongolian Independence," *Pacific Affairs* 10(2) (June 1937): 176; Paine, *Imperial Rivals,* 287.

response was a radical movement in the form of *duguilan* (rebellious circles). These "circles" were led by popular leaders and often targeted local Mongol aristocrats who collaborated with China's central authorities. Unlike their Outer Mongol kindred, Inner Mongol aristocrats tended to face a much graver threat from underneath. During China's revolutionary crisis in 1911, consequently, many of them opted to continue collaborating with whatever new authorities were emerging in China to protect their own class interests. In early 1912, Yuan Shikai, the first formal president of the Republic of China (ROC), reciprocated the sentiment and issued a nine-article decree. It reconferred on Mongol princes and lamas all their old titles and privileges under the Qing.[30]

This is not to say that Inner Mongol aristocrats did not respond to Urga's call for a unified Mongolian state. A number of them actually went to Outer Mongolia and served in the Urga government. During the uncertain months of Chinese politics from December 1911 to February 1912, the Inner Mongol nobility assembled at least twice to discuss whether or not they should follow Urga's example and secede from China. A number of Inner Mongolian leagues and banners sent petitions to Urga for support. Eventually, however, the princely interests behind these moves proved too narrow to support decisive and bold action. When China's revolutionary crisis was over, the historical moment for erasing the old divide between Inner and Outer Mongolia also passed. Once the ROC settled in as a new status quo, most Inner Mongol elites sought comfort in the continuation of old arrangements promised by the politically conservative Yuan Shikai government, not throwing in their lot with the uncertain destiny of the Urga regime.

Belatedly, in July 1912, two banners in Jerim League of eastern Inner Mongolia rebelled and proclaimed their allegiance to the Urga regime. This was, however, not greeted by Urga with any effective support. Only six months later did the Urga regime dispatch an expeditionary force of 2,000 to attack Guisui (today's Hohhot) and Kalgan (Zhangjiakou) in western Inner Mongolia. According to one estimate, before Urga terminated the effort

---

30. Owen Lattimore, "Mongolia Enters World Affairs," *Pacific Affairs* 7(1) (March 1934): 18; Chang Ch'i-hsiung, *Waimeng,* 35, 46; Literature and History Committee of the Political Consultative Council of the Yekejuu League, "Sini Lama and the *Duguilan* Movement under His Leadership," *Neimenggu Wenshi Ziliao* (Literary and Historical Materials of Inner Mongolia; hereafter *NWZ*) 19 (1985): 4–17; Buyantu, "Brief Chronicle of Wandannima's Career," ibid., 36-41; Henry Serruys, "Documents from Ordos on the 'Revolutionary Circles,' Part I," *Journal of the American Oriental Society* 97(4) (October–December 1977): 482–507.

in the fall of 1913, the expedition force increased to 7,000. These "wars of unification" achieved some brief success but in the end were foiled by Yuan Shikai's troops. Witnesses' recollections put refugees from these conflicts in the tens of thousands. In eastern Mongolia alone, the civilian casualties exceeded 2,500, many of whom were killed by Chinese troops when following the routed Mongol troops into Outer Mongolia.[31] After these events, military effort to "liberate" the Inner Mongols would not be attempted again by Outer Mongolia until 1945, when Outer Mongol troops entered China at the side of the Soviet Red Army in the name of war against Japan.

In the 1930s, Lattimore attributed the Mongols' failure to unify in 1911 to geographical factors, tribal traditions within Mongolian society, and political conditions in Central Asia, suggesting that the Mongols' internal division was almost a "normal condition." The Manchu court's "artificial" unification and the actual division of the Mongols in a "Great Wall-Inner Mongolia-Outer defense walls-Gobi-Outer Mongolia" stratification was not surmounted by Mongolian independence of 1911, which was narrowly constructed around princely interests.[32] Before Mongolian unification in the modern sense could be attempted again, the Mongols had to live through

31. Lu Minghui, "Revolution of 1911 and Feudal Mongolian Princes" (in Chinese), in *Opuscula Altaica: Essays Presented in Honor of Henry Schwarz,* ed. Edward H. Kaplan and Donald W. Whisenhunt (Bellingham: Center for East Asian Studies, Western Washington University, 1994), 427–35; Baabar, *Twentieth Century Mongolia,* 138–39, 153–54; Balgud, "The Rebellions in the Zasagtu and Zhenguogong Banners," *NWZ* 1 (1979): 63–82; Buyanmandukhu, "The Incident of Prince Wutai's Rebellion," ibid., 83–94; Shi Bo, *Waimenggu Duli Neimu* (The Inside Story of Outer Mongolia's Independence) (Beijing: Renmin Zhongguo Chubanshe, 1993), 152–55; Onon and Pritchatt, *Asia's First Modern Revolution,* 19–21; Friters, "Prelude to Outer Mongolia Independence," 185–86.

32. Lattimore's relevant discussions can be found in his *Manchuria: Cradle of Conflict* (New York: Macmillan, 1932), 36–52, *The Mongols of Manchuria* (New York: John Day, 1934), 18, and "Historical Setting of Inner Mongolian Nationalism," in *Studies in Frontier History,* ed. Lattimore (London: Oxford University Press, 1962), orig. pub. *Pacific Affairs,* September 1936, 440–55. Mei-hua Lan, "China's 'New Administration' in Mongolia," in *Mongolia,* ed. Kotkin and Elleman, 39–53, is a recent effort to explain Inner Mongolia's failure to join Urga's separation from China in 1911. The study confirms Lattimore's view on Inner Mongolian princes' selfish calculations and points out that at the time of the Urga independence the partially sinicized Inner Mongolian princes "lacked secular or ecclesiastic leaders who could unify them for a higher political cause." Onon and Pritchatt, *Asia's First Modern Revolution,* 22–40, offers a detailed account of various Inner Mongolian banners' response to the Urga independence of 1911. It should be noted that Prince Demchugdongrob, who would lead the second wave of autonomous movement in Inner Mongolia in the 1930s, was just nine years old in 1911.

their division in a nontraditional way. As Christopher Atwood points out in his detailed study of the genesis of Inner Mongolian nationalism, after 1911 the Inner Mongols for the first time realized that they now lived in the "Middle Realm" (China) and outside the "Mongolian Realm" represented by the separate Outer Mongolia. A socially more progressive program in Urga would have attracted more young Inner Mongols to the latter.[33]

The demise of the Qing Empire was thus followed by two unfinished political enterprises. The republican revolution in China brought down an imperial system of two millenniums but neither replaced it with functional governance nor accomplished any meaningful social transformation. Meanwhile, the secessionist movement in Outer Mongolia broke the territorial domain of a three-century-old empire but could neither organize the new state according to national principles nor make it a full-fledged entity of independence. The two burgeoning national states in China and Mongolia would continue to compete for the Qing legacy on their own terms—if both could stay in their chosen courses, respectively.

Independence for the Second Time

Just as the Yuan Shikai presidency would not continue the republican system of China (he attempted abortively to enthrone himself in 1915), neither could the Urga regime maintain Mongolian independence for long. The difference is that in the Mongolian case, external factors were crucial. After Outer Mongolia easily broke its flimsy tie to China, its road from geopolitical separation to internationally sustainable independence proved more difficult. Whereas China's persistent claim to sovereignty continued to impede the Urga regime's international outreach, the foreign policy of Russia wielded a decisive influence over the Mongols' independence struggle. Irrespective of the Urga regime's and its successors' efforts, for a long period Outer Mongolia could not escape its fate as a buffer in Russia's geostrategic schemes. Both Tsarist and Soviet policymakers in Russia did not hesitate to put Outer Mongolia on the bargaining table of great power diplomacy if doing so could serve Moscow's purposes. Only briefly, between 1917 and 1920, Russia's own revolutionary crises created an interval when its influence in Outer Mongolia declined. The opportunity, unfortunately for leaders

---

33. Christopher Atwood, *Young Mongols and Vigilantes in Inner Mongolia's Interregnum Decades, 1911–1931* (Leiden: Brill Academic Publishers, 2002), 1: 40–41, 95–96.

in Urga, just allowed the Chinese government to use force in 1919 to abolish Mongolian independence.[34]

Unable to duplicate the Manchus' imperial patronage of Outer Mongolia, the Chinese intervention of 1919 gave rise to a second Mongolian independence revolution. The historical significance of this second revolution has been debated among historians, and different interpretations have either stressed the event's populist nature or ethnonationalist characteristics.[35] Historians nevertheless agree that after the aristocratic secessionists of 1911 discredited themselves by capitulating to the Chinese in 1919, the second round was initiated by partisans of commoner backgrounds. Amid the pandemonium of Chinese interventions and spillover effects of the Russian Revolution, a new thread of political activists came into the political arena of Outer Mongolia. In the spring of 1920, a Mongolian People's Party (MPP, later renamed the Mongolian People's Revolutionary Party) emerged and started a new phase of struggle for Mongolian independence.

By early July 1921, assisted by the Soviet Red Army, these MPP partisans captured Urga and established a Mongolian People's Revolutionary Government. Outer Mongolia, taking the name of the Mongolian People's Republic (MPR) after 1924, thus declared for the second time its independence from China.[36] Yet again, the meaning of independence was ambiguous. Although the 1921 revolution might satisfy progressive Inner Mongols as a movement in the right direction, the MPP's reliance on Soviet support marked 1921 as the year when Soviet Russia's "oldest political satellite" was born. Mongolian historians prefer to view the event as their country's second revolution for national liberation, though they also have to face the dark period that ensued.[37]

---

34. Chang Ch'i-hsiung, *Shoufu Waimeng Zhuquan, 1917–1920* (Restoration of Sovereignty in Outer Mongolia, 1917–1920) (Taipei: Meng Zang Weiyuanhui, 1998), is a study of the process from a Chinese perspective.

35. See Hiroshi Futaki, "A Re-Examination of the Establishment of the Mongolian People's Party, Centering on Dogsom's Memoir," *Inner Asia* 2 (2000): 37–61, for a detailed analysis of different sources on which historians have based their interpretations of the 1921 revolution in Outer Mongolia.

36. Fujiko Isono, "Soviet Russia and the Mongolian Revolution of 1921," *Past and Present* 83 (March 1979): 116–40; Baabar, *Twentieth Century Mongolia,* 201–2, 218–20; Shi Bo, *Waimenggu,* 214.

37. For Inner Mongols' reaction to the event, see Atwood, *Young Mongols,* 110–11. A typical Western view of the MPR's dependence on the Soviet Union is George G. S. Murphy, *Soviet Mongolia: A Study of the Oldest Political Satellite* (Berkeley: University of California, 1966). Baabar, *Twentieth Century Mongolia;* and Shagdariin Sandag

In his erudite study of Russian geopolitics, John P. LeDonne states that "geopoliticians consider a boundary a 'political isobar' along which the competing pressures of political rivals reach a temporary balance." By this logic, between 1911 and 1917, when seeking a "line of an optimum of conquest" in their eastern frontier, the policymakers of Tsarist Russia decided to accommodate the Chinese interests "while obtaining for Russia the role of mediator between China and Mongolia." The policy turned Mongolia into a contradictory international phenomenon, a "Russian protectorate under Chinese suzerainty."[38] The Soviet Russian government followed the same policy and formalized Mongolia's ambiguous status in a 1924 agreement with the Chinese government. Only this time the distance between legality and reality was further increased by the Soviets' apparently "correct" but actually craftier foreign policy. In the agreement, the Soviet government "recognizes Outer Mongolia as an integral part of the Republic of China and respects China's *sovereignty* in that territory." Meanwhile, in a secret protocol, Moscow managed to maintain the old Tsarist arrangements and treated Outer Mongolia as a Russian protectorate.[39]

In current scholarly references to Outer Mongolia's status between 1921 and 1945, it is common to point out the divergence between China's de jure sovereignty and Mongolia's de facto separation. Yet the latter's de facto separation can be easily interpreted as Russia's actual hegemony. The situation continued in these years more because of imperial intrigues among big powers than the national competition between the ROC and the MPR. A consistent Russian policy was to keep the Mongolian affair "private" in the

---

and Harry H. Kendall, *Poisoned Arrows: The Stalin-Choibalsan Mongolian Massacres, 1921–1941* (Boulder, Colo.: Westview Press, 2000) are two Mongolian accounts of Mongolia's sufferings under Soviet control. The debate in Mongolia about the historical crimes of the Communist period is reported in "Mongolia Faces Its Communist Past," *Moscow Times,* 16 May 2000.

38. LeDonne, *Russian Empire,* 181, 211, 218, 220. Peter S. H. Tang, *Russian and Soviet Policy in Manchuria and Outer Mongolia, 1911–1931* (Durham, N.C.: Duke University Press, 1959), 271–358, discusses in detail Russia's Mongolian diplomacy between 1911 and 1917. It is updated by Paine, *Imperial Rivals,* 287–313.

39. "Agreement on the Outline for Solving the Pending Cases between China and Russia, March 14, 1924," in *Zhong Su Guojia Guanxi Shi Ziliao Huibian* (Collected Documents on the History of Sino-Soviet Interstate Relationship), 4 vols., comp. Xue Xiantian et al. (Beijing: Shehui Kexue Chubanshe, 1993–97) (hereafter *ZSGG*), 1: 217–19. Bruce Elleman, "Secret Sino-Soviet Negotiations on Outer Mongolia, 1918–1925," *Pacific Affairs* 66 (Winter 1993–94): 554–58, describes the cunning Soviet diplomacy in 1924.

sense that it would not attract undue international attention. Between 1907 and 1916, Tsarist Russia and Japan concluded a string of secret deals for carving out their respective spheres of influence in Mongolia and Manchuria.[40] A 1915 tripartite agreement among the Chinese, Russian, and Outer Mongolian governments continued an administrative practice of the late Qing and designated the regions of the four Khalkha *aimags* as the territory of the "autonomous" Outer Mongolia.

The Soviets basically maintained the established power balance after Mongolia's second independence. From 1936 to 1941, the MPR and Japan's puppet state "Manchukuo" held negotiations to demarcate their boundaries, with Moscow and Tokyo pulling all the strings behind their respective client states and making secret deals between themselves.[41] All these diplomatic moves had the effect of entrenching the Mongolian state within Moscow's private domain and hardening the traditionally "soft" divide between the Outer Mongols and their southern kith and kin. The MPR in the meantime remained incommunicado with the international community.

Indeed, Mongolia's landlocked geographic position was difficult, but, until the late 1920s, it was by no means isolated internationally. At the time, Mongolia hosted several hundred foreign companies, including an American-financed gold-mining firm named Mongolor. Between 1925 and 1929, the MPR government sent trade and education delegations to Western European countries. An education delegation visited Germany and arranged in Berlin for the manufacturing of the first Mongolian typewriter and the printing of 10,000 copies of a Mongolian atlas for school students back home. Such outreach was soon terminated. By the early 1930s, the only occasions for the Mongols to see images of "foreign capitalists and generals" were in party-staged plays, who were denounced together with "greedy Chinese traders" and "cruel feudalists and shrewd lamas."[42] No one else but Joseph Stalin himself best depicted the MPR's predicament. On an

---

40. Tang, *Russian and Soviet Policy in Manchuria and Outer Mongolia,* 61–67.

41. Chang, *Shoufu Waimeng Zhuquan,* 254–61; Bruce A. Elleman, "The Final Consolidation of the USSR's Sphere of Interests in Outer Mongolia," in *Mongolia,* ed. Kotkin and Elleman, 126–29; Baabar, *Twentieth Century Mongolia,* 93–94, 139, 162–67, 340–42, 390.

42. Sandag and Kendall, *Poisoned Arrows,* 28–29; Baabar, *Twentieth Century Mongolia,* 299–300; Serge M. Wolff, "Mongols in Western Europe in 1925–1929," *Man* 45 (March–April 1945): 41–42; Bazaryn Shirendev, *Through the Ocean Waves: The Autobiography of Bazaryn Shirendev,* (Bellingham: Western Washington University Press, 1997), 62.

occasion in 1936, he shouted down at the MPR prime minister Genden, who wished for a greater degree of Mongolian autonomy: "No other country except us recognizes Mongolia. You are still part of China. We have no obligation to help you at all."[43] What Stalin did not say was that the MPR's international predicament was largely Soviet made. The Russian–Soviet policy first isolated Mongolia and then used this isolation to throttle any Mongolian aspirations for meaningful international independence.

The conception of the MPR as the Soviets' protectorate is not without a certain irony. After the 1920s, Moscow offered Outer Mongols its bear's embrace only for the protection of the Soviet Union itself. Under the circumstances, the MPR easily became a brutalized beneficiary of Soviet guardianship. In recent years, information has surfaced in Mongolia, revealing the heavy price that the Mongolian people paid for this long protectorate relationship. It is clear now that in the 1920s, having just achieved freedom from Chinese overlordship, Mongol revolutionaries were reluctant to go under Soviet rule. When the MPP was established in 1920, it was a far cry from the Soviet standard for a revolutionary party. The "Party Oath" was a mixture of cultural conservatism and social egalitarianism, which commanded its members to "recall the lost Mongolian law, to strengthen the State and the religion," and "in every way to protect the interests of the *arat* [herder] masses . . . and put an end to the sufferings of the working people."[44] Inevitably, their policies for national development engendered conflicts with Moscow's political-strategic calculations. Even when they were cooperating with Moscow, the MPR leaders still could not avoid being a scapegoat in Moscow's often brutal readjustments of orientation.[45]

Soviet influence in the MPR became finally entrenched only through ruthless the "Sovietization" of Mongolian society supervised by Comintern and Soviet agents. Eventually, all but one of the leading revolutionaries of 1921 were physically eliminated by repeated purges. Horoloogiin Choibalsan, the remaining leader, adhered to Moscow's line loyally from the 1930s

---

43. According to Baabar, *Twentieth Century Mongolia,* 347–48, on that occasion the angered Genden called Stalin a "bloody Georgian" and a "virtual Russian Tsar." The quarrel led to Genden's arrest and execution in 1937.

44. Cited in Thomas T. Hammond, "The Communist Takeover of Outer Mongolia: Model for Eastern Europe?" *Studies on the Soviet Union* 11(4) (1971): 115.

45. A case in point is the Soviet-directed purge of the MPR leadership in 1932, when Stalin decided to change the Comintern's radical social and economic policies in the country. See Tsedenbambyn Batbayar, "Stalin's Strategy in Mongolia, 1932–1936," *Mongolian Studies* 22 (1999): 1–17.

to his death in 1952. From their cooperation with Moscow, the leaders of the 1921 generation learned enough to see that the Soviet government was pursuing a "policy of colonizing Mongolia just like other big powers."[46] Prominent leaders who fell victim to persecutions after the 1930s would not have their names cleared until the end of Communist rule in Mongolia in the early 1990s. The scope of ordinary people's sufferings can be known only through statistics. Between 1928 and 1931, the Comintern-directed radical social and economic policies in the MPR caused a "nationwide flight." From 30,000 to 50,000 refugees entered Inner Mongolia and Xinjiang in China.[47] The more vigorous elements in the society staged an armed resistance that continued into the better part of 1932. Some lamas' involvement in the uprising provided Stalin with an excuse to order MPR leaders to terminate the religious practices in the country. By the end of the 1930s, Mongolia's lama population simply disappeared from this pastoral country. It has been estimated that about 17,000 lamas were among the 29,800 people executed during the purges of the mid-1930s.[48]

The continuity between the Tsarist and Soviet policies toward Outer Mongolia granted, the "Sovietization" of the MPR should not be interpreted as a usual process of "Russification" that Russian tsars applied to their imperial territories before 1917. "Sovietization" was a peculiar variant of Russification conducted under a supposedly supranational, supracultural, and class-oriented ideology. Specifically, to the new occupants of the Kremlin, the MPR's international isolation was necessary because the first successful proletarian revolution in Russia needed a cordon sanitaire against

46. This is from the last words of Anandiin Amar, who served as prime minister of the MPR from 1936 to 1939 and was executed in the USSR in 1941, quoted in Baabar, *Twentieth Century Mongolia,* 367–68. For a chilling account of the political persecution in the MPR, see Sandag and Kendall, *Poisoned Arrows.*

47. Baabar, *Twentieth Century Mongolia,* 309, 315–17; Sandag and Kendall, *Poisoned Arrows,* 63; Benson Bobrick, *East of the Sun: The Epic Conquest and Tragic History of Siberia* (New York: Poseidon Press, 1992), 421–22. Bulag, *Nationalism,* 14, puts the number even higher, at 10 percent of the total Outer Mongolian population. Different estimates put the size of the population between 647,500 and 800,000 from the late 1910s to the early 1930s. See Murphy, *Soviet Mongolia,* 180; and Batbayar, "Stalin's Strategy in Mongolia," 4, 11.

48. "Mongolia Faces Its Communist Past," *Moscow Times,* May 16, 2000. According to contemporary information cited in Batbayar, "Stalin's Strategy in Mongolia," 11, in the early 1930s the MPR had a lama population of 85,677, or 11.7 percent of the total population. Sandag and Kendall, *Poisoned Arrows,* 121, estimate that if the persecutions in the 1920s were counted, a total of 50,000 lamas were executed.

the hostile capitalist world. So the Soviet domination of the MPR differed from traditional colonization in confining the Mongols to a burgeoning "socialist bloc" that would not expand until after World War II.[49] By the same token, radical social changes were engineered in Mongolia not so much to Russify the Mongols as to make the nomadic society politically and ideologically compatible with the Soviet Union. For instance, in the late 1920s the Comintern ordered leaders in Ulaanbaatar to "prepare a united and principled policy on the Lamaist question" because, to Soviet leaders, the lama clergy were the only remaining organized group in the Mongolian society that could pose a challenge to Communism.[50]

Paradoxically, it was the "Sovietization" of Outer Mongolia that helped keep the Mongolia question part of China's nation building. Outer Mongolia's "Sovietization" had two ethnopolitical consequences pertinent to China. First, the process contributed to the split of modern Mongolian identity into a desolated, "noncapitalist" nationhood of Outer Mongolia and a "bewildered" ethnicity of Inner Mongolia. The latter, according to Uradyn Bulag, rejected the "assimilationist ideology of the modern [Chinese] nation-state" while pursuing in vain "completeness" with the MPR.[51] The Inner and Outer Mongols' respective struggles for convergence between the two identities in the post–World War II period will be discussed below. Here, it is necessary to clarify the second consequence of Outer Mongolia's entry into the Soviet orbit—by channeling the MPR into their world revolutionary strategy, Soviet leaders unwittingly left the door open for a revolutionary China to reclaim the MPR's allegiance. In the 1920s, the Nationalist Revolution under Sun Yat-sen tried to reincorporate Outer Mongolia into China through this revolutionary passage. In 1949, the Communist Revolution under Mao Zedong would try again.

Ethnic Separation and National Revolution

Although Chinese nationalism in its embryonic form had a strong ethnic, Han-oriented, anti-Manchu connotation, the mainstream of modern Chinese ethnopolitics began with a "five-race republic" creed, which was advocated

---

49. Elleman, "Secret Sino-Soviet Negotiations on Outer Mongolia, 540, suggests that Soviet domination in Outer Mongolia in the 1920s was actually the "beginning of the Soviet-led bloc," though his focus is on the diplomatic aspect.
50. Sandag and Kendall, *Poisoned Arrows,* 120.
51. Bulag, *Nationalism,* 2–4.

by victorious Chinese nationalists after the Revolution of 1911. The successive Chinese "central" governments in the republican period continued to uphold the idea.[52] In meshing values of modern nationalism with Confucian culture and a political legacy of the polyethnic Qing Empire, the creed fit Chinese nationalists' purposes well. This imaginary, "Pan-Chinese" common family was, however, not cherished by all the designated member "races" of the ROC. From the outset, although the ROC adopted a five-strip color to denote officially the birth of a new multiethnic entity, the Tibetans in the west and the Mongols in the north manifested their intentions of staying out of the scheme.[53]

When Sun Yat-sen's Guomindang (GMD, Nationalist Party) and the Soviets forged a partnership in advancing China's Nationalist Revolution in the 1920s, Chinese Nationalists briefly saw some advantages in a Soviet-controlled Mongolia. In August 1922, in a letter to Soviet representative Adolf Joffe, Sun Yat-sen accepted Moscow's disclaimer of any territorial ambition in Outer Mongolia and agreed that the Soviet Red Army should continue to be stationed in the territory to forestall foreign imperialist intrigues.[54] In the next few years, Soviet military assistance to the GMD was phenomenal. Buttressed by their alliance with Moscow, Sun and his associates envisioned "immediate unification of the revolutionary Chinese forces in South China, Central Asia and the Far East," and they planned to use Mongolia or Xinjiang as the training base for a Chinese nationalist army or as a launching pad for direct Soviet military interventions on behalf of the Chinese revolution.[55]

---

52. For the anti-Manchu phase of Chinese nationalism, see Kauko Laitinen, *Chinese Nationalism in the Late Qing Dynasty: Zhang Binglin as an Anti-Manchu Propagandist* (London: Curzon Press, 1990). John Fitzgerald, *Awakening China: Politics, Culture, and Class in the Nationalist Revolution* (Stanford, Calif.: Stanford University Press, 1996), 67–102, offers a detailed discussion of the evolution of modern Chinese consciousness from "ethical awakening to national emancipation."

53. Fitzgerald, *Awakening China,* 180–81. Anthony D. Smith, *National Identity* (Reno: University of Nevada Press, 1991), 171, defines "pan-nationalisms" as "movements to unify in a single cultural and political community several, usually contiguous, states on the basis of shared cultural characteristics or a 'family of cultures.'"

54. "Sun Yat-sen's Letter to Joffe, 27 August 1922," in *Gongchan Guoji, Liangong (Bu) yu Zhongguo Geming Dangan Ziliao Congshu* (Selected Archival Materials on the Comintern, Soviet Communist Party [Bolshevik] and the Chinese Revolution; hereafter *GLZD*), 12 vols., comp. First Research Department of the Research Office on the Party History of the CCP Central Committee (Beijing: Beijing Tushuguan Chubanshe, 1997–98, vols. 1–6; Beijing: Zhongyang Wenxian Chubanshe, 2002, vols. 7–12), 2: 393.

55. "Simolanchev's Comment's on the Plan for material assistance to the Nationalist Army and Guangzhou [Canton], 7 October 1925," *GLZD,* 1: 707–9; "Minutes no. 13

At the time, the Mongolia question appeared rather benign to the Soviet–GMD relationship not only because Sun Yat-sen tolerated the Soviet presence in Outer Mongolia in order to get desperately needed Soviet assistance but also because certain pro-China calculations did exist in Soviet foreign policy. At first, to win over Chinese nationalism in their struggle against Western powers, Soviet policy toward China, in the words of Comintern agents, appeared to "have absolutely nothing similar to imperialist powers." In July 1919, in a declaration under the name of Soviet vice commissar for foreign affairs Lev Karakhan, Soviet Russia made a friendly gesture toward China by unilaterally renouncing Russia's old treaty privileges in China.[56]

After Moscow supported Mongolian partisans to gain power in Urga in 1921, Soviet and Comintern agents in China seriously questioned the wisdom of Moscow's Mongolian policy, which stood contradictory to the spirit of 1919. To assuage Chinese anxieties, in late 1923 Karakhan sent a letter to Michael Borodin, the Soviet envoy to Sun Yat-sen, spelling out how Mongolian independence should be explained to the Chinese revolutionaries: The Mongols were driven to independence by China's current conditions and "once China has a democratic and honest government, the Mongols may be willing to join the [Chinese] republic on the basis of some kind of autonomy."[57]

The Karakhan démarche did not prevent the Mongolia question from becoming a cancer in the Soviet–GMD relationship. As long as its cooperation with Moscow and the Chinese Communist Party (CCP) continued, the GMD leadership promised a liberal policy toward the Mongols and China's other non-Han peoples and did not openly fault the Soviet military presence in Outer Mongolia. But with respect to Mongolia's destiny, Sun's attitude

---

of the Meeting of the China Committee of the Russian Communist Party (Bolshevik) Central Politburo, 19 October 1925," ibid., 1: 716–18; Alexander Yurkevich, "History: Military Schools in Sun Yat-sen's Army and Soviet Advisers," *FEA* 2 (2001): 67–82; Mikhail Kriukov, "Once Again about Sun Yatsen's Northwest Plan," *FEA* 5 (2000): 69–84; "Borodin's Notes on the Situation in South China, 10 December 1923," *GLZD*, 1: 366.

56. "On Our Work in Colonies and Semi-Colonies—Especially China; An Outline by Joffe and Snevlit (No Later Than December 1922)," *GLZD*, 2: 405; "Declaration Signed by Karakhan to the Chinese People and to the Governments of North and South China, 25 July 1919," in *Soviet Documents on Foreign Policy,* 4 vols., ed. Jane Degras (New York: Octagon Books, 1978), 1: 158–61.

57. "Joffe's Telegram to Chicherin, 7 and 8 November 1922," *GLZD,* 1: 148; "Karakhan's Letter to Borodin, 27 December 1923," ibid., 1: 389.

was fundamentally in agreement with the then-warlord-controlled Chinese government in Beijing, which was, according to a Comintern agent, "firmly opposed to Mongolian independence." As for Soviet leaders, Japan's activities in Manchuria and Inner Mongolia were sufficient to cause them to reconsider the 1919 policy toward China. In August 1922, Moscow instructed its representatives in China that any negotiations with the Chinese government must *not* be based directly on the Karakhan declaration of 1919 and its corollaries, and that any international discussion of the Mongolia question must include the Mongolian government. Also noteworthy was that the same concern about Japan caused Soviet leaders to decide not to support any element in the GMD military strategy that might be provocative to the Japanese, such as aggressive movements in the direction of Inner Mongolia.[58] Together, these decisions added a complex layer to the Bolsheviks' revolutionary diplomacy toward China and quietly brought back Tsarist Russia's geopolitical stratagems.

In the final analysis, Mongolia became one of the wedges between the GMD and the Soviets because, from the very beginning, the two partners knew that they were just temporary co-travelers pursuing their separate journeys. In April 1927, just a week before Jiang Jieshi turned his guns against the CCP, at a party conference in Moscow Stalin defended the policy of cooperation with the GMD in China in a rather cynical way. Although admitting that the current Chinese revolution under the GMD leadership was "bourgeois" in nature and that the right wing of the party was gaining ground, Stalin argued nevertheless that "I think suchlike people as the rightists should be used to the dregs. Squeeze what you can squeeze out of them, and then throw [them] away like a lemon squeezed dry. Whoever does otherwise, he is stupid, I think."[59] Stalin won the debate in Moscow but, in his Machiavellian contest with Jiang in China, Stalin was the one who was soon thrown out like a juiceless lemon.

Although Jiang shared Sun Yat-sen's conviction that the GMD needed Soviet help to become a viable force in Chinese politics, he was among

58. "Joffe's Telegram to Chicherin"; "Wu Peifu's Letter to Joffe, 20 November 1922," *GLZD,* 1: 160; "Minutes no. 24 of the Meeting of the Russian Communist Party (Bolshevik) Central Politburo, 31 August 1922," ibid., 1: 114–15; "Minutes no. 53 of the Meeting of the Russian Communist Party (Bolshevik) Central Politburo, 8 March 1923," ibid., 1: 225–26.

59. "Joseph Stalin's Unpublished Speech on China [5 April 1927, at a Meeting of Party Activists of the Moscow Committee of the All-Union Communist Party (Bolshevik)]," *FEA,* 1 (2001): 64–79.

those GMD principals who harbored an innate distrust of Bolshevism and Moscow's motives. Given the Soviets' disingenuous rhetoric about their intention in Mongolia after conducting a successful military intervention there, it was no accident that Jiang's abhorrence of the Bolsheviks was brought to the surface by the Mongolia question. A military professional and a staunch nationalist, Jiang regarded Chinese sovereignty over China proper and the borderlands alike as a matter of power. When Tibet and Outer Mongolia became estranged from China upon the formation of the ROC, Jiang called these developments "treason" on the Mongols' and Tibetans' part and advocated military expeditions to restore China's control.[60]

In late 1923, Jiang led a GMD delegation to Russia to promote Sun Yat-sen's strategic plan for cooperating with Moscow in borderlands such as Xinjiang and Mongolia. Disheartened by Soviet leaders' aloofness toward the strategy and offended by their lectures on how the Chinese should reform their dealings with frontier ethnic minorities, Jiang returned to China an angry man. In a letter to a GMD colleague, he asserted that Moscow's China policy was to "turn Manchuria, Mongolia, Hui territory [Xinjiang], and Tibet into its soviets, and probably to have a hand in China proper as well." In his opinion, Moscow's "so-called internationalism and world revolution are not different from Caesar's imperialism except their deceitful names."[61]

Yet, as long as the GMD was still in need of Soviet assistance, it remained part of an amorphous antiwarlord coalition that Moscow helped organize. In northern China, this coalition included the GMD, the CCP, Mongolian partisans from both Outer and Inner Mongolia, and, for a while, the "Christian general" Feng Yuxiang.[62] This artificial coalition came to an end in April

60. Jiang Jieshi, "A Fundamental Solution of the Mongolia-Tibet Question" and "A Preliminary Discussion of Military Expedition against Mongolia," in *Xian Zongtong Jiang Gong Sixiang Yanlun Zongji* (Complete Works of the Late President Jiang [Jeshi]), 40 vols., comp. Historical Council of the Guomindang (Taipei: Guomindang Dangshi Weiyuanhui, 1984), 35: 16–22, 37–55. These essays were originally published in *Junsheng Zaizhi* (Military Forum Magazine) in 1912.

61. "Balanovskii's Report on the Meeting between the GMD Delegation and Sklianskii and Kamenev, 13 November 1923," *GLZD*, 1: 309–13; "Shorthand Minutes of the Meeting of the Comintern Executive Committee Participated by the GMD Delegation, 26 November 1923," ibid., 330–38; "Balanovskii's Report on the GMD Delegation's Visit of Trotsky, 27 November 1923," ibid., 339–41; Second Historical Archives of China, *Jiang Jieshi Nianpu Chugao* (Preliminary Draft of the Chronicle of Jiang Jieshi's Life) (Beijing: Dang'an Chubanshe, 1992), 137–38, 140, 167.

62. "Qijia's [code name for the CCP center] Opinion on the Work of Inner Mongolian GMD, December 1926," *Minzu Wenti Wenxian Huibian* (Collected Documents on

1927, when Jiang surprised the CCP with a bloody purge in Shanghai. The GMD/CCP split marked the beginning of a deadly struggle between the two wings of Chinese nationalism. An ethnopolitical consequence of the event was that, by turning against the Soviet bloc, the GMD severed its revolutionary ties to Outer Mongolia. From then on, the GMD authorities could only make some hollow legal claims on the northern territory.

After Jiang Jieshi launched his "National Government" in Nanjing in 1928, the ROC remained an administrative sham. In many provinces, the GMD regime's "central" authority existed in name only and was maintained by a delicate balance of political and military power between the GMD and local forces. In the meantime, Outer Mongolia and Tibet were designated by the government as the ROC's two "special districts," even though to these areas Nanjing's authority did not exist even in name. In mid-1929, a resolution of the GMD Central Committee admitted that the party-state's "tutelage" was yet to cover these borderlands. In the document, the Mongols and Tibetans were defined as part of *zhonghua minzu* (the Chinese nation) and as two peoples that should be salvaged with the Three People's Principles and be enlightened to regain "consciousness of [their Chinese] ancestral origins" (*shizong*).[63]

The GMD's 1929 resolution revealed a painful admission by its authors that neither the party's political indoctrination nor its military prowess could reach these estranged borderlands. While achieving an upper hand in its military campaigns against the CCP and other local Chinese forces, Nanjing watched helplessly the radicalization of the Outer Mongolian society. In early 1931, alarmed by the rapid communization of Mongolia, Nanjing's military authorities warned the GMD Central Committee that if the trend continued, in the near future the Soviet Union would be able to use a red Mongolian military force to threaten China's northern frontiers. For the moment, however, the question facing the Chinese government was how

---

the Nationality Question; hereafter *MWWH*), comp. United Front Department of the Central Committee of the Chinese Communist Party (Internal circulation; Beijing: Zhonggong Zhongyang Dangxiao Chubanshe, 1991), 50; "Letter from Inner Mongolian GMD to Chinese GMD, 8 November 1926," ibid., 51.

63. Resolution by the Second Conference of the Third Executive Committee of GMD Central Committee on Mongolia and Tibet, 17 June 1929, Quanzonghao (general record number; hereafter QZH) 141 / 72. The usual translation of *zhonghua minzu*, "Chinese nation," should not be confused with the Han nationality (*hanzu*). In modern China's political discourse, as shown in this document, *zhonghua minzu* is often used as a collective but nonetheless Han-centric identity for all ethnic groups of China.

to deal with a wave of refugees who were fleeing Sovietizing Mongolia. The situation gave certain confidence to GMD officials that the ROC could lure Outer Mongols back after all. For the purpose, Nanjing adopted certain "preliminary steps to recover Outer Mongolia," including the establishment of secret liaison posts along the border, favorable treatment for refugees from Outer Mongolia, and a lenient policy for Inner Mongol students who returned from Outer Mongolia and showed no obvious "reactionary" (pro-communist) tendencies.[64] Given the GMD government's focus on the war against the CCP, a more aggressive reaction to the situation in the MPR was impractical. Shortly after, Ulaanbaatar stabilized conditions in the MPR and thus rendered Nanjing's measures irrelevant.

During the rest of the 1930s, the GMD government's policy toward Outer Mongolia changed gradually. The assertive irredentism that characterized the GMD's earlier revolutionary years proved hollow, because the party had no power to implement the goal. Now GMD leaders' bitterness toward Moscow's cynical revolutionary diplomacy was replaced with a political realism. None other than Jiang Jieshi himself called for a pragmatic approach in dealing with China's frontier crises. In March 1934, in a speech to a small circle of GMD officials, he told those present that all China's frontier crises were entangled with diplomacy with certain great powers and China was not ready to settle these issues from a position of strength. Therefore, according to Jiang, while continuing to strengthen itself materially, the GMD government must be able to win over the hearts of the frontier peoples, for "when people come, their land will come as well." Noticeably, in Jiang's opinion, Moscow's policy toward its own ethnic minorities, though wily and hypocritical, could serve as a successful model for China to settle its ethnic and territorial problems. He suggested that China "learn from Soviet Russia's 'free federation'" scheme and substitute the earlier formula of "five-race republic" with one of "five-race federation."[65]

The GMD's ethnopolitical approach, however, would not enter history as

64. Secretariat of the GMD Central Executive Committee to the National Government, 3 April 1931, and Enclosure: General Staff, "The Communists' Activities in Mongolia and Inside China," QZH 1(2) / 441; Executive Yuan to National Government, 7 April 1931, and Enclosure: Mongolian and Tibetan Affairs Commission, "Outline on Preliminary Steps to Recover Outer Mongolia," ibid.

65. Jiang Jieshi, "China's Frontier Problems, 7 March 1934," speech made at his official residence in Nanchang, Historical Council of the Guomindang, *Xian Zongtong Jiang Gong Sixiang Yanlun Zongji* (Complete Works of the Late President Jiang [Jieshi]), 40 vols. (Taipei: Guomindang Dangshi Weiyuanhui, 1984), 12: 105–10.

a variant of the Soviet model. Caught in a dilemma between continuing his "annihilation campaigns" against the CCP in interior China and staging a resistance against the aggressive Japanese in Manchuria, Jiang was attracted to the Bolshevik precedent as a temporary, passive tactic, which could hopefully anaesthetize the pain caused by China's frontier crises before the supposed cure, or strong Chinese power, became ready. This tactic was destined to fail on two counts: First, Jiang misunderstood the Bolshevik formula as conciliatory rhetoric, whereas it was an aggressive revolutionary strategy for cultivating and controlling "socialist elements" within the minorities; second, as of the 1930s, the ethnopolitical aspirations of the frontier groups had already passed the stage at which they might be sedated by limited, symbolic concessions from the Chinese authorities.

A case in point was the Inner Mongolian autonomous movement under Prince Demchugdongrob (Prince De). The movement was an Inner Mongolian response to the Chinese authorities' intensified effort of sinicization and political centralization and to the critical situation of northern China caused by Japan's aggression after 1931. In late September and early October 1933, delegates from Inner Mongolian banners met in Beile-yin sume (Bailingmiao) of Ulanchab League and organized an "Inner Mongolian Autonomous Government." Although Jiang Jieshi adopted what he believed was a very "accommodating" attitude toward the Inner Mongols' autonomous demands, Prince De was soon frustrated by the Chinese authorities' intransigence and turned to the Japanese for assistance.[66] To the GMD authorities, Prince De's decision to collaborate with the Japanese only proved the futility of the government's conciliatory approach to ethnic autonomists. After the experience, Jiang would never make reference to the Soviet model again, though occasionally he still received such advice from individual GMD officials or foreign advisers. The GMD's new party line was that none of the existing models in the world was suitable for China's ethnic frontier problems and these problems must be settled solely in accordance with the needs of China's national defense and other interests.[67]

66. Sechin Jagchid, *The Last Mongol Prince: The Life and Times of Demchugdongrob, 1902–1966* (Bellingham: Western Washington University Press, 1999), 60–124, discusses Prince De's movement in detail. In his March 1934 speech, Jiang actually used Prince De as an example of his new liberal treatment of the frontier minorities.

67. Sun Fo to Chiang Kai-shek, 7 August 1938, in *Zhonghua Minguo Zhongyao Shiliao Chubian: Dui Ri Kangzhan Shiqi* (Preliminary Compilation of Important Historical Records of the Republic of China: The Period of the War of Resistance against Japan; hereafter *ZZSC*), 7 vols., comp. Historical Council of the Guomindang (Taipei:

Meanwhile, to the GMD regime, the Soviet Union became the lesser evil in comparison with Japanese aggression. In March 1936, Moscow and Ulaanbaatar concluded a pact of mutual assistance in violating Chinese sovereignty in Outer Mongolia as prescribed by the Sino-Soviet treaty of 1924. Afterward, the Chinese government only made a restrained protest to Moscow. The GMD's official organ, *Zhongyang Ribao* (Central Daily), told its readers that the "principal purpose of the pact is of course for Soviet assistance to Outer Mongolia's defense against foreign aggression. . . . So far as its motive and function are concerned, the pact should not be compared with the Japanese–puppet [Manchurian] agreement of 1931."[68] From this point onward, the meaning of the Mongolia question to GMD officials seemed to have changed. Nanjing rediscovered a certain value in the Soviet domination of Outer Mongolia.

Soon the GMD government tried to put the value to use. In October 1937, Jiang Jieshi instructed his representatives in Moscow to find out whether or not, at the forthcoming international conference in Brussels on the Far Eastern crisis, China's and Soviet Union's interests in Outer Mongolia could serve as basis for their "common action" against Japan. By this time, the GMD and the CCP had already stopped their civil war for the sake of a national war against Japan. The prospect of Nanjing–Moscow cooperation in containing Japan became more promising than ever. Although the Brussels conference ended in failure, the Soviet Union soon became the principal supplier of the Chinese government's war effort. In the meantime, Stalin sent words to Jiang that the Soviet Union had absolutely no ambitions in Outer Mongolia and Xinjiang. He asked Jiang to trust him on this.[69]

In July–August 1938 and then again in May 1939, Soviet–Japanese military conflicts broke out at Zhanggufeng and Nomonhan, two locations along

---

Guomindang Dangshi Weiyuanhui, 1981), 3(2): 408–9; Owen Lattimore's memo for Chiang Kai-shek, "Memorandum on Outer Mongolia, September 1941," Jiang Zhong-zheng Zongtong Dang'an: Geming Wenxian (Kangzhan Shiqi), Academia Historica, Taipei (Archives of President Jiang Jieshi: Revolutionary Documents [Period of the War of Resistance]; hereafter JZZD / GW [KZS]), 35: 55–61; position paper by the Mongolian and Tibetan Affairs Commission, "Outline Plan for Postwar Frontier Administrative Reconstruction, 1943," QZH 141/112.

68. "Pact of Mutual Assistance with the Mongolian People's Republic, 12 March 1936," in *Soviet Documents,* ed. Degras, 168–70; "Editorial of *Zhongyang Ribao:* Protest against Soviet–Mongolian Agreement, 8 April 1936," *ZSGG,* 3: 27–28.

69. Jiang Jieshi to Jiang Tingfu (ambassador to Moscow), 22 October 1937, *ZZSC,* 3(2): 333; Sun Ke (Sun Fo) to Jiang Jieshi, 7 February 1938, ibid., 407–8.

the Soviet–Manchurian and MPR–Manchurian borders. Jiang seized these occasions to urge Moscow not to reach any compromise with Japan. Furthermore, he asked Stalin to use Soviet military forces along the Mongolian–Manchurian border to distract the Japanese Army from China.[70] During the Nomonhan conflict, Stalin informed the Chinese government that the Soviet Red Army was fighting the Japanese in pursuance of the Soviet–Mongolian pact of 1936. The military and legal implications of these events would later lead historians to conclude that the brief Soviet–Japanese conflicts between 1938 and 1939 resulted in the "final consolidation of the USSR's sphere of influence in Outer Mongolia." At the time, however, the ominous implications of these events to the Chinese claim of sovereignty in Outer Mongolia seemed secondary to the GMD government. The utmost important matter was to keep the Russians and Japanese apart. As Jiang told Soviet leaders, as long as they did not reach an agreement with the Japanese on the boundaries between Mongolia and the "Manchukuo," the Chinese would believe that the "Soviet Union has always stood for justice."[71]

The Sino-Soviet intimacy during China's war against Japan, however, did not restore the quasi-bloc relationship between the two sides in the 1920s. The wartime geopolitics only helped deprioritize the GMD government's opposition to Soviet involvement in China's ethnic frontiers. In the war years, China's northwestern province Xinjiang, which had been controlled by local warlords in close collaboration with the Soviet Union, became a principal gateway for the GMD government to receive assistance from Moscow. In the meantime, a line between Ulaanbaatar and Lanzhou, the capital city of China's Gansu Province, was designated as an alternate route for Soviet convoys to reach China. To take advantage of the new Chinese–Soviet rapprochement, some of Jiang's close advisers proposed to him that a new road via Outer Mongolia be opened to connect Soviet Siberia with

70. Jiang Jieshi to Yang Jie (ambassador to Moscow), 27 July 1938, *ZZSC,* 3(2): 342; entries on 20 and 22 September 1939, Wang Shijie, *Wang Shijie Riji* (Wang Shijie Diaries) (Taipei: Zhongyang Yanjiuyuan Jidaishi Yanjiusuo, 1990), 2: 153, 154–55; Jiang Jieshi's Conversation with the Soviet Ambassador, 8 November 1939, *ZZSC,* 3(2): 350–55.

71. Sun Ke to Jiang Jieshi, 24 June 1939, *ZZSC,* 3(2): 422–23; He Yaozu to Jiang Jieshi, 28 April 1940, ibid., 373; Bruce A. Elleman, "The Final Consolidation of the USSR's Sphere of Influence in Outer Mongolia," in *Mongolia,* ed. Kotkin and Elleman, 123–36. The Soviets, of course, did not maintain "justice" for long. In May 1942, a border agreement was reached between the MPR and the "Manchukuo." The Chinese government watched the development helplessly. See entry on 15 May 1942, Wang Shijie, *Wang Shijie Riji,* 3: 296–97.

Ningxia province in China. Intended to facilitate transportation of Soviet materials to China, such a project would require tabling the question of Outer Mongolia's legal status. Yet, according to supporters of the idea, in the long run, the proposed road could reintroduce Chinese influence into Outer Mongolia.[72] Eventually, the scheme was not implemented, partly because the proposed route was too close to Japan's military force in Inner Mongolia and partly because the Soviet leadership did not want to involve the MPR prematurely in China's war with Japan.

April 13, 1941, was one of the darker days during the GMD government's resistance against Japan. On that day, Moscow and Tokyo concluded a treaty of neutrality and declared mutual respect for the "territorial integrity" of the MPR and the "Manchukuo." The next day, GMD principals met for three hours to deliberate how to react. In the end, they decided to continue the low-key approach. The Chinese government would reiterate its sovereignty over the two territories in question but would make the statement unprovocative to Moscow.[73] This orientation was adopted, despite the fact that GMD leaders were really saddened by Moscow's acceptance of neutrality with Japan and failure to "stand for justice," as expected by Jiang.

During the war years, the GMD government and the MPR had very little contact with each other. The divide between Inner and Outer Mongolia became significantly formalized in these years because of the policies enforced by both sides. The GMD regime tightened border control, reversing its earlier policy of accommodating Outer Mongols who crossed the border without permission. Incremental punitive measures were adopted to deal with violators and repeated violators, regardless of whether these were common criminals, smugglers, or political refugees. Generally, all captured perpetrators would be expelled back to the MPR. Only occasionally were exceptions made for educated political dissidents who might provide useful intelligence to the Chinese military. Because the border between the

---

72. Yuri Gradov, "A Convoy on the Pass," *FEA* 3 (1990): 175–87, and 4 (1990): 107–20; Liu Tangling, "Recollections on the Trip to the Soviet Union to Purchase Weapons for the Resistance against Japan," *Xinjiang Wenshi Ziliao* (Literary and Historical Materials of Xinjiang) 24 (1992): 1–21; Wu Zhongxin to Jiang Jieshi, 19 March 1941, QZH 141/223.

73. "Soviet–Japanese Neutrality Pact and Joint Declaration, 13 April 1941," in *Soviet Documents,* ed. Degras, 3: 486–87; entry on 14 April 1941, Wang Shijie, *Wang Shijie Riji,* 3: 57; Chinese Foreign Ministry's Statement on the Soviet–Japanese Neutrality Pact, 14 April 1941, *ZZSC,* 3(2): 390; Stalin to Jiang Jieshi, 12 December 1941, ibid., 391–92.

two parts of Mongolia was long and difficult to guard by regular forces, the Chinese authorities stationed "self-supplied" Mongolian families along the border to undertake tasks of border patrol and information collection, a method used first by the MPR with certain effectiveness.[74] Thus, although the border was watched over by Mongols on both sides, the distinction between the "Chinese side" and the "Mongolian side" of the artificial line increasingly adopted an "international" appearance.

In November 1941 and again in January 1942, the MPR sent an envoy, named Baatarhu, to the Chinese side of the border and met with Chinese officials in Ejine Banner, the westernmost banner of Inner Mongolia. These were followed by a Chinese mission to an unidentified location on the Mongolian side. In the official records of the Chinese government, these were the only Chinese–Mongolian official contacts throughout the war. Initially, the Chinese side was led to think that the MPR was interested in discussing with China common defense measures against Japan. But later it became clear that, with or without Ulaanbaatar's knowledge, the government of Gobi Altai, a frontier province of the MPR, initiated the contact and was solely interested in reaching some understanding with the local Chinese authorities about border control.

These encounters are nevertheless interesting in revealing how far apart the two societies on the different sides of the border had become since the 1920s. As astonishing was the two sides' mutual ignorance about each other's "achievements" in Sovietization and in "nationalization" of the GMD sense. In their conversations, Chinese officials barraged Baatarhu with questions about the political, economic, and military systems in the MPR. As for Baatarhu, he had some idea about the Three People's Principles as the official creed of the ROC but was ignorant about who was the current leader of the Chinese government. He brought some communist literature to his Chinese counterparts as gifts, apparently unaware of his hosts' political orientation. He seemed genuinely puzzled by the material poverty on the Chinese side of the border and by lamas' continued existence under the party government of the GMD.[75]

74. Council of Military Affairs, "Measures for Dealing with Outer Mongols who Crossed the border," 11 July 1940, QZH 141/1202; Alashan Banner to the Mongolian and Tibetan Affairs Commission, "Measures to Prevent Outer Mongolian Intrusion," 21 April 1942, QZH 141/1783.

75. Reports by the "Hehuang Investigative Group," 11 and 12 March 1942, and enclosures: (1) Chinese translations of Outer Mongol Baatarhu's passport and official letter, and (2) "Record of Interrogation of Baatarhu from Outer Mongolia by Officials of the

Partisan, National, and Imperial Interests

Power, no matter whether perceived as Soviet prowess or China's weakness or Soviet–Japanese balance, was certainly a most important factor contributing to Outer Mongolia's separation from China. But it was the diverging sociopolitical developments as exposed by the Baatarhu episode that eventually engraved a "Chinese" or a "Mongolian" identity onto the Mongolian groups separated by the border.[76] In the 1930s, Owen Lattimore wrote the best-informed essays of the time about historical and tribal distinctions among different Mongolian groups and about how the "Chinese" and the "Mongols" had "turned" into each other, or adopted each other's identities, as part of the Inner Asian frontier experience.[77]

In 1941, however, when advising Jiang Jieshi on the Mongolia question in his capacity as Jiang's political adviser, Lattimore became very conscious that the sociopolitical divergence between the MPR and Mongolian society on the Chinese side far exceeded their historical and tribal differences. He suggested to Jiang that the GMD government liberalize its ethnic policies to pave the way for Outer Mongolia's reunion with China. But, Lattimore argued, because communist influence in Outer Mongolia was so strong, Inner and Outer Mongolia should remain segregated even after Outer Mongolia's independence was abolished. He told Jiang that continued Outer Mongolian autonomy would actually be beneficial to China as a quarantine measure against the spread of communism.[78]

In accepting Lattimore's diagnosis about the distance between China and a socially and politically transformed Outer Mongolia, GMD officials were nevertheless unequivocal about erasing the distance. In the GMD

Ejine Banner and the Special Military Office in the Ejine Banner," QZH 141/1220. The "Hehuang Investigative Group" seems part of the GMD's secret service.

76. The "Hybridity" of the Mongolian identity is the subject of Uradyn E. Bulag's fascinating anthropological study, *Nationalism and Hybridity in Mongolia* (Oxford: Oxford University Press, 1998), in which (pp. 4–5) the author, a Mongol born in China, tells his own puzzling experience of being regarded not as a "Mongol, but an Inner Mongol" or "worse still . . . as Chinese" during his visit in Mongolia in 1990.

77. Owen Lattimore, "The Geographical Factor in Mongol History" (orig. pub. *Geographical Journal,* January 1938) and "The Historical Setting of Inner Mongolia Nationalism" (orig. pub. *Pacific Affairs,* September 1936), in Lattimore, *Studies in Frontier History,* 241–58, 440–55.

78. Owen Lattimore's memo to Jiang Jieshi, "Memorandum on Outer Mongolia, September 1941," JZZD / GW (KZS), 35: 55–61.

government, two distinct schools of thoughts existed with respect to the problem's solution. Echoing Jiang's prewar idea about winning Mongolian "hearts" before recovering Mongolian "land," the Ministry of Foreign Affairs stressed that the abolition of Outer Mongolia's independence would hinge on the growth of its population's centripetal tendency toward China. Conceding that Chinese diplomacy would have an uphill fight against Soviet influence in Mongolia, the Ministry of Foreign Affairs identified domestic political efforts in China as the most effective means to lure the Mongols back. Necessarily, this line of action would require patience and could not be implemented when China was still in the middle of war.[79]

Sharply against this domestic-political approach was a diplomatic-military position held by some officials in the military sector. According to these officials, the frontier peoples' strong ethnopolitical aspirations were partially fostered by the Chinese government's own inconsistent policies in the past, which in different times were either overly harsh or excessively loose toward the minorities. Especially harmful to China's purpose was the idea of self-determination that "actually put the weak and small nations in a position superior [to the Han]." In their opinion, the Mongolia and Tibet questions were not about "people" but about "territory." By nature, these were not "domestic" but "diplomatic" problems, whose solution had to rely on diplomacy backed by military strength. Accordingly, the best timing for solving the Mongolia question would depend on how the war and international alignments in Europe and Asia could weaken the Soviet Union and strengthen China. In this regard, a catastrophe for the Soviet Union, either from its current war with Germany or caused by a Japanese invasion, would be a welcome development.[80]

Obviously, the two groups were pursuing the same goal, which, expressed in typical GMD terminology, was to "establish a unitary culture of the state nation [*guozu*], dissolve the parochial barriers between the clans [*zongzu*], and complete the construction of an integral great *zhonghua minzu* [Chinese nation]."[81] As long as China's long and arduous war against Japan continued,

79. Memo by the Ministry of Foreign Affairs, "Achieve Territorial and Sovereign Integrity of our Country, 7 June 1943," Victor (Shize) Hoo Papers, box 3.

80. Counselors Office of the National Military Council to Jiang Jieshi, September 1944, QZH 761/171, Second Historical Archives of China; He Yingqin to Jiang Jieshi, 13 July 1942, *ZZSC*, 3(2): 438–40.

81. Mongolian and Tibetan Affairs Commission, "Outline Plan for Postwar Frontier Administrative Reconstruction, 1943," QZH 141/112. In the war years, the GMD regime no longer use *minzu* (nation) to refer to China's non-Han ethnic groups. Instead, Jiang

neither of the two proposed lines of action had a chance. The vicissitudes of the Soviet Union's military fortunes in World War II never created an opening in Outer Mongolia for the GMD government to step in. Nor could the GMD regime even begin serious "party work" toward either Mongolia or Tibet when it was itself pressed by the Japanese Army into China's southwestern corner. Thus, the only area left for the GMD government to maneuver was the unpredictable arena of wartime diplomacy.

Unlike its predecessors during the Qing and the early years of the ROC, the GMD government engaged the international community extensively in dealing with its continual domestic and foreign crises. China's war of resistance against Japan especially led to an unprecedented activism of Chinese diplomacy in the international scene. In World War II, as a member of the Grand Alliance against the Axis Powers, the GMD government assumed a new international persona and had to act accordingly. A question could not be evaded by GMD officials: Though fighting against the Axis Powers' aggression and championing deliverance of the Asian peoples from Japanese imperialism as well as Western colonialism, how should the Chinese government reconcile its public foreign policy with its "private" domestic policy toward China's frontier regions?

Generally, in the war years, the GMD government avoided raising questions concerning the status of Mongolia and Tibet on international occasions lest such discussions provoke the British and the Russians or unnecessarily force China itself to commit to a public stand. Yet in inter-Allied consultations about a postwar peace order, subjects such as "ethnic minorities' rights," "independence against aggressions," and "decolonization" could have important ramifications for China's own frontier problems. One view in the GMD government regarded China as a repressed national state and considered all these subjects as part of China's foreign affairs. Accordingly, after the war, foreign governments' treatment of "Chinese minorities" overseas must be improved, China's security against foreign aggression must be guaranteed, and foreign encroachment on Chinese territories, including those ethnic borderlands, must be redressed. A dissenting opinion argued that while working toward decolonizing Western colonies, the Chinese government could not pretend that China did not have its own problems of colonialism in Tibet and Mongolia. In the war years, GMD diplomacy forged

---

Jieshi's *China's Destiny* (1943) established a new practice of defining all these groups as branch *zongzu* (clans) of the Chinese nation.

ahead largely according to the first view. But the second view often gave GMD diplomats pause about how to proceed with Western allies in advancing a rather assertive Chinese agenda for the causes of China and Asia's colonial peoples.[82]

Because the Western allies' war effort in Asia was anchored in China's cooperation and ability to stay in the war, they, especially the United States, promoted China's image as a "great power." This allowed the GMD government to present the ROC on the international scene as an integral entity and to trumpet its legal sovereignty over all territories bequeathed by the Qing Empire. In late 1944 and early 1945, however, the trend of international politics changed in East Asia with the Western allies' active quest for Soviet participation in the Pacific war. In February, 1945, a secret tripartite pact was concluded at Yalta, in which the American and British governments supported a string of territorial demands made by Stalin in return for his agreement to enter the war against Japan. In this deal, the pretensions about China's great power status were discarded, and the ROC's de jure sovereignty over Manchuria and Mongolia did not prevent the "Big Three" from allocating "rights" in these territories to the Soviet Union. Then, in August, after a series of strenuous negotiations in Moscow, the GMD and Soviet governments concluded a treaty that basically confirmed the result of the Yalta agreement.

An immediate consequence of the Sino-Soviet treaty was a plebiscite held in the MPR in October 1945, which was designed more for China's procedural approval of MPR independence than for testing the popular will in Mongolia. In January 1946, the Chinese government recognized the legality of the plebiscite. Thus, as far as the protracted ROC–MPR competition for the Qing heritage was concerned, World War II produced a remarkable result: The internationally solitary MPR prevailed in its defiance of one of the wartime "Big Four," the supposed Chinese "great power." Yet, surely, ever

---

82. "Draft Memo for Chinese Delegation to the Institute of Pacific Relations Conference," 7 November 1942, V. K. Wellington Koo Papers, box 58; memo by the Ministry of Foreign Affairs, "Postwar International Peace Organization and Other Related issues," (1944), Victor Hoo Papers, box 7; Jiang Jieshi to the Chinese Delegation to the Dumbarton Oaks Conference, 19 August 1944, Koo Papers, box 70; "Notes of the Chinese Delegation's Private Meetings at Dumbarton Oaks," 30 September 1944, Koo Papers, box 75; Hsu Shu-hsi to T. V. Soong, 20 January 1945, T. V. Soong Papers, box 30; "Notes of Conversation with Commander Harold E. Stassen," 18 May 1945, Koo Papers, box 77; Gu Weijun (Wellington Koo), *Gu Weijun Huiyilu* (Memoirs of Gu Weijun), 12 vols. (Beijing: Zhonghua Shuju, 1983–93), 5: 532.

since the 1920s, the Chinese government had mainly competed with Moscow, not Ulaanbaatar, over Outer Mongolia. The Mongolian plebiscite in October 1945 would not have taken place without the bargaining between the Chinese and the Russians in Moscow.

   Sino-Soviet diplomacy at the end of the war has been the subject of several detailed studies, and there is no need to recycle the information here.[83] The historical significance of the event to the Mongolia question should, however, be clarified. At first glance, the success of Soviet diplomacy seemed to indicate a sudden change in China's legal fortune. Until the Moscow negotiations, legally speaking, the Chinese government had stood on rather solid ground. Despite its long separation from China, the MPR was not recognized by the international community as an independent state. As mentioned above, even the Soviet Union regarded Outer Mongolia as under Chinese sovereignty in its 1924 treaty with China.[84] At a time when the world was divided by war, the series of bilateral agreements between Moscow and Ulaanbaatar certainly could not make the MPR's independence more legal than the statehood of Japan's puppet "Manchukuo." The "legality" of both would depend on how the war would conclude. In 1932, a public memorandum issued by the American Council of the Institute of Pacific Relations defined Outer Mongolia as "one of the peripheral provinces of China . . . being absorbed by neighboring states," and compared the Soviet position in Outer Mongolia with Japan's in Manchuria.[85] Such a view was probably typical in the West, and it was also the very reason why Stalin included Mongolia in his bargaining with the American and British leaders at Yalta.

---

83. For three different interpretations of the Moscow diplomacy, see John W. Garver, *Chinese–Soviet Relations, 1937–1945: The Diplomacy of Chinese Nationalism* (New York: Oxford University Press, 1988), 214–30, Odd Arne Westad, *Cold War and Revolution: Soviet–American Rivalry and the Origins of the Chinese Civil War, 1944–1946* (New York: Columbia University Press, 1993), 31–56, and Xiaoyuan Liu, *A Partnership for Disorder: China, the United States, and Their Policies for the Postwar Disposition of the Japanese Empire, 1941–1945* (Cambridge: Cambridge University Press, 1996), 258–86. Outer Mongolia was an important item in the Sino-Soviet negotiations.

84. Memo by the Ministry of Foreign Affairs, "Chairman's [Chiang Kai-shek] Directives on Diplomacy" (1944), Hoo Papers, box 3, suggested that China must not negotiate with the British over Tibet lest compromise its previous legal standing on the matter, but that a Sino-Soviet talk over Outer Mongolia could be conducted with the 1924 treaty as a guideline.

85. American Council of the Institute of Pacific Affairs, "Memorandum on Outer Mongolia," *Memorandum,* 1 (14) (August 3, 1932): 1–3.

The result was the Western allies' support for continuation of the ambiguous "status quo" of Mongolia. The secret Yalta agreement, therefore, neither changed the legal status of the MPR nor obliged the Chinese government to include the Mongolia question in its own diplomatic agenda with Moscow. Shortly after the Yalta diplomacy, President Franklin D. Roosevelt told the Chinese ambassador that "Outer Mongolia's status quo does not seem to present any problem because the sovereignty will remain Chinese." This provided the GMD government with a safety margin so that its leaders decided not to include Mongolia in their agenda for the Moscow diplomacy.[86]

Yet, as soon as the negotiations in Moscow began, Stalin insisted on including MPR independence in the prospective Sino-Soviet treaty and thereby forced the GMD leaders to discuss the problem hastily among themselves. In the end, the Chinese reluctantly agreed to make Mongolian independence part of their concessions to Moscow. These concessions were made as trade-offs for certain legal restraints on Soviet expansion in northeastern and northwestern China and for Moscow's "correct" behavior regarding the GMD–CCP power struggle in China. In their agreements with the GMD regime, the Soviets indeed pledged to respect China's sovereignty in Manchuria and Xinjiang as well as to give "moral, military, and other materials assistance" only to the "Nationalist Government" of China. With these understandings in the background, the MPR plebiscite was held according to the script prepared by Sino-Soviet diplomacy in Moscow.[87]

Without question, in Moscow, the GMD diplomacy made concessions on the Mongolia question under duress. Historians, however, cannot agree to what extent the diplomacy was opportunistic and sacrificed China's national interests in exchange for the GMD's partisan advantages.[88] The question about the GMD regime's "national" or "partisan" identity aside,

86. Wei Daoming to Jiang Jieshi, 12 March 1945, *ZZSC*, 3(2): 542; entry on 25 June 1945, Wang Shijie, *Wang Shijie Riji*, 4: 111–12.

87. Liu, *Partnership for Disorder*, 258–86; Shirendev, *Through the Ocean Waves*, 114–18, offers an interesting discussion of the author's personal experience in organizing the October plebiscite. It should be pointed out that during the GMD regime's confused deliberation about China's postwar interests, Jiang once considered a different kind of trade-off in offering some privileges in Manchuria to the Soviet Union in exchange for its "good attitude" toward China's sovereignty in Outer Mongolia. See Jiang Jieshi to Song Meiling (Madam Chiang), 18 June 1943, *ZZSC*, 3(1): 853–54.

88. Garver, *Chinese–Soviet Relations*, 214–30; and Westad, *Cold War and Revolution*, 31–56.

it should be noted that like all of China's previous humiliating diplomatic experiences since the mid–nineteenth century, the Moscow diplomacy performed a role in clarifying China's *national* interests.

During the first half of the twentieth century, Chinese political discourse extensively publicized two cardinal goals of China's national struggle: abolition of the "unequal treaties," and recovery of the "lost territories." These were two marks of *national* humiliation because China was projected as a national state in the twentieth century. In reality, as policy objectives, these had also been targeted by the Qing government's "imperial" struggle since the Opium War. A paradox of Chinese nationalism was that it sought historical legitimacy in claiming an ability to "restore" completely its imperial enemy's, or the Qing's, political and territorial domains. In this sense, China's "national interest" as defined by Chinese Nationalists was actually a new name for the "imperial interest," including "lost imperial interest," bequeathed by the Qing Dynasty. While focusing on the dual stigma of national humiliations, the Nationalist diplomacy actually concealed the greatest embarrassment for power holders of the ROC—their unsubstantiated claim for a "five-race republic" within the officially delineated national boundaries. Although the late Qing could be blamed for concluding bad treaties and losing territories, it could not be readily blamed for the ROC's failure to continue the Manchus' "five-race empire" under a republican cloak. The estrangements of Mongolia, Tibet, and, in a different manner, Xinjiang did not take place until the end of the Qing. Reestablishment of Chinese authority in these borderlands was indeed part of Chinese political discourse, but the goal never achieved the same status as the two goals mentioned above. It was in this ethnopolitical arena that the Chinese Nationalists faced the most serious challenge in translating the late Qing's "imperial interests" into the "national interests" of a modern Chinese national state.

Whereas the Qing court had maintained its reign over the empire's ethnic frontiers with a combined prowess of superior military power, supraethnic appeal of imperial ideology, and skillfully administered indirect control, the ROC was found wanting in all departments. Aside from military weakness, China's successive "central governments" in the republican period lacked an inclusive ideology and corresponding policies to rally the non-Han frontiers. Both Sun Yat-sen's "five-race republic" doctrine and Jiang Jieshi's "one nation, many clans" creed were efforts for patching up China's fragmented ethnographic landscape. However, as official Chinese ideologies, these were ethnocentric, unilateral, and therefore repulsive to non-Han groups. Last, as a nation-building force, the GMD did not just seek to restore the Qing-type nominal or hegemonic reign over the ethnic frontiers. As stated in a position paper of the Council of Military Affairs, which was the GMD regime's policymaking body in the war years, China did not seek in Mongolia and Tibet merely "sovereignty on paper" but "actual control."[89] The fact, however, was that the ROC's actual authority and power never went beyond the Han ethnographic zones in southern and eastern China. At the time of the Sino-Soviet diplomacy in Moscow, this had been a basic reality of the GMD's party state.

After a short-lived wartime euphoria about China's ability to regain its greatness, Jiang and his associates had to come to terms with this reality. Even though some GMD officials still cherished a hope that China's ambiguous "sovereignty" over Outer Mongolia could be used as a stopgap measure to counter Soviet pressure, such a position was completely divorced from the international political relations emerging at the end of World War II.[90] At least in East Asia and Europe, the international political trend pointed to a two-bloc confrontation that demanded states' unambiguous affiliations and tolerated no murky middle ground. Stalin certainly would not allow the ROC, a close ally of the United States, to retain any lingering legal claim on his first satellite, the MPR. Because the GMD government's domestic and international conditions would not allow it to extend "actual control" into the MPR, its only realistic option was to give up Outer Mongolia in order to consolidate its *actually controlled* political domain.

Consequently, after arguing among themselves for many years about Outer Mongolia's importance to and inseparability from China while delaying a decision, GMD leaders could no longer circumvent the issue when the Moscow diplomacy imposed it on them. They made the choice of relinquishing this "imperial" outer land for the sake of consolidating the "national interests" of the ROC. After the Chinese delegation put up an ineffective resistance to Stalin's pressure in Moscow, Jiang, in a directive to his delegates, agreed to let Outer Mongolia go with these words: "If our country can indeed achieve domestic unification (including the Northeast and Xinjiang), and territory, sovereignty and administration can indeed remain

89. Counselors Office of the Council of Military Affairs to Jiang Jieshi, September 1944, QZH 761/171.

90. Ministry of Foreign Affairs, "Proposed Agendas to be Discussed with America, Britain, and the Soviet Union Outside the San Francisco Conference," 25 March 1945, Koo Papers, box 81, included a "half-independence" formula for Outer Mongolia. Jiang Jieshi also tried the idea with Soviet ambassador in a conversation in late June, as indicated in "Jiang Jieshi–Petrov Converstions, 26 June 1945," *ZZSC,* 3(2): 569–71.

intact, then Outer Mongolia's independence may be considered."[91] Thus, in terms of the GMD's nation-building effort, the Moscow diplomacy performed a historic function in externalizing Outer Mongolia from China's sovereignty and therefore making a landmark distinction between modern China's national interests and traditional China's imperial interests.

In 1945, however, this significance was by no means clear. The Moscow diplomacy did not end the Mongolia question, to say nothing of the troubles in China's other frontier regions. As in the case of the Yalta diplomacy, in Moscow the deal was made between two great powers, but the price was paid by a third, weaker party that had no voice in the negotiations concerning itself. In Moscow, the Mongols' interests and destiny were bargained and decided, and the result, as it has been called, was the "second partition of Mongolia."[92] In retrospect, the partition was a necessary condition for the MPR to continue, which, until the collapse of the Soviet Union, made the Outer Mongols the "only Central Asian people with internationally recognized independence."[93] Yet the 1945 partition of Mongolia was not final to some concerned groups, including the Mongols on both sides of the "border" and the CCP, whose victory in China four years later would put all of China's foreign agreements in question. The Mongolia question was therefore a tangled web woven together with many threads. Its Moscow connection will be explored further in the next chapter.

91. Jiang Jieshi to T. V. Soong, 6 July 1945, *ZZSC*, 3(2): 593–94.

92. Christopher P. Atwood, "Sino-Soviet Diplomacy and the Second Partition of Mongolia, 1945–1946," in *Mongolia,* ed. Kotkin and Elleman, 137–62.

93. Elizabeth E. Green, "China and Mongolia: Recurring Trends and Prospects for Change," *Asian Survey* 26(2) (1986): 1344.

2

"Red Protective Deity":
World Revolution and Geopolitics

When the physical and political maps of any continent are juxtaposed, it can be easily seen how the stylus of human activities has willfully engraved its mark on the natural canvas of the earth. The "geopaths" of these activities may or may not be congruous with the earth's physical features, and, in comparison with the latter, can be easily interrupted, altered, and even obliterated by the eraser of time. At the threshold of the twentieth century, commenting on Asia, the American geostrategist Alfred T. Mahan showed an astute awareness of great powers' wrestling in the ring of space and time: "The division of Asia is east and west; movement is north and south. . . . [There] is assurance that there will continue to be motion until an adjustment is reached, either in the satisfaction of everybody, or by the definite supremacy of some one of the contestants."[1] Mahan's commentary was typical of the high time of imperialism, and his two scenarios for Asia denoted but two modes of great power relationship—balance or hegemony. To historians, China's and Russia's respective positions in this contest seem clear. Whereas "China has been the proving ground for the greatest variety of imperialisms in history" and China's receding boundaries "became the physical incarnation" of the country's repeated frustrations in the hands of Western powers, the continuous aggrandizement of the Russian Empire in modern times, to the Russians, "enshrined their country's great power status."[2]

---

1. A. T. Mahan, *The Problem of Asia and Its Effect upon International Politics* (Port Washington, N.Y.: Kennikat Press, 1970; reprint of 1900 ed.), 23.
2. David Shimmelpenninck van der Oye, *Toward the Rising Sun: Russian Ideologies of Empire and the Path to War with Japan* (Dekalb: Northern Illinois University Press, 2001), 196; S. C. M. Paine, *Imperial Rivals* (Armonk, N.Y.: M. E. Sharpe, 1996), 9.

Yet, in both Mahan's macro-landscape of great power movements and historians' dichotomy between the predatory Western powers and the victimized China, a school of "baby otters between two rocks," or the peoples along China's peripheries, are omitted. These were peoples who had engaged China's central authorities in an erratic relationship over centuries before bearing the brunt of modern imperialism. From the perspective of this third party, the offensiveness of modern imperialism and the righteousness of China's anti-imperial nationalism immediately assumed rather different meanings.

Although seemingly indiscernible to the likes of Mahan's, the Mongols were certainly qualified as "contestants" in modern Asia's political arena. Although their fight was in no way reminiscent of their thunderous ancestors' more than a half millennium before, the Mongols' quest for "satisfaction" was nevertheless among the factors that set modern Asian geopolitics in motion. In both Inner and Outer Mongolia, power politics, national struggles, and revolutions became helplessly intertwined. In the former, the Mongols were by no means passive in the intricate competitions among the Chinese, Russians, Japanese, and Americans. In the latter, however, the Mongols had to face the Russians alone, who were poised to be the successor of Genghis Khan's Eurasian empire.

Bolsheviks and Mongolian Partisans

Tsarist Russia—"one of the most effective mechanisms for territorial expansion ever known"—expanded its domain more than 560 times (from 24,000 to 13.5 million square kilometers) from the fifteenth century to the beginning of the twentieth century.[3] The geography of the Eurasian land mass certainly played a role in determining the paths and directions of the "forward policy" of the Russian Empire, but it was the completion of the Siberian Railway in the late nineteenth century that especially endeared northeastern Asian territories to Russian imperialists.[4] Unlike Genghis Khan, who used

3. Dominic Lieven, *Empire: The Russian Empire and Its Rivals* (New Haven, Conn.: Yale University Press, 2000), 262.

4. V. Avarin, *Diguozhuyi zai Manzhou* (Imperialism in Manchuria) (Beijing: Shangwu Yinshuguan, 1980; translation by Beijing Foreign Trade Institute of the 1934 Russian edition), 24, 31, 34, 93, 345, 350; John P. LeDonne, *The Russian Empire and the World, 1700–1917: The Geopolitics of Expansion and Containment* (Oxford: Oxford University Press, 1997), 7–8.

his cavalry to terrify states into submission, Russian expansionists patiently chipped away territories of their neighboring states and encouraged the internal "rotting process" of their targets. They succeeded over the centuries because most of the time they made the right judgment about the question as to "where a line of an optimum conquest lay."[5]

After taking power in 1917, Russian Bolsheviks believed that they had not only broken away from Russia's Tsarist past but also opened a new future to the entire world. By the end of World War II, however, it became clear that just like its Tsarist predecessor, the Soviet Union remained a "symbiosis of imperial expansionism and ideological proselytism." Only Soviet expansion was carried out in the name of security for the Mecca of the international proletarian class, not just of "Mother Russia," and the ideological mission was to spread a Russian brand of Marxism, not Orthodox Christianity.[6] The Soviet Union was born a challenger to the existing international order. Its quest for power and security surpassed Tsarist Russia's in both energy level and sense of urgency. And as Russia's immediate neighbor in the south, Mongolia could hardly avoid encountering revolutionary Russia, one of the most potent and contagious international phenomena of the twentieth century.

Although historical memories can indeed give powerful impetus to state or societal behaviors, it is yet to be documented how the nightmare of the ancient "Mongol yoke" still hounded Soviet leaders during the first half of the twentieth century.[7] Obviously, modern Mongolia featured prominently in Soviet security not because of its power status but because of its geographical location. After the Chinese Revolution of 1911, China could no longer hold its outer frontiers. Soviet strategists, like their Tsarist predecessors, were convinced that a new arrangement had to be made about Mongolia either to advance Russia's strategic advantages in Central and Northeast Asia or to prevent other powers from doing so.

This should not obscure the fact that in both 1911 and 1921 the Outer Mongols themselves were initiators of Mongolian independence and that they

5. LeDonne, *Russian Empire,* 180–81.

6. Vladislav Zubok and Constantine Pleshakov, *Inside the Kremlin's Cold War: From Stalin to Khrushchev* (Cambridge, Mass.: Harvard University Press, 1996), 2–3; Vladimir Shlapentokh, "The World Revolution as a Geographic Instrument of the Soviet Leadership," *Russian History,* 26(3) (Fall 1999): 315.

7. Richard Soloman, "Coalition Building or Condominium? The Soviet Presence in Asia and American Policy Alternatives," in *Soviet Policy in East Asia,* ed. Donald S. Zagoria (New Haven, Conn.: Yale University Press, 1982), 284.

actively sought Russian assistance. For all practical purposes, the satellite relationship between Russia and Outer Mongolia did not begin until the second Mongolian revolution of 1921. Remarkably, the relationship began with much incongruity between the two sides. To the Bolsheviks, the Mongol revolutionaries' sociopolitical and nationalist agendas were respectively too conservative and flamboyant. At the beginning, the founding members of the Mongolian People's Party were at most populists politically and remained pious religiously. In 1919, when they took a vow to fight Chinese forces intent on abolishing Mongolian autonomy, Mongol revolutionaries prayed for protection from their traditional "Red Protective Deity," named Jamsran. By that time, although the Russian Bolsheviks had already successfully conducted their revolution for two years, these Mongol partisans still contemplated seeking assistance from the White Russian forces. Only after meeting with Soviet agents in early 1920 did the Mongol revolutionaries find their "Red protector" in Soviet Russia, which would dominate the Mongols' worldly life in the next seven decades as Jamsran overshadowed their spirituality.[8]

At the beginning, however, the Russian Bolsheviks' attention to Mongolia was more expedient than strategic. Unlike all the "national" communist revolutions in Asia that evolved under its inspiration, the Bolshevik Revolution of 1917 was conceived and conducted as an igniter of a world proletarian revolution. Being ideologically committed to Karl Marx's internationalist worldview, the Bolsheviks, at least initially, did not believe that an isolated revolution by Russia's small working classes could survive the encirclement by the capitalist world. The havoc engendered by World War I provided opportunities for them to make a world revolution. When the Bolsheviks organized their military and state apparatuses, these were intended as much for providing assistance to a socialist revolution in Europe as for building a new soviet state in Russia. Vladimir Lenin, who always wanted to bring Russia up to the "Western" and "European" level of the "ethnic hierarchy in his revolutionary politics," declared in March 1919 that "the working masses of Paris, London and New York have translated the word 'soviets' into their own languages. . . . We'll soon see the birth of the World Federal Soviet Republic."[9]

8. For an effort to demythicize the original participants of the 1921 revolution, see Hiroshi Futaki, "A Re-Examination of the Establishment of the Mongolian People's Party, Centering on Dogsom's Memoir," *Inner Asia* 2 (2000): 37–61.

9. Robert Service, *Lenin: A Biography* (Cambridge, Mass.: Harvard University Press, 2000), 337–39.

Yet the situation in Europe soon indicated that a revolution there might just be an unreachable mirage. In a report to the Russian Communist Party Central Committee, Leon Trotsky, the commissar for military affairs, admitted that on the stage of European politics the Russian Red Army was a rather weak force in both offensive and defensive senses. But he was very optimistic about the situation in Asia:

> In the Asian arena of world politics, without doubt our Red Army constitutes a strength incomparably stronger than it is in Europe. . . . At this moment, the road to India is probably easier and shorter than that to a soviet Hungary. Our force is insignificant according to European standards but may be able to break the unsteady balance in Asia's colonial relations, to promote directly the uprisings by suppressed peoples there, and to guarantee the victory of these uprisings. . . . Revolutions in Europe seem to have been postponed. Unquestionably we have already shifted from the West to the East.[10]

Shortly after seeing Trotsky's report, Lenin authorized operations to set up an "independent base" in Turkestan that would be used to cultivate ties within India and Persia and to transmit weapons, in Lenin's words, "in an extremely conspiratorial manner" from America or Europe to the Asian peoples who were fighting imperialism.[11]

At the time, however, Lenin did not necessarily agree with Trotsky's view on a strategic shift. According to a recent study, in the summer of 1920, "Europe remained the key to Lenin's strategic calculation."[12] If not all Lenin's colleagues shared his optimism about a European revolution in the near future, at least Joseph Stalin was an enthusiastic supporter. In July 1920, encouraged by the Red Army's progress in Poland, Stalin telegraphed Lenin and suggested that the Comintern now consider organizing uprisings in weak European countries such as Italy, Hungary, the Czech lands, Rumania, and Germany. He contended:

---

10. "Document 00957: Trotsky to the Russian Communist Party Central Committee, 5 August 1919," in *Sulian Lishi Dang'an Xuanbian* (Selected Historical Archives of the Soviet Union; hereafter *SLDX*), 34 vols., ed. Shen Zhihua (Beijing: Shehui Kexue Wenxian Chubanshe, 2002), 3: 364–68.

11. Mikhail Kiukov, "Once Again about Sun Yat-sen's Northwest Plan," *Far Eastern Affairs* (hereafter *FEA*) 5 (2000): 83–84; Richard Pipes, ed., *The Unknown Lenin: From the Secret Archive* (New Haven, Conn.: Yale University Press, 1996), 74.

12. Service, *Lenin,* 406–7.

Simply put, we should take advantage of this opportunity when imperialism has not had the time to repair its broken war chariot—it can be repaired in time and start attack again; [let's] weigh anchor and set sail.[13]

In less than a month, the Polish army's effective resistance would have shattered the Soviet leaders' dream about a Soviet Federal Union of Europe. Consequently, instead of weighing anchor in Europe, the Bolsheviks' revolutionary boat set sail for Asia. Between 1919 and 1921, Russian military personnel and money were allocated to clandestine operations in Persia, Turkey, and Afghanistan, aiming to create or foster pro-Soviet forces and regimes. In these places, however, the Bolsheviks created nothing that could last except the wreckage of their adventure.[14]

It was in the Far East, the opposite direction from Europe, that the Bolsheviks' schemes of exporting revolution achieved some tangible results. In this direction, instead of organizing an offensive against British imperialism, the perceived archenemy of the Soviet revolution, Lenin and his associates were preoccupied with a defensive concern about Japan, which since 1918 had occupied Vladivostok. Aside from playing a pragmatic balancing game in inviting American influence into the Russian Far East as a counterweight to the Japanese, in February 1920 Trotsky instructed the Siberian Revolutionary Committee to establish a non-Soviet buffer state as soon as possible. As spelled out by Trotsky and Lenin, such an entity could exercise control of the region on behalf of Moscow, maintain a democratic appearance appealing to American public opinion and commercial interests, and in the meantime avoid any incident between the Russian Red Army and Japanese occupation forces. In April 1920, a Far Eastern Republic (FER), the incarnation of Lenin's "concession strategy," was established.[15]

Yet Moscow's decision to postpone the "sovietization" of the Russian Far

13. "Document 04202: Stalin to Lenin, 24 July 1920," *SLDX,* 1: 420–21.

14. "Document 04188: Trotsky to Laskornikov, 26 May 1920," *SLDX,* 1: 401–2; "Document 04189: Laskornikov to Trotsky, Lenin, and Chicherin, 7 June 1920," ibid., 403–6; "Document 04194: Chicherin to the Russian Communist Party Central Politburo, 28 June 1920," ibid., 409-410; "Document 04196: Chicherin to Krestinsky, 5 July 1920," ibid., 412–13; "Documents 04213 and 04288: Karakhan to the Russian Communist Party Central Politburo, 9 September 1920 and 26 January 1921," ibid., 424–26, 427–28.

15. Bruce Elleman, *Diplomacy and Deception: The Secret History of Sino-Soviet Diplomatic Relations, 1917–1927* (Armonk, N.Y.: M. E. Sharpe, 1997), 29–30, 32–33; "Document 11210: Trotsky to Smirnov, 18 February 1920," *SLDX,* 3: 476; John Stephan, *The Russian Far East: A History* (Stanford, Calif.: Stanford University Press, 1994), 141, 164.

East did not prevent the Bolsheviks in Siberia from intensifying activities of spreading revolution in East Asian countries. In July 1920, to facilitate the training of Japanese, Korean, and Mongolian revolutionaries, the Siberian Bureau of the Russian Communist Party in Irkutsk established an "Oriental Peoples Section." Among its tasks, the section was to organize struggles in Mongolia, Manchuria, and Tibet against "Chinese imperialism." Plans were drafted for opening China as a revolutionary arena and for sending military expeditions into Korea. In seeing these plans as directly contradictory to their original defensive purpose in creating the FER, the leaders in Moscow had to restrain the revolutionary enthusiasm of their Siberian comrades.[16]

This is not to say that the Bolshevik central leadership was not interested in exporting revolution to the Far East. Especially on the issue of Mongolia, there was little disagreement between the Central Committee and its Siberian Bureau. Throughout 1920, a series of reports to the Siberian Bureau suggested that revolutionary agitation in Mongolia could achieve results relatively easily and without much risk. This was so because the adversaries in Mongolia were not Japanese imperialists but just "Japan-loving" Chinese officials and their ineffective forces. Allegedly, the Mongols were eager to throw off Chinese control with help from Soviet Russia. It was expected that "Mongolia will be ours within two or three months."[17] In March 1920, after meeting with a Soviet agent named I. A. Sorokovikov in Urga, the Mongolian partisans established the Mongolian People's Party and decided to send a delegation to Soviet Russia. Although the Mongolian delegation's experience in Soviet Russia was not as smooth as expected, they received due attention from top Bolshevik leaders, including an interview with Lenin

---

16. Li Yuzhen, "Sun-Joffe Proclamation Reconsidered," in *Sulian, Gongchan Guoji yu Zhongguo Geming de Guanxi Xintan* (New Studies of the Relationship between the Soviet Union, the Comintern, and the Chinese Revolution), ed. Huang Xiurong (Beijing: Zhonggong Dangshi Chubanshe, 1995), 236; Moisei Persits, "A New Collection of Documents on Soviet Policy in the Far East in 1920–1922," *FEA* 5 (1997): 82–85; "Report to the Comintern Executive Committee on the Structure and Work of the Oriental Peoples Section of the Siberian Bureau of the Russian Communist Party Central Committee, 21 December 1920," *Gongchan Guoji, Liangong (Bu) yu Zhongguo Guomin Keming Dang'an Ziliao Congshu* (Series of Archival Materials on the Comintern, the Soviet Communist Party [Bolshevik], and the Chinese Revolution; hereafter *GLZD*), 12 vols., comp. and trans. First Division of the Party History Research Office of the Chinese Communist Party Central Committee (Beijing: Beijing Tushuguan Chubanshe, 1997, vols. 1–6; Beijing: Zhongyang Wenxian Chubanshe, 2002, vols. 7–12), 1: 49–57.

17. Persits, "New Collection of Documents," 86–87.

himself. At the time, trying to cultivate a workable relationship with the Chinese government, the Bolsheviks did not immediately satisfy the Mongols' every request for help. Still, in treating the Mongols Moscow was generous enough to cause the Siberian Bureau to complain afterward that the Mongolian delegation had received "a huge amount of silver and other valuables" from the Commissariat of Foreign Affairs, and this made it very difficult for the Bureau's Oriental Peoples Section to control unauthorized activities by Mongol partisans.[18] Despite misgivings like this, Irkutsk and Moscow clearly agreed that the Mongolian cause was worth supporting.

In the summer of 1920, Soviet Russia's Mongolian enterprise began even before the Bolshevik leadership ascertained the strategic value of this sparsely populated pastoral land. The land was added to the Bolsheviks' canvas because they did not want to omit a single stroke of any significance in painting their worldwide landscape. But in October, the relatively easily created artwork was marred by the invasion of Mongolia by "Mad Baron" Roman von Ungern-Sternberg, a runaway general from G. M. Semenov's "white" army, which had recently been smashed by the Red Army in southeastern Siberia. To the revolutionaries in Irkutsk, the consequence of this "Mongolian incident" was graver than the revolution in Mongolia itself. By then, the Oriental Peoples Section of the Siberian Bureau had maintained regular communications with its agents in China through Urga. Because of Ungern's invasion, the connection between Soviet Russia and its China work was temporarily cut off.[19]

But the crisis could also be an opportunity for using Soviet force not only to secure the eastern border but also to dislodge Chinese influence in Mongolia. In early February 1921, leaders of the FER were ready to change their state from a buffer to a launch pad. They suggested to Moscow that the FER send its army into Mongolia to destroy Ungern and to install the Mongolian People's Revolutionary Party (MPRP) in power in an independent Outer Mongolia. The Far Eastern Secretariat of the Comintern also resolved to

18. Baabar, *Twentieth Century Mongolia* (Cambridge: White Horse Press, 1999), 200–1; Futaki, "Re-Examination," 45–53; O. Edmund Clubb, *China and Russia: The "Great Game"* (New York: Columbia University Press, 1971), 177; "Report to the Comintern Executive Committee on the Structure and work of the Oriental Peoples Section of the Siberian bureau of the Russian Communist Party Central Committee, 21 December 1920," *GLZD,* 1: 56-57; Fujiko Isono, "Soviet Russia and the Mongolian Revolution of 1921," *Past and Present,* 83 (March 1979): 116-140.

19. Baabar, *Twentieth Century Mongolia,* 207; "Report to the Comintern Executive Committee on the Structure and Work of the Oriental Peoples Section," 54–55.

recover Outer Mongolia as a "revolutionary base" and identified Ungern's adventure as part of Japan's effort to set up a series of "black buffer zones" around the Soviet Far East that therefore must be thwarted.[20] Thus, the "Mongolia incident" helped Soviet and Comintern strategists to clarify Mongolia's role as a "red buffer" against Japan's "black buffer." Unlike the FER, which had been formed as part of Lenin's "concession strategy," Mongolia would be revolutionized both to serve Soviet Russia's security goal vis-à-vis the alleged Japanese threat and to facilitate the Comintern's revolutionary schemes in the Far East.

On June 16, 1921, the Russian Communist Party's Politburo decided to send the Red Army into Outer Mongolia to destroy Ungern. In the meantime, it rejected FER's proposition that Mongolia be detached from China and made independent.[21] In retrospect, Moscow's decision on intervention proved one of the most critical events in modern Chinese and Mongolian histories. The Russian intervention of 1921 not only guaranteed the political victory of a small group of Mongol partisans over all other forces in Mongolia but also laid the groundwork for transforming Mongolia from a dependency of the falling Chinese empire to a satellite of an emerging Soviet superpower. In 1921, however, Bolshevik leaders would not have made the decision unless they believed that the action was relevant to either of their two principal concerns at the time. One was the momentum of their revolution, and the other was the security of their new state. In late 1920 and early 1921, Lenin and his associates were in a bind to determine the priority between the two.

Eurasian Federation versus Soviet Empire

As the Red Army's Poland adventure foundered in the summer of 1920, a serious crisis was mounting within Russia. Continuous warfare and the Bolsheviks' stringent and radical wartime economic policies were pushing ordinary people to the verge of desperation. Urban chaos and peasants uprisings were threatening the revolution from within. Sensing the danger, Lenin persuaded his party to suspend its revolutionary offensive on the economic

20. Persits, "New Collection of Documents," 88–90; Sergei Luzianin, "Mongolia: Between China and Soviet Russia," *FEA* 2 (1995): 54–58; Baabar, *Twentieth Century Mongolia,* 210.
    21. Luzianin, "Mongolia," 56–58.

front and to revive private commerce and the normal exchange of products between rural and urban areas. The result was the so-called New Economic Policy. This internal security measure also led to drastic changes in Soviet foreign policy. Now that business deals with Western countries were welcomed again, in a March 1921 trade agreement with the United Kingdom the Soviet authorities promised to stop all subversive activities within the British Empire.[22] Thus, the Bolshevik Revolution appeared on retreat on both international and domestic fronts. In retreat, Moscow needed something to show the world that its revolutionary ideal and Red Army remained valid forces on the international scene. Mongolia became the chosen location for this demonstration, even though it was in a negligible corner of world politics in the 1920s. The "whites" in Mongolia provided the perfect excuse for Moscow to take action. A Soviet expedition against the "whites" in Mongolia could be explained as a necessary extension of the civil war in Russia. The expected effects were to demonstrate Soviet power and to reconnect the Soviets with their interrupted China work.

On June 1, 1921, officials of the Far Eastern Bureau of the Russian Communist Party, the Commissariat of Foreign Affairs, the FER, and the Red Army held a joint meeting to discuss the Mongolia question. The final resolution of the meeting favored a military expedition with this justification: "The Mongolia operation is important as a display of power of the Far Eastern Republic and Soviet Russia, as a means of ensuring security in our rear, and as a way of taking action against Zhang Zuolin and preparing revolutionary strata in China and Mongolia".[23] Zhang was identified here because at the time the Manchuria-based warlord dominated the Chinese government in Beijing, with which the Soviet Russian and FER governments had been conducting difficult negotiations for diplomatic recognition and commercial arrangements. A Soviet military presence in Outer Mongolia would therefore significantly enhance Moscow's diplomatic leverage with Beijing.[24]

To meet these revolutionary and diplomatic goals, a Soviet expedition to destroy "Mad Baron" Ungern in Urga was just the means. By this time, the "whites" in Mongolia no longer posed a security problem to Soviet Russia. In late March 1921, I. N. Smirnov, the head of the Siberian Revolutionary

22. Service, *Lenin,* 421–34.
23. Luzianin, "Mongolia."
24. Peter S. H. Tang, *Russian and Soviet Policy in Manchuria and Outer Mongolia, 1911–1931* (Durham, N.C.: Duke University Press, 1959), 114–47, 371–77; Elleman, *Diplomacy and Deception,* 34–49.

Committee, reported to Lenin that the "white bandits" in the western area of "China's Mongolia" were disintegrating, and that some 5,000 of them had requested permission to return to Soviet Russia and had been allowed to do so after disarmament. As for Ungern's force in Urga, the Red Army command in southern Siberia also attested that it did not pose any threat to Soviet Russia.[25] Because of the lack of an immediate military threat from the direction of Mongolia, a disagreement emerged among Soviet and FER strategists about whether or not the Red Army was really needed to remove Ungern. This did not appear to be a problem for Lenin. On June 15, E. M. Sklyanski, the deputy commissar for military affairs, asked Lenin what was the central leadership's decision on the proposed Mongolian expedition. In response, Lenin readily attached his approval to the military plan and asked the Politburo to adopt it the next day.[26]

During the last couple of years of his life, Lenin was cautious not to repeat the Poland fiasco and wanted to avoid any direct conflict with Western powers. But Lenin, in his own words, was still "dreaming" about the "great tasks" of undermining European imperialism through a circuitous eastern way. Surely Lenin's strategic focus was always on the "advanced West." In Mongolia, what began under Lenin was a tactical incursion mainly to perfunctorily display the validity of the Soviet ideal of world revolution, though later Stalin would turn the undertaking into part of a deadly serious strategy to enhance Russia's geopolitical environment.

The difference between Lenin and Stalin was not about Soviet expansionism; both favored an advance policy for the Russian Revolution. But whereas Lenin visualized Russia's "revolutionary hegemony" in a sovietized world, Stalin was bent on creating a "red empire." A revolutionary opposing not only the Tsarist system in Russia but also the entire existing world order, Lenin expected that a wave of soviet revolutions in many national states would fundamentally change the international system. In 1920, Lenin engaged Stalin in a debate about how Europe should be reorganized as the revolution was advancing in the continent. Lenin's idea was to form an open-ended Federal Union of Russia that would first incorporate other soviet republics into the former domain of the Russian Empire and then continuously receive other European countries whenever they achieved their own

25. "Document 01431: Smirnov to Lenin, 25 March 1921," *SLDX,* 5: 38; Baabar, *Twentieth Century Mongolia,* 211.

26. "Document 01449: Notes Exchanged between Lenin and Sklyanski on the Question of Advancing into Mongolia, 14 and 15 June 1921," *SLDX,* 5: 45.

soviet systems. Stalin harbored a serious doubt about this internationalist scheme, arguing that "old national pride" would continue to exist in these countries even after they went through their own soviet revolutions. Soviet Russia could serve itself better by grabbing whatever it could and holding tightly its acquisitions in a world that would continue to be divided by national differences for a considerable time. For this view, Stalin was accused of chauvinism by Lenin.[27]

In the second half of 1922, when the Bolshevik leadership considered the constitutional structure of Soviet Russia, the conflict between "internationalist" Lenin and "chauvinist" Stalin flared up again. Contending that the party's liberalism in the civil war "unexpectedly fostered a group of real and thorough social independent elements among communists," Stalin proposed to reduce independent soviet republics into "autonomous" components of the Russian Soviet Republic. If "autonomization," meaning independent republics' "joining" Soviet Russia, was not implemented now, Stalin argued, the unification of these soviet republics would become extremely difficult in the future, and Soviet Russia would never be able to include them in a "genuine economic entity."[28] Lenin stood firm on his ground and proposed to organize a "Eurasian Federal Union of Soviet Republics." In countering Stalin's "autonomization" formula, Lenin suggested that all independent republics and Soviet Russia together organize the new union on an equal footing. Thus, according to Lenin, "We neither encourage the 'independent elements' nor abolish their independence. We just build a higher level—an equal federation of republics." Lenin's formula received support from communists in several independent republics. They argued that internally, the new union must reconcile with the multiethnic fact of the member republics, and externally, the new union could exercise the strongest revolutionary influence possible abroad only if its member republics retained their independence.[29]

27. Service, *Lenin,* 12.

28. "Document 02406: Stalin's Draft Program on the Relationship between Russian Socialist Federal Soviet Republic and the Independent Republics," no later than 11 August 1922, *SLDX,* 5: 329–30; "Document 07308: Stalin's Letter to Lenin, 22 September 1922," ibid., 5: 340–43.

29. "Document 01527: Lenin to Kamenev, 27 September 1922," *SLDX,* 5: 356–58; "Document 02408: Excerpts from the Minutes of the Seventh Plenum of the Azerbaijani Communist Party Central Committee, 11 September 1922, ibid., 5: 333; "Document 07307: Excerpts from the Minutes of a Meeting of the Georgian Communist Party Central Committee, 15 September 1922, ibid., 5: 334–35; "Document 02412: Excerpts from

In late September, in an exchange of notes, Lev B. Kamenev, a member of the Politburo, told Stalin that "Ilich [Lenin] is prepared to fight for independence [of the republics]." Stalin responded: "In my opinion, determination is needed in opposition against Ilich."[30] What eventually helped Stalin was not determination but Lenin's illness, which had prevented him from attending the party's routine work since mid-1921. The Soviet Union that emerged from the dispute between Lenin and Stalin was a symbolic concession to the former but an actual victory for the latter. On December 16, the Russian Communist Party's Central Committee adopted a "Treaty for Establishment of the Eurasian Union of Soviet Socialist Republics" to be signed by all members of the new union. But in the draft constitution of the new union and Stalin's related report made two days later, "Eurasian" disappeared from the name of the union. The constitution included Lenin's demand for "equality" and stipulated that the union was organized together by all member soviet republics, and that every republic retained the right of secession. Conversely, the authority and power to deal with all foreign and domestic affairs were centralized in the newly organized All Soviet Congress and Central Executive Committee.[31]

Lenin was outraged by the result. But he could do nothing except dictate his thoughts in a series of secret memoranda. In a memo titled "The National and Autonomization Questions," Lenin described the unifying government of Russia as an "inheritance of the Tsarist system with some soviet color." Under the circumstances, Lenin continued, "our self-justification, the 'freedom of secession from the union,' is but empty words. They cannot protect other nationalities within Russia from violations by real Russians such as Russian bureaucrats and Russian chauvinists who are really thugs

---

the Minutes of the Second Meeting of the Belorussian Communist Party Central Bureau, 16 September 1922, ibid., 5: 338; "Document 02423: Rakovsky to Stalin, 28 September 1922," ibid., 5: 362–66.

30. "Document 02422: Notes Exchanged between Kamenev and Stalin at a Meeting of the Russian Communist Party Central Bureau, 28 September 1922," *SLDX,* 5: 361.

31. "Document 07805: Draft Constitution of the Soviet Union Adopted by the Sub-committee of the Russian Communist Party Central Committee, 5–16 September 1922," *SIDX,* 5: 401–5; "Document 07806: Minutes of a Meeting of the Russian Communist Party Central Committee, 16 December 1922, Appendix 1: Treaty for the Establishment of the Eurasian Union of Soviet Socialist Republics, and Appendix 2: Proclamation of the Eurasian Union of Soviet Socialist Republics," ibid., 5: 406–14; "Document 07807: Excerpts of the Minutes of a Plenum of the Russian Communist Party Central Committee, 18 December 1922," ibid., 5: 416–17.

and scoundrels."[32] Stalin would see to it that Lenin's prediction became reality. What Lenin did not admit is that his feeble "fight for independence" helped create one of the most hypocritical imperial systems in world history, one that combined a liberal exterior charm with a brutal innate obsession.

The formation of the Soviet Union had an immense impact on the revolutions in China and in Mongolia. Unaware of the Lenin-Stalin dispute, the Chinese and Mongolian revolutionaries were fascinated by this novel form of state organization that appeared to treat weak and oppressed peoples justly and generously. Respectively interpreting the Russian Soviet experiment to their own advantage, centralizing Chinese revolutionaries and independence-seeking Mongol partisans competed with each other as tensely as founders of the Soviet Union maneuvered with nationalistic communists in Ukraine, Georgia, and Byelorussia. By sending Red Army troops into Outer Mongolia in June 1921, the Bolsheviks put themselves right in the middle of one of China's most intricate ethnic conflicts in the twentieth century.

In the 1920s, however, Soviet policymakers could not reach a consensus on how the Mongolian affairs could best serve their purposes. Moscow's policy priorities in the East also kept changing. After the Red Army's successful intervention in Mongolia, the Soviets were elated now that a friendly regime had been created along their eastern border. In October 1921, with a certain degree of exaggeration, Georgy V. Chicherin, people's commissar for foreign affairs, reported to Lenin:

> The revolutionary government [of Outer Mongolia] is a major trump card in our hands. Its creation has utterly thwarted Japan's plans of setting up a counter-revolutionary belt between the Pacific and the Caspian Sea. Our borders are perfectly safe for miles and miles, covered as they are by a friendly Mongolia.[33]

Having helped alter Mongolia's *political* orientation, Moscow was, however, not yet ready to change the territory's *legal* status. To the Chinese government, Chicherin's Commissariat of Foreign Affairs pledged that the Red Army's Mongolian incursion was solely intended to purge the "whites" and that Soviet Russia would continue to respect China's sovereignty in the

32. "Document 01545: Lenin's Letters to the Party Congress, December 1922," and appendix, "On the National and Autonomization Questions, 31 December 1922," *SLDX,* 5: 440–42.

33. Luzianin, "Mongolia," 61.

territory. In the meantime, Soviet and Comintern agents urged Chinese and Mongolian revolutionaries to accept a two-phase formula. In phase one, a revolutionary Mongolia would maintain actual autonomy in the Republic of China, which was still dominated by reactionary forces; in phase two, after the Chinese revolution succeeded, Mongolia and other frontier ethnic regions would unify with China in a Chinese federation. The idea was roundly opposed in China and did not please leaders in Urga either. The only receptive group was the newly organized Chinese Communist Party (CCP).[34]

Inserting Soviet influence into the Mongolia situation, Moscow had to juggle several objectives. The 1921 intervention could showcase Soviet Russia's revolutionary prestige, reopen a channel of communications with Chinese revolutionaries, and preempt potential Japanese penetration into Mongolia. Yet the action might also distract Moscow's New Economic Policy toward Western countries and damage its post-tsarist diplomatic image in China created by the famous Karakhan proclamation of 1919. Actually, increased Soviet influence in Mongolia had already caused Western governments to be concerned. Shortly after the Soviet incursion, the U.S. consul general in Zhangjiakuo (Kalgan), Samuel Sokobin, visited Urga. Afterward, he reported to Washington that the new Mongolian government was in no position to negotiate with the Russians.[35]

More troubling to Moscow was the adverse effect of the Mongolian intervention on its efforts in China. To serve their overall strategy in the Far East of "using all possible means to intensify interest conflicts among Japan, the United States, and China," Soviet and Comintern strategists cultivated a friendly relationship with China's "central government" in Beijing while secretly fostering revolutionary forces in southern China. The revolutionary connection was a two-pronged effort. Since the summer of 1920, Comintern agents had assisted Chinese radicals in organizing their own communist party, which was established in July 1921. And in the early months of 1921, the Soviets identified Sun Yat-sen's Guomindang (GMD, Nationalist Party) as their principal ally. In November, Lenin directed Chicherin to establish a secret working relationship with Sun Yat-sen's government in Guangzhou

34. Li Yuzhen, "Sun-Joffe Statement Reconsidered," in *Sulian,* ed. Huang, 236; Baabar, *Twentieth Century Mongolia,* 250. According to Luzianin, "Mongolia," 59–62, before August 1921 the Mongolia partisans were receptive to the Chinese federation idea but then had a change of heart because they disliked a reference to Mongolia as "autonomous" made in Soviet communications.

35. Baabar, *Twentieth Century Mongolia,* 229; Paine, *Imperial Rivals,* 321, 326.

(Canton) and to deal with Sun "as warmly as possible."[36] Yet, except for the young CCP, Moscow's Mongolian adventure caused across-the-board objections in China, including that from Sun Yat-sen, who was then actively seeking assistance from the Russians. In comparison with Moscow's effort in China, Mongolia was just a sideshow. In 1921, in the Comintern's 80 million ruble subsidy to revolutionary activities in the Far East, Mongolia was worth merely an insignificant 3 million (3.75 percent).[37] After the Mongolian incursion, therefore, Moscow had serious repair work to do in China.

Adolf Abramovich Joffe, who became Moscow's plenipotentiary to China in July 1922, bore the unpleasant responsibility of convincing the Chinese how the Russian Red Army's occupation of Mongolia differed from imperialist encroachment on Chinese territories in the past and how Soviet objectives were actually compatible with China's progressive interests.[38] Joffe believed that in terms of the worldwide struggle against capitalism, China provided a much better chance for success than Central Asia, an area favored by Lenin. In 1923, he accomplished a remarkable diplomatic feat for Moscow in forging a revolutionary alliance with Sun Yat-sen. But Joffe's job was marred by his own government's démarche in Mongolia. While dutifully carrying out instructions from Moscow, Joffe was troubled by what he called a "new edition of the Tsarist policy," meaning Moscow's detachment of Outer Mongolia from China by way of "sovietization."

Diagonally opposing Chicherin's acclamation that Mongolia was a "trump card" for Soviet Russia, Joffe called the Mongolia question the "only trump card imperialists have against us." In favoring a policy of returning Outer Mongolia to China, Joffe contended in his reports to Moscow that "we are perfectly justified at times in betraying the interests of a small nation" and that "it is not worthwhile, for the sake of two million Mongols who do not have any role to play in the world, to damage our entire policy and relationship with four hundred million Chinese who are having such a huge impact." In Joffe's opinion, the issue of Mongolia should be settled through negotiations between the Russian and the Chinese governments, and

---

36. "Vilenskii-Sibiriakov's Report to the Comintern Executive Committee, 1 September 1920," *GLZD*, 1: 38–42; "Sokolov-Stlahov's Report on the Guangzhou Government, 21 April 1921," ibid., 1: 58–64; "Likin's Report to the Comintern Far Eastern Department, 20 May 1922," ibid., 1: 81–96; "Chicherin's Letter to Lenin, 6 November 1921," ibid., 1: 66; "Lenin's Note to Chicherin, 7 November 1921," ibid., 1: 67.

37. Baabar, *Twentieth Century Mongolia*, 215.

38. "Joffe's Letter to Wu Peifu, 19 August 1922," *GLZD*, 1: 99–102; "Joffe's Letter to Sun Yat-sen, 22 August 1922," ibid., 1: 103–6.

Moscow should "not require the participation by the Mongolian People's Revolutionary Government, basically not speak on behalf of Mongolia, and state that Mongolia is China's internal affair."[39]

Joffe's willingness to abandon the Mongols to the Chinese has been defined as "revolutionary cynicism."[40] Yet his cynicism toward Mongolia was surpassed by his superiors' cynicism toward China. In a telegram to Joffe drafted by Stalin, the Russian Communist Party's Central Bureau pointed out that "in negotiations with China, it is impermissible to derive guidelines directly from the general [Karakhan] proclamations of 1919 and 1920. . . . As for Mongolia, the questions of its state status and Red Army's withdrawal should be settled through Russian–Chinese–Mongolian agreements. The solution of these questions must not exclude Mongolia itself. This policy does not contradict our recognition of China's sovereignty over Mongolia."[41]

Clearly, as a diplomat, Joffe at this time was out of step with his government. To Moscow's China policy, which was now under Stalin's close supervision, the self-denial rhetoric of the Karakhan proclamations of 1919 and 1920 was outdated. Joffe also mistook Moscow's Mongolia policy for a principled defense of a weak nation's interests. The fact was that when deciding on using Mongolia to showcase Soviet power in the summer of 1921, the Bolshevik leaders already jeopardized the Mongols' most important political interest—independence. Furthermore, because Moscow had not taken Mongolia away from China in a legal sense, Joffe's proposition for "returning" Mongolia to China appeared both naive and irrelevant to Soviet leaders. Whereas Joffe's formula was unacceptable to Moscow, Stalin's directive could not be sold to the Chinese government either. The Mongolia question between China and Russia thus entered an impasse between 1922 and 1923. Aside from Mongolia, Joffe also had disagreements with Moscow on other issues related to China. In late 1922, Joffe began to complain to Moscow that he did not have the trust of the Russian Communist leadership and that his actions were too restrained by Moscow. In March 1923, Moscow finally decided to recall its despondent envoy from China.[42]

39. Luzianin, "Mongolia," 64–68; Joffe's telegrams to Karakhan, 25 and 30 August 1922, *GLZD*, 1: 107–9, 112; Joffe's telegrams to Chicherin, 1 and 7–8 November 1922, ibid., 1: 142–43, 147–50.

40. Luzianin, "Mongolia," 66.

41. Minutes no. 24 of the RCP Central Bureau meetings, 31 August 1922, *GLZD*, 1: 114–15.

42. "Trotsky's Letter to Joffe, 20 January 1923," *GLZD*, 1: 200–2; minutes no. 53 of the RCP Central Politburo meetings, 8 March 1923, ibid., 1: 225–26.

Stalin and his associates never got a tripartite agreement on Mongolia. Instead, Soviet Russia's post-1921 position on the Mongolia question was anchored on two separate agreements with the Mongols and the Chinese, concluded respectively in 1921 and 1924. It has been suggested that Moscow gave up the idea for a Soviet–Chinese–Mongolian settlement because the Soviet leadership reluctantly conceded to Joffe's argument about the value of winning over the Chinese at the expenses of the Mongols.[43] As a matter of fact, the tripartite formula was not implemented simply because it was rejected by both the Mongols and the Chinese. Neither side wanted to re-peat the same mistake of accepting the Tsarist government's tripartite agree-ment in 1914 that did not give independence to Mongolia while seriously compromising Chinese sovereignty.[44] In concluding two bilateral agree-ments, the Bolsheviks did not retreat from their original plans about Outer Mongolia. Rather, the separate dealings with the Mongols and the Chinese served Moscow's objective well in severing contacts between the two sides. If in 1914 the Tsarist government still respected the norms of international relations and wanted to penetrate Mongolia with the blessing of a binding tripartite agreement, in the 1920s the Bolsheviks were using international agreements as a tool of deception and manipulation. In its 1921 agreement with the Mongols, Moscow treated Mongolia as a "free" entity without rec-ognizing Mongolian independence. And in its 1924 treaty with China, Mos-cow recognized China's sovereignty over Mongolia without relinquishing its own control there.[45]

The mastermind behind this "new" diplomacy was Chicherin, a revolu-tionary from "an old and distinguished aristocratic Russian family" whose members had served in the Tsarist government, including the foreign service. This background made Chicherin the right person to supervise the transition of Russian foreign policy from Tsarist imperialism to Soviet expansionism.[46] Under his stewardship, Soviet diplomacy meant diplomatic sovietization wherever possible. When sending the Soviet representative P. N. Nikiforov to Ulaanbaatar, the renamed Mongolian capital, Chicherin instructed him that "while proclaiming our recognition of Outer Mongolia's autonomous

43. Luzianin, "Mongolia," 68.

44. Tang, *Russia and Soviet Policy,* 336–40; Baabar, *Twentieth Century Mongolia,* 162–67.

45. Baabar, *Twentieth Century Mongolia,* 220–26; Elleman, *Diplomacy and Decep-tion,* 100–4; Tang, *Russia and Soviet Policy,* 378–79.

46. Timothy Edward O'Connor, *Diplomacy and Revolution: G. V. Chicherin and Soviet Foreign Affairs, 1918–1930* (Ames: Iowa State University Press, 1988), 3.

status under Chinese sovereignty, we will be working for the former's political and economic rapprochement with the Soviet form."[47]

The question now was how the Soviet enterprise in Mongolia should be reconciled with Moscow's bigger project in the south, the Chinese revolution. After all, to a large extent the Mongolian enterprise was started to fortify Soviet strategy in China. Until early 1927, even Moscow's financial assistance to Outer Mongolia was decided by a "China Committee" under the Politburo.[48] Joffe's warning about the danger of losing 400 million Chinese did not materialize in a politically divided China. A good sign for Moscow was that Sun Yat-sen, who from early 1923 became the pivot of Soviet strategy in China, seemed to have changed his attitude toward the Mongolia question. In 1922, Sun had expressed a strong objection to Mongolian autonomy and the inclusion of the Mongolian government in any Sino-Soviet negotiations. But in 1923, he appeared more interested in taking advantage of Soviet military presence in Outer Mongolia and wanted to coordinate the GMD's northward strategy with Soviet assistance through either Mongolia or Chinese Turkestan (Xinjiang).[49]

But, between 1923 and 1927, the heyday of Moscow's strategic partnership with the Chinese Nationalist revolutionaries, Outer Mongolia did not serve as a base for creating "strata of Chinese revolutionaries" as planned. When the goal of Moscow's revolutionary advance policy shifted from seeking a Leninist hegemonic sphere to ascertaining a Stalinist imperial domain, Soviet influence in Outer Mongolia became increasingly incompatible with the respective ethnopolitical connotations of the Chinese and Mongolian revolutions. In hoping to use Outer Mongolia as a principal portal for exporting revolution to China, Soviet policymakers would have to face the ethnopolitical implications of reconnecting the two regions. The connection, even though in a "revolutionary" form without legal or administrative implications, would provide opportunities to the Chinese and the Mongols. Chinese Nationalists would want to use the connection to realize their dream of a Chinese national state of the Qing Empire's proportions. Mongol partisans, conversely, would seize any chance to extend their new

47. Baabar, *Twentieth Century Mongolia,* 255.
48. Minutes no. 84 of the Soviet Communist Party Politburo meetings, 5 February 1927, *GLZD,* 4: 103.
49. Joffe's telegraphs to Chicherin, 7 and 8 November 1922, *GLZD,* 1: 148; Joffe's letters to leaders of the RCP, Soviet government, and Comintern, 13 and 26 January 1923, ibid., 1: 197, 214.

state into Inner Mongolia in the south, Urianhai (Tannu Tuva) in the north, and even the Buryats' territories in Russia. Thus, from the Soviet strategists' perspective, although the Chinese ideal of national unification posed a common challenge to both Moscow and Ulaanbaatar, the Mongols' pan-Mongol tendency must be contained as well.

The issue of curbing Mongolian nationalism was as controversial as that of blocking Chinese Nationalists' territorial ambitions. In the early 1920s, leaders in Ulaanbaatar went along with Moscow's China policy and sought political and military ties with Sun Yat-sen's GMD. Yet they were more interested in establishing contacts with the Mongols in different areas of China.[50] Between 1923 and 1927, they had certain freedom to do so because Soviet and Comintern officials could not agree among themselves about what role the MPR should play in China and who should decide that matter. While Moscow kept a watchful eye on Ulaabaatar's pan-Mongol tendency and was unwilling to "reactivate" the MPR's role in China, certain Comintern agents in Mongolia saw the advantage of using Outer Mongols' ethnic ties with Mongolian areas in China to promote revolutionary activities on the Chinese side of the border. In 1925 and after, agents from the MPR were involved in organizing and assisting the Inner Mongolian People's Revolutionary Party (IMPRP). Although the IMPRP also cooperated with the GMD and the CCP as directed by the Comintern, agents from Ulaanbaatar and the Comintern easily maintained a stronger influence. A CCP document dated May 1926 indicated that its work in the three provinces of Inner Mongolia (Rehe, Chahar and Suiyuan) was under the guidance of a "Mongol representative" sent by the Comintern. Until the end of the 1920s, the CCP would not try to take the lead among the Inner Mongols.[51]

---

50. Baabar, *Twentieth Century Mongolia,* 274–75; S. G. Luzianin, *Rossiia–Mongoliia– Kitaii v pervoi polovine XX v.: Politicheskie vzaimootnosheniia v 1911–1946 g.* (Russia, Mongolia, and China in the first half of the twentieth century: Political relations, 1911– 1946) (Moscow: Far Eastern Institute of Russian Academy of Sciences, 2000), 129.

51. Luzianin, *Rossiia–Mongoliia–Kitaii,* 130, 133–34; Baabar, *Twentieth Century Mongolia,* 274–75; "Comrade Liu Bojian's Report from Kulun [Ulaanbaatar], 8 September 1926," United Front Department of the Central Committee of the Chinese Communist Party, *Minzu Wenti Wenxian Huibian* (Collected Documents on the Nationality Question; hereafter *MWWH*) (Beijing: Zhonggong Zhongyang Dangxiao Chubanshe, 1991), 76–77; "IMPRP's Letter to the GMD Central Committee, 8 November 1926," ibid., 51; "Some Questions about the Work in the Three Special Districts, May 1926," Central Archives, *Zhonggong Zhongyang Wenjian Xuanji* (Selected Documents of the Chinese Communist Party Central Committee), 18 vols. (Beijing: Zhonggong Zhongyang Dangxiao Chubanshe, 1989), 2: 64–65; Christopher Atwood, *Young Mongols and*

At the time, some members of the Comintern Executive Committee favored accommodating pan-Mongolism with pan-Sovietism, suggesting that all Mongolian sectors organize a unified republic at present and join the Soviet Union in the future.[52] The proposition had a precedent in Lenin's idea about an ever-expanding "Eurasian Union of Soviet Republics," though there is no evidence that Lenin had considered Mongolia as a prospective member republic. In the mid-1920s, however, a Comintern-sponsored pan-Mongol program would have immediately demolished what Soviet diplomacy had hitherto achieved with the Chinese government. Besides, the proposition also contradicted the Comintern's routine extenuation with the GMD and the CCP that Outer Mongolia was not really detached from China—it was "liberated" ahead of China and would be a member of a new Chinese federal state in the future. As a matter of fact, when Soviet influence became entrenched in the MPR, any doctrinal prediction of a unified Mongolia as part of a federal system, either Chinese or Soviet, became increasingly superfluous to policymakers in Moscow.

Under the circumstances, Nikiforov, the Soviet representative in Ulaanbaatar, in 1926 proposed to his superiors in Moscow a "two-Mongolia" scheme, which was designed to nullify the old rhetoric about a liberated and unified Mongolia as part of a certain federation and at the same time to counter both China's irredentism regarding Outer Mongolia and Ulaanbaatar's pan-Mongol craving for Inner Mongolia. According to the formula, the MPR should be made an outright independent state under Soviet influence while Inner Mongolia remain as an autonomous region of China. But Nikiforov was ahead of his time by two decades. In 1926, Moscow preferred ambiguity to clarity with respect to Outer Mongolia's legal status. Besides, the concerns of the Nikiforov scheme could be addressed in a different manner. In January 1927, after prolonged deliberation, the Comintern Executive Committee adopted a three-point resolution to this effect:

1. The national revolutionary movement of Inner Mongolia was part of China's "general national liberation movement" led by the GMD and the CCP.
2. The movement of Inner Mongolia was not under direct guidance of Outer

---

Vigilantes in Inner Mongolia's Interregnum Decades, 1911–1931 (Leiden: Brill Academic Publishers, 2002), 2: 537.

52. Luzianin, *Rossia–Mongolia–Kitaii,* 132.

Mongolia because its leading organ, the IMPRP, was working under the Comintern's supervision.

3. The IMPRP's work must be conducted under slogans against feudalism and for an autonomous Inner Mongolia as part of a revolutionary Chinese federal republic.[53]

Thus, by defining the "revolutionary identity" of and the "revolutionary responsibility" for Inner Mongolia, the Comintern resolution rejected the notion of an inclusive Mongolian national identity. By explicitly designating Inner Mongolia as part of the Chinese revolution, the resolution also implicitly excluded Outer Mongolia from the Chinese state.

Divided Nation and Split Revolution

The division of Mongolia into an inner and an outer zone was a trademark practice of the late Qing court's ethno-geopolitics. In the twentieth century, Chinese and Mongolian nationalists wanted to revoke that tradition by unifying Mongolia in their own ways, though neither got the chance to do so. It was Russia, under both the Tsarist and Soviet governments, that inherited the Manchus' divisive orientation toward Mongolia. There was, however, an important difference between the Manchu and Russian stratagems: Whereas the Manchu court had rendered both Inner and Outer Mongolia centripetal toward a same political center, Tsarist and Soviet policies were aimed at turning the two places away from each other and putting them separately under Chinese and Russian influence. In this regard, the divisive significance of the 1927 Comintern resolution cannot be exaggerated. Despite its revolutionary terminology and internationalist format, the resolution actually ended the Bolsheviks' initial idealistic search for a new Asia policy and reconnected the Soviet regime with the Tsarist geopolitical tradition.

In the early 1920s, as Lenin was debilitated politically by illness, Stalin already exerted strong influence on the direction of Moscow's Mongolia policy. Yet other Bolshevik principals, including some of Stalin's arch-rivals such as Trotsky, basically agreed with the policy of detaching Outer Mongolia from China and keeping the Mongols divided. At a March 1927 Comintern conference, Nikolai Bukharin, another top Bolshevik, made a flimsy argument for unifying all Mongols into a revolutionary political en-

---

53. Luzianin, *Rossiia–Mongoliia–Kitaii,* 135-136.

tity. This proved to be the last dissenting voice about the issue among Soviet leaders.[54]

Soon, Jiang Jieshi's bloodbath against the CCP in April 1927, stressful as the development was to Stalin and his associates, proved convenient for Moscow to perpetuate Outer Mongolia's separation from China. Before Jiang Jieshi turned his guns against the Chinese Communists and Comintern agents, the GMD and Outer Mongolia were in the same "revolutionary bloc" fostered by Moscow. The Soviet leaders could not simply reject the GMD's demand for Mongolia's "return" to China upon the victory of China's revolution. After April 1927, the GMD's open hostility toward the Soviet Union made it much easier for Moscow to consolidate its Mongolian enterprise. There was no more need for comradely maneuvering with the GMD. Now, the Comintern informed the leaders in Ulaanbaatar that their former ally, the GMD, was actually Mongolia's worst enemy. Those Mongol leaders who were suspected of pro-Chinese inclinations were quickly removed. From the reshuffling, Choibalsan emerged as a firm follower of Moscow. Once he taunted his less convinced colleagues that any behavior deviant from the Comintern was the same as "nibbling the earth with one's teeth."[55]

Nevertheless, nationalism was an emotion hard to suppress. Despite Moscow's misgivings, some leaders in Ulaanbaatar continued to advocate a Mongolian federation in Central Asia that should include not only all Mongolian sectors but also Tibet and Turkestan. This was not entirely an original Mongolian idea. Moscow had also pondered briefly using Mongolia's cultural and religious connections with Tibet to advance Soviet influence in the highland of snow. In early 1926, the Politburo even approved a plan for sending a "unofficial representative" to Tibet in the name of the MPR.[56] But Moscow would not tolerate any action in this direction initiated by the Mongols themselves. Meanwhile, Japanese-fostered pan-Mongol tendencies seemed on the rise in the direction of Inner Mongolia. Beginning with the late 1920s, Soviet leaders suspected that a Japanese conspiracy against the Soviet Union was unfolding in northern China and Inner Mongolia. After the Japanese military created its Manchukuo puppet state, Moscow was alarmed

54. "Baranovsky's Written Report on the GMD Delegation's Interview with Trotsky, 27 November 1923," *GLZD,* 1: 339–41; Luzianin, *Rossia–Mongolia–Kitaii,* 136.

55. Baabar, *Twentieth Century Mongolia,* 283, 285–87; Luzianin, *Rossia–Mongolia–Kitaii,* 151; Sergei Luzianin, "The Yalta Conference and Mongolia in International Law before and during the Second World War," *FEA* 6 (1995): 34–35.

56. Baabar, *Twentieth Century Mongolia,* 278; minutes no. 5 of the Soviet Communist Party Politburo meetings, 21 January 1926, *GLZD,* 3: 23–24.

that Japan's next step was to unify Inner and Outer Mongolia into an independent state and thus to achieve a "strategic edge in war" against the Soviet Union.[57]

The perceived or real threat from Chinese "counterrevolutionaries" and Japanese imperialism partially explained the frenzy under which the Soviets implemented steps for incorporating Outer Mongolia into their orbit. The process, innocently defined as "reciprocal political adaptation" by Russian scholarship today, began in the mid-1920s.[58] Through a series of bilateral agreements on trade and economic development, Outer Mongolia was integrated into the "genuine economic entity" about which Stalin had so forcefully argued in his earlier debate with Lenin. The reliability of Ulaanbaatar was guaranteed with Moscow's appointments of Russian officials and Buryat Comintern agents to important positions in the MPR government and military establishment. In the meantime, repeated purges of the MPR leadership eliminated leaders of the 1921 revolution one after another until Stalin identified Choibalsan as his alter ego to rule Mongolia in 1939.[59]

Choibalsan's ascendance to power coincided with an important structural change in the Soviet–Mongolian relationship. In March 1932, after a three-year disaster of radical social and economic reforms supervised by the Comintern, the Soviet leadership decided to put Mongolian affairs under its direct command. To deal with the rebellious situation in the MPR and to expedite the policymaking process, the Soviet Communist Party's Politburo set up a standing committee in charge of all questions related to Mongolia. Stalin considered the work of the committee important enough to have himself included. The committee decided that the Soviet Union needed Mongolia as a stable protectorate. Therefore, the road of development for the MPR would not be socialism but a "non-capitalist way rejecting imperialism and

57. Luzianin, *Rossia–Mongolia–Kitaii,* 156–57; Baabar, *Twentieth Century Mongolia,* 341.

58. Luzianin, *Rosisia–Mongoliia–Kitaii,* 155.

59. Luzianin, *Rossiia–Mongoliia–Kitaii,* 155; Baabar, *Twentieth Century Mongolia,* 299, 326–27; Shagdariin Sandag and Harry H. Kendall, *Poisoned Arrows: The Stalin-Choibalsan Mongolian Massacres, 1921–1941* (Boulder, Colo.: Westview Press, 2000), 89–103. For different appraisals of Soviet personnel and tactics in the MPR, see Thomas T. Hammond, "The Communist Takeover of Outer Mongolia: Model for Eastern Europe?" *Studies on the Soviet Union* 11(4) (1977): 107–44; Zotan Barany, "Soviet Takeovers: The Role of Advisers in Mongolia in the 1920s and in Eastern Europe after World War II," *Eastern European Quarterly* 28 (4) (January 1995): 409–33, and I. I. Kuznetsov, "The Soviet Military Advisors in Mongolia, 1921–1939," *Journal of Slavic Military Studies* 12(4) (December 1999): 118–37.

feudalism." Afterward, although radical economic measures were suspended, attacks against perceived class enemies were intensified. Between 1935 and 1939, Stalin repeatedly admonished leaders in Ulaanbaatar for their "lack of will" in fighting lamas' influence with a "tough policy." According to Stalin, tolerance of Lamaism at home was incompatible with defense of Mongolian independence, for "the lamas living in your country have become enemies of its independence, [and] they are ready to help Japanese aggressors."

As of March 1939, Choibalsan's political victory over his rivals finally gave Stalin a Mongolian leader who was willing to translate the Soviet ruler's logic into policy steps in Mongolia. On March 17, 1939, or ten days after Choibalsan became the prime minister of the MPR, the Soviet Politburo abolished its standing committee on Mongolia and divided its responsibilities among several ministries of the Soviet government.[60] The significance of this development was twofold: First, to Moscow the Mongolia question had changed from a party, or "revolutionary" affair to a matter of routine bureaucratic management; second, the emergence of the Stalin–Choibalsan patronage rendered all committee works redundant.

Ideologically proselytizing, Soviet and Comintern officials could not appraise the value of their Mongolia project without lauding its demonstrative function as a model of "non-capitalist development" for other "backward colonial states." But, in reality, only tangible benefits could sustain Moscow's interest in the Mongolian protectorate. Aside from supplementing the Soviet economy with its animal husbandry, Mongolia's sheer size provided the Soviet Union with an extensive strategic buffer in the east and the south. In the words of a Comintern agent in Mongolia, the country's territory was more important than its population, and control of the territory was therefore "more important than to build socialism in a country of eight hundred thousand herdsmen."[61] After the Sino-Japanese war began in July 1937, Mongolia was immediately turned into a Soviet military barricade. Within a year Moscow's military subsidy to Ulaanbaatar was increased from 6 to

---

60. "Document 02052: Politburo Resolution on the Mongolia Question, 16 March 1932," *SLDX,* 11: 33; "Document 02054: Politburo Resolution on Comrade Eliava's Report on the Mongolia Question, 1 September 1932," ibid., 11: 39; Baabar, *Twentieth Century Mongolia,* 318; Togoochiyn Lkhagva, "What Was Stalin's Real Attitude to the Mongols?" *FEA* 4 (1991): 123–25; Luzianin, *Rossiia–Mongoliia–Kitaii,* 204. Tseden-dambyn Batbayar, "Stalin's Strategy in Mongolia, 1932–1936," *Mongolian Studies* 22 (1999): 1–17, details a "new turn policy" in the MPR supervised by Stalin.

61. Soviet Politburo member Sh. Z. Eliava and Comintern agent Bogumiral Smeral are quoted in Baabar, *Twentieth Century Mongolia,* 288, 325.

8 million rubles, and 30,000 troops of the Soviet Red Army were dispatched to the MPR to fend off possible invasion by the Japanese Army. These were soon consolidated into the 57th Special Rifle Corps, consisting of a motorized rifle division, a cavalry brigade, a tank brigade, and three motorized armored brigades.[62]

In the summer of 1941, Germany's attack on the Soviet Union from the west further tightened the knot between Moscow and Ulaanbaatar in the east. The German invasion forced Moscow to relocate its military industries to Siberia and to turn the remote area into its most important rear base. These developments put pressure on Ulaanbaatar to beef up its defenses against Japan. Between 1941 and 1945, half of the MPR's state budget was spent for defense purposes, and the size of its military force increased fourfold.[63] By the end of World War II, although not a formal part of the Soviet Union, the MPR's economic, political, and military ties with the Soviet Empire were as close as any member republic of the Soviet Union.

Thus, after more than two decades' effort, the "outer" part of Moscow's "two-Mongolia" formula was accomplished. Yet from the outset, the formula was asymmetric. Although able to force the Outer Mongols to accept a fragmentary Mongolian nationhood, the Soviets had no means of convincing the Inner Mongols about their "Chinese" identity. If the Qing division of Mongolia had been feudal, the twentieth-century version of Mongolia's division was "international" and characterized by Outer and Inner Mongolia's domination by different powers. In curbing the Outer Mongols' pan-Mongol tendencies and preserving the internationalized division of Mongolia, Soviet leaders were always cunning in avoiding turning the anti-Chinese premise of Mongolian nationalism into an anti-Soviet one. Over the years, one way deployed by Stalin to tame nationalistic Mongol leaders was to keep reminding them that no other power but the Soviet Union protected Mongolian independence from the Chinese.[64] Nevertheless, the territorial perimeter of Moscow's geopolitical strategy could only circumscribe Ulaanbaatar's activities but not the ethnopolitical reach of the Mongolian revolution. As a region that had the largest Mongolian population, Inner

62. Kuznetsov, "Soviet Military Advisors," 127–28.
63. Stephan, *Russian Far East,* 183–86, 190, 235, 241; Luzianin, *Rossiia–Mongoliia–Kitaii,* 197; Baabar, *Twentieth Century Mongolia,* 357–58; Benson Bobrick, *East of the Sun: The Epic Conquest and Tragic History of Siberia* (New York: Poseidon Press, 1992), 445; Ch. Purevdorzh, "Soviet–Mongolian Cooperation during the Second World War," *FEA* 4 (1985): 35–43.
64. Lkhagva, "What Was Stalin's Real Attitude to the Mongols?"

Mongolia remained a hotbed of Mongolian nationalism. Its connections with Outer Mongolia could neither be severed by convenient arrangements among great powers nor by the Comintern's two-Mongolia resolution.

As a matter of fact, soon after the resolution was adopted, the revolutionary hierarchy prescribed in it was ruined by the GMD–CCP split in April 1927. The designated leader of the Inner Mongolian revolutionary movement, the GMD, turned into a counterrevolutionary, and the CCP, which had never been strong in northern China, had to recover from the GMD's onslaught and was less likely than before to lead the Inner Mongolian movement. Leaders in Ulaanbaatar immediately seized the chance to regain some influence in Inner Mongolia. In June, they convinced Moscow, which had not yet recovered from the shock of its recent China debacle, to send some weapons secretly to the IMPRP, which was in chaos because of the GMD–CCP conflict.[65] Yet, the Comintern ban on Ulaanbaatar's leading role in Inner Mongolia was not lifted. At this juncture, the Inner Mongols took the initiative. The result was a military uprising in eastern Inner Mongolia led by Merse (a.k.a. Guo Daofu), a founding member of the IMPRP and a "radical communist revolutionary" according to one definition.[66]

Only recently, the background of the Merse insurrection has been unveiled by scholars with access to Soviet and Mongolian archival materials. Briefly, after the IMPRP fell into internal feuds in the wake of the GMD–CCP split, Merse reorganized the party's left wing into an Inner Mongolia Youth Party. In July 1928, after consulting with a Comintern agent named A. Klimov in Ulaanbaatar, Merse and his associates adopted a program for launching a new stage of revolution in Inner Mongolia. The steps would include mass mobilization, the organization of a local self-government and a self-defense force, and preparations for calling a people's *hural* (assembly). But, after returning to his home region, Hulunbuir of eastern Inner Mongolia, Merse believed that the situation warranted a more drastic action, namely, a military insurrection. His action was either encouraged or fully approved by another Comintern agent in the area, Ivan P. Stepanov, who promised the conspirators that weapons and financial assistance would soon arrive from the Comintern. Yet when the news about the Hulunbuir insurrection arrived in Ulaanbaatar, Comintern representatives there, including Klimov,

65. Minutes no. 107 of the Soviet Communist Party Central Politburo meetings, 2 June 1927, *GLZD*, 4:297; Luzianin, *Rossia–Mongolia–Kitaii*, 138.

66. Uradyn E. Bulag, *The Mongols at China's Edge: History and the Politics of National Unity* (Lanham, Md.: Rowman & Littlefield, 2002), 144.

denounced the action as a violation of Comintern policies and accused agent Stepanov of committing a serious error. Without support from the Comintern and the MPR, the uprising managed to last just about a month (from August 7 to September 12) before it was crushed by the Chinese authorities. In public, both Moscow and Ulaanbaatar denied any connection to the Merse group. Soviet propaganda even denounced the event as a Japanese plot intent on creating an excuse for Japanese interference in northern Manchuria. To conceal the connections between the Merse's group and the Comintern, the Soviet government ordered the arrest of Merse's associates who had arrived in Outer Mongolia during and after the uprising. They were conveniently accused as Japan's secret agents.[67]

As for Merse, rejected by Moscow and Ulaanbaatar, he had to accept the Manchurian warlord Zhang Xueliang's peace offer to save his people from further destruction. Before Japan took over Manchuria, he served in the local government of Hulunbuir but did not stop planning for new actions. In August 1930, a translated article of Merse's appeared in the American journal *Pacific Affairs,* which advocated "fusion of the two races" of China and Mongolia. Although admitting significant socioeconomic improvements in the MPR because of its collaboration with the Soviet Union, Merse had these words about his former sponsor, the Soviet Union: "Her words are honey but her intentions are the sword. . . . She is stealing a bell with her own ears stuffed," meaning that self-deceivingly, Moscow had monopolized the MPR in the name of friendship.[68] In the years to come, Merse would remain a controversial figure in Inner Mongolian politics and history. Aside from being a political embarrassment to Moscow after 1928, Merse's "Daur-Mongol" identity would warrant his receiving a triple denunciation for treachery in the orthodox revolutionary historiographies of the CCP, the Inner Mongols, and the Daurs.[69] Yet, clearly, in the episode of the Hulunbuir uprising, treachery was committed by Moscow alone.

67. Luzianin, *Rossiia–Mongoliia–Kitaii,* 139–41. Atwood, *Young Mongols,* 2: 853–60, hypothesizes that Moscow initially encouraged but then abandoned the Merse group for two reasons: (1) The uprising could not prevail because of bad timing; and (2) the uprising was not stopped because it could create a manageable war scare to isolate the MPR from outside contacts, especially with Japan.

68. Guo Tao-fu (Merse), "Modern Mongolia," *Pacific Affairs* 3(8) (August 1930): 754–62. The editorial note indicates that this article was first published in a Chinese journal, *Progress.*

69. Merse's treatment in post-1949 historiographies in China and the ethnopolitics around Daur identity are detailed in Bulag, *The Mongols at China's Edge,* 137–76.

The Hulunbuir uprising had two consequences in the revolutionary politics of Inner Mongolia. In the short run, it prompted Comintern agents in Ulaanbaatar and Soviet leaders in Moscow to reaffirm the established Comintern démarche that Ulaanbaatar ought to refrain from any direct responsibility for the movement in Inner Mongolia. In hoping to counter Japanese influence based in Manchuria and meanwhile to prevent provocative, militant actions by the Inner Mongols, Moscow asked the CCP to intensify its work in Inner Mongolia and to coordinate with Ulaanbaatar closely. At the time, the CCP indeed endeavored to take the helm of the Inner Mongolian movement. Ever since its split with the GMD, the CCP tried to step out of the GMD's shadow and, in the words of a CCP document dated March 1928, "to obtain with determination the leadership of the revolution in Inner Mongolia and to get all controlling power, including military power, of the IMPRP." CCP leaders believed that slogans like "national independence" and "Inner Mongolian National Republic" could effectively mobilize ordinary Inner Mongols and expedite the transformation of the IMPRP's left wing into a "national organization for mass struggle."[70] In contrast to Moscow, they actually had a rather positive estimate of the Merse group's effort. In early 1929, in a letter to its Inner Mongolian branch, the CCP Central Committee pointed out:

> Some young left-wing members [of the IMPRP] have paid close attention to mass work and can consistently pursue revolutionary objectives of Inner Mongolian national independence and opposition to China's GMD warlords. In eastern Mongolia they have quite a bit of popular support.[71]

Thus, when Moscow encouraged the CCP to set the tempo for the Inner Mongols' struggle, the CCP, thinking and acting in a context rather different from Moscow's perceived geopolitical interests, did not feel prohibited at all in exploiting the Inner Mongols' "revolutionary nationalism" and pitting them against China's political authorities. It is significant that the CCP

70. Luzianin, *Rossiia–Mongoliia–Kitaii,* 141–42; Hao Weimin, "The IMPRP during the First and Second Domestic Revolutionary Wars," in *Zhongguo Menggu Shixuehui Chengli Dahui Jinian Jikan* (Collected Essays Commemorating the Establishment of the Mongolian Studies Society of China), comp. and pub. Zhongguo Menggu Shixuehui (1979), 595–96; "CCP Central Committee's Letter to the Special Branch of Inner Mongolia, 23 October 1928," *MWWH,* 91.

71. "CCP Central Committee's Letter to the [Inner] Mongolian Committee, 30 February 1929," *MWWH,* 100–7.

leadership identified eastern Inner Mongolia as the most advanced area in terms of revolutionary preparedness, though a meaningful contact between the CCP and eastern Mongols would take place only after World War II and in a rather different context. In the late 1920s, neither could the Inner Mongol revolutionaries put their movement back on track nor was the CCP effective enough to start a "Mongolian national movement" of its own design. Hard pressed by GMD troops in southern China, the CCP, a party committed to and sustained by the "mass line," had first to survive in China's Han ethnographic zones before it could exert any meaningful influence on the Inner Mongols.

In sum, after the GMD–IMPRP collaboration of the mid-1920s collapsed, the CCP was unable to replace the GMD and to resuscitate the Chinese aspect of the 1927 Comintern resolution on "two Mongolias." In 1930, the CCP Central Committee adopted an outline for Inner Mongolia work that set an "Inner Mongolian Commoners Republic" as the goal. In the meantime, the CCP leadership accepted the party's impotence in Inner Mongolia. Contrary to the Comintern decision on the CCP leadership of the Inner Mongolian movement, the outline recommended that the IMPRP accept the leadership of the MPR.[72]

During the 1930s, the central stage of Inner Mongolian politics was no longer occupied by the IMPRP or its offspring. Rather, an autonomous movement around Prince De held the attention of the Chinese government and the outside world. Being neither from radical eastern Mongolia nor the sinicized western Mongolian province Suiyuan, Prince De represented the more conservative and traditional Mongolian values entrenched in central, pastoral Inner Mongolia, a region that had largely been bypassed by the Comintern-directed movement in the 1920s. In 1933, when Prince De issued his open message to the Chinese authorities demanding Mongolian autonomy, a political Inner Mongolia suddenly came to life. This Inner Mongolia acted in reaction to the new Chinese–Japanese conflict and was difficult for the Comintern to penetrate.[73]

Nevertheless, in the long run, the Hulunbuir uprising fostered a thread of Inner Mongolian radicalism that would become a focal point of Inner Mon-

72. "CCP Center's Outline Plan for Inner Mongolia Work, 5 November 1930," *MWWH,* 136–41.

73. Sechin Jagchid, *The Last Mongol Prince: The Life and Times of Demchugdongrob, 1902–1966* (Bellingham: Center for East Asian Studies, Western Washington University, 1999), 26, 66–69.

golian politics again after World War II. In its post-1927 history, the IMPRP assumed a phoenix-like character and would become one of the most mysterious political parties in world history because of its repeated disappearance and reappearance. After the Hulunbuir fiasco of 1928, Merse did not retire politically. In late September 1931, or less than two weeks after the Japanese Army manufactured the Mukden incident in Manchuria, Merse instructed his associates and young followers, including two would-be leaders of the post–World War II eastern Mongolian movement, Khafengga and Buyanmandukhu, to take advantage of Japan's stated sympathy toward Inner Mongolian autonomy and organize a military force in eastern Mongolia. According to the plan, after receiving weapons from the Japanese Army, the Mongolian force, in the name of "Mongolian autonomous army," should march to a base in western Inner Mongolia and start anti-Japanese and autonomous activities. Those involved believed that the plan was from the IMPRP leadership, not realizing that both Moscow and Ulaanbaatar had already disavowed Merse. According to some accounts, after the military plan failed in 1932, Merse made a trip to Ulaanbaatar. It cannot be ascertained whether or not Merse ever reached his destination, because he would never be heard from again.[74]

To Moscow, Merse's action was again disconcerting. As a matter of fact, shortly after the Mukden incident, the Comintern instructed its two Inner Mongol agents in Manchuria, Temurbagana and Pungsug, to involve themselves in organizing a "Mongolian autonomous army." But Moscow's purposes were rather different from Merse's military plan. Instructing the Inner Mongols to focus on political and intelligence activities, the Comintern explicitly prohibited them from carrying out any military activities. In the spring of 1932, Temurbagana and Pungsug decided to enlarge their circle and inducted some twenty people, including Khafengga and Askhan, into their IMPRP cell. This must have been a strange occasion to these people, because at least some of them had already been working under Merse's "IMPRP leadership" for some time. At the time, the central leadership of the IMPRP no longer existed, except for an empty headquarters in Ulaanbaatar. Shortly after expanding his group, Pungsug traveled to Ulaabaatar and then to Moscow to meet with Pavel Mif, the deputy head of the Oriental Secretariat of the Comintern Executive Committee. Pungsug's trip was

---

74. Buhe and Sain, *Boyanmandu Shengping Shilue* (Buyanmandukhu's Life and Times) (Internal circulation; Hohhot: Neimenggu Daxue Tushuguan, 1999), 50–53; Jagchid, *Last Mongol Prince,* 46–47; Hao Weimin, "IMPRP," 591–97.

probably related to a plan to move the IMPRP headquarters back to Inner Mongolia. But the plan was never implemented. Then, in 1933, the IMPRP establishment in Ulaanbaatar was simply abolished.

During most of the 1930s, the Temurbagana–Pungsug group received directives mainly through two Comintern liaisons named "Pankov" and "Delger," who were hiding in the French concession in Beiping (Beijing). Under this arrangement, the "IMPRP" of the 1930s was reduced from a leading body of the Inner Mongolian national movement to a secret cell of Moscow's intelligence network in northeast China. But even this situation did not last. In 1936, Temurbagana was arrested by the Japanese authorities in Manchuria and would be kept under close surveillance until the end of war. In the fall of 1939, when traveling to Ulaanbaatar to solicit instructions from the Comintern, Pungsug was detained by the Mongolian authorities, which were caught in a frenzy of political purges. He would not be allowed to return to Inner Mongolia until the end of World War II. In the meantime, other members of the group worked either in the administration of Manchukuo or in Prince De's regime in collaboration with Japan, believing that they were underground IMPRP members and were carrying out "long-term secret work" under Comintern directives.[75]

To these Inner Mongol partisans, this conviction was vitally important. In the war years, the belief sustained their hope that one day their IMPRP phoenix would fly again. Indeed, right after Japan's surrender, Khafengga and Temurbagana would declare the resurrection of the IMPRP from ashes. Although during the 1930s and 1940s Mif and other Comintern handlers of the Temurbagana–Pungsug group successively became victims of the Stalinist purges in the Soviet Union and the MPR, the group's Comintern connection warranted its legitimacy in postwar politics in China and East Asia. Unlike Prince De and his associates, whose golden age ended together with Japan's military empire in the summer of 1945, the eastern Mongol partisans' wartime

75. Oljeiochir, "Tidal Waves in the Sea of Deserts," *Keqi Wenshi Ziliao* (Historical and Literary Materials of Khorchin Banner) 1 (1985): 21–26; Jiang Mingsheng, "Brief Biography of Temurbagana," *Xing'an Dangshi Wenji* (Essays on the Party History in the Xing'an [League]) 1 (1993): 229; Tumen and Zhu Dongli, *Kang Sheng yu Neirendang Yuan'an* (Kang Sheng and the Unjust Case of the IMPRP) (Beijing: Zhongyang Dangxiao Chubanshe, 1995), 111–17; Bukho and Sayin, *Boyanmandu Shengping Shilue* (A Brief Biography of Buyanmandukhu) (Hohhot: Neimenggu Daxue Tushuguan, 1999), 54, 92, 100. All relevant sources from China indicate that in 1934 Pungsug brought a Comintern directive on secret works to the group; however, after 1949, in a different political atmosphere of China, Pungsug was reluctant to admit his role in this regard.

service under the Japanese authorities became part of their "revolutionary credentials" and put them in the right position to start a new Inner Mongolian movement. What these people did not realize was that, with an established "two Mongolias" orientation, Moscow had ceased to be a supporter of Mongolian nationalism a long time before. It was Moscow's long-term ally in China, the CCP, that maintained a constant interest in both Inner and Outer Mongolia out of its particular concerns.

3

Dialectics of Brotherhood:
The Chinese Communist Party
and the Mongolian People's Republic

In the history of the Chinese Communist movement, the issue of Outer Mongolia remains largely an unwritten page. In 1993, a group of writers in China put out a semihistorical and semifictional work on Mongolian independence, which was soon taken out of circulation by the authorities.[1] In the West, although Edgar Snow's famous interview with Mao Zedong in 1936 has often been cited in scholarly works as evidence of Mao's ethnocentrism, no systematic study has been done about the Chinese Communist Party's (CCP's) relationship with the issue of Mongolian independence. This historiographical omission is unfortunate, because the issue of Outer Mongolia was a constant factor in the CCP's political journey before 1949 and has continued to vex the Chinese psyche to this very day.[2]

The CCP's historical relationship with the Mongolia question is neither linear nor simple. Like the party itself, the relationship has evolved in phases.

---

1. Shi Bo, *Waimenggu Duli Neimu* (Inside Story of Outer Mongolian Independence) (Beijing: Renmin Zhongguo Chubanshe, 1993). "Shi Bo" is a collective pseudonym for a group of unknown academics in Beijing led by Zhang Guoan, Song Dachuan, and Wang Xinguang. The book's publication was noticed in both Mongolia and Russia. Baabar's *Twentieth Century Mongolia* (Cambridge: White Horse Press, 1999) cites information from an unpublished, handwritten Mongolian translation of the book.

2. For some "news sites" on the Internet that reflect opinions of Chinese "Netizens" about the Mongolia question, including outright irredentism and misinformed understandings of history, see *Junshi Tiandi* (Military Domain) of the "Wanwei" news group (http://www.creaders.net) and the *Qiangguo Luntan* (Strong Power Forum) of *People's Daily* online (http://www.people.com.cn). The former is a nongovernmental site outside China, and the latter is an official Chinese site of the government.

Michael Hunt's study of the genesis of Chinese Communist foreign policy identifies the years from 1920 to 1934 as a period in which the Chinese Communists, under the aegis of the Comintern, developed their "international affairs orthodoxy." From 1935 onward, the CCP's ideology and policymaking gradually came under the predominant personality of Mao Zedong—hence the beginning of the famous Maoist variant of communism.[3] Although not discounting personality and ideology as important factors in the CCP's decisionmaking, Yang Kuisong's detailed survey of the CCP–Moscow relationship examines the subject as a process of trials and readjustments on both sides in the context of China's internal and foreign crises. The result is a different periodization, which is characterized by the CCP's hesitant trust of the Comintern in its formative years and incomplete autonomy from Moscow even after Mao took charge.[4] Undoubtedly factors like ideology, personalities, and China's general political conditions stressed in these studies are extremely important for understanding the CCP's relationship with the Mongolia question. In this regard, however, the CCP, as a revolutionary movement, a nation-building force, and an ethnopolitical agent, should be positioned particularly on China's multiethnic canvas so that its shifting stance in China's ethnopolitics can be revealed, which in history played out in a center-versus-periphery fashion.

Until the end of World War II, the center–periphery conception proved a twisted one for the CCP. As a Han-centric movement striving to gain the ruling position of China, the CCP naturally was inclined to adopt the "central" position in China's ethnopolitics; yet as an emulator of the Russian Bolshevik Revolution, the CCP was a "revolutionary periphery" revering the Soviet Union as the "revolutionary center." The revolutionary connection not only introduced Marxist-Leninist doctrines into the CCP movement, which significantly modified its participants' ethnocultural proclivities, but also made Moscow's satellite, the Mongolian People's Republic (MPR), a secondary "revolutionary center" to the CCP. A position of centrality was also hard for the CCP to hold because the Guomindang (GMD, Nationalist Party) government, China's official center, spared no effort to drive the CCP

---

3. Michael H. Hunt, *The Genesis of Chinese Communist Foreign Policy* (New York: Columbia University Press, 1996), esp. 83–158.

4. Yang Kuisong, *Zhonggong yu Mosike de Guanxi, 1920–1960* (The CCP's Relationship with Moscow, 1920–1960) (Taipei: Dongda Tushu Gongsi, 1997), separates the relationship into three overlapped periods: a confidence-building period (1920–30), a contradiction-burgeoning period (1929–36), and a loose-connection period (1937–60).

to the fringe of China's political life, or to the verge of extinction. Especially after the early 1930s, the CCP had to find a new lease on life in a location between China's ethnopolitical center in the south and the international "revolutionary center" in the north.

Revolutionary Paradox

Before the Chinese Communist Party was organized in 1921, the would-be CCP founders' attitudes toward the Mongolia question were as diverse as political groupings in China, though this diversity reflected a shared sense of urgency about China's national crises. In their anxious search of a way out for China, for instance, Li Dazhao and Chen Duxiu, two leading radical intellectuals who would together launch the CCP in 1921, engaged each other in a debate about whether or not the current republican state was worth saving.[5] It is also not surprising that after upholding a typical statist stand in sounding alarms about China's possible loss of Mongolia and Manchuria in 1916, Mao switched to a totally iconoclast argument in 1920 that China did not deserve to be a "big country" and that its "twenty-two provinces, three special districts and two dependent regions . . . should be broken into twenty-seven states." The three "special districts" were divided regions of Inner Mongolia, and the two "dependent regions" were Outer Mongolia and Tibet.[6] These divergent personal views were generated by what is deftly called a "patriotic impulse" and would, after 1921, be replaced by a disciplined party line.[7]

During its first decade or so, the CCP publicly issued its "unconditional recognition" of Outer Mongolia's independence. The attitude was especially manifested by the CCP when the Sino-Soviet diplomacy over Outer Mongolia stalled in the early 1920s.[8] During the Chinese–Soviet negotiations over

5. John Fitzgerald, *Awakening China: Politics, Culture, and Class in the Nationalist Revolution* (Stanford, Calif.: Stanford University Press, 1996), 89–91.

6. Documentary Research Office of the CCP Central Committee, *Mao Zedong Nianpu* (Chronicle of Mao Zedong's Life), 3 vols. (Beijing: Zhongyang Wenxian Chubanshe, 1993), 1: 24; Mao Zedong, *Mao Zedong Zaoqi Wengao* (Early Writings of Mao Zedong) (Changsha: Hunan Chubanshe, 1995), 503–8, 530–33.

7. Hunt, *Genesis,* 53–82.

8. "Chen Duxiu's Report to the Comintern, 30 June 1922," United Front Department of the CCP Central Committee, *Minzu Wenti Wenxian Huibian* (Collected Documents on the National Question; hereafter *MWWH*) (Internal circulation; Beijing: Zhonggong

Outer Mongolia in 1924, CCP apparatuses in Beijing orchestrated letter writing, demonstrations, and direct petitions to the government. The CCP was even possibly behind a terrorist bombing to pressure the Beijing government to conclude an agreement with Moscow on Outer Mongolia. Wellington Koo, who was then foreign minister of the Beijing regime and therefore the main target of the bomb attack, later remembered a rather emotional exchange between himself and Li Dazhao. On this occasion, Li argued that Outer Mongolia would be better off even if it came under Soviet domination. At the time, both the radicals and the government in Beijing understood that the agreement under negotiation was not about China's sovereignty in Outer Mongolia in name but was about Soviet influence there in substance. Obviously, in 1924 the CCP acted in coordination with Soviet foreign policy, though the effect of its action on Chinese diplomacy was not clear. The issue nevertheless marked a clear cleavage between the CCP and the Beijing regime and its GMD successor.[9]

It would, however, overly simplify the problem to define the CCP's behavior as the slavish following of Moscow's orders. Although growing out of the same patriotic roots as the GMD, the CCP followed a very different path of national salvation. Whereas the GMD made a commitment to jump-starting the moribund Chinese republic, the CCP wanted to remake China from the bottom up and from inside out. As revolutionaries against what they perceived as a suppressive system of China, the Chinese Communists had at least a theoretical empathy for ethnic minorities' resistance against the Chinese authorities. In this regard, impulsive ideas like Mao's earlier proposition for breaking up China into many states certainly received refinement from the CCP's alliance with the Soviet Union. Lenin's phased strategy on the "national question" prescribed that revolutionaries would

---

Zhongyang Dangxiao Chubanshe, 1991), 6; "Resolution on the Question of National Minorities in Chinese Territories Adopted by the First Congress of the Chinese Workers, Peasants, and Soldiers Soviet, November 1931," ibid., 171; "CCP Central Committee's Letter to Party Comrades and All Laboring People on Support to the Soviet Union and Opposition against the Imperialists' and GMD's New Provocation, 15 May 1933," Central Archives, *Zhonggong Zhongyang Wenjian Xuanji* (Selected Documents of the CCP Central Committee; hereafter *ZZWX*), 18 vols. (Beijing: Zhonggong Zhongyang Dangxiao Chubanshe, 1992), 9: 181.

9. Gu Weijun, *Gu Weijun Huiyilu* (Memoirs of Gu Weijun [Wellington Koo]), 12 vols. (Beijing: Zhonghua Shujun, 1983–93), 1: 330–49; Chen Duxiu, "Our Answer, 17 September 1924," *MWWH*, 60–61; Xiao Chunu, "Xingshi Clique under the Microscope, October 1925," ibid.

first make use of ethnic minorities' secessionist tendencies to facilitate their own rebellion against the current ruling regime, and then employ a federalist formula to optimize the newly created revolutionary power in the largest territorial domain possible.

At the time, the Soviet model seemed to suit the CCP well. The CCP's pledge of allegiance to that model could fulfill a Comintern requirement that all its member parties oppose both foreign and their own government's imperialist oppressions of colonial peoples. Meanwhile, the CCP formula about a "Chinese federal republic" in the future could satisfy China's nationalistic public with a promise that sooner or later those alienated ethnic frontiers would rejoin China on a new basis. Thus, the CCP was able to argue with the GMD that they did not disagree on China's sovereignty over Outer Mongolia or any other frontier territory but on how and when these territories should be reincorporated into a reformed China.[10]

For the CCP's political strategy, Mongolia stood as a unique case among the ethnic borderlands. Among China's territorial ethnic minorities, the Mongols constituted the only group that had actually developed its own "socialist" revolutionary movement and thus could supposedly facilitate the downfall of China's old regime in accordance with the Leninist strategy. Furthermore, Outer Mongolia had achieved ahead of China the kind of "liberation" for which the CCP itself was still struggling. This was why, unlike the GMD, the CCP did not have a generic antiseparatist stance in China's ethnopolitics. Although sharing an animosity with the GMD against the British-encouraged Tibetan alienation, the CCP did not lament the Soviet-supported Outer Mongolian separation. To the CCP, because of its "liberation," independent Outer Mongolia became a revolutionary ally in the north and therefore constituted a gain for the CCP's own cause as well.

In embracing the Leninist orthodoxy on the "national question," the CCP renounced the old Chinese regime's "imperial" sovereignty over Mongolia and other ethnic frontiers and also, naturally *and* doctrinally, expected that these territories would voluntarily reunify with a revolutionized new China. To the Chinese Communists, self-denying anti-imperialism and voluntary federal reunification were two inseparable components of the Soviet model. In the 1920s, they did not think that China's reunification could happen only in a distant future. The GMD–CCP united front helped maintain a sense of

10. Qu Qiubai, "Leninism and Chinese Revolution, 21 January 1926," *MWWH,* 71; "CCP Central Committee's Letter to GMD Members on the Anniversary of Mr. [Sun] Yat-sen's Death, 12 March 1926," ibid., 43.

ethnopolitical centrality in the CCP. The coming tidal wave of the Nationalist Revolution kept the Chinese Communists optimistic.

Thus, unsurprisingly, in 1925 Li Dazhao advocated that once the Soviet Army completed its withdrawal from Outer Mongolia, the Chinese and Mongolian nations would be able to achieve their "brotherly coordination" either through an agreement between their national liberation movements or through Outer Mongolia's "free unification" with the Republic of China. Soon, a delegation from Ulaanbaatar came to Beijing and met with Li. However, they found Li's "sympathetic" stand as offensive as the GMD's outright rejection of MPR independence.[11]

Two years later, the GMD/CCP split drove the CCP off the central stage of Chinese politics. Although the event did not necessarily change the party principals' assumption about how a new China should be configured territorially and ethnically, the party's timetable had to be reset and its political strategy became uncertain. Under the circumstances, the CCP's earlier rosy anticipation about Mongolia's "return" was replaced by the party's anxiety about getting assistance from its revolutionary allies in the north. Yet, although the CCP's homage toward the Soviet Union was complete, its respect for the MPR was equivocal.

The CCP's ethnopolitical orthodoxy was based on a double-negative premise. Whereas the party repudiated Chinese imperialism and supported ethnic minorities' right to self-determination, its deprecating opinion about minorities' socioeconomic conditions led to a conclusion that these ethnic groups would have to make significant progress before they could catch up and join with the supposedly more advanced Chinese nation in a united states of China. Unlike their GMD counterparts, who upheld Chinese superiority in an ethnocultural sense, CCP theoreticians employed the "scientific" approach of Marxist political economics. Accordingly, the frontier peoples in "nomadic, primitive conditions" were even more backward than China's "immature capitalist production system."[12] Under this argumentation, the sovietized Outer Mongolia became a revolutionary paradox, which was best illustrated in Chen Duxiu's rhetorical question to those in China who faulted

11. Li Dazhao, "The Liberation Movement of the Mongolian Nation, 1925," *MWWH,* 69; Atwood, *Young Mongols and Vigilantes in Inner Mongolia's Interregnum Decades, 1911–1931* (Leiden: Brill Academic Publishers, 2002), 1: 405–6.

12. "The CCP's and the Central Bureau of the Chinese Socialist Youth League's Opinion on the GMD's National Congress, December 1923," *MWWH,* 23; "The CCP's Plan for Current Practical Questions, 1923," ibid., 24–25; "Proclamation of the CCP's Second National Congress, July 1922," ibid., 17.

Moscow for spreading communism in Outer Mongolia: "How can a nomadic Outer Mongolia practice a communist system?"[13]

Indeed, the *Han* leadership of the CCP and the party's small number of *Mongol* members had rather different perceptions of the MPR revolution. To Inner Mongol revolutionaries who operated within the CCP orbit, the MPR was a model of successful "socialist new life" as well as of the Mongolian people's national liberation.[14] The predominantly Han leadership of the CCP, however, never admitted that the MPR successfully conducted a socialist revolution ahead of China. In the CCP's political discourse, the MPR's demonstrative significance was therefore limited to a "model of genuine self-determination and independence," in contrast to some other ethnic regimes in China that received support from imperialist countries like Japan and the United Kingdom.[15]

Before allying itself with the GMD again in a national war of resistance against Japan, the CCP encouraged China's ethnic minorities to follow the precedent of the MPR in setting up their own revolutionary governments against the repressive GMD regime. In the early 1930s, its political agitation toward the Inner Mongols went so far as to suggest that an "Inner Mongolian People's Republic" should be established to struggle for a national restoration in "entire Mongolia." In pursuance of the Leninist formula, the CCP also proposed that the prospective Inner Mongolian people's republic alone have the right to decide whether it should join the MPR or a "Chinese soviet federation" under the CCP.[16]

In view of the CCP's quasi-pan-Mongol agitation among the Inner Mongols in the 1930s, its negative attitude toward a spontaneous pan-Mongol

13. Chen Duxiu, "The October Revolution and China's National Liberation Movement, 7 November 1925," *MWWH,* 67.

14. This is how Ulanhu, the highest-ranking Mongolian CCP member, recalled the impression about the MPR among young Inner Mongolian radicals in the 1920s. See Ulanfu, *Wulanfu Huiyilu* (Memoirs of Ulanfu) (Beijing: Zhonggong Dangshi Ziliao Chubanshe, 1989), 56–57.

15. Liu Chun, "How to Unite with the Mongolian Nation in Resistance against Japan," 20 March 1940, *MWWH,* 819.

16. "CCP Central Committee's Plan for the Mongolian Work, 5 November 1930," *MWWH,* 138; "CCP's Sichuan Provincial Committee's Proclamation to the Tibetan Nation and the Laboring Mass of the Yi Nation along the Sichuan Border, 20 June 1932," ibid., 185; "CCP Central Committee's Letter to Manchurian Party Organizations and Party Members, 26 January 1933," *ZZWX,* 9: 37; "CCP Central Committee's Directive Letter on Inner Mongolian Work, 24 August 1936," *MWWH,* 418; "Program for the Activities of the Anti-Japanese and Mongolian Salvation Society, July 1937," ibid., 550.

tendency in postwar Inner Mongolia would seem an about-face change. Actually, in its early years the CCP continually invoked the MPR model, not to promote a greater Mongolian state but to bring China's ethnic minorities into a perceived international, revolutionary bloc consisting of the Soviet Union, the CCP, and the MPR. With a consistent conviction about the MPR's eventual reunion with China, the CCP's advocacy for the Inner Mongols' right to self-determination was part of a phased strategy. Noticeably, while propagating the MPR model among China's ethnic minorities, the CCP kept silent on the MPR's general revolutionary implications.

This issue reflected a Han-centric conviction among CCP leaders that was reinforced by the Soviet model: Although China's ethnic minorities should emulate the MPR in achieving *national* emancipation, their eventual *social* deliverance—a higher level of liberation, according to Marxist historicism—would have to be achieved as part of the larger Chinese revolution. As indicated by the Soviet model, a socioeconomically more advanced core nation had to lead the relatively backward ethnic minorities in their odyssey toward the ideal realm of communism. Whereas the Russians made up such a core nation in the Soviet Union, in a Chinese federation the core nation would have to be the communized Han Chinese. Obviously, in the CCP leaders' mind, this would also be the core to which the MPR would rally.

Thus, although deriving its ethnoterritorial vision about a new China from the cocoon of the late Qing Empire, the CCP wanted to reweave the cocoon with a different thread. The GMD envisaged the Republic of China as a modern nation-state, but its narrowly construed Chinese nationalism, the chosen agent for binding China together, actually helped rip the multiethnic fabric of the Qing Empire. By contrast, in upholding communism in a class-based sociopolitical revolution, the CCP managed to fashion an ideology that in a sense had a supra-ethnic appeal, similar to the Manchu imperial authority's, for Inner Asian peoples. With this ideology, the CCP attempted to achieve what the GMD could not—reunification of China as bequeathed from the Qing. Years later, for this very reason, the CCP's Mongolian enterprise would become one of the root causes for schism between the CCP and the Soviets.

Yet, in the long period from 1921 and 1949, the CCP's historical connection with the Qing Empire was often obscured by its ideological affiliation with the Soviet Union. In the early 1920s, Mao observed: "As for the [Mongolian] People's Party and Chinese Turkestan, we of course believe that they should have the right to self-determination because [in these areas] we and the Soviet Union have a common front. But in Tibet the slogan of self-determination can become an instrument for the British because at present we do not have any influence there."[17] Still struggling for power in China, the Chinese Communists prioritized Mongolia's "bloc identity" over its national identity. For the time being, the CCP leaders were turning a blind eye to the fact that Mongolia's bloc identity was consequential for its national identity as well.

As long as the CCP remained a rebellious movement struggling for national power, its amorphous bloc relationship with the Soviet Union and the MPR seemed to work well. During the 1920s and the early 1930s, Inner Mongolia became a fitting ground for such a three-sided collaboration. The CCP accepted the natural link between the revolutionary activities of the Inner and Outer Mongols and collaborated with the Comintern and Ulaanbaatar in deciding political strategies regarding Inner Mongolia.[18] Often it was difficult or, from the CCP's point of view, unnecessary to ascertain which operation in Inner Mongolia was under whose direction. The early career of Yun Ze (a.k.a. Ulanhu), who would become the most important Mongol member of the CCP after the 1930s, was a case in point.

In 1929, Yun concluded his training in Moscow and returned to Inner Mongolia to launch underground activities. Many years later, he and his biographers could not agree whether he returned to China under a decision by the CCP or by the Comintern. Having returned to China, Yun was unable to establish direct contact with the CCP center until 1938. Until then, he received directives from his superiors in the MPR. A similar case was Wang Ruofei, a senior CCP cadre who in 1930 arrived in Inner Mongolia from Moscow. Wang's mission, in the name of a "CCP northwestern special committee," had no connection at all with the CCP Central Committee's Inner Mongolian work conducted through its Manchurian apparatus.[19]

Unlike the GMD, which was extremely sensitive about its own "revolu-

17. "Meeting of the CCP Delegation [to the First National Congress of the GMD], 18 January 1924," *Gongchan Guoji, Liangong (Bu) yu Zhongguo Geming Dangan Ziliao Congshu* (Selected Archival Materials on the Comintern, Soviet Communist Party (Bolshevik) and the Chinese Revolution; hereafter *GLZD*), 12 vols., comp. First Research Department of the Research Office on the Party History of the CCP Central Committee (Beijing: Beijing Tushuguan Chubanshe, 1997–98, vols. 1–6; Beijing: Zhongyang Wenxian Chubanshe, 2002, vols. 7–12), 1: 469.

18. "[Minutes of] the Special Conference of the CCP Central Committee, 21 February 1926," *MWWH,* 42.

19. Ulanfu, *Wulanfu Huiyilu,* 105–8, 130–31, 151, 157–58, 199; Wang Shusheng and Hao Yufeng, *Wulanfu Nianpu* (Chronicle of Ulanfu's Life) (Beijing: Zhonggong Dangshi Ziliao Chubanshe, 1989), 47, 51, 56, 59.

tionary jurisdiction" in Mongolia during its cooperation with the Soviets in the 1920s, the CCP's priority was the effectiveness of the movement. In the dark years of the CCP movement after 1927, the CCP Central Committee stressed more than before the importance of maintaining contact with the Mongolian People's Revolutionary Party (MPRP) of the MPR. It is most interesting that while qualifying the MPRP as a "foreign" organization, the CCP urged Chinese laborers in Outer Mongolia to become its members or to adopt Mongolian nationality. For, by becoming "foreigners" in this manner, these Chinese laborers would actually join the CCP's side in its struggle against China's counterrevolutionaries.[20]

The CCP leaders never admitted that the CCP might suffer from a potential disadvantage in its tripartite revolutionary partnership with Moscow and Ulaanbaatar. Among the three, the CCP was the only nonruling party, while Moscow and Ulaanbaatar were state governments with well-defined national territories and interests to defend or expand. Although in the early stage of its revolution the CCP was inclined to postpone the issue of China's national jurisdiction in Outer Mongolia and was willing to share "revolutionary jurisdiction" in Inner Mongolia with Moscow and Ulaanbaatar, the latter two did not view the two types of jurisdictions as disconnected. Often restrained by Moscow, the MPR leaders nevertheless maintained their pan-Mongol idealism. Just like the CCP principals who were waiting for Outer Mongolia's return to a communist China, leaders in Ulaanbaatar were expecting to complete their own cause of reunifying all Mongols.

In the Comintern's division of revolutionary responsibilities for East Asian countries, the CCP was never granted a share for Outer Mongolia. In 1920, when the Comintern just started organizing its operations in East Asia, an "East Asian Secretariat" was established to include three branches respectively responsible for China, Korea, and Japan. A year later, the agency was replaced by a "Far Eastern Secretariat" with an additional "Mongolia and Tibet branch." The same structure was also adopted by the Soviet Communist Party's Siberian Bureau, which was involved in many activities in East Asian countries.[21] When the Comintern assigned the responsibility for

---

20. "Political Resolution of the CCP's Sixth National Congress, 9 July 1928," *ZZWX,* 4: 327; "CCP's Letter to Chinese Workers in Mongolia, October 1929," *MWWH,* 113–14.
21. "Valensky-Sibilyakov's Report to the Comintern Executive Committee on the Work among East Asian Peoples, 1 September 1920," *GLZD,* 1: 38–39; "Report to the Comintern Executive Committee on the Organization and Work of the Oriental National Division of the Siberian Bureau of the Soviet Communist Party Central Committee,

Taiwan, then Japan's colony, to the Japanese Communist Party, its exclusion of Mongolia and Tibet from the CCP's realm of operations was significant. For the moment, the division of labor spared the newly formed CCP the burden of helping Outer Mongolia's and Tibet's "national liberation." In the long run, however, the arrangement would have implications for a communist China's sovereignty in these regions as well. Furthermore, until the end of World War II, Moscow would continue to use the MPR, not CCP bases in China, as a preferred scheming ground for Inner Mongolia. From time to time, the leaders in Moscow also contemplated using the MPR as a front for expanding Soviet influence into Tibet or for exerting pressure on Xinjiang.[22]

Sooner or later, the Soviet leaders' obsession with the Mongolian buffer and their penchant for maximizing Soviet influence by sponsoring dissident ethnic groups in China's borderlands would cause conflicts with the CCP revolution, which, like any other national revolutionary movement in history, was self-centered. The CCP endured tremendous losses when its Comintern-guided partnership with the GMD failed in 1927. Yet the split with the GMD also allowed the CCP to emerge from the GMD's shadow and become an independent force in China's political arena. In the next three years, the CCP would launch military attacks against the GMD government, aiming to create a new "revolutionary high tide" in China. In 1931, the CCP created a "Chinese soviet republic," an embryonic revolutionary state power, out of its bases in southern China. These developments, as understood by the CCP, demanded devotion from its international allies in the north and also reset the issue of revolutionary jurisdiction.

In August 1930, an expectation emerged in the CCP Politburo that when the CCP was promoting uprisings in southern Chinese cities, Inner and Outer Mongolia should dispatch expeditionary forces southward to attack the enemy. The CCP leaders found the existing relationship between their

---

21 December 1920," ibid., 49–57; "E. Linchin" and "I. K. Mamayev" in "Index of Personalities," ibid., 4: 543, 547–48.

22. "Minutes Number 5 of the Meeting of the Soviet Communist Party Central Politburo, 21 January 1926," *GLZD*, 3: 23–24; "Qijia's [code name for the CCP center] Opinion on the Inner Mongolian People's Party, December 1926," *MWWH*, 50; Christopher Atwood, "A. I. Oshirov (c. 1901–1931): A Buriat Agent in Inner Mongolia," in *Opuscula Altaica: Essays Presented in Honor of Henry Schwarz,* ed. Edward H. Kaplan and Donald W. Whisenhunt (Bellingham: Center for East Asian Studies of Western Washington University, 1994), 53–64, 77–87; Xiaoyuan Liu, *A Partnership for Disorder: China, the United States, and Their Policies for the Postwar Disposition of the Japanese Empire, 1941–1945* (Cambridge: Cambridge University Press, 1996), 161.

movement and the MPR unsatisfactory and urged the Comintern to make arrangements for "the Mongolian party to develop a brotherly inter-party relationship with the CCP." Li Lisan, who was then in charge of the CCP Central Committee's routine operations, further suggested that once the uprisings in southern China achieved success, Outer Mongolia should immediately declare its merger with the Chinese soviet republic and send a sizable force into northern China. In addition, the Soviet Union should also send troops into Manchuria to fight the Japanese. Li Lisan asserted this offensive strategy unequivocally: This was a strategy loyal to the Chinese revolution and must be implemented even if the Comintern was opposed to it.[23] In the eyes of Soviet leaders, this outright China-centric line of action would throw their foreign policy in East Asia into chaos. Unsurprisingly, Stalin regarded Li's position as "absurd" and "mischievous." The "Lisan line" was soon repudiated by the Comintern as "adventurous opportunism" that would endanger the Chinese revolution. But, although criticizing Li for erroneously pitting loyalty to the Chinese revolution against that to the Comintern, Moscow completely evaded the issue of the CCP–MPR relationship.[24]

Rally toward Periphery

From late 1930 to the spring of 1931, the CCP leadership went through a reshuffle orchestrated by the Comintern. The new leadership was dominated by a group of returnees from Moscow. The most prominent among these was Wang Ming (a.k.a. Chen Shaoyu), who between 1932 and 1937 headed the CCP delegation to the Comintern. The new leadership, in the words of Wang, was "hundred-percent loyal to the Comintern's general line."[25] This

23. "[Wen] Yucheng's Presentation at the CCP Provisional Politburo Meeting That Continued to Discuss the Current Political Situation and the National Work Arrangements, 3 August 1930," *MWWH*, 482; "Stoliyar's Letter to Lozovsky, 5 August 1930," *GLZD*, 9: 258–62; "Oriental Secretariat of the Comintern Executive Committee's Circular to the Political Secretariat on the Internal Conditions of the CCP, 9 October 1930," ibid., 365–66.

24. "Stalin's Telegram to Molotov, 13 August 1930," *GLZD*, 9: 300; "Comintern Executive Committee's Letter to the CCP Central Committee on the Question of the Lisan Line,16 November 1930," *ZZWX*, 6: 645; "Far Eastern Bureau of the Comintern Executive Committee to the CCP Central Politburo, 10 December 1930," *GLZD*, 9: 525–29.

25. "Chen Shaoyu's Letter to Safarov, Mif, Majyar, and Mayer, 17 December 1930," *GLZD*, 9: 540–41; "Kucheumov's Records on the Mistakes of Qu Qiubai and Zhou Enlai, 22 December 1930," ibid., 550–54; "Qu Qiubai's Letter to Mif, 4 January 1931," ibid.,

was an awkward moment to reassert the CCP's internationalist devotion. After manufacturing the Mukden incident in September 1931, the Japanese Army continued to turn China's northeastern provinces into a puppet "Manchukuo" state and to expand into northern China and Inner Mongolia. China entered a period of acrimonious nationalism, under which any distracting ideology would suffer.

With its principal bases confined to the countryside of southern China, the CCP could do little about the crises in northern China. Still, it was remarkable that at the moment of China's national crisis, the CCP should reassert its devotion to Moscow. In the first few years after Japan's occupation of Manchuria, aside from blaming the GMD regime for selling out Manchuria and Inner Mongolia to Japan, the CCP leadership repeatedly called upon the Chinese people to carry out the "glorious mission" of defending the Soviet Union and the MPR from Japanese intervention.[26] This "revolutionary peripheral" position, rallying around the Soviet–MPR bloc, understandably fell out of sync with most Chinese people's nation-centered anxieties. As of late 1934, Jiang Jieshi's successive "annihilation campaigns" finally squeezed the CCP out of its bases in southern China, physically marginalizing the CCP in China's political life. Indeed, had the CCP perished during these campaigns with its "hundred-percent loyalty" to Moscow, it would not have been missed in China's national war against Japan.

Between 1934 and 1935, the CCP managed to escape from the GMD's deadly encirclement by embarking on a strategic retreat, later known as the Long March. It has been established in historiography that during the Long

---

589–90; Yang, *Zhonggong yu Mosike,* 277–80; Wang Ming, "Revolution, War, Military Intervention and the CCP's Task, 31 November 1933," *ZZWX,* 9: 597.

26. Yang Kuisong, *Mao Zedong yu Mosike de En En Yuan Yuan* (Gratitude and Grievances between Mao Zedong and Moscow) (Nanchang: Jiangxi Renmin Chubanshe, 1999), 197; "Outline of the CCP Central Committee's Report to the Comintern, 20 June 1933," *Zhonggong Zhongyang Zhengzhi Baogao Xuanji, 1927–1933* (Selected Political Reports of the CCP Central Committee) (Beijing: Zhonggong Zhongyang Dangxiao Chubanshe, 1983), 135; "CCP Central Committee's Letter to the Hebei Provincial Committee on Carrying Out the Spirit of the Northern China Conference, 22 July 1932," *ZZWX,* 8: 330; "CCP Central Committee's Letter to the Chinese People on the Imperialist Partition of China and the GMD's Fifth Encirclement and Annihilation Campaign, 5 August 1933," ibid., 9: 283; "CCP Central Committee's Letter to the Masses on the Japanese Imperialists' New Offensive against Northern China, 10 April 1934," ibid., 10: 201; "CCP Central Committee's Urgent Notice on the Party's Task at Various Levels during the Current Crisis in Northern China, 12 April 1934," ibid., 10: 221.

March, the CCP leadership shifted into the hands of the unorthodox Mao Zedong, and that from the point onward the CCP movement began to achieve distinctively Chinese characteristics. In reality, what the Long March did to the CCP was much more than change its leadership. For the first time in its history, the CCP was not only forced out of the central areas of China's political life but also to the margins of the Han ethnographic zones. Thus the CCP lost its clinch of centrality in China in both political and ethnogeographic senses. Eventually, the CCP's destiny would depend on its ability to regain centrality in Chinese politics. In 1934, however, it was in the direction of China's ethnic frontiers that the CCP had to find a chance for survival.

The northward retreat by the CCP's central leadership and the Red Army immediately reversed the significance of the Mongolia question for the CCP. If in the past the CCP had regarded Mongolia as a revolutionary paradox in which a nomadic society had leapt into the "socialist stage" of development, or as a "liberated" periphery waiting for return to the fold of a Chinese soviet federation in the making, now the MPR became a safe haven toward which the uprooted CCP must rally. Among the CCP leaders, the northern direction of the Long March was a rather controversial choice. In mid-1935, the decision actually caused a temporary split between the CCP Central Committee and the Fourth Front Army under Zhang Guotao, who preferred a southern march to the Tibetan areas. The rationale for the northern direction was to "break through" to Soviet assistance by reaching either the Chinese–Soviet border in Xinjiang or the border of the MPR. Between the two locations, Outer Mongolia always appeared the more attractive option to CCP strategists.[27]

In late 1935, at a meeting of senior party cadres held in southern Gansu,

---

27. "The Significance of Attacking the Song-Li-Mao Area and Our Current Task, 23 May 1935," in *Ganbu Bidu* ("Compulsory Readings for Cadres," issued by the Red Fourth Front Army), *Zhongguo Gongnong Hongjun Disi Fangfianjun Zhanshi Ziliao Xuanbian, Changzheng Shiqi* (Selected Materials on the Fighting History of the Fourth Front Army of the Chinese Workers' and Peasants' Red Army, the Long March Period; hereafter *DFZZ*) (Beijing: Jiefangjun Chubanshe, 1992), 4; "Take Offensive to Destroy the Enemy and Create a New Soviet Region in Sichuan, Shaanxi, and Gansu, 10 July 1935" (editorial), *Hongxing* ("Red Star," the Red Army daily), *MWWH,* 296; "Political Department of the Red Army University's Propaganda and Education Materials on the Current Situation, Tasks, and Work, 1 June 1936," *DFZZ,* 529; Documentary Research Office of the CCP Central Committee, *Zhou Enlai Nianpu* (Chronicle of Zhou Enlai's Life) (Beijing: Zhongyang Wenxian Chubanshe, 1989), 287; Yang, *Zhonggong yu Mosike,* 341–48, 355–82.

Mao made the following remark to justify the Red Army's northward movement, which was rather revealing about the changed meaning of Mongolia:

> [Our] current basic orientation is to use guerrilla warfare to fight to the borders of the Soviet Union. . . . The distance from our current location to the Soviet border is just five thousand li, . . . and in terms of population conditions, we can win over the minorities through our work. The land from here to the north is a Han region, in Mongolia the Han and the Mongols live together, and Mongolia is our brother. . . . We can still possibly fight a mobile war, but not without restrictions. Therefore we must prepare equipment for trench and fortress warfare, such as aircraft and artilleries, so we can coordinate mobile warfare with trench warfare. . . . In this regard, . . . we can always ask for help because we are not an independent communist party. We are a branch of the Comintern and the Chinese revolution is part of the world revolution. We may first create a base area along the Soviet border and then expand eastward.[28]

Mao certainly did not give up hope that the CCP would eventually be able to come out of its predicament and return to the main stage of Chinese politics. He was nevertheless pragmatic in recognizing the CCP's marginalization and intended to make the best of a desperate situation.

Although Mao was talking about the old Moscow–Ulaanbaatar–CCP axis, the CCP's position in this tripartite bloc became explicitly subsidiary. The Long March would position the CCP physically closer to its northern allies, but, as indicated by Mao's words, the party's reliance on direct Soviet–Mongolian support would just accentuate its lack of credibility as a native political force of China. This was one of the reasons why Zhang Guotao opposed Mao's "opportunism" of "relying on Soviet aircraft and big guns." Zhang's choice was to lead the Red Army to the Tibetan regions in the southwest. Interestingly, Zhang also used Outer Mongolia in his argument, suggesting that the Tibetans might follow the example of the MPR and

---

28. "Mao Zedong's Report and Conclusion at the Ejie Conference, 12 September 1935," *DFZZ*, 151. Mao's calculation of distance is inaccurate. The direct distance from Ejie in southern Gansu to the Soviet–MPR border in the north was about 1,800 kilometers or 3,600 li, and to the Soviet–Xinjiang border in the west was about 2,250 kilometers or 4,500 li. The distance from Ejie to the MPR's southern border was less than half of that to its northern border.

make their "backward" areas hospitable to the CCP, as if the CCP were still in an advantageous "central" position to rally less-developed frontier ethnic groups.[29]

Obviously, even though before the Long March Mao proved himself a creative and independent-minded revolutionary, his installation into the CCP's leading position during the Long March did not guarantee that in the years to come the CCP would become a self-reliant communist movement free from Soviet domination. In the 1935 debate, Zhang was the one who argued for the CCP's self-reliance in a desolate location, whereas Mao insisted on seeking the party's salvation in the direction of the Soviet and Mongolian allies. The majority of the CCP principals rejected Zhang's argument along with his choice of location. Yet the CCP would soon be forced by political circumstances to rely on itself after following Mao abortively in seeking a new lease on life on the fringe of Soviet–Mongolian power.

The CCP was not the first political force in China that tried to set up a base along the northern borders in order to receive direct assistance from the Soviet Union. As mentioned above, in the early 1920s Moscow cold-shouldered Sun Yat-sen's "northwestern strategy." Then, in 1935, a group of anti-Japanese GMD generals in Fujian, disenchanted with Jiang Jieshi's obsession with the civil war against the CCP, also sought in vain Moscow's endorsement of a scheme for setting up an anti-Japanese base in China's northwestern borderlands. If the Soviet leaders were reluctant to foster a Chinese nationalist force along China's northern borders, their attitude toward the CCP's northward movement was very different. As a matter of fact, when the CCP just started its Long March without a clear destination, the Comintern had already begun to contemplate reinvigorating the Chinese Communist movement through direct Soviet assistance. The plan called for organizing a CCP northwestern bureau somewhere in Soviet Central Asia, launching guerrilla expeditions into China via Xinjiang and Outer Mongolia, and establishing a secret military school and an arsenal in Central Asia that could train and equip at least 50,000 troops for the CCP. In 1935, Soviet strategists studied the plan's feasibility, and then, in early 1936, Stalin sent a personal message to the CCP: "The main force of the Red Army

---

29. "Zhang Guotao's Report at a Cadre Conference on the Prospect of China's Soviet Movement, 15 March 1936," *DFZZ*, 399; "Zhang Guotao's Report at an Activists' Conference on the Prospect of China's Soviet Movement and Our Current Tasks, 1 April 1936," ibid., 423.

can expand toward the northwest and north, and its movement toward the Soviet Union is not objected."[30]

Then why, after marching more than 7,000 miles from southern China, did the Chinese Red Army stop in northern Shaanxi, which was less than 500 miles from the border of the MPR? What prevented the CCP from marching directly into the embrace of the "brotherly" arms of the Soviet Union and the MPR? Surely, the enormous loss of the Red Army during the Long March and CCP leaders' surprising yet pleasant discovery of an existent CCP base in northern Shaanxi were among the reasons why the CCP leadership chose the area as its new home base. The strategic plan for seeking Soviet assistance via Outer Mongolia was not abandoned, but the way of approaching the MPR border was changed. Mao decided that the Red Army should move toward the MPR along with an expanding new base, not as a band of rootless vagrants. Hence the Red Army ended its—in the view of the Comintern leadership—"nomadic" movement in northern Shaanxi.[31]

Still, having just overcome the extremes of natural and human-made obstacles along the way of the Long March, the Red Army should have been able to cross the Inner Mongolian Plateau relatively easily. But the Red Army stopped short of going into Inner Mongolia and stayed largely on the southern side of the Great Wall. Aside from the reasons given above, the modification of the CCP's northern strategy was also based on an important ethnopolitical consideration that has been overlooked by previous studies. More than any other CCP leaders, Mao was very conscious of the Chinese Communist movement's ethnopolitical origins in and ties to the Han society. Even when arguing at a desperate moment about the necessity for the Red Army to temporarily relinquish its pride of independence and to seek a chance of survival on the verge of Soviet power, Mao still believed that the "[CCP] center should stay in an area from which it can direct the revolution of the whole country."[32] China's ethnographic configuration made northern Shaanxi the last Han region verging on an ethnic fault line in northern China. Crossing the line, the CCP and the Red Army would have completely severed their own ethnographical roots and lost contact with the Han

30. Qiu Lu, "Secret History of Sun Yat-sen's Request for Soviet Assistance," *Baini-anchao* (Centennial Tidal), 6 (1997): 55–57; Yang, *Zhonggong yu Mosike,* 351–54; "Telegram from Lin Yuying and Zhang Wentian to Zhu De and Zhang Guotao on the Fourth Front Army's Strategy and Other Matters, 24 January 1936," *DFZZ,* 371–72.

31. Yang, *Zhonggong yu Mosike,* 354–61; Ivo Banac, ed., *The Diary of Georgi Dimitrov, 1933–1949* (New Haven, Conn.: Yale University Press, 2003), 37.

32. "Mao Zedong's Report and Conclusion at the Ejie Conference," 151–52.

population. Therefore, to Mao and his associates, the northern Shaanxi base was important not only because it provided the Red Army with a replenishing station before its further effort to reach the revolutionary "brothers" in Mongolia and the Soviet Union but also because it gave the CCP movement a last chance to stay with the ethnic "family" of the Han Chinese mass.

In retrospect, when the CCP decided to preserve what it had left in its *qunzhong jichu* (mass foundation) and not to become a rootless military group relying on foreign support, it actually forfeited its opportunity to get much desired assistance from the Moscow–Ulaanbaatar bloc. Circumstances did not allow the CCP to have it both ways. In December 1935, the CCP leadership adopted a strategic plan for approaching Outer Mongolia by extending its new base eastward into Shanxi and northward into Suiyuan in Inner Mongolia. According to Mao's estimate, it would need about six months to implement the plan. The Suiyuan direction was crucial for making a connection with the MPR, and the Inner Mongols of the region must be enlisted for the effort.[33] What the CCP activities tried to accomplish in the next few months resembled to a significant degree the pentangular alliance of the 1920s involving the Soviets, the MPR, the CCP, the GMD, and the Inner Mongols. The combined results of military and political operations were expected to create a new soviet region that would include Shanxi, Shaanxi, Gansu, Suiyuan, and Ningxia Provinces and "merge into an integral piece [*lian cheng yipian*] with the Soviet Union and the MPR."[34] No matter what had been the CCP leaders' previous opinions on the MPR as a revolutionary model, their strategic plans, if they materialized, would have made the CCP base in northern Shaanxi an MPR-type region and have reinvited the Soviets into the Chinese Civil War.

The problem for the CCP's northern strategy was that, unlike in the 1920s, no Inner Mongolian and Chinese nationalist groups were cooperating with the CCP in the effort. The CCP had to seek out potential partners. On December 20, 1935, a "proclamation to the Inner Mongolian people by the central soviet government of China" was issued under Mao's name. The document asked the Inner Mongols to reject the Japanese-sponsored pan-Mongolism and to join the CCP and the MPR in an effort to "rejuvenate the nation" and to "preserve the glory of Genghis Khan's time." Conspicuously,

---

33. Mao Zedong's Letter to Zhang Wentian, 1 December 1935, Chinese Military Museum, *Mao Zedong Junshi Huodong Jishi* (Records of Mao Zedong's Military Activities) (Beijing: Jiefangjun Chubanshe, 1994), 180.

34. Chinese Military Museum, *Mao Zedong Junshi Huodong Jishi,* 179.

on this occasion the CCP did not attack Prince De, who, frustrated by the GMD's rigid frontier policies, was about to establish a separatist Mongolian government with Japan's support. Instead, the CCP promised cooperation with the Inner Mongols in rolling back the GMD government's assimilation schemes in Inner Mongolia.[35]

The CCP also sought to forge a regional partnership with GMD generals in the northwest. In early 1936, the CCP negotiated with Zhang Xueliang to stop hostilities between the Red Army and Zhang's Northeast Army in the region. By "upgrading the Mongolian nation's anti-Japanese struggle into a military one" and including Zhang's force in a "grand northwestern alliance," the CCP hoped that its own passage to Soviet aid could be opened and then its two-pronged war against the GMD regime and the Japanese could be significantly enhanced.[36] However, it soon became clear that the CCP had overestimated its ability to win over the Inner Mongols and underestimated Zhang's loyalty to Jiang Jieshi. The effect of the CCP's propaganda toward the Inner Mongols was minimal, and its negotiations with Zhang resulted in a local truce but not an anti-Nanjing front.

In the meantime, the CCP's military operations for expanding the northern Shaanxi base also stalled. According to the logic of the Red Army's post–Long March strategy, only by "expanding the soviet area vigorously" could the Red Army "get closer to Outer Mongolia gradually." In March 1936, when Moscow and Ulaanbaatar concluded a pact of mutual defense and assistance, leaders in Yan'an interpreted the development to their own advantage and regarded it as part of Moscow's preparations for giving aid to the Chinese Red Army.[37] During much of 1936, the CCP made efforts to push its base in eastern, northern, and western directions and to open a corridor to the MPR either through Suiyuan or Ningxia. But all the operations encountered tremendous difficulties and eventually failed.

---

35. "Proclamation to the Inner Mongolian People by the Central Soviet Government of China, 20 December 1935," *MWWH*, 322–24.

36. "CCP Center's Resolution on Military Strategy, 23 December 1935," *ZZWX*, 10: 592, 597; Wang Jiaxiang, "Oppose Japan's Occupation of Inner Mongolia, 22 July 1936," *MWWH*, 508; "Lin Yuying, Zhang Wentian, Mao Zedong, and Zhou Enlai to Zhu De, Zhang Guotao, Liu Bocheng, and Xu Xiangqian on Domestic and Foreign Conditions, 20 May 1936," *DFZZ*, 519; Documentary Research Office of the CCP Central Committee, *Zhou Enlai Nianpu* (The Chronicle of Zhou Enlai's Life) (Beijing: Zhongyang Wenxian Chubanshe, 1989), 316–17; Yang Kuisong, *Xi'an Shibian Xintan* (New Study of the Xi'an Incident) (Taipei: Dongda Tushu, 1995), 32–50.

37. "CCP Center's Telegram to the Second and Fourth Front Armies on the Current Situation and Strategic Orientation, 25 May 1936," *DFZZ*, 524.

Exasperated by repeated frustrations, the CCP leaders unwittingly revisited Li Lisan's ground and thought that Moscow might be willing to put the interests of the Chinese revolution above its own foreign policy calculations. At one point in the summer, Mao hoped that the MPR could dispatch an army to Ningxia to coordinate the Red Army's operation there. In late August, the CCP Central Committee instructed its representative in Moscow, Wang Ming, to make a request to the Soviet leaders for direct military support. It was proposed that Moscow send airplanes and artillery units to the CCP via Outer Mongolia or Xinjiang. The Central Committee stressed that without such support, the CCP's northward campaign to open a Ningxia corridor would fail and the party would then have to turn to the south again, a direction that would mean civil war with the GMD, disengagement from resistance against Japan, and increased distance between the CCP and the Soviet–MPR bloc.[38]

Given the increasingly delicate political situation in northwestern China, it was more unlikely than ever that Moscow would become openly involved in China's internal struggle. Still, in the fall and winter of 1936, the Soviet–Comintern leadership contemplated assisting the CCP via the MPR. A plan was made to concentrate military materials along the southern border of the MPR and then, through a certain foreign firm, to transport the materials to CCP troops in Ningxia.[39] In mid-October, the Comintern notified the CCP that 150 trucks were ready to transport 550 to 600 tons of materials to the Red Army but that a strong Red Army force must come to the MPR border to receive the convoy. This could not be done because by that time the Red Army's Ningxia campaign had already failed. In early November, the Comintern finally decided to move the operation of aiding the CCP away from the sphere of Japan's military power in Inner Mongolia. The CCP was now told that Xinjiang, not Outer Mongolia, was the designated venue for receiving Soviet assistance. In early December, the Soviet Politburo resolved to allocate "1,166 tons of freight for the 'nomads' [i.e., the CCP]."[40] Yet the CCP's western expedition to Xinjiang in the winter of 1936 and spring of 1937 ended as one of the worst military catastrophes in its history.[41]

---

38. Mao Zedong's Telegram to Peng Dehuai, 1 July 1936, *Mao Zedong Nianpu,* 1: 555; "CCP Center to Wang Ming on the Red Army's Operation Plan, 25 August 1936," *DFZZ,* 661–62.

39. Banac, *Diary of Georgi Dimitrov,* 30–31.

40. Banac, *Diary of Georgi Dimitrov,* 37.

41. "CCP Center to Zhu De, Zhang Guotao and Ren Bishi on the Plan to Occupy Ningxia, 14 September 1936," *DFZZ,* 696; "CCP Military Committee to Zhu De and

In the end, despite these efforts, the CCP's bloc relationship with Moscow and Ulaanbaatar remained largely ideological and never achieved territorial and material substantiation. The CCP's abortive efforts to substantiate its bloc relationship with the Soviet–MPR allies, from the Ningxia operation to the western expedition, indicated that its renowned self-reliant orientation during China's eight-year war against Japan was really forced upon it by circumstances.

It was in this context that Mao granted personal interviews to the American reporter Edgar Snow. Snow's resulting book, *Red Star over China,* publicized the CCP movement and its leaders for the first time to the outside world. But, as information about the CCP's policymaking and about Mao himself, the book was both enlightening and misleading. Making an effort to reach out to both foreign and Chinese audiences, Mao carefully presented images of the CCP movement and himself to Snow, and none of his words should be taken at face value. As such, Mao's remarks in these interviews relating to Mongolia must be examined in the context of the CCP's activities at the time.

Snow raised the question of Mongolia in two interviews. On July 16, 1936, unaware of the CCP's eagerness at the time to involve Soviet and MPR troops in its military effort to open a corridor to the MPR border, which was part of the ongoing Civil War in China, Snow asked Mao a hypothetical question—that in case of China's war against Japan, whether or not the Soviet Union and Outer Mongolia would become involved. In retrospect, a better informed question would have been about Mao's invitation for Moscow to compound Japan's aggression against China with its own hostile action against the Chinese government. Spared such a tough query, Mao indulged himself in harmless speculation about Soviet belligerence against Japan once China began its own war of resistance. Mao also ignored the Outer Mongolia part of Snow's question and just talked about autonomy for Inner Mongolia in responding to Snow's other questions.[42]

Zhang Guotao on Seizing Ningxia and Breaking Through to the Soviet Union, 19 September 1936," ibid., 707; "Zhu De and Zhang Guotao to the CCP Center on the Fourth Front Army's Westward Movement, 26 September 1936," ibid., 721–22; "Comintern Secretariat and Wang Ming and Chen Yun to the CCP Center Secretariat on the Change of Way of Assistance, 3 November 1936," ibid., 862; "Presidium of the CCP Military Committee to Xu Xiangqian and Chen Changhao on the Western Route Army's Operational Plan, 17 March 1937," ibid., 966; Yang, *Mao Zedong yu Mosike,* 198–99.

42. "Conversations with American Reporter Snow, 16 July 1936," Mao Zedong, *Mao Zedong Wenji* (Manuscripts of Mao Zedong), 5 vols. (Beijing: Renmin Chubanshe,

A week later, Snow raised the question of Outer Mongolia again in a more pointed way: When the Chinese revolution was victorious, would the Chinese–Soviet relationship be maintained through the Comintern, or under a combination of the Soviet and Chinese governments, or in the same way as that between Outer Mongolia and the Soviet Union? Although Snow was posing the question in the future tense, he was close to the crux of the CCP's current policy predicament: While vanquishment, not victory, was the immediate concern of the CCP, should it follow the MPR precedent in becoming an appendix of the Soviet Union? But again Mao was not asked about the CCP's current position. Mao rejected the assumptions in Snow's question that the Comintern controlled national communist movements and that the Soviet Union dominated Outer Mongolia now and would dominate a Communist China in the future. His assertion of equality between Moscow and other communist movements brought out the following remark:

> The relationship between Outer Mongolia and the Soviet Union, now and in the past, has always been based on the principle of complete equality. When the people's revolution has been victorious in China, the Outer Mongolian republic will automatically become a part of the Chinese federation, at its own will. The Mohammedan and Tibetan peoples, likewise, will form autonomous republics attached to the China federation.[43]

Mao's defense of the allegedly equal Soviet–Mongolian relationship might have sounded delusional to Snow. But because the focus of Snow's question was the CCP–Moscow relationship in the future, Mao's assertion about the CCP's equality with the Russians must have sounded reassuring to Snow and his Chinese and foreign readers. Had Snow been privy to the CCP's desperate effort at the moment to get Soviet aid and to merge its northern Shaanxi base with the MPR and the Soviet Union "into an integral piece," he might have put his question in the present tense and interpreted Mao's justification for Soviet domination over the MPR as an allusion to a CCP–Moscow relationship in the making.

Mao's statement on Mongolia, Tibet, and China's Islamic northwest as "autonomous republics" of a Chinese federation in the future, because of

---

1993–96), 1: 402–3; Edgar Snow, *Red Star over China* (New York: Random House, 1938), 110.

43. Snow, *Red Star,* 443–44.

its publication in Snow's book, would become better known to outside observers than the CCP's other similar statements before and after. In the evolving course of the CCP's ethnopolitics, however, Mao's profession to Snow did not stand out as a major policy manifestation. As mentioned above, the CCP had always supported Outer Mongolia's independence from the Republic of China *and* had always believed that the MPR would reunify with a Chinese federation under the CCP. In other words, as far as Mongolia was concerned, the CCP leaders' belief in ultimate Chinese national centrality and their acceptance of the party's momentary revolutionary periphery position was never much of a contradiction. Mao did not make any departure from the stand.

Nevertheless, Mao's statement is historically interesting in two senses. First, it is ironic that he should reiterate the CCP's standard prophecy about Outer Mongolia's "automatic" reunion with China at this peculiar moment, when the CCP was struggling desperately to accomplish its own rallying to the MPR. Second, this was the last time that the CCP could unequivocally defend the MPR's independence and predict its reunion with China at the same time. The preconditions for the CCP's Mongolian dialectics were the party's rejection of the GMD's official China and projection of itself as the revolutionary China. When Mao talked to Snow, the CCP's theoretical bifurcation of China was about to come to an end.

Return to Centrality

December 12, 1936, would be remembered as one of the most important turning points in modern Chinese history. Zhang Xueliang's abduction of Jiang Jieshi on that day in Xi'an, however, was neither a coup d'état nor a revolution. It was a "military petition" (*bingjian*) typical of traditional Chinese politics, in which a loyal military commander used force to co-opt his reluctant master to take action along a certain direction. In such an event, the mutual political obligations between the two sides were not broken. Yet the famous Xi'an incident did turn China in a drastically new direction. The resulting truce between the GMD and the CCP made a national war of resistance against Japan possible. The CCP was also able to come out of its most arduous decade since 1927 and for the first time to become legal on China's official political stage.

During China's eight-year war (1937–1945) against Japan, the CCP accomplished what had been impossible during its ten-year war (1927–37) with the GMD—a "vigorous expansion" of its military-political bases. On the eve of Japan's surrender, the CCP had a regular force of more than a million troops, plus another 2 million in militias. The "liberated regions" under the CCP's control spread from northern to southern China, including a total area of nearly a million square kilometers and a population of about 100 million. As of this time, China clearly was no longer an amorphous geopolitical conception with a weak central regime that could not rule. China had become a country with two entrenched, experienced, and powerful military-political groups that shared the same dream of restoring its great power status in East Asia. The problem was that they did not want to share China with each other or any third party.

As far as the CCP's relationship with Outer Mongolia was concerned, two wartime readjustments in the CCP's political orientation and military strategy were crucial. Politically, the CCP reached reconciliation with the GMD's official China, which, as precarious as it was, significantly modified the CCP's ethnopolitical orientation in general and its stand on the Mongolia question in particular. Militarily, the CCP substituted its earlier northward thrust to reach the MPR and the Soviet Union with southward and eastward expansions to reach more Chinese population. These maneuvers ended the CCP's marginalization and restored its centrality in China's political life.

It is well known that the wartime GMD–CCP relationship was a continued confrontation wrapped in the cloak of a national united front. It was made up of successive, small partisan wars within China's national war against Japan. However, although the CCP's reconciliation with the GMD regime was superficial, its resubscription to Chinese nationalism was substantive. The party's newly gained legitimacy in Chinese political life relied less on its "legalization" by the GMD government after 1937 than on its assumption of leadership in the ordinary daily struggle of Chinese against Japan, though the CCP was able to assume this role only after the Civil War in China was suspended. Given the CCP's commitment to a class-struggle-oriented revolution in China and its pledged internationalist obligations, its wartime reorientation was by no means a "natural" turn. The course necessarily involved the suspension of certain fundamental elements in the party's previous policies.

In March 1937, Liu Shaoqi, who was then in charge of the CCP's underground work in "white areas," made a sharp criticism of the party's orientation since Japan's 1931 invasion of Manchuria. In a letter to the CCP Central Committee, Liu pointed out that since Japan had openly violated

China in the Mukden incident, the party's political analysis of the development had not mentioned Japan's colonization of Manchuria and China's loss of sovereignty but instead had stressed support for the Soviet Union and the Chinese revolution. This approach, according to Liu, had prevented the CCP from leading China's anti-Japanese struggle. Liu's diagnosis of the CCP's problem was that the party had too often echoed the Comintern's opinions on China's conditions "for years without much thinking" by itself.[44] In the CCP's history, Liu's was certainly not the first contention that contrasted the Comintern line with "Chinese thinking." For instance, Li Lisan had voiced a much harsher objection to the Comintern's advice. But Liu's timing was right, and his opinion had Mao's personal support.

Thus, beginning with Liu's advocacy for "Chinese thinking," the CCP launched itself into a new kind of competition with the GMD. The competition was no longer defined as one between revolutionary and counter-revolutionary classes, but one between true patriots and those who were undermining China's national cause. The CCP shelved its "proletarian internationalism" and vied with the GMD in the arena of Chinese public opinion in championing Chinese nationalism. Before the war, the CCP had attacked the GMD regime for promoting "nation supremacy and state supremacy" (*minzu zhishang guojia zhishang*). In the war years, the CCP propaganda made an about-face and faulted Jiang Jieshi's government for not carrying out these "principles." It was declared that the CCP alone was the "loyal guard of the Chinese nation," "glorious savior of the Chinese people," and true practitioner of "nation supremacy and state supremacy." It was asserted that much of the GMD's nationalism had been lost since the Northern Expedition in the mid-1920s while the CCP "firmly takes the national stand."[45]

Similar to the CCP's wartime nationalism, which had a significant domestic angle and was not single-mindedly anti-Japanese, Yan'an's adjusted military strategy was a double-edged sword that would cut both outward and inward. In its original agreement with the GMD about stopping the Civil War for the sake of national resistance against Japan, the CCP promised to use the main force of the Red Army to fight the Japanese. But, after the GMD–CCP cease-fire was achieved, Mao had second thoughts. Now he

44. "Liu Shaoqi's Letter to the CCP Center on the Work in White Areas in the Past, 4 March 1937," *ZZWX*, 11: 806.

45. "Nation Supremacy and State Supremacy" (editorial), *Xinhua Ribao* (New China Daily), 15 June 1941, *Zhou Enlai Nianpu*, 507; "The GMD and Nationalism" (editorial), *Jiefang Ribao* (Liberation Daily), 18 September 1943, *ZZWX*, 14: 566–76.

believed that only a third of the Red Army should be used in small operations against Japan, lest any large-scale Red Army operations shift the brunt
of Japan's offensive from the GMD to the CCP. Zhou Enlai, the CCP's principal interlocutor with the GMD regime in the war years, disagreed initially.
In an August 1937 telegram to Mao, Zhou and some other CCP principals
pointed out the inconsistency between Mao's idea and the party's earlier
promise, arguing that if the Red Army's main force attacked the Japanese
in the north, the CCP would score politically and would also have a better
chance to make a connection with Outer Mongolia.[46]

Mao obviously believed that the CCP's public relations were less important than its military situation in the war, and that Zhou's point on Outer Mongolia was no longer valid because of the post-Xi'an political landscape in
China. After Japan injected its military force into China and pushed from the
north to the south, the CCP's geostrategic location in the remote northwest
became an advantage. The Red Army could leave the frontal warfare to the
GMD government in the south while starting a guerrilla war on the flank of
the Japanese offensive and expanding its bases behind Japanese lines. In the
rest of the war, Mao would stick to this guerrilla strategy, even when, in mid-
1941, he was urged by the Comintern to "take all possible vigorous action to
counter the Japanese offensive, no matter what difficulties you face."[47]

The CCP's successful wartime expansion behind Japanese lines proved
that in the prewar years what had prevented the CCP's growth was not so
much the GMD's military power as the existent sociopolitical fabric of local
Chinese communities. In the war years, the Japanese Army succeeded in destroying both. But, as an intruding foreign force, it lost to the CCP in a competition to fill in the political vacuum created by itself. If in the prewar years
the CCP's Long March toward China's ethnic frontiers and rally toward the
MPR were caused by its failure to amass enough revolutionary loyalty from
the Chinese populace, the war against Japan generated so much nationalistic
and communal loyalty to the CCP among ordinary Chinese that its old strategy for "breaking through to the Soviet Union" was no longer needed.[48]

46. Zhou Enlai et al. to Mao Zedong and Luo Fu, "Opinion on Sending Out the Red
Army's Main Force to Resist Japan, 4 August 1937," in *Zhou Enlai Junshi Wenxuan* (Selected Military Works of Zhou Enlai) (Beijing: Renmin Chubanshe, 1997), 2: 10–11.

47. Jiang Kefu, *Minguo Junshishi Luegao* (Brief Military History of the Chinese
Republic) (Beijing: Zhonghua Shuju, 1991), 3(1): 193–203; Banac, *Diary of Georgi
Dimitrov,* 164.

48. Chalmers A. Johnson's classic, *Peasant Nationalism and Communist Power* (Stanford, Calif.: Stanford University Press, 1962), is still useful but can be supplemented by

Throughout the war years, the only CCP effort reminiscent of its earlier northern strategy was a costly base in the Daqingshan Mountain area between Guisui (Hohhot), Inner Mongolia's political center, and the border of Outer Mongolia. In the spring of 1938, Mao posed a question to his military commanders: "Is it possible to establish a nomadic guerrilla cavalry acting along the range of the Daqingshan Mountain? If feasible, the unit can reach the border of Xinjiang in the west and Manchuria in the east and use the entire border region between Inner and Outer Mongolia as its guerrilla area." A base in the Daqingshan Mountain area would be established afterward but would never achieve the extensiveness that Mao had envisioned. The base's preservation in the war years, according to the words of a CCP commander, cost "countless people's lives." The two principal justifications for the sacrifice, as revealed in CCP internal correspondence, were to open an alternative line of communications with the Soviet Union and to keep a CCP foothold in Inner Mongolia for facilitating its coordination with the Soviet–MPR bloc in the event of a Japanese–Soviet war.[49] Yet on both counts the Daqingshan base did not function as expected.

The CCP's abandonment of the northern strategy did not mean that it was no longer longing for Soviet assistance. During China's war with Japan, the Chinese (GMD) and Soviet governments cooperated in maintaining a transportation line of some 3,000 kilometers between the Soviet border with Xinjiang and Lanzhou in Gansu Province. Over the years, about 4,000 Soviet personnel and 5,000 trucks were involved in transporting aid materials from

more recent regional studies, e.g., Ralph A. Thaxton, *Salt of the Earth: The Political Origins of Peasant Protest and Communist Revolution in China* (Berkeley: University of California Press, 1997) and the essays in *North China at War: The Social Ecology of Revolution, 1937–1945,* ed. Feng Chongyi and David S. G. Goodman (Lanham, Md.: Rowman & Littlefield, 2000).

49. Mao Zedong and Teng Daiyuan to He Long, Xiao Ke and Guan Xiangying, 30 March 1938, *Daqingshan Kangri Youji Genjudi Ziliao Xuanbian: Lishi Dang'an Bufen* (Selected Materials on the Anti-Japanese Guerrilla Base in the Daqingshan Mountain: Archival Materials), comp. Committee on the Collection of Party History Materials of the CCP Committee of the Inner Mongolian Autonomous Region and the Archives of the Inner Mongolian Autonomous Region (Huhhot: Neimenggu Renmin Chubanshe, 1987), 3; "CCP Center's Opinion on the Work in Daqingshan, 9 August 1941," ibid., 14; Zhou Shidi and Gan Siqi to Yao Ji, Zhang Dazhi and Bai Chengming, 20 August 1942, ibid., 94; "Directive from Mao Zedong et al. on the Establishment of the Daqingshan Guerrilla Base and the Party's Policy, 1938," *MWWH,* 590–91; Wang Tingbi, "One Year's Struggle in Daqingshan," in *Zhan Dong Zonghui Wenxian Ziliao Huiyilu* (Materials and Recollections of the General Society for Wartime Mobilization), comp. Party History Research Office of the CCP Shanxi Committee, 655.

the Soviet Union to China. After 1938, an unknown number of truckloads of these materials, guided by a CCP office in Lanzhou, were secretly diverted to the CCP area.[50] Thus, a material connection with Moscow, which the CCP had failed to achieve in its war with the GMD regime, was realized to a certain degree during its wartime collaboration with the GMD.

Yet, in general, during the war years the CCP's relationship with the Soviet–MPR bloc was not enhanced. Officially cooperating with the GMD regime in containing Japanese expansion, Moscow had to maintain at least a "correct" face in its contact with the CCP. This was the reason that Moscow could only deliver some material aid to the CCP by devious means. The CCP's own agreement to operate under the GMD government's authority further limited its ability to benefit from its "brotherhood" with the Soviets and Outer Mongols. However, what was more important was that World War II not only brought unprecedented destruction and sacrifice to every nation involved but also rearranged the prewar international alignment. On both counts, the old communist bloc organization, the Comintern, became outdated. In 1943, the Comintern dissolved itself, not only because it had become increasingly incompatible with Moscow's wartime diplomacy with the Western Allies but also because its usefulness in guiding national communist movements had declined drastically.

Before the war, a truism learned by the CCP from its subordinate relationship with the Comintern was that Moscow's interests were supposedly higher than those of the Chinese revolution. World War II provided the Chinese Communists with an opportunity to turn the tables and let the masters in the Kremlin know that Chinese interests were second to none. Surely the CCP still differed from the GMD government in maintaining a significant degree of camaraderie with Moscow. For instance, during the Soviet–Japanese border conflicts in 1938 and 1939, the CCP did not ask Moscow to intensify its confrontation with Japan. When the Soviet–Japanese neutrality pact was concluded in April 1941, the CCP's open reaction was also mildly positive. The party propaganda suggested that Moscow's agreement to not invade Manchukuo was logical, for it was China's duty to recover that region in the first place, and that the agreement was also beneficial in guaranteeing Outer Mongolia's security.[51]

50. S. Tikhvinsky, "China in My Life," *Far Eastern Affairs* 4 (1989): 92; Yuri Gradov, "A Convoy on the Pass," *Far Eastern Affairs* 3 (1990): 185; Wu Xiuquan, *Wo de Jingli* (My Experience) (Beijing: Jiefangjun Chubanshe, 1984), 36.

51. "CCP's Opinion on the Soviet–Japanese Neutrality Pact, 16 April 1941," *ZZWX*, 13: 76.

At first glance, this attitude seemed to continue the CCP's previous partisan stand that every step of Soviet foreign policy was correct. In reality, Mao's interest after 1938 in opening and preserving a costly guerrilla base in the Daqingshan area indicated a high hope that a Soviet–Japanese war would soon begin. Such a war would have released China from its isolated resistance against Japan. The expectation was also shared by GMD officials, though the CCP would have been the immediate beneficiary of such an event because of its ideological affinity with and geographical proximity to the Soviet Union. Therefore, the CCP's reaction to Soviet–Japanese neutrality probably concealed a disappointment as deep as that felt in Chongqing. The statement's central message was, however, not concealed: China had to fight its own war and must not wait for deliverance by others. It is most interesting that a few months later, Mao applied the same standard to the Soviet Union.

Nazi Germany's effective blitzkrieg against the Soviet Union in June 1941 indicated to Yan'an that even the almighty homeland of socialist revolutions was not immune to devastating defeat. In July, in a series of anguished telegrams to other CCP leaders, Mao Zedong laid down a policy principle, anticipating an even worse scenario in which the Soviet Union could be caught in a two-front war against Germany and Japan. Certainly, Mao told his comrades, the CCP would assist the Soviet Union if Japan entered the anti-Soviet war, but the assistance would be provided in a long-term and strategic, not operational, way. This meant that the CCP would continue its own strategy of expanding anti-Japanese bases and launching guerrilla warfare in current directions. The CCP force would not move northward "even if Japan attacks the Soviet Union and Jiang Jieshi tries to force us to move northward." Now the meaning of the Daqingshan base also changed. In the near future, it would not be a welcoming station for receiving a southward offensive by the Soviets but would serve as a distracting force against a northward attack by the Japanese. In an August directive, Mao told party operatives in the area that in case of a Soviet–Japanese war the base would be most significant in giving assistance to the Soviets.[52]

But this was not the kind of assistance that Moscow expected from the CCP. In early September, the Soviet Ministry of Defense asked the CCP to send troops to southern Manchuria in the event of Japan's attack on the Soviet Union.[53] Then, according to the recollections of Shi Zhe, Mao's Russian-

52. Chinese Military Museum, *Mao Zedong Junshi Huodong Jishi,* 455–56.
53. Chinese Military Museum, *Mao Zedong Junshi Huodong Jishi,* 457–58.

speaking secretary, between the late fall of 1941 and early 1943 Stalin himself sent three telegrams to Mao, suggesting three ways in which the CCP could help the Soviet Union contain Japan's possible anti-Soviet move. Stalin—obviously unable to trust the defense of his Mongolian buffer to the small MPR army, and hoping to reduce the Soviet Red Army's burden in maintaining both the internal and external security of the MPR—wanted to add some CCP troops to the outer zone of Soviet security.[54] He first suggested that two CCP divisions be sent to the border between the MPR and Inner Mongolia to receive modern weaponry. After Mao demurred on the ground of logistical difficulties and threat from Japan's air force, Stalin requested small CCP guerrilla units that would take turns receiving weapons from the Soviet Union and operate along the border between the MPR and Manchuria. Again, Mao's reply was negative. In early 1943, Stalin finally got a sense of what Mao was willing to do and asked him to deploy a sizable CCP force along the Great Wall as deterrence against Japan. This time Mao agreed, because such an operation would not contradict the CCP's military plan for an eastward projection.[55]

Shi Zhe, a Russian-trained "internationalist" persona, for a while was unable to comprehend how Mao could repeatedly reject these requests from Stalin himself. Not until the spring of 1945 did Shi Zhe get a clue. During the CCP's seventh national congress, Shi was enlightened by Mao's diagnosis of the defects of those "internationalists" within the CCP: "Wang Ming's problem was that he thought too little about his own [meaning China's] business and too much about other people's [meaning the Soviet Union's]."[56] In rejecting Stalin's requests, Mao was obviously thinking about the CCP's business. Mao's obsession with the CCP's "own business" in the war years

54. According to Marko Milivojevic, "The Mongolian People's Army: Military Auxiliary and Political Guardian," in *Mongolia Today,* ed. Shirin Akiner (London: Kegan Paul International, 1991), 142, 149–50, the Mongolian People's Army (MPA) numbered about 9,000 in 1929 and after 1944 increased to 80,000. The MPA's involvement in a rebellion in 1932 led to the return of large Soviet forces to Outer Mongolia to police the country as well as to deter the Japanese Army in Manchuria. About Soviet control of the MPA, also see I. I. Kuznetsov, "The Soviet Military Advisors in Mongolia, 1921–1939," *Journal of Slavic Military Studies,* 12(4) (December 1999): 118–37.

55. Shi Zhe, *Zai Lishi Juren Shenbian: Shi Zhe Huiyilu* (At the Side of Historical Giants: Memoirs of Shi Zhe) (Beijing: Zhongyang Wenxian Chubanshe, 1995), 214–15; Shi Zhe, *Feng yu Gu: Shi Zhe Huiyilu* (Peaks and Valleys: Memoirs of Shi Zhe) (Beijing: Hongqi Chubanshe, 1997), 96.

56. Shi Zhe, *Feng yu Gu,* 97–98.

let pass what could be an opportunity for the CCP to establish certain influence in the MPR.

Probably because of a similar consideration of self-interest, a few years earlier the MPR leadership had let pass an opportunity to control Yun Ze, who would later prove to be the CCP's most effective Mongol cadre. Before he could make contact with the CCP center in early 1938, Yun contacted the MPR authorities about leading an "independent Mongolian brigade," consisting of mutinied units from Prince De's force, to cross the border. Only after being rejected by Ulaanbaatar did Yun receive instructions from Yan'an directing him to change his narrow focus on military work and to use secret CCP cells to rally broader support among ordinary Inner Mongols. Yun, a Moscow-trained communist with extensive ties within the MPR, was then at an important juncture in his political career. The national coloration of his communism could be either more "Mongolian" or more "Chinese." Either way, he would continue to qualify as a loyal party member. Ulaanbaatar's decision certainly made the choice much easier for Yun. In May 1938, Yun made his first trip to Yan'an and was received by Mao himself. Then, beginning with August 1941, Yun became part of the CCP's central echelon in northern Shaanxi and started his rapid rise within the CCP organization.[57]

Mao's refusal to move as requested by Stalin and Ulaanbaatar's avoidance of involvement with Yun's group indicated how low the communist bloc relationship dropped in a time of war for national survival. The ascendance of nationalist tendencies in both Yan'an and Ulaanbaatar pointed to further divergence between these communist partners' views on the future of the Mongolia question. To the leadership of the MPR, Japan's invasion of China and entanglement with Inner Mongolia further darkened the already uncertain prospect for Mongolian national unification. During the war years, the MPR had no alternative but to closely follow Soviet foreign policy, which was to preserve the current Soviet–Japanese balance of power in Central Asia. For the CCP's part, its wartime nationalism only strengthened the old conviction that the MPR would rejoin China as a brother republic. There was, however, an important change in the CCP's wartime discourse: The MPR was not only linked to a Communist China in the future but also to the GMD's official China at present.

---

57. Wang and Hao, *Wulanfu Nianpu,* 92–93, 96, 101–4, 119. Uradyn E. Bulag, *The Mongols at China's Edge: History and the Politics of National Unity* (Lanham, Md.: Rowman & Littlefield, 2002), 207–44.

The CCP's wartime cooperation with the GMD government did not mean that it had abandoned its class-struggle orientation. In the war years, Mao's own thinking about the GMD–CCP relationship moved from a conciliatory agenda for the two parties' "long-term cooperation and common effort in national construction" to a confrontational objective of using the CCP's "new democratic republic" to replace the GMD's "republic of Three People's Principles."[58] The two parties' wartime "united front" was therefore just a new phase in the CCP's struggle to gain power in China. Nevertheless, because in the war years the CCP had openly recognized the GMD government as the legitimate central government of China and used the banner of nationalism to win the broadest possible support for its own programs in China, its class-based bifurcation of China was no longer appropriate.

Now China had to be construed and constructed in terms of the Chinese nation, which used to be the GMD's ideological turf. In the war years, the CCP made a special effort to establish its own definition of *zhonghua minzu* (Chinese nation). In criticizing Jiang Jieshi's idea about "one Chinese nation, many branch clans," which was publicized in his 1943 book, *China's Destiny,* the CCP deployed a plural conception of "Chinese nations" (*zhonghua ge minzu*) to affirm the non-Han ethnic groups' own "Chinese national" status. But on a fundamental point the CCP did not disagree with the GMD: All the ethnic groups living within the political map of the Republic of China were members of the Chinese nation. In other words, the CCP's wartime radical, populist nationalism concurred completely with the GMD's official, elitist nationalism in respect to the geobody and ethnic configuration of the Chinese nation.

Along with this general reorientation, the CCP's conception of the MPR as a "class brother" had to be substituted by a brotherhood of national connection. Consequently, in the war years CCP documents defined the Mongolian nation as a member of the *zhonghua minzu* while treating the MPR as its "liberated" half. In the party's propaganda toward the minorities, the MPR's role as a model of struggling against the GMD authorities was also replaced with one of unifying with China in the war against Japan.[59] Could this part of the Chinese nation not be part of the Chinese state, or the GMD-

---

58. Yang, *Zhonggong yu Mosike,* 436, 446.

59. Yang Song, "On Nation, 1 August 1938," *MWWH,* 767; Liu Chun, "How to Unite with the Mongolian Nation in the Resistance against Japan, 20 March 1940," ibid., 819; "Outline on the Mongolian Nation in the War of Resistance by the Northwestern Working Committee of the CCP Central Committee, July 1940," ibid., 657.

ruled Republic of China? For a while, the CCP seemed self-contradictory on this point. In December 1939, the CCP Central Committee issued a pamphlet under Mao's name. The first section, on the Chinese nation, described "China's current boundaries" and stated that China "in the north shares a common border with the Mongolian People's Republic," as if the MPR were a foreign country. But in another textbook issued by the CCP's Eighth Route Army in the same month, China was described as a state with twenty-eight provinces, plus Mongolia and Tibet as two "special administrative districts." This was exactly how the GMD government defined the territories of the Republic of China. After reading the text, Mao commended the CCP officials responsible for its compilation while ignoring the discrepancy between the two texts.[60]

Because the intended audience for both documents were CCP cadres and troops, their inconsistency on the MPR was not deliberate. The discrepancy just reflected a momentary confusion among CCP officials when the party was shifting its gears from class struggles to a national war of resistance. Mao's own oversight of or indifference toward the obvious contradiction was not surprising—for as either a "liberated" nation or as part of the Chinese "motherland," Outer Mongolia could fit well into the CCP's political education program in the war years.

The CCP, which was neither in charge of the Chinese central government nor responsible for Chinese diplomacy, did not need to be overly concerned with the legal and diplomatic ramifications of its political literature. At the time, the outside world did not know the CCP well enough to question the party about these internal party materials. In the meantime, in its limited wartime contact with the West, the CCP was rather consistent on the prospect of the Chinese–Mongolian relationship. In 1944, the U.S. government sent a military observers' group, dubbed the "Dixie Mission," to Yan'an. Mao and his associates took advantage of the new contact and let the Americans know, among other things, about their criticism of the GMD government's repressive policies toward China's minority peoples and their own support for the minorities' status as "nations." As for Outer Mongolia, the CCP leaders were confident that the unification of Inner and Outer Mongo-

---

60. Mao Zedong, "Chinese Revolution and the Chinese Communist Party, December 1939," *MWWH,* 625; Political Department of the Eighth Route Army, "Political Textbook for Soldiers Resisting Japan, December 1939," ibid., 807; "To Xiao Xiangqian, 1940," Mao Zedong, *Mao Zedong Shuxin Xuanji* (Selected Correspondence of Mao Zedong) (Beijing: Renmin Chubanshe, 1983), 161.

lia would be "inevitable" and that the unified Mongolian nation would certainly join a Chinese federation.

At the time, America's China hands were impressed by the CCP's "high nationalist spirit" with regard to China's territorial integrity and sovereignty. Meanwhile, they were also baffled by the CCP leaders' seemingly indifferent attitude toward Soviet encroachments on Chinese territories in the past and possibly in the near future if the Russians entered the war against Japan.[61] Soon enough, when the Soviet–MPR forces entered the war against Japan through the areas of Inner Mongolia and Manchuria, they were greeted by a new wave of Inner Mongolian autonomous movements. Postwar Inner Mongolian politics therefore became the first occasion to force the CCP leaders to quit equivocating about the bedeviling contradiction between their nationalist practices and internationalist pronouncements.

61. "Clarence E. Gauss to the Secretary of State, 1 September 1944," in *Foreign Relations of the United States: Diplomatic Papers, 1944: China,* ed. U.S. Department of State (Washington, D. C.: Government Printing Office, 1967), 536–37; John P. Davies' memo on Yan'an, 7 November 1944, ibid., 667–69; John Service, "Communist Views in Regard to Mongolia," 16 March 1945, General Records of the U.S. Department of State Central Files: China, 893.00 / 3-1645.

Part II

Autonomy and Civil War, 1945–1950

4

"National Fever": The Genesis of
an Autonomous Movement

As of the end of World War II, Inner Mongolia was a geopolitical puzzle and a demographic maze. In the first half of the seventeenth century, the name "Inner Mongolia" was first used by the Manchu rulers of the Qing Dynasty to denote a group of Mongolian tribes and their territories that pledged allegiance to the Qing court. Along with "Outer Mongolia," it has remained a divisive conception ever since. At the onset, the conception covered a vast region. From east to west, the area stretched from modern Jilin to the Qilian Mountains; its northern rim was marked by a natural feature, the Gobi Desert, and its southern extension was blocked by a human-made barrier, the Great Wall. Yet, during the first few decades of the twentieth century, successive efforts by China's central authorities to "establish provinces and install counties" (*jiansheng shexian*) in border regions effectively nullified Inner Mongolia as a distinctive ethnopolitical territory. Afterward, the geographical features depicted above remained merely in the Inner Mongols' self-image. To China's central authorities, the issue of "Inner Mongolia" was replaced by one that involved a number of remaining Mongolian banners scattered in seven provinces. In the early 1930s, Japanese influence penetrated deeply into northern China and the area of Inner Mongolia. Though the Japanese promoted anti-Chinese emotions among the Inner Mongols, they nevertheless did not want to restore Inner Mongolia as a unified entity. In the war years under the Japanese occupation, the authorities for the area became part of *manmeng* (Manchuria–Mongolia), a nebulous geostrategic region that the Japanese invented and arbitrarily shaped.[1]

---

1. During the republican period, Inner Mongolia was divided and incorporated into Heilongjiang, Jilin, Liaoning, Rehe, Chahar, Suiyuan, and Ningxia provinces. The

Yet during the long history of Inner Mongolia, the movement of people was a development more serious than how the area was named and renamed. The Chinese government did not have reliable vital statistics for Inner Mongolia as a region. An official Chinese yearbook of 1946 put the total population of the three Inner Mongolian provinces, Rehe, Chahar, and Suiyuan, at 6.3 million without indicating the size of the Mongol population, which the compilers of the volume admitted was declining. According to a 1948 report by the Mongolian and Tibetan Affairs Commission, China's Mongol population, which was scattered in eleven provinces, was one and a half million in total. A Manchukuo source cited in a Chinese official report of 1947 indicated that the ratio between the Mongol and Han populations in the puppet regime's seven principal Mongolian provinces was about one to nine. Clearly, since the late Qing period, waves of Han migration and agricultural cultivation had rendered the Inner Mongols a "minority" people in their own land.[2]

In such a constant interethnic contest, assimilation and alienation were two possible directions for the Han–Mongolian relationship, and evidence of both was abundant. For instance, in both western and eastern Inner Mongolia, elementary education was available for Mongol pupils in both Mongolian and Han languages. Many parents started their children in the former but, recognizing the irreversible trend of sinicization of Inner Mongolia, they also viewed the latter as a much-sought-after skill that their children

---

situation was altered one more time during Japan's occupation. After 1932, the Japanese authorities put three eastern leagues (Jerim, Juu-uda, and Josotu) and Hulunbuir under its puppet government of Manchuguo as parts of a "general Xing'an Province." In 1939, an "Associated Autonomous Government of Mongolia" under Prince Demchugdongrub (Prince De) emerged with Japan's blessing at Zhangjiakou (Kalgan), whose nominal authority covered Shilingol, Ulanchab, Bayantala, Yekejuu, southern Chahar, and northern Shanxi. See Zhou Qingshu, *Neimenggu Lishi Dili* (Historical Geography of Inner Mongolia) (Hohhot: Neimengu Daxue Chubanshe, 1993), 156–58, 238–39, 241–42.

2. *China Handbook, 1937–1945: New Edition with 1946 Supplement* (New York: Macmillan, 1947), 2, 29; Mongolian and Tibetan Affairs Commission, "Demographic Chart of Frontier Nationalities," December 1948, Jiang Zhongzheng Zongtong Dang'an: Geming Wenxian (Kanluan Shiqi) (Archives of President Jiang Zhongzheng [Jiang Jieshi]: Revolutionary Documents [the Period of Rebels' Suppression]), 39: 444; "Facts about the Inner Mongolian Autonomous Government," 3 June 1947, Zongtongfu Dang'an (Records of the Presidential Palace; hereafter ZD), 055/1657, Sinica Historica; Ge Jianxiong et al., *Jianming Zhongguo Yiminshi* (A Brief Migration History of China) (Fuzhou: Fujian Renmin Chubanshe, 1993), 474–82.

must learn to the degree of perfection. The situation proved consequential to the Chinese Communist Party's (CCP's) postwar work in Inner Mongolia. Among participants in the postwar Mongolian autonomous movement, it was at first scandalous that Yun Ze, the most prominent Mongol member of the CCP, could not even speak the Mongolian language. This was, however, quite common among Yun's fellow bannermen in Tumed, which was sometimes referred in the Chinese official language simply as *guihuaqi,* or "assimilated banner." In the postwar years, this banner supplied many of the CCP's first group of young Mongol activists. Yet the party leadership found it necessary to teach these often reluctant youths how to speak and write Mongolian. Sometimes Han instructors had to be used.[3]

Although there were cultural and linguistic distinctions among the Mongols, there were also personalities who bridged the Han/Mongolian ethnic gap. Assimilation was never a one-way street. A most significant development in the history of China's northern frontier was the emergence of a great number of intercultural and even interethnic personalities, such as sinicized Mongols and "Mongolized" Han. For instance, Li Shouxin, the number two figure in Japan's puppet Mongolian regime at Zhangjiakuo, was not, in his own words, of "genuine Mongolian" (*zhen menggu*) origin. His ancestors belonged to a category of "adapted Mongols" (*sui menggu*), that is, Han migrants who were assimilated into Mongolian banners.[4] In the postwar years, Yun and the leaders of the eastern Mongolian movement started from different positions in Inner Mongolian politics, but they shared the same important quality—their cross-ethnic and intercultural faculties. In a purely Han or Mongolian environment, they might or might not have been able to excel in their undertakings. But under interethnic circumstances, the more complicated the situation was, the more powerful these people's management or manipulative skill would appear. These were the people who were positioned at the very center of the power struggle for Inner Mongolia in the postwar years.

3. Dawa-ochir, "My Experiences," *NWZ,* 31: 106; Hao Yufeng, *Wulanfu Zhuan* (Biography of Ulanfu) (Hohhot: Neimenggu Renmin Chubanshe, 1990), 5, 12; Buyante, "Comrade Ulanfu and translation works," *Wulanfu Jinian Wenji* (Memorial essays on Ulanfu) (Hohhot: Neimenggu Renmin Chubanshe, 1990), 2: 318; Wang Duo, *Wushi Chunqiu* (Eventful fifty years) (Hohhot: Neimenggu Renmin Chubanshe, 1992), 115–116.

4. Li Shouxin, "*Li Shouxin Huiyilu*" (Autobiography of Li Shouxin), *Neimenggu Wenshi Ziliao* (Literary and Historical Materials of Inner Mongolia; hereafter *NWZ*), 20: 2–3.

From Colonialism to National Fever

War is a time of taking sides. In an article written in 1936, Owen Lattimore concisely presented his view on why Prince De (Demchugdongrub), the most visible Inner Mongol leader in the prewar period, became a collaborator with Japan during the deadly Chinese–Japanese conflict. He wrote: "Te Wang [Prince De] . . . has not 'gone over' to Japan; he has been tied hand and foot and thrown to the Japanese [by the Chinese government]."[5] The folly of the Guomindang (GMD, Nationalist Party) government's policy in Inner Mongolia not only alienated ambitious figures like Prince De but was also an important reason for many Inner Mongols' passiveness toward China's struggle for survival. Even the Chinese Communists, who were usually effective in mobilizing popular support in their undertakings, were frustrated with their abortive efforts among the Inner Mongols, complaining that "basically, the Mongolian nation has maintained a vacillating and neutral attitude toward the anti-Japanese war. . . . The crux of today's Mongolian question is whether the Mongolian nation will take the side of China's war of resistance or the side of the Japanese invader."[6]

During China's war of resistance, although there were Inner Mongols in the ranks of both the CCP and the GMD, many Inner Mongols chose to remain dormant. It therefore appeared surprising at the war's end that popular political activism erupted suddenly in Inner Mongolia. A GMD official warned his government that although in the past Inner Mongolian leagues and banners had never been able to work together, now they seemed to rise as one. In this official's opinion, this dangerous phenomenon arose under the stimulation of China's recognition of Outer Mongolia's independence and agitation by Russian and Outer Mongolian agents.[7]

---

5. Owen Lattimore, "The Eclipse of Inner Mongolian Nationalism," in his *Studies in Frontier History* (London: Oxford University Press, 1962), 438. The essay originally appeared in *Journal of the Royal Central Asian Society* (London) 33 (July 1936).

6. Northwestern Working Committee of the Chinese Communist Party, "Outline on the Question of the Mongol Nation during the War of Resistance," July 1940 (approved by the secretariat of the CCP Central Committee), *Minzu Wenti Wenxian Huibian* (Collected Documents on the Nationality Question; hereafter *MWWH*), comp. United Front Department of the Central Committee of the Chinese Communist Party (Internal circulation; Beijing: Zhonggong Zhongyang Dangxiao Chubanshe, 1991), 664.

7. "Memorandum by Sun Fushen, 19 July 1947," Waijiaobu Yaxisi Dang'an (Records of the Western Asian Division of the Ministry of Foreign Affairs): 112/93, Waijiaobu Dang'an Zisunchu (Desk of Archives of the Ministry of Foreign Affairs), Taipei.

The Mongolian People's Republic (MPR) and the Soviet Union were certainly the most potent external influence for the new wave of ethno-nationalist activities in postwar Inner Mongolia. Yet in comparison with pre-war autonomous movements, the new activism was particularly internally motivated. It was best represented by the spontaneous mass movement in eastern Mongolia, which had minimal influence from old aristocrats and highly positioned lamas. This "modern" feature had much to do with the social and political conditions created by Japan's occupation since the 1930s.

Like all modern colonial encounters, Japan's rule in Inner Mongolia, which started in eastern Inner Mongolia in 1931 and extended to the west after 1935, performed the role of a suppresser and that of a modernizer at once. If, to borrow Lattimore's metaphor, the Chinese government had thrown the Inner Mongols to the Japanese with their hands and feet tied up, the Japanese occupation authorities had no intention of untying the knots. The Japanese never approved Prince De's demand to establish an independent Mongolian state. After 1939, Prince De became president of an "associate autonomous government of the Mongolian frontier," sharing power with a Japanese "supreme adviser." A year before the war ended, Japanese policymakers in Tokyo further decided to treat the "Mongolian frontier [*mengjiang*]" as China's internal problem.[8]

Had Japanese rule merely functioned to curb Prince De's ambitions, its position in the modern history of Inner Mongolia would not have differed much from the GMD's. But the Japanese occupation had another set of effects on Inner Mongolian society that was directly relevant to the region's postwar political conditions. Japanese rule not only created its potential enemies among Inner Mongols but also exerted a "modernizing" effect on the society. With respect to the latter, even GMD officials marveled at the "rather progressive" programs implemented by local Mongolian regimes under Japanese control. According to a 1939 GMD government report, under the Japanese, government finance in Inner Mongolia was managed in an orderly way and achieved a favorable balance, highway constructions progressed impressively, and livestock was improved in quality and increased

---

8. *Demuchukedonglupu Zishu, NWZ,* 13: 59, 65, 81, 83, 93, 95–102, 105; Supreme War Council, "Implementation of the Working Plan toward Chongqing," 5 September 1944, in *Riben Diguozhuyi Duiwai Qinlue Shiliao Xuanbian* (Selected Historical Documents on Japanese Imperialist Foreign Aggression), comp. and trans. Japanese History Group of the History Department of Fudan University (Shanghai: Renmin Chubanshe, 1975), 474–78.

in quantity. In 1941, factories were opened in Zhangjiakuo and Guisui (Hohhot) that used sheep intestines to produce catgut and strings for musical instruments. This was unheard of for the local people and had significant implications for the pastoral economy.[9]

To serve its military empire in China, the Japanese authorities also took measures to foster an echelon of Inner Mongolian civil servants. The resultant impact on the social psychology of the region was profound. The originally Han-dominant social atmosphere was the first to disappear. In Japanese-controlled Suiyuan and Chahar areas, a popular saying among the Han people depicted a new Japanese-centered ethnic relationship: "The Mongols become soldiers, the Manchus run errands, the Hui serve as informants, and the Han are suffering." This was probably an exaggerated expression of the Han's bitterness. Nevertheless, a reversal of relations between the Han and the other ethnic groups did take place under Japan's rule. Although a subjugated people under the Japanese, ordinary Mongols got a boost in their self-esteem vis-à-vis the Han from such Japanese policies as rolling back the Chinese county system and allowing Mongol herdsmen to reclaim land from Han farmers.[10]

Perhaps nothing was more morale enhancing for an oppressed people than the reclamation of their history and culture. Because of the GMD government's record in the past, it did not take much for the Japanese to assuage the Mongols' cry for a self-identity. The Japanese occupation authorities took pains to foster a pro-Japanese mentality among the Mongols, especially among the young people. In school curriculums, all references to China were eliminated and the alleged historical, cultural, and geographical ties between the "Mongolian frontier" and the Japanese Empire were emphasized.

9. "Conditions of the Puppet 'Associate Autonomous Government of Mongolia," April–September, 1939, *Zhonghua Minguo Zhongyao Shiliao Chubian: Dui Ri Kangzhan Shiqi* (Preliminary Compilation of Important Historical Records of the Republic of China: The Period of the War of Resistance against Japan; hereafter *ZZSC*), 7 vols., comp. Historical Council of the Guomindang (Taipei: Guomindang Dangshi Weiyuanhui, 1981), 6(2): 261–73; Chahar–Mongolian Special Office, "The Situation of the Japanese Enemy's Economic Aggression in Puppet Mongolia," 1941, ibid., 393.

10. Suiyuan–Chahar Administrative Office (CCP), "Open Letter to All Nationalities in the Suiyuan–Chahar area," 1 October 1941, *Daqingshan Kang Ri Youji Genjudi Ziliao Xuanbian* (Selected Materials on the Anti-Japanese Base in the Daqing Mountains) (Hohhot: Neimenggu Renmin Chubanshe, 1987), 1: 268; Tan Wenbin (director of the Civil Affairs Department of the Reha government [GMD]), "Three Present and Serious Problems of Rehe," March 1946, Xingzhengyuan (Executive Yuan [chamber]; hereafter XZY), 067/523, Archives of Academia Historica.

The Chinese language was abolished in school instruction, and the Japanese language became a required course in elementary and middle schools. Yet, despite these colonizing features of the "new" education, Inner Mongols could find certain satisfaction in the fact that Mongolian history, distorted as it was in the new curriculum, could be taught and that the Mongolian language had become the "national language" to study in school.[11] To the Chinese authorities, these developments were part of a Japanese conspiracy to subjugate the "Chinese nation," of which the Inner Mongols were members. To some Inner Mongols, the Japanese rule could be a chance for at least a conditional rehabilitation of the Mongolian nation.

The fourteen-year period Japanese occupation (1931–45) was long enough for a newborn to grow into a teenager and an adolescent into adulthood. By the time the Japanese Empire crumbled, the effects of its colonial rule in the Mongolian Plateau began to manifest. The generation that matured in the war years did not grieve over the eclipse of the Japanese sun in the Pacific. Instead, August 15, 1945, was generally hailed as a day of liberation by Genghis Khan's descendants. To Inner Mongolia's postwar politics, the immediate legacies of Japanese rule were the retreat of Chinese influence and the decline of the old elites of the Mongolian society. The political stage was thus swept clean for a new breed of autonomist leaders.

This was so not only because Prince De's collaboration with a losing power badly damaged the reputation of the old elites. It was so also because in the war years the Japanese made a deliberate effort, for the sake of government efficiency, to replace medieval figures in local administrative structures with new blood from the commoners' crowd. In the Mongolian leagues and banners of western Inner Mongolia, Japan's collaboration with Prince De allowed the traditional power structure to survive to a certain degree. Socially the most conservative sector was, however, the region in the middle of Inner Mongolia. In these "pure Mongolian" areas such as the Shilingol grassland, many old aristocrats maintained predominant positions, and their privileges were barely touched by the laws of the Republic of China or by Japanese rule. At the war's end, these princes were still in their official uniforms of the Qing period and wielded official seals issued by Manchu emperors. But after Japan's defeat, the center of Inner Mongolia's autonomous movement shifted to the Xing'an area in the east, which in the war years

---

11. Office of the Commissioner to Mongol Banners in Chaha'er, "General Military and Political Conditions of Puppet Mongolia," after 1939, *ZZSC,* 6(2): 453–54.

was under the "Manchukuo." It was in this area that Japan's policies of fostering a new elite class had the most conspicuous effect.[12]

Dawa-ochir, an autonomist in the postwar years, was typical among eastern Mongol activists who came from a commoner's background and achieved political prominence during the Japanese period. He was born to a poor herdsman's family in Jerim League, schooled in his home banner and the nearby county, and accepted by Beijing University in 1930. While still a college student, he was once a house guest in Prince De's palace in Western Sunid, Shilingol; took part in activities to promote Mongolian culture; and befriended Owen Lattimore. A conviction of young Dawa-ochir's, for which he would feel quite "scared" in later years, was that if the Mongolian nation was destined for subjugation, it would rather become a slave of a strong foreign power than as a tamed subject of the weak China. With this thought, Dawa-ochir worked with the Japanese in Xing'an for twelve years. On the eve of Japan's surrender, he was promoted to the position of councilor of the Xing'an "general province" and also became a research fellow at the "Great Harmony Institute" of Manchukuo. Japan's defeat convinced Dawa-ochir that Inner Mongolia had to follow in the footsteps of Outer Mongolia. So he joined with a group of autonomists in Wangyemiao (Wang-un Sume, today's Ulanhote) who seemed to be doing just that.[13]

About the newly found prestige of Wangyemiao, the political center of the Xing'an region, Zhang Ce, the secretary of the CCP committee for Xing'an province, made the following observation:

> During the 14 years of the puppet "Manchukuo," Wangyemiao became a ruling center of the Mongols. Since the liberation they have centered their independence movement here. Until now Wangyemiao remains the head of the Mongols, just like how our liberated areas look up to Yan'an.[14]

---

12. Oljeinaren, "In the Mighty Torrent of Inner Mongolia's Liberation Movement," *NWZ*, 50: 194–96; Yun Shiying and Chao Luomeng, "Recollections of Works in the Shilingol League," ibid., 156–75; Budebara, "Recollections and Memories," *Xilinguole Shi Wenshi Ziliao* (Literary and Historical Materials of the Shili-yin Gool Municipality), 1: 46–72; report by Jin Chongwei (member of the "Propaganda and Comforting Mission to Mongol Banners" in Liaoning), 31 May 1946, ZD, 055/1623.

13. Dawa-ochir, "What I Witnessed and Experienced," *NWZ*, 31: 104–25, 130–57.

14. Zhang Ce, "The Conditions and Experiences of Works in the Eastern [Inner] Mongolian Region (Xing'an)," 15 August 1946, *MWWH*, 1315–21.

The geographical shift of Inner Mongols' political activities from Prince De's palace in Western Sunid to Wangyemiao in Xing'an reflected a generational transition. Now at the forefront of the autonomous movement were no longer princes and old *jasags* (banner leaders). The new vanguards were modern bureaucrats and young intellectuals.

The situation of Xing'an was eye opening for Chinese officials. A GMD report that reached Jiang Jieshi's desk described the new Mongol leaders in the region with a language completely devoid of the condescending tone that was prevalent in official papers on Mongolian affairs in the past. According to the report, all these leaders in eastern Mongolia had received higher education in China, Japan, or the Soviet Union, and these were "of first-class quality and Genghis Khan's ambitions." To the report's authors, it was simply "astonishing" that the movement in Wangyemiao gathered around itself so many well-trained military officers (about 6,800) and civil officials (about 24,300). What about ordinary people? The question was answered by the CCP, the mass-line practitioner. According to one of its documents, "In this place, generally speaking, the Han people are more backward than the Mongols who can learn new ideas very quickly under the spirit of a national fever [*minzure*]."[15]

"National fever" was a term originating in eastern Inner Mongolia. The term was never mentioned in the GMD government's documents. CCP operatives learned about it just a few months after Japan's surrender. In November 1945, autonomous leaders in Wangyemiao sent an envoy named Bao Yukun to contact Mongol activists in western Inner Mongolia. In Zhangjiakou, Bao met with Yun Ze and his CCP colleagues, who were there organizing an Inner Mongolian Autonomous Movement Association. Bao confessed to Yun that he did not have many ideas about how the Mongolian people should proceed with their cause, and that he acted purely out of a "national fever." Bao nevertheless had an unequivocal understanding of the conception: "We of the Mongolian nation are now doing things by ourselves and we need to cultivate relations with all sides. Outer Mongolia and we belong to the same nation and will unify in the future."[16] These simple words revealed just about all the thoughts in many Mongols' minds.

15. "Facts of the Inner Mongolian Autonomous Government," 3 June 1947, ZD, 055/1657; Zhang Ce, "Conditions and Experiences," 1319.

16. Ulanfu, *Wulanfu Huiyilu* (Memoirs of Ulanfu) (Beijing: Zhonggong Dangshi Ziliao Chubanshe, 1989), 215–16; Liu Chun, "Works in Inner Mongolia Remembered," *NWZ*, 50: 41–42.

"National fever" best captured the phenomenal eruption and widespread character of Inner Mongolian ethnonationalism in postwar months, a prominent feature of which was a heightened group identity. A people of ancient origins and unique culture, the Inner Mongols easily recognized commonalities that bonded them into a national community. During the postwar years, the most popular slogan among the Inner Mongols was "Genghis Khan's descendants, unite!" This slogan was aimed not only at overcoming regional divisions of Inner Mongolia wrought by Chinese authorities' administrative policies but also at projecting a general unification of all Mongols, including the MPR. In their official documents, the eastern Mongol leaders identified common "historical, blood, geographic, linguistic, cultural, and religious" origins and practices as the denominators of the modern Mongolian nation. But for ordinary people, the Mongolian language was the insignia of their self-group. In the politically charged atmosphere of postwar Inner Mongolia, language alone sometimes could decide political grouping. Yun's deficiency with the language at first caused a rumor among eastern Mongols that he was actually a Han. Wang Zaitian (a.k.a. Namjil-Sileng), another sinicized CCP cadre from Jerim, could not reestablish his Mongolian identity with young activists in his own home area because of his poor spoken Mongolian. The barrier was broken only after he asked his aged mother, who spoke the "national language" perfectly, to move in with him.[17]

Another conviction held feverishly by all political groups of Inner Mongolia was the need for a Mongolian government for the entire Inner Mongolian region. This idea included two basic components: First, the division of Inner Mongolia among several Chinese provinces should be abolished; and second, the original region of Inner Mongolia should be restored. Whereas Inner Mongolian autonomists had no consensus on the idea of Inner Mongolia's unification with the MPR and the degree of Inner Mongolian autonomy, their shared aspiration for Mongolian governance of Inner Mongolia stood out as a unifying agenda. This agenda appeared in the documents of the relatively radical eastern Mongolian movement, in conservative Mongol figures' petitions to the GMD government, and also in Mongol party mem-

---

17. Hao, *Wulanfu Zhuan,* 445; "Principal Slogans for the Conference of May 1st," *Neimenggu Dang'an Shiliao* (Historical Materials from Archives of Inner Mongolia), 1: 22; "Constitution of the People's Autonomous Government of Eastern Mongolia," February 1946, Quanzonghao (general record number; hereafter QZH) 4/1 (2); Wang Zaitian, "Recollections on My Work in the Social Department before and after the Establishment of the Autonomous Government of Inner Mongolia," *NWZ,* 50: 131–32.

bers' advice to the CCP leadership. More than anything else, this aspiration constituted the basis for cooperation among different Mongolian groups.[18]

The GMD's and CCP's policies toward the Inner Mongols' autonomous aspirations will be discussed below. It is sufficient to point out here that the two parties made rather different estimates of the "national fever." Always careful about spontaneous tendencies of the mass, CCP observers admitted that the phenomenon represented a prevalent passion for progressive changes among the Inner Mongols. At least initially, the CCP differentiated the Inner Mongols' political activism from "narrow Mongolian nationalism," a CCP conception for "Inner Mongolia's reactionary fantasy."[19]

GMD officials' opinions about the situation varied. In early 1946, Fu Zuoyi, the commander of the GMD forces in western Inner Mongolia, reported to Jiang Jieshi that, having been incited by Outer Mongolia's independence, autonomy was now a "central popular demand" among the Inner Mongols. Yet a warning like this tended to be diluted by reports asserting that the noises in Inner Mongolia were made only by a small group of ambitious Mongolian figures who were maneuvering for self-promotion. According to a report from the GMD's Rehe apparatus, the southern part of Inner Mongolia had already melted into the Han society and therefore the Mongols there were not enthusiastic about autonomy; herdsmen in the still primitive north rarely had contact with the Han people and therefore remained passive politically. It was therefore only in the middle region around Wangyemiao that "partially assimilated" Mongols acted as self-appointed vanguards of a Mongolian autonomous movement.[20]

18. Bai Yunti to Jiang Jieshi, 15 December 1945, ZD, 055/1645; Secretariat of the Office of Aides to Jiang Jieshi, 12 March 1947, ZD, 055/1657; "Declaration on the Establishment of the Autonomous Government of Eastern Mongolia," 19 January 1946, QZH 4/1 (5); minutes of Sui-Meng government's (CCP) discussion of the Mongolian work, 11 August 1945, *Daqingshan,* 2: 292–95; Hao, *Wulanfu Zhuan,* 394–98.

19. Directive of Ji-Re-Liao Branch Bureau of the CCP on the Mongolian work in Rehe, 14 December 1946, in *Neimenggu Tongzhan Shi: Dang'an Shiliao Xuanbian* (History of the United Front in Inner Mongolia: Selected Archival Materials), comp. United-Front Department of the CCP Committee of Inner Mongolia and Archives of the Inner Mongolian Autonomous Region (internal circulation, 1987), 1: 355; Hu Shaoheng, "Excerpts from Hu Shaoheng's Diary," entry of 11 March 1947, *Xing'a Geming Shihua* (Historical Literature on the Revolution in Xing'an) (Xing'an Meng Dangshi Ziliao Zhengji Bangongshi, 1990), 3: 230.

20. Fu Zuoyi to Jiang Jieshi, 25 March 1946, Jiang Zhongzheng Zongtong Dang'an: Tejiao Wendian (Edi Yinmou Bufen) (Archives of President Jiang Zhongzheng: Specially Submitted Telegrams [Part on Russian Imperialist Conspiracy]; hereafter JZZD /

Although there are no overall statistics to show the scale of mass partic-ipation in Inner Mongolian autonomous movements during the early postwar months, autonomist leaders' effort to mobilize the masses can be docu-mented.[21] The Inner Mongols had a strong tradition of preserving and spread-ing ideas and memories orally. Without a printed press, mass mobilization would have been difficult but not entirely impossible. Yet a sign indicating the coming of age of Inner Mongolian nationalism was that in eastern Mon-golia autonomist leaders not only sent letters of intentions to banner authori-ties but also used newspapers to reach as wide an audience as possible.

During the brief four years of the Chinese Civil War (1945–49), ninety-four new publications appeared in Inner Mongolia. The distribution of these publications' affiliations was, roughly, fifty-two to the CCP, nineteen to the GMD, thirteen to eastern Mongolian organizations, two to Soviet military authorities, and eight to nonpartisans. The GMD authorities did not seem interested in competing for readership in the Mongolian language. In these years it had only three new Mongolian publications, while the CCP had seventeen. The eastern Mongolian movement started nine Mongolian jour-nals and newspapers during its less than two years of existence. In the same period, the CCP started twelve newspapers and journals, but only four were in Mongolian. On the basis of these figures, the conclusion can only be that to literate Mongols, the eastern Mongolian movement had the strongest voice among all the political forces present.[22] Surely, the postwar Inner Mongolian autonomous movement was driven by an "imagined" common identity rooted in an ancient ethnic history, not by a "printed" nationalism based on modern mass schooling. But if "a Man without a Shadow was the Man without a Nation," in the postwar years the Inner Mongols could easily

---

TW [EY]), 35023332; Suiyuan Councilors' Conference to Jiang Jieshi, 11 March 1946, ZD, 055/1657; Tan Wenbin, "Three Present and Serious Problems of Rehe."

21. Christopher Atwood, "East Mongolian Revolution and Chinese Communism," *Mongolian Studies* 15 (1992): 45–46, makes an effort to show the popularity of the eastern Mongolian movement by comparing the 2,200 participants in the assembly that inaugurated the eastern Mongolian government with the much smaller numbers of dele-gates who had attended some previous historical occasions for Inner Mongolian autonomy in the 1920s and 1930s.

22. The figures are computed with information from Temle, *Jianguo qian Neimenggu Difang Baokan Kaolu* (Investigation and Classifications of Newspapers and Journals in the Area of Inner Mongolia before the Foundation of the State) (Hohhot: Neimenggu Tushuguan, 1987).

find their "shadow" through the printed media—the eastern Mongolian autonomists' journalistic effort to spread "national fever."[23]

Liberation through Unification

Japan's surrender to the Allied Powers on August 15, 1945, was one of the "liberation" moments in twentieth-century Chinese history. This moment kindled high hopes in the Chinese people that were soon followed by new sufferings and disappointments. A new round of civil war, before sending the CCP to the ruling position in China, would inflict tremendous agonies on ordinary people. While China was torn apart by a struggle for central power, the Inner Mongols strove to tear themselves away from China. Hence continued the contest between centralizing Chinese nationalism and separatist Mongolian nationalism that had begun in the 1900s.

Yet unlike the Outer Mongolian independence of 1911 and the autonomous drive in Inner Mongolia in the 1930s, both of which were reactions to distressful situations, the autonomous activities in postwar Inner Mongolia assumed an upbeat quality from the outset. Aside from stimulation from the MPR example, the initial optimism among Inner Mongol autonomists arose also from the facts that the Soviet–MPR troops were present in Inner Mongolia and Manchuria in the initial postwar months and that a good portion of Inner Mongolian population and territories had been beyond Chinese control for more than a decade. Thus postwar Inner Mongolian politics was sharply antithetical to Chinese politics in both its GMD and its CCP versions. To Inner Mongolian autonomists, the moment of "liberation" started as a test of their ability to replace Japan's imperial separation of Inner Mongolia from Chinese governance with a national form of Mongolian self-government.

The necessary internal coherence for an inclusive Inner Mongolian movement, however, was not automatically ushered in by "national fever." Old and new political cleavages continued to prevent the Inner Mongols from rising in one. Badly discredited after Japan's defeat, Prince De joined a Mongolian crowd in the GMD-controlled areas, petitioning and plotting on the

23. Both Ernest Gellner, *Nations and Nationalism* (Ithaca, N.Y.: Cornell University Press, 1983), and E. J. Hobsbawn, *Nations and Nationalism since 1780* (Cambridge: Cambridge University Press, 1990), emphasize the modern industrial basis of a truly national consciousness. The quotation is from Gellner, p. 6.

verge of GMD power to regain influence in Mongolian affairs. Meanwhile, an autonomous government in Hulunbuir, a "Provisional Government of the Inner Mongolian People's Republic" in Shilingol, and an eastern Mongolian movement centered in Wangyemiao separately brought to the surface the Inner Mongols' unequivocal aspiration for self-government. Among these, the eastern Mongolian movement alone occupied the central stage of Inner Mongolian politics for about two years and had a singularly important impact on the GMD–CCP power struggle in China.

More than any other political projections in postwar Inner Mongolia, the eastern Mongolian movement represented the beginning of a popular phase of Inner Mongolian nationalism. This was decided by several factors. First, the movement derived its popular character from the effects of some modern changes imposed on Mongolian society by Japanese rule. On the one hand, the Japanese authorities used preferential treatments for the Mongols to foster pro-Japanese feelings, and on the other it abolished the Mongolian aristocracy in favor of efficient administration. In Xing'an Province, the Japanese authorities imposed universal education on the Mongols. According to Dawa-ochir, who in the late 1930s was in charge of school education in southern Xing'an, before 1931 the area had just a few hundred elementary school students. In the next few years, however, the number increased to 20,000, and many middle and professional schools were also set up.[24]

These measures eventually brought about not only a reversal of the symbiosis between the Mongols and the Han but also a change in the internal configuration of Mongolian society: Ordinary Mongols' self-esteem vis-à-vis the Han was immensely enhanced, and a new, egalitarian appearance, if not reality, of the Mongolian society was created. Although these developments did not really bring the Mongols into an "age of universalized clerisy," they nevertheless helped strengthen the ties among different social strata of the Mongols. This proved extremely important for the postwar mass movement.[25]

Second, the movement took place in a region densely populated by Mon-

---

24. Dawa-ochir, "What I Witnessed," 138–41.
25. See Atwood, "Eastern Mongolian Revolution," 11–25, for a detailed treatment of the impact of Japanese policies on eastern Inner Mongolia. In his *Nations and Nationalism,* 8–38, Gellner compares the stratified agrarian society and the egalitarian industrial society with real or illusive social mobility, contending that only the latter can make the transition to the age of nationalism. Although this may be the case in the history of most Western societies, the argument is difficult for most non-Western societies.

gols. By the end of World War II, the total Mongolian population in the area of Inner Mongolia was probably less than 1.5 million. Of these, 1.16 million (or about 77 percent) lived in the four eastern Mongolian leagues, Hulunbuir, Jerim, Juu-uda, and Josotu. In this sense, the eastern Mongolian movement *was* the Inner Mongolian movement. A degree of territorial and administrative coherence existed among these leagues, largely because of a Japanese decision in 1943 that combined them into a "general Xing'an province." Although in this region the Mongols were still a numerical minority vis-à-vis the Han population, the interethnic ratio here was very different from that in western Inner Mongolia. In the postwar years, a CCP cadre working in Xing'an made a rough estimate of the population in the eleven banners around Wangyemiao. In six of these banners, Mongols accounted for 42 percent or more of the total population, including two banners in which the Mongolian population was more than 80 percent. It is important to note that these were not thinly populated pastoral banners like those in Shilingol, where ten banners together had a total population of 50,000. Agricultural or semi-agricultural banners in the east had much larger populations. Khorchin Left Center Banner alone, for instance, had more than 79,000 Mongol residents. Under the circumstances, a politically highly motivated Mongol populace could easily achieve a majority-like momentum over their politically inert Han neighbors.[26]

Third, the triumvirate of the movement, including Buyanmandukhu, Khafengga, and Temurbagana, had enough populist elements in their ideological backgrounds that made their nationalist ideals both ethnic and civil. All three were bilingual, had been exposed to modern education, had a commoner background, and were connected in their prewar careers to Inner Mongolia's first revolutionary party, the Inner Mongolian People's Revolutionary Party (IMPRP). Buyanmandukhu (1894–1980), the most senior of the three, was a reform advocate and a veteran of the IMPRP movement of the 1920s. His career as a newspaperman and an educator made him a well-known figure in the intellectual circles of Manchuria. Perhaps this was the reason that after the Mukden incident he was inducted by the Japanese into their Mongol staff in Xing'an. Before Japan's defeat, he rose continually in

26. Mongolian History Compiling Group, *Mengguzu Jianshi* (Brief History of the Mongolian Nationality) (Hohhot: Neimenggu Renmin Chubanshe, 1985), 402–3, 421; Hu Shaoheng, "Excerpts from Hu Shaoheng's Diaries," entry of 29 January 1948, in *Xing'an Dangshi Wenji* (Collected Essays on the Party History of Xing'an) 1 (1993): 73–74; Budebara, "Recollections and Memories."

the puppet bureaucracy and eventually became governor of the Manchukuo's "General Xing'an Province." Although at the war's end he was one of the organizers of the autonomous movement in eastern Mongolia, Buyanmandukhu was quite conscious that his prominent position in Japan's puppet government had stained his career. This made him politically vulnerable in the intricate ethnopolitical struggle in postwar Inner Mongolia. To some participants in the struggle, Buyanmandukhu's inclusion in the eastern Mongolian leadership was not for guiding the movement into the future but for cultivating the movement's connection to the past.[27]

For the eastern Mongolian movement, Temurbagana (1901–69) played a different kind of role in making connections. His earlier political career was almost identical with Yun Ze's. As a student from Kharachin Banner near Chifeng, Temurbagana first became involved in political activities at the Mongolian–Tibetan School in Beijing during the May Fourth period. In 1925, the CCP sent Temurbagana to Outer Mongolia's central party school to study. From there he proceeded to the Oriental University in Moscow. During his stay in the Soviet Union, he made Yun's acquaintance and also became a member of the Soviet Communist Party.

In 1929, when the Comintern sent Inner Mongol students back to China, Temurbagana went to eastern Inner Mongolia, while Yun went to the west. In March 1932, following Comintern directives, Temurbagana organized a secret cell in the name of the dormant IMPRP, which included Pungsug, Khafengga, Askhan, and some others. The group managed to maintain its contact with the Comintern till 1939. Temurbagana's activities attracted the attention of the Japanese authorities, and he was imprisoned briefly in 1936. After his release, he remained inactive under close Japanese police surveillance through the end of the war. These circumstances basically paralyzed the IMPRP group in the war years. When the Soviet Army entered Manchuria in August 1945, and especially when the eastern Mongolian group met with Yun and other CCP cadres in early 1946, Temurbagana's background enabled him to serve as the linchpin between the eastern Mongols and the Moscow–MPR–CCP bloc. The social reform agendas adopted by

---

27. Gan Fengling, "Brief Biography of the Eleven Members of the Political Council of Inner Mongolia," *NWZ*, 50: 335; Buyanmandukhu, "Recollections of My Participation in the Mongol Conference in Nanjing," *NWZ*, 16: 150–61; Dawa-ochir, "What I Witnessed," 125–30; Bukho and Sayin, *Boyanmandu Shengping Shilue* (Buyanmandukhu's Life and Times) (Hohhot: Neimenggu Daxue Tushuguan, 1999), 6–8, 26–32, 115–16.

the eastern Mongolian movement should probably be attributed to Temur-bagana's Comintern background as much as to the MPR's examples.[28]

Among the prominent three, Khafengga (1908–70) was the youngest and was also the central figure of the movement. Charismatic and especially popular among young Mongol activists, he even impressed the CCP cadres with his dynamic personality. After meeting with Khafengga for the first time, one of Yun's close associates recorded his impression of Khafengga as an enthusiastic and perspective leader for the Mongolian cause well deserving his popularity among the eastern Mongols.[29] Khafengga was a native of Khorchin Left Center Banner of Jerim League, the same banner that produced Gada Meiren, Inner Mongolia's folk hero who in 1929 sacrificed his life in leading a rebellion against forced land cultivation in the region. During the republican period, Khorchin Left Center Banner had the largest Mongolian population among Mongolian banners. It was also a principal interethnic battleground over sinicization. By the end of World War II, agriculture had made enough advances in the banner, but the Mongols remained the overwhelming majority of its population.[30]

The local environment and history helped shape young Khafengga's ethnonationalist consciousness, which grew further under the influence of Merse, his mentor at the Northeast Normal School for the Mongolian Banners in Mukden. After the Mukden Incident of September 1931, Khafengga became involved in an abortive military conspiracy to organize a Mongolian force that would fight for Mongolian autonomy. The next year, Khafengga joined with Temurbagana in the secret IMPRP cell. Then, acting in accordance with Comintern directives, he penetrated the Manchuguo government.

28. Jiang Mingsheng, "A Brief Biography of Temurbagana," in *Xing'an Dangshi Wenji*, 1: 226–36; Gan Fengling, "Brief Biographies of the Twenty-One Members of the Inner Mongolian Autonomous Government," *NWZ*, 50: 316; Tumen and Zhu Dongli, *Kang Sheng yu Neirendang Yuan'an* (Kang Sheng and the Unjust Case of the Inner Mongolian People's Party) (Beijing: Zhonggong Zhongyang Dangxiao Chubanshe, 1994), 114–19, 123–24.

29. Kho'erge, "Recollections of the Unification of the Inner Mongolian Autonomous Movement," *NWZ*, 50: 156.

30. Hu Shaoheng, "Excerpts from Hu Shaoheng's diaries," entry of 29 January 1948, *Xing'an Dangshi Wenji*, 1: 73-74. According to Hu Shaoheng, a CCP official working in the Wangyemiao area after the war, the Mongols accounted for 90 percent of the banner's 88,000 population. As of the late 1980s, according to *Neimenggu Zizhiqu Dituce* (Atlas of the Inner Mongolian Autonomous Region) (Hohhot: Neimenggu Zizhiqu Cehuiju, 1989), 61–63, the Mongols remained about 65 percent of the banner's total population of 450,000.

After Temurbagana was arrested in the late 1930s, Khafengga became the actual leader of the IMPRP group. Khafengga must have appeared as impressive to the Japanese authorities as to his IMPRP comrades, for, after serving in different positions in the Manchukuo government, he was inducted into its elite policy study body, the "Great Harmony Institute." After a stint serving in the Manchukuo Embassy in Tokyo between 1941 and 1943, he became a counselor in the governor's office of Xing'an province to the end of the war.[31]

In the postwar years, these eastern Mongolian leaders' complicated backgrounds were a mixed blessing for their cause. Their positions in the Manchukuo bureaucracy enabled them to take charge of a spontaneous mass movement as authoritative figures at a chaotic moment of regime change, and their Comintern connections helped legitimize the "friendly" status of their movement in the eyes of the invading Soviet Red Army. Yet, in the long run, these leaders' legitimacy in postwar politics based on their Comintern background meant that from the outset they were not really free agents for an Inner Mongolian cause and would be subject to party-line manipulation from Moscow, Ulaanbaatar, or Yan'an. Their wartime records, even though authorized by the Comintern, would also continue to cast a long shadow on these leaders' relationship with the CCP.

The beginning of the eastern Mongolian movement was not a textbook version of revolutionary conspiracies. Its "first shot" was fired by student cadets of the Xing'an Military School on August 11, 1945, killing some Japanese officer-instructors. The event, named the "August Eleventh Uprising" by its participants, involved minimal planning in which the secret IMPRP group had only an indirect role. The mutineers had a rather simple purpose before and after the uprising—to go over to the Soviet–Mongolian Army. The Soviet Red Army at first greeted them with suspicions and collected and destroyed their weapons. In early September, however, a working relationship between the two sides began, with these student cadets serving as the core of a newly organized, Soviet-endorsed police force for the Wangyemiao area. An "Inner Mongolian People's Revolutionary Youth League" was also organized a month later and began to play a major role in political agitation.[32]

31. Gan Fengling, "Brief Biographies of the Twenty-One Members," 315; Dawaochir, "What I Witnessed," 125–28, 155; Tumen and Zhu Lidong, *Kang Sheng yu Neirendang Yuan'an,* 114–19, 123–24; Bukho and Sayin, *Boyanmandu Shengping Shilue,* 10, 49–54.

32. Bayantu, "Awakening before Dawn: The August 11th Uprising Remembered," *Xing'an Geming Shihua,* 3: 192–201; Butegechi, *Fengyu Jiancheng Wushinian* (Ad-

After the August 11 uprising, a series of events unfolded in Wangyemiao that led to an organized ethnopolitical movement in eastern Mongolia. On August 14, the secret IMPRP group surfaced in Wangyemiao under the name of the Eastern Mongolian Branch of the IMPRP. The same group also announced themselves as an "Inner Mongolian People's Liberation Committee (eastern Mongolia)" and issued a "Declaration of Inner Mongolian People's Liberation" on August 18. During the remaining days of August, the committee dispatched messengers to different locations in eastern Mongolia to disseminate the declaration and to start a mass campaign of collecting signatures supporting Inner Mongolia's unification with Outer Mongolia. Then, either in late August or early September, an IMPRP conference was held in Wangyemiao, which elected a party executive committee with Khafengga as its secretary general. In addition, the conference adopted a "Provisional Constitution" for the IMPRP that clarified the party's immediate tasks and long-term goals. Probably it was also at this meeting that the eastern Mongol leaders decided to send a messenger to western Inner Mongolia to contact like-minded Mongols. Temurbagana drafted a letter in Chinese addressed to two old friends from his time in Moscow, not knowing where they were and whether or not they were still alive. Bao Yukun went to the west with the letter and, as mentioned above, met with Yun in Zhangjiakou in December.[33]

The "Declaration of Inner Mongolian People's Liberation" and the "Provisional Constitution" of the IMPRP expressed the same cluster of ideas. The former, however, deserves special attention because it was intended as an instrument to mobilize popular support throughout Inner Mongolia, not just in the eastern area. The preface of the document articulated three points. First, since its establishment in 1925, the IMPRP had not stopped its struggle for the goals of the Soviet Revolution of October 1917—to liberate weak

---

vance in Trials and Hardships for Fifty Years) (Hohhot: Neimenggu Renmin Chubanshe, 1997), 12–23.

33. Butegechi, *Fengyu Jiancheng Wushinian,* 14, 17, 20; Khafengga's interview with *Dongbei Ribao* (Northeast Daily) on 28 September 1946 as reported in "Eastern Mongolian People's Leader Khafengga on the Unification of Inner Mongolian People's Autonomous Movement after the Removal of the Long Suppression," *Woguo Minzu Quyu Zizhi Wenxian Ziliao Huibian* (Collected Documents on the Nationality Regional Autonomy of Our Country), comp. Institute of Nationalities of Chinese Academy of Social Sciences (n.p., n.d.), 3: 65–68; Dawa-ochir, "What I Witnessed," 157; Kho'erge, "Recollections of the Unification of Inner Mongolian Autonomous Movement," *NWZ,* 50: 145; Tuman and Zhu Dongli, *Kang Sheng yu Neirendang Yuan'an,* 120.

nations of the world and to implement proletarian revolution. Second, during the difficult fourteen years of Japanese occupation, the party was active both among the people and within the puppet army. It worked to undermine Japan's plan to encircle the MPR and the Soviet Union and to pave the way for Inner Mongolia to receive guidance from the two revolutionary countries. Third, since the Soviet Red Army started its offensive against Japan, the party had led military rebellions against Japan and assisted the Red Army's operations.[34] Clearly, the eastern Mongol leaders intended to make these points for establishing their credentials with both the Soviet military authorities and the Mongol mass. For this purpose, they needed to impress upon the intended audience that the largely invisible IMPRP had actually been an active revolutionary body—socialist, nationalist, and resistant all in one.

Then the Declaration launched into a detailed discussion of the IMPRP's goals and means, which deserves a complete quotation here:

(1) Under the IMPRP's leadership, Inner Mongolia from now on comes under the guidance of the Soviet Union and the MPR and becomes part of the MPR in order to gain complete liberation. Before a state body can be organized, to restore the local order speedily, a temporary Inner Mongolian People's Liberation Committee has been set up according to the principle of people's front. [The committee] will follow the established practices of the MPR in conducting all its works in education, industry, domestic affairs, diplomacy, finance, health, and transportation construction, strengthening the basis for cooperation [with the MPR].

(2) Inner Mongolian Liberation Army continues to help the [Soviet] Red Army and actively participate in the war of liberation in order to fulfill its mission and in the meantime to provide a comprehensive assistance to the Red Army's operations.

(3) All feudal vestiges must be eliminated and the rights and freedom of the laboring people protected. In the future the social economy will develop in high speed along a "non-capitalist development" road.

(4) All people in the territory are equal regardless of their races. The Mongolian–Han relationship has always been very close and friendly. In the future the Han nationality's liberation movement will be given active

---

34. "Declaration of Inner Mongolian People's Liberation, 18 August 1945," QZH 4/1 (6); "Provisional Constitution of the IMPRP," n.d., ibid.; Tan Wenbin, "Three Current and Serious Problems of Rehe, March 1946."

assistance. [We] believe that the Han population in Mongolian territories can achieve liberation only after the liberation of the Mongolian people. Therefore, we will closely cooperate with revolutionary parties in our friendly neighbor, China, anticipating a just and thorough solution of the Mongol–Han [inter-]nationality problem.

The above items have been decided upon. We deeply hope that the world's weak nations' savior Soviet Union and the world's peace-loving democracies can understand clearly our heartfelt feelings and provide us with sympathetic and positive advice and assistance.[35]

As expressed clearly in point 1 above, the eastern Mongols not only wanted to emulate the MPR in sociopolitical development but also tied their "complete liberation" to Inner Mongolia's accession to the MPR. The goal echoed an unfulfilled dream of the Mongolian Revolution of 1911. Since then, it had never been endorsed in Moscow; and in 1945, the pan-Mongol agenda was again rendered unlikely by the newly concluded Sino-Soviet treaty. Hence Khafengga and his associates headed toward a political impasse. Obviously, these people's wartime isolation on the Japanese side of the war deprived them of relevant information about international conditions, without which they were unable to adopt a more practical agenda.

Also noteworthy was the eastern Mongolian leaders' reference to China and the Han in point 4 above. Calling China a "friendly neighbor," they did not even bother to petition any Chinese authorities to release Inner Mongolia. This sense of separation was probably derived from the years of the Manchukuo. After Japan's defeat, for a moment it was by no means certain that the Chinese government would be able to reestablish itself in Manchuria anytime soon. Also, in view of the Han–Mongolian population ratio in eastern Mongolia, which was not unfavorable to the Mongols in every banner, the eastern Mongolian leaders found an edge in treating the Han residents in their region as a weaker nationality. At least politically if not numerically, in the document the Mongols and the Han switched their "minority" and "majority" positions. Probably unwittingly yet quite naturally, in contending that the Han's liberation had to come as a corollary of the Inner Mongols' liberation, the eastern Mongolian leaders reversed one of the most important arguments made by the CCP on why the ethnic minorities had to be part of China.

35. "Declaration of Inner Mongolian People's Liberation, 18 August 1945," QZH 4/1 (6).

In taking such an audacious ethnopolitical stance challenging the entire spectrum of Chinese political forces, Khafengga and his associates were, however, tardy in one aspect of preparing themselves for the difficult struggle ahead. The essence of twentieth-century Chinese politics was best summarized by Mao Zedong's famous saying, "Power comes from the barrel of the gun." From this perspective, the eastern Mongolian leaders' initial steps were dangerously devoid of a serious effort to establish a Mongolian military force. The "Inner Mongolian Liberation Army" mentioned in point 2 of the "Declaration" quoted above did not exist at the time, and the point was made only to impress the audience. An objective obstacle in this respect was the restrictions imposed by the Soviet military authorities on any unauthorized military activities. Even the organization of a local police force in Wangyemiao had to be approved by the Soviets. Still, Khafengga and other leaders did not appear eager to equip their movement with a military arm.

Not until early November, after Askhan returned from Jerim, did a serious effort begin to establish a unified military force for eastern Mongolia. For the purpose, a "Department of Internal Defense" was set up with Askhan as the chief. Because Askhan was also a member of the secret IMPRP cell in the war years, he had received a military education in Japan in the late 1930s before taking military positions in Manchukuo. His insight about military power was probably the most important factor in Wangyemiao's achievement of a military force. As a matter of fact, at the time Khafengga, Buyanmandukhu, and Temurbagana were leading a mission in the MPR and would not return to Wangyemiao until late November.[36] Obviously, to most eastern Mongol leaders, Moscow's and Ulaanbaatar's endorsement of Inner Mongolia's accession to the MPR was the key to their movement's success, not the movement's own military ability to survive the forthcoming Chinese civil war.

Although Mongolian unification was a widely shared goal among the Mongols, Inner Mongolia's accession to the MPR was not universally accepted among the Inner Mongols at the end of World War II. Mongol officials and intellectuals in the GMD camp resented the sovietized MPR, if not "Outer Mongolia" as they remembered it. The Inner Mongolian cadres of the CCP were also receptive to the CCP formula of Mongolian unification

36. Gan Fengling, "Brief Biographies of the Twenty-One Members," 318; Bayantu, "Awakening before Dawn," 201; Dawa-ochir, "What I Witnessed," 158, 161; Tuman and Zhu Dongli, *Kang Sheng and Neirendang Yuan'an,* 120–21.

by way of a Chinese federation. Still, along China's northern borders where the Soviet–MPR entry into the war against Japan exerted a direct impact, the accession idea was quite popular among the Mongols. This was evident even in the still stratified society of Shilingol, where herdsmen's mass meetings voted to join the MPR and some princes practiced accession by simply taking their subjects and livestock to the other side of the border. A former member of Prince De's wartime regime explained the pro-MPR feelings as "envy of Outer Mongolia's independence."[37]

For members of the restored IMPRP in eastern Mongolia, however, the MPR did not stand merely for an ethnonational ideal of the Mongolian people. Supposedly modeled after the Soviet Union, the MPR also represented the best social system on earth. Regarding themselves as communist revolutionaries, Khafengga and his closest collaborators viewed the MPR as the fountainhead of their own revolution. This attitude was also shared by Yun Ze and other Inner Mongol members of the CCP, at least before they shed their "internationalist" trace and converted to the Maoist brand of communism.[38] Therefore, as far as the core leadership of the eastern Mongolian movement was concerned, its accession program was compatible with the goal of Inner Mongolian revolution. Social as well as national emancipation was therefore fully implied in the phrase about Inner Mongolia's "complete liberation" as "part of the MPR." But, soon enough, the eastern Mongol leaders learned that in their case state sovereignty and revolutionary cause did not go hand in hand.

This was what the eastern Mongolian delegation found out in Ulaanbaatar. Having been constrained on the other side of World War II too long, the eastern Mongol leaders were largely ignorant about the wartime inter-Allied diplomacy, in which the Chinese government was not only treated as a nominal member of the "Big Four" but also managed to strike deals with other great powers about China's postwar status. China's territorial integrity minus Outer Mongolia was sealed with the last wartime international agreement, which was the Sino-Soviet treaty concluded in August 1945. Consequently, when the eastern Mongols came to knock on the door of the MPR,

37. Fu Zuoyi to Jiang Jieshi, 15 March 1946, JZZD / TW (EY), 6: 35022506; Budebara, "Recollections and Memories"; Wang Zongluo's Report at the Enlarged Meeting of the Executive Committee of the Alliance of the Inner Mongolian Autonomous Movement, 16 April 1947, *Neimenggu Zizhi Yundong Lianhehui Dang'an Shiliao Yuanbian* (Selected Archival Materials on the Alliance of the Inner Mongolian Autonomous Movement) (Beijing: Dang'an Chubanshe, 1989), 210–11.

38. Ulanfu, *Wulanfu Huiyilu,* 56–57.

they were greeted with a huge lock that had been forged by the Chinese and the Soviets together.

Degrees of Self-Government

During the first three months after Japan's surrender, Ulaanbaatar received many groups of visitors from Inner Mongolia, invited and uninvited. The delegation from Wangyemiao was just one of these. The delegation departed for Ulaanbaatar in mid-October and stayed there through November, seeking the MPR leaders' endorsement of Wangyemiao's programs. Unlike the situation in West Sunid and Hulunbuir, where MPR troops were part of the Soviet offensive, central Xing'an was in the direction of the Soviet Red Army's principal attack without MPR participation. Consequently, the eastern Mongolian leaders did not get a chance to contact MPR officials immediately. In early October, Sangjaijab, Wangyemiao's liaison in Changchun, learned from a Buryat officer of the Soviet Far Eastern Army Headquarters that under the new Sino-Soviet treaty, Inner Mongolia's accession to the MPR was impossible and should not be pursued. During the initial postwar months, the transportation and communication systems in Manchuria collapsed, and the condition probably prevented the advice from reaching Wangyemiao before its delegation's departure for Ulaanbaatar. But there was also a possibility that the knowledge about the treaty just made the eastern Mongolians even more anxious to meet with the MPR leaders.[39]

Khafengga assumed the main responsibility for making preparations for the mission. His chosen approach to securing a relationship with the MPR was to reestablish an organizational tie between the IMPRP and the Mongolian People's Revolutionary Party of the MPR. For this purpose, he drafted a detailed report on the IMPRP's activities in the past fourteen years. The effort proved a futile exercise. Choibalsan left no doubt in the minds of his visitors that their request for accession to the MPR was impossible. He repeated the point many times in his talks with the visiting Inner Mongols: The current international circumstances meant that a solution of the Inner

---

39. Tan Wenbin's report, March 1946, XZY, 067/523; Dawa-ochir, "What I Witnessed," 158–59; Zhahalofu (M. B. Zakharov) *Jieju: 1945 nian Dabai Riben Diguozhuyi Lishi Huiyilu* (The Finale: A Historical Memoir of the Defeat of Japanese Imperialism in 1945), trans. Jun Qing (Shanghai: Shanghai Yiwen Chubanshe, 1978), 68–80; Atwood, "East Mongolian Revolution," 33–34, 39.

Mongolia question must be achieved under the leadership of the CCP, and the solution should be Inner Mongols' national self-rule in the form of a people's autonomous government. Choibalsan told his visitors that "national self-government under the CCP's assistance will be as good as national independence."[40] Choibalsan's encumbered interpretation of "self-government" and "independence" on this occasion appeared consistent with the MPR's own "independent" relationship with the Soviet Union. As a matter of fact, as this study will show later, the MPR leader was acting according to a party line handed down from Moscow.

As for Choibalsan's reaction to the eastern Mongol leaders' attempt to reestablish the IMPRP, relevant reminiscent materials are contradictory. One version suggests that Choibalsan refused to recognize the existence of the IMPRP before Japan's surrender at all and that he asked the eastern Mongols to dissolve their current party organization in favor of the CCP's leadership. Another version indicates that the MPR leader only criticized the current IMPRP for inducting "complicated elements" in its membership, lest the party be handicapped in its struggle against the GMD. The first version does not seem likely because, at the time, the dissolution of the IMPRP in eastern Mongolia would in practice have nullified the leading body of the eastern Mongolian movement. Refusing to shoulder any responsibility for the ethnopolitical upheaval in Inner Mongolia, Choibalsan would probably not dictate such a decisive step to the eastern Mongols. The two versions, however, can be reconciled if Choibalsan's advice on IMPRP's dissolution was actually a suggestion for the party's reorganization. This was exactly what Khafengga and his associates would do after they returned to Wangyemiao.[41]

Although failing to achieve its main purpose in Ulaanbaatar, the Wangyemiao delegation did not make its trip in vain. An important message was learned. It was, in Khafengga's words, that "Mongolia, the CCP, and the Soviet Union are all in one with regard to the future of Inner Mongolia;

40. Dawa-ochir, "What I Witnessed," 161–62; Wang Deyuan, "The Establishment of the Eastern Mongolian General Branch of the Alliance of the Inner Mongolian Autonomous Movement," *Neimenggu Tongzhan Lilun Yanjiu* (Inner Mongolian Studies of the Theories on the United Front) , 1987, 2: 24; Jin-Cha-Ji Central Bureau to the Central Committee of the CCP, 8 November 1945, *MWWH,* 975.

41. Dawa-ochir, "What I Witnessed," 161–62; Wang Deyuan, "Establishment of the Eastern Mongolian General Branch," 24; Tuman and Zhu Dongli, *Kang Sheng yu Neirendang Yuan'an,* 121, 123–24; Office for Party History Research of the CCP Committee of Inner Mongolia, *Neimenggu Dang de Lishi he Dang de Gongzuo* (The Party's History and Works in Inner Mongolia) (Hohhot: Neimenggu Renmin Chubanshe, 1994), 176, 178.

accordingly we should implement high-degree self-government [*gaodu zizhi*] within China." The eastern Mongol leaders, however, did not regard "high-degree self-government" as their final goal. In mid-January 1946, when a people's assembly was held in Wangyemiao to launch an Eastern Mongolian Autonomous Government (EMAG), Buyanmandukhu explained to the delegates that the liberation of Inner Mongolia would go through three phases: (1) the establishment of eastern Mongolian self-government, (2) unification between the eastern and western areas of Inner Mongolia, and (3) the combination of Inner Mongolia with the MPR.[42] This proved wishful thinking. A few months later, the eastern Mongol leaders had to re-define their goal. The original goal of "complete liberation" through a simple and clear-cut step, accession, had to be postponed indefinitely; and the new goal, "high-degree self-government" (*gaodu zizhi*), though easy to promulgate, proved elusive in meaning and manipulable in practice.[43]

When visiting in Ulaanbaatar, Buyanmandukhu self-consciously apologized to Choibalsan for his wartime collaboration with Japan: "I was like a housewife who was abducted by a local tyrant and then, for fear of death, lived with him for years and even had a few children together. Now I came to admit guilt." Choibalsan replied with a laugh: "You are forgiven." After the change of goals of the eastern Mongolian movement, Buyanmandukhu must have realized that he would have to repeat the same ritual to a higher authority in China.[44] The problem for him and for the entire movement was, which one? For the moment, the Soviet Red Army was the strongest military force in Manchuria, and the policies of the Soviet Far Eastern Army Head-quarters could directly affect the conditions under which the postwar polit-ical struggle for Manchuria would unfold. But the Soviet occupation would end sooner or later, and the eastern Mongols would be compelled to take a

---

42. Dawa-ochir, "What I Witnessed," 161; Liu Chun, "Works in Inner Mongolia Remembered," 50.

43. *Gaodu zizhi* should probably be translated into "high-degree self-government" but not "high-degree autonomy." "Autonomy," like "self-determination" [*zijue*], con-notes a condition of self-governance defying limitation by others' force or will and therefore should not be modified by "degrees." For definitions of "autonomy" and "self-determination," see Gordon Marshall, *The Concise Oxford Dictionary of Sociology* (Ox-ford: Oxford University Press, 1994); and Joel Krieger, ed., *The Oxford Companion to Politics of the World* (New York: Oxford University Press, 1993). Walker Connor, *Ethno-nationalism: The Quest for Understanding* (Princeton, N.J.: Princeton University Press, 1994), 150, uses "autonomy" and "self-determination" interchangeably.

44. Hu Shaoheng, "Excerpts from Hu Shaoheng's Diaries," entry on 16 January 1947, *Xing'an Geming Shihua,* 3: 220–21; Hao, *Wulanfu Zhuan,* 401.

stand in the brewing GMD–CCP conflict. Now the question facing leaders in Wangyemiao was whether their movement should maintain its ethno-political character and stay neutral in the Chinese Civil War or should let its social revolutionary aspect flare up and join the side of the CCP.

In early September 1945, the GMD government, still sitting in China's southwestern corner, issued orders to redivide Manchuria into nine provinces with newly appointed provincial heads. A Northeastern Military Field Headquarters was set up to take over the whole area. Most of these measures turned out to be just exercises on paper. In October, the Northeastern headquarters entered Changchun only briefly before retreating to Beiping (Beijing), protesting the Soviet military authorities' irregular behavior. Just a small number of the newly appointed provincial officials managed to reach their posts. However, their tenures, as described by Xiong Shihui, the chief of the Northeast headquarters, were like an "illusive epiphyllum that flowered only briefly." Wu Huanzhang was appointed governor of a new Xing'an Province, which included the eastern and northern areas of the puppet "General Xing'an Province." He was never able to reached his post in Hailar. In late 1945 and early 1946, therefore, the so-called GMD influence in eastern Mongolia was mainly made up by complicated local elements that lacked either internal coherence or external contacts.[45]

In Manchuria, the CCP also had to start from scratch. At the war's end, the CCP did not have any organized guerrilla force in Manchuria that could prepare the groundwork for the party's postwar penetration of the region. The CCP made its first political effort in eastern Mongolia in October 1945, when some cadres went to Tongliao of Jerim League to start a county government. The operation was easily frustrated by local pro-GMD forces. The CCP did not become a respectable influence in the region until late November, when 32,000 troops of the New Fourth Army's Third Division arrived. This force of southern troops had started their journey northward from northern Jiangsu and had marched on their feet through five provinces for two months. After the troops reached their destination, Huang Kecheng, the division commander, telegraphed Mao that in the region the troops were

---

45. Order of the National Government to appoint nine governors and two mayors in the Northeast, 4 September 1945, *ZZSC,* 7(1): 36–37; Supreme Council of National Defense to Civil Officials' Department of the National Government, 9 September 1945, ibid., 47–53; Report on Political Takeover in the Northeast, March 1946, ibid., 82; Jiang Jieshi to Wang Chonghui, 30 March 1946, Guofang Zuigao Weiyuanhui Dang'an (Records of the Supreme Council of National Defense): 004/1441.

facing a situation of "seven no's"—no CCP party organization, no mass support, no government, no food, no fund, no medicine, and no clothing. In other words, in eastern Mongolia the CCP force was an army without roots, and it would take time and arduous efforts for the CCP to gain a foothold in the area.[46]

Because it had started in the first hotbed of the postwar GMD–CCP conflicts, the eastern Mongolian movement had to militarize itself to survive. When the movement's principal leaders were still in Ulaanbaatar, Wangyemiao's small "police regiment," which was started mainly to assist Soviet occupation, already was engaged in some operations that would prove vital to the movement's later development. In late October, the regiment successfully abolished a local branch of the GMD and a GMD county government in Solon, the site of Shijagar Banner east of Wangyemiao. Then, in mid-November, the regiment destroyed a hostile force under Yan Zhenshan. Yan was a professional brigand. After Japan's surrender, he accepted the GMD's appointment and became an underground "peace preservation commander" in central Xing'an area. Yan openly challenged the Wangyemiao movement in the name of the "preservation society," a common form of pro-GMD local organizations in postwar China. Because Yan and most of his followers were Han Chinese, Askhan decided to ask assistance from the New Fourth Army nearby, lest any action of his own force against Yan lead to interethnic hostilities. The New Fourth Army unit in Baichengzi, some 70 kilometers southeast of Wangyemiao, was happy to oblige. A dozen CCP soldiers participated in the successful operation of the Wangyemiao force. They also became the first CCP troops to enter the Wangyemiao area.

These two operations eliminated the immediate GMD threat to Wangyemiao and guaranteed that the self-government movement would develop in a relatively peaceful environment. A month later, the New Fourth Army command in Baichengzi asked Askhan to return the favor and to rescue Hu Bingquan, a CCP cadre captured by GMD's local "restoration army" when he was trying to organize a pro-CCP government in Tuquan. In late December, Askhan's troops not only rescued Hu but also took Tuquan, a strategic location on the main road that connected Xing'an League to the other three eastern Mongolian leagues in the south and the west. After this operation,

---

46. Zhao Shi, "The Victory of the CCP's Nationality Policy," in *Shuguang Zhaoyao Zhelimu* (Dawn upon Jerim), ed. Geng Binying (Beijing: Minzu Chubanshe, 1988), 4; Wu Xinquan and Fang Zhida, "The Third Division of the New Fourth Army in Jerim," ibid., 34–35; Huang Kecheng, *Huang Kecheng Zishu* (Autobiography of Huang Kecheng) (Beijing: Renmin Chubanshe, 1994), 195, 196.

Askhan proceeded to Jerim and recruited a division of troops there.[47] Thus, even before an eastern Mongolian government was established, the Mongolian force based in Wangyemiao had already won a reputable position for the eastern Mongolian movement in regional politics.

All these and other similar developments indicate an important fact overlooked by previous studies of the Chinese Civil War: The eastern Mongolian movement was the first and only organized local force in Manchuria that offered any assistance to the CCP's initial effort to gain a foothold in the region. The CCP's Northeast Bureau was quick to grasp the significance of the Wangyemiao movement. In mid-November 1945, the Northeast Bureau called a "conference of northeastern people's representatives" in Shenyang (Mukden) and invited Wangyemiao to send a delegation. During the conference, still unaware of Ulaanbaatar's policy intention, the delegation from Wangyemiao asked the Northeast Bureau to support unification between Inner Mongolia and the MPR. Lin Feng, a member of the Northeast Bureau presiding over the conference, responded that although the CCP supported self-determination by the Mongolian people, the MPR might not be able to accept Inner Mongolia under the current international circumstances and domestic conditions of China. Therefore he advised the eastern Mongols to work for more pragmatic objectives. In February 1946, the Northeast Bureau reported the situation to the CCP Central Committee, indicating that the eastern Mongols had apparently heeded Lin's advice and that their activities, including an assembly in January to start an autonomous government, were "basically correct."[48]

This was probably the most positive endorsement that the CCP could give to a spontaneous ethnonationalist movement. To the CCP cadres of the Northeast Bureau, the eastern Mongols' collaboration with CCP troops seemed natural because both were struggling against the same central authorities in China. A "correct" line of action, however, was not easy to find from the point of view of the eastern Mongolian leaders, whose ethnopolitical objectives were rather different from the CCP's. Having switched to the goal of self-government within China after the Ulaanbaatar mission, the leaders in

47. Dugurjab, "Recollections of the Days and Nights of the First Division of the Inner Mongolian Cavalry," *Xing'an Dangshi Wenji*, 2: 199–213; Wang Haishan, "Recollections of the Bandits Suppression Operations of the First Division of the Inner Mongolian Cavalry," *Xing'an Dangshi Wenji*, 1: 51, 56; Lowangjab, "Night Attack on Tuquan," *Xing'an Dangshi Wenji*, 2: 218.

48. Dawa-ochir, "What I Witnessed," 160–61; Tuman and Zhu Dongli, *Kang Sheng yu Neirendang Yuan'an*, 121–22; Northeast Bureau of the CCP to the CCP Central Committee, 20 February 1946, *MWWH*, 1002–3.

Wangyemiao had to strive to define the goal in clear terms and in the context of Chinese politics. Yet it was by no means clear how a definition could be found that could be acceptable to both the GMD and the CCP, two parties that appeared to have different criteria about almost everything in China.

After one and a half months' preparations, including the drafting of autonomous documents by a "documents examination committee" under Temurbagana, in mid-January 1946 an "Assembly of Eastern Mongolian People's Representatives" was held in Gegenmiao, a small village near Wangyemiao. Two thousand participants, of whom about 300 were voting delegates, came to the conference from thirty-six eastern Mongolian banners. The assembly discussed and approved four documents, including a "manifesto on the establishment of the Eastern Mongolian People's Autonomous Government [EMPAG]," "administrative program of the EMPAG," "autonomous constitution of the eastern Mongolian people," and "organizational law of the EMPAG." A "peasant-herdsman banner," which had first appeared during the August 11 uprising, was officially adopted as the "colors of the eastern Mongolian autonomy." Using the MPR as a model, the eastern Mongols adopted a bicameral system consisting of a great assembly (*da hui* in Chinese; *ih hural* in Mongolian) and a small assembly (*xiao hui; bag hural*). The delegates also elected their first government with Buyanmandukhu as chairman and Khafengga as secretary general. According to the organizational law, the government included four ministries separately in charge of the economy, civil administration, internal defense, and justice. Hu Bingquan, the CCP cadre member who was earlier rescued by Askhan's troops, spoke to the delegates on behalf of the CCP. Aside from praising the growth of the Mongolian people's movement for self-determination, Hu pointed out that the CCP, not the GMD, was the true supporter of the movement.[49]

In spite of the explicit partisan message in Hu's speech, the divisive Chinese politics was not reflected in the inaugurating documents of the EMPAG. In comparison with the first liberation declaration of August 1945, these documents situated the eastern Mongolian movement in a very different context. Whereas the earlier declaration was intended to convince the MPR that the eastern Mongolian movement and the MPR belonged to the same Mongolian revolutionary tradition, these January documents were now

---

49. Dawa-ochir, "What I Witnessed," 162–63; Liu Chun, "Works in Inner Mongolia Remembered," 50; "Transcript of Comrade Hu Bingquan's Speech, 16 January 1946," QZH 4/1 (9). According to Dawa-ochir, Hulunbuir could not send delegates to the assembly because of difficult travel conditions.

intended to justify to a broader audience that a Mongolian political entity had the right to exist within the Chinese state. In other words, with these documents the Wangyemiao regime started its interethnic negotiations with China's principal political forces.

In its manifesto, the EMPAG identified itself with the international trend of national self-determination and independence and found its legal basis in several instruments, including the Atlantic Charter, the principles of the United Nations, the Chinese government's approval of the de jure independence of the MPR, and a recent speech by Jiang Jieshi on equality for all nationalities in China. The authors of the manifesto were careful in directing the Inner Mongols' grievances only against local tyrants in frontier provinces but not the Chinese central authorities. Their sole complaint about the GMD was that its good doctrines on nationalities had never reached the Mongolian areas. The manifesto actually expressed gratitude to Jiang Jieshi's "great revolutionary spirit" in granting independence to the MPR, for Jiang's act "simultaneously vests Inner Mongolia with the right to establish a free government." Presented as such, the "high-degree national self-government" pursued by eastern Mongolia did not seem contradictory to the GMD government's official ethnopolitics.

The key conception in these documents was the reference to the Republic of China (ROC) as the "suzerain state," which marked the "degree" of self-government sought by the eastern Mongolian movement. The ROC authority in diplomacy and national defense was respected in the fact that the EMPAG did not set up its own foreign office and had only an "internal" defense ministry. In the meantime, the autonomous constitution did stipulate that the EMPAG organize an "eastern Mongolian people's autonomous army" and have the right to conclude trade agreements with foreign countries, provided that the practice did not violate the sovereignty of the ROC. As for the EMPAG's territory, for the moment the Wangyemiao regime claimed the entire eastern Mongolian region, including Jerim, Juu-uda, Josotu, Hulunbuir, and Butekha (Naun Muren) "provinces," plus three banners east of Qiqihar. As a long-term objective, according to the "autonomous constitution," Mongolian self-government would be extended to a larger region demarcated by "historical and current fundamental elements of blood, geographic, linguistic, customary, and religious commonalities."[50]

50. "Manifesto on the Establishment of the Eastern Mongolian People's Autonomous Government," QZH 4/1 (5); "Political Programs of the EMPAG," QZH 4/1 (2); "Eastern Mongolian People's Autonomous Constitution," ibid.

The theoretical neutrality of eastern Mongolia in the Chinese Civil War was underscored by an entangled reality. As suggested in the EMPAG's inaugural documents, eastern Mongolian autonomy was implemented within the limits of the ROC's nationality policies. The propaganda outline adopted by the EMPAG avoided any explicit criticism of the GMD regime and only vaguely attacked the "dark policies under the feudal society and the fascist imperialist government."[51] Yet the EMPAG's stated homage to the ROC and intentional silence on the GMD–CCP conflict proved futile as far as the GMD government was concerned. As will be shown in chapter 6, the GMD regime regarded the eastern Mongolian movement as an open challenge to its authority and power. But for the EMPAG, a more immediate concern was its relationship with the CCP, which was vigorously expanding in Manchuria. From late 1945 to early 1946, the initial encounters between the two sides already caused mutual misgivings over the issue of territorial control. Ideologically, not all military forces in eastern Mongolian banners viewed the CCP and its troops as a "friendly party and a friendly army." Essentially, however, the two sides' simultaneous assertions of population and territorial controls in the same region duplicated the prewar controversy between Han counties and Mongolian banners. This time, however, each side of the controversy claimed the priority of its own revolution, and the two revolutionary forces seemed to turn a chronic dispute into an urgent crisis.

In early 1946, the CCP cadres in western Manchuria reported to their superiors a series of local incidents that threatened to develop into open conflicts between Mongolian and CCP forces. On the Mongolian side, Wang-yemiao's administrative policy was designed not to deal with these current incidents but, as an important part of the eastern Mongolian revolution, to overturn the earlier divisions of the Mongolian region by the GMD and Japanese authorities. To achieve coherent Mongolian governance within its claimed territories, the EMPAG decided to use a new structure of seven provinces to replace the old league system. On the CCP side, to facilitate its strategic competition with the GMD in Manchuria, the Northeast Bureau wanted to confine Wangyemiao's influence to the areas of the four Xing'an provinces of the Manchukuo period, and it was especially concerned about Wangyemiao's intention to expand into the Chifeng (Ulaankhada) area in

---

51. "Eastern Mongolian People's Autonomous Constitution"; "Propaganda Outline of the EMPAG," QZH 6/1 (3).

the southwest and the four "outside banners" (Yekhe-Minggan, Durbote, and Front and Rear Gorlos) in the east.[52]

Thus, when pursuing their own revolutionary objectives, the EMPAG and the CCP found themselves treading on each other's toes. For the moment, however, the common military threat from the GMD government forced the two sides to avoid open friction between themselves and to reach some temporary compromises. Even before the EMPAG was established, the eastern Mongolian and CCP forces made certain ad hoc agreements for the purposes of suppressing bandits and resisting GMD influence. In early February 1946, a formal agreement was concluded between Askhan on behalf of the EMPAG and Lü Zhengcao on behalf of the CCP's Western Manchurian Military District. According to the agreement, the CCP and the EMPAG would separately assume administrative responsibilities for counties and banners, CCP troops would not be stationed in Mongolian residential areas, and the two sides would coordinate operations against bandits and "reactionary armed forces," whether Mongolian or Han. Then, armed with the agreement and a letter of introduction from Lü's headquarters, Askhan traveled to areas under the CCP's control and recruited troops for the newly organized Eastern Mongolian People's Autonomous Army. In return, he helped local CCP officials smooth out difficulties in the CCP–Mongolian relationship in these areas.[53]

Yet troubles between the CCP and eastern Mongols continued. For instance, the EMPAG's efforts to recruit troops for a third division of the Autonomous Army in the Chifeng area and to organize a government in Josotu were blocked by the CCP Committee of Rehe Province. The reason given by Hu Xikui, the secretary of the Rehe committee, was simple: Chifeng should be closed to eastern Mongols because it had been "liberated" by the Eighth Route Army and because a local government under the CCP already

52. "Eastern Mongolian People's Autonomous Constitution"; Ni and Guo to Western Manchurian Branch Bureau and Northeast Bureau of the CCP, 20, month unknown, 1946, *MWWH,* 1086; Northeast Bureau to Cheng Zihua et al., 21, month unknown, 1946, ibid., 1085.

53. "Minutes of a Meeting between the Southern Area of the General Xing'an Province and the CCP Commissioner's Office in Liaoyuan," 10 November 1945, enclosure 4 of Tan Wenbin report, March 1946, XZY: 067/523; Wu Xinquan and Fang Zhida, "The Third Division of the New Fourth Army in Zhirim," *Shuguan Zhaoyao Zhelimu,* 35–36, 44–45; "Order Number 5 of the Western Manchurian Military District, 1 February 1946," *Neimenggu Dang'an* (Inner Mongolian Archives), 4 (1991): 35.

existed. In the end, Bai Yunhang, Wangyemiao's commissioner, had to modify his original plan, and he agreed to organize a Mongolian column under the unified command of the Eighth Route Army.[54] The situation was quite different in places where the CCP did not have the upper hand. In postwar Juu-uda, Chinjorigtu (a.k.a. He Zizhang), a local notable, emerged as a strongman. In November 1945, at Khafengga's suggestion, he organized a government in Balin Left Banner and also set up a Mongolian force of several hundred troops. After the EMPAG was established, Chinjorigtu was appointed commander of the autonomous army's fourth division.

Chinjorigtu was determined to exclude Han troops of any political affiliation from the territory north of the Shilamulun River that ran through the middle of Jerim and Juu-uda from east to west. It was said at the time that Chinjorigtu was such a strong figure that even the Soviet commander in Chifeng had to lend a respectful ear to what he had to say. When a CCP regional committee for northern Rehe, based in Linxi, was expanding its strength simultaneously with Chinjogtu's, conflicts could not be avoided. In several cases of military friction between the two sides, CCP troops suffered some casualties; but the CCP Central Committee was more concerned that such friction could drive Chinjogtu and the like into the GMD's arms. In realizing that the Chinjogtu case was not an isolated local phenomenon, the CCP leadership sought a general solution through negotiations with the EMPAG. In March 1946, the CCP sent its principal interlocutor with the Inner Mongols, Yun Ze, on a mission to meet with Khafengga and his associates.[55]

The eastern Mongol leaders did not wait idly. In the early months of 1946, they embarked on a two-pronged diplomatic effort with the GMD government and the CCP leadership. The démarche for direct negotiations with the GMD government was a result of Khafengga's meeting with a Buryat Mongol, Major Sangjai of the Soviet Far Eastern Army Headquarters. The meeting was suggested by Sangjai through Wangyemiao's liaison in Changchun. Khafengga attached such great importance to the meeting that from early December 1945 to early February 1946 he traveled between Wang-

---

54. Liu Chun, "Works in Inner Mongolia Remembered," 47–49.

55. Liu Chun, "Works in Inner Mongolia Remembered," 46–47; Ji-Re-Liao Branch Bureau of the CCP to Northeast Bureau and Central Committee of the CCP, 15 January 1946, *MWWH,* 989; Ji-Re-Liao Bureau of the CCP's Report on the Mongolian Problem in Northern Rehe, 26 January 1946, ibid., 995; Lin Anmin, "Ulanfu Led the Mongolian People on a New Path," *Wulanfu Yanjiu Jinian Wenji,* 193–94; *Neimenggu Dang de Lishi he Dang de Gongzuo,* 180.

yemiao and Changchun and consequently missed the EMPAG's inauguration assembly in January. In Changchun, Sangjai suggested that after an autonomous government was established in eastern Mongolia, it should send a delegation to Chongqing, the GMD government's wartime capital. Whatever the GMD government's attitude might be, Sangjai advised, the step was necessary for a "lawful struggle."[56] Consequently, on February 22, a small "Eastern Mongolian Petition Delegation," headed by EMPAG vice chairman Manibadara (a.k.a. Ma Mingzhou), departed for Chongqing. Manibadara was chosen for the mission because, among eastern Mongol leaders, he was known for having a "legitimate tendency," meaning a pro-GMD attitude.

Manibadara's chance was poor for either carrying out the EMPAG's "lawful struggle" or pursuing his own belief in a constructive relationship with the GMD government. After his delegation arrived in Beiping, the GMD authorities there refused to allow it to proceed further south. In Beiping, Manibadara could make only two inconsequential contacts: He talked to two American intelligence officers, and he was able to connect with the GMD's secret police, the notorious Juntong (Bureau of Military Investigation and Statistics) under Dai Li. When Manibadara returned to Wangyemiao in May, two Juntong agents traveled with him. The action proved politically suicidal for Manibadara, because at the time a close collaboration between the EMPAG and the CCP was already emerging. Three months later, Manibadara would be arrested on a charge that he was a secret GMD agent himself.[57]

The failure of the Manibadara mission had a graver significance than Manibadara's personal calamity. When the mission was sent, the EMPAG also decided to dispatch another, led by Khafengga and Temurbagana, to Yan'an. The second mission was canceled when the leaders in Wangyemiao learned that Yun Ze was traveling eastward to meet with them. At the time, Wangyemiao's simultaneous dealings with the GMD and the CCP were able to offer something to both the radical and moderate elements in the eastern Mongolian leadership. Yet, for most participants of the movement, the orientation mainly reflected an ethnopolitical desire that the Inner Mongols stay

56. Dawa-ochir, "What I Witnessed," 158, 161–63, 164–65.

57. Demchugdongrob, "Autobiography of Demchugdongrub," *NWZ*, 13: 144; "Historical Materials on the Puppet Mongol Army," *NWZ*, 38: 92–94; Jiang Jieshi to the Mongolian and Tibetan Affairs Commission, 10 April 1946, QZH 141/3626; Dawa-ochir, "What I Witnessed," 164, 169–70, 173–74.

neutral in the Chinese Civil War. Or, to some scheming minds in Wang-yemiao, the parallel relationship with the two Chinese parties could facilitate an ethnostrategic calculation of playing one Chinese party against the other. No matter what original motives were behind the orientation, Manibadara's fruitless trip to the south effectively ended any double play on the part of the eastern Mongolian leadership. The danger of playing a two-sided game was sensed by eastern Mongol leaders even before Manibadara's return. Some time in March, after meeting with Yun in Chifeng, Buyanmandukhu sent a secret letter to Manibadara, asking him to discontinue at once any petition with the GMD government.[58]

Thus, in the spring of 1946, more than three years before Mao Zedong issued his famous "leaning to one side" statement and put the CCP on the Soviet side of the superpower confrontation, the eastern Mongols made their own decision to lean to the CCP's side in China's power struggle. If the CCP chose to ally itself with the Soviet Union out of ideological and geopolitical considerations, the question is why in 1946 the eastern Mongolian movement, during a struggle for ethnic self-government within China's existing political system, decided to take the side of a rebellious Chinese force whose victory was far from certain. This question will be explored in the next chapter.

---

58. Wang Deyuan, "Establishment of the Eastern Mongolian General Branch," 24; Demchugdongrob, "Autobiography," 144.

5

Ethnic Strategy:
The Eastern Mongolian Experience

If politics is defined as the "social application of power" and political development as "stages of the increased complexity of the state," it is necessary to understand the encounter between Inner Mongolian ethnopolitics and Chinese politics in 1945–49 as a power relationship and to explain how the political development of Inner Mongolia during the "decisive encounter" between the Guomindang (GMD, Nationalist Party) and the Chinese Communist Party (CCP) contributed to the increased complexity of the Chinese state.[1] From April 1946 to May 1947, the eastern Mongolian movement's gradual absorption by the CCP indicated convergence between Inner Mongolian ethnopolitics and Chinese politics. The process was paralleled by disappearance from China's political stage of an independent "third force," the Democratic League between the GMD and the CCP. The Democratic League was a "third force" within the *Chinese* politics of 1945–49 characterized by the GMD–CCP power struggle, and it has been a subject in every study of the civil war period. In contrast, political movements and regimes in Inner Mongolia, Xinjiang, and Tibet in this period constituted a "third force" outside *Chinese* politics, and they have been overlooked by the existing historiography. The omission of Inner Mongolian politics from the civil war historiography is especially troubling because—unlike Xinjiang and Tibet, where direct GMD–CCP competitions almost did not exist—the

---

1. Tony Smith, "Political Development," in *The Oxford Companion to Politics of the World,* ed. Joel Krieger et al. (New York: Oxford University Press, 1993), 713–15. "Decisive Encounter" is Odd Arne Westad's conception of the Chinese Civil War. See his *Decisive Encounters: The Chinese Civil War, 1946–1950* (Stanford, Calif.: Stanford University Press, 2003).

Inner Mongols' movement not only "entered" the *Chinese* power struggle but also had a direct impact.

As a liberal alternative to the GMD and the CCP brands of authoritarian politics, the Democratic League, without its own military-territorial base, could not sustain an independent position for long under the GMD regime's police persecution and the CCP's political competition. The eastern Mongolian movement was a challenge to mainstream Chinese politics in a different sense. Aside from being an armed territorial force, Wangyemiao posed a challenge to the "hardware" of the Chinese state as well as to its "soft values." As was shown in the previous chapter, the eastern Mongols' northward mission to Ulaanbaatar in October 1945 and southward missions to Chongqing and Yan'an in February 1946 respectively manifested intentions of externalization and of internalization in their relationship with China. As China became split between two irreconcilable forces, the questions for the eastern Mongols were from which China should Inner Mongolia externalize and with which internalize. To answer these questions, eastern Mongolian leaders not only had to make a military judgment between the GMD and the CCP as to which would more likely emerge from the civil war as the power holder of China, they also had to make an ethnopolitical decision between the two as to which had the greater potential to increase the complexity of the Chinese state to accommodate the Inner Mongolian people's group rights and interests. The eastern Mongols, however, proved far from free agents in making these judgments and pursuing their goals.

Chengde Concession

As residents of a region where the GMD and the CCP forces fought ferociously, the Inner Mongols, whether politically active or not, could hardly avoid taking sides. Surely, there was no uniform "Inner Mongolian reaction" to the Chinese Civil War. Ideologies, social statuses, personal circumstances, and regional conditions were among the factors affecting different behaviors. For instance, during the first two postwar years, Mongol aristocrats in Shilingol tended to act mercurially as the GMD–CCP military contest in the area fluctuated. There were also cases in which Mongol youths followed the CCP just because the GMD propaganda, misleadingly, accused the CCP of supporting Inner Mongolian independence.[2] For the

2. Yun Shiying and Chao Luomeng, "Recollections of Works in the Shili-yin Gool League," *Neimenggu Wenshi Ziliao* (Literary and Historical Materials of Inner Mongolia;

principal leaders in Wangyemiao, however, especially Khafengga and Temurbagana, the decision on forging a partnership with the CCP did not come
impulsively. In the past decades, the GMD regime repressed frontier non-
Han peoples and was on record as denying the very existence of non-Han
nationalities in China. By contrast, the CCP appeared sympathetic toward
"minority nationalities" and was willing to work with the eastern Mongolian movement. More important, to the members of the eastern Mongolian
Inner Mongolian People's Revolutionary Party (IMPRP), the CCP had an
ideological affinity with the Soviet Union and the Mongolian People's Republic (MPR). It therefore came from the same roots and belonged to the
same revolutionary bloc as the IMPRP. In addition, the MPR's and Soviets'
postwar advice also helped convince eastern Mongol leaders about the necessity of cooperation with the CCP.

In a sense, it was the eastern Mongol leaders themselves who led the CCP
to them. Bao Yukun, the liaison they sent to western Inner Mongolia, did not
find any independent autonomous movement other than the CCP-organized
Inner Mongolian Autonomous Movement Association (IMAMA) in Zhangjiakuo. Yun Ze and his CCP colleagues welcomed the arrival of Bao because
he brought to them important information about the developments in eastern Mongolia and provided a lead to further contacts. In late December
1945, upon Yun's proposal, the CCP's Jin-Cha-Ji (Shanxi-Chahar-Hebei)
Central Bureau sent an "eastern Mongolian work group" to travel eastward
with Bao. Uncertain about the situation of eastern Mongolia and the policies
of the Northeast Bureau, the group went in the name of IMAMA. Its mission was to discuss with eastern Mongol leaders how the two movements
could unify their activities. The group was headed by Liu Chun, a Han cadre
who had started working on minority nationality issues in Yan'an during the
war. Its principal members included Kho'erge, a Tumed Mongol and longtime associate of Yun's, and several Han and Mongol cadres. In addition, to
facilitate the group's work, some nonparty Mongol youths originally from
eastern Mongolia were also included.

In Liu Chun's mind, the trip to Wangyemiao was not different from his
wartime trips to GMD-occupied "white areas." Therefore, he prepared a
secret code for making contact with underground CCP members who presumably existed in Wangyemiao. But he did not get a chance to test his

---

hereafter *NWZ*), 50: 165–75; Zhao Zhenbei, "Glorious Model and Immortal Achievements," *Ulanfu Jinian Wenji* (Memorial Essays on Ulanfu) (Hohhot: Neimenggu Renmin
Chubanshe, 1990), 2: 94.

underground skills in Wangyemiao because, after reaching Chifeng, he fell ill and could no longer travel. Consequently, Kho'erge led several members of the group to complete the journey and to deliver a meeting invitation to eastern Mongol leaders. In late February or early March 1946, Kho'erge arrived in Wangyemiao. Years later, Kho'erge remembered that in Wangyemiao he was both horrified by a still rampant bubonic plague and moved by young Mongols' enthusiasm about a unified autonomous cause. Around March 10, Kho'erge headed back to Chifeng with Wangyemiao's big three, Buyanmandukhu, Khafengga, and Temurbagana.[3] It can be recalled that during the months between Bao Yukun's arrival in Zhangjiakou and Kho'erge's visit in Wangyemiao, the "national fever" in eastern Mongolia already took solid form in the Eastern Mongolian People's Autonomous Government (EMPAG).

Before the big three's departure, no formal government meetings were held in Wangyemiao to discuss an agenda or a negotiation strategy. Instead, eastern Mongol leaders just held two brief "cabinet" meetings and made some administrative decisions, including one on sending forty young Mongol students to the MPR and another on appointing acting officials who would keep the government running in the absence of the principals. It is nevertheless clear that the eastern Mongols did not entertain the slightest doubt about the continuation of their government. At one of these meetings, steps were decided about taking over the railroads in the EMPAG-controlled territories, a measure stipulated by the "Eastern Mongolian Autonomous Constitution."

Another telling sign of these leaders' thinking about the talk with CCP representative was an open letter drafted by Buyanmandukhu in the name of "Eastern Mongolian People's Congress." On their way to Chifeng, they asked the CCP's Western Manchurian Military District to help release the letter through the New China News Agency. Addressed to "Chairman Jiang [Jieshi], Chairman Mao [Zedong]," and all political and military organizations and nationalities of China, the letter blamed "high-positioned fascists" in the Chinese government for starting a civil war and attacking the "Northeastern People's Autonomous Army," a name used by the CCP forces under Lin Biao in Manchuria. This was the first public sign that, in the expanding conflict between the GMD and the CCP, eastern Mongolia took the side of

3. Liu Chun, "Works in Inner Mongolia Remembered," *NWZ,* 50: 43–47; Kho'erge, "Recollections of the Unification of the Inner Mongolian Autonomous Movement," ibid., 143–54; Dawa-ochir, "What I Witnessed and Experienced," *NWZ,* 31: 165.

the latter. In taking such an action, eastern Mongol leaders actually forfeited any ethnopolitical strategy of pitting the two Chinese parties against each other and unequivocally preset their talk with the CCP on a common anti-GMD basis.[4]

The CCP, however, did not reciprocate the eastern Mongols' gesture with an unconditional endorsement of their movement. In March 1946, the CCP Central Committee decided that Yun Ze should proceed eastward and negotiate with the eastern Mongols. The CCP leadership wanted the Wang-yemiao regime to be reduced in territory and modified in form. Ideally, the authority of the eastern Mongolian government should be confined to administering only the Mongols residing in the new Liaobei and Xing'an provinces set up recently by the GMD government (an area including Xing'an, Hulun-buir, and part of Jerim). The form of the government should be changed from Mongolian autonomy to Mongolian–Han coalition. By the fall of 1945, Yun Ze had already succeeded in abolishing a "Provisional Government of the Inner Mongolian People's Republic" in West Sunid, Shilingol. Although his mission to the east differed significantly from the one in West Sunid and the popular eastern Mongolian movement could not be simply abolished, Yun still understood these two missions in the same terms; his tasks in both cases were to "overcome two independence movements."[5] Thus, in their brief autonomous history, after being told by Ulaan-baatar to retreat from their initial goal of accession to the MPR, the eastern Mongol leaders would be asked for the second time to reorient, and again by a presumed ally.

Chifeng was southwest of Wangyemiao, and the straight-line distance between the two locations was about 500 kilometers. Because of the military situation between the CCP and the GMD in the area, however, the eastern Mongolian delegation had to travel southeastward before heading toward

4. Dawa-ochir, "What I Witnessed," 165–66; Office for Party History Research of the Chinese Communist Party Committee of Inner Mongolia, *Neimenggu Dang de Lishi he Dang de Gongzuo* (The Party's History and Works in Inner Mongolia) (Hohhot: Neimenggu Renmin Chubanshe, 1994), 186; Liu Chun, "Works in Inner Mongolia remembered," *NWZ,* 50: 52; Li Fuchun to Northeastern Bureau of the CCP, 12 March 1946, *Minzu Wenti Wenxian Huibian* (Collected Documents on the Nationality Question; hereafter *MWWH*), comp. United Front Department of the Central Committee of the Chinese Communist Party (Internal circulation; Beijing: Zhonggong Zhongyang Dangxiao Chubanshe, 1991), 1026.

5. CCP Central Committee's Directive on the Question of Eastern Mongolia, 10 March 1946, *MWWH,* 1023; Yun Ze's Report to the CCP Central Committee on the Land and Autonomy Problems of Inner Mongolia, 1 August 1946, ibid., 1057–58.

the west. The journey took more than ten days. After reaching Chifeng, they learned that there had been a change of venue. Now Chengde, an extra 100 kilometers in the south, was selected as the new location for the meeting. According to Liu Chun, the change was made for a protocol reason: Chengde was a middle point between the two sides. But in reality Chengde was much closer to Zhangjiakou, where Yun was stationed, than to Wangyemiao. This "middle point" theory makes sense only from the perspective of ethnic diplomacy: Chengde was the southernmost city of Rehe, and between it and the Great Wall lying further south there were no more Mongolian banners. Therefore Chengde was on the fault line between the Han and Mongolian ethnographic zones, whereas Chifeng was in the heart of Juu-uda, an eastern Mongolian league. A more important reason, which could not be revealed to the eastern Mongolian delegation, was that Chengde was the site of the CCP's Ji-Re-Liao (Hebei-Rehe-Liaobei) Branch Bureau. The location allowed the CCP leadership to closely supervise the negotiations, even though Yun was a trusted operative and had proven his effectiveness in dealing with Inner Mongol autonomists.[6]

Both in Chifeng and on their way to Chengde, Liu Chun and eastern Mongol leaders informally sounded out each other's positions. It became clear that both the IMAMA and the EMPAG expected the other side to follow its own lead. The leaders from Wangyemiao insisted that their ultimate goal remained Inner Mongolia's accession to the MPR but, because of the current circumstances, they were willing to settle for an autonomous government for all Inner Mongols. In their opinion, such a government should be organized immediately, and thereafter all autonomous movements, including the IMAMA in Zhangjiakou, would become unnecessary. Although seeking the CCP's assistance at present, they believed that Inner Mongolia would be able to stand on its own feet in the future. To these views, Liu countered that only under the CCP's leadership could the Inner Mongols achieve national liberation, and that this was the "correct road" taken by the IMAMA.

These exchanges indicated to both sides that difficult negotiations were waiting for them in Chengde. Yet the eastern Mongol leaders had no reason to feel distressed for, after all, Liu was a Han who, once told face to face by an eastern Mongol official, could not possibly understand the Mongols' na-

---

6. Oljeinaren, "In the Mighty Torrent of Inner Mongolia's Liberation Movement." *NWZ*, 50: 193–206 (the citation here is on 202); Liu Chun, "Works in Inner Mongolia Remembered," ibid., 45, 52.

tional emotions. Supposedly, Yun, a fellow Mongol, should support the Inner Mongols' aspirations.[7] The eastern Mongols would soon be surprised.

On the surface, the Chengde conference was an equal dialogue between two Mongolian autonomous organizations, the IMAMA and the EMPAG. It followed a parity protocol in having seven delegates from each side.[8] In reality, this was the first formal, interethnic negotiation between the CCP and the eastern Mongols. On March 28, the eastern Mongols and Yun first met briefly. Yun and Temurbagana immediately recognized each other as old acquaintances from their times in Moscow. On the occasion, Buyanmandukhu repeated his self-deprecating routine in telling Yun that he was a "remarried daughter in law" now returning to the home of her original in-laws.

These developments would prove attenuating to the eastern Mongols' negotiating position.[9] Between March 30 and April 3, five so-called preparatory meetings were held. Buyanmandukhu did not participate in any of them. The hard bargaining was mainly done between Liu and Khafengga. Temurbagana appeared more receptive to the other side's arguments, and his attitude was continuously swayed by Yun in their private conversations. Inevitably, the discussions bogged down on whether the autonomous cause of Inner Mongolia should be led by the CCP or the IMPRP. This hurdle was overcome after the Ji-Re-Liao Branch Bureau decided that Khafengga and Temurbagana should be inducted into the CCP.[10]

As an old member of the Soviet Communist Party, Temurbagana's reconnection with the CCP was easy to understand. Khafengga's motives were more complicated. He always believed that a communist party was not suitable for the economically backward Inner Mongolia. As defined in the relevant documents of the IMPRP and the EMPAG, the current revolution in

7. Liu Chun, "Works in Inner Mongolia Remembered," 49, 52–54.

8. The names listed in Liu Chun, "Works in Inner Mongolia Remembered," 61, were Ulanhu (Yun Ze), Liu Chun, Kho'erge, Buyan, Tian Hu, Ulijinaren, and Chingeltu for the IMAMA, and Buyanmandukhu, Khafengga, Temurbagana, Bao Yukun, Bai Yunhang, Yidegasureng, and Hasbatu for the EMPAG.

9. Wang Shusheng and Hao Yufeng, *Wulanfu Nianpu* (Chronicle of Ulanfu's Life) (Beijing: Zhonggong Dangshi Ziliao Chubanshe, 1989), 142–43; Liu Chun, "Works in Inner Mongolia Remembered," 54–55.

10. Liu Chun, "Works in Inner Mongolia Remembered," 52–59; Wang and Hao, *Wulanfu Nianpu,* 143–45; Hao Yufeng, *Wulanfu Zhuan* (Biography of Ulanfu) (Hohhot: Neimenggu Remin Chubanshe, 1990), 401–10; Kho'erge, "Recollections of the Unification of Inner Mongolian Autonomous Movement," *NWZ,* 50: 154–55; Liu Jieyu, "The Necessary Path for the Inner Mongolian Autonomous Movement," ibid., 225–31.

Inner Mongolia was to implement nationalist goals appealing to both the laboring mass and the upper strata of the Mongolian society. More important, the IMPRP supremacy was to guarantee the Mongolian core values of the movement while accommodating other ethnic groups. In other words, whereas in Chinese politics the class-struggle-oriented CCP was promoting its ascendancy by wielding Mao's famous idea about a class-inclusive "new democracy," in Inner Mongolia, the eastern Mongol leaders were struggling to gain the IMPRP's ethnopolitical dominance through a nationality-inclusive "new nationalism."[11]

Yet, at the Chengde conference, Khafengga's leftist tendencies and his historical, even though indirect, connection to the Comintern led him to discuss Inner Mongolian autonomy with Yun and Liu in the context of the international communist revolution. Once accepting such a premise for the Inner Mongolia question, Khafengga could not uphold his "new nationalism" for long. Almost undetectably, the Chengde conference changed from a two-sided, "diplomatic" negotiation about reciprocal policy readjustments to a "party-line" debate over which side was more "correct" according to the communist dogmas. Compared with Liu and Yun, Khafengga was too green to match their mastery of communist doctrines and clichés. His application for or induction into the CCP membership in Chengde was therefore a way to register the eastern Mongols' setbacks on both ideological and organizational fronts.

However, this did not mean—as some CCP participants would later claim—that the Chengde conference conclusively channeled eastern Mongolia's ethnonationalist movement into the CCP's orbit. To Khafengga, his CCP membership could mean Yan'an's official approval of his wartime record. Because at the time the CCP had by no means achieved predominance in eastern Mongolia, it was hoped that he could continue what he had been doing in the name of a more powerful political organization. What Khafengga and Temurbagana did not seem to understand then was that as CCP members, from now on they would be subject to the CCP's internal discipline.

On April 3, after the so-called preparatory discussions had removed disagreements, a formal conference of the fourteen delegates from the two sides was held. This was merely an occasion to announce what had already

11. "Provisional Outline for Party Work during the Political Construction Period," n.d., Quanzonghao (general record number; hereafter QZH) 6/1 (11); "Eastern Mongolian People's Autonomous Constitution," QZH 4/1 (2).

been decided. In his opening speech, Yun emphasized that the two sides had "agreed without prior consultation" that only the CCP could lead Inner Mongolia to liberation. The meaning of the leadership was laid out in the resolution adopted by the conference. The principal items included the following:

1. The orientation of Inner Mongolian national movement was autonomy for equality, not autonomy for independence; liberation could be achieved only under the CCP's leadership and assistance. The IMAMA was the unified leading body of the Inner Mongolian autonomous movement.

2. Now that western and eastern Mongolia were unified under the IMAMA, the EMPAG would be dissolved upon eastern Mongol representatives' return to Wangyemiao. A general branch of the IMAMA would be established to lead the work in eastern Mongolia.

3. Separate administrations for Mongol and Han residents would be established in areas where the two peoples lived together. Democratic autonomy should be implemented in Mongolian areas and Han enclaves within these areas, and these areas must accept the leadership of relevant democratic league governments. The Eighth Route Army could mobilize the masses and reform the governments in Han counties inside Mongol areas.

4. The IMAMA alone held a unified leadership over all Mongolian armed forces. But under the current circumstances, Mongol troops in different areas should follow the direction of the Eighth Route Army's military districts in these areas.

5. The original organization of the IMAMA was expended to include eight departments and one office. The Eastern Mongolian General Branch of the alliance was responsible for the work in four eastern leagues (Jerim, Xiang'an, Naun Muren, and Hulunuir); Josotu, Juu-uda, Shilingol, and Chahar were under the IMAMA's direct leadership; and the Western Mongolian General Branch was in charge of the three western leagues (Ulanchab, Bayantala, and Yekejuu) plus the Mongols in Ningxia.

6. Representatives of the National Congress in liberated areas should pay attention to the issue of Mongolian representation and make an effort to elect Mongol representatives to replace those named by the GMD.

7. The governments of liberated areas and military districts should help solve problems concerning Mongolian relief, cadre and army training, supplies, and government funding; western Manchuria should send many cadres to Wangyemiao to help the Mongolian work.

8. The central work of the IMAMA at present was to mobilize the mass to participate in the movement for democratic autonomy and to defeat GMD reactionaries' activities against Inner Mongolia's autonomous movement.
9. Chifeng was selected as the temporary center of Inner Mongolia and the site of the IMAMA headquarters.[12]

Through these items, the eastern Mongolian movement, at least on paper, became part of the CCP's front organization in Inner Mongolia. Although a principle of parity was adopted in dividing the official positions of the IMAMA between its original members and the eastern Mongols, the CCP's decisive influence was maintained through Yun's position as the chairman of the reorganized IMAMA and CCP members' control of the organization's military and organizational departments and the secretariat. Buyanmandukhu became the vice chairman of the IMAMA, while Khafengga concurrently held three positions, deputy secretary-general of the IMAMA secretariat, propaganda minister, and director of a new Eastern Mongolian Branch of the IMAMA. Two other decisions of the conference were not included in the resolution. One was to dissolve the IMPRP, and the other was to adopt eastern Mongolia's "peasant–herdsman flag" as the colors of the IMAMA.[13]

The merger between the IMAMA and the EMPAG was a resounding success for the CCP. The success in Inner Mongolian politics would be directly translated into assets in the arena of Chinese politics. The items of the Chengde resolution were carefully tailored to meet the CCP's political and military needs at the time. Still playing the game of "political consultation" with the GMD, the CCP, by dissolving the eastern Mongolian government, deprived GMD propaganda of material evidence that the CCP was selling Inner Mongolia out to the Russians. The merger also opened the territories controlled by the Wangyemiao regime for CCP troops, which would soon prove a vital condition for the CCP's military strategy against the GMD in western Manchuria. The Chengde conference also constituted a personal triumph for Yun. Before the Chengde conference his IMAMA was a CCP front apparatus without a popular following. Now, by incorporating the east-

    12. Yun Ze's speech at the April 3 conference, 3 April 1946, *Neimenggu Zizhi Yundong Lianhehui Dang'an Shiliao Xuanbian* (Selected Archival Materials on the Inner Mongolian Autonomous Movement Association; hereafter *NZYL*) (Beijing: Dang'an Chubanshe, 1989), 49; Principal Resolution of the Chengde Conference on the Unification of the Inner Mongolian Autonomous Movement, 3 April 1946, ibid., 51–53.
    13. Liu Chun, "Works in Inner Mongolia Remembered," 62.

ern Mongolian movement, the IMAMA was no longer just a bodiless head. As a result, Yun made a connection to the majority of the Inner Mongolian population and began to assume an aura of the Inner Mongols' leader. The Chengde conference further enhanced Yun's standing with the CCP leadership. Again, he proved himself an effective operative in dealing with complicated nationality issues.

With their government abolished, party dissolved, and territory modified by the Chengde resolution, eastern Mongol leaders did not seem to have much to celebrate. Back in February, when considering sending missions to contact both the GMD and the CCP, they had probably expected a failure in petitioning with the GMD government. However, they did not foresee that their five-day meeting with another Inner Mongol (Yun), even though one representing the CCP, would end with the invalidation of much of what they had accomplished during the eight months since the end of the war. They came to Chengde to discuss the expansion of their autonomous government throughout Inner Mongolia. Instead, they were inducted into the amorphous IMAMA and saw their regional government swallowed.

It would overly simplify the event to suggest that the CCP forced the eastern Mongols to make concessions. If force played a role in Chengde, it was eastern Mongols' need of CCP power to counterbalance the GMD. Along with this power calculation, another principal reason for the Chengde concession was ideological. In addition to the CCP's apparent sympathy with Inner Mongolian autonomy, the leading figures of eastern Mongolia (Temurbagana and Khafengga) shared with Yun the same revolutionary pedigree. Thus, during the conference, the central theme of the talks shifted easily from a clear-cut ethnopolitical goal of autonomous government to a figurative revolutionary topic, the "correct road of liberation." The eastern Mongols might believe that their concessions were mainly tactical and therefore eventually remediable. Still, the Chengde conference taught them a lesson: They could not avoid compromising their ethnonationalist stand when joining one side of the Chinese power struggle which, ethnopolitically, was Han-centric. These leaders recovered from the Chengde surprise quickly enough. After they returned to Wangyemiao, they began to carry out the Chengde resolution without relinquishing their independence, just as suspected by their fellow Mongol, Yun Ze.[14]

14. Yun Ze's Report to the CCP Central Committee on the Chengde Conference, 5 April 1946, *NZYL*, 54–55.

Xing'an Interval

Back in Wangyemiao, the eastern Mongol leaders made their best defense of the Chengde concession in stressing the achievement of Inner Mongolian unification, an object desired by all Inner Mongols for many years. But the unification forged at Chengde was illusive. Nothing was unified there except the "movement," and even that was achieved only on paper. As a region, Inner Mongolia remained divided politically and administratively. Even the CCP continued to divide its Mongolian work among its different regional bureaus. Yun Ze's organizational affiliation was with the Jin-Cha-Ji Central Bureau, whereas eastern Mongolia was the responsibility of the Northeast Bureau. Yun's interbureau operation at Chengde did not change the CCP's organizational structure regarding the Mongolia work, which, ironically, followed the provincial divisions of Inner Mongolia made by the GMD government. After the Chengde conference, Yun returned to Zhangjiakou as Khafengga's group returned to Wangyemiao. Chifeng's position as the "temporary center" of Inner Mongolia would never be substantiated.[15] Another irony is that, although back in Wangyemiao the eastern Mongol leaders used Inner Mongolian unification to defend their concessions at Chengde, they actually tried to maintain as much as possible the freedom of action of the eastern Mongolian movement after the Chengde conference.

Yet Khafengga and his associates were obliged to adapt their movement to the Chengde resolution. Under the new circumstance, this had to be done in close collaboration with CCP cadres in western Manchuria. When the eastern Mongol principals were still in Chengde, the CCP's West Manchurian Branch Bureau sent Zhang Ce to Wangyemiao to open an "Office of the Western Manchurian Military District." As a seasoned CCP cadre from Shaanxi, Zhang was familiar with all the traditions and methods of the CCP's mass-line work. Yet he knew nothing about Inner Mongolian affairs before his assignment to Wangyemiao. When he first arrived in Wangyemiao, Zhang and his twenty soldiers were subject to isolation, harassment, and even surprise attacks after dark. Cautiously following advice from his superiors against "Han chauvinism," Zhang was able to make some friends among young people and was invited by Askhan to become political commissar of Wangyemiao's internal defense department. In mid-April,

15. Wang and Hao, *Wulanfu Nianpu,* 146; CCP Western Manchurian Bureau to the CCP Central Committee, 20 May 1946, *NZYL,* 63; Yun Ze to Yang Zhilin and Wang Duo, 23 May 1946, ibid., 64–65.

after the Khafungga group returned from Chengde, Zhang began to work with them in the capacity of secretary of the CCP Working Committee for Eastern Mongolia, and, within the CCP hierarchy, he was the direct superior of Khafengga and Temurbagana.[16]

Upon the delegation's return, a joint meeting of the EMPAG and the Executive Committee of the Eastern Mongolian People's Congress was called to discuss the result of the Chengde conference. Khafengga and Temurbagana did most of the explanation and justification of the Chengde decisions. Dawa-ochir and several participants in the meeting argued that the EMPAG had been established by the Eastern Mongolian People's Congress and should not be canceled simply by a decision made in Chengde. In the end, it was decided that a temporary session of the congress would be called to vote on the issue. After much lobbying for the Chengde decisions by Khafengga and others within the establishments of the EMPAG, the congressional session was held in Wangyemiao between May 25 and 29.

More than 300 delegates attended the session, plus about 1,000 "observers and guests." Zhang and several of his CCP colleagues participated in the meeting as "special representatives." The session had some tense moments when a number of delegates accused the leadership for "selling out eastern Mongolia" or "being fooled in Chengde." Although in the end the majority of the delegates voted to support the Chengde resolution, they also made an important revision: The EMPAG should be dissolved as decided, but a new government should be organized to administer the four eastern Mongolian leagues assigned to the eastern branch of the IMAMA. Sensing the dynamics of the meeting, Zhang suggested a compromise in organizing a Xing'an provincial government, instead of a reduced Mongolian government. This would suit the CCP's concern about "legality" at the time, for Xing'an was one of the new provinces in Manchuria that the GMD government had instituted since the end of the war.[17]

<hr />

16. Zhang Ce, "My Onerous Lifetime," in *Xing'an Geming Shihua* (Historical Literature on the Revolution in Xing'an) (Xing'an Meng Dangshi Ziliao Zhengji Bangongshi, 1990), 3: 86–87; Zhang Ce, Hu Shaoheng, and Fang Zhida, "Some Events from the Time of the Eastern Mongolian Autonomous Government to the Establishment of the Inner Mongolian Autonomous Government," *Xing'an Dangshi Wenji* (Essays on the Party History in Xiang'an [League]) 1 (1993): 3–4.

17. Dawa-ochir, "What I Witnessed," 168–69, 171–72; Khafengga's Report to the IMAMA on the Work in Eastern Mongolia, 25 July 1946, *NZYL,* 87–88; Zhang Ce, "Work and Experiences in the Eastern Mongolian (Xing'an) Area, 15 August 1946," *MWWH,* 1316.

   After the meeting, the eastern Mongolian movement issued its third declaration since Japan's surrender. The "Declaration of the Eastern Mongolian
People's Congress's Temporary Session" explicitly put eastern Mongolia
on the CCP side of the Chinese Civil War. It explained that the dissolution
of the EMPAG was for the purpose of repudiating the "vicious smears"
spread by the "GMD reactionaries," and that the establishment of the Xing'an
government was to implement the goals of the National Political Consultative Conference, a political arena in Nanjing used by the CCP to win public
support. The document clearly stated that "we firmly oppose the GMD reactionaries' absurd policy of 'armed takeover in the Northeast.'" When such
a stand was taken in public, the military and political establishments of eastern Mongolia were no longer separate ethnic organizations but became part
of a coalition with the CCP. Indeed, after the reorganization, CCP personnel
began to take important positions in these establishments. Buyanmandukhu
was removed from policymaking positions and became the figurehead
of the provincial political council; Temurbagana was elected chairman of
the Xing'an government with Zhang as his "deputy"; and a Xing'an military district was set up with CCP cadres' extensive participation.
Khafengga, as director of the IMAMA's eastern branch, shared responsibility with the CCP's "Northeast People's Government" for guiding the
Xing'an government's operations. In addition, the CCP exercised control of
the eastern Mongolian movement through its working committee for
Xing'an Province, which was headed by Zhang and included Khafengga,
Temurbagana, Askhan and other members.[18]

   As the ethnic character of the eastern Mongolian movement was thus
being diluted, its policies became increasingly class oriented. The radicalization of social policies was an inevitable consequence of Wangyemiao's
cooperation with the CCP. When CCP cadres first came to Wangyemiao,
their first impression was that the regime had been established without
people's, meaning laboring classes', revolutionary struggle. Unsurprisingly,
such a struggle was started after the Chengde conference. The CCP Central
Committee's directive on the land problem arrived in Xing'an in June 1946.
Although the CCP leadership cautioned that the land problem in Mongolian
areas should be investigated first, the land struggle started immediately anyway. From August 1946 to June 1947, 246 households of "tyrannical land-

   18. Declaration of the Eastern Mongolian People's Temporary Congress, 27 May 1946,
NZYL, 68–69; Wang Duo, *Wushi Chunqiu* (Fifty Eventful Years) (Hohhot: Neimenggu
Renmin Chubanshe, 1992), 278–79; *Neimenggu Dang de Lishi he Dang de Gongzuo,* 189.

lords" were struggled against, 72 labeled as such were executed, and 412 households of "feudal landlords" were dispossessed of their properties in the process of "account settlements." Beginning in October 1946, "democratic reforms," CCP jargon for the process of overthrowing the existing socioeconomic order, were introduced into the pastoral areas of Xing'an League to "eliminate feudal privileges."[19]

It should be noted that antifeudalism, always part of progressive Inner Mongolian nationalism, was reflected in the initial programs of the eastern Mongolian movement. For instance, the second item of the EMPAG's political programs stipulated "demolishing feudal influence, eliminating unjust special privileges, and destroying all reactionary forces that interfere with the sound development of the EMPAG." Yet originally the eastern Mongolian leadership mainly targeted at the social and political privileges of the aristocrats and upper lamas, differing from the CCP's "antifeudalism," which entailed a complete economic redistribution and social reorganization in the countryside. The eastern Mongolian IMPRP's provisional platform was explicitly opposed to "commercial capitalism," a Han-dominated phenomenon, but it was vague about what constituted "unequal social organizations" that allegedly impaired "poor workers, farmers, and herdsmen" and should therefore be abolished.[20] In other words, class struggle was not an unequivocal feature of the original eastern Mongolian movement. Especially after their visit in Ulaanbaatar in late 1945, during which Choibalsan advised against conducting class struggles in Inner Mongolia, the eastern Mongol leaders did not want to incite class antagonisms.[21]

After the Chengde conference, the taboo of waging class-oriented reforms in eastern Mongolia was rescinded. Leaders like Khafengga and Temurbagana enthusiastically followed the new direction. When rent reduction was introduced into the region, some people became concerned that the measure

19. CCP Central Committee's Directive on the Solution of the Land Problem in the Northeast and Rehe, 6 May 1946, *Zhonggong Zhongyang Wenjian Xuanji* (Selected Documents of the CCP Central Committee), 16: 155; "General Discussion of the Land Reform in the Xing'an League," *Xing'an Dangshi Wenji* 2 (1993): 1–13; "General Discussion of the Democratic Reforms in the Pastoral Areas of the Xing'an League," ibid., 115–23.

20. "Political Programs of the EMPAG," QZH 4/1 (2); "Provisional Platform of the IMPRP," in Tan Wenbin's Report to the Executive Yuan, "Three Current Serious Problems in Rehe, March 1946," Xingzhengyuan (Executive Yuan [chamber]), 067/523.

21. Bukho and Sayin, *Boyanmandu Shengping Shilue* (Buyanmandukhu's Life and Times) (Hohhot: Neimenggu Daxue Tushuguan, 1999), 79.

would only benefit Han peasants and hurt Mongol landowners, and that such a development would damage the Mongolian "national economy." Khafengga was firmly in favor of rent reduction in both the Han and the Mongolian communities. He countered opposition opinion in this remark:

> "Recovery of national economy" . . . does not mean to preserve stubbornly the economic privileges and positions of feudal landlords and local tyrants; maintenance or bankruptcy of the Mongolian nation's economy must not be judged with the increase or decline of these people's properties. An opposite perspective should be adopted: If feudal economy continues, the national economy will never be able to get out of bankruptcy and will only become worse.

This opinion was informed by his understanding of "people" and "nation" that hardly differed from the CCP's:

> By basic masses we mean the poor peasants and herdsmen who account for more than 90 percent of our region's population. They are largest in number and poorest in life, and only they constitute the main body of the nation. In the past a small number of princes, aristocrats, and feudal lords appointed themselves as the masters of the nation, perpetrating a fraud of stealing and usurping. After clarifying this, we can know that the poor herdsmen's emancipation is a precondition of national liberation. Without their political, economic, and cultural emancipation, national liberation would become a empty phrase and a hoax.[22]

Although having insisted in Chengde on the independence of the Inner Mongolian autonomous movement, Khafengga did not seem to view the CCP brand of social reforms as contradictory to the Inner Mongolian cause for autonomy. He actually urged eastern Mongolian cadres to learn from their CCP colleagues in this regard. Still believing in the internal unity of the Mongolian nation and not wanting to "make a big noise about class struggles," Khafengga, a mass-line practitioner himself, nevertheless conceded that "peasants' struggle for power and land is indeed class struggle" and was willing to support it. Under his leadership, the eastern branch of

---

22. Khafengga to Jegmude, 19 July 1946, *NZYL,* 78–80; Khafengga's Speech at the Conference on the Work of the Mass Work Team to West Khorchin Front Banner, 24 July 1946, ibid., 80–86.

the IMAMA actively participated in land and democratic reforms in Xing'an League. As a matter of fact, in advocating "land to all toilers" regardless of nationalities, Khafengga went even farther than the CCP's orientation at the time.[23]

These developments indicated that the ethnonationalist movement centered in Wangyemiao was capable of class-oriented radicalism, though the CCP encouragement from the outside was obvious. The movement's radicalization after April 1946 must, however, not be construed as evidence of its complete absorption by the CCP. After the Chengde conference, frequent contacts between the CCP personnel and the Mongols actually caused new tensions between the two sides. A principal reason was that the dissolution of the EMPAG neither nullified the existent banner and league governments in eastern Mongolia nor prevented these local authorities from continuing to treat Wangyemiao as their capital and the IMAMA's eastern branch as their sole leading body. In other words, the CCP leadership of the Inner Mongolian autonomous movement as theorized by the Chengde conference at best remained an abstract idea to the lower echelons of the eastern Mongolian movement. When CCP cadres and troops entered the region in large numbers, leaders in Wangyemiao began to receive disgruntled reports from various banners. The main complaint was that CCP cadres, though completely ignorant about conditions of Mongolian communities, often took over local affairs on behalf of the Mongols (*baoban daiti*) and pushed policies without consulting local Mongolian governments. In receiving CCP troops as a "friendly force," not a leading authority, these Mongolian banner governments were upset by CCP cadres' arbitrary behavior.[24]

The misgivings were mutual. CCP cadres in eastern Mongolia felt that their work was hindered by two kinds of barriers. One was the ethnic barrier that prevented them from establishing a cordial relationship with the Mongolian mass. The other was the class barrier. The CCP's principal collaborators in eastern Mongolia were social elites and this complicated revolutionary tasks. A few months after the Chengde conference, the CCP Committee for Tongliao District, Jerim, professed in a report that "it is not that we distrust the Mongolian mass; we just cannot trust those new bureaucrats and

    23. Khafengga to Ulitu and Shierobjengga, 25 August 1946, *NZYL,* 120–24; "General Narrative on Land Reform in the Xing'an League," *Xing'an Dangshi Wenji* 2 (1993): 4–5.
    24. "Alliance of the Inner Mongolian Autonomous Movement: Mass Work in Banners, 1946," QZH 6/1 (14).

young intellectuals who have no [laboring] class consciousness." A special complaint was directed at the second division of the Eastern Mongolian Autonomous Army: "[These troops] wear [uniforms with] red stars and look very revolutionary in appearance, but in essence most of these are reactionary landlords' forces but not people's forces." The Tongliao committee predicted that "if conditions change to the worse, our today's 'friends' will likely turn into enemies and join the GMD offensive against us." The proposed remedy to the situation was to emphasize "democratic revolution" over "national revolution" in order to mobilize the true "Mongolian revolutionary forces," which, according to the report, consisted of Mongolian *and* Han laboring masses. Under such a policy, there would be little need for the current delicate and difficult "united front" with the Mongolian elites.[25]

Although this line of thinking was soon criticized within the CCP as an "extreme leftist and wrong orientation," the report unmistakably reflected the difficulties in converging the two revolutions respectively under Yan'an and Wangyemiao.[26] The frustration about the conditions of the Mongolian–Han relationship in eastern Mongolia was widely shared among CCP cadres. Zhang Ce, the top CCP official in Wangyemiao, believed that eastern Mongol leaders like Khafengga, Askhan, and Temurbagana were sincere in cooperating with the CCP and loyal to the revolutionary cause. But in his opinion, there were some highly positioned Mongol officials who continued to distrust or even oppose the CCP. The problem was that in the eastern Mongolian leadership, "internal conflicts have not yet flared in the open." Thus, the Chengde conference did not really make the CCP leadership the rulers of the land in eastern Mongolia. Although a regional CCP committee secretaryship usually carried tremendous decisionmaking power, Zhang often felt helpless. In his own words, he "could not decide everything and issue orders as in Han regions," and "in this place the Mongol comrades played the decisive role." Also, their role did not always meet Zhang's standard. In his opinion, the eastern Mongolian authorities' practices in economic, social, educational, and civil affairs showed a strong pro-Mongol tendency and treated the Han people unfairly. Consequently, the so-called government–people and army–people relations in eastern Mongolia were in essence re-

25. CCP Committee of Tongliao District of Jerim, "Self-Criticism on the Mongolian Work in the Past and Report on Work Orientation and Tasks in the Future, 31 July 1946," *MWWH,* 1305–12.

26. CCP Western Manchurian Bureau's Directive on the Work in Eastern Mongolia, 13 September 1946, *NZYL,* 127–29.

lations between the Mongols and the Han.[27] In other words, these were relations between a ruling Mongol minority and a ruled Han majority.

While the CCP's leading official in Wangyemiao held such a perspective, the CCP-encouraged "class struggles" in eastern Mongolia inevitably intensified interethnic vendettas. In contrast to the eastern Mongol leaders' view that the Han population was secondary in the Mongolian liberation cause, the CCP operatives identified the Han people as the "basic mass." Thus the Mongol–Han antagonism became a favorable condition for them to mobilize the "mass" to participate in land and democratic reforms, and the "bad elements" that were struggled against were often Mongols. Yet the work along this line did not achieve its desired result and its consequences were perplexing to the CCP cadres. The "bad elements" naturally hated the CCP for agitating the struggles against them, but these people were often defended by other Mongols of "good class" backgrounds simply because they were all Mongols. Progressive Mongols were often frustrated because they did not receive credit for their reform effort from the "mass" who only trusted the "old Eighth Route." Even the "masses" were not satisfied because they were allowed to struggle against only those petty targets while the CCP cadres themselves were collaborating with the big ones. Caught in this self-made vicious circle of class conflict and ethnic friction, Zhang admitted that for a while he and his comrades felt "very depressed."[28]

Less than a half year after the Chengde conference, the CCP's Liao-Ji (Liaoning and Jilin) Provincial Committee warned that because of the CCP's own wrong policies and the GMD's military offensive, "the entire Mongolian area now appears very unreliable." The West Manchurian Branch Bureau concurred. A major policy readjustment, therefore, was in order. In early October 1946, the Xing'an Provincial Government issued a directive that stopped the struggle of "account settlements."[29]

By this time, mere readjustments of socioeconomic policies were no longer enough to stabilize the CCP–Mongolian relationship. A fundamental issue, ethnic authority and power, had poked a big hole in the "revolutionary" wrapper of that relationship and reappeared with all its thorny aspects.

27. Zhang Ce, "My Onerous Lifetime," 88; Zhang Ce, "Work and Experiences in Eastern Mongolian (Xing'an) Area," 15 August 1946, *MWWH*, 1318–19.
28. Zhang Ce, "Work and Experiences," 1316–17.
29. CCP Liao-Ji Provincial Committee's Opinion on Works in the Mongolian Area, 15 September 1946, *MWWH*, 1072; CCP West Manchurian Branch Bureau's Supplementary Directive on the Mongolian Work, 21 September 1946, ibid., 1073–74; Xing'an Government's Directive on the Method of Mass Work, 8 October 1946, *NZYL*, 133.

Now the Chengde formula had to be reconsidered. The CCP, not yet the ruling party of China, was forced to consider concessions to the eastern Mongols largely because of the changing military-political conditions in China. In April 1946, the Soviet Red Army pulled out of Manchuria. Soon, the military contest for Manchuria between the GMD and the CCP was seriously under way. The war turned Jerim into a front line, and Xing'an was also under constant pressure from pro-GMD forces. As a result, some Mongol notables changed their friendly attitude toward the CCP and rallied to the GMD. Even within the eastern Mongolian movement, some people began to question the wisdom of cooperating with the CCP. Pressed from the outside, there were two threads of events in the movement, and together these events set up an eastern Mongolian agenda for changing the status quo of the CCP–eastern Mongolian partnership.

The first was a decision by the IMAMA's eastern branch to strive to establish an autonomous government for all Inner Mongolia. Either in late September or early October of 1946, an enlarged conference of the eastern branch's executive committee adopted several resolutions on the most urgent issues facing eastern Mongolia. One of these demanded that the IMAMA immediately call an Inner Mongolian people's assembly for the purpose of creating a "supreme autonomous political power of Inner Mongolia." According to the resolution, the new Inner Mongolian government should lead the Mongolian people to achieve both national liberation and democracy, and under such a government "the people will defend it to the bitter end and die for it with no regret." The resolution was careful to state that these goals could be achieved only if the Mongolian nation trusted the CCP and accepted its leadership.[30] The idea of an Inner Mongolian government had always been dear to the eastern Mongolian leaders. It was now presented to the CCP at an opportune moment. Soon the CCP leadership would realize that such an Inner Mongolian power could serve as a defiant response to the GMD's recent military offensives in Manchuria and its political mischief in calling a GMD-monopolized national congress in mid-October.

Yet the eastern Mongols' defiance of the GMD also required concessions on the part of the CCP. In another resolution on democratic reforms in the countryside, the leaders in Wangyemiao called for substituting the earlier ethnicity-blind orientation of class struggles with a policy of differential treatment for Mongol and Han "feudalists." To the former, a "relatively mild

---

30. "Resolution on Establishment of a Supreme Inner Mongolian Autonomous Government," late September or early October 1946, *NZYL*, 150.

and lenient policy" should be applied to induce them to participate in the "national struggle"; to the latter, the policy was to "thoroughly destroy their rule in the countryside" so that "the social basis of great Hanism [Han chauvinism] can be demolished."[31] More upsetting to Han CCP cadres was a resolution on the reorganization of the Mongolian Self-Defense Army. Since the Chengde conference, the eastern Mongolia's military forces had gone through rectifications, in which CCP cadres had participated. The process resulted in dissolving units that were deemed unreliable. Now, aside from calling for the continued "purge of bad elements," the resolution's main purpose was to "dismiss with gratitude those Han officers and soldiers (except Eighth Route Army personnel) in our self-defense army and send them home, so a genuine national army can be created." The resolution called for "conducting immediately national education among the troops to enhance their national consciousness and to foster their morale in the struggle against great Hanism." This agenda was particularly interesting because earlier, during the months of "national fever," such indoctrination was hardly necessary. Since then, Wangyemiao had collaborated with the CCP on the basis of class struggles, and resultantly some eastern Mongols' "national consciousness" might have been diluted.[32] Although these resolutions attributed "great Hanism" only to the GMD, the CCP cadres nevertheless could feel their stings through daily contacts with the Mongols.

By adopting these highly charged nationalistic resolutions, the eastern Mongol leaders did not mean to split from their CCP associates. In Chengde, they had already accepted the necessity of long-term cooperation with the CCP. Especially now, under the GMD's intensified offensive, parting with the CCP would be suicidal for the eastern Mongolian movement. Conversely, in the past few months, the association with the CCP had also proven a principal cause of internal disarrays in the rank and file as well as in the leadership of the movement. Contrary to Zhang Ce's expectation of letting the "internal [meaning class] conflicts" flare up, the leaders in Wangyemiao resorted to a different social-political glue, nationalism, to patch up the cracks in their movement. A half year after the Chengde conference, the eastern Mongol leaders did not attempt to rebargain with the CCP from a

31. "Resolution on Mass Mobilization," late September or early October 1946, *NZYL*, 151; "IMAMA Eastern Mongolian General Branch's Directive on the Current Conditions and Work in Eastern Mongolia," *NZYL*, 144–49.

32. "Resolution on Strengthening the Inner Mongolia People's Self-Defense Army," late September or early October 1946, *NZYL*, 152.

stronger position. Instead, in distress, they raised the stake in their partnership with the CCP. Threatened by internal friction and GMD's military pressure, they decided that only by rehabilitating to a certain degree their original ethnopolitical stance could the eastern Mongolian movement survive the current crisis.

The second development was Buyanmandukhu's new political activism, which led to the conclusion of an agreement between him and Li Fuchun, the commissar of the CCP's Western Manchurian Military District. After Khafengga and Temurbagana were inducted into the CCP at Chengde, Buyanmandukhu was practically excluded from the policymaking process of eastern Mongolia. He held honorary chairmanship of Xing'an Province's political council only because, to the CCP, Buyanmandukhu remained a principal "object of the united front." In the summer of 1946, when Xing'an was threatened by GMD's military offensives, the CCP's West Manchurian Branch Bureau became concerned that some elements in the Xing'an government would be affected and lose confidence in the CCP. This led to the relocation of the Xing'an government and some politically vulnerable members of the IMAMA's eastern branch northward and away from the GMD's direct threat. In late June, the Xing'an government moved first to Hailar, and in early October it moved again to Zhalantun, both in Hulun-buir. Buyanmandukhu was among those who were relocated. While in Hailar, Buyanmandukhu did not have much to do until mid-August, when Manibadara was arrested by the Hailar Public Security Bureau under an order originated from the CCP's West Manchurian Branch Bureau. Aside from the fact that Manibadara had been a close associate of Buyanmandukhu's since the 1930s, the arrest of a member of the political council, in Buyanmandukhu's view, was illegal. Together with Dawa-ochir and some local leaders from Naun Muren, he started a concerted effort for Manibadara's release.[33]

In late September, Buyanmandukhu traveled from Zhalantun to Qiqihar to meet with Li Fuchun. Li did not accept his request for Manibadara's release but agreed to discuss with him other problems of mutual concerns. The result was an understanding in the form of a "summary of negotiations on the Mongolia question" dated October 15. The topics discussed between

---

33. Zhang Ce, Hu Shaoheng, and Fang Zhida, "Some Events from the Time of the Eastern Mongolian Autonomous Government to the Establishment of the Inner Mongolian Autonomous Government," *Xing'an Dangshi Wenji* 1 (1993): 6–7; Dawa-ochir, "What I Witnessed," 172–77.

the two included an Inner Mongolian autonomous government, CCP personnel in the Xing'an government, mass work in Mongolian areas, finance and trade in eastern Mongolia, and CCP aid to eastern Mongols consisting of weapons and railway carriages. The demands raised by Buyanmandukhu clearly reflected his misgivings about the current arrangements between the CCP and eastern Mongolia. In following the usual script of the CCP's united front policy, Li granted some of Buyanmandukhu's demands and deferred some others. Buyanmandukhu's immediate gain from the negotiations was the removal from the Xing'an government of two CCP cadres he disliked. Encouraged by the success, a few days later Buyanmandukhu wrote a letter to Li Fuchun and asked him to expedite the transfer of the Manibadara case to the Xing'an government and to replace CCP troops with Mongolian units as the guards of the Chinese Changchun Railway near Zhalantun.[34]

Buyanmandukhu's bargaining with Li, however, was viewed by other eastern Mongol leaders as a disaster, because his action showed a tendency to exclude the CCP from eastern Mongolian affairs and was thus in violation of the Chengde resolution. The result of the Buyanmandukhu–Li negotiations was disseminated as a new official understanding between the CCP and eastern Mongolia through local channels of the Xing'an government and its organ, the *Xing'an Daily.* But pro-CCP elements in the movement regarded it as Buyanmandukhu's personal behavior. A few days after the *Xing'an Daily* published the "summary of the negotiations," the leading officers of the eastern Mongolian army's fifth division, probably goaded by CCP cadres, forced the newspaper to publish a statement of their own that sharply attacked Buyanmandukhu's "recent words and deeds detrimental to revolution."[35]

These developments threatened to split the eastern Mongolian movement at the top. To prevent further deterioration of the situation, Khafengga sent Pungsug to Zhalantun to mediate. Pungsug was a founding member of the eastern Mongolian IMPRP and also a student of Buyanmandukhu's who had just recently returned from a long sojourn or detention in the MPR. His

34. Summary of the Negotiations on the Mongolian Question between Western Manchurian Military District Commissar Li Fuchun and IMAMA Vice-Chairman Buyanmandukhu, 15 October 1946, *NZYL,* 135–36; Buyanmandukhu's Letter to Li Fuchun, 25 October 1946, ibid., 136–37.

35. Joint General Order of the Alliance of the Inner Mongolian Autonomous Movement and the Xing'an Government, 21 October 1946 (signed by Buyanmandukhu and Temurbagana), *NZYL,* 134; Dawa-ochir, "What I Witnessed," 176–77.

mediation proved effective. In mid-December, Pungsug brought Buyan-mandukhu and his associates back to Wangyemiao to have two-day "heart-to-heart conversations" with Khafengga and Temurbagara. Only five people participated in these conversations, with Khafengga and Temurbagana on one side and Buyanmandukhu and Dawa-ochir on the other. Again, Pungsug was in a mediating position. These leaders discussed their disagreements caused by the dissolution of the EMPAG, Manibadara's arrest, radical mass movements in southern Xing'an, and the recent *Xing'an Daily* incident. Although the dialogue did not necessarily change their opinions on these events in the past, they agreed to work as one for the goal of organizing an Inner Mongolian autonomous government. At this point, therefore, this common goal became the most important factor holding the original leadership of the eastern Mongolian movement together.[36]

Between December 20 and 23, an "enlarged joint conference of the eastern Mongolian general branch of the IMAMA, the political council and the administrative committee of the Xing'an government" was held in Wangyemiao. The old triumvirate presided over the conference in unity. The conference denounced the GMD for "launching a mad offensive against the Chinese people with American imperialists' assistance." The eastern Mongolian people's counter measure was to strive for an Inner Mongolian autonomous government. The conference also clarified the movement's policies toward certain fundamental issues that had been in question the past few months. These were summarized as "four great revolutionary policies":

1. Alliance with the CCP—accept the CCP leadership and assistance, trust the CCP, discard all suspicions of the CCP, and regard the CCP as the best friends of the Mongols.

2. National equality—grant equal political, economic, and cultural rights to all nationalities within the [eastern Mongolian] territory, and unit Mongolian and Han democratic forces within the territory in a common struggle to prevent the Mongolian nation's isolation.

3. Class equality—mobilize the mass to gain political and economic equality for poor peasants and poor herdsmen, and reform the feudal [Inner] Mongolia into a democracy in order to unleash the strength of the entire nation.

4. Elimination of traitors—thoroughly purge Mongol traitors, Han traitors,

36. Dawa-ochir, "What I Witnessed," 177–79.

and GMD agents in order to consolidate internal [security] and to strengthen the national united front.[37]

In comparison with the resolutions adopted by the IMAMA's eastern branch two months earlier, these policies appeared positively pro-CCP and devoid of anti-Han sharp edges. These refinements reflected the moderating effect of the recent consultations among the top eastern Mongol leaders themselves. Nevertheless, their central demand remained an Inner Mongolian autonomous government.

Despite the Inner Mongols' repeated invocation of "Genghis Khan's glory," neither in ancient nor in modern times had the Inner Mongols lived under unified governance as an integral people. Although the Mongolian historical memory of the Mongolian unification under Genghis Khan and tribal alliances under other strong Mongolian leaders could help glorify the current cause, "Inner Mongolia" was really a stigma left by the Qing conquest. Furthermore, the idea of integral Mongolian governance for the region was a twentieth-century invention. Whereas the "autonomous" qualification of "government" indicated the Inner Mongol nationalists' compromise with the Chinese state, the idea could nevertheless qualify the Inner Mongols' postwar movement as a nationalist effort to make their territory congruous with governance.

Meanwhile, because of a half-century of Han migration, even "Inner Mongolia" as a Mongolian territory was more imaginary than real. Ever since the eastern Mongol leaders started their movement, they had been conscious of the ethnodemographic reality of Inner Mongolia and had advocated a "new nationalism" in justifying Mongolian governance of a region in which the Han already constituted the majority. This reality partially explained why the postwar Inner Mongolian movement was never bloodied by the interethnic massacres that often characterized ethnic conflicts in Chinese history. Under the circumstances, the eastern Mongols' demand for Mongolian governance over the Han population in Inner Mongolia was actually a trade-off for their agreement to remain an autonomous entity within the Chinese state. In late 1946 and early 1947, Chinese politics and Inner

37. "Victorious Conclusion of the Enlarged Conference of the Eastern Mongolian General Branch and the Political Council: The Conference Demands in One Voice the Establishment of an Inner Mongolian Autonomous Government and a National United Front in Alliance with the CCP against Jiang [Jieshi]," 23 December 1946, *Neimenggu Tongzhan Shi Dang'an Shiliao Xuanbian* (Selected Archival Materials on the History of the United Front in Inner Mongolia) (internal circulation, 1987), 1: 357–58.

Mongolian politics became intricately entangled over this issue. At the time, it was by no means clear which side would get the better part of the bargain. During these months, the eastern Mongol leaders made one more try to formalize a relatively independent position for their movement within the framework of their cooperation with the CCP. This proved the last visible, organized effort of this kind in Inner Mongolian history.

Wangyemiao Finale

As always, the CCP response to the eastern Mongolian initiative followed its own reading of the general military-political situation in China. In early August 1946, Yun Ze reported to the CCP Central Committee that in Inner Mongolia, although the CCP had in the past months "overcome two independence movements," the issue of "unified autonomy" remained the central demand of the people. To the CCP leadership, which specialized in land revolution, Yun made a point that "how to satisfy the Mongolian people's demand is as important as the solution of the land problem."

The CCP Central Committee did not respond to this observation until almost four months later, when the military-political struggle with the GMD made a response necessary. On November 26, the Central Committee issued a directive to Yun and its regional bureaus in Manchuria and Inner Mongolia, instructing them to make preparations for "combining eastern and western Mongolia and establishing a local government of high-degree self-government." The directive made it clear that in the past the eastern Mongolian government was dissolved to meet the need of political maneuvering with the GMD, but now the circumstances had already changed. Accordingly, a high degree of self-government for the Inner Mongols would be in concert with public opinion in China and could better unify the Mongols in the anti-GMD struggle.[38]

Thus, when the eastern Mongols' December conference put forward their "four great revolutionary policies" and demanded the establishment of an Inner Mongolian autonomous government, the CCP was ready to endorse the idea and was organizationally prepared to control the process. In mid-

---

38. Yun Ze's Report to the CCP Central Committee on the Questions of Land and Autonomy in Inner Mongolia, 1 August 1946, *MWWH,* 1057–58; CCP Central Committee's Directive on the Establishment of an Inner Mongolian Autonomous Government, 26 November 1946, ibid., 1081.

January 1947, Yun again sent Liu Chun to Wangyemiao to sound out the eastern Mongols' ideas. Liu's findings were alarming. Khafengga and Buyan-mandukhu spoke in one voice that in the proposed Inner Mongolian government the eastern Mongols should have a stronger position than those from the west, and that the IMPRP should be rehabilitated with the eastern Mongols in charge. During a dinner party, Liu was challenged by Medurtu, commander of the eastern Mongolian army's first division. Medurtu laid his pistol on the table and pointed a finger at Liu while accusing "people from the west" of meddling in eastern Mongolia. A month later, Yun himself arrived in Wangyemiao and was warmly received. But from two parallel slogans shouted by the welcoming crowd, "long live Yun Ze" and "long live Khafengga," any observant bystander could sense that a competition was on.[39]

Having just lost to GMD forces their areas of activities in western Inner Mongolia, Yun and his colleagues working at IMAMA headquarters were forced to relocate to eastern Mongolia in February 1947. Yet, because the CCP Central Committee decided to physically combine the western and eastern components of the Inner Mongolian movement, Yun's move assumed the appearance of a strategic initiative. Coming to Wangyemiao to implement the CCP's new stratagem, Yun's group did not behave as modest guests humbled by their recent frustrations in the west.

The aggressiveness of Yun and other "western Mongol comrades" was sensed even by some Han CCP cadres that had been working in Wangyemiao since early 1946. Hu Shaoheng, a member of the CCP's Xing'an working committee, recorded in his diary that Yun's group did not waste any time and put some "very sharp" questions to their eastern Mongol hosts at the welcoming meeting and a dinner party in honor of Yun. These, not surprisingly, caused displeasure and disappointment among the eastern Mongols. Hu became very concerned with what seemed to him factional bickering between the western and eastern Mongols. He suggested to Liu Chun that Yun should be advised that the top priority at the moment was the anti-GMD struggle but not "account settlement regarding policy lines in the past" and that "western Mongol representatives should not have a sense of superiority."[40]

39. Liu Chun, "Works in Inner Mongolia Remembered," 73–76; Wang Zaitan, "Recollections of My Work in the Social Department before and after the Establishment of the Inner Mongolian Autonomous Government," ibid., 130–31.

40. Wang, *Wushi Chunqiu,* 235–36; Hu Shaoheng, "Excerpts from Hu Shaoheng's Diaries, 1 January to 31 December 1947," entries on 26, 27, and 28 February, in *Xing'an Geming Shihua* 3: 224–25.

The so-called east–west misgivings may have reflected certain vestiges of old tribal or regionalist divergences between Yun's group, core members of which were sinicized Tumed Mongols and the Xing'an Mongols. The divergences, however, often went beyond internal friction. At the time, the western group in the eyes of many eastern Mongols must have resembled the "Inner Mongols" in the eyes of the "Outer Mongols" during the Qing Dynasty or the Buryat Mongols in the eyes of the rest of the Mongolian population in the twentieth century. In other words, "Inner," "Buryat," and "western" modifications of certain Mongols represented their association with non-Mongolian forces "earlier" than other Mongols. "Earlier," Hu Shaoheng warned in respect to Yun's group, must not mean "superior" to other, or eastern, "Mongolian comrades."

Either because of some predetermined plans or because of the rough start of Yun's group in Wangyemiao, the most important groundwork for launching Inner Mongolia's autonomous government was laid under the close supervision of the CCP's Northeast Bureau in Harbin. In early March, Yun and the principal eastern Mongol leaders arrived in Harbin. After a courtesy meeting with the CCP officials of the Northeast Bureau—including Lin Biao, Luo Ronghuan, Gao Gang, and Li Fuchun—the visitors from Wangyemiao entered intensive discussions to decide the structure, programs, and personnel of the future government for Inner Mongolia. Again, as in the Chengde conference, the principle of parity was followed. The eight conferees included four from the west (Yun Ze, Liu Chun, Kuibi, and Kho'erge) and four from the east (Khafengga, Temurbagana, Buyanmandukhu, and Oljeiochir). Although at the beginning Northeast Bureau officials told the conferees that Mongolian affairs were for Mongol comrades to decide and that they themselves were there only to assist, eventually all the bureau's officials named above, except Lin Biao, participated in the meetings. This time Yun's skill of suasion appeared much less effective than before.

The conferees spent much of March arguing about who should be "elected" into the future government and political council. From time to time, the Northeast Bureau officials had to offer their "advice" to keep the discussions on the right track. In the end, a so-called election accord was hammered out, which included a list of names to be included in the future government. It was decided that Yun, Khafengga, and Buyanmandukhu would respectively take the positions of chairman and vice chairman of the government and president of the political council. The purpose of this pre-election understanding was to ensure a proper balance between the two groups and also to commit the eastern Mongols in advance. Before they came to Harbin, the western group had decided that under Yun, the vice chairman in the future government should be a Han. Such an arrangement would have significantly diminished eastern Mongolian influence in the government and also made the government a Mongol–Han coalition. Even Hu Shaoheng thought the idea excessive, and, obviously, it was not approved by the Northeast Bureau either.[41]

During the Harbin conference, the CCP Central Committee offered its "assistance" as well. On March 23, the Central Committee sent a six-point directive on Inner Mongolian autonomy to the Northeast Bureau. Some of these points would later be included in the programs of the Inner Mongolian Autonomous Government, such as the government's "temporary" structure pending the "liberation" of western Mongolia and its "recognition of the Inner Mongolian national autonomous region still as part of China." The Central Committee's suggestions on the relationship between the Inner Mongolian government and CCP-controlled "liberated areas" and on the organization of an Inner Mongolian communist party were intended for future implementation. As far as the Central Committee's advice on the fate of the IMPRP was concerned, as will be shown below, it only caused confusion.[42]

The Harbin decisions would not stand if they were not adopted by the forthcoming assembly of eastern Mongolian people's representatives. At the time, Khafengga's prestige in eastern Mongolia was very high. CCP cadres were often impressed by how spontaneously the eastern Mongols viewed Khafengga as their leader and "teacher" and how his words decisively influenced people of different political persuasions. In contrast, as of 1947 Yun remained largely an unfamiliar figure to ordinary people in the region. The CCP had to use its mass work and propaganda organs to deliberately foster his reputation as *the* leader of the Mongolian people.[43] Viewed by

41. Wang and Hao, *Wulanfu Nianpu,* 158–59, 161; Liu Chun, "Works in Inner Mongolia Remembered," 76–78; Wang Zaitian, "Recollections of My Work in the Social Department before and after the Establishment of the Autonomous Government of Inner Mongolia," *NWZ,* 50: 118–42 (the citation here is on 136–38); Hao, *Wulanfu Zhuan,* 451–64; Liu Chun, "How Was the Inner Mongolian Autonomous Government Started," *Neimenggu Dang'an Shiliao* 1 (1992): 66–68; Hu Shaoheng, "Excerpts from Hun Shaoheng's Diaries, 1 January to 31 December 1947," entry on 28 February, in *Xing'an Geming Shihua,* 3: 225.

42. CCP Central Committee's Directive on the Question of Inner Mongolian Autonomy, 23 March 1947, *MWWH,* 1094–96.

43. Zhang Ce, "My Onerous Lifetime," 87–88; Wang Zaitian, "Recollections," 130–31, 132, 139; Wang Haishan, "Comrade Ulanfu's Great Contribution to Nationality Work," in *Wulanfu Jinian Wenji* (Memorial Essays on Ulanfu) (Hohhot: Neimenggu

eastern Mongol leaders as the linchpin of their alliance with the CCP, Yun's position in the future Mongolian government was secure. But this did not mean that he would be able to control the majority in the government. To implement the Harbin decisions, now Yun and his associates again needed to muster all their skills as party operatives to achieve solid control of the electoral politics in Wangyemiao.

Before his trip to Harbin, Yun had already gained an important advantage by setting a procedure for selecting assembly delegates. The eastern Mongols' oversight in this regard indicated a lack of political experience. The most prominent feature of the procedure was that the selection of representatives was not proportional to regional populations but was based on the organizational structures of CCP's influence in Inner Mongolia. This approach nullified in one stroke the eastern Mongols' advantage in the size of their population. After being approved by their local governments and CCP organizations, the delegates would come to Wangyemiao and be screened one more time by a "representative qualification examination committee." Temurbagana was the head of the committee, but the committee's work was supervised closely by Yun and other CCP cadres. The process weeded out people disliked by the CCP. For instance, He Zizhang (a.k.a. Chinjorigtu) was disqualified as a formal representative, despite the fact that he was a prominent local leader in Juu-uda and a division commander of the eastern Mongolian army. Not long before, He had been praised by the IMAMA's eastern branch as a "national model of integrity" for his execution of three GMD agents who tried to persuade him to rally to Nanjing. Nevertheless, He lost his representative status because, after arriving in Wangyemiao, he began to draw a crowd around him by openly advocating the restoration of the IMPRP.[44]

In the end, the selection process confirmed 393 voting delegates. Seventy-one, or 18 percent of them, were members of the IMAMA's executive

Renmin Chubanshe, 1990), 1: 181; Dugarzhab, "Recollections of Works under Comrade Ulanfu's Leadership," ibid., 194; Gowanbozhab, "The Glittering Light of Spirit," ibid., 212; Wang, *Wushi Chunqiu,* 285.

44. "IMAMA's Notice on the Assembly of Inner Mongolian People's Representatives and the Procedure of Selecting Representatives," *Neimenggu Dang'an Shiliao* 1 (1992): 9; "Temurbagana's Report on Behalf of the Representative Qualification Examination Committee, 25 April 1947," ibid., 32; "IMAMA Eastern Mongolian General Branch's Directive on the Current Situation and Work in Eastern Mongolia," late September or early October 1946, *NZYL,* 147; Oljeinaren, "In the Mighty Torrent," 205.

committee and its other direct affiliates. Another 71 came from the four western leagues, even though these leagues accounted for less than 13 percent of the total Inner Mongol population. Eastern Mongolia, accounting for about 83 percent of the Inner Mongol population, got 249 delegates, or 63 percent of the total. Among them, only 95 did not have any organizational affiliation or social insignia attached. Surely the intended composition of the forthcoming assembly was not designed by "western Mongols" in opposing "eastern Mongols." Yun Ze's group and the eastern Mongol leaders were in an accord to prevent any rightist group from commandeering the assembly. Still, Yun and his associates wanted to make sure that the "progressive elements" had an "absolute superiority" in the voting body so that they would be able to deal with any contingency, including potential disagreements between themselves and the original eastern Mongolian leadership. This goal was secured by carefully screening the eastern Mongol delegates to ensure that pro-CCP activists made up a majority. Then, the only thing that they needed to do next, in the words of a CCP cadre, was to "prevent any blind optimism among party members and progressives" lest an easy victory slip away.[45]

The Harbin conferees returned to Wangyemiao in late March. From April 3 to 21, an enlarged conference of the IMAMA executive committee was held to review the organization's work in the past year and to adopt the Harbin decisions regarding the establishment of an Inner Mongolian autonomous government. Then, on April 23, the people's assembly was launched with great fanfare. Some 600 guests and delegates participated in the ceremony outside the Genghis Khan Temple in Wangyemiao. Portraits of Mao, Yun, Stalin, and Choibalsan were displayed. The GMD regime was of course absent from the scene, except that the IMAMA's "peasant-herdsman" flag flew side by side with the national colors of the Republic of China. Congratulatory posters were everywhere. For the occasion, a presidium was elected and Khafengga was named the secretary general of the assembly. Yun and Buyanmandukhu made speeches to call the assembly into session.

The most popular speech of the day was delivered by Zhang Pinghua on behalf of the CCP's West Manchurian Branch Bureau. According to one account, when he presented the assembly with four phrases—"unify ourselves, overcome the enemy, practice self-government, and strive for self-

45. "Name List of the May the First Conference (393 Names)," *Neimenggu Dang'an Shiliao* 1(1992): 15–21; "Fang Zhida's Opinion on the Party Corps's Leadership, 5 April 1947," ibid., 12.

determination"—the meeting ground was shaken by "thunderous applause" from the audience. As a matter of fact, since China's war against Japan, the CCP leadership had already ceased supporting minority nationalities' right to "national self-determination" for the sake of promoting the territorial and national unity of the Chinese nation. Yet, as shown in Zhang Pinghua's case, CCP operatives in the field could still occasionally use the slogan of "national self-determination" to promote the CCP's popularity among the non-Han peoples.[46]

Zhang's public-pleasing rhetoric however had a more concrete function in promoting Yun. At the assembly Yun's position was lifted by CCP officials to an unprecedented height. His portrait was watching over the delegates along with those of Mao, Stalin, and Choibalsan. A connection between Yun and Genghis Khan was made by two official slogans of the assembly, "Genghis Khan's descendants, unite to shatter the aggression of American–Jiang reactionaries and to strive for the victory of the self-defense and liberation war of the Mongolian nation of Inner Mongolia," and "Unite under the banner of Inner Mongolian people's leader Ulanhu [Yun] to construct a new Inner Mongolia and to gain Inner Mongolian nation's complete liberation." These were stressed in Zhang's speech. From now on, in public Yun would more frequently use his Mongolian name "Ulanhu" (Ulanfu in Chinese pronunciation). In contrast, no individual eastern Mongol leader was invoked to incite public enthusiasm.

On the second day of the assembly, it was Yun who delivered the meeting's main political report. In summarizing the history of Inner Mongolian autonomous movements, he mentioned the postwar eastern Mongolian movement only in one sentence in connection with the Chengde conference. He asserted that before the IMAMA was established, Inner Mongolia did not have any mass organization except the yearly gatherings of the lamas' ghost dance.[47] Thus he had already begun to write Inner Mongolia's post-

---

46. "Congratulation to the Beginning of the Assembly of People's Representatives" (editorial), *Neimeng Zizhibao* (Inner Mongolian Autonomy Daily), 23 April 1947, *Neimenggu Dang'an Shiliao* 1 (1992): 26; "Representative of the West Manchurian Branch Bureau and Military District Zhang Pinhua's Congratulatory Speech at the Opening Ceremony of the Assembly of Inner Mongolian People's Representatives," ibid., 25; "Unprecedented Grand Opening Ceremony of the Assembly of Inner Mongolian People's Representatives," *Neimeng Zizhibao,* 26 April 1947, *MWWH,* 1325–26.

47. "Assembly's General Slogans," *Neimenggu Dang'an Shiliao* 1 (1992): 22; "Outline of the Political Report by Ulanhu at the Assembly of Inner Mongolian People's Representatives," ibid., 27–31.

war history with the intention of relegating the spontaneous eastern Mongolian movement to historical oblivion.

The assembly would have been a model operation of the CCP's self-centered "new democracy" if it had followed the tone set by Yun's speech during its six-day convention. During the convention, however, a genuine political contest took place over two subjects. One concerned the election of a political council, and another was the issue of the IMPRP. Years later, participants in the assembly would offer different accounts of the election. According to Liu Chun, on the eve of election, which was held April 29, Buyanmandukhu initiated an effort to alter the Harbin "election accord" and put out a "three-not-to-elect" principle: not to elect Mongol cadres from Yan'an (except Yun and Kui Bi), not to elect radical young eastern Mongols who joined the movement after Japanese surrender, and not to elect Han Chinese. Although operating on a different track, Khafengga, Temurbagana, Oljeiochir, and Pungsug also tried to modify the "election accord" and thus perpetrated serious irregular behavior unbecoming their CCP membership. In an "internally circulated" biography, Buyanmandukhu's offspring reject Liu Chun's story about Buyanmandukhu's transgression. In identifying Khafengga's group as the schemers against "western Mongolian" and CCP influence during the assembly, Buyanmandukhu's children depict their father as at least a passive supporter of the Harbin "election accord."[48]

A third version of the situation is upheld by Dawa-ochir and Teguschogtu, both of whom were members of the IMAMA Executive Committee and separately associated with Buyanmandukhu and Khafengga. In their accounts, the so-called efforts to alter the Harbin list of candidates for the political council involved merely different groups' open or secret campaigns to elect their favorite candidates from the list. According to a "temporary organizational guideline of the Inner Mongolian autonomous government," which was approved by the assembly on April 27, the assembly would elect a temporary political council of 99 to 121 members. This gave the delegates room to cross some names off the Harbin list. Actually, the list was officially released to the delegates only one day before the election, and the delegates were not given much time for campaigning. Some participants in the Harbin conference might have leaked the list to their supporters before the official release to give them more time. Such an action may have looked conspiratorial to people like Liu Chun but it did not really violate the limits set by

---

48. Liu Chun, "Works in Inner Mongolia Remembered," 78–81; Bukho and Sayan, *Boyanmandu Shengping Shilue,* 94–97.

the Harbin conference. Furthermore, because the CCP delegates to the assembly forged caucuses and decided on their own "campaign list" three days before the election, Liu's accusation against the eastern Mongol leaders' similar activities clearly followed a double standard.[49]

What seems to have really happened during the election was that, accustomed to channel unorganized mass into a political direction set by themselves, Yun and his fellow CCP operatives were surprised by the effect of their own "democratic" formula of a "multicandidate election" when dealing with an organized eastern Mongolian movement. What they could do to prevent their preferred candidates from being voted down was to order implicitly or explicitly CCP and Youth League delegates and other reliable delegates to vote only for the candidates on their "campaign list."

It is said that after the votes were cast on April 29, Yun had a sleepless night, waiting for the result of the election and worrying about whether or not the political council would be elected as planned. What was intended was a body that could at once be "representative" of all social and political circles and put Yun's group in control. As it turned out, the CCP caucuses' "campaigning" was so effective that the control aspect of the election almost marred the facade of its representativeness: Buyanmandukhu, the principal target of the CCP's united front policy in eastern Mongolia, got just a half the votes and had to compete for the last seat of the political council with three other candidates who got the same number of votes. In the end, he was politically resuscitated only by successfully, and reluctantly, drawing lots.[50]

Yun and his CCP colleagues succeeded in the election partially because the eastern Mongols did not make a coherent effort to compete with the "western" group. After the eastern Mongolian movement entered the GMD–CCP struggle and adopted radical social policies, its initial internal unity based on ethnicity disintegrated gradually. This was both anticipated and

49. Tegus (Teguschogtu), "My Second Thought about the May the First Conference," *NWZ*, 50: 212; Dawa-ochir, "What I Witnessed," 182; "Temporary Organizational Guideline of the Inner Mongolian Autonomous Government, Adopted by the Assembly of Inner Mongolian People's Representatives on 27 April 1947," *Neimenggu Dang'an Shiliao* 1 (1992): 35–36; Hu Shaoheng, "Hu Shaohen Diaries, 1 January–31 May 1947," entry on 26 April 1947, ibid., 60. There is no direct information about the number of names in the Harbin list. According to Dawa-ochir, about 20 names on the list, all from his "conservative group," were voted down. Because eventually 121 people were elected as members of the political council, this means that the official list included more than 140 names.

50. Hao, *Wulanfu Zhuan*, 471–76; Bukho and Sayan, *Boyanmandu Shengping Shilue*, 96–97.

desired by CCP operatives. Obviously, the "heart-to-heart" conversation between Khafengga and Buyanmandukhu in December 1946 did not really restore the internal coherence of the leadership. Before the people's assembly, disagreements among eastern Mongols over the issue of cooperation with the CCP often showed in forms of factional friction. During the election, factionalism among the eastern Mongols further intensified and thus provided an opportunity for CCP operatives to maneuver between what they classified as "backward" and "progressive" elements.[51]

The "progressive" elements of the eastern Mongolian movement, however, presented a more difficult question to their CCP collaborators. Their persistent demand for rehabilitating the IMPRP posed such a challenge to the basis of the CCP–eastern Mongolian cooperation that both the Northeast Bureau and the CCP Central Committee became involved in searching for a solution. As mentioned above, after their trip to Ulaanbaatar in late 1945, the eastern Mongol leaders purged and reorganized the IMPRP. During the process, "conservative elements," including Buyanmandukhu, were excluded and young activists were inducted into the party. During the Chengde conference, after being "overcome" by Yun's argument on the "correct road" of Inner Mongolian liberation, Khafengga and Temerbagana agreed that upon their return to Wangyemiao, they would dissolve the IMPRP for the second time. Later, Yun and his CCP colleagues became convinced that although the IMPRP was not officially dissolved, its activities had indeed stopped.[52]

In reality, after returning to Wangyemiao, Khafengga and his closest associates took advantage of the CCP's regional bureau system and proposed to the West Manchuria Branch Bureau that the IMPRP continue as a peripheral organization (*waiwei zuzhi*) of the CCP. They promised that with the eastern Mongol members of the CCP as its core, the IMPRP would recruit

51. Li Fuchun et al. to the Northeast Bureau and the CCP Central Committee, 15 April 1946, *MWWH,* 1040; Northeast Bureau's Opinion on the Orientation of Work in Eastern Mongolia, 17 April 1946, ibid., 1042–43; Hu Shaoheng, "Excerpts from Hu Shaoheng Diaries, 1 January to 31 December 1947," 16 January and 19 March entries, in *Xing'an Geming Shihua,* 3: 219–20, 231–32; Bukho and Sayan, *Boyanmandu Shengping Shilue,* 94–97; Dawa-ochir, "My Experiences," 181–83.

52. Butegechi, *Fengyu Jiancheng Wushinian* (Advance in Trials and Hardships for Fifty Years) (Hohhot: Neimenggu Renmin Chubanshe, 1997), 20; *Neimenggu Dang de Lishi he Dang de Gongzuo,* 178, 284; Tumen and Zhu Dongli, *Kang Sheng yu Neirendang Yuan'an* (Kang Sheng and the Unjust Case of the IMPRP) (Beijing: Zhongyang Dangxiao Chubanshe, 1995), 123–24; Liu Chun, "Works in Inner Mongolia Remembered," 55–58, 62.

new members only from laboring people and young intellectuals. Its members would devote themselves to the liberation of Inner Mongolia "according to Marxist-Leninist nationality policy," to struggle against imperialism, feudalism, and GMD reactionaries, and to accept the "comprehensive leadership of the CCP." The CCP regional leadership in Manchuria was receptive to the proposition. In mid-April 1946, after receiving the West Manchurian Branch Bureau's report on the matter, the Northeast Bureau emphasized that as the "vanguard of the Mongolian people," the IMPRP's quality was more important than its size and it must have a tight organization to "fulfill its historical task." Even in late September 1946, the West Manchurian Branch Bureau continued to view the IMPRP as valid as the Xing'an government and the IMAMA's eastern branch. Until early 1947, or before Yun's group moved to eastern Mongolia, it was obviously unnecessary for eastern Mongol leaders to emphasize the IMPRP's party function. The combination between "western" and "eastern" Inner Mongols in early 1947 had the effect of abolishing the relative independence of Wangyemiao and consequently pushed the party question to the fore. At the time, however, the real question was not to reestablish the IMPRP but to reactivate it from hibernation.[53]

The issue was first brought up by Khafengga to Liu Chun when the latter visited Wangyemiao in mid-January. Then it was widely discussed among the eastern Mongols during the preparations for the Inner Mongolian autonomous government. According to Hu Shaoheng's diary, Khafengga, Temurbagana, Pungsug, and Oljeiochir were united in an effort to persuade Yun to support the rehabilitation of the IMPRP and even Inner Mongolia's eventual accession to the MPR. Heated debate on the IMPRP question occurred between Yun's group and these eastern Mongol leaders throughout April. After the Inner Mongolian Autonomous Government was officially launched in early May, the debate continued but mostly in the form of the eastern Mongol leaders' reluctant self-criticism.[54]

53. West Manchurian Branch Bureau's Report to the Northeast Bureau on the Organization of an Inner Mongolian Party, 12 April 1946, *MWWH,* 1039; Northeast Bureau's Opinion on the Orientation of Work in Eastern Mongolia, 17 April 1946, ibid., 1044; West Manchurian Branch Bureau's Supplementary Directive on the Mongolian Work, 21 September 1946, ibid., 1073.

54. Liu Chun, "Works in Inner Mongolia Remembered," 75–76; Hu Shaoheng, "Excerpts from Hu Shaoheng's diaries, 1 January to 31 December 1947," entries on 30 March, 8 April, 8 May, and 21 October 1947, in *Xing'an Geming Shihua,* 3: 235, 238, 244, 280.

The reasons for the eastern Mongol leaders' perseverance with the IMPRP were not difficult to fathom. After the Chengde conference, although the government structure of eastern Mongolia was changed and more CCP personnel entered the area, eastern Mongolia was still run by the same group of people who had started the eastern Mongolian movement. After a year of cooperation with the CCP based on the Chengde formula, the eastern Mongols felt that their concessions at Chengde not only did not reduce the GMD's offensive against their region but instead allowed a group of very assertive Han Chinese, or CCP cadres, to meddle in their local affairs. The backlash of the partnership with the CCP therefore caused a strong demand among the eastern Mongols to realize an original goal of their movement, an Inner Mongolian autonomous government, as a means of mitigating CCP influence.

Soon enough, however, it became clear to the eastern Mongol leaders that the so-called unification of western and eastern Mongolia under such a government would most likely mean further dilution of the ethnic character of their movement. When Yun Ze and his CCP colleagues homed in on Wangyemiao, the autonomous days of eastern Mongolia were numbered. Having let their "movement" be incorporated into the IMAMA, the eastern Mongol leaders now realized that they were going to lose the "autonomous government" to the CCP as well. Under the circumstances, an Inner Mongolian party seemed the last device left for them to preserve the ethnic character of the movement. Although Khafengga, Temurbagana, Pungsug, and Oljeiochir were leaders making the argument with Yun on behalf of the IMPRP, they had many supporters in eastern Mongolian governmental, military, and youth organizations. It is ironic that this ethnopolitical effort had to be made in a form that excluded a fellow Mongol: These leaders contended that because of Yun's high position within the CCP, he should not become a member of the IMPRP.[55]

This time Khafengga, and his colleagues appeared more determined than they were in Chengde. To warnings from CCP cadres that they were perpetrating "anti-party (CCP)" activities and "making a reckless move," they responded by expressing willingness to give up their CCP membership. Yet, again, the eastern Mongol leaders made the same mistake as they did in Chengde in allowing themselves to engage Yun's group in a theoretical

55. Hu Shaoheng, "Excerpts from Hu Shaoheng's Diaries," entries on 19 March, 30 March, and 8 April 1947, in *Xing'an Geming Shihua,* 3: 232, 235, 238; Liu Chun, "Works in Inner Mongolia Remembered," 82–84.

debate in Marxist terms. Aside from using the MPR as the example for Inner Mongolia, they basically shied away from making any ethnic argument, probably for fear of being labeled as "parochial nationalists." Instead, they argued that, because it was economically backward and lacked the social-class conditions necessary for a proletarian communist party, Inner Mongolia with its many social classes needed the IMPRP as its leading body. Inevitably, in this line of dogmatic debate, Yun and his associates again proved superior to their eastern Mongol counterparts. In one of the meetings attended only by CCP members, Oljeiochir was so frustrated by the other side's reasoning that he roared at Liu Chun, the only Han present at the meeting, and accused him of being a fascist who "messed up everything in Inner Mongolia."[56]

Unable to make any advance on the theoretical front, eastern Mongol leaders nevertheless persisted. Interestingly, not only the MPR but also Yan'an were the sources of their intransigence. As mentioned above, before the end of World War II, the political careers of Temurbagana and Pungsug were connected to the MPR but not the CCP. In the war years, Oljeiochir was a secret Comintern agent in Prince De's army and, when Japan surrendered, he led a mutiny and took some troops into the MPR. During the debate, the MPR was certainly not neutral about this "internal disagreement" of the CCP's. At the time, an MPR agent named Banchigle was in close contact with Khafengga in Wangyemiao and communicated with the MPR authorities through a transceiver. At least Yun's group suspected that he was encouraging Khafengga and the others in the name of the MPR leadership. Soon, at Yun's request, Ulaanbaatar recalled Banchigle. Another bit of circumstantial evidence of MPR involvement in the dispute was that Khafengga and his colleagues did not begin to admit their "mistakes" within the CCP until Temurbagana returned from a trip to the MPR some time in May.[57]

More likely, however, it was the CCP Central Committee's interference that made the eastern Mongols' argument for the IMPRP seemingly defensible. As mentioned above, in March, during the Harbin conference the Central Committee sent a directive to the Northeast Bureau as a policy guid-

---

56. Hu Shaoheng, "Excerpts from Hu Shaoheng Diaries, 1 January to 31 December 1947," entry on 6 July 1947, in *Xing'an Geming Shihua,* 3: 258–59; Liu Chun, "Works in Inner Mongolia Remembered," 82–84.

57. Wang Zaitian, "Recollections," 136; Hu Shaoheng, "Excerpts from Hu Shaoheng Diaries, 1 January to 31 December 1947," entry on 30 May 1947, in *Xing'an Geming Shihua,* 3: 250.

ance for the planned Inner Mongolian government. One of the items in the directive reads:

> If the activists among the Mongolian people demand dissolution of the IMAMA and organization of the IMPRP, we should support them and have CCP members enter the party to become its leading core. But if it is inopportune [to implement the step], the IMAMA may be preserved for the moment and be used as a mass organization to conduct activities in western Mongolia.[58]

Among the eastern Mongol participants in the Harbin conference, at least Khafengga learned about the content of the directive. He must have concluded that as long as they, the "activists," insisted on their demand, the CCP leadership would endorse the IMPRP as indicated in the directive. This was why during the debate, to show their seriousness, Khafengga and the others indicated that if the CCP refused to lead the IMPRP they would have to consider withdrawing themselves from the CCP. Khafengga also used the content of the directive to convince some of his hesitant colleagues that the IMPRP was attainable.[59]

Unable to overcome the IMPRP problem with reasoning and concerned that the debate within the progressive wing of the movement could create opportunities for conservatives, Yun had no alternative other than resorting to the higher authorities. He communicated with Ulaanbaatar directly and got a disclaimer signed by Choibalsan, which denied categorically any responsibility for supporting the IMPRP idea. After Yun showed the telegram to young activists in Wangyemiao and discredited the notion that the CCP Central Committee was willing to adopt the IMPRP as a front organization, Khafengga's credibility was seriously damaged. He could not produce a copy of the CCP directive to back up his story. Now convinced that Khafengga had lied to them about the CCP leadership's endorsement of the IMPRP, many young Mongols turned against their "teacher."[60]

Although in the debate in Wangyemiao Yun and his colleagues often

---

58. CCP Central Committee's Directive on the Question of Inner Mongolian Autonomy, 23 March 1947, *MWWH*, 1095.

59. Tegus, "My Second Thoughts about the May the First Conference," *NWZ*, 50: 212–13; "Excerpts from Hu Shaoheng Diaries, 1 January to 31 December 1947," 8 April entry, in *Xing'an Geming Shihua*, 3: 238.

60. Tegus, "My Second Thoughts," 212–13.

accused supporters of the IMPRP of committing an "antiparty" crime, there was no consensus on the matter within the CCP's higher echelons. In its reports to the Central Committee, the Northeast Bureau now attributed selfish and cryptic motives to eastern Mongol leaders and defined their promotion of the IMPRP as an "action of excluding the CCP disguised in a national form." In contrast, the West Manchurian Branch Bureau believed that a concession to the Khafengga group should be made to channel, not suppress, the eastern Mongol leaders' nationalist tendency under the CCP leadership.[61] The CCP Central Committee did not regard the IMPRP as a matter of principle and was willing to grant the eastern Mongols their own organization. In a late April directive to the Northeast Bureau and Yun, the Central Committee admitted the advantage of using the IMAMA to replace the IMPRP as the mass organization in Inner Mongolia, but it noted that

> if the [Inner Mongolian] People's Revolutionary Party has not been openly dissolved and these people [eastern Mongol leaders] are strongly demanding its restoration and cannot be dissuaded for the moment by our comrades, it would be better for us to adopt a positive attitude in establishing the party around ourselves and leading its revolutionary development. It is unnecessary to harbor a preset intention that the party has to be abolished.[62]

Such a "preset intention" was indeed harbored by Yun and his colleagues in Wangyemiao because, better than the CCP's central leadership, they understood that the eastern Mongols were making the IMPRP the last stronghold of their autonomy. In the end, the CCP's policymaking mechanism produced a compromise formula that did not contain much of a concession from the CCP's side: The IMPRP should not be organized, but a working committee should be established to make preparations for an Inner Mongolian communist party. The formula highjacked eastern Mongols' idea that Inner Mongolia needed a party of its own, and, in the meantime, it left hardly any room for Inner Mongolian nationalism. In putting Yun in charge of the

61. Northeast Bureau's Report to the CCP Central Committee on its Opinion on the Problem of Inner Mongolian Autonomy, 1 April 1947, *MWWH*, 1097–98; West Manchurian Branch Bureau's Letter (to the Northeast Bureau) on the Issue of IMPRP, 10 April 1947, ibid., 1099; Northeast Bureau's Report to the Central Committee on the Issue of IMPRP, 18 April 1947, ibid., 1100–1.

62. CCP Central Committee's Directive to the Northeast Bureau and Yun Ze on the Policy toward the IMPRP, 23 April 1947, *MWWH*, 1103.

working committee, the formula also prevented the eastern Mongols from controlling the planned Inner Mongolian communist party.

Ironically, the formula also had an advantage over the eastern Mongol leaders' argument in their own domain, nationalism. In contrast to Khafengga and his associates, who asked their supporters to accept the "backwardness" of Inner Mongolia as the main reason against a communist party in the region, the CCP formula told the Inner Mongols that Inner Mongolia was as "advanced" as the rest of China and was therefore qualified to have its own proletarian party. Thus, the last "victory" that the eastern Mongols gained in their bargaining with the CCP over the question of an Inner Mongolian party ended with the loss of their last ethnopolitical ground, the IMPRP. Once the CCP formula turned many of Khafengga's supporters against him and isolated the staunchest supporters of the IMPRP, the planned Inner Mongolian communist party also became unnecessary. It was never organized, because such a party would be redundant to the CCP in the first place and was meaningless to the eastern Mongols from the very beginning.[63]

The IMPRP episode during the founding assembly of the Inner Mongolian Autonomous Government in 1947 was the last effort by the eastern Mongols to rescue their independent ethnic movement, though Khafengga and his colleagues were naive in believing that having entered the CCP orbit, they could still maintain a realm of their own. In name, the Inner Mongolian Autonomous Government launched on May 1, 1947, gave a high degree of self-government to the Inner Mongols. In practice, the event completed the CCP's domestication of the most effective autonomous movement in postwar Inner Mongolia. From 1947 to the foundation of the People's Republic of China in late 1949, the Inner Mongolian Autonomous Government held a very interesting place in Chinese politics. Solemnly announcing itself as the highest authority in a yet-to-be-defined Inner Mongolia, the autonomous government put itself under the sovereignty of the Republic of China but

63. Liu Chun, "Works in Inner Mongolia Remembered," 84–86; Hu Shaoheng, "Excerpts from Hu Shaoheng's Diaries, 1 January to 31 December 1947," entries on 11, 12, 18, and 19 April 1947, in *Xing'an Geming Shihua,* 3: 239, 240; Wang and Hao, *Wulanfu Nianpu,* 167; Wang, *Wushi Chunqiu,* 290–91; *Neimenggu Dang de Lishi he Dang de Gongsuo,* 287, 293. A preparatory "Working Committee of the Inner Mongolian Communist Party" was set up on 26 May 1947 with Yun Ze as the secretary and Khafengga and Temurbagana among its nine members. On 13 December 1949, the CCP Central Committee decided to establish a CCP Inner Mongolian Branch Bureau and thereby ended any chance for an Inner Mongolian party.

not under its "central government," the GMD regime. From the GMD's perspective, the Inner Mongols under the autonomous government committed
a high crime of splitting the state. Yet, because of the CCP's interference
and maneuvering, the Inner Mongols accomplished at most a "revolutionary independence" comparable to the CCP's political separation from the
GMD government. In the meantime, between 1947 and 1949, the Inner
Mongolian Autonomous Government and its territories constituted an "internal protectorate" of the CCP. From this point onward, the Inner Mongols'
ethnic autonomy had to be measured against the CCP's ethnic sovereignty
over them.

Such a result was dictated by circumstances of the time. A right combination of power and passion is a prerequisite for any successful nationalist
movement. The eastern Mongolian movement suffered from want of the
former. Despite its leaders' territorial claims, the eastern Mongolian movement did not have a region definable, much less defensible, in demographic,
geographical, political, and strategic senses. Nor did the movement possess
the necessary means to create such a region for itself. Moreover, the leaders
in Wangyemiao never intended to confine their movement to the eastern part
of Inner Mongolia. Their goal of creating a unified Mongolian government
over all Inner Mongolia's "original territories" can be viewed as a kind of
"internal irredentism" in China. The goal was far beyond the eastern Mongolian movement's reach. In practice, it only created opportunities for the
CCP's Inner Mongolian drive and let Yun Ze's group to make inroads into
eastern Mongolia.

In addition, the movement took place in a location that, depending on
circumstances, could be deemed either highly advantageous or extremely
detrimental. Had the MPR not been a mere satellite of the Soviet Union, the
eastern Mongols might have had a better chance of obtaining assistance
from their fellow Mongols on the other side of the border. The reality was
that, unable to enjoy the ethnopolitical advantage in the north, the eastern
Mongols mainly suffered from a geopolitical disadvantage in the south. Unlike Xinjiang and Tibet, which were far away from the central stage of Chinese politics, at the end of World War II Inner Mongolia became one of the
first regions where the GMD–CCP power struggle turned into devastating
warfare. The eastern Mongolian movement was able to take shape and expand only briefly during the Soviet Red Army's temporary occupation of
Manchuria. After the Russians left, the movement came under constant
threat from the GMD's colossal fighting machine and the CCP's mass-line
political campaigns.

A lack of power led the eastern Mongols to compromise their nationalist passion: They had to cooperate with one side of the Chinese Civil War to survive. Here ideology entered the equation. The inborn qualities of the movement—its leaders' Comintern connections and the progressive tendency of most of its participants—decided that the CCP was the chosen partner. Departing from Prince De's autocratic nationalism, the eastern Mongols conducted an ethnic movement while upholding a social-revolutionary agenda. The eastern Mongol leaders believed that only by accession to the MPR could their ethnic and revolutionary tasks be accomplished simultaneously. That denied, cooperation with the CCP became the movement's second best choice. It should be pointed out that the independence of Inner Mongolia was never a goal of the movement. As partisans of the communist thread themselves, the principal leaders of eastern Mongolia constantly submitted themselves to a higher authority, whether the Comintern, the MPR, or the CCP. Consequently, at every important juncture, the higher authority decided the direction of the movement. These leaders subscribed to the Soviet-type nationality policy as a way out for China's minority peoples, and they believed in socialism as the necessary road to national development. These convictions helped forge their ideological bond with the CCP. In the years of revolutions and the Cold War, relationships based on ideologies could be as tenacious as those based on interests. This explains why the CCP did not need to use force to subdue the eastern Mongols and could always use ideology to co-opt them into submission.

By May 1947, the eastern Mongolian movement had been completely absorbed by the Chinese Communist movement. Many years later, Yun Ze evaluated the "positive significance" of the former with these words: "Practically speaking, the existence of the Eastern Mongolian Autonomous Government at least allowed us to negotiate for unified autonomy with one organization; otherwise an anarchic eastern Mongolia would have cost us who knows how much more time, energy, and resources."[64] This tactical estimate from the point of view of a CCP operative, of course, was intended to discount the accomplishment of the eastern Mongolian movement as a genuine nationalist drive in the modern sense. The movement articulated the Inner Mongols' aspirations and tested different ways to realize them. In the People's Republic of China, the Inner Mongolian Autonomous Region would be hailed as the CCP's model solution of China's "national question."

---

64. Liu Jieyu, "The Necessary Path of the Inner Mongolian Autonomous Movement," 230.

Yet the model adopted its shape mainly because the CCP responded to the initiatives of a powerful autonomous movement centered in Wangyemiao.

After 1947, the "national fever" in Inner Mongolia was replaced by the CCP's political operations, but this did not mean the end of national spirit of Inner Mongolia. During the preparations for the autonomous government, the organizers of the people's assembly asked the delegates to write and select a song for the government. This song, with the following lyric, like many other contributions, reflected how the Mongolian national spirit continued in the tide of the Chinese revolution:[65]

> Great war of liberation bestows grace,
> Vicious enemies are struck down and we control our own destiny;
> Autonomous government is established by hope and efforts of many
>   years,
> It is the first fruit of our struggle.
> —Truth shines for ever:
> Struggle and struggle again for the nation's thorough liberation;
> Advance with courage and gain victory with determination,
> Rise! Fellow Mongols, patriots, and revolutionaries.
> —Unite all classes and strata,
> Support democratic government and militia;
> Defeat hateful sinicization and enslavement,
> Protect our motherland and joyous Mongolia will be free completely.
> —Carry herdsman's lasso and farmer's hoe,
> Develop pastoral economy and agriculture;
> Study sciences and new ideas and march along with the world,
> New government always develops and new society always advances.
> —Rise! Genghis Khan's warriors,
> Follow Choibalsang's will and Ulanhu's leadership;
> Loyal to the nation and faithful to the people,
> For ever carry forward our glorious history,
> Mongolia! Mongolia's future is limitless.

65. Lyrics for the song of the Inner Mongolian Autonomous Government, April and May 1947, QZH 6/1 (3).

6

"Restoration": The Guomindang's Administrative Endeavor

In the summer of 1945, when negotiating with Guomindang (GMD, Nationalist Party) diplomats, Stalin made a point that an Outer Mongolia lingering under China's sovereignty would become a rallying center to unify all Mongolian sectors, implying that China could secure Inner Mongolia only if it let the Mongolian People's Republic (MPR) go.[1] Outer Mongolia's independence, however, did not secure Inner Mongolia for the GMD government. Soon after Japan's surrender, a new wave of autonomous movements took place in Inner Mongolia, to which the MPR's newly minted legal statehood stood as a model. As a matter of fact, the postwar situation in northern China was so complex that the GMD government watched helplessly when the MPR extended its plebiscite for independence into certain areas of Inner Mongolia.[2]

The significance of the MPR's de jure independence in 1945 was not limited to legalizing a state that had existed for twenty-four years. The event had a demonstrative effect on the Inner Mongols and China's other frontier ethnic groups, such as the Tibetans and the ethnic groups of Xinjiang. In

1. T. V. Soong to Jiang Jieshi, 2 July 1945, in *Zhonghua Minguo Zhongyao Shiliao Chubian: Dui Ri Kangzhan Shiqi* (Preliminary Compilation of Important Historical Records of the Republic of China: The Period of the War of Resistance against Japan; hereafter *ZZSC*), 7 vols., comp. Historical Council of the Guomindang (Taipei: Guomindang Dangshi Weiyuanhui, 1981), 3(2): 578.

2. Report by the Mongolia and Tibetan Affairs Commission, "Delegation to Outer Mongolia to Observe the Plebiscite and the Preparation for receiving the Outer Mongolian Delegation," 2 October 1945, Quanzonghao (general record number; hereafter QZH) 141/1223; Mongolian and Tibetan Affairs Commission to the Ministry of Foreign Affairs, 29 November 1945, ibid.; Jiang Jieshi to Wang Chonghui, 5 October 1945, ibid.

this sense, the Sino-Soviet diplomacy of 1945 was truly a defining moment in China's long journey to become a modern national state. Its ramifications might work in two opposite directions: MPR independence might prove a terminus that completed China's parting with its unrecoverable "imperial" territories, or it could become a starting point for a new round of territorial and sovereignty reductions from China.

Eventually, a range of factors would decide where China was heading. But in the postwar years, the GMD "central government," which should have been the most important determinant in China's territorial and ethnographic development, did not appear to be able to prevent China's further decline in territoriality and sovereignty. Arguably, the GMD government was a central authority of twentieth-century China that pursued political centralization with the most explicit rhetoric and the most ruthless means. Yet throughout its rule of China, the GMD government was doomed to preside only nominally over a disintegrated country. Like many southern dynasties in Chinese history that had ruled only part of the country but assumed pretentiously the "central authority," in its successive capitals in southern China the GMD regime proclaimed complete sovereignty over the late Qing's imperial domain. Ironically, during China's eight-year war with Japan, when cornered in China's southwestern city Chongqing and unable to project its authority beyond the immediate neighboring provinces, the GMD government found its loudest voice on the international stage as a "great power." This Washington-buttressed diplomatic success in image making proved in the long run unfortunate for the GMD regime. The success helped entrench GMD leaders' determination to substantiate the Chinese Republic's "great power" image with geopolitical gains, but it did not really amplify the regime's ability to achieve the goal.

In the postwar years, as the "central government" of China, the GMD government's immediate task was to extend its authority not only to all Chinese provinces but also to China's ethnic borderlands. Although the two types of territories called for different policies, mere control of these regions, not to say stabilization of them, would similarly require a combination of military power, administrative acumen, and moral strength. Debilitated by corrupt and incompetent officials and restrained by rigidly conservative ideologies, the GMD regime was superior to its competitors only in the department of naked military force. In the last months of the war, the GMD diplomacy with the Soviet Union over Outer Mongolian independence was basically a power move from which no ethnopolitical lessons were learned by GMD policymakers. Thus, in the postwar years, when challenged by the new tide of the Inner Mongolian autonomous movement, the GMD regime's "solution" was as unimaginative as ever. Yet unlike previous encounters between the Chinese authorities and frontier ethnic groups, which had always ended with the latter's further victimization, the GMD–Inner Mongolian confrontation in the postwar period was a case study of a peripheral ethnic uprising that helped bring about a regime change at the center. This time the GMD regime was the historical victim of its own obstinacy.

In August 1945, when peace broke out in Asia upon Japan's surrender, the GMD, the Chinese Communist Party (CCP), and the Inner Mongols were three competing forces in North China and Manchuria. Soon, the GMD regime's categorical rejection of the Inner Mongols' autonomous movement made itself the most disadvantageous side of the ethnostrategic triangle. The CCP–Inner Mongolian cooperation significantly strengthened the former's military position vis-à-vis the GMD in North China and Manchuria. As history has shown, the GMD's eventual expulsion from these areas left the door wide open for the CCP to come to power in China. Thus, though it was problematic that the GMD government's Outer Mongolia diplomacy at the war's end improved in any way its domestic security, the regime's postwar Inner Mongolia policy definitely contributed to its own demise in China.

Delusive "Frontier Administration"

During the republican period, Outer Mongolia was never officially declared a "lost territory" by any Chinese government, though privately Chinese officials admitted that the solution of the "Mongolia question," meaning Outer Mongolia's "return," would have to involve diplomacy with Moscow. Meanwhile, successive Chinese governments, either in the hands of warlords or GMD partisans, took steps to erase the "inner" part of the question, that is, Inner Mongolia, from China's political landscape. The result was the complete disappearance of any reference to Inner Mongolia on China's political maps after 1928. Meanwhile, forced sinicization continued in the area. So, at the end of World War II, the question of Inner Mongolia as such did not even exist as far as the GMD regime was concerned. Yet, like any other ethnic questions of the modern times, although the question of Inner Mongolia could be renamed, painted in different colors, or wrapped up in various forms, it could not be entirely obliterated.

As mentioned in earlier chapters, the Inner Mongols' prewar drive for autonomy developed around Prince Demchugdongrub (Prince De), the *jasag* of West Sunid Banner. In the 1930s, when China was struggling alone against Japanese aggression, the GMD leaders became briefly willing to use the "way of mollifying the remote" (*rou yuan zhi dao*) to appease frontier regimes and ethnic groups. In September 1933, one and a half years after Japan created its puppet Manchukuo, the GMD government reluctantly permitted Prince De to set up a powerless "Mongolian Autonomous Political Council." Such a meager allowance did not satisfy the Mongolian prince and, two years later, he began to openly collaborate with the Japanese.[3]

Noticeably, at about the same time, having just survived its arduous Long March and relocated to the foot of the Great Wall, the CCP learned to appreciate the value of the Mongolia question to revolutionary agitation. In December 1935, Mao Zedong, in the name of a "Chinese soviet republic government," issued a "proclamation to the Inner Mongolian people," calling upon the Inner Mongols to join China's war against Japan and committing the CCP to the Inner Mongols' struggle for self-determination in a "restored" Inner Mongolian territory. Throughout the war against Japan, the CCP would continue to view the issue of Inner Mongolia as an important component of its overall strategy.[4]

By contrast, the GMD regime viewed the war with Japan as a reason to intensify its effort to extinguish any ethnonationalist aspiration on the non-Han people's part, which, like the continual challenge from the CCP, was deemed detrimental to the already weak Chinese state. During the 1930s and 1940s, the Chinese–Japanese conflict constituted a powerful stimulus to Chinese nationalism, which was always a Han-centered phenomenon. When the undeclared Sino-Japanese war began in the summer of 1937, the GMD's presentation of Chinese nationalism had already gone through several versions. The time had long since passed when the GMD supported a "five-race republic" (*wu zu gonghe*) in China and the non-Han peoples' right to

---

3. Demchugdongrob, "*Demuchukedonglupu Zishu,*" in *Neimenggu Wenshi Ziliao* (Literary and Historical Materials of Inner Mongolia; hereafter *NWZ*), 13: 6–17, 88–95.

4. "Chinese Soviet Central Government's Proclamation to the Inner Mongolia People, 20 December 1935," *Minzu Wenti Wenxian Huibian* (Collected Documents on the Nationality Question; hereafter *MWWH*), comp. United Front Department of the Central Committee of the Chinese Communist Party (Internal circulation; Beijing: Zhonggong Zhongyang Dangxiao Chubanshe, 1991), 322–24; "CCP Center's Directive on the Mongolian Work, 10 July 1937," ibid., 545–47; "Northwestern Work Committee of the CCP Center's Outline on the Mongolian Nationality Question in the War of Resistance, July 1940," ibid., 657–67.

national self-determination.[5] Under Jiang Jieshi, the GMD had become a largely partisan sheath for a military power driving toward political centralization. China's war with Japan provided the GMD with one more justification to pursue its "one nation, one state" doctrine.[6] In the war years, Jiang Jieshi assumed personal responsibility for the party's official rhetoric, which denied China's multinational character. His theory on racial nationality was spelled out in the notorious book, *China's Destiny,* issued in 1943, in which Jiang arbitrarily depicted China as a one-nation country that in history had absorbed many "clans" (*zongzu,* or *zongzhi*).[7]

Under this assumption, those undeniable interethnic situations in China became mere "frontier problems" involving some peculiar, undefined groups. To GMD officials, the Inner Mongols' demand for autonomy was no more than some Mongolian aristocrats' self-promoting scheme. Thus, officially the GMD government did not have an ethnic or nationality policy as such, and it handled all interethnic affairs under a vague bureaucratic conception called "frontier administration" (*bianzheng*). In the government, the Mongolian and Tibetan Affairs Commission (MTAC) existed also as a peculiar agency to deal with these two "exceptional" regions, not one responsible for general interethnic matters. In the war years, GMD documents categorized the borderlands as "remote frontiers" (*yuan bian*) and "near frontiers" (*jin bian*). The distinction between the two types was by no means made in a geographical sense. Rather, it was based on the degrees of the borderlands' political, economic, and cultural assimilation with China proper. For instance, Inner Mongolia was defined as a "near frontier," even though it was geographically more remote to Chongqing, the GMD's wartime capital in southwest China, than was Tibet that, by definition, was a "remote frontier."[8]

During World War II, the GMD regime supported the principle of national self-determination in the international scene to promote Chinese prestige

---

5. Minority "Nationalities' Right to Self-Determination," included in the "Proclamation of the First National Congress of the GMD, 23 January 1924," *MWWH,* 28.

6. For the racial discourse of Chinese nationalism, see Kauko Laitinen, *Chinese Nationalism in the Late Qing Dynasty: Zhang Binglin as an Anti-Manchu Propagandist* (London: Curzon Press, 1990); and Frank Dikotter, *The Discourse of Race in Modern China* (Stanford, Calif.: Stanford University Press, 1992). John Fitzgerald's *Awakening China: Politics, Culture, and Class in the Nationalist Revolution* (Stanford, Calif.: Stanford University Press, 1996) offers a nuanced analysis of Chinese nationalism in the first half of the twentieth century.

7. Chiang Kai-shek, *China's Destiny* (New York: Roy Publishers, 1947), 29–43.

8. "Outline of the plan for postwar construction of frontier political establishments," n.d. (later than 1943), QZH 141/112.

among Asian nations vis-à-vis Western colonial powers. Meanwhile, the leaders of the GMD regime denied any relevance of the principle to China's "frontier affairs." Their experiences had convinced them that any government concession to "frontier" groups would only invite more troubles. A case in point was the GMD government's prewar abortive mollification of Prince De, which ultimately seemed to prove the folly of the conciliatory approach. The government's double standard on the issue of national self-determination abroad and at home eventually caused a sense of embarrassment among Chinese diplomats. Late in World War II, officials of the Chinese Ministry of Foreign Affairs began to argue that China should restrict its interference with Western powers' colonial problems. They were also opposed to inclusion of the principle of national self-determination in the United Nations charter, lest China's aggressiveness in these matters invite foreign governments' meddling in China's alienated ethnic frontiers, such as Mongolia, Xinjiang, and Tibet.[9]

In Owen Lattimore's view, the GMD regime did not have to be caught in such a self-made predicament. During his one-and-half-year tenure as Jiang Jieshi's political adviser beginning in the summer of 1941, Lattimore engaged GMD leaders in discussing China's frontier questions. In several memoranda, he criticized the Chinese government's policy of sinicization in the past and urged GMD officials to pay close attention to the importance of minority nationalities.[10] Because he was sensitive to the GMD regime's drive for national unification and political centralization, Lattimore suggested that a change of the government's orientation might well serve its own purposes. The key was to attract the peoples of Mongolia and Xinjiang with correct policies but not to alienate them further by coercive means. Among Lattimore's concrete policy suggestions, measures for fostering non-Han peoples' cultural autonomy stood out. He recommended that the GMD learn

9. Gu Weijun, *Gu Weijun Huiyilu* (Memoirs of Gu Weijun), 13 vols. (Beijing: Zhonghua Shuju, 1982–94), 5: 532; Ministry of Foreign Affairs, "Organization for Postwar International Peace and Other Related Questions," 1944, Victor Hoo (Hu Shize) Papers, box 7; Xu Shuxi to T. V. Soong, 20 January 1945, T. V. Soong Papers, box 30.

10. Lattimore to Lauchlin Curry, 27 July 1941, Owen Lattimore Papers, box 27; "Chungking, 7 November 1941: Chu Chia-hua, Head of the Organizational Board of the Guomindang," ibid.; "Chungking, 14 November 1941: Dined with Generalissimo [Jiang Jieshi]," ibid.; "Chungking (Huangshan), 5 December 1941: Generalissimo," ibid.; "Chungking, 2 November 1942: Weng Wen-hao," ibid; Owen Lattimore, *China Memoirs: Chiang Kai-shek and the War against Japan,* comp. Fujiko Isono (Tokyo: University of Tokyo Press, 1990), 105–6, 110–11.

from the Soviet model, citing Moscow's method of dealing with minority nationalities as "one of the most successful Soviet policies." One of his memoranda on Inner Mongolia began with these words: "Settlement of all Inner Mongolian problems is inseparably connected with the full recovery of the Northeast."[11] This would prove prescient for the postwar GMD–CCP contest in Manchuria.

Lattimore, however, made only a limited impact on the GMD's thinking about the frontier question. After reading Lattimore's memoranda, Wang Chonghui, the secretary general of the Supreme Council of National Defense, commented that although making some good points, Lattimore underestimated the Soviet factor in the Xinjiang and (Outer) Mongolian situations, which, in Wang's opinion, was the "cause of the particularization" (*teshuhua*) of these regions.[12] Wang was in charge of the GMD government's wartime policy planning, and his emphasis on "foreign factors" in China's "frontier affairs" was shared by many GMD officials. By the same token, because Japan occupied a large portion of Inner Mongolia during the war, GMD officials insisted that the Inner Mongols' continuous aspiration for autonomy was actually a new question created by the Japanese. Indeed, as a wartime CCP document observed, Japan's policies among the Inner Mongols were effective by simply reversing the GMD's prewar measures.[13] But, when contemplating postwar policies toward the Mongolian populace, the GMD government did not begin with a reevaluation of its earlier orientations. Instead, its policy planning focused on how to accomplish the task of overcoming the Japanese legacy, meaning Japanese-organized political and cultural institutions and Japanese-incited anti-Chinese social psychology in Inner Mongolia.

In the GMD regime's wartime planning documents, the official reference

11. Lattimore, "Memorandum on Outer Mongolia," September 1941, Jiang Zhongzheng Zongtong Dang'an: Geming Wenxian (Kangzhan Shiqi), Academia Historica, Taipei (Archives of President Jiang Jieshi: Revolutionary Documents [Period of the War of Resistance]; hereafter JZZD/GW [KZS]), 35: 55–61; Lattimore, "Memorandum on Sinkiang Province," before September 1941, Lattimore Papers, box 28; Lattimore, "Memorandum on Inner Mongolia," n.d., ibid.

12. Wang Chonghui, "Supplementary Comments on the Xinjiang Question," 1 September 1941, JZZD/GW (KZS), 3: 53–54.

13. Committee on Frontier General Mobilization for the National Revolutionary War in the Second War Zone, "How the Anti-Japanese Guerrilla Base in the Daqing Mountains was Created," July 1939, in *Daqingshan Kang Ri Youji Genjudi Ziliao Xuanbian* (Selected Materials on the Anti-Japanese Base in the Daqing Mountains) (Hohhot: Neimenggu Renmin Chubanshe, 1987), 2: 63.

to the government's postwar goal in Inner Mongolia, "restoration of the Mongolian banners" (*mengqi fuyuan*), precluded any consideration of meaningful reforms in frontier policies. The whole issue was reduced to an insignificant component of China's postwar demobilization. Toward the end of the war, when a disagreement did emerge among GMD officials about the meaning of "restoration" in Inner Mongolia, it happened between those who wanted a complete return to the prewar (pre-Japanese) conditions and those who favored a selective preservation of Japanese establishments for the sake of more effective governmental control over Mongolian banners. Unsurprisingly, neither side of the debate went beyond the ideological limits set in Jiang Jieshi's *China's Destiny.*[14]

Between late 1944 and early 1945, the MTAC, in pursuance of the fundamentals set forth in Jiang's book, produced a guideline for the government's postwar policymaking in relation to frontier regions. Accord to the guideline, the postwar frontier policy would hold the "interest of national defense as the criterion, national equality as the basis, and formation of all racial groups [*zu*] into one state-nation [*guozu*] as the ultimate goal." Under this formula, any frontier peoples' autonomous aspiration would be viewed as antithetical to the GMD's nation-building objective. As for Outer Mongolia and Tibet, two regions that for all practical purposes were already separate from China, the committee suggested that the government promise them "high-degree self-government" to lure them back to China's fold. As far as the Inner Mongols and other non-Han frontier peoples were concerned, they should remain under the authorities of various Chinese provinces. Or, at most, they could seek "local autonomy" in the same manner as the local Han communities. In disputing the proposition made by Lattimore and some liberal elements in the GMD that the Soviet federation of republics or the British Commonwealth should serve as a model for China's readjustment of its internal ethnic relations, the committee contended that only its own formula was suitable for China's particular conditions and needs.[15]

---

14. Office of the Commissioner to Chahar Mongolian Banners, "Military and Political Conditions of the Puppet Mongolia," 1940, *ZZSC,* 6(2): 422–72; Mongolian and Tibetan Affairs Commission, "Draft Plan for the Recovery in [Mongolian] Leagues and Banners," August 1944, QZH 141/3663; Memorandum by the Counselors' Office of the Military Council, December 1944, QZH 761/171.

15. Wu Zhongxin to Jiang Jieshi, "Plan for Recovering the Lost Mongolian Banners and for Postwar Political Establishment in Mongolia and Tibet," 27 August 1944, Zongtongfu Dang'an (Archives of the Presidential Palace; hereafter ZD), 055/1631; Wu Zhongxin and Luo Liangjian to Jiang Jieshi, 26 May 1945, ZD, 055/0501; GMD Polit-

Throughout the war, the GMD government's general attitude toward non-Han peoples' autonomy was summarily expressed in a rhetorical question posed by Zhu Jiahua, the head of the GMD's organizational department in the early 1940s: "With the skin gone, where can the hair adhere to?" The "skin" was the supposedly solid Chinese interior, and the "hair" the vacillating ethnic frontiers.[16] To the GMD officials' dismay, when World War II concluded in Asia, their government did not hold a "skin" position to attract the "hair." As far as the "Mongolia question" was concerned, the GMD government found in its hand a situation far more intricate than a mere "Japanese legacy."

The reality was that at the war's end, Inner Mongolian nationalism was released from the straitjacket of the Sino-Japanese war and got a new breath of life. Several Inner Mongolian groups of different political persuasions took action to seek a new future for their people. To the GMD authorities, the eastern Mongolian movement posed the most serious challenge because it threatened to alter both the hard international border between China and the MPR and the soft interethnic fault line between the Han and the Inner Mongols within China.

The GMD regime did not learn about the situation immediately. During the first few months of peace, the GMD government lacked reliable information about the conditions in North China and Manchuria. Its intelligence network only began to catch up in early 1946. The initial intelligence reports pointed to an international conspiracy involving the Russians, the Outer Mongols, and the CCP. For instance, according to a GMD "top secret" report dated March 1, 1946, Soviet leaders, including Stalin himself, allegedly discussed the issue of Inner Mongolia early in the year and decided that "no matter how our [GMD] government would evolve, the Soviet Union will continue its established orientation toward Inner Mongolia that is to lure Inner Mongolia into independent autonomy (*duli zizhi*)."

---

ical Conference, "Principles on Mongolian Local Autonomy," 28 March 1934, Jiang Zhongzheng Zongtong Dang'an: Tejiao Dang'an (Zhengzhi) (Archives of President Jiang Zhongzheng: Specially Submitted Documents [Political]), vol. 051; Chen Bulei to Jiang Jieshi, 13 March 1937, Jiang Zhongzheng Zongtong Dang'an: Tejiao Dang'an (Jiao Fei) (Archives of President Jiang Zhongzheng: Specially Submitted Documents [Banditry Suppression]), vol. 002; Sun Fu to Jiang Jieshi, 7 August 1938, *ZZSC,* 3(2): 408–9.

16. Zhu Jiahua, "Frontier Problems and Frontier Works," 21 October 1942, Guofang Zuigao Weiyuanhui Dang'an (Archives of the Supreme Council of National Defense; hereafter GZWD), 510/3.

The same report also included Moscow's "directive" to a "puppet eastern Mongolian autonomous republic and communist league." Allegedly, Moscow ordered these organizations to control as large a portion of Manchurian territory as possible. If in the process they encountered difficulties with GMD troops, the "directive" advised, the Mongols could count on the assistance of the Soviet Red Army. Another piece of intelligence reported Moscow's instruction to the MPR leaders that they provide military assistance to the CCP and to a "Comintern's army" in Inner Mongolia and Manchuria in the event that the GMD government failed to produce "proper solutions" in these areas soon. It was also reported that eastern Inner Mongols had already received from the Russians 150,000 Japanese rifles, 3,000 Soviet automatic rifles, and other light weapons.[17]

Reports like these, though credible to GMD leaders, were misleading or erroneous. For instance, by 1946, the Comintern had been dissolved for three years. There was no autonomous republic, communist league, or Comintern army in eastern Inner Mongolia. In January 1946, the eastern Mongolian autonomous government declared its "high-degree self-government" (*gaodu zizhi*) but still named China as its "suzerain state" (*zongzhuguo*). It never identified itself as a "republic."[18] The alleged Soviet policies for Inner Mongolian independence and for the MPR's involvement in the GMD–CCP civil war were inconsistent with Moscow's China policy of the time, which was to maintain a "correct" stand in the Chinese turmoil. As for Soviet military assistance to eastern Inner Mongols, it occurred only on a small scale during Soviet occupation of Manchuria. Otherwise, in October 1945, Wangyemiao's small security garrison recovered on their own an unknown number of weapons abandoned by the Japanese near Solon. Because the region was under Soviet control at the time, the GMD agents might have

17. Party-Administration-Army Joint Office, "Research Report on Current Conditions in the Northeast and Inner Mongolia, 1 March 1946," "Weekly Report on Current Conditions in the Northeast and Inner Mongolia, 17–23 March 1946," and "Special Report on Current Conditions in the Northeast and Inner Mongolia, 16–30 March 1946," Waijiaobu Yaxisi (West Asian Division of the Ministry of Foreign Affairs; hereafter WJB/YXS), 197/1. The term "national autonomy" (*minzu zizhi*) was never used in GMD documents. "Independent autonomy" (*duli zizhi*) was sometimes used in contrast to "local autonomy" (*difang zizhi*), an ethnic-blind program promoted by the GMD authorities.

18. "Manifesto on the Establishment of the Eastern Mongolian People's Autonomous Government," QZH 4/1 (5); "Administrative Program of the Eastern Mongolian People's Autonomous Government," QZH 4/1 (2); "Eastern Mongolian People's Autonomous Constitution," ibid.

blown up this episode into a story about Soviet aid to the eastern Mongols.[19] As for the many alleged meetings between CCP, Soviet, and MPR officials, the GMD intelligence simply did not possess viable sources for such sensitive information.

By nature, intelligence cannot be completely free of misinformation or misconstruction of facts. Yet the GMD intelligence about Inner Mongolia was exceptionally biased and self-deceptive. According to the recollection of a GMD intelligence officer, except for making some contact with Prince De's regime in western Inner Mongolia, during World War II the GMD intelligence organizations' knowledge about eastern Mongolia and the vast pastoral area was "almost a blank." After the war, the GMD government was anxious to find out Soviet and MPR intentions in Inner Mongolia. In the process of doing so, it adopted a predetermined syllogism: The Soviet Union dominated Mongolia and coveted Manchuria; the CCP was Moscow's instrument and was penetrating into Inner Mongolia and Manchuria; therefore Moscow must have conspired to duplicate the MPR story in Inner Mongolia. The intelligence network's task was to verify these assumptions. Consequently, intelligence operatives in the field concerned themselves mainly with answering uniform questionnaires from their superiors sitting in the capital. Exaggeration, distortion, and the fabrication of "facts" became necessary practices for intelligence officers to provide recipes catering to their superiors' particular tastes.[20] This so-called intelligence, consequently, was more reflective of GMD policy makers' own mindset than of the actual developments in Inner Mongolia and Manchuria.

Surely there was international involvement in the ethnopolitics of China's northern frontiers. During the Soviet–MPR occupation of Inner Mongolia and Manchuria, MPR personnel were especially active in agitating among Inner Mongols for a unified Mongolia.[21] The problem was that GMD leaders

19. Dugurjab, "Memories about the Days and Nights of the Inner Mongolian First Cavalry Division," in *Xing'an Dangshi Wenji* (Essays on the Party History of Xing'an) (Ulanhot: Office of the Party History of the CCP Committee of the Xing'an League, 1993), 2: 210.

20. Shen Zhongyu, "The Jiang Jieshi Clique and Demchugdongrub's Reactionary Force of Inner Mongolia," *NWZ,* 15: 136–37.

21. Fu Zuoyi to Jiang Jieshi, 15 March 1946, Jiang Zhongzheng Zongtong Dang'an: Tejiao Wendian (Edi Yinmou Bufen) (Archives of President Jiang Zhongzheng: Specially Submitted Telegrams [Part on Russian Imperialist Conspiracy]; hereafter JZZD/TW [EY]), 6/35022506; Fu Zuoyi to Jiang Jieshi, 25 March 1946, JZZD/TW (EY), 6/35023332.

were so anxious to blame international irregularities that they failed to see the intra-ethnic nature of the MPR's activities. In other words, the Inner Mongols hardly needed the Outer Mongols' agitation to feel alienated by the policies and practices of China's "central governments" and to be sympathetic to the MPR. In addition, the GMD's constant accusations of international conspiracies did not accord with the actual international situation in Inner Mongolia, which was constantly changing. Toward the end of 1945, according to a piece of information obtained by the GMD's Northeast Field Headquarters, the Soviet military authorities in Manchuria informed eastern Mongolian leaders that the Soviet government, because of a concern about international criticism, would be unable to provide assistance to Inner Mongolia's "independence movement."[22] This information proved accurate, but it did not alter the GMD authorities' overall estimate of the Soviet intention in Inner Mongolia.

With or without the Soviets' direct involvement with the Inner Mongols, the GMD leaders were convinced that an international conspiracy was at work. For one thing, after recognizing MPR independence, the GMD officials saw Outer Mongolia changing from a thorny "internal problem" into a constant source of external threat. For another, as long as the CCP, a mere instrument of Moscow's in the GMD leaders' eyes, had a hand in Inner Mongolia, the international conspiracy was a present and real danger to China's integrity. From the point of view of the GMD officials, there was no lack of evidence to incriminate the CCP for agitating among the "ignorant and poor Mongolian masses." The GMD reportage on CCP–Inner Mongolian relations, however, often contained massive misrepresentations of CCP intentions. It stubbornly refused to admit that the Inner Mongols were capable of spontaneous nationalist aspirations. Yet, again, accuracy was unimportant as long as the intelligence seemed to bear out the GMD leadership's convictions.[23]

The GMD policymakers' obsession with international conspiracies should be understood in historical context. After all, the GMD government had just signed Outer Mongolia away under Soviet pressure, a result of the recent

---

22. Xiong Shihui to Wang Shijie, 25 December 1945, QZH 18/1094.

23. Memorandum by Sun Fushen, 19 July 1947, WJB/YXS: 112/93; Executive Yuan to Ministry of Foreign Affair, 6 July 1947, QZH 18/106 (4); GMD Department of Organization to the Supreme Council of National Defense, 9 August 1946, GZWD, 004/114.2; Bai Chongxi and Wang Shijie to Jiang Jieshi, 31 December 1946, JZZD/GW (KLS), 39: 411–13; Secret Bureau to Jiang Jieshi, 4 May 1947, JZZD/GW (KLS), 39: 419; Chen Cheng to Jiang Jieshi, November 1946, JZZD/GW (KLS), 8: 439.

Moscow negotiations. Foreign influence continued to loom large over the GMD regime's relations with Tibet and Xinjiang. In addition, during the initial postwar months, the government's "takeover" operations in North China and Manchuria ran into serious difficulties because of the CCP rivalry and Soviet entanglement. But it should be pointed out that these frustrations could also have led to a different reaction.

Actually, different opinions did exist within the GMD. Between the summer of 1945 and the spring of 1946, a so-called reform group became quite active during the GMD's sixth national congress and the following second plenary session. The development was called by some GMD high officials a serious "deterioration of party discipline."[24] On these occasions, appalled by the tumultuous conditions of the northern frontier, the "reformers" demanded democracy within the party, advocated for an overturn of the Sino-Soviet treaty of August 1945, and they urged Jiang Jieshi to dismiss the apparently ineffective Xiong Shihui, commander of the Northeast Field Headquarters. Notably, they also favored a renovation of the party's frontier policies. Jiang had to reason with these people, but at times he felt it necessary to use intimidation to keep them in line.

In the end, the "reformers" proved ineffectual in most of their demands. With respect to frontier policies, their dissension nevertheless brought about some results on paper.[25] The sixth congress acknowledged the party's lack of effort in the past in helping "frontier peoples" (*bianjiang gezu*) and agreed to add a phrase, "realization of high-degree self-government by the Mongols and Tibetans," to the party's current interpretation of the Three People's Principles. Then, in early 1946, the second plenum adopted a more detailed resolution on frontier issues, which included a promise to restore the prewar Mongolian political council.[26]

24. *Wang Shijie Riji*, entries on 1–17 March 1946, 5: 279-287. The group included Chen Lifu, Liang Hancao, Liu Jianqun, Zhang Daofan, Bai Chongxi, Wang Zhengting, Hu Qiuyuan, and others.

25. Ministry of Interior to the MTAC, 3 Autust 1945, QZH 141/3178; *Zai Jiang Jieshi Shenbian Ba Nian: Shicongshi Gaoji MuliaoTang Zong Riji* (With Jiang Jieshi for Eight Years: Senior Member of the Aides' Office Tang Zong's Diary), comp. Ministry of Public Security Archives (Beijing, Qunzhong Chubanshe, 1992), entries on 5–21 May 1945 and 1–17 March 1946, 507–12, 595–600.

26. Executive Yuan to the MTAC, 24 August 1945, QZH 141/3179; Executive Yuan to MTAC, 24 August 1945, ibid.; MTAC to the Executive Yuan, 2 October 1945, ibid.; "Resolution on the Political Report," passed by GMD's Sixth National Congress, 17 May 1945, *Geming Wenxian* (Revolutionary Documents), comp. Historical Council of the GMD (Taipei: Zhongyang Wenwu Gongyingshe, 1976–), 76: 410; "Resolution on the

In such an atmosphere, Jiang was compelled to defend his foreign policy in front of the Chinese public and also to make some tantalizing gestures toward the non-Han peoples of China. In modern China, perhaps nothing else was more shameful to China's collective memory than "unequal treaties" and "lost territories." Understandably, the Sino-Soviet treaty of August 1945, with Outer Mongolia on the price tag, was not well received by members of the GMD and the Chinese public. With the GMD's turbulent national congress in the background, Jiang was anxious to polish the public image of his recent concessions to the Soviets. In late August, 1945, he delivered a speech at the Supreme Council of National Defense. Concealing from his audience that GMD negotiators in Moscow had used Outer Mongolia as a bargaining chip in exchange for the Soviets' cooperation on the CCP question, he described the Moscow concession as a noble and logical step to implement the GMD's promise to support weak nations' right to autonomy. To make himself sound more convincing, he promised to "ensure equality for all the nationalities (*minzu*) within the country" and to give a sympathetic consideration to demands for self-government or independence by "frontier nationalities situated in regions outside the provinces."[27] For a moment, "high-degree self-government" seemed not utterly impossible for frontier ethnic groups.

The Inner Mongols were responsive to the gesture. In January 1946, in its inaugural manifesto, the eastern Mongolian autonomous government cited Jiang's speech to justify its legality and expressed gratitude to the GMD leader.[28] Soon, an eastern Mongolian delegation proceeded from Wang-yemiao to Chongqing with a petition for recognition. Seeing what was coming, the GMD government held an interdepartmental meeting and decided to receive the delegation in the capital. But Xiong Shihui, then squatting in Beiping (Beijing) and fuming over the Soviets' uncooperativeness in Manchuria, intercepted the mission and turned it away. He did not believe that the government would be able to accomplish anything in receiving the delegation.[29] Thus, as often happened in the GMD power structure, a central

Party's Constitution and Policies Passed by the Sixth National Congress," 18 May 1945, *Geming Wenxian,* 70: 395; Bai Yunti et al. to Jiang Jieshi, 17 October 1946, ZD, 055/1655.

27. *Xian Zongtong Jianggong Sixiang Yanlun Zongji* (General Collection of the Late President Jiang's Thoughts and Words), 40 vols. (Taipei: Guomindang Dangshi Weiyuanhui, 1984), 21: 170–75.

28. "Manifesto on the Establishment of the Eastern Mongolian People's Autonomous Government," 19 January 1946, QZH 4/1 (5).

29. Demchugdongrob, "Autobiography," *NWZ,* 13: 144; "Historical Materials on the Puppet Mongolian Army," *NWZ,* 38: 92–94; Jiang Jieshi to the Committee on Mongolian–

government decision made by civil bureaucrats was easily overturned by a powerful regional official. A chance for the GMD regime to maneuver directly with the eastern Mongols was thus lost.

The episode was, however, never much of a chance for the eastern Mongols. The delegation would not in any case have been able to accomplish its mission, which was to get the GMD government's recognition of eastern Mongolia autonomy, even if it had reached Chongqing. First, Jiang's speech, one of the inspirations of the eastern Mongolian mission, was a propaganda piece that did not break any new ground for the GMD's ethnic policy. The speech's terminology indeed sounded fresh. For instance, unlike Jiang's earlier book, *China's Destiny,* in which the term *minzu* (nation or nationality) was used exclusively to denote the state-nation (as in *zhonghua minzu*) and the term *zongzu* (clan) to refer to the non-Han peoples in China, Jiang's speech used *minzu* throughout to refer to the non-Han peoples. This seemed a good sign to the Chinese-reading eastern Mongolian leaders. Yet the new usage did not change the GMD government's policy of denying a nationality status to Inner Mongols or any other non-Han peoples. As a matter of fact, when Jiang's speech was issued in English, its official translators carefully converted all the references of non-Han peoples as *minzu* into "racial groups" but not "nations" or "nationalities."[30]

Jiang's speech also treated these "racial groups" differently. Its special reference to peoples in "regions outside the provinces" effectively excluded the Inner Mongols and the Muslim peoples of Xinjiang, both of which were "within the provinces," from the benefit of the so-called new policy. In other words, the so-called new policy was not designed to give a chance of autonomy to ethnic groups inside the provinces but to dupe Tibet (the only remaining territory outside the provinces after MPR independence) into rescinding its de facto separation from China. The speech therefore continued the old policy of differentiating between the "remote" and "near" frontiers.

Second, even if the central government had been willing to make a change of policy regarding frontier peoples' autonomy, it would have encountered strong resistance from its regional apparatuses. At the time, GMD officials in Manchuria and Inner Mongolia tried to convince the central government that eastern Mongolia's "peculiar autonomy" (*teshu zizhi*) must not be

---

Tibetan Affairs, 10 April 1946, QZH 141/3626; MTAC to the Executive Yuan, 20 March 1946, QZH 141/1060.

30. *The Collected Wartime Messages of Generalissimo Chiang Kai-shek, 1937–1945,* comp. Chinese Ministry of Information (New York: Kraus Reprint Co., 1969), 854–60.

tolerated, lest it undermine the government's anti-CCP operations. Wu Huanzhang, the designated governor of Xing'an Province who never reached his post, argued that in Manchuria the Mongols and the Han had long become economically and culturally interdependent, and that political difficulties in the region could be reduced if the Mongolian league system—in his opinion, the last barrier between the Han and the Mongols—was completely liquidated. The GMD authorities in Rehe agreed, contending that the real problem in the area was the obsolete Mongolian banner system blocking the government's anticommunist pacification campaigns.[31] A report from Suiyuan repudiated the notion that in the area the Han was the ruler or oppressor and the Mongols the ruled or oppressed. Instead, the report asserted that it was the Mongols who were privileged in many aspects, and, without the incitement from a small group of ambitious elements, they would have lived together with the Han "harmoniously like brothers." Authors of the report warned against any encouragement by the central government to the Inner Mongols' autonomous tendency, maintaining that "the beneficiary will learn to appreciate the allowances from his patron only after the patron's power is established."[32]

GMD officials, however, did have an inkling about the difference between the postwar popular upsurge in Inner Mongolia and the prewar movement around Prince De. For instance, they asserted that autonomous aspirations were high in certain Mongolian areas not because the Inner Mongols longed for autonomy but because the "fainthearted Mongolian youth" had fallen for the "CCP's temptation," thus identifying the youth, not the traditional elites, as the core of the postwar movement. Unlike the CCP, whose knowledge about the popular character of the Inner Mongolian autonomous movement entailed the party's diligent effort to channel the mass movement into its own orbit, the GMD officials ironically used the knowledge to fortify their self-complacent attitude. Fu Zuoyi was the commanding officer of the GMD government's "takeover" operations in Suiyuan and Chahar. He did not believe that Inner Mongolia's autonomous movement deserved much attention because, as he once insisted to Jiang, "there is absolutely no problem among the Mongol princes of Suiyuan." In Manchuria, Xiong Shihui was of the same mind and was sternly opposed to a proposition that the

---

31. Jiang Jieshi to Wang Chonghui, 30 March 1946, GZWD, 004/144.1; Executive Yuan to the Civil Officers' Division of the National Government, 20 March 1947, GZD, 213/1212; Executive Yuan to Supreme Council of National Defense, 16 April 1947, GZWD, 004/144.3.

32. Congress of Suiyuan to Jiang Jieshi, 11 March 1946, ZD, 055/1657.

GMD government change its reliance on Mongol princes in managing Inner Mongolian affairs. He advised Jiang that "the gravity of the Mongolian society still rests on its honest members," meaning the upper echelon of the Inner Mongolian society.[33]

In sum, despite its resolutions and public statements on frontier matters at around the end of the war, the GMD government did not for a moment give up its invariable drive to forge a "Great Chinese Nation" (*da zhonghua minzu*) by assimilating non-Han peoples. Except for Outer Mongolia and Tibet, "self-government" for frontier non-Han peoples was qualified as "local," a term that in the GMD's official terminology meant merely communal autonomy below the county level. Under this definition, the Mongolian political council promised by the resolution of the GMD's second plenum, if ever established, would have been a mere titular body.[34] As a matter of fact, in early September 1945, just ten days after Jiang's well publicized speech, the Ministry of the Interior quietly modified the wording of its internal planning documents. The controversial phrase "high-degree self-government" was replaced with the conventional "local autonomy." The original use of the ethnic–territorially specific term "Inner Mongolia" was also replaced with a general term "frontier." Soon, the Executive Yuan (chamber) instructed its branches that the term "Inner Mongolia" be avoided altogether in government documents because it had been used by the Japanese in promoting the Inner Mongols' separation from China.[35] Thus, under the GMD's postwar statist drive, in the name of "restoration," even this originally China-centric term became politically incorrect.

Abortive "Restoration"

"Restoration" (*fuyuan*) was a term widely used in postwar China. Yet, to different groups of people, its meaning varied tremendously. To most Inner Mongols, "restoration" connoted the rollback of Chinese provinces in

33. "Society to Promote Restoration of Mongolian Banners in the Northeast" to the GMD Central Committee and Jiang Jieshi, 18 March 1947, GZD, 128/0233; Fu Zuoyi to Jiang Jieshi, 11 July 1946, JZZD/TW (EY), 6/35010309; Xiong Shihui to Jiang Jieshi, 12 August 1946, ZD, 055/1635.

34. *Zhonghua Minguo Shi Neizheng Zhi (Chugao)* (History of the Republic of China: A Chronicle of Domestic Administration), comp. Sinica Historica (Taipei: Guoshiguan, 1992), 32–44.

35. Ministry of Interior to the MTAC, 4 September 1945, QZH 141/3178; Executive Yuan to the Ministry of Foreign Affairs, 27 March 1946, WJB/YXS, 197.1.

Inner Mongolia and the establishment of an Inner Mongolian political entity according to the region's "original" ethnogeographic features. To GMD provincial and county officials concerned, the term meant the resumption of their prewar posts. And, to the GMD central authorities, the "restoration" of the Mongolian banners was actually an operation to expand its control because, before the war, its authority had never been able to reach all these banners. In this sense, the GMD government's Inner Mongolia policy became less about Inner Mongolian ethnicity than about Chinese nationalism. In other words, the GMD government's takeover operations in the northern frontier renewed the Chinese nationalists' Northern Expedition, which had started in the mid-1920s but fallen short of reaching its destination. For the GMD regime, however, the problem was that the CCP, a collaborator in the Northern Expedition of the 1920s, also revived its northward effort after Japan's surrender. This time it was the GMD's deadly competitor.

Pursuing a long-standing dream of national unification and battling along the way an "international communist fifth column," the GMD leadership found the theme of Chinese nationalism vitally important. This can be illustrated with an effort of Jiang Jieshi's in March 1948. At this difficult moment of the war against the CCP, Jiang used his small air force to carry out an airborne propaganda campaign, seeking to use "cardinal principles of righteousness" and "national consciousness" to censure the CCP and to expose it as a mere tool of Moscow. Later in the year, Jiang told his generals that "national consciousness can overcome the fifth column that relies on foreign influence," and that, therefore, the government troops must "strengthen their national consciousness and use the spirit of resistance against Japan to annihilate the bandits [meaning the CCP]."[36] Many years later, a former GMD official would recall the rigid and unimaginative policies of the GMD government in this period, saying that by sticking to Chinese nationalism, the GMD government tramped into a "dead-end street" and "could not strike out in new directions."[37] The diagnosis was certainly applicable to the GMD regime's postwar policies toward the Inner Mongols.

Typical of its propensity to rely on military approaches in solving complicated social-political problems, the GMD regime's initial operations for "restoring" Mongolian banners were appendages of its military thrust. Xiong

36. Zheng Wenyi to Jiang Jieshi, 7 March 1948, JZZD/GW (KLS), 13: 324; Jiang Jieshi's Speech at a Military Conference, 2 August 1948, JZZD/GW (KLS), 13: 391–94.
37. "Reminiscences of Chen Kuang-fu," Oral History Project of Columbia University (1961), 89.

Shihui, the commanding officer of the Northeast Field Headquarters (responsible for Manchuria and Rehe), and Fu Zuoyi, commander of the Twelfth War Zone (responsible for Suiyuan and Chahar), were the supreme authorities in their regions. Jiang Jieshi vested these two with tremendous authority in both civil and military affairs. Shortly after Japan's surrender, the GMD government abolished the administrative structure of Manchukuo and redivided Manchuria into nine provinces (three before Japanese occupation). At Xiong's headquarters, a "Northeast Committee on Recovery of the Mongolian Banners" was set up. In September 1945, the government adopted an act titled "Urgent Measures and Solutions in the Recovered Areas," under which "commissions of propaganda and consolation" (*xuan wei tuan*) and "commissions of propaganda and direction" (*xuan dao tuan*) were sent to Mongolian banners in Suiyuan, Chahar, Rehe, and Manchuria. These commissions were charged to convey to the local populace the "center's benevolent intentions," to issue emergency relief, to escort former league and banner officials back to their posts, to investigate Mongolian officials' wartime behavior, and to assist the government's chief regional officials in dealing with puppet organizations and restoring local order.[38]

All these steps were taken under the assumption that the so-call Mongolia problem was just a short-term effect of wartime politics. Presumably, when the government's political and military takeover was completed, the problem would either vanish or diminish. These steps were hurriedly put into place also to create an appearance of GMD control in Mongolian banners so that, it was hoped, it could prevent the Russians and the CCP from fishing in troubled water. These measures were bound to fail exactly because their precondition, the GMD's solid military control of the areas concerned, had not been established. Upon Japan's surrender, the GMD government was unable to get out of its seclusion in China's southwestern corner. Its influence with the Inner Mongols could not be established simply by sending to them propaganda teams. In addition, because of the uncertain military situation between the GMD and the CCP, many GMD appointees never

---

38. Jiang Kefu, *Minguo Junshi Shiluegao* (Brief Military History of the Republic of China), 4 vols. (Beijing: Zhonghua Shuju, 1987), 4(1): 7–8; Jiang Jieshi to Chen Bulei, 5 August 1945, GZWD, 003/3350; National Government's appointment of Xiong Shihui as Director of the Northeast Field Headquarters, 1 September 1945, *ZZSC*, 7(1): 34; National Government's Appointment of Governors of Nine Northeast Provinces and Two Mayors, 4 September 1945, *ZZSC*, 7(1): 36–37; "Urgent Measures and Solutions in Recovered Areas," September 1945, *ZZSC*, 7(4): 401.

reached their posts, and some Mongolian notables simply declined to accept GMD appointments. In a more fundamental sense, the GMD regime's measures would not be able to produce lasting results under any circumstances: They failed to directly address Inner Mongols' autonomous demands; these could not be appeased easily by the GMD's stated "benevolent intentions" and usually stalled relief operations.

A few months into peacetime, it became clear that the Mongolia question was not closer to a solution, and that the Soviets could not be directly blamed for it. The issue maintained its magnitude and momentum in the GMD's policymaking circles because the CCP seemed to have taken full advantage of the Inner Mongols' discontent. Therefore, in early 1946, the MTAC proposed a stopgap measure to tackle the problem from its ethnic roots. It was suggested that the administrative authorities of the Chinese counties and Mongolian banners in Inner Mongolia be clearly defined and separated. The assumption was that separation would reduce Han–Mongolian friction and consequently deprive the CCP of its opportunity to conduct anti-GMD agitation among the Mongols.[39] In making the proposal, the committee massively underestimated the difficulties that such a segregation operation would incur. By this time, many counties and banners had already become intricately intertwined, and, in some cases, counties and banners were just different names for the same areas. Therefore, in practice, a segregation program would only intensify, not alleviate, the county–banner conflict.

In mid-March 1946, the Mongolia question, especially the situation in eastern Mongolia, caused enough concern in the GMD government that an interdepartmental meeting was called to find solutions. Blaming the eastern Mongols for dividing the country, the participants in the meeting nevertheless admitted that a decision on Mongolian autonomy should not be delayed any longer. But the issue was so sensitive and controversial within the GMD government that—except for urging the Northeast Field Headquarters to speed up its takeover operations in Manchuria and to prevent the eastern Mongolian autonomous movement from spreading to the west—the meeting did not generate any new policy. Seeing no clear way out, Jiang Jieshi concluded that a solution to the Mongolia question would have to wait still longer.[40]

---

39. Wang Shijie and Xiong Shihui to Jiang Jieshi, November 1945, Waijiaobu Yataisi (Asian-Pacific Division of the Ministry of Foreign Affairs), 019.48; MTAC to the Administrative Bureau (of the Executive Yuan?), 28 February 1946, QZH 141/1080.

40. Luo Liangjian to Jiang Jieshi, 12 August 1945, ZD, 055/1653; Zhang Zhongwei to Luo Liangjian, 15 March 1946, and MTAC to the Executive Yuan, 20 March 1946,

But the issue could not stay on the back burner for long. In the spring of 1946, the Soviet troops left Manchuria and, consequently, an international restriction on the GMD–CCP conflict in the region was removed. In the two parties' ensuing military scramble for Manchuria, the GMD at first had the upper hand. By the summer of that year, having occupied all the major cities in southern Manchuria, the GMD forces pushed northward and at one point forced the CCP to abandon Harbin and Qiqihar. In Rehe, Chahar, and Suiyuan, the GMD forces also made progress. Before mid-October, Fu Zuoyi's troops entered Zhangjiakou, which since Japan's surrender had been the site of the CCP's Jin-Cha-Ji (Shanxi-Chahar-Hebei) Military District and Yun Ze's Inner Mongolian Autonomous Movement Association. A full-scale civil war between the GMD and the CCP was well under way, even though America's mediation effort under General George C. Marshall continued to linger for a while. On November 15, over the objection of the CCP and some other lesser parties, the GMD government confidently called into session a national congress to decide on a new constitution. Amid these seemingly encouraging developments, the time seemed to have arrived for the GMD regime to find a solution for the Mongolia question.[41]

In July 1946, Chen Cheng, the chief of staff of the Defense Ministry, contended to Jiang that reorganization of the government's frontier establishment was not only an urgent task for the present but would also have vital and lasting significance for the future. He proposed that the matter be considered immediately. Sharing Chen's sense of urgency, Jiang gave the task to the Supreme Council of National Defense (SCND), instructing the SCND to call a meeting of relevant ministries and departments to study the question of Mongolian autonomy and find a solution within ten days. The SCND passed the ten-day deadline without finding any solution.[42] In late August,

---

QZH 141/1060; Jiang Jieshi to Wang Chonghui, 22 April 1946, GZWD, 004/144.1. The conference involved MTAC, the Ministries of the Interior and Foreign Affairs, the Military Administrative and Military Ordinance Departments, and GMD Propaganda and Organizational Departments.

41. Jiang Kefu, *Minguo Junshishi Luegao* (Brief Military History of the Chinese Republic), 4 vols. (Beijing: Zhonghua Shuju, 1991), 4(1): 87–88, 105, 111, 180–86, 230–31; "Zhou Enlai's Press Release on the GMD's Opening of the National Congress, 16 November 1946," in *Zhou Enlai Yijiusiliu Nian Tanpan Wenxuan* (Selected Documents on Zhou Enlai's Negotiations in 1946), comp. Documentary Research Office of the CCP Central Committee and the CCP Committee of Nanjing (Beijing: Zhongyang Wenxian Chubanshe, 1996), 689–91.

42. Jiang Jieshi to Wang Chonghui, 27 July 1946, GZWD, 004/144.1.

another push for a decision came from the GMD's party organization. On the recommendation of the party's "supervisory committee on implementation of the second plenum resolutions," the GMD Central Committee's Standing Committee adopted a decision on overhauling the government's frontier establishment. The decision was again handed to the SCND for consideration. In September, Jiang gave the SCND and relevant ministries a week to complete their deliberation. But, once again, the second deadline passed without any result.[43]

The GMD government's tardiness in reaching a decision was due to an insurmountable internal disagreement on whether, or how much, concession should be made to the Inner Mongols. Officials from agencies directly involved in making Mongolian policies, such as the MTAC, the Ministry of Interior, the Executive Yuan, and the GMD's Organizational Department, were willing to make at least some symbolic concessions to the Inner Mongols. These agencies either had Mongolian appointees or shouldered the burden of reducing the discrepancy between the GMD's public statements and actual policies. The concessions under consideration included the elevation of Mongolian leagues to the same level as provincial governments, establishment of a Mongolian political council as a coordinating body for the Mongolian areas, appointment of more Mongol figures at the provincial and national levels of government, and reorganization of the MTAC into a full-fledged ministry. These, clearly, remained far distant from the kind of ethnopolitical reforms demanded by the Inner Mongols, who wanted first and foremost an autonomous territory under a Mongolian government.[44]

Even these minimal concessions proved unacceptable to another group of GMD officials. In opposition was a front of diehard "irreconcilables," including mainly officials of the Defense Ministry, the Department of Military Ordinance under the Military Council, and those responsible for executing the government's Mongolian policies in the field, namely, people like Xiong Shihui in Manchuria and Fu Zuoyi in Suiyuan and Chahar. As ever, in denying any true ethnic character in the Inner Mongols' demands, they directed their strongest objection to any concession to Inner Mongols at the

---

43. Organizational Department of the GMD to the Supreme Council of National Defense, 28 August 1946, GZWD, 004/144.2; Jiang Jieshi to Wang Chonghui, 23 September 1946, GZWD, 004/144.1.

44. Organizational Department of the GMD to the Supreme Council of National Defense, 28 August 1946, GZWD, 004/144.2; Jiang Jieshi to Wang Chonghui, 23 September 1946, GZWD, 004/144.1; Secretariat of the Executive Yuan to the MTAC, 22 November 1946, QZH 141/1085.

expense of the existing provincial structure. Categorizing Mongolian leagues and banners as medieval and ineffective administrative systems, they accepted no other policy alternatives than enforcement of political and cultural assimilation whenever and wherever possible.[45]

Fu proved the single most effective regional administrator and military commander in blocking the central government's move toward what he deemed an unwise frontier policy. Ever outspoken in contesting any "soft" Mongolian policies originating in central government agencies, he could in practice invalidate the central government's policy decisions by procrastination. In the summer of 1946, he delayed the government's deliberation of a plan for local Mongolian autonomy simply by not responding to the Executive Yuan's request for his comments on the plan. Then, in early 1947, the Executive Yuan adopted a legislation on the same issue and again asked him to second the act. Once again, he used his old tactic to interrupt the legislative procedure.[46]

Fu's ability to counteract the GMD central government's Mongolian policies revealed as much about the GMD's power structure as about its frontier policy. Originally a renowned general in Yan Xishan's "Jin-Sui" (Shanxi and Suiyuan) clique, which remained semi-independent from Jiang Jieshi over the years, Fu did not rally to Jiang until the late 1930s. Before the Japanese–American war began in the Pacific in 1941, Fu's troops won several battles against the Japanese-backed puppet army in Suiyuan and, during the rest of the war, he became Jiang's indispensable commander to keep the Japanese at bay in the area. At the war's end, Jiang needed Fu more than ever in "restoring" the central government's authority in Suiyuan, Chahar, and Rehe. Like any other strong local figure in the GMD power structure, Fu's strength lay in his regionalism, not his connection to the GMD center. The Mongolia question was not the first occasion in which he went his own way. His actual veto power on the Mongolia question was evidence of the fact that he and the center both knew that any decision on the matter could not be implemented without his cooperation. His notorious record against ethnopolitical reforms in Inner Mongolia made him one of the "frontier

45. Department of Military Ordinance to Wang Chonghui, 30 March 1946, GZWD, 004/144.1; Fu Zuoyi to Song Ziwen, 5 February 1946, GZWD, 004/144.1; Wang Wenhao to Wang Chonghui, 19 April 1946, GZWD, 004/144.1.

46. Fu Zuoyi to the National Government, 24 September 1946, ZD, 055/1632; *Wang Shijie Riji,* entry on 1 December 1946, 5: 436–37; MTAC Report on Important Works in 1947, QZH 141/3243; MTAC, "Plan for Important Central Work during the First Half of 1948," 27 January 1948, QZH 141/3200.

mandarins" most hated by the Inner Mongols. In the view of the Inner Mongols, the GMD central government's reluctance to overrule him made it an accomplice of the Mongol-phobic general.[47]

Jiang, who was more sensitive than any other top GMD leader to the need of maintaining the delicate balance between the center and the local forces, pushed the government to find a solution to the Mongolia question without sacrificing the central–regional balance of power. The balance was especially vital during the war against the CCP. Thus, in early November 1946, after his own deadline was ignored for the second time, Jiang readily approved a solution which, the SCND promised, would be a better alternative to the policies preferred by the two opposing groups discussed above. Although granting that both groups had good intentions, either to placate the "Mongolian situation" (*meng qing*) or to preserve the state's integrity, the SCND felt that neither offered a suitable remedy to the current problem. A proper solution had to pass two tests: It would have to promote Mongolian autonomy, and at the same time it would be able to preserve the existing administrative system at the provincial level.

Accordingly, the SCND offered a seven-point formula. The primary ingredient of the formula was to use a political accommodation scheme to dissuade Mongolian activists from pursuing their separatist agendas. The central and local governments should include more Mongol figures and "certain concrete authority" should be vested in these appointments. In lieu of the Mongolian political council sought by some Mongol petitioners, a "Mongolian local autonomy promotion committee" should be established to propagate the GMD doctrines and help implement local Mongolian autonomy within provinces. Once the leading Inner Mongols' thirst for power was satisfied, the SCND reasoned, the proposed stratagem would be able to induce the Inner Mongols to "lean inward and not fall into the temptation of the Soviet Union, Outer Mongolia, and CCP."[48] Jiang deemed the formula

47. Jiang Shuchen, *Fu Zuoyi Zhuanlue* (Biography of Fu Zuoyi) (Beining: Zhongguo Qingnian Chubanshe, 1990), 65–72, 75–101, 104–5, 113–19, 123–24; Secret Bureau to Jiang Jieshi, 1 August 1947, JZZD/GW (KLS), 39: 437; Investigation and Statistics Bureau of the GMD Central Committee to Jiang Jieshi, 11 February 1947, ZD: 055/1657; "A Brief Narrative of the 19 September [1949] Peaceful Uprising in Suiyuan," in *Suiyuan "Jiu Yi Jiu" Heping Qiyi Dang'an Shiliao Xuanbian* (Selected Archival and Historical Materials on the 19 September Peaceful Uprising in Suiyuan), comp. Inner Mongolian Archives (Hohhot: Neimonggu Renmin Chubanshe, 1986), 1–14.

48. Wang Chonghui to Jiang Jieshi, 7 November 1946, and Jiang Jieshi to the Supreme Council of National Defense, 19 November, 1946, GZWD, 004/144.2.

"feasible" and approved its implementation. But even with Jiang's support, the SCND did not get a chance to test its political-bribery scheme. Bai Chongxi, the defense minister, effectively intercepted the proposed policy measures by contending that the opinions of the Inner Mongols and, especially, of the provincial governments concerned should be consulted first.[49]

Unsurprisingly, the provincial authorities' opinions were that currently (late 1946 and early 1947) the government had even fewer reasons to worry about the Mongolia question than in the early postwar months. In a March 1947 report on work regarding Mongolian banners, Xiong Shihui's Northeast Field Headquarters listed many "achievements." Reportedly, in the past year or so the headquarters had implemented military, political, cultural, and economic measures in Mongolian areas without much difficulty. By the time of the report, according to the headquarters, "a great number of people from the puppet [meaning eastern Mongolian] and the bandit [meaning CCP] troops have rallied to the government, Mongol compatriots' (*mengbao*) determination to lean inward has become increasingly firm, and the puppet eastern Mongolian organization in Wangyemiao is on the verge of collapse." The only remaining problem was Yun Ze's group in western Mongolia, and it was "obviously incited and controlled by Outer Mongolia."[50]

The reality was that, having entered into a partnership with the CCP in the spring of 1946, the eastern Mongols pushed the CCP leadership into agreeing to establish a unified Inner Mongolian autonomous government. Such a government was set up in May 1947, and the event marked the Inner Mongols' "revolutionary independence" from the GMD government after the CCP model. The Inner Mongols finally obtained a unified government and were poised to reclaim Inner Mongolia's original area. But the development was an even greater victory for the CCP. In skillfully playing the autonomy card, the CCP consolidated its relationship with the eastern Mongols by co-opting them into accepting its own leadership. Thereby the CCP not only secured much needed strategic bases in western Manchuria and Rehe but also predetermined the Inner Mongols' position in the emerging Communist China.

The MTAC evaluated the situation more honestly than Xiong Shihui's

49. Wang Chonghui to Jiang Jiehsi, 13 April 1947, GZWD, 004/144.3; Xu Shiying's Memorandum on Principles for Local Mongolian Autonomy, 7 June 1947, ZD, 055/1632.

50. "Report on takeover in Northeast Mongolian banners," from Report by the Chairman of the National Government (Jiang Jieshi) on the Work of the Northeast Field Headquarters, March 1947, *ZZSC,* 7(1): 88–93.

office. In its yearly report for 1947, the committee pointed out that because of the intense struggle with the CCP, the government had to stop implementing certain measures intended to establish its authority among the Inner Mongols. One such measure was the government's "reform" attempt to collect from local Mongol officials old official seals that had been issued to them by the late Qing court. Despite the fact that traditional Mongol elites were largely swept aside by the turbulent events in recent years, both the GMD government and the old Mongolian ruling class still took the issue of seals seriously. Symbolic as the matter might look, the GMD government deemed it necessary to use new seals to demonstrate to the Inner Mongols that the GMD's long overdue authority finally arrived in the Mongolian areas. But the old Mongolian elites were deeply suspicious and wanted to keep the old seals as proofs of their own power and status. The government also had plans for further sinicization of the Mongolian banners through measures such as organized Han migration, readjustment of the relationship between the Mongolian banners and the Han counties, and promotion of economic development in Mongolian areas. All these were ethnically provocative in the first place, but it was the uncertainty caused by the GMD–CCP military conflict that effectively prevented their implementation.[51]

Between the summer of 1947 and the spring of 1948, the CCP successfully conducted a series of military operations in Manchuria. As a result, the GMD's military influence in the region diminished rapidly. Then, between September 1948 and January 1949, the CCP launched three massive offensives (the Liao-Shen, Huai-Hai, and Ping-Jin Campaigns) that effectively ended the GMD's power in Manchuria and North China. As accessories to the GMD's military policy in these areas, the GMD government's Mongolian measures had no chance of survival after the regime's military defeat.

The MTAC's reports in early 1948 already saw the writing on the wall. It was reported that since the GMD government had achieved "restoration" in forty-seven banners at one point or another, most of them had now re-

---

51. MTAC, "Report on Important Works of the MTAC in the Thirty-Sixth Year [1947]," n.d., QZH 141/3243; Central Planning Bureau, "National Defense Construction," 21 December 1943, Hsiung Shihui (Xiong Shihui) Collections, box 1. During the first few month of peace, the GMD government considered seriously a plan to move a few millions of Han people to fill in the "population blanks" in the vast northeastern and northwestern border regions. In late 1945, acting upon Jiang Jieshi's directive, the Executive Yuan proposed to move immediately 100,000 discharged troops to the northern border areas. It was also proposed that 20,000 households be moved to the northwest in the next five years.

turned to "chaos," meaning that they had "betrayed the state" again and rallied to the CCP. According to the committee's estimate, three tenths of the Inner Mongolian population, or approximately 600,000 people, had become refugees of war.[52] In March 1948, troubled by the inescapable bankruptcy of the government's "restoration" measures in Mongolian banners, Chen Lifu, the head of the GMD's Organization Department, wrote a letter to Jiang Jieshi, urging him to make an "early decision" on Mongolian autonomy "in order to pacify the Mongolian people."[53] But it was already too late for any "early decision," either on Inner Mongolian autonomy or on the GMD's own fate in China.

Nevertheless, during the last two years of its lingering on the mainland, the GMD government continued to fumble in vain for guiding principles to solve its Mongolian imbroglio. Even after the GMD government fled to Taiwan in late 1949 and thus lost any practical contact with Inner Mongolia, the MTAC would not become delinquent in its homework. For instance, in 1951, the committee drafted a "plan for temporary measures of frontier administration in case of a counteroffensive on the mainland." Typically, the plan proposed no countermeasures to the CCP's Inner Mongolian Autonomous Region but stingily offered to the Inner Mongols six league governments under a temporary "Mongolian political council in the battlefield."[54]

Elusive "Loyalists"

The reference to the "battlefield" in the MTAC's 1951 document indicated a belated admission by GMD officials that during the gruesome GMD–CCP scramble for North China and Manchuria, the GMD regime had suffered from a vital weakness in not having a functional contact with the Inner Mongols "in the battlefield." While the CCP enhanced its reputation and connection with the Inner Mongols through a group of deft Mongol and Han

---

52. Chu Minshan's Report on Work of the Committee on Restoration in Northeast Mongolian Banners, 4 March 1948, ZD, 055/1633; MTAC (Xu Shiying) to the Executive Yuan (Zhang Qun), 27 January 1948, QZH 141/3200; "MTAC' Report on Its Work in the Past Year," 14 April 1948, QZH 141/131. The figures are from the document by Xu Shiying. It is not clear whether they meant only the Mongols or the entire population also including the Han.

53. Chen Lifu to Jiang Jieshi, 3 March 1948, ZD, 055/0500.

54. MTAC, "Plan for Temporary Measures of Frontier Administration in Case of a Counteroffensive on the Mainland," December 1951, WJB/YXS, 019/48.

operatives under Yun Ze, the GMD authorities' image was constantly damaged by its own rigid policies and by "frontier mandarins" such as Fu Zuoyi and Xiong Shihui. At the beginning, the government indeed sent out some Mongol figures to the field. Bai Yunti (a.k.a. Serengdonrub), a longtime collaborator with the GMD, made a brief trip to the north with a "commission of propaganda and consolation." But he soon returned to the comfort of the capital without much accomplishment. The GMD government also used Li Shouxin and Wu Heling, two wartime collaborators with Japan, to turn their old subordinates into anti-CCP forces. The usefulness of these figures' military effort was limited, and their impact on GMD–Inner Mongolian relations, because of their wartime records, was detrimental rather than constructive.

After turning away the eastern Mongolian delegation in early 1946, the GMD government did not have any channel to influence the most popular and energetic movement in Inner Mongolia. During the rest of the Chinese Civil War, GMD policymakers' only Mongolian contact was a small group of Inner Mongols who were long-term residents in the capital. The phenomenon was indicative of two facts. First, the Inner Mongol elites were as divided as the Chinese politics characterized by the GMD–CCP conflict. Second, the GMD regime had its own Inner Mongol "loyalists," who were mostly elements brushed aside by the postwar Inner Mongolian autonomous movement.

During the Chinese Civil War, a small Mongolian pressure group in the GMD's capital, first Chongqing and then Nanjing, was conducting an old game of court politics reminiscent of the Qing period. In this period, there were probably several hundred Inner Mongols residing in the GMD areas, mostly in Peiping and Nanjing. These were Mongol officials in the GMD government, displaced aristocrats, unemployed and out-of-school students, and petitioners who came to the GMD-controlled areas after Japan's surrender. Bai Yunti and Rong Xiang were two leading figures among these people. Bai was a founding member of the Inner Mongolian People's Revolutionary Party in the 1920s and joined the GMD camp after the GMD/CCP split in 1927. As a member of the MTAC, Bai was one of the highest positioned Inner Mongols in the GMD government. Rong Xiang, the chief steward (*zongguan*) of Tumed Banner, Suiyuan, belonged to Inner Mongolia's traditional ruling class. During World War II, he played a role in the GMD's Mongolian policy as a leading member of the Suiyuan Mongolian political council. In the summer of 1946, to appeal to the GMD government for Inner Mongolian autonomy, Rong, along with some others from Mongolian banners in Suiyuan, Chahar, and Rehe, organized a "delegation from the anti-Japanese Mongolian banners to celebrate the government's victorious return to the capital." In May 1948, these Inner Mongols held their largest meeting in Nanjing, in which some 200 people assembled to discuss Inner Mongolian autonomy.[55]

In comparison with the Uigur and Tibetan figures in the GMD capital, the Inner Mongols were much better organized and were defter lobbyists in the GMD political arena. During the twentieth century, although no longer able to maintain a power position comparable to that in the Manchu–Mongolian dyarchy of the Qing period, the Inner Mongols at least held a more prominent position than other non-Han groups in China's central government. Many of them had a good Chinese education and some held high positions in the GMD regime. They were familiar with the political culture of the GMD and could craft memoranda either in elegant Chinese or in typical GMD jargon. While Yun Ze's group was negotiating between the Inner Mongols and the CCP to prepare for Inner Mongolian autonomy as a new basis of interethnic cooperation between the two sides, the Mongol lobbyists in the GMD court petitioned for a policy to redress the Inner Mongols' old grievances. On the ethnopolitical front, these two groups shared certain goals vis-à-vis the Chinese authorities, even though they represented very different forces within Inner Mongolian society.

Unsurprisingly, the Inner Mongols on the GMD side at most had a moderate social agenda, whereas those on the CCP's side were convinced that Inner Mongolia's national liberation had to be accompanied by a social revolution, and that the privileged old ruling class, to which many "GMD Mongols" belonged, must be abolished. The "GMD Mongols" stood on an impossible ethnopolitical ground—only by separating themselves from the autonomists in Inner Mongolia could they maintain a tenable loyalist position with the GMD authorities. But exactly because these Mongols lacked a popular basis in Inner Mongolia, the GMD authorities easily dismissed their petitions as self-seeking maneuvers that could be appeased with small personal favors.

During the postwar months, the Mongol petitioners stressed two themes in the GMD capital. First, as far as their attitude toward the GMD "central

55. Bai Yunti to Li Zongren, 23 December 1945, ZD, 055/1645; Guo Zichen's Report on the Inner Mongols' Meeting in the Capital, 10 May 1948, ZD, 055/1657; "Suiyuan in the War of Resistance," November 1940, *Daqingshan Kang Ri Youji Genjudi Ziliao Xuanbian,* 2: 384.

government" was concerned, the Inner Mongols remained "loyal" and "inwardly inclined" (*nei xiang*). Second, Outer Mongolia and the CCP were indeed making troubles in Inner Mongolia, but they were not the fundamental causes of the Inner Mongolian problem. The real causes, according to the petitioners, were the local Han authorities' tyrannical treatment of the Mongols and the central government's failure to honor its own long-standing promise to support the non-Han peoples' self-government (*zizhi*). Contrary to GMD officials' theory on an international communist conspiracy, the group suggested that the Inner Mongols' autonomous demand reflected a genuine ethnic aspiration. Failing to treat the demand as such, they warned, the GMD authorities would soon have on its hands a "second Outer Mongolia."[56]

Yet the GMD authorities acted as callously toward this "loyal" petition as toward the eastern Mongols' unauthorized autonomy. This finally compelled the "loyal" Inner Mongols to take more drastic action. In mid-October 1946, after sending a "joint declaration by all Inner Mongolian groups and organizations in the capital" to Mongolian banners in Rehe, Suiyuan, and Chahar, seven Inner Mongolian organizations in the capital selected ten representatives to bring their case to Jiang himself. The declaration listed a series of misgivings of the Mongolian people while focusing on the sufferings of the Inner Mongolian league–banner system from the expanding Chinese province–county structure. In discharging a volley of harsh criticisms against those "frontier mandarins," or GMD governors in frontier provinces, and holding them personally responsible for all the ills and sufferings of the Mongolian society, the petition made only a feeble complaint about the central government's tardiness in carrying out promises. The petitioners told Jiang that the situation in Inner Mongolia could be remedied only with the Inner Mongols' "unified autonomy."[57]

It may be recalled that about the same time, but under different circumstances, the eastern Mongols also made their demand to the CCP for a unified Inner Mongolian autonomous government. In contrast to the eastern Mongols' demands, the "loyal Mongols" in Nanjing had a rather conservative

---

56. Bai Yunti to the MTAC, 16 December 1945, QZH 141/1080; Jin Chongwei's Report, 31 May 1946, ZD, 055/1632; Rong Xiang et al. to Jiang Jieshi, 18 July 1946, ZD, 055/1637.

57. Bai Yunti to Li Zongren, 15 December 1945, ZD, 055/1645; Sechin Jagchid et al. to the Supreme Council of National Defense, 5 and 16 January 1946, *ZZSC*, 7(2): 333–34; Society of Fellow Mongols in Peiping to the Supreme Council of National Defense, 16 January 1946, ibid., 334–35; Bai Yunti et al. to Jiang Jieshi, 17 October 1946, ZD, 055/1655.

goal of "unified autonomy," which was to implement the aforementioned resolution passed by the second plenum of the GMD's sixth congress in March 1946. The resolution promised "restoration of the original political council on Mongolian local autonomy and a clear division of authority between the league–banner governments and the provincial–county governments." These petitioners believed mistakenly that the resolution could remove the provincial barrier between the GMD central authorities and local Mongolian governments, stopping short of demanding the organization of Inner Mongolia into a unitary autonomous region free from harassment by any Chinese provincial authorities. Anticipating difficulties in getting the GMD authorities' endorsement, the petitioners threatened that in the event of a rebuttal from the government, "all Mongolian banners' loyal [GMD] party members and activists who have participated in the war of resistance and national reconstruction will return to the grassland to share the same fate with our compatriots there and will no longer submit ourselves to the inhuman treatment."[58]

Clearly, the petitioners' audacity did not go beyond calling upon the GMD authorities to implement their own programs. Identifying themselves as "loyal" and "anti-Japanese," the group wanted to show the GMD regime that they were different from wartime collaborators with Japan and postwar fellow travelers with the CCP. Hence they posed no threat to the central government's sovereignty over Inner Mongolia. Limiting their efforts to the rejuvenation of the Inner Mongols' ethnic power embedded in the traditional league–banner system but showing no interest in socioeconomic reforms, the petitioners easily allowed GMD officials to view them as a group of old timers who were mainly concerned with their own privileges.

The GMD authorities' typical way of dealing with "loyal" Mongols was appeasement without meaningful concessions. Earlier, in mid-1946, after receiving a memorandum submitted by the Inner Mongols in the capital, Jiang allowed himself to be "shocked" only by the document's reference to the local GMD authorities' willful use of corporal punishment against Inner Mongols but not by its other complaints. He issued a stern order to reprimand the provincial and county authorities involved in these cases: "Prejudice against and illegal torture of Mongol compatriots are absolutely prohibited, and violators will be severely punished." Meanwhile, Jiang completely

58. Bai Yunti et al. to Jiang Jieshi, 17 October 1946, ZD, 055/1655; Investigation and Statistics Bureau of the GMD Central Committee to Jiang Jieshi, 11 February 1947, ZD, 055/1657.

ignored the memorandum's principal recommendations for policy changes.[59]
In late 1946, the similar approach was deployed to placate those Inner Mongol representatives who directly petitioned Jiang.

Jiang did not receive these representatives, Rong Xiang among them, until December. He conducted the interview by following an advice from Chen Bulei, one of his most trusted advisers: Although the Mongols needed to be encouraged and their demands promised consideration, Jiang must avoid expressing any consent on implementing the second plenum resolution. Not only refraining from endorsing the petitioners' demands, after the interview Jiang also instructed the GMD authorities in Suiyuan, Chahar, and Rehe to closely watch those Mongol activists who might be connected to the recent petition. In the meantime, the Investigation and Statistic Bureau of the GMD Central Committee (*zhongtong*), the twin agency of Dai Li's secret police (Investigation and Statistic Bureau of the Military Council, or *juntong*), devised a scheme to split the Mongols in the capital and isolate the leading figures.[60]

The "loyal" Mongols' threat to return to the grassland turned out to be a bluff. With their demands rejected, they nevertheless decided to stay on in the GMD capital and continued to hold inconsequential meetings and to file petitions. In 1949, when GMD rule in China was coming to an end, some of these Mongols would follow the ousted GMD regime to cross the Taiwan Strait, and some others would join Prince De in his last attempt to jump-start an autonomous movement in a remote location in northwestern China.[61] Although information is not available about how many Inner Mongols followed the GMD regime to Taiwan in 1949, it is clear that the most vigorous elements of the Mongol "loyalists" did not quit the stage of Chinese politics without trying to find a third alternative outside the GMD–CCP matrix.

In the postwar years, these people's activities were not limited to petitioning the GMD government for a change of its Inner Mongolian orientation. As will be discussed in chapter 8, a group of young Mongols organized a youth alliance and tried to enlist American support to what they termed a

59. Jiang Jieshi to Wang Chonghui, 20 July 1946, GZWD, 004/144.1.
60. Chen Bulei to Jiang Jieshi, 3 December 1946, JZZD/GW (KLS), 39: 405–7; reports by the Office of Investigation and Statistics on Mongolian banners, 27 January and 11 March, 1947, ZD, 055/1657; Jiang Jieshi to Dong Qiwu, Fu Zuoyi, and Liu (?), 3 March 1947, ZD, 055/1657; Secret Bureau to Jiang Jieshi, 6 April 1948, JZZD/GW (KLS), 10: 237–38.
61. Zhang Qun to the National Government, 17 April 1948, GZD, 241/0736; Demchugdongrob, "Autobiography," *NWZ,* 13: 164–65.

"racial movement." This thread of Inner Mongolian politics, as reflected in the eastern Mongols' search for assistance from Outer Mongolia and the Soviet Red Army in Manchuria, indicated the degree of mutual penetration among international, Chinese national, and ethnic-regional politics during the Chinese Civil War and the early Cold War. In comparison with any other moment in modern times, this period seemed to offer the Inner Mongols several options for political allies in a divided China and a confrontational international scene. In the end, however, the situation proved disadvantageous to the Inner Mongols, for it encouraged Mongolian groups of different political persuasions to seek their own ideological allies at the expenses of national unity.

To make their "racial movement" credible, the young Mongols in Nanjing and Beiping upheld Prince De as their leader. By making this choice, these "loyal" Mongols proved that their loyalty to the GMD regime was as equivocal as the regime's patronage of ethnic minorities was deceitful. Although sojourning silently in Beiping during the better part of the GMD–CCP war, Prince De was nevertheless viewed as the most important Inner Mongol by the GMD authorities. His treatment by the GMD government best illustrated the latter's fear of incurring an insolvent policy in tolerating the Inner Mongols' autonomist tendencies. Yet, in focusing on the prince and other upper-strata Mongolian figures as the objects of its Mongolian policy, the GMD regime lagged behind Inner Mongolian politics by at least a decade.

Conscious of the government's unpopularity among the frontier peoples, the GMD officials tended to believe that the CCP enjoyed an "invisible support" in the borderlands. At the end of World War II, Prince De, the most conspicuous individual in wartime Inner Mongolian politics, proved this assumption erroneous by leading his troops and associates to rally to the GMD side. Their collaboration with the Japanese was exonerated by a wartime act of the GMD government titled "Regulations on Rewards to and Settlement of Mongolian League and Banner Officials in the Front Who Returned with Subordinates," which was still in effect in the initial months of peace.[62]

---

62. Department of Military Ordinance, "A Brief Narrative on the Russian Revolution of 1917 and a Comparison between the Objective Conditions of the Russian Communist Party and Those of Our Country's Treacherous Puppets Now," 1942, Jiang Zhongzheng Zongtong Dang'an: Tejiao Dang'an (Fang Gong) (Archives of President Jiang Zhongzheng: Specially Submitted Documents [Defense against the Communists]), vol. 006; "Historical Materials on the Puppet Mongolian Army," *NWZ*, 38: 72, 81–82; Jiang Jieshi to the National Government, n.d., and enclosure, "Regulations on the Rewarding and

Prince De's rally, however, was not followed by a working relationship between him and the GMD regime. Instead, to the GMD authorities, this was an opportunity to put a tiger back into the cage.

The GMD authorities' negative veneration of Prince De was derived from a basic perception of Inner Mongolian society. The GMD authorities viewed ordinary Inner Mongols and their princely leaders as an "ignorant and inadequate" group unworthy of cooperation until they could be indoctrinated with "political consciousness and a sense of state." Accordingly, meaningful progress in Inner Mongolian communities was unlikely until a new generation of Inner Mongols could be nourished with the GMD ideology. Before such a new generation could be fostered, the GMD government saw no other alternative but to control the ruling princes. After World War II, the GMD officials still believed that Mongolian society revolved around these princes, even though this belief was contradicted by the reality of postwar Inner Mongolia and contradicted by liberal Inner Mongols in the GMD camp.[63] During its fierce fight against the CCP, the GMD government's effort to "win over" Mongol princes often entailed the latter's physical confinement within the government's reach. For instance, in the spring of 1946, Fu Zuoyi was concerned that Mongolian banner officials in Suiyuan and Chahar might be influenced by political agitation by the MPR and the CCP, so he moved most of them to Guisui (Hohhot) "for protection."[64] In this regard, Prince De was a more prominent case.

When the Japanese empire collapsed, Prince De's political star was eclipsed but did not fall completely. At least the Mongol princes continued to take their cue from him, and ordinary Mongols speculated and debated

---

Settling of Mongolian League and Banner Officials in the Front Who Return with Subordinates," GZD, 331/0001. By the end of the war, Prince De's regime had six regular cavalry divisions, three brigades, and a regiment, plus five "defense divisions" or local forces. Some of these dissolved upon Japan's surrender, and the ninth division and part of the seventh division went over to the Soviet-Mongolian Army. The "regulations" for exonerating Inner Mongols who had collaborated with Japan were not suspended until November 1945.

63. Counselors' Office of the Military Council to Jiang Jieshi, 30 December 1944, QZH 761 (JW) 171; MTAC Report on Recent Work, July 1945, QZH 141/128; Jiang Jieshi to Li Zongren, 30 March 1946, ZD, 055/1663; Xiong Shihui to Jiang Jieshi, 19 February 1946, JZZD/TW (EY), 6/35032144; Xu Yongchang to Jiang Jieshi, April 1946, and Xiong Shihui to Jiang Jieshi, 4 October 1946, JZZD/GW (KLS), 8: 79, 359; MTAC to Jiang Jieshi, 17 February 1946, QZH 141/1080; Organizational Department of the GMD to the Supreme Council of National Defense, 3 August 1946, GZWD, 004/144.2.

64. Fu Zuoyi to Jaing Jieshi, 25 March 1946, JZZD/TW (EY), 6/35023332.

among themselves in which direction the prince would turn once he recovered from his embarrassing failure in wartime collaborative politics. Some in the eastern Mongolian movement wanted to invite Prince De to Wangyemiao. The GMD and the CCP also competed secretly for his allegiance. In October 1945, even after Prince De had already gone over to the GMD, Yun Ze personally talked to the prince's wife in West Sunid, expressing a hope that the prince could return and work with the Mongolian people for the Mongolian nation's future. Only when it became clear that Prince De would not make the switch did the CCP begin to call him a "Mongol traitor" and try to purge his lingering influence among the Inner Mongols.[65]

In twentieth-century China, it was difficult for an ethnonationalist movement to maintain a purely ethnic political stand. Such a movement, always a weaker force challenging the dominant Chinese central authority, often sought to ally itself with a stronger foreign or rebellious Chinese force. The history of Inner Mongolian autonomy shows that in the historical confrontation between Chinese nationalism and foreign imperialism, the Inner Mongols could not avoid taking sides in advancing their own causes—in the Chinese–Japanese war of 1937–45, the GMD–CCP power struggle of 1945–49, and the superpower rivalry in post–World War II China.

Prince De, whose aristocratic background did not prepare him to be a master of mass movements, made side taking in China's military-political tumults the sine qua non of his political career. When Japan was defeated, members of Prince De's wartime regime were at a loss for what to do next. At first, Prince De acted in accordance with his ethnic instincts and made efforts to contact the advancing MPR army. When he found out that the Soviet–Mongolian army listed him as Japan's "running dog," he threw himself back into Jiang Jieshi's arms. Actually, during the war Prince De had maintained contacts with the Chinese government through Jiang's secret agents. At the war's end, Jiang's promise to give more freedom to non-Han

65. Oljeinaren, "In the Mighty Torrent of Inner Mongolia's Liberation Movement," *NWZ,* 50: 194–96; Demchugdongrob, "Autobiography," *NWZ,* 13: 138, 144–47; Zhao Tongru to Gao Gang, 27 August 1945, *Neimenggu Tongzhan Shi Dang'an Shiliao Xuanbian* (Selected Archival Materials on the History of the United Front in Inner Mongolia) (internal circulation, 1987), 1: 266; Bao Fuming, "Conversation between Ulanfu and Prince De's Wife," *Neimenggu Dang'an Shiliao* (Historical Archives of Inner Mongolia), 2 (1993): 62; "Ulanfu's Report on the Mongolian Work, July 1946," *Neimenggu Zizhi Yundong Liaohuhui Dang'an Shiliao Xuanbian* (Selected Historical Archival Materials on the Alliance of the Inner Mongolian Autonomous Movement) (Beijing: Dang'an Chubanshe, 1989), 94.

peoples, the GMD regime's alliance with the powerful United States, and Prince De's own anticommunist politics were factors affecting his action. In the end, in terms of his quest for Inner Mongolian autonomy, Prince De's decision to rally to the GMD side in postwar Chinese politics proved one more disaster following his wartime collaboration with Japan.[66]

In late August 1945, Prince De first traveled to Peiping, and from there he proceeded to Chongqing to petition Jiang Jieshi for Inner Mongolian autonomy. During September, he met with Jiang twice and also lobbied other GMD leaders. Throughout their meetings, Jiang maintained a polite posture but was firm and clear on a point that at least for the moment Mongolian autonomy could not be properly included in the government's agenda. Jiang also advised Prince De to keep a low profile, clearly telling the prince not to involve himself in the vortex of postwar Inner Mongolian politics. Yet merely by petitioning Jiang, Prince De had already caused some GMD officials in the capital to view him as one who "has steeped in evil yet refuses to repent." In detecting the Mongol prince's "untamed wild heart," these officials advised Jiang that he must never be allowed to enter Mongolian politics again. Consequently, Prince De was kept in Chongqing until November, while his two wartime associates, Li Shouxin and Wu Heling, were immediately sent to Rehe and Manchuria to collect their old troops or to carry out "comforting" missions. During the next three years, Prince De's residence was moved to Peiping, where he lived under the secret police's close surveillance.[67]

During his first one and a half years in Peiping, Prince De heeded Jiang's warning and kept a low profile. He seemed to have accepted his fate as an involuntary houseguest of the Juntong and was content with a monthly pension of 500,000 yuan. In Nanjing, Jiang did not forget the prince and regularly read the Juntong's reports on the prince's activities. According to one of these reports, Prince De led a simple and destitute life. He studied Buddhist scripts every day and met only occasionally with Inner Mongols from the north. Then, beginning with the midsummer of 1947, probably incited by the establishment of the Inner Mongolian autonomous government under

66. Demchugdongrob, "Autobiography," 95–102, 135–36, 138.
67. Chen Shaowu, "The Relationship between Jiang Jieshi and Demchugdongrub," *NWZ,* 1: 50–51; Demchugdongrob, "Autobiography," 138–42; Shen Zhongyuan, "The Jiang Jieshi clique and Demchugdongrob's Reactionary Inner Mongolian Force," *NWZ,* 15: 131–34; Department of Military Administration to the MTAC, 30 September 1945, QZH 141/1202; *Tang Zong Riji,* entries on 8 September and 31 December 1945, 538, 569; MTAC to Li Shouxin, 18 October 1945, QZH 141/1202; Xiong Shihui to Jiang Jieshi, 4 October 1946, JZZD/GW (KLS), 8: 79, 359.

Yun Ze, Prince De seemed tired of his Buddhist life aloof from worldly matters. During the next one and a half years, Juntong's reports covered his open
and secret activities aimed at pressuring the GMD government to make
concessions over Inner Mongolian autonomy. Fearing that Beiping was becoming a new "center of the Inner Mongolian independence movement," the
GMD authorities called upon some "more loyal" Inner Mongols to counter
Prince De's influence. Yet, at the time, the GMD government could not even
keep secondary figures such as Wu Heling in line. After finding out that he
was under surveillance by the secret police, Wu used the discovery to bargain recklessly with the embarrassed GMD authorities for a high position
in the central government. Annoyed by Wu's self-serving behavior but unwilling to openly offend "loyal" Inner Mongols, Jiang Jieshi ordered his
subordinates to "find a way fast to deal with this guy."[68]

When 1949 began, the GMD's influence in North China declined rapidly. For fear of being left behind in a CCP-controlled territory, Prince De
flew to Nanjing and met with Jiang for the last time. On the occasion, in
responding to the prince's old theme of Inner Mongolian autonomy, Jiang
remarked: "If the CCP cannot be terminated, there will be no more nations
and states." But to Prince De, the GMD government's disarray was his opportunity to get away from Juntong's grip. In April, he traveled a long way
to Dingyuanying (today's Bayanhot), the site of Alashan Banner in Ningxia
and a dilapidated town of 3,000 residents. Unrepentant as ever about his
ambition to lead an autonomous Inner Mongolia, Prince De immediately
started to make preparations for a Mongolian government. Privately, he
praised Yun Ze for unifying the Inner Mongols into a coherent force, though
regretting that Yun Ze took a wrong path in cooperating with the CCP. His
own path was, however, by no means clear. Lacking meaningful support
from the local people, Prince De soon felt that he again had to turn to his
nemesis, the GMD government, for recognition and assistance.[69]

68. MTAC to Jiang Jieshi, 10 November 1945, and Jiang Jieshi to the Committee,
19 November 1945, QZH 141/1202; Secret Bureau to Jiang Jieshi, 5 July 1947, JZZD/
GW (KLS), 39: 430; Secret Bureau to Jiang Jieshi, 1 August 1947, JZZD/GW (KLS),
39: 433; Xu Shiying to Jiang Jieshi, 9 August 1947, JZZD/GW (KLS), 39: 437; Secret
Bureau to Jiang Jieshi, 9 September 1947, JZZD/GW (KLS), 39: 438; "Information about
Prince Te's Promotion of Inner Mongolian Autonomy and the Background and Activities of the Society for the Assistance of Mongolian Banners' Restoration," 30 March
1948, ZD, 055/1657; Yu Jishi to Jiang Jieshi and Jiang's handwritten directive, 17 June
1948, JZZD/GW (KLS), 39: 446–47.

69. He Zhaolin, "The Beginning and the End of the Western Mongolian Autonomous
Movement," *NWZ*, 1: 6–7, 15–16; Demchugdongrob, "Autobiography," 142, 156–64;

The last episode of the GMD–Prince De melodrama was brief. In May 1949, after setting up a preparatory committee for his government in Ding-yuanying, Prince De traveled to Guangzhou (Canton) to plea his case with the GMD government, which was on the run. There he got support from Bai Yunti, who briefly assumed the chairmanship of the MTAC. He also obtained a small amount of money and some light weapons from Zhu Jiahua, then vice president of the Executive Yuan. In addition, as will be discussed in chapter 8, he received some encouragement from American diplomats in Guangzhou.

In the main, however, the prince's visit to Guangzhou was a chilling experience. He was severely berated by Yan Xishan, an old foe who had recently become the president of the Executive Yuan. Refuting the prince's reference to Sun Yat-sen's Three People's Principles as a justification of Inner Mongolian autonomy, Yan lectured the prince that the late GMD leader's "principles" must not be confused with "policies." Prince De's principal purpose for making the trip, an official GMD endorsement of his activities in Dingyuanying, was not achieved. Rebuffed but undaunted, the recalcitrant prince went back to the northwestern desert and launched his government anyway. At the time, already putting one foot in the East China Sea to cross the Taiwan Strait, the GMD government could no longer restrain Prince De, other than fuming internally that his action violated the Chinese Republic's constitution. In this manner, the GMD and Prince De staged their last standoff widely apart from each other, and both would soon be swept away by the unstoppable power of the CCP.[70]

Dalizhaya, "Ma Hongkui's Brutal Exploitation and Suppression of the Alashan Banner," *NWZ*, 1: 1–5. According to He Zhaolin, the GMD government did make a feeble effort to persuade the prince to go to Qinghai but not further north.

70. Demchugdongrob, "Autobiography," 156–64, 165, 170, 172, 182–85, 189–211; Bai Yunti to He Yingchin, 24 May 1949, QZH 141/1048; MTAC to the Northwestern Field Headquarters, 3 July 1949, QZH 141/1049; W u Heling, et al. to the MTAC, 20 August 1949, QZH 141/1049; Memorandum by the Mongolian Branch of the MTAC, 2 October 1949, QZH 141/1089; Wang Duo, *Wushi Chunqiu* (Fifty Eventful Years) (Hohhot: Neimenggu Renmin Chubanshe, 1992), 386–87; "Special Issue of Historical Materials on Dalizhaya and His Wife Jin Yuncheng," *Bayannuo'er Wenshi Ziliao* (Literary and Historical Materials of Bayannuo'er), 9: 140–45; Lu Minghui, *Menggu "Zizhi Yundong" Shimo* (The Beginning and End of the Mongolian "Autonomous Movement") (Beijing: Zhonghua Shuju, 1980), 359–409. Prince De left Dingyuanying in late September, refusing to accept "liberation" by CCP's troops. After wandering for awhile in the desert, he and a few followers entered the territory of the MPR, hoping that Mongols would treat Mongols well. But he was soon arrested by the MPR government and

The GMD regime's postwar ethnopolitics with regard to the Inner Mongols proved counterproductive to its own principal objective, which was to establish once and for all the central government's authority throughout China. The GMD's loss of the Inner Mongols' support in a critical strategic region bridging North China and Manchuria created opportunities for its deadly enemy, the CCP. The connection between the GMD's failures in the ethnopolitical arena and in the battlefield should be clear. As history has shown, after being ousted from Manchuria and North China, the GMD government's days in China were numbered.

A conclusion can therefore be drawn from this episode: Even to a Han-centric government like the GMD regime, "peripheral" problems actually assumed central importance, and "gray" areas like ethnic borderlands were not obscure but dangerously obtrusive. This was so in spite of the GMD regime's diligent effort to eradicate the nationality question from China's social and political life. In the final analysis, the "peripheral" questions in the "gray" frontier regions were always at the very hub of Chinese nationalist ideology and played a defining role in the formation of China's self image. This was true for both the GMD and the CCP. Though by and large sharing a conception about China as far as its "hard," international borders were concerned, the two parties' different approaches toward the "soft boundaries" between the Han and non-Han peoples proved consequential to their competing claims to China's political power.

During the Chinese Civil War of 1945–49, one of the most intense power struggles in Chinese history, the GMD, as the official power holder of China, seriously erred in denying the genuine ethnic character of the Inner Mongolian autonomous movement. Instead, having just signed Outer Mongolia away and being threatened by the CCP, the GMD government became readily suspicious of the origins of the concurrent Inner Mongolian movement. When Chinese society was in a revolutionary upheaval, the Inner Mongols were conducting their own revolution and could hardly maintain a neutral or purely ethnonationalist stand without becoming entangled in China's mainstream politics. Indeed, after the CCP-sponsored Inner Mongolian Autonomous Government was established in May 1947, the autonomous movement in Inner Mongolia finally turned partisan in the Chinese

---

expatriated to the People's Republic of China in September 1950. In 1964 he was pardoned by Beijing and assigned to the Inner Mongolian House of Historical Literature (Neimenggu Wenshiguan). He completed a self-deprecating autobiography between mid-1963 and the spring of 1966. He died of an illness in May 1966.

sense, and Inner Mongolia was lost to the GMD government for all practical purposes. Yet the continued policy debates within the GMD government and the existence of a group of "loyal" Inner Mongols in the GMD regions indicated that other courses of action were still possible for the GMD regime. Ethnocentrism, rigid ideology, and the awkward power structure of the regime prevented it from taking even a tiny step toward meaningful ethnopolitical reforms in China. As shown in the episode of Prince De, it was remarkable that top GMD officials did not relax their defense of their government's "central authority," even when the government itself was heading toward a permanent peripheral position in Taiwan. In retrospect, the GMD's intransigence about Chinese political centrality only benefited its Communist successors.

7

"Liberation": The Chinese Communist Party's Interethnic Approach

According to the official history of the People's Republic of China, its system of "minority nationalities' regional autonomy" began in 1947 with the establishment of the Inner Mongolian Autonomous Government. That event has been acclaimed as a model of the Chinese Communist Party's successful application of Marxist-Leninist theory on the "national question" to the Inner Mongolian situation, or the Chinese Communist Party's (CCP's) achievement in leading the Inner Mongols to embark on the "correct road to national liberation." Unsurprisingly, according to this historiography, the spontaneous Inner Mongolian autonomous movement in the postwar years automatically falls into the "incorrect" category and its historical significance is hardly acknowledged. This party-line history can be so rigid that even the CCP's own Inner Mongolian operation, or "Mongolian work" in the party jargon, has been carefully treated so as to conceal its intricate and often contradictory features. Much, therefore, is yet to be said about the CCP's postwar relationship with the Inner Mongols.

Referring to the period between 1945 and 1949 in China as the Chinese Civil War may oversimplify the extremely complex political processes of postwar China. From this study's perspective, at least three simultaneous contests involving six conflicting sides need to be examined: the power struggle between the Guomindang (GMD, Nationalist Party) and the CCP, the hegemonic rivalry between the Soviet Union and the United States, and the ethnopolitical conflicts between centralizing Chinese nationalism and several autonomy-seeking non-Han ethnonationalisms. These struggles became hopelessly intertwined. Together, they created a "Rubic's Cube effect" in China's postwar political arena. A definition of that popular puzzle reads:

The challenge in solving the Rubic's Cube comes from the fact that each move affects one third of the puzzle pieces, so even after you work hard to fix the first layer you have to temporarily "mess" it up in order to fix other layers. The trick is to find sequences of moves which allow you to manipulate a smaller number of pieces at any one time.[1]

From China's postwar contests, the CCP eventually emerged a winner not because it was able to manipulate all the "layers" and fix all the "sides" of the puzzle. But the CCP did manage to avail itself of opportunities to prioritize its objectives, and it made fewer missteps than its adversaries in postwar China's multilateral contests.

Inner Mongolian ethnopolitics in the postwar years presented both opportunities and challenges to the CCP. In these years, as the CCP made its final dash toward national power in China, Inner Mongolia existed as a singularly important area. Militarily, the area was vital to the CCP's strategy for controlling Manchuria, which would finally decide the CCP's victory in China. Politically, Inner Mongolia was the CCP's first arena of engaging in intricate interethnic and frontier politics. The experience would help shape the territorial and ethnographic structure of the future Communist China. A seasoned revolutionary force, the CCP was nevertheless ill prepared for Inner Mongolia. At the beginning, the CCP leadership was caught in a surprise by the Inner Mongols' spontaneous autonomous movement. The CCP's eventual success in co-opting the Inner Mongols into its orbit therefore came only after a learning process for the party.

In its ethnopolitical competition with the GMD in Inner Mongolia, the CCP's principal advantage was not communist ideology but pragmatism. At different times, various aspects of the Inner Mongolia question, such as state sovereignty, national power, ethnic equality, and social justice, were prioritized in CCP policies to achieve opportunely "proper" stances. In the meantime, the CCP never deviated from its strategic goals of replacing the GMD as the ruling party of China and reasserting China's internal and external sovereignties to their fullest meanings.

1. See http://www.csua.berkeley.edu/~innami/rubic/frame2.html.

Decide on a Strategy

During China's war against Japan, Mao Zedong told his comrades that "we must capture China" after this war.[2] When Japan surrendered in August 1945, however, the CCP's chance to "capture" China remained murky, even after its phenomenal wartime expansion.[3] It should be noted that as of the end of war, the CCP's geostrategic position in China had not improved in any fundamental way since its Long March in the mid-1930s. It remained a force in China's impoverished northwestern corner. Although during the Sino-Japanese war the CCP managed to enlarge its northwestern base and to insert a number of guerrilla enclaves behind Japanese lines in eastern and southern China, these territorial gains were too scattered to improve the CCP's geostrategic situation. In mid-1945, Mao defined the CCP base in northern Shaanxi as a "foothold and a departure point."[4] Having served as a haven of survival for the CCP in the past decade, the base's economic backwardness and geographic remoteness from the hubs of modern China could handicap the CCP's contention for power in the future.

Yan'an had two strategic options from its northwestern position. One was a full-scale competition with the GMD in taking over Japanese-occupied territories in both northern and southern China. The degree of this strategy's success would decide the extent to which the CCP was able to replicate Japan's wartime strategic posture. Although this was Yan'an's initial preference, the CCP leadership soon realized that without a modern army, it was not in position to repeat Japan's urban-centered strategy. The GMD–Soviet treaty of August 1945 dashed Yan'an's hope for modernizing its troops with material assistance from Moscow. A self-reliant and less ambitious strategy had to be devised, which must have a regional priority and be supplemented

2. Cited in Yang Kuisong, *Zhongjian Didai de Geming* (A Revolution in the Intermediate Zone) (Beijing: Zhonggong Zhongyang Dangxiao Chubanshe, 1992), 391.

3. Chen Lian, *Kang Ri Genjudi Fazhan Shilue* (A Brief History of the Growth of the Anti-Japanese Bases) (Beijing: Jiefangjun Chubanshe, 1987), 4–5.

4. "Mao Zedong's Report on the Working Orientation of the Seventh Congress, 21 April 1945," *Zhonggong Zhongyang Wenjian Xuanji* (Selected Documents of the CCP Central Committee; hereafter *ZZWX*), 15: 102–3; "Center's Directive to the Xiang-E-Gan Party Committee on the Strategy of Establishing Southern Bases, 24 June 1945," ibid., 171–73.

with political maneuvers.[5] As a result, Manchuria, Rehe, and Chahar were marked out as the first prizes to seize. In late August 1945, the CCP Central Committee (CCPCC) ordered its troops in Shandong and the Jin-Cha-Ji (Shanxi-Chahar-Hebei) area to enter Manchuria, Rehe, and Chahar immediately because these areas were distant from the GMD power center and close to Soviet help. Restrained by the recent Sino-Soviet treaty, Soviet assistance could not be offered to CCP troops openly. Still, the CCP leadership expected the Soviet forces in Manchuria to act sympathetically toward the Chinese comrades. As for Rehe and Chahar, because they were not covered by the Sino-Soviet treaty, CCP leaders considered them fair game.[6]

Still, the CCP's military strategy did not become firmly anchored in the northern direction until Mao, beseeched by Joseph Stalin, went to Chongqing to negotiate with Jiang Jieshi for peace. At the time, Stalin was worried that a Chinese civil war would be detrimental to both the militarily weaker CCP and to the Soviet–U.S. relationship in Asia. The political maneuvering in Chongqing compelled the CCP to withhold a southern pincer of military operations. In mid-September, the CCPCC settled for a national strategy of "advance in the north and defense in the south." Scrambling for Manchuria, Rehe, and Chahar thus became its highest priority. To make its negotiation stance in Chongqing convincing, the CCP leadership was prepared to withdraw its forces from a vast region in southern China. But the concession would hinge on Jiang's acceptance of the CCP's predominance in North China. Unsurprisingly, this proposed division, albeit a momentary one, of China's internal sovereignty was unacceptable to Jiang. Nonetheless, while the Chongqing negotiations were still stumbling ahead, the CCP began to move its main forces south of the Yangtze River toward Manchuria.[7]

5. "Center's Decision on Our Party's Tasks after Japanese Surrender, 11 August 1945," *ZZWX,* 15: 228; "CCP Center's and CCP Military Committee's Directive on the Revision of Strategic Orientation: Current Policy Stresses the Seizure of Small Cities and the Vast Countryside, 22 August 1945," ibid., 243; "Center's Directive on Conduct of Legal Struggles in GMD-Occupied Big Cities and Important Transportation Lines, 29 August 1945," ibid., 256.

6. "Center's Directive on Rapid Entry into the Northeast and Control of the Vast Countryside and Medium and Small Cities, 29 August 1945," *ZZWX,* 15: 257–58.

7. "CCPCC's Telegram to the CCP Delegation to the Chongqing Negotiations on the Determination of a Strategic Orientation of Advance in the North and Defense in the South, 17 September 1945," *ZZWX,* 15: 278–80; "CCPCC's Directive to the Central China Bureau on the Question of Withdrawing Troops from the South of the [Yangtze] River and Marching Northward, 20 September 1945," ibid., 286–87; Office of Documentary Study of the CCP Central Committee, *Mao Zedong Nianpu* (Chronicle of Mao Zedong's

Eventually, what began as Yan'an's reluctant strategic readjustment would prove a realistic and masterful move. The essence of the strategy, as spelled out by Huang Kecheng, a CCP strategist, was to "give up some territories voluntarily (though guerrilla warfare will continue), concentrate the main forces for decisive battles, and create a large, integral strategic base (that includes railroads and cities)." Only by creating such a new powerful "general base" in Manchuria, which would be buttressed by other strongholds in North China, could the CCP fundamentally change its weak, northwestern posture and force the GMD government to make meaningful concessions. In addition, the new orientation would allow the CCP to maintain its strategic self-reliance and to prevent an "extremely dangerous" tendency within the party of "depending on negotiations or international interference" to achieve peace. As the Mao–Jiang talks continued, the CCP's withdrawal from the south was carried out with great fanfare for propaganda purposes. Meanwhile, the northern advance was implemented in secrecy. The approach at once satisfied international and domestic desires for peace in China and proceeded to deploy CCP troops in a geostrategic location from which the Manchus and the Japanese had prepared their southward conquests.[8]

Earlier, Mao informed his party that the economically highly developed Manchuria would be vitally important to the CCP's "regularization" (*zhengguihua*), meaning its transformation from an agrarian and rural-oriented revolutionary movement into a ruling party based in industrial and urban centers. Yet, Manchuria was first and foremost attractive to the CCP because of its geostrategic advantages. In an August conversation with Mao, Liu Shaoqi summarized these advantages in this way: Mongolia, the Soviet Union, and Korea were the western, northern, and eastern neighbors of the region, all friendly toward the CCP; and even though under current international conditions the Soviet Union could not provide aid to the CCP, the CCP's forces, once positioned in Manchuria, would achieve secure flanks and face the enemy from only one direction, the south.[9]

Life; hereafter *Mao Zedong Nianpu*) (Beijing: Zhongyang Wenxian Chubanshe, 1993), 3: 7, 9, 10–12, 14–16; Shi Zhe, *Zai Lishi Juren Shenbian: Shi Zhe Huiyilu* (At the Side of a Historical Giant: Shi Zhe's Memoir) (Beijing: Zhongyang Wenxian Chubanshe, 1995), 307–8.

8. "Huang Kecheng's Proposal about the Current Situation and Strategic Orientations, 14 September 1945," *ZZWX*, 15: 282–85;"Center's Directive on Our Party's Tasks and Orientations after the Double Ten Agreement, 12 October 1945," ibid., 324–25.

9. *Mao Zedong Nianpu,* 2: 600, 601, 603–4; Shi Zhe, *Zai Lishi Juren Shenbian,* 307.

Liu's estimation of Manchuria indicated that in formulating their military strategy in China's forthcoming civil war, the CCP leaders consciously made geopolitical calculations informed by an understanding of postwar international bloc politics. In his conversation with Mao, however, Liu did not mention that the western flank of Manchuria would be safe only if the CCP could also control Inner Mongolia. A strategic linkage between Inner Mongolia and Manchuria had already been demonstrated in the Japanese Kwantung Army's westward expansion from Manchuria in the 1930s. In seeking a satisfactory "zone contiguous to Manchuria," the Japanese pushed westward until they captured Guisui (Hohhot) and Baotou in Suiyuan (western Inner Mongolia).[10] In the war years, the CCP made arduous efforts to maintain a guerilla base in the Daqingshan range close to the military fault line between Japanese and GMD forces in Suiyuan. At the time, the purpose was to keep an Inner Mongolian corridor open between the Mongolian People's Republic (MPR) and the CCP's northern Shaanxi base. These efforts eventually paid off. In the final stage of the war against Japan, CCP troops were able to expand rapidly in Rehe, Chahar, and Suiyuan in collaboration with the invading Soviet–MPR army.[11]

Yet, after the war, as the CCP's strategic center was shifting from northern Shaanxi to Manchuria, the significance of Inner Mongolia changed from

10. James W. Morley, ed., *The China Quagmire: Japan's Expension on the Asian Continent, 1933–1941* (New York: Columbia University Press, 1983), 216, 217, 318–20.

11. Chen Lian, *Kang Ri Genjudi Fazhan Shilue,* 66–72; Zhou Shidi and Gan Siqi to Yao Ji et al., 20 August 1942, in *Daqingshan Kang Ri Youji Genjudi Ziliao Xuanbian* (Selected Materials on the Anti-Japanese Base in the Daqing Mountains) (Hohhot: Neimenggu Renmin Chubanshe, 1987), 1: 94; "Sui-Meng Military District's Order on Military Operations before the Signing of the Instrument for Japanese Surrender, 12 August 1945," ibid., 491–93; "Yan'an Headquarters' Order Number Two, 11 August 1945," *ZZWX,* 15: 219; "Yan'an Headquarters' Order Number Three, 11 August 1945," ibid., 220; "Military Committee's Directive to He Long and Others on Controlling the Entire Sui-Cha-Re Territories with All Efforts, 30 August 1945," ibid., 260–61; Office of Documentary Research of the CCP Central Committee, *Liu Shaoqi Nianpu* (Chronicle of Liu Shaoqi's Life; hereafter *Liu Shaoqi Nianpu*) (Beijing: Zhongyang Wenxian Chubanche, 1996), 1: 490–91; "Center's Telegram to the CCP Delegation to the Chongqing Negotiations on the Determination of a Strategic Orientation to Advance in the North and to Defend in the South, 17 September 1945," *ZZWX,* 15: 278–80; "Center's Telegram to the CCP Negotiation Delegation to Chongqing on Current Situation and Arrangements, 26 September 1945," ibid., 295. The last two documents indicate that in September 1945 the Soviet–Mongolian command in Rehe and Chahar demanded three times that the CCP take over the territories under its control, including important cities like Chengde and Chifeng.

a northerly route of international communication to a westerly buffer for domestic defense. Until the GMD thrust into Manchuria and North China could be irreversibly frustrated, Inner Mongolia would remain strategically crucial to the CCP. After the abortive Mao–Jiang negotiations, Yan'an continued to cultivate international and domestic sympathy in pursuing "peaceful transition" in GMD-controlled southern China while striving to achieve "exclusive control" (*duzhan*) in Manchuria and superiority in North China. The success of this two-pronged stratagem would depend on whether or not the seaports of Manchuria in the east and Inner Mongolia in the west could be sealed to deny GMD troops any access to Manchuria.[12]

Therefore, by November, the CCP leaders' plan for monopolizing Manchuria had proven untenable. CCP troops' "transportation warfare" (destruction of roads, bridges, and railways) outside Manchuria only slowed down but did not stop the GMD forces' northward movement via land. Meanwhile, a large number of GMD troops were transported to the north via sea and air with American assistance. The CCP could not get similar assistance from the Soviet Red Army, which at the time took a bystander's position in the brewing GMD–CCP war for Manchuria. In late October, the CCPCC urgently requested the Soviet Red Army's assistance in blocking GMD troops' landing on Manchuria from the sea and the air. The Soviets were sympathetic and used various excuses to delay the GMD landing. But Stalin would not allow his treaty with Jiang and his understandings with Western leaders about China to collapse over the CCP's plan for Manchuria. Bound by the recent Sino-Soviet treaty, the Soviet Red Army was obliged to turn Manchurian cities under its control over to the GMD authorities.[13]

12. *Liu Shaoqi Nianpu*, 1: 495–96, 498, 499; "Military Committee's Directive on the Strategic Orientation and Concrete Deployment in the Northeast, 28 September 1945," *ZZWX*, 15: 299–301; "Military Committee's Directive on Thorough Destruction and Control of Railways and Highways in Order to Delay the Movement of Jiang's Troops, 29 September 1945," ibid., 306–7; "CCPCC's Directive to the Northeast Bureau on the Strategic Orientation and Deployment in the Northeast, 2 October 1945," ibid., 309–10; "CCPCC's Directive to Peng Zhen, Chen Yun et al. on the Question of Preventing the GMD Army from Entering the Northeast, 16 October 1945," ibid., 351–52; "CCPCC's Directive to the Northeast Bureau on Concentrating the Main Force to Block Jiang's Troops' Landing, 19 October 1945," ibid., 364–66; "CCPCC's Directive on the Situation and Tasks during the Transition Period, 20 October 1945," ibid., 370–72.

13. "CCPCC's Directive on Conduct of Transportation Warfare in Order to Stop the Advance of the GMD Army, 15 October 1945," *ZZWX*, 15: 345–48;"CCPCC's Directive to the Northeast Bureau on Controlling the Northeast with All Forces and Blocking Jiang's Troops' Landing, 28 October 1945," ibid., 388–89.

Thus denied help from the Soviets, the CCP leaders had to drastically downgrade their goal in Manchuria from "exclusive control" to "a certain position" (*yiding diwei*). This meant that CCP personnel had to give up all the big cities and important railways in the Soviet occupation zone in order to allow the Soviets to turn these over to the GMD government. For a moment, the CCP had to stay agrarian and rural even in Manchuria, dropping its timetable for "regularization" within six months. In mid-November, exhausted from tense military and political maneuvering, Mao was hospitalized and would not attend routine work for more than a month.[14]

Now that CCP troops had to leave urban centers, Inner Mongolia became even more important. While Mao remained hospitalized, Liu Shaoqi took over the daily policymaking responsibility at the CCPCC, as he had done earlier during the Mao–Jiang negotiations in Chongqing. On November 22, on behalf of the CCPCC, Liu cabled a directive to Nie Rongzhen and the other leading CCP officials of the Jin-Cha-Ji Bureau:

Restrained by treaty obligations, the Soviet Union must guarantee Jiang Jieshi's takeover of big cities in Manchuria. For the moment this will dash our hope to strive for big cities in the Northeast. Consequently, the importance of Rehe, Chahar, and Suiyuan to our national strategy has been enhanced. To have a relatively secure rear, entire Suiyuan must be controlled, and the flanks of Zhangjiakou must be protected. A passage to Xinjiang should be opened to be used in the future if necessary (if a solid strategic base cannot be established in the Northeast, it may still be possible in Xinjiang).

This was a defensive posture preparing for the worst scenario. Having thrown themselves into the scramble for Manchuria zealously just a few months before, the CCP cadres and troops in Manchuria were now reluctant to let the prize of "regularization" out of their hands. In late December,

---

14. "Directive by the CCPCC Military Committee on Military Operation Deployment in November, 1 November 1945," *ZZWX,* 15: 394–96; "CCPCC's Directive to Peng Zhen and Lin Biao on Organizing a Field Army and Opposing GMD Army's Landing in the Northeast under American Warships' Protection, 4 November 1945," ibid., 400; "CCPCC's Directive on Increasing Troops to Control the Northeast, 4 November 1945," ibid., 401–2; "CCPCC's Directive to the Northeast Bureau on Developing Works in Eastern and Northern Manchuria after Giving Up Big Cities and the Changchun Railway, 20 November 1945," ibid., 431–32; "CCPCC's Directive to the Northeast Bureau on the Development Orientation in the Northeast after Leaving Big Cities and Main Railroads, 28 November 1945," ibid., 447–48; *Mao Zedong Nianpu,* 3: 49.

therefore, Liu had to sternly reiterate the CCPCC's new strategy to the Northeast Bureau, which was still deploying troops to seize cities: "Sit your bottom to reliable areas in eastern, northern, and western Manchuria, and establish bases with your back relying on the Soviet Union and Outer Mongolia."[15]

Thus, during the few months after Japan's surrender, the CCP made two vital strategic readjustments. The first was the switch from a nationwide to a regionally prioritized military strategy aimed at seizing the resource-rich and industrialized Manchuria as the party's new power base. The second was the modification of the originally urban-oriented Manchurian strategy to one that stressed control of rural and frontier areas first. These decisions established the CCP's sociostrategic and geostrategic postures in the postwar years: The CCP would continue to encircle and eventually to seize urban centers from its rural bases, and its conquest of China would follow the Manchu and Japanese precedents starting from Manchuria. Under the circumstances, because of Inner Mongolia's prominent position in the CCP's road map to power, it became imperative for the CCP to devise an ethnopolitical strategy regarding the Inner Mongols. In a late November 1945 telegram, Liu pointed out to CCP officials in Manchuria that "in western Manchuria and Rehe, the Mongolian nation's [*menggu minzu*] attitude toward us is one of the conditions that will decide our success or failure in these areas."[16]

Awake to Spontaneity

In contrast to the GMD government's objection to the term "Inner Mongolia," the CCP used the conception frequently in its public and internal documents in referring to Rehe, Chahar, and Suiyuan Provinces. In early 1946, western Manchuria was included in the conception after the CCP "discovered" the powerful eastern Mongolian movement. Although readily recognizing Inner Mongolia's strategic significance in connection with Manchuria, the CCP leadership was slow to form an ethnopolitical policy toward the Inner Mongols as a people. As a matter of fact, when the postwar period began, the CCP leaders in Yan'an were clueless about the dynamics of Inner Mongolian politics and where they were heading.

To continue the party's wartime effort in Suiyuan, in mid-September

15. *Liu Shoqi Nianpu,* 1: 507–8, 532, 546; "Liu Shaoqi's Telegram to Peng Zhen on Use of Main Force to Establish Eastern, Western, and Northern Manchurian Bases, 24 December 1945," *ZZWX,* 15: 512–14.

16. *Liu Shoqi Nianpu,* 1: 533.

1945 the CCP Central Committee instructed its Suiyuan apparatuses to organize local Mongolian governments and military forces. Yun Ze left Yan'an and traveled northward to work among Inner Mongols. After arriving in the Jin-Cha-Ji Bureau in Zhangjiakou, he and the bureau leadership proposed to the CCPCC that the party start working for Inner Mongolian autonomy and put Yun Ze in charge of the work in western Inner Mongolia. Aside from believing that the Inner Mongols needed CCP mobilization and guidance in starting an autonomous movement, Yun Ze and the bureau also regarded such a movement mainly as a means of "facilitating a close [CCP] connection with Outer Mongolia." Then, only in late September, perhaps in a bit of surprise, the Jin-Cha-Ji Bureau informed Yan'an that a certain "Inner Mongolian Liberation Committee (western Mongolia)" already existed in West Sunid.[17]

In reaffirming Inner Mongolia's "extremely important strategic position," the CCPCC's reply asserted that a proper solution of the national question of Inner Mongolia would not only liberate the Mongolian people but could also strengthen the CCP's rear area and its connection to the Soviet–Mongolian Army. For the moment, the Central Committee pointed out, the basic policy in Inner Mongolia was to implement "regional autonomy" by organizing local Mongolian autonomous movements in leagues and banners. This meant that a unified operation for Inner Mongolia was unnecessary and that the CCP's regional organizations would continue to handle Mongolian affairs in their own areas under the CCPCC's direction. As for Yun Ze, he was directed to act as a liaison between the Jin-Cha-Ji and the Jin-Sui Bureaus without independent policymaking responsibility. In general, however, the CCPCC's response to the Inner Mongolia question was rather tentative, emphasizing that the party could not put its Inner Mongolia policy in more concrete terms before it had better ideas about Outer Mongolia's attitude, Inner Mongols' intentions, and the consequences of Japanese and GMD policies in Inner Mongolia.[18]

This initial CCP deliberation about postwar Inner Mongolia resembled

17. "CCP Center's Directive to He Long and Lin Feng on Organizing Local Mongolian Autonomous Governments and Armed Forces, 16 September 1945," *Minzu Wenti Wenxian Huibian* (Collected Documents on the Nationality Question; hereafter *MWWH*), 960; "Jin-Cha-Jin Bureau's Request for Direction on Policy toward the 'Inner Mongolian Liberation Committee,' 29 September 1945," *ZZWX*, 15: 377–78; "Request to the CCPCC for Direction by Nie Rongzhen et al. with Regard to Work Orientation in Inner Mongolia, 29 September 1945," ibid., 378–79.

18. "CCPCC's Directive to the Jin-Cha-Ji and Jin-Sui Bureau on Work Orientation in Inner Mongolia, 23 October 1945," *ZZWX*, 15: 375–77.

the GMD's way of thinking in two aspects. First, like the GMD government, the CCP viewed the question largely in connection with Outer Mongolia. But the CCP and the GMD took opposite stands on the matter: Whereas the GMD feared MPR agitations for autonomy among the Inner Mongols, the CCP was inclined to encourage Inner Mongolian autonomy as a means of enhancing its own relationship with the MPR. Second, also like the GMD, the CCP leadership failed to anticipate the Inner Mongols' political prowess and spontaneity. Yet again, the two parties diverged on this score: Whereas the GMD was opposed to Inner Mongolian political activism and tended to attribute any such phenomenon to outside manipulations, the CCP was worried about the Inner Mongols' political passiveness and wanted to propel them into action through its own "Mongolian work." Considering that the CCP was usually masterful and positive in estimating the power and potential of the "masses," its initial misreading of Inner Mongolian politics was astonishing. A lack of information about Inner Mongolia was just one of the reasons for the CCP's misjudgment. Another and more important reason was the CCP leadership's low opinion of Inner Mongols' "political consciousness."

Informed by the Marxist linear view of history, the CCP classified the Mongols as a "backward" nation in terms of socioeconomic development and social class configuration. During World War II, CCP officials were especially frustrated by the ineffectiveness of their own effort to mobilize the Inner Mongols to participate actively in China's war against Japan. One of the CCP's wartime documents stated:

Today, apathy, decadence, and corruption are prevailing within the Mongolian nation; these phenomena have deprived the Mongolian people, upper and lower classes alike, of confidence in their own nation. Feeling powerless and seeing no way out, they become fully dispirited, weak, and dependent. These conditions indicate that the Mongolian nation's liberation must rely on assistance from outside revolutionary force, and that the Mongolian nation's liberation movement can be successful only by combining itself with the Chinese revolution.[19]

In this view, Prince De personified this "dispirited and weak" nation's dependence on Japanese imperialism. His postwar rally to the GMD government certainly did not help improve the CCP's opinion of Inner Mongol elites. The

---

19. "Outline by the Northwestern Work Committee of the CCPCC with Regard to the Question of the Mongolian Nation in the War of Resistance, July 1940," *MWWH*, 659.

wartime estimate cited above thus continued in the postwar period, and the CCP leadership remained convinced that only "outside assistance" from the CCP itself could initiate the Inner Mongols into a movement to achieve "regional autonomy."

Despite its theoretical subscription to Marxist-Leninist dogmas on the "national question," the CCP's practical ethnopolitical stance was shaped mainly during its intricate political-military struggle with the GMD and war against Japan in the 1930s. In comparison with these two adversaries, the CCP ethnopolitics was characterized by two peculiar features. First, as a revolutionary power contender against the present Chinese central government, the CCP contradicted the GMD government's pacification orientation toward ethnic frontiers and endeavored to incite the non-Han peoples' participation in the revolution. Second, because it was a contender for China's national power, the CCP was in favor of political centralization. Its agitation among the non-Han peoples, unlike that of the Japanese, was against ethnic and territorial separatism. In the postwar years, such a revolutionary-preservationist symbiosis, designed mainly to differentiate the CCP from the GMD and the Japanese in the party's propaganda toward ethnic minorities, was soon challenged by the reality of Inner Mongolian politics. In the postwar scramble for Manchuria and Inner Mongolia, the Inner Mongols proved that they were neither passive recipients of the Chinese parties' propaganda nor mere objects for others to "mobilize." Rather, they constituted a valid "third force." Thus, for the first time in its history, the CCP was faced with an organized revolutionary movement of ethnic, not class, motivations. In coping with this novelty, the CCP relied on its principal Inner Mongol operative, Yun Ze.

From 1941 to 1945, Yun spent most of his time in Yan'an, helping with training programs for "minority cadres" and with the management of Mongolian affairs in the CCP base area. These endeavors earned him a reputation as the party's expert in nationality affairs and speeded his rise within the party. During the CCP's seventh national congress in the summer of 1945, Yun was elected an alternate member of the CCPCC. When Japan surrendered, the CCP immediately sent him back to the field in a fashion typical of the CCP–GMD takeover competition at the time—he was appointed governor of Suiyuan and mayor of Guisui (Hohhot). Also like GMD's absentee officials, Yun's titles soon became irrelevant as the GMD established control in Guisui ahead of the CCP. Yun could only reach Zhangjiakou, where he became affiliated with the Jin-Cha-Ji Bureau.[20]

    20. Hao Yufeng, *Wulanfu Zhuan* (Biography of Ulanfu) (Hohhot: Neimenggu Remin Chubanshe, 1990), 337–40, 342, 355–56, 359–60.

Before familiarizing himself with the situation of postwar Inner Mongolia, Yun already had some ideas about how to start. In an internal discussion of the party's Mongolian work, he stressed several points: The work should not be limited to upper-class people but must make an effort to reach the lower strata of society; the CCP should help the Inner Mongols but must not repeat a mistake of the past by taking over Mongolian affairs; a Mongolian government should be established to win over puppet troops from Prince De's wartime regime; propaganda must be carried out in the Mongolian language (even though Yun himself could not speak the language); taxation should be lighter than the GMD's and Japan's. Remarkably, although at the time Yun wanted to focus his attention on former puppet troops, his points regarding a mass movement, the Mongols' management of their own affairs, and the idea of a Mongolian government were essentially in agreement with the eastern Mongols' programs. In listing ideas shared by progressive Inner Mongols in the postwar years, Yun obviously also believed that his proposition was in concert with the CCP's ethnopolitical stance in general and orientation toward the Inner Mongols in particular.[21]

Years later, one of Yun's colleagues from the period recalled that Yun took very seriously the CCP's 1935 proclamation for the Inner Mongols undersigned by Mao. The proclamation supported restoration to the Inner Mongols of their "original territories" and also supported Inner Mongolia's "independence and freedom" as similar to that of Turkey, Poland, Ukraine, and Caucasus. But by the end of the war, the 1935 document was ten years old, and during the decade the CCPCC already quietly shelved "national self-determination" as a party program for gaining non-Han allies. Yun's refusal to accept the document's obsolescence would eventually get him into serious trouble with the CCP leadership in the 1960s and 1970s.[22] In 1945,

21. "Sui-Meng Government's Discussion of the Mongolian Work, 11 August 1945," in *Daqingshan Kang Ri Youji Genjudi Ziliao Xuanbian: Lishi Dang'an Bufen* (Selected Materials on the Anti-Japanese Guerrilla Base in the Daqingshan Mountain: Archival Materials), comp. Committee on the Collection of Party History Materials of the CCP Committee of the Inner Mongolian Autonomous Region and the Archives of the Inner Mongolian Autonomous Region (Huhhot: Neimenggu Renmin Chubanshe, 1987), 2: 292–95.

22. Yang Zhilin, "A Pioneer of the Chinese Revolution and a Model of Nationality Work," in *Wulanfu Jinian Wenji* (Memorial Essays on Ulanfu) (Hohhot: Neimenggu Renmin Chubanshe, 1990), 1: 38; "The Chinese Soviet Central Government's Proclamation for the Inner Mongolian People, 20 December 1935," *MWWH*, 322–24; Tumen and Zhu Dongli, *Kang Sheng yu Neirendang Yuan'an* (Kang Sheng and the Unjust Case of the Inner Mongolian People's Party) (Beijing: Zhongyang Dangxiao Chubanshe, 1994, 13–14. In the mid-1960s, Ulanfu (Yun Ze) reissued the document in the Inner Mongolian

however, Yun's conviction was still allowable within the CCP, though at the time the CCP leadership did not necessarily support an Inner Mongolian government. Meanwhile, Yun's proposed policy priority regarding the puppet troops soon proved off the mark. After Japan's defeat, most of Prince De's troops rallied to the GMD government and thus left Yun nothing to "focus on." Obviously, having stayed in the CCP central base for seven years (1938–45), Yun lost touch with conditions in Inner Mongolia and was not much better informed than the rest of the CCP leadership about the postwar political trend in the region.

Soon, Yun had his opportunity to learn about the trend firsthand. On August 16, 1945, immediately after Japan's surrender, an "Inner Mongolian Liberation Committee" emerged in West Sunid Banner, site of Prince De's original residence. On September 9, the same group of people organized a "provisional government of the Inner Mongolian People's Republic." The nominal head of the government was Buyandalai, the former chief justice in Prince De's wartime regime, but the real driving force behind this self-appointed government was a group of young intellectuals and low-ranking officials who a year before had organized themselves into a "Mongolian Revolutionary Youth Party." When the Soviet–Mongolian troops entered the area, these young people captured two alleged Japanese spies and sent them to the Soviets. Having hereby proved their standing on the Allied side of the war, the Youth Party declared war on Japan, not knowing that the war had already ended.

During its brief life span, this Youth Party "government" received encouragement and advice from Outer Mongol personnel and carried out mass propaganda on Soviet trucks. Like many other Inner Mongol activists at the time, the group dispatched a delegation to Ulaanbaatar to petition for assistance. The MPR leaders told the delegation to go back and to contact the Chinese Communists. Consequently, the West Sunid group sent a delegation to Zhangbei to request the CCP's recognition. They were told there that the chairman of the CCP's Suiyuan–Mongolian government would soon pay their government a visit. This "chairman" was none other than Yun Ze. Some time in October, Yun and five other CCP cadres arrived in West Sunid. In Yun's own words, his mission was to "abolish" the self-appointed government.[23]

Autonomous Region. The action was soon interpreted by the CCP leadership during the "Cultural Revolution" as evidence of Ulanfu's crime of "splitting the nation."

23. Uljinaren, "Comrade Ulanfu and Inner Mongolian Autonomous Movement," in *Wulanfu Jinian Wenji,* 1: 256–57; Delgerchogtu, "The Mongolian Youth Revolutionary

Many years later, Yun's trip to West Sunid would be acclaimed within the CCP as a heroic deed of "going to a dangerous meeting with a single broadsword [*dandao fuhui*]."[24] As a matter of fact, not much danger was awaiting Yun's group in Sunid, which was then controlled by the CCP's Soviet ally. Yun did not bring troops with him, lest they cause suspicions on the part of the local Soviet military authorities. It turned out that the commander of the Soviet–Mongolian regiment there, a Soviet major general, was the principal obstacle to Yun's mission. The general insisted that Inner Mongolia be allowed to exercise the right to national self-determination. After a "three-day verbal battle," Yun failed to dissuade the Soviet officer from his position. He had no choice but to resort to the higher authorities on the other side of the border. A few days later, the Soviet officer in question was recalled and his replacement completely cooperated with Yun's mission.

In contrast, Yun's dealings with the members of the Youth Party and the "provisional government" were much easier. He only needed to make two points to them: First, the Soviet Union, Outer Mongolia, and the CCP were actually the same; second, the "provisional government" and the Youth Party had the wrong leaders. According to Yun, Buyandalai was a "Mongol traitor" (*mengjian*) and a wanted war criminal, and Delgerchogtu, the leader of the Youth Party, was a secret Japanese agent. With their hope for MPR support dashed and their political confidence undermined, these inexperienced young Mongols accepted Yun's proposal for reorganizing the government. As a result, Yun became chairman of the government. Having secured the leadership, he now ordered the government to be moved to Zhangbei, where it would soon wither away. Altogether, Yun spent fewer than three weeks in abolishing the West Sunid "government." Later, when recalling this experience to his associates, Yun said that he had used only two trucks to tow the "provisional government" back to Zhangbei.[25]

Party as I Knew It," in *Wulanchabu Wenshi Ziliao* (Literary and Historical Materials of Ulanchab), 2 (1984): 89–115; Liu Jieyu, "The Role and Contributions of Inner Mongolia's [Minority] Nationalities in the War of Liberation in the Northeast: Recorded Recollections by the Late Vice President Ulanfu," *Neimenggu Wenshi Ziliao* (Literary and Historical Materials of Inner Mongolia; hereafter *NWZ*), 50: 239–40; Liu Chun, "Works in Inner Mongolia Remembered," *NWZ*, 50: 38.

24. Hao Yufeng, *Wulanfu Zhuan,* 369. *Dandao fuhui* is a story about Guan Yu in the classic Chinese novel, *Sanguo Yanyi* (Romance of the Three Kingdoms). A few decades after the event, Zhou Enlai used the phrase to praise Ulanhu.

25. Liu Jieyu, "Role and Contributions of Inner Mongolia's [Minority] Nationalities"; Oljinaren, "In the Mighty Torrent of Inner Mongolia's National Liberation Movement,"

It did not come as a surprise that a self-appointed government fostered by Soviet trucks could be easily abolished by CCP trucks that were probably made by the Soviets as well. Yet this short-lived West Sunid regime had a significant position in Inner Mongolia's postwar history. It was a wakeup call to both Yun Ze and CCP leaders in Zhangjiakou and Yan'an. Three things became abundantly clear. First, in spite of the CCP's unflattering view of the Inner Mongols as a politically impotent people, a strong autonomous tendency was obviously seething in Inner Mongolia. Evidently, in the war years, the CCP had misconstrued the Inner Mongols' reluctance to become involved in China's war against Japan as political numbness. Second, now that a reevaluation of the Inner Mongols' political activism was in order, the CCP did not want to see any ethnonationalist movement in Inner Mongolia to run outside the party's orbit. For such a movement might be manipulated by the GMD, or create difficulties for CCP operations on its own, or grow into an unstoppable separatist movement to harm China's territorial integrity. Third, the West Sunid affair educated the CCP leadership that an ethnic separatist movement might be encouraged by a supposedly friendly foreign influence, such as the Soviet–Mongolian army in Inner Mongolia. For the moment, even though the affair's solution seemed to indicate compatibility between the MPR's and the CCP's policies toward the Inner Mongols, there was no guarantee for the two sides' cooperation in the future.[26]

This last point was extremely important to the CCP. After the West Sunid episode, an understanding emerged among the CCP, the MPR, and the Soviets that the Inner Mongolian revolution was China's internal affair and therefore should come under the CCP's responsibility. To CCP officials,

NWZ, 50: 294–95; Liu Chun, "Works in Inner Mongolia remebered," ibid., 38–40; Ji-Cha-Ji Central Bureau to the CCPCC, 27 October 1945, *MWWH,* 966; Ulanfu, *Wulanfu Huiyilu* (Memoirs of Ulanfu) (Beijing: Zhonggong Dangshi Ziliao Chubanshe, 1989), 213–14; Yun Shiying, "Unforgettable Memories," in *Wulanfu Jinian Wenji,* 1: 83. After he prevailed, Yun Ze allowed Buyandalai to remain in the reorganized government as a "united front" figure. The accusation against Delgerchogtu was baseless, but his name would not be cleared until 1957.

    26. Wang Shusheng, "Great Deeds Recorded in History and Valuable Legacy to the Coming Generations," in *Wulanfu Jinian Wenji,* 1: 375–76; "Jin-Cha-Ji Central Bureau's Telegram to the CCPCC on the Situation and Policies in Chahar Mongol Area, 27 October 1945," *Neimenggu Zizhi Yundong Lianhehui Dang'an Shiliao Xuanbian* (Selected Archival Materials on the Inner Mongolian Autonomous Movement Association; hereafter *NZYL*), 3–5.

nevertheless, their Soviet–MPR allies initially created more problems in Inner Mongolia than did the GMD. According to reports by the Jin-Cha-Ji Bureau, more than 60 percent of Shilingol League's livestock and most of Chahar League's were taken away by the Soviet–Mongolian army. In CCP officials' words, the heist was an "unprecedented calamity in a long time" and "now people in [Mongolian] banners are in great panic and the society is in chaos." This human-made disaster put an extra burden on CCP operatives in these Mongolian communities who had to devote tremendous energy to arranging reliefs. The situation, however, helped in a negative way the CCP's effort to organize local governments in these areas. For instance, in early October 1945, the *jasags* (banner rulers) of Chahar League agreed to set up a joint office under the CCP's leadership. The office was soon changed into a league government. In this case, an important reason for Mongol officials' willingness to collaborate with the CCP was that, plagued by Soviet–Mongolian troops, these banner officials were anxious to have a unified and effectual body to shield their areas from the occupation force.[27]

Although the CCP's political-military units in Inner Mongolia often had to function in the name of the "Chinese authorities" in helping the local people fend off the predatory foreign occupation force, this was not their original mission. Their charge was to prepare the land and populace of Inner Mongolia for the CCP's power struggle against the real Chinese "central authorities" of the time, the GMD regime. For this purpose, the Jin-Cha-Ji Bureau at first organized a "Mongolian people's liberation committee" as an intermediary to work among the Inner Mongols. But the West Sunid affair proved that the device was inadequate. At the juncture, Yun proved himself a valuable field operative in helping the CCP leadership readjust its perception of Inner Mongolian politics. When reporting to the CCPCC about Yun's mission to West Sunid, Han-Chinese cadres in the Jin-Cha-Ji Bureau still believed that because of Outer Mongolian troops' predatory behaviors in Inner Mongolia, the local people's central concern at the time was relief. The West Sunid experience taught Yun differently. He realized that the central issue in postwar Inner Mongolia was a competition among various political forces for the "banner of the [Mongolian] nation." The insight led him, along with his superiors in the Jin-Cha-Ji Bureau, to propose to Yan'an

27. "Request for Instruction with Regard to the Question of Establishing the 'Provisional Government of the Inner Mongolian People's Republic in the Chahar League,' 27 October 1945," *MWWH,* 972–73; "Recent Conditions in the Leagues and Banners of Chahar and the Work in Chahar and Shilingol Leagues, 27 October 1945," ibid., 966–71.

that an "Inner Mongolian Autonomous Movement Association" (IMAMA) be organized immediately. The proposal was approved by the CCPCC in early November 1945.[28]

On November 26, the IMAMA was officially launched in Zhangjiakou with Yun Ze as chairman of its executive committee. The inauguration assembly supposedly represented thirty-seven banners scattered in six provinces from Ningxia in the west to Heilongjiang in the east. Some of the delegates indeed came directly from banners, but there were also banners that could not send their delegates in time or were not aware of the assembly at all. In the latter case, the seats were assigned to people already working with the CCP in Zhangjiakou. The IMAMA charter subscribed to the "new democracy" creed that was issued by Mao not long before, targeted "reactionaries within the GMD" as Inner Mongols' enemies, and proclaimed a current goal in forming a "local, democratic, and autonomous political power" that would "grant equality to all nationalities and accommodate all classes." Right after the assembly, the IMAMA sent a congratulatory message to Yan'an and announced its existence to the outside world through the CCP's New China News Agency.[29]

As defined by a CCP participant in these events, the IMAMA was designed to function simultaneously as a party, a government, a military establishment, and a mass organization. At this stage, the CCP's Mongolia policy needed such an amorphous amalgam to maintain enough flexibility. Within the CCP, the IMAMA served as a switchboard to coordinate the party's Mongolian work in different areas; for the Inner Mongols, the IMAMA format was broad enough to attract people of different social strata and political orientations and seemed a promising step toward a full-fledged Inner Mongolian government. The loose form of "association" was especially suit-

28. Jin-Cha-Ji Central Bureau to the CCPCC, 27 October 1945, *MWWH,* 966–68; Wang Shusheng, "Great Deeds Recorded in History and Valuable Legacy Bequeathed to Generations to Come," in *Wulanfu Jinian Wenji,* 1: 375–76; Wang Shusheng and Hao Yufeng, *Wulanfu Nianpu* (Chronicle of Ulanfu's Life) (Beijing: Zhonggong Dangshi Ziliao Chubanshe, 1989), 134; CCPCC Secretariat to the Jin-Cha-Ji Central Bureau, 10 November 1945, *MWWH,* 976.

29. Wang Duo, *Wushi Chunqiu* (Fifty Eventful Years) (Hohhot: Neimenggu Renmin Chubanshe, 1992), 197; "Name List of the Delegates of the IMAMA, 25 November 1945," *NZYL,* 14–17; "Charter of the IMAMA, 27 November 1945," ibid., 27–31; "Proclamation of the Inaugural Assembly of the IMAMA, 28 November 1945," ibid., 32–34; "Message of Greeting to Chairman Mao and Commander-in-General Zhu from the Delegates to the Inaugural Assembly of the IMAMA, 28 November 1945," ibid., 34–35; "Bulletin of the Inaugural Assembly of the IMAMA, 29 November 1945," ibid., 41–43.

able to the CCP's need in its political maneuvering with the GMD at the time. Before a full-scale war with the GMD government began, the CCP needed to maintain its "legal" facade and did not want to challenge the existing administrative structure of the Republic of China. Therefore the IMAMA must not claim itself to be a body of governance for an integral Inner Mongolia.

Even within the CCP's organizational structure, the IMAMA was not vested with policymaking authority for the entire area of Inner Mongolia. The CCP apparatuses in Suiyuan, Chahar, Rehe, and western Manchuria continued to be responsible for Mongolian work in their own regions.[30] At the time, however, the most important significance of the IMAMA was to mark the CCP's public commitment to Inner Mongolian autonomy. "Autonomy" was an ambiguous term. Whereas the IMAMA's public acceptance of Yan'an's leadership clearly put it on the CCP side in China's postwar rivalry, its position in Inner Mongolian politics was yet to be clarified. Mainly because of the existence of a powerful autonomous movement in eastern Inner Mongolia, the establishment of the IMAMA officially started the CCP's contest for the "banner" of the Inner Mongolian nation.

Perhaps more than other types of politics, ethnopolitics involves a craft of emotion invocation. As the CCP's leading operative in Inner Mongolia, Yun understood this thoroughly. From the moment of the IMAMA's existence, he invoked the Inner Mongols' historical memories in identifying the new organization with a long line of ethnic heroes from Genghis Khan to famous members of the Inner Mongolian People's Revolutionary Party of the 1920s.[31] Similarly, a proper location of the IMAMA headquarters would symbolically serve to justify the organization's legitimacy as the leading body of the Inner Mongols. Zhangjiakou was improper because of its Han character. Guisui (Hohhot), though deemed by many as the political center of Inner Mongolia, was unsuitable either. Guisui, meaning "submission and pacification," was associated historically with the Inner Mongols' subjugation by outside authorities. In the 1630s, the Manchus incorporated the

---

30. "Ji-Cha-Ji Cental Bureau's Report about Establishment of the IMAMA, 8 November 1945," *MWWH*, 974; "Jin-Cha-Ji Central Bureau's Report to the CCPCC on Political Power in Chahar and Suiyuan Leagues, 9 November 1945," ibid., 975; Wang Duo, *Wushi Chunqiu*, 198; Wang Shusheng, "Great Deeds Recorded in History and Valuable Legacy to the Coming Generations," in *Wulanfu Jinian Wenji*, 1: 375–76; Jin-Cha-Ji Central Bureau, "Important Points in Current Policies toward Inner Mongolia, 23 November 1945," ibid., 981.
31. "Yun Ze's Speech at the Inaugural Assembly of the IMAMA, 26 November 1945," *NZYL*, 17–19.

Inner Mongols into their empire by expanding to the place; in World War II, Prince De's puppet regime under Japan made the city its capital. When Japan surrendered, the city regained its capital status in Suiyuan Province and was occupied by Fu Zuoyi's forces on behalf of the GMD government.[32]

Denied access to Guisui, Yun and his associates made a bold plan to move the IMAMA to Prince De's old residence in West Sunid. Despite the fact that the CCP denounced Prince De as a *mengjian* and Yun called him "devil prince" in public, Prince De's palace was situated in one of the least sinicized Mongolian leagues, Shilingol, and, because of Prince De's prewar autonomous activities and the recent West Sunid affair, the location seemed able to catch the Inner Mongols' attention. The plan was delayed because, soon after the establishment of the IMAMA, Yun and its other leading members had to travel eastward to deal with the eastern Mongolian autonomous movement. When they returned to Zhangjiakou in the late spring of 1946, the CCP's military situation in Suiyuan and Chahar deteriorated rapidly. By late September 1946, the Jin-Cha-Ji Bureau had to abandon Zhangjiakou to GMD troops and retreat southward into Hebei.[33]

To maintain the IMAMA's ethnic authenticity, Yun convinced the bureau leadership that his group should not retreat into Hebei, a Han province, but should instead march northward into the grassland of Shilingol as originally planned. Ethnopolitically, Yun's choice made good sense, but it proved a poor strategic move in the context of the CCP–GMD military struggle. Soon after separating from the CCP's main force, in pastoral Shilingol the IMAMA had to struggle for survival against GMD troops and local anticommunist aristocrats. Nor did the IMAMA benefit ethnopolitically from moving into Shilingol. The region's "pure" Mongolian character turned out to be an obstacle to the IMAMA's work. As members of the IMAMA recalled later, Shilingol's Mongol herdsmen viewed the IMAMA cadres, most of whose members either did not speak Mongolian or spoke different dialects of the language, as *manzi* (southern savages) and outsiders. The lack of Chinese

32. Rene Grousset, *The Empire of the Steppes: A History of Central Asia* (New Brunswick, N.J.: Rutgers University Press, 1970), 517; Zhou Qingshu, *Neimenggu Lishi Dili* (Historical Geography of Inner Mongolia) (Hohhot: Neimenggu Daxue Chubanshe, 1993), 225, 227.

33. "CCP Jin-Cha-Ji Central Bureau's Report about Establishment of the IMAMA, 8 November 1945," *MWWH,* 974; "Yun Ze, Chairman of the Sui-Meng Government, Discusses the Question of Inner Mongolian Autonomy," from the 16 November 1945 issue of the *Jin Cha Ji Ribao* (Jin-Cha-Ji Daily), *NZYL,* 8–11; Wang Duo, *Wushi Chunqiu,* 210–12.

influence in the region also meant that local princes and *jasags* still held undisputable authority over the population. These ruling elites adopted an opportunist stand in the CCP–GMD struggle and made it very difficult for the IMAMA to create a reliable base in the area. Soon the CCPCC and the Jin-Cha-Ji Bureau recognized the IMAMA's perilous situation and ordered Yun to take his group to eastern Inner Mongolia where CCP influence was strong enough to protect them.[34]

Secure "National Banner"

The direct distance from Zhangjiakou to Wangyemiao was about 820 kilometers. Because the IMAMA first moved from Zhangjiakou to Beizimiao (today's Shilinhot) in Shilingol, it actually covered more than 900 kilometers to move from its birthplace to the center of the eastern Mongolian movement. Although not comparable to the Chinese Red Army's Long March of the mid-1930s, which traversed 12,500 kilometers, the eastward journey by Yun's group nevertheless resembled the Long March as a turning point. As with the Red Army in the 1930s, they escaped a danger of elimination and thrived later in a new base.

The ethno-geopolitical significance of the two events, however, were rather different. In the mid-1930s, the CCP moved away from China's political centers and became marginalized from the Han-Chinese ethnographical zone; in 1947, the IMAMA moved right into the center of the postwar Inner Mongolian autonomous movement and came to eastern Inner Mongolia, where the largest number of Inner Mongols resided. Had the IMAMA been an independent organization, its relocation to eastern Mongolia would have been recorded as a turning point of Long March magnitude in Inner Mongolia's revolutionary history. But, as a CCP front, the IMAMA's arrival in Wangyemiao has to be evaluated mainly in the context of the CCP's "Mongolian work."

Charged to carry out unprecedented and urgent mass work among the Inner Mongols, the IMAMA had to rush in preparing a cadre. While still in Zhangjiakou, Yun told young Mongol trainees in the IMAMA's military-political school that they should not attempt to grasp Marxism during their

---

34. Hao Yufeng, *Wulanfu Zhuan,* 431–38; Wang Duo, *Wushi Chunqiu,* 213–36, 242–52; Yun Shiying and Chao Luomeng, "Recollections of Work in the Shili-yin Gool League," *NWZ,* 50: 156–75.

brief training period and that for now it was sufficient for them to have just "a taste of the CCP." By this he meant a sense of the basic differences between the CCP's and GMD's nationality policies. Some of the quicker learners got their "taste" within ten days, were inducted into the CCP, and were then sent to the "mass" as party operatives.[35] At the time, the GMD regime's intransigence on Inner Mongolian autonomy made it easier for the CCP to promulgate its programs among the Inner Mongols. Nevertheless, as Yun and his colleagues found out in their encounter with eastern Mongol leaders, the CCP did not monopolize the key to the autonomy question.

In late December 1945, when CCP troops pushed into northern Rehe and western Manchuria, they were greeted with the problem of the eastern Mongolian movement. Due to the size of the Mongolian population involved, which was presumed to be 2 million by CCP cadres, and the strategic location that the eastern Mongols occupied, Yan'an immediately understood the magnitude of the matter. But during the next month, the CCP leaders could not decide how to deal with the situation. The Jin-Cha-Ji Bureau's experiment with the IMAMA in western Inner Mongolia could not be readily emulated by the Northeast Bureau. In the west, the IMAMA was set up to start a CCP-led Mongolian movement and to preempt any Mongolian initiative outside the party's orbit, whereas in the east a well-organized popular movement had already taken root before the CCP's arrival.

As viewed by CCP officials, this popular movement centered in Wang-yemiao had many "incorrect" features: It stressed the Mongolian–Han contradictions but ignored class struggles within the Mongolian society; it pursued "great Mongolism" (*da menggu zhuyi*) in insisting on Mongolian governance for territories where the Han population already constituted the majority; it showed a neutralist tendency in the current GMD–CCP struggle; and it strove for ethnic independence or combination with Outer Mongolia. Even more troublesome, these "mistakes" could not be "corrected" in haste as Yun had done to the West Sunid group. For one thing, the movement seemed to have the sympathy of the Soviet–Mongolian Army in Manchuria; for another, any abrasive move by the CCP might tip the delicate Mongolian–GMD–CCP triangle in the region in favor of the GMD.[36]

35. Zhao Zhenbei, "Glorious Model and Immortal Achievements," in *Wulanfu Jinian Wenjin,* 2: 96–97.
36. "Policy Suggestion on Mongolian Banners by the Western Military District of the Northeastern People's Autonomous Army, 22 December 1945," *MWWH,* 983; "Report by the CCP Committee in Western Liaoning on the Discovery of the Organization

The CCP leadership did not wait long to decide that the eastern Mongolian movement must not be encouraged in its current form. Yan'an was unhappy about the recent events in Wangyemiao, on two counts. First, as a *Chinese* party the CCP could not endorse Wangyemiao's separatist tendency. The CCP leadership, as will be shown in chapter 10, did not completely give up hope for Outer Mongolia's return to a "liberated" China in the future. The eastern Mongols' explicit intention of accession to the MPR only complicated China's task of territorial consolidation. Second, as a *partisan* contender of national power, the CCP was currently conducting a legal political struggle with the GMD in the arena of Chinese public opinion, which was highly nationalistic. In mid-January 1946, the CCP initiated a political stratagem in presenting to the National Political Consultative Conference in the GMD's capital a "draft program for peaceful reconstruction of the state." The program advocated a unified, democratic, and constitutional new China under the leadership of Jiang Jieshi. Measured within such a frame, the eastern Mongols' programs for independence and self-determination appeared to the CCP as "excessively leftist." Thus, in mid-February, Yan'an instructed responsible officials of the Jin-Cha-Ji and Northeast Bureaus that the CCP must not support the eastern Mongolian programs, lest the party be accused by the GMD of splitting the country.[37]

The Northeast Bureau, which was directly responsible for CCP operations in Manchuria but distant from Yan'an's political maneuvering with the GMD in the south, preferred a more positive response to the eastern Mongols. After receiving Yan'an's cautionary directive, the bureau responded with a report dated February 20, pointing out that the eastern Mongols had earlier expressed the hope of joining Outer Mongolia without the benefit of knowing about the Sino-Soviet treaty and about the CCP's and Ulaanbaatar's policies. In the last few months, the report claimed, the Northeast

of the 'Inner Mongolian People's Revolutionary Party,' 24 December 1945," ibid., 1293; "CCPCC's Directive to Lin Biao et al. on Policies toward the Mongolian Nationality, 25 December 1945," ibid., 984; "Ji-Re-Liao Branch Bureau's report to the Northeast Bureau and the CCPCC on Mongolian and Han Governments in Northern Rehe, 15 January 1946," ibid., 989; "Ji-Re-Liao Branch Bureau's Report on the Mongolia Question in Northern Rehe, 26 January 1946," ibid., 995; "Report on Conditions of Inner Mongolia from the Seventh Division of the Northeastern Anti-Japanese Allied Army to the Northeast Bureau, 29 January 1946," ibid., 996–97.

37. "Draft Program for Peaceful Reconstruction of the State, 16 January 1946," *MWWH,* 990–91; "CCPCC's Directive on a Necessary Cautious Attitude toward the Nationality Question of Inner Mongolia, 18 February 1946," ibid., 1000.

Bureau and the West Manchurian Branch Bureau, assisted by the MPR leadership, had already brought the movement around. Now the eastern Mongols adopted a pro-CCP stance and agreed to pursue autonomy within China. To address Yan'an's concern about public reaction, the report indicted that in an assembly held in mid-January the eastern Mongols adopted "basically correct" programs. Their "automatic recognition of China as the suzerain state" should be able to rebuff effectively the GMD's disinformation that the movement was inspired by the CCP and aspired to Inner Mongolian independence. On the same day, Peng Zhen, the secretary of the Northeast Bureau—after further consultation with Lü Zhengcao, the deputy commander-in-chief of the CCP's "Northeast Democratic Allied Army," who had recently concluded a working agreement with the eastern Mongols—sent another message to the CCPCC, asserting confidently that "now the eastern Mongolian people's autonomous movement is basically under our influence, and their principal armed force of two thousand troops is under the leadership of the youth league and may be subject to our command." Peng and Lü urged Yan'an that "we must accept" the eastern Mongols' demand for including in their jurisdiction territories of Rehe that in the war years had been part of Xing'an Province.[38]

To a significant degree, the Northeast Bureau's favorable impression of the eastern Mongolian movement was derived from the experiences of Lü and members of other CCP cadres in western Manchuria who had positive encounters with pro-CCP eastern Mongol figures, such as Askhan. CCP officials in Rehe had a rather different perspective because of their experience in dealing with different personalities. In southern Rehe, CCP officials met Bai Yunhang and regarded him as a nuisance. His attitude toward his brother Bai Yunti, a highly positioned official of the GMD regime, appeared ambiguous, and his attempt to recruit Mongol troops and to establish Mongolian governments in CCP-controlled areas was utterly unacceptable. In northern Rehe, He Zizhang proved a tough local contender who tried to squeeze CCP influence out of his region. Both Bai and He were creating problems for the CCP in the name of the Eastern Mongolian Autonomous Government.

Unsurprisingly, CCP officials in Rehe reported negatively to Yan'an about

---

38. "Northeast Bureau's Report to the CCPCC on the Mongolian Question, 20 February 1946," *MWWH,* 1002–3; "Request from Peng Zhen and Lü Zhengcao for the CCPCC's Directive on the Region of Eastern Mongolia Autonomy, 20 February 1946," ibid., 1004; "Order Number 5 of the Western Manchurian Military District, 1 February 1946," *Neimenggu Dang'an* (Inner Mongolian Archives), 4 (1991): 35.

the eastern Mongolian movement, calling it a de facto autonomous Mongolian state led by a group of "upper-class bureaucrats" and ex-collaborators with Japan. Allegedly, this group showed no concern with ordinary people's welfare and their party, the "Inner Mongolian People's Revolutionary Party" was "very leftist in programs but very rightist in action." As for the most urgent issue of strategic territories, the Ji-Re-Liao (Hebei-Rehe-Liaobei) Branch Bureau strongly objected accepting the eastern Mongols' demand for incorporating former Xing'an territories into their region, contending that the step would destroy the "integrity of Rehe" and would be opposed by the majority, or Han, populace of the area.[39]

The stark contrast between the perspectives of the Northeast Bureau and the Ji-Re-Liao Branch Bureau was sensed by the eastern Mongols. Among them there was a saying that the "Eighth Route Army" in the east was better than that in the west. To Yan'an, however, operational problems at the regional level were less imperative than what the eastern Mongolian movement might mean to its own political maneuvering at the national and international levels. After receiving Peng Zhen's reports, the CCPCC decided to maintain its earlier opinion that the movement in Wangyemiao could not be supported in its current form. Its new directive, dated February 24, deserves a complete quotation:

Northeast Bureau, West Manchuria Branch Bureau, and Rehe Branch Bureau:

Having studied the programs and activities of the eastern Mongolian people's autonomous government, we believe that under current domestic and international circumstances, the establishment of such an autonomous-republic type of government is still *excessively leftist* and disadvantageous to the Mongolian nationality, the Chinese people, and the Soviet and Outer Mongolian diplomacy. It can only provide an anti-Soviet and anti-communist excuse to the reactionaries, and create *a fear among the parochial nationalists [xia'ai minzuzhuyizhe] among the Chinese people.* Today eastern Mongolia should pursue local autonomy in

39. "Hu Xikui's Materials and Opinions about the Eastern Mongolian Question, 3 March 1946," *MWWH,* 1013–14; "Huang Kecheng's Report on Conditions of Eastern Mongolian Autonomy, 3 March 1946," ibid., 1015–16; "Ji-Cha-Re-Liao Branch Bureau's Report on How to Deal with the Eastern Mongolian Question, 3 March 1946," ibid., 1017; "Ji-Re-Liao Branch Bureau's Report to the CCPCC on the Question of the Mongolia Work in Rehe, 7 March 1946," ibid., 1021.

accordance with article six, section three of the "program for peaceful reconstruction of the state." This is to set up an autonomous region under the Liaobei and Rehe provincial governments, or *at most to require for organizing a single province as an ordinary local government.* It should not form a relationship with China as one between a suzerain state and an autonomous republic, and there is no need for it to have a separate currency, a separate army, and even a separate national color (there is a rumor about this, please verify), etc. If they want to have an autonomous region below the provincial level, our liberated area can already guarantee its implementation; if they demand to establish a province, we can also help them to achieve the goal. These are realistic and feasible approaches, and can in essence satisfy their demands. Now they made a big fanfare in issuing declarations, despatching delegates, and filing petitions. This way, they cannot achieve anything in practice and will only run into a stone wall. Please patiently persuade them to change orientation along this line. In addition, *they should be warned that if they insist on the current orientation, we will not be able to support them and, if necessary, will have to renounce publicly any relationship with them.* PS. To our knowledge, the Soviet Union is not aware and not supportive of their action in question. Please investigate and report *what on earth is the origin of their activities.*[40] (emphasis added)

The message is self-explanatory. As seasoned revolutionaries, CCP leaders calculated and carefully executed policies through the party system. Although stressing the "mass line," they welcomed spontaneity from the mass only if it could be channeled into the party's orbit. They therefore naturally felt discomfort about the independent-minded Wangyemiao. Still, it was remarkable that CCP leaders in Yan'an could easily imagine and be sensitive to a "fear" among "parochial" Chinese nationalists but could not grasp the magnitude of a genuine mass movement of the Inner Mongols. In defining the eastern Mongolian movement as "excessively leftist," the CCPCC used CCP jargon to express disapproval of Wangyemiao's challenge to the GMD regime outside the matrixes of the Chinese state and the Han-centric Chinese nation. Like the document's agreement to support only an "ordinary local government" by the Mongols, the jargon indicated CCP leaders' intention

---

40. "CCP Center's Directive to the Northeast Bureau on the Impropriety of Organizing the East Mongolian People's Autonomous Government, 24 February 1946," *MWWH*, 1011.

to curtail Wangyemiao's ethnopolitical character. During the Chinese Civil War, although unhappy about Moscow's admonitions and restrictions on their own revolution, which were often justified by the Soviets with "higher" revolutionary interests (meaning Soviet interests) in a "bigger" picture, the CCP leaders found themselves conducting a similar containment of a "lower" revolution in a "smaller" situation of eastern Mongolia.

Again, the CCP turned to Yun Ze to implement the operation. On March 10, 1946, Yan'an issued a directive to its regional bureaus concerned with policy coordination in western and eastern Inner Mongolia through Yun. The directive laid out a general orientation toward eastern Mongolia:

> The policy toward the eastern Mongolian autonomous government should be cautious; as the opportunity arises they should be persuaded to accept regional autonomy [*quyu zizhi*]. But the policy should stress unity [with eastern Mongols] and not be executed with undue haste lest it alienate them and push them toward the GMD.[41]

It has been discussed in chapter 5 how Yun, in his own words, "overcame" the eastern Mongolian movement through negotiations with leaders from Wangyemiao in late March and early April, 1946. If Yun's biographer is believable, Yun had anticipated this mission because of his ethnic conviction that the western and the eastern regions of Inner Mongolia should become one.[42] Yet in April 1946, Yun pursued an integral Inner Mongolia by ushering the eastern Mongols into collaboration with the CCP. In changing the eastern Mongolian autonomous government into an "ordinary" provincial government of Xing'an, the CCPCC's "regional autonomy" formula was implemented. Yet, although in April 1946 the eastern Mongols accepted the nominal leadership of Yun's IMAMA, a unified autonomous Inner Mongolia did not materialize. It is therefore necessary to explain the meaning of the CCP's "regional autonomy" formula in 1946.

---

41. "Hu Xikui's Materials and Opinions on the East Mongolian Question, 3 March 1946," *MWWH,* 1013–14; "Huang Kecheng's Report on the Situation of East Mongolian Autonomy, 3 March 1946," ibid., 1015–16; "Ji-Cha-Re-Liao Branch Bureau's Report on How to Deal with the East Mongolian Question, 3 March 1946," ibid., 1017; "Northeast Bureau's Telegram on East Mongolian Work, 11 March 1946," ibid., 1024; "[Jin-Cha-Ji Bureau's] Telegram to the Northeast Bureau on the East Mongolian Question, 13 March 1946," ibid., 1027; "CCPCC's Directive on the East Mongolian Question, 10 March 1946," ibid., 1023.

42. Hao Yufeng, *Wu Lanfu Zhuan,* 394–95.

As GMD officials were juggling terms like "nation" (*minzu*) and "clan" (*zongzu*) in referring to the non-Han peoples of China, the CCP cadres had their own terminological challenges. One pair of difficult terms was "regional autonomy" (*quyu zizhi*) vis-à-vis "local autonomy" (*difang zizhi*), and another was "self-determination" (*zijue*) and "self-government" (*zizhi*). All these were concerned with non-Han peoples' right to self-government: The words "regional" and "local" indicated the territorial reach of autonomy, and "self-determination" and "self-government" connoted the intensity of political power. CCP definitions of these terms varied from time to time. By the end of World War II, with regard to non-Han peoples' political rights, CCP thinking had traveled a long way from adherence to the Leninist dogma recognizing minority nationalities' right to secession to adoption of the Chinese nationalist stand demanding unity of all nationalities in China on equal basis. This shifting only had a limited impact on China's interethnic relations because, until the end of World War II, the CCP in practice had no contact with any ethnic-separatist movement.[43]

During the initial postwar months, the CCP's encounter with Inner Mongolian separatism changed the context of its ethnopolitical deliberations. Now practical political actions took priority over lofty propaganda. Clearly, in 1946 the CCP leadership's goal was to limit the territorial region and decrease the power intensity of the eastern Mongolian movement. Its "regional autonomy" formula therefore differed drastically both from the "territorial autonomy" aspired to by the Inner Mongols at the time and from the "autonomous regions" practiced by the People's Republic of China after 1949. The conception did not particularly connote an ethnoterritorial content but was generally in concert with the CCP's advocacy for "people's autonomy" against the GMD dictatorship. For the Inner Mongols, such a formula meant only a low-level self-government by Inner Mongolian residents in separate provinces.[44]

43. I have discussed the CCP's changing ethnopolitical stance between 1921 and 1945 in my *Frontier Passages: Ethnopolitics and the Rise of Chinese Communism, 1921–1945* (Washington, D.C., and Stanford, Calif.: Woodrow Wilson Center Press and Stanford University Press, 2004).

44. "CCPCC's Directive to Peng Zhen and Lin Biao on Organization of a Field Army and Opposition to the GMD Troops' Landing in the Northeast under the Protection of American Warships, 4 November 1945,"*ZZWX*, 15: 400; "CCPCC's Directive on Increasing Troops to Control the Northeast, 4 November 1945," ibid., 401–2; "Chairman of the Sui-Mongolian Government Yun Ze Discusses the Question of Inner Mongolian Autonomy," *Jin-Cha-Ji Ribao* (Jin-Cha-Ji Daily), 16 November 1945, in *NZYL*, 8–11.

After China's war against Japan, support for ethnic separatism, even if only in rhetoric, was out of the question for the CCP. With the GMD regime again as its principal adversary, Yan'an had two overriding concerns in contemplating actions to gain ground with both Chinese nationalism and non-Han ethnonationalism. One was to maintain the CCP's anti-GMD yet nevertheless "legitimate" standing in the forum of Chinese, principally Han, public opinion. As indicated in its February 24 directive, the CCPCC tried painstakingly not to offend the feelings of "parochial Chinese nationalists," which, probably shared secretly by many in the CCP, were most potent in postwar China's public forum. Another was to maintain the CCP's liberal ethnopolitical reputation, in contrast to the GMD's rigid image, among the non-Han peoples. Always careful to avoid a head-on confrontation with Inner Mongols' postwar movements, Yan'an opted for an approach of co-optation and incorporation. In this sense, between 1945 and 1949, the CCP did not just follow an anti-GMD path of partisan politics to power; it was also walking on a tightrope of ethnopolitics and constantly maintaining its balance between Chinese nationalism in China's central political stage and non-Han ethnonationalisms along China's ethnic frontiers.

In the early months of 1946, the CCP balanced its "constitutional" struggle against the GMD with a "regional autonomy" formula for the Inner Mongols. Then, before the year ended, as its legal struggle in the GMD capital became deadlocked and its military situation in Manchuria deteriorated, a new balancing move was in order. This time, along with renouncing the GMD regime's legitimacy, Yan'an tilted its balancing pole toward the Inner Mongols' demand to establish a unified Inner Mongolian autonomous government. The episode of Yun Ze's operation of incorporating eastern Mongolia into the CCP orbit in 1947 has been considered in chapter 5. Two points should, however, be further clarified here.

First, although as early as in August 1946 Yun suggested to Yan'an that its Inner Mongolian strategy concentrate on the issue of autonomous government, the CCPCC did not accept the idea until almost four months later. When the decision was made, Yan'an acknowledged the merit of Yun Ze's recommendation mainly in the context of Chinese, not Inner Mongolian,

---

Quyu zizhi in the CCP terminology of the 1940s meant autonomy below the provincial level. After the IMAMA was established, Yun Ze explained to the CCP press that *quyu zizhi* was a necessary preparatory stage *before* autonomy for the entire Inner Mongolia. Since 1949, however, *quyu zizhi* has been used in the PRC to refer to its "autonomous region" practice, as if the practice was intended by the CCP all along.

politics. In other words, it was the GMD regime's recent actions, not the Inner Mongols' long-standing aspiration, that compelled the CCP leadership to take new steps. In November, the GMD regime decided to hold a national congress unilaterally, regardless of objections from the CCP and the Democratic League. The move rendered meaningless any further legal maneuvering by the CCP, and, in addition, it might lead to some placating gestures by the GMD government toward ethnic minorities. Meanwhile, having asserted political authority at the center, the GMD regime also intensified its military offensive in Manchuria and Inner Mongolia.

In response, the CCPCC used endorsement of an Inner Mongolian autonomous government to consolidate the party's cooperation with the Mongolian populace, which had been deteriorating because of the CCP's own radical social policies as well as new GMD offensives. In supporting an Inner Mongolian autonomous government against the official Chinese state, the CCP was no longer inhibited by a concern about international reactions. By that time, the Soviet Army already left Manchuria and Inner Mongolia, and consequently Moscow could not be held responsible for developments in these areas. General George C. Marshall, who had been leading a frustrated mission for a year to mediate between the CCP and the GMD, was also about to give up and return to the United States.[45]

Second, although the CCP gained tremendous ethnopolitical advantage over the GMD by supporting the Inner Mongolian Autonomous Government in May 1947, the relationship between the CCP and Inner Mongolian nationalism remained ambiguous and unsteady. It was yet to determine to what extent the "autonomous government" could satisfy Inner Mongols' desire for self-government and what would be the territorial limits of Inner Mongolian autonomy. In February 1947, at a cadre conference in eastern Inner Mongolia, Yun Ze used Outer Mongolia as a model for the Inner Mongols'

---

45. "Yun Ze's Report to the CCPCC on Land and Autonomous Questions of Inner Mongolia, 1 August 1946," *MWWH,* 1057–58; "CCPCC's Directive on Consideration of Establishing an Inner Mongolian Autonomous Government, 26 November 1946," ibid., 1083. Many years later, as recorded in Liu Jieyu, "The necessary path for Inner Mongolian autonomous movement," *NWZ,* 50: 230, Ulanfu (Yun Ze) recalled the connection between the ethnopolitics of Inner Mongolia and the mainstream politics of China, saying that as long as the GMD and the CCP were still talking to each other, Inner Mongolia could have an autonomous movement but not an autonomous government. This raises a question as to whether or not in 1946 Yun Ze was aware of such a connection. If he was, then his August recommendation was a conscious call for Yan'an to treat Inner Mongolian politics on its own terms.

phased autonomy, suggesting that just as Outer Mongolia, Inner Mongolian autonomy would grow from an autonomous movement into an autonomous government. Then, he contended, the third phase for Inner Mongolia would differ from MPR independence and would be one of "free federation" with China. In the following month, he actually suggested to the CCPCC that in China's new constitution all nationalities' right to self-determination should be recognized and an equal, democratic federation based on these peoples' "free unification" should be established. To Yun, the Inner Mongolian autonomous government would coincide with "regional autonomy," waiting for a higher-level autonomy based on national self-determination. Such a periodization was also accepted by the CCP's Western Manchurian Branch Bureau. For instance, in May 1947 Zhang Pinghua, the bureau's representative to the inaugural assembly of the Inner Mongolian Autonomous Government, told the assembly that the CCP "firmly supported national self-determination," and that the Inner Mongols should "implement autonomy" for now and "strive for self-determination" in the future (*shixing zizhi, zhengqu zijue*).[46]

In retrospect, however, Yan'an's endorsement of the Inner Mongolian Autonomous Government in May 1947 proved to be the CCP's last concession to Inner Mongolian nationalism during its war with the GMD. The hollow promise of national self-determination indicated both the extent to which the CCP needed the Inner Mongols' cooperation at the moment and the fact that the CCP never in practice granted such a right to China's national minorities. The "autonomy first, self-determination later" formula of May 1947 was actually intended to circumscribe, not encourage, the Inner Mongols' demand for self-determination. Unsurprisingly, when the CCP's political and military crises were over, there would be no more incentive for the CCP even to repeat its 1947 promise to the Inner Mongols.

---

46. "Yun Ze's Report at a Cadre Conference in Lindong, February 1947," *Neimenggu Tongzhanshi Dang'an Shiliao Xuanbian* (Selected Archival Materials on the History of the United Front in Inner Mongolia), comp. United Front Department of the CCP Committee of the Inner Mongolian Autonomous Region and the Archives of the Inner Mongolian Autonomous Region (internal circulation, 1987), 1: 368; "Yun Ze's Opinion on the Constitutional Question of the Minority Nationalities, 17 March 1947," *MWWH*, 1324; "Assembly of Inner Mongolian People's Representatives Opens and the Grand Ceremony Has No Precedent," from *Neimeng Zizhi Bao* (Daily of Inner Mongolian autonomy) of 26 April 1947, *MWWH*, 1325–26; "Chairman of the Inner Mongolian Autonomous Government Yun Ze Interviewed by Reporters," from *Neimeng Zizhi Bao* of 10 May 1947, *MWWH*, 1327.

In January 1948, obviously in a good mood about the direction of Chinese politics, Mao Zedong made this remark to Chen Yi:

When Japan just surrendered, we were at once happy and afraid. We were happy about Japan's surrender but afraid of the unsettled superiority [between the CCP and the GMD]. We had not gained much and Jiang Jieshi remained strong. When a serious civil war fell upon us, the possibilities of victory and failure struggled against each other. Now the situation is good because our superiority has been established. This is not an estimate, but a fact.[47]

In the next two years, as the CCP's military superiority vis-à-vis the GMD increased steadily, its ethnopolitical need of the Inner Mongols in the power contest decreased proportionally. When the CCP's final victory was approaching, the CCPCC was obliged to clarify its stand on what should be the highest form of non-Han peoples' autonomy and what should be their relationship with the incoming Chinese Communist state. CCP cadres involved in the nationality work at local levels held a range of views.[48]

The confusion soon ended. In September 1949, during the preparatory conference for a new "People's Political Consultative Conference" (PPCC), Mao assigned Li Weihan, a senior CCP official who had been involved in the CCP's nationality work in the Yan'an period, the task of studying the question of multinational federation. Because this was not really a new question for the CCP, it did not take Li much time to report that China's nationality question in history and at the moment was different from that of the Soviet Union. Therefore, Li recommended, a unitary state system was more appropriate than a federal system. The CCP leadership readily accepted the conclusion. Then, explaining the decision to representatives of the PPCC, Zhou Enlai reaffirmed the minorities' right to self-determination. But, he added, the question was whether or not in China, where the Han population was the overwhelming majority, the nationality policy should go beyond the goal of national self-government. Zhou's principal reason against doing so

---

47. *Mao Zedong Nianpu,* 3: 275.
48. "Excerpts from Hu Shaoheng's Diaries," entry on 15 March 1949, *Xing'an Dangshi Wenji* (Collected Essays on the Party History of Xing'an) 1 (1993): 185; "Cao Diqiu's Speech on the Minority Nationality Question, 21 September 1949," *MWWH,* 1347–50; Yang Song, "On Nationalist Movement and National Question in the Age of Imperialism, August–October 1938," ibid., 794–801.

was external: "Today imperialists again want to split Tibet, Taiwan, and even Xinjiang from us. . . . Because of this situation our state is named as the People's Republic of China, not as a federation." In this republic, therefore, the nationalities would exercise their "right to self-government" but not that to "self-determination."[49]

Thus, Zhou used the external thrust of Chinese nationalism, or anti-imperialism, to dilute any impression that the real reason for the CCP to reject a multinational federal system was internal. No matter how external and internal considerations weighed respectively in the CCP decision, it would not change the fact that the decision was made in contradiction to the CCP's 1947 promise to the Inner Mongols and to Yun Ze's different opinion on the matter. In this manner, when the People's Republic of China was about to begin, its founders set a precedent to settle the issue of "self-determination" by way of "other-determination."[50]

In the CCP's postwar ethnopolitics, Yun occupied a very influential but ultimately impossible position. It was the CCP that made him a "leader of the Inner Mongols" so that he could help the CCP to incorporate and digest the eastern Mongolian movement. Therefore, although having an edge in occupying a cross-ethnic position, Yun was unable to switch from his role

49. Jiang Ping et al., eds., *Zhongguo Minzu Wenti de Lilun yu Shijian* (Beijing: Zhonggong Zhongyang Dangxiao Chubanshe, 1994), 170–72. A speech made by Li Weihan many years later revealed the CCP's basic reasoning against a federal system in China: (1) In its long history, China had already become a Han-centric, unified, and multi-nationality state; (2) the struggle against imperialism, feudalism, and bureaucratic capitalism required unity of all nationalities of China; and (3) the Chinese revolution had to be led by the proletariat, a class that did not exist within minority nationalities, and therefore these peoples' separation from the Han would mean their deprivation of sound leadership. In the same speech, Li also insisted that in China the "right to self-determination" could only be exercised by the Han and other nationalities together against foreign imperialism but not by the non-Han nationalities against the Han. See, "A Few Questions in the Nationality Work, September 1961," in *Li Weihan Xuanji* (Selected works of Li Weihan), ed. Li Weihan (Beijing: Renmin Chubanshe, 1987), 366–68, 372.

50. According to Wang and Hao, *Wulanfu Nianpu,* 209–11, Yun Ze did not arrive in Beijing until September 17, 1949, ten days after Zhou Enlai's explanatory speech. *Wulanfu Nianpu,* 322, also reveals that Yun Ze did not sort out his thoughts on the matter, perhaps along the party line, until five years later, when he wrote a series of "study notes" regarding the "way of reference to the nationality question, the question of self-determination vis-à-vis self-government, and the differences and similarities in Chinese and Soviet solutions of their domestic nationality questions." A study of a possible disagreement between Yun Ze and the CCPCC over "self-determination" and "federation" has to wait for further declassification of the CCP archives.

as a "loyal party member" vis-à-vis the Inner Mongols to that as an "Inner Mongolian leader" vis-à-vis the party. Consequently, his opinion within the CCP hierarchy would not be treated by the party leadership much differently from other CCP cadres'.

Within the CCP, however, Yun did score on another controversial question, which concerned demarcation of Inner Mongolia as an autonomous territory. When the Inner Mongolian Autonomous Government was launched in May 1947, its political program stipulated that the new government's authority cover "every Inner Mongolian league and banner." According to a map published by the autonomous government four months later, these leagues and banners stretched from the northeastern corner of Manchuria to Ningxia in the west. In an earlier speech to a CCP cadres' meeting in Rehe, Yun Ze asserted that "generally speaking, Inner Mongolia includes the region north of the Great Wall, basically meaning the three areas of Rehe, Chahar, and Suiyuan." He told his audience that the GMD policy to convert original Inner Mongolian leagues and banners into provinces was the "earliest demonstration of great Hanism [*da hanzu zhuyi*]." This view was shared by Inner Mongols of all political persuasions but was opposed by some CCP officials. As mentioned above, in defending the "integrity of Rehe," the CCP's local organization in Rehe objected to the eastern Mongols' intention to extend their influence into the province. The Northeast Bureau also cautioned the CCPCC that restoration of an Inner Mongolian region might cause disagreements within the party and that such a policy was difficult to implement anyway while the civil war continued. By no means neutral on the matter, the bureau ridiculed the opinion that north of the Yellow River or north of the Great Wall should be regarded as Inner Mongolian territories.[51]

As in the GMD power structure, the real obstacle to establishing an integral Inner Mongolian region came from the CCP's middle-level organizations. At least in a territorial sense, Mao wanted to be consistent with his

---

51. "Political Program of the Inner Mongolian Autonomous Government, 27 April 1947," *NZYL*, 231–33; "Map on the Locations of Inner Mongolian Leagues and Banners," orig. pub. in *Neimenggu Jianying* (Profile of Inner Mongolia) by the Inner Mongolian Autonomous Government in September 1947, reprinted in *Neimenggu Dang'an Shiliao* 1 (1992): 2; "Yun Ze's Speech on a Few Questions in the Inner Mongolian Autonomous Movement at an Enlarged Cadre Conference of the [CCP] District Committee in Northern Rehe, 3 February 1947," *NZYL*, 157–58; "CCP Ji-Re-Liao Branch Bureau's Report to the CCPCC on the Mongolian Work in Rehe, 7 March 1946," *MWWH*, 1021; "Northeast Bureau's Opinion on the Question of Inner Mongolian Autonomy and Request for direction from the CCPCC, 1 April 1947," ibid., 1097.

1935 proclamation to the Inner Mongols. In 1947, he approved the Northeast Bureau's suggestion for delay. But, in early 1949, during the second plenum of the CCP's seventh congress, Mao personally promised Yun that Inner Mongolia's original area would be restored. He also asked Yun to pick a capital city for Inner Mongolia among Chifeng, Zhangjiakou, and Guisui (Hohhot). Yun understood the conversation as Mao's commitment to the abolition of Rehe, Chahar, and Suiyuan Provinces. Yet it would take six more years before the People's Republic of China could erase the "first demonstration of great Hanism" of the GMD regime. In the meantime, Yun's effort to restore regional integrity of Inner Mongolia was interpreted by some of his Han colleagues in the CCP as evidence of an "excessive desire for leadership."[52]

Mao, however, knew better than these officials about trade-offs. In early 1952, during a CCP conference in Beijing, some provincial officials continued to argue against Suiyuan's merger with Inner Mongolia. Their obtuseness about Mao's intention was described by Nie Rongzhen as "at eleven o'clock in the morning still not knowing from which direction the sun rises." Reportedly, on one occasion Mao slapped the table angrily and threatened to remove these opponents from their positions. Later, nevertheless, Mao, via the always tactful Zhou Enlai, laid out his quid pro quo formula for these blunt local officials: "The Suiyuan–Inner Mongolia merger must open two doors. One door is for the Mongols to welcome the Han to enter [Inner Mongolia] for the sake of exploring the iron mines [of Baiyun'ebo] and developing the steel enterprise of Baotou; another door is for the Han to support Suiyuan's merging into the Inner Mongolian Autonomous Region for the sake of Inner Mongolia's unified autonomy."[53]

Again, as in the case of the Inner Mongolian Autonomous Government, the demarcation of Inner Mongolia's regional territory was an interethnic compromise struck under conditions suitable to the CCP's policy need. Under Mao's formula, the historical region of Inner Mongolia would be restored, but the cultural, demographic, and economic sinicization of the region would continue at present and in the future. As the new ruling party

52. "CCPCC's Reply to the Northeast Bureau on the Question of Inner Mongolian Autonomy, 20 April 1947," *MWWH*, 1102; Wang and Hao, *Wulanfu Nianpu*, 200–1, 297–98, 302–3, 306.

53. Liu Jieyu, "Restoration of Inner Mongolia's Historical Feature: Late Vice President Ulanfu's Recollections Recorded," *NWZ*, 50: 258–72; Wang Duo, *Wushi Chunqiu*, 368–69. The dates for the abolition of Chahar, Suiyuan, and Rehe provinces are separately October 1952, January 1954, and July 1955.

of China, the CCP's first and foremost task was to impose its political culture on Chinese society. In China's ethnic frontiers including Inner Mongolia, this became the CCP brand of political sinicization.

Enact "Leftist Excessiveness"

Rarely did Mao and other top CCP leaders evaluate the Han–minority relationship with a purely interethnic perspective. In 1952, both the Inner Mongolian and the Suiyuan governments were part of the CCP administrative system, and Mao's quid pro quo was really for the CCP system to operate smoothly. As a rule, CCP leaders viewed ethnic matters through the lense of "class analysis." In their ideological chart, the vertical structure of social classes was solid and principled, and the horizontal relationship of ethnic groups was unsubstantial and maneuverable. The CCP valued the class-struggle doctrine not only because it was a Marxist dogma but also because it proved effective in the party's mass mobilization operations. While pushing for a land revolution in China's countryside, Mao and his colleagues demonstrated tremendous imagination and creativity in identifying and differentiating the rural "classes" of China. The Marxist perception of a two-class struggle between bourgeoisie and proletariat in the Western capitalist world was replaced with a more elaborate, multistrata, Maoist maneuvering in China's rustic society.[54]

Yet in Inner Mongolia, where interethnic antagonism intertwined with and compounded socioeconomic contradictions, even the CCP's elaborate class analysis became inadequate. During the Chinese Civil War, the overwhelming concern of the CCP's political strategy in Inner Mongolia, as in other regions, was to enlist popular support. But here the CCP's single-plank agenda for land reform (also named "democratic reform"), as Yun Ze pointed out to the CCPCC, had to be modified and supplemented with another reform of ethnopolitical significance. The problem was that the two reforms tended to interfere with each other. In addition to deciding a balanced strategy at the national level in struggling against the GMD and maneuvering with the Inner Mongols, the CCP had to develop a proportional policy in its Mongolian work in alternately promoting "social justice" and "ethnic justice."

---

54. See Mao Zedong's model "Analysis of All the Classes in Chinese Society," December 1925, in *Mao's Road to Power,* ed. Stuart R. Schram (Armonk, N.Y.: M. E. Sharpe, 1992), 2: 249–62.

During the initial postwar months, the CCP followed a cautious social policy in Inner Mongolia that was aimed at forging an "extensive united front" of "all social strata, all religious beliefs, and all nationalities." In focusing on enlisting the Inner Mongols in its struggle against the GMD, the CCP intended to spare no effort in "properly mediating the internal contradictions" of the Mongolian society. In comparison, the newborn eastern Mongolian movement appeared much more radical than the CCP in announcing its goals of enhancing workers' and farmers' welfare and avoiding a "capitalist future." At the time, the CCPCC advised its operatives in Manchuria and Inner Mongolia that Mongol princes should probably not be struggled against and that Mongol youths' activities in that direction must not be supported by the party unconditionally.[55] But, by March 1946, when CCP operatives sensed that "autonomy" pursued by the eastern Mongols was not totally in concert with the party's military and political strategies, they began to seek a remedy in the familiar class-struggle approach.

Lin Biao, who was in command of the CCP's military operations in Manchuria, was at the time disheartened by the Mongolian situation and cabled the CCPCC to express his discontent with the party's current moderate policy. Lin contended that the current policy was ill advised in "solely focusing on canvassing the upper classes and dealing with the independent autonomous movement." Aside from providing the GMD with propaganda materials, he pointed out, the orientation harvested no benefit for the CCP but Mongols' "closed-door and rejective attitude toward us." This was because, when the CCP courted the upper classes in vain, the lower-class Mongols were ignored and became disillusioned. Lin proposed a policy readjustment whereby the CCP would only pay lip service to the autonomous movement in order to placate the upper classes and would meanwhile carry out serious work among the lower strata of Mongolian society.[56]

About a month later, the Northeast Bureau presented its first detailed

55. "Recent Conditions in Various Leagues and Banners of Chahar and the Process of Work in Chahar and Shilingol Leagues, 27 October 1945," *MWWH*, 971; "Jin-Cha-Ji Central Bureau's Report on the Establishment of the IMAMA, 8 November 1945," ibid., 974; "Northwest Bureau's Opinion on the Question of Erdos Banner, 15 February 1946," ibid., 998; "Report to the Northeast Bureau on Conditions of Inner Mongolia by the Seventh Division of the Northeast Anti-Japanese Allied Army, 29 January 1946," ibid., 996; "CCPCC's Directive to Lin Biao, Huang Kecheng, Li Fuchun, Cheng Zihua et al. on the Policy toward the Mongolian Nationality, 25 December 1945," ibid., 984.

56. "Lin Biao's Opinion on the Policy toward the Mongolian Question, 21 March 1946," *MWWH*, 1032.

analysis of the eastern Mongolian movement to the CCPCC. Unlike Lin Biao, who defined autonomy as a hobby of Inner Mongolian upper classes, the bureau suggested that neither the traditional elite nor the ordinary folks cared much about autonomy, and that the real driving force of the autonomous movement was made up mainly of young intellectuals. In disagreeing with Lin's dismissive attitude toward the Inner Mongols' ethnopolitical aspirations, the bureau held the question of autonomy, therefore its young intellectual advocates, as the key to enlisting the Inner Mongols into the CCP-led struggle against the GMD. The bureau, however, shared Lin's central argument on the importance of the "lower-stratum basic masses," seeing their "rise" as the precondition for a thorough solution of the Mongolia question. As for the upper classes, the bureau went even further than Lin and recommended that they be treated with a "isolating, weakening, and attacking" course. In sum, the bureau wanted to use class struggles to knock the eastern Mongolian autonomous movement into the "correct direction."[57]

Lin's and the Northeast Bureau's recommendations on radicalizing the CCP's Inner Mongolian policy came at a time when the CCPCC was ready to abandon its moderate social policies in the countryside, which had been in effect during the anti-Japanese war. In early May 1946, the CCPCC held a meeting to evaluate the general conditions of China's countryside and concluded that the CCP's land policy had lagged behind the mass' demands. A decision was adopted to switch the current moderate policy of "rent and interest reduction" back to the party's prewar, radical orientation of land revolution. Thus, with the slogan of "land to the tiller," the CCP was poised to involve the vast rural population of China in its power struggle against the GMD. CCP operatives in Manchuria and Rehe were immediately informed of the decision and were instructed to carry out the new policy "resolutely." Still mindful of a cautionary advice from the field that the land question in Mongolian areas was intricately entangled with the historically unjust Han–Mongolian relationship, the CCPCC suggested that these areas be exempted from the new policy for now. But in reality, the new land policy had such a sweeping effect that none of the Inner Mongolian areas under CCP influence was spared.[58]

57. "Northeast Bureau's Opinion on the Working Orientation toward Eastern Mongolia, 17 April 1946," *MWWH*, 1041–45.

58. *Liu Shaoqi Nianpu*, 2: 42–43; "CCPCC's Directive on the Solution of the Land Question in the Northeast, Rehe, and Other Areas, 6 May 1946," *ZZWX*, 16: 155; "CCPCC's Directive to the Ji-Re-Liao Branch Bureau on Furthering the Campaign for

Although available information cannot support a macro evaluation of the land reform campaign in Inner Mongolia, CCP documents dated a few months after the CCPCC's land policy directive reveal that the campaign progressed violently. In many areas, "full-scale class struggle" was carried out, and "land to the tiller" was creatively supplemented with "livestock to the herdsman" and "housing to the dweller." For the first time, people in the countryside found themselves being classified into groups named "farm laborers," "poor peasants," "middle peasants," "rich peasants," "landlords," and "tyrannical landlords." Many learned quickly to behave accordingly during the campaign.

According to a CCP material published years later, in the Xing'an area, the land reform campaign identified 3,610 households as "landlords" or "rich peasants" out of the total 74,110 households (4.9 percent). These two categories were targeted for "accounts settlement." More than a quarter of the landlord households were struggled against during the first ten months of the campaign, and, according to the same source, seventy-six of the "most vicious" landlords were "suppressed," or executed. But the real picture was much more severe because of the inevitable excessiveness of such mass campaigns. In a CCP internal meeting in 1948, Yun Ze revealed that the class identification in Inner Mongolia had been carried out in a chaotic way, resulting in initially "attacking a very wide range of people." According to Yun, the attack was extended to 20.8 percent of the households and 25.6 percent of the region's population. The "attack range" would later be narrowed down, but the imprint on the society left by the initial impact was hard to erase. Furthermore, Yun admitted, a "serious mistake" was that "beating occurred at every struggle session and too many people were killed."[59]

Excessive deeds and "extreme leftist mistakes" were recurring phenomena

Accounts Settlement and Solving the Land Problem for the Peasants, 17 May 1946," ibid., 164–65; "Ji-Re-Liao Branch Bureau's Report to the CCPCC on the Mongolian Work in Rehe, 7 March 1946," *MWWH*, 1021–22; "General Narrative on the Land Reform in Xing'an League," *Xing'an Dangshi Wenji*, 2: 4; "Zhang Ce on the Conditions and Experiences of Working in the Eastern Mongolian Region, 15 August 1946," *MWWH*, 1317.

59. "Northeast Bureau's Directive on Correcting and Preventing a Leftist Tendency in Current Mongolian Work, 1 September 1946," *MWWH*, 1065; "West Manchurian Branch Bureau's Conclusion on the Mongolian Work and Regulations on Some Policies, 13 September 1946," ibid., 1068–69; "General Narrative on the Land Reform Campaign in Xing'an League," *Xing'an Danshi Wenji* (Essays on the Party History of Xing'an) 2 (1993): 1–13; "Outline of Comrade Yun Ze's Report at Inner Mongolian Cadres' Conference, 30 July 1948," *Neimenggu Tongzhanshi Dang'an Shiliao Xuanbian*, 1: 422.

throughout CCP history. These were tolerated or even encouraged by the party at the initial stage of a campaign in order to obtain sufficient "enthusiasm of the mass" that would sustain the campaign for a long enough period. But to mark more than a quarter of a population as the targets of a single campaign was exceptionally excessive, even for the CCP standard.[60] Although the CCP's land policy was harvesting popularity among Chinese peasants elsewhere, in Inner Mongolia the same policy was counterproductive: It was undermining the party's interethnic united front with the Inner Mongols. There was only one reason for the excessive "excessiveness" of the CCP policy in Inner Mongolia, the intertwined ethnic and class relationships. CCP operatives, who were inventive in launching peasants movement in the Chinese countryside but ignorant about interethnic social conditions of Inner Mongolia, were presumably initiating a class struggle but were actually aggravating the region's chronic ethnic conflict. Years later, Mao would make a remark that "in the final analysis, the question of national struggles is that of class struggles."[61] But, in the late 1940s, CCP cadres in Inner Mongolia learned that underneath violent class struggles a deep interethnic hatred might be burning.

In the so-called agricultural and semipastoral areas, Han peasants' historical encroachment on the Inner Mongols' land had created different socioeconomic terrains, whereas those "pure" pastoral areas remained a category distinct from both. Such a complicated situation was completely novel to many CCP operatives, who were accustomed to function according to the CCP's established perceptions about the rural class structure. As a CCP document pointed out, some CCP cadres "applied mechanically their experience of mass struggle gained in the Han areas to the Mongolian areas." These cadres' conducting of the Han-type class struggles in the Mongolian region was inevitable because the CCPCC did not have any different guidelines for them to follow. For instance, in April 1946, the Northeast Bureau used the CCP's established method of class analysis to ascertain the rural class struc-

---

60. This proved to be just the first such case in Inner Mongolia. During the "Cultural Revolution" of the late 1960s, 346,000 people were identified as members of an imaginary underground "new Inner Mongolian people's revolutionary party" and were subject to persecution. At the time, the total Mongolian population of Inner Mongolia was about 1.6 million. In other words, one out of every five Inner Mongols were persecuted. See Hao Weimin, *Neimenggu Zizhiqu Shi, 1947–1987* (History of the Inner Mongolian Autonomous Region) (Hohhot: Neimenggu Daxue Chubanshe, 1991), 285, 313.

61. Mao Zedong, *Mao Zedong Waijiao Wenxuan* (Selected Diplomatic Works of Mao Zedong) (Beijing: Zhongyang Wenxian Chubanshe, 1994), 495.

ture of eastern Mongolia. On the basis of data from two villages, the bureau's verdict was that in the area 30 percent of the households were "landlords" who exploited the other 70 percent, defined as "serf-like" population.[62]

After the land campaign in Inner Mongolia continued for several months, Yun Ze urged the CCPCC to make some policy readjustments. He pointed out that land ownership in different areas of Inner Mongolia, depending on the degree of agricultural development and demographic sinicization, existed in various forms and carried no uniform socioeconomic significance. Yun suggested that land reform be suspended altogether in those semi-pastoral and pure pastoral areas. Even in areas where agriculture was predominant, land reform must first and foremost be tailored in relation to the nationality question, which, according to Yun, involved the Han–Mongolian relationship and the issue of "right to the land." By "right to the land," Yun meant the Inner Mongols' collective ownership of the territory vis-à-vis the Han population, including the ownership of farm land, mineral resources, mountains, forests, and idle spaces. He also believed that class struggles within the Mongolian society must be conducted by the Inner Mongols themselves and that the Han people could use the properties listed above through renting but not owning.[63]

At the time, Yun's ethnopolitical interpretation of the land question in Inner Mongolia was praised by the CCPCC. After September 1946, alarmed by erosion of the CCP–Mongolian cooperation caused by the party's land policy, which in some areas caused Mongol residents' collective exodus, the Northeast Bureau and other CCP regional bureaus involved in Mongolian

62. "West Manchurian Bureau's conclusion on the Mongolian work and regulations about several policies, 13 September 1946," *MWWH*, 1069; "Northeast Bureau's Opinion on the Work Orientation in Eastern Mongolia, 17 April 1946," ibid., 1041.

63. "Yun Ze's Report to the CCPCC on the Questions of Land and Autonomy in Inner Mongolia, 1 August 1946," *MWWH*, 1057–58. It should be noted that Yun Ze's policy suggestion for differentiating the Han and the Mongols in land reform sounded even more "nationalistic" than what the eastern Mongolian leaders advocated. Khafengga, as evidenced in "Khafengga's Letter to Jigemude, 19 July 1946," *NZYL*, 78–80, and "Khafengga's Speech at the Meeting to Conclude the Mass Work by the Work Team in Khorchin West Front Banner, 24 July 1946," ibid., 80–86, supported an ethnicity-blind policy in land reform. Yun Ze was thinking more as a CCP operative than as an Inner Mongol and recommended to the CCPCC a tactful way, or a favorable treatment of a "minority people," for consolidating the party's standing with the Inner Mongols. Khafengga, by contrast, considered the Inner Mongols as the host nationality of the land and was thinking like a Mongolian revolutionary who wanted to treat the Han peasants fairly.

work began to take steps to correct "leftist mistakes." By early 1947, the first wave of class struggles seemed to be over, and the Inner Mongols' ethno-nationalist agenda could again take priority in the CCP's Mongolian work. The result was the establishment of the Inner Mongolian Autonomous Government. The new government's political program actually pledged that it would protect "all Inner Mongolian people's human rights and property rights." In the program, "landlords, herd owners, industrialists and merchants, and lamas and former princes" were listed along with "farmers, herdsmen, workers" and others as part of the "people."[64]

Yet, the "excessiveness" of the CCP policy did not end here. In August 1946, after making his suggestion to the CCPCC about how to conduct land reform in Inner Mongolia, Yun advised his Han colleagues in western Inner Mongolia that in the Mongolian banners of Suiyuan, where more than 90 percent of the Mongolian population lived on rents collected from tenant farmers who were mostly Han, the land question should not be interpreted as the same landlord–tenant relationship as in the Chinese countryside. A few months later, at a party conference in Rehe, he further outlined a policy for differentiating the Han and the Mongols socioeconomically. Despite the CCPCC's approval, Yun's advice must have fallen on deaf ears among many of his Han colleagues, for, two year later, in both the eastern and western regions of Inner Mongolia, the CCP's regional bureaus were still trying to correct exactly the same kind of "mistakes" that he had cautioned against. By 1948, even he had to change his ethnopolitical analysis of the Inner Mongols' right to "Mongolian land," and he embraced the standard CCP view that the Inner Mongolian people would automatically become "masters" in their land after the success of the Chinese revolution.[65]

---

64. "CCPCC's Telegram to Yun Ze, the Branch and Central Bureaus on the Land Question of Inner Mongolia, 10 August 1946," *NZYL*, 106; "Northeast Bureau's Directive on Correcting and Preventing a Leftist Tendency in Current Mongolian Work, 1 September 1946," *MWWH*, 1064–66; "West Manchurian Branch Bureau's Conclusion on the Mongolian Work and Regulations on Several Policies, 13 September 1946," ibid., 1067–69; "CCP Committees of Liao-Ji Provinces' Opinion on the Work in Mongolian Areas, 15 September 1946," ibid., 1072; "Jin-Cha-Ji Central Bureau's Conclusion on the Mongolian Work, 1946," ibid., 1087–92; "Political Program of the Inner Mongolian Autonomous Government, 27 April 1947," ibid., 1111–13.

65. "Yun Ze's Letter to Comrade Gao [Kelin], Yao [Ji], and Others on the Mongolian Work in Suiyuan–Mongolia, 19 August 1946," *NZYL*, 107–9; "Yun Ze's Speech on Certain Questions in the Inner Mongolian Autonomous Movement at the Enlarged Cadre Conference of the CCP Committee of Northern Rehe District, 3 February 1947," ibid., 157–61; "Northeast Bureau's Report to the CCPCC on the Implementation of the

In reversing Mao's "in the final analysis" perspective, one can see that although the CCP preferred to "elevate" the Inner Mongols' struggle for autonomy to the level of its own revolution of "class struggles," it could not avoid the ultimate question in the Han–Mongolian relationship, which was about power. The GMD confronted the question in a rigid and condescending manner and paid a high price of losing Inner Mongols to the CCP. The CCP first tried to deal with the question by partially accommodating the Inner Mongols' aspirations but eventually tried to go around it with a class-struggle compass. In the late 1940s, the compass did not function well. The Inner Mongols put the question to the CCP in clear terms, contending that "Mongolian territories, Mongolian interests, and Mongolian rights" must not be violated by the Han any longer in the future. Experiences taught the CCP leadership that these matters must be reckoned with to avoid "leftist mistakes." But, in the CCP's terminology, a "leftist tendency" might simultaneously mean an inopportune move for the present and a desirable direction for the future. The Inner Mongols' aspirations of the late 1940s needed to be dealt with patiently for the moment. Yet, because these were basically misguided ideas reflective of "narrow nationalism," they should eventually be overcome with the spirit of working-class revolution.

The problem for such an approach was that posing as supranational warriors of class struggles, CCP operatives themselves could hardly overcome their own Han predispositions, which were often disguised as excessive revolutionary enthusiasm. In a mid-1948 report to the CCPCC, the Northeast Bureau admitted that CCP cadres working in the Mongolian areas were "generally excessively leftist." They "disregarded the differences between [the two] nationalities, economies, customs, and religions, forcefully applied Han people's way of doing things, and attacked and discriminated against many Mongolian cadres." This kind of interethnic friction within the CCP ranks had disastrous consequences for Mongolian society:

CCPCC's Directive on Land Reform and Party Rectification, 23 June 1948," *MWWH,* 1139; "Northwestern Bureau's Decision on the Question of Rent Reduction in Jungar Banner, 27 October 1948," ibid., 1169–70; Wang Duo, *Wushi Chunqiu,* 257–63, 272; "Yun Ze's Conclusive Report at the Inner Mongolian Senior Cadres' Conference, 30 July 1948," *Neimenggu Tongzhan Shi Dang'an Shiliao Xuanbian* (Selected Archival Materials on the History of the United Front in Inner Mongolia) (internal circulation, 1987), 1: 420; "Ulfanfu's Speech at Xing'an League's Conference on the Mass Work, 15 November 1948," ibid., 476.

In agricultural areas, aside from the general leftist bias, most Lamaist temples were destroyed, and even the worship of the Buddha was banned. In troops, if a Mongol spoke the Mongolian language, he would be cursed as "crying like a donkey." In pastoral and semi-pastoral areas, livestock husbandry suffered from serious destruction; most herds were divided and distributed, and were slaughtered and eaten extravagantly. The death rate [of livestock] was very high.

But the alternative policy suggested by the same document was merely one of "slow advancement," not change of goals.[66]

In early 1947, when the CCP decided to embrace the idea of a unified autonomous government for Inner Mongolia, Yun Ze made an effort to persuade the Inner Mongols to forgive the CCP's earlier ethnic misdeeds in the area: "We need to view the CCP's policy toward minority nationalities with a long-term perspective and also view it in practice. At the same time we have to understand that since its formation, for the first time in history the CCP has been faced with such a vast Mongolian region and has made contact with so many Mongols. It is therefore not surprising that some mistakes have occurred."[67] Yet, in the CCP–Inner Mongolian partnership, the latter's alleged mistakes would neither be forgiven nor forgotten. Eastern Mongol leaders, for instance, were not really accepted by the CCP as its own cadres. In CCP documents produced in the late 1940s, they were named as "former puppet officials," "new bureaucrats," and "pure nationalists." Not only these leaders' pre-1945 experiences were indefensible; even their cooperation with the CCP after Japan's surrender was described as "sneaking into" the CCP and "speculating in revolution." Thus the mass movement of eastern Mongolia was reduced to a few individuals' opportunistic endeavor out of their upper-class motivations.[68]

66. "Report [by the CCP Committee in Tongliao District] on the Mongolian Work in the Past and the Work Orientation and Tasks in the Future, 31 July 1946," *MWWH,* 1306; "Jin-Cha-Ji Central Bureau's Conclusion on the Mongolian Work, 1946," ibid., 1091; "Northeast Bureau's Report on the Implementation of the CCPCC's Directive on Land Reform and Party Rectification, 23 June 1948," ibid., 1139.

67. "Yun Ze's Report at a Cadres' Conference in Lin Dong, February 1947," *Neimenggu Tongzhanshi Dang'an Shiliao Xuanbian,* 1: 370.

68. "Hu Xikui's Opinion on the Materials Pertinent to the Question of Eastern Mongolia, 3 March 1946," *MWWH,* 1013; "Ji-Re-Liao Branch Bureau's Report to the CCPCC on the Question of the Mongolian Work in Rehe, 7 March 1946," ibid., 1021; "Northeast Bureau's Opinion on the Orientation of Eastern Mongolian Work, 17 April 1946," ibid.,

Yun Ze, although willing to make excuses for the CCP's wrongdoings, did not appear more understanding than his Han colleagues about eastern Mongol leaders' "mistakes." Twice in 1948, he mercilessly repudiated eastern Mongol leaders at senior cadre conferences of Inner Mongolia, labeling them "national isolationists." He contended that although in history Inner and Outer Mongolia had been one nation, today the Inner Mongols' destiny became irrevocably tied to the revolution under the CCP. His logic was that "if the Chinese revolution fails, the Inner Mongolian revolution would also fail even if it succeeds." Thus, according to him, eastern Mongol leaders were blind about history in refusing to recognize the connection between Inner Mongolia and Chinese society; their nationalism was bourgeois by nature, and their effort to organize an Inner Mongolian party was to split the proletarian leadership of the revolution.[69]

Belonging to the same ethnonational "self group," the difference between Yun and eastern Mongol leaders reflected a debate among the Inner Mongols about how they should participate in China as an ethnopolitical group. A similar disagreement also existed among those Inner Mongols who in the postwar years continued to tie their political future to the GMD regime. So this was a question of across-the-board significance to the Inner Mongols. Yun's upbringing and political career made him a complete devotee of the Inner Mongols' cooperation with the CCP. As the principal manager of CCP–Inner Mongol partnership in the postwar years, he understood better than eastern Mongol leaders about under what conditions such a partnership would be acceptable to the CCP. He worked for Inner Mongols' complete integration into the new state system that the CCP was striving to create, and he managed to bring the eastern Mongols along. Although he was negotiating with Inner Mongolian autonomists on behalf of the CCP most of

---

1042; "Western Manchurian Branch Bureau's Letter on the Question of the IMPRP [Inner Mongolian People's Revolutionary Party], 10 April 1947," ibid., 1099; "Northeast Bureau's Report for Direction on the Organization of the People's Revolutionary Party in Inner Mongolia, 18 April 1947," ibid., 1100; "Conclusion on the Work of Army Construction in Inner Mongolia by the Political Department of North China Military District of the Chinese People's Liberation Army, 14 February 1949," ibid., 1225.

69. "Ulanfu's Opening Speech at the Inner Mongol Senior Cadres' Conference, 2 July 1948," *Neimenggu Dang'an Shiliao* (Historical Archival Materials of Inner Mongolia), 1993 (2): 4–6; "Yu Ze's Conclusive Report at the Inner Mongol Senior Cadres' Conference, 30 July 1948," ibid., 13–14. When Yun Ze's speech of 2 July 1948 was published in 1993, four eastern Mongol leaders' names—probably Khafengga, Temurbagana, Pungsug, and Oljeiochir—were omitted.

the time, he also negotiated with the CCP from an Inner Mongolian stance in a most subtle way. Both eastern Mongols' and Yun's orientations can therefore be defined as ethnopolitical and Inner Mongolian. The fundamental disagreement between the two was over the possibility of an Inner Mongolian ethnopolitical stance within the CCP system. On this score, Yun would eventually prove the naive one.

It would trivialize both Yun's group and the eastern Mongol autonomists by defining them as two Inner Mongolian factions struggling for power or depicting the former as true revolutionaries (or, negatively, the tool of the CCP) and the latter as separatists (or, positively, true Mongols). The disagreements between the two groups should not discount the sincerity of their respective ethnopolitical stands. The real divide in postwar Inner Mongolian politics was interethnic, not intraethnic: It existed between the principal Chinese political forces' (the GMD and the CCP) effort to internalize estranged ethnic frontiers and the Inner Mongols' assorted reactions to the effort. Yet, like the Chinese Civil War, postwar Inner Mongolian politics did not just involve forces within China. The CCP's eventual success in internalizing the Inner Mongolian autonomous movement, as will be shown in part III of this study, was also facilitated by certain international conditions of the postwar years.

Part III

Ethnicity and Hegemony, 1945–1950

8

"New Frontier": America's Encounter with Inner Mongolia

Shortly after World War II ended, U.S. Navy secretary James V. Forrestal proclaimed at a Cabinet meeting that "China now is our eastern frontier."[1] This was a Eurocentric assertion erroneously characterizing the geostrategic relationship between China and the United States. Unlike the British and Soviet empires, which made overland contacts with China from the west and the north and therefore perceived China as an "eastern" or "southern" territory, the United States approached China from the east across the Pacific Ocean. The rapid ascendance of American power in the Asia-Pacific region during World War II and the American occupation of Japan in the postwar years made China an immediate neighbor of the United States in the "Far Far West." Forrestal's assertion nevertheless reflected an enthusiasm among American policymakers about the new opportunities in China that came with the end of World War II.

At the threshold of peace, China indeed stood as a "new frontier" for American foreign policy. Although American exploration of this frontier during the next four years (1945–49) would eventually prove fruitless, the scope and depth of the expansion of American influence in China in these years had no precedent. To verify this point, it is only necessary to mention that American foreign policy not only was deeply involved in China's partisan power struggle but also for the first time became a factor on China's ethnopolitical stage. American entanglement in postwar Inner Mongolian politics was therefore a landmark development in the history of U.S.–Chinese relations.

---

1. Cited in Walter LaFeber, *The Clash: U.S.–Japanese Relations throughout History* (New York: W. W. Norton, 1997), 257.

In the international history of East Asia, Inner Mongolia served as a geographical link between the "Great Game" for Central Asia in the west and the Manchurian "cradle of crises" in the east. Yet, during most of the first half of the twentieth century, the region itself assumed little independent significance. In World War II, the Japanese Army in China used Inner Mongolia as a corridor to push toward Xinjiang and also as a protective flank for its puppet Manchukuo. In the western direction, Japan's "Greater East Asia" enterprise was never powerful enough to supersede the old "Great Game" between the British and Russia influence. In the war years, therefore, the two contested Asian regions in the east and the west remained two separate arenas. In the summer of 1945, when the Japanese Empire was finally brought to its knees by America's nuclear blast and by the Soviet invasion of Manchuria, the two-game situation was about to change. The Soviet thrust into Inner Mongolia and Manchuria immediately created an unprecedented circumstance. For the first time in the twentieth century, a great power poised to achieve predominance in a vast stretch of land between the Yalu River in the east and the Tianshan Mountain in the west. At the time, when foreign policy "pioneers" in Washington envisioned China as a "frontier" for the United States, they encountered a strong competitor along China's northern borderlands.

The stretch of the Soviet shadow over China's northern borderlands, of course, first and foremost posed a serious challenge to the Chinese government's long effort for national unification. The challenge was, however, also directly contradictory to a fundamental goal of American foreign policy in postwar East Asia, which was to maintain a strategic partnership with a unified, stable, and strong Chinese state. Although at the global strategic level America's China policy was designed to compete with Moscow, at the regional operational level the policy had to deal with a civil war political landscape in China—compounded by frontier ethnic groups' autonomous movements. Thus, during the first few years after World War II, the vast area encompassing Manchuria and Inner Mongolia became a converging ground for the interbloc rivalry of global significance around the two superpowers, the interpartisan struggle for national power between the Guomindang (GMD, Nationalist Party) and the Chinese Communist Party (CCP), and the interethnic conflict over nationhood and territoriality between the Inner Mongols and the Han Chinese authorities. These three threads of political affairs became so intertwined that involvement with one would necessarily lead to entanglements with the other two. Under the circumstances, the Americans' postwar encounter with the Inner Mongolian frontier became inescapable.

At no point during the Chinese Civil War were American officials in China or in Washington misled by the GMD regime's self-serving interpretation of the Inner Mongolian situation. In general, they maintained a healthy critical attitude toward the GMD's repressive ethnopolitics. In the meantime, America's China policy rarely saw the Inner Mongolia question as an "ethnopolitical" one. Washington's bloc politics vis-à-vis the Soviet Union and its "partisan" bias between the warring GMD and CCP determined the angles from which it approached the Inner Mongolian frontier. For U.S. foreign policy, this was a period of involvement in China's ethnopolitics without an ethnopolitical perspective.

Partisan Mongols

Months before the Japanese surrendered, the U.S. Embassy in Chongqing learned from a GMD source that the CCP was agitating among the disgruntled Inner Mongols for Inner Mongolia's unification with the Mongolian People's Republic (MPR). The alleged purpose was to connect the CCP's northwestern bases with Soviet-controlled territories.[2] Then, in early 1946, when an anti-Soviet and anti-CCP students riot took place in Chongqing, the CCP and Moscow were again identified by the rioters as the culprits of a separatist movement in western Inner Mongolia. On these occasions, American officials in the embassy were not convinced. When reporting the Chongqing riot to the State Department, the embassy pointed out that among all the local newspapers only the CCP's *Xinhua Ribao* (New China Daily) made an effort to explain that what the Mongols wanted was no more than maintaining their banner system. Considering the CCP's explanation "reasonable," the embassy commented that the Inner Mongols probably acted spontaneously and were neutral to the GMD–CCP rivalry.[3]

As already indicated in part II of this study, the event in western Inner Mongolia (West Sunid Banner) was only an initial spark of Inner Mongolian nationalism, which, ironically in view of Chongqing rioters' accusations, was extinguished by the CCP. In late November 1945, shortly after Yun Ze

---

2. Edward Rice to the Secretary of State, 21 May 1945, General Records of the U.S. Department of State Central Files: China (hereafter GRDS), 893.00/5-2145.

3. The Counselor of Embassy in China (Smyth) to the Secretary of State, 23 February 1946, *Foreign Relations of the United States: Diplomatic Papers* (hereafter *FRUS*), 1946, 9: 439-441.

and his associates established the "Inner Mongolian Autonomous Movement Association" (IMAMA) in Zhangjiahou, four American officers arrived in the area, identified by the CCP as "officers of the intelligence bureau of the U.S. Department of State." Because the CCP Central Committee was extremely suspicious of the purpose of these officers' visit, it directed its Jin-Cha-Ji (Shanxi-Chahar-Hebei) Bureau to provide "necessary propaganda materials" to the Americans but not to permit them to conduct any intelligence gathering operation.[4] It was under such an atmosphere that, in mid-February 1946, Yun Ze—accompanied by some other CCP officials, including Nie Rongzhen, commander of the CCP's Jin-Cha-Ji military district—granted an interview to one of the American officers named Frank Bessac (a.k.a. Bai Zhiren). What was discussed on this occasion has not yet been clarified by available historical records. According to an official chronology of Yun Ze's life published in China, Bessac "spared no effort to sow discord in the Sino-Soviet, Sino-MPR, and Han–Mongolian relationships, raised many provocative questions, and made many absurd suggestions." To these, allegedly, Yun Ze and his comrades "gave a potent refutation with many facts."[5]

As Yun Ze and other CCP cadres were making efforts to incorporate Inner Mongol autonomists in western Inner Mongolia into a front organization for the CCP, the blaze of Inner Mongolian nationalism began to spread in the east. By January 1946, the autonomous movement in eastern Inner Mongolia had achieved enough momentum to launch an autonomous government in Wangyemiao. A genuine local force thus appeared in the middle of the already intricate international and partisan scrambles for Manchuria.

This development in eastern Inner Mongolia immediately caught the attention of the official U.S. community in China. In late February 1946, an eastern Mongolian petition mission to Chongqing was intercepted by the GMD authorities in Beiping (Beijing). This provided American intelligence officers with an opportunity to learn about the eastern Mongolian movement by interviewing its participants. On February 25, two American intelligence officers, whose names were listed in GMD documents as "Sima Xiao" and "Der-si-de-jia-li," met with Manibadara, a leading figure of the Wangyemiao movement and head of the delegation. During the conversation, Manibadara

---

4. "CCPCC's Directive on the Tactics for the Struggle with the Americans and Jiang," 28 November 1945, *Zhonggong Zhongyang Wenjian Xuanji* (Selected Documents of the Chinese Communist Party Central Committee; hereafter *ZZWX*), 15: 456.

5. Wang Shusheng and Hao Yufeng, *Wulanfu Nianpu* (Chronology of Ulanfu's Life) (Beijing: Zhonggong Dangshi Ziliao Chubanshe, 1989), 140–41.

presented the Wangyemiao regime as an anti-CCP force that sought ethnic autonomy under the GMD "central government." However, most of his remarks were made to answer the Americans' pointed and pregnant questions.

Unsurprisingly, although the Americans were interested in learning about the organization and scope of the eastern Mongolian movement, the central thrust of their inquisition was about the eastern Mongols' relationship with the Soviet–Mongolian Army, the MPR, and the CCP. During the interview, the Americans showed a strong suspicion that the Wangyemiao movement was actually under the Soviet aegis. They encouraged Manibadara to reveal how the eastern Mongols "welcomed" alleged Soviet assistance and to what extent Wangyemiao's actions were directed by the Soviet military authorities in the region. Not satisfied with what they heard, the Americans challenged Manibadara: "Given the complex conditions in the Northeast, how can you not be used by the Soviet Union [as] feared by [the Chinese government]?" Genuinely or not, they seemed puzzled by the fact that although the Soviet Red Army controlled Manchuria at the moment, Wangyemiao did not petition Moscow for permission of autonomy but instead sent a delegation to Chongqing. Furthermore, to ascertain Wangyemiao's "partisan" affiliation, they asked Manidabara to clarify which between the GMD and the CCP was "more suitable" to Mongolian autonomy and whether or not Wangyemiao would make its next move without the GMD regime's authorization.

Disappointed by the Americans' barely concealed distrust, Manibadara lauded the United States as a "benefactor" to the Inner Mongols but offered his interviewers this advice:

I have certain hopes in you [Americans]. You are concerned and interested in the Mongolian autonomous issue, which we appreciate very much. I hope that you can understand Mongolia correctly and provide us with effective guidance and assistance. You all ought to view Mongolia as [Owen] Lattimore does; then we would be extremely grateful. Minority nationalities' demand for autonomy is for national survival and development. Because of this trend in the world and the conditions in the Northeast [Manchuria], autonomy [for Inner Mongolia] should be implemented as soon as possible. Please help us achieve the goal in an early date.[6]

6. Jiang Jieshi to Luo Liangjian, 10 April 1946, and appendix: "Minutes of a Conversation between Der-si-de-jia-li of the American Office of Strategic Services and the Easter Mongolian People's Delegation," Quanzonghao (general record number; hereafter QZH) 141 / 3626. The real names of the two American officers cannot be verified.

The meeting proved the only direct encounter between U.S. officials and the eastern Mongols, and Manibadara's statement quoted above was the only appeal for American help made by an eastern Mongol leader. Apparently, Manibadara's invoking of Lattimore's scholarship indicated that the eastern Mongols were uninformed of Washington's Cold War agenda, just as the Americans were unfamiliar with or indifferent toward Wangyemiao's ethnopolitical stance. The first encounter between the Americans and the Inner Mongolian frontier was inconsequential.

Yet the effort of the U.S. government to learn about conditions in China's borderlands continued. During the initial postwar months, America's intelligence establishment was going through a transitional period. In October 1945, the wartime Office of Strategic Services was disbanded and its personnel were divided between an Interim Research and Intelligence Service under the State Department and a Strategic Service Unit (SSU) directed by the War Department. After the Central Intelligence Group, predecessor of the Central Intelligence Agency (CIA), was created in early 1946, it incorporated the SSU and renamed the SSU's China branch unremarkably as External Survey Detachment 44 (ESD 44). In 1947, after U.S. foreign policy finally found its "hidden hand" for the Cold War, the CIA, ESD 44 agents would continue to operate but under deeper covers as diplomats or personalities of various trades.[7] The shifting geography of the GMD–CCP struggle and the perceived directions of Soviet expansion in China determined the regional priorities of American intelligence operations. A 1946 State Department tabulation of intelligence priorities in China stressed that "special attention" ought be given to information about the developments in China's borderlands such as Manchuria, Inner Mongolia, and Xinjiang, where Soviet influence loomed large.[8]

---

7. Yuri Totrov, "American Intelligence in China," *Far Eastern Affairs* (hereafter *FEA*) 2 (2002): 100–16; Matthew M. Aid, "US Humint and Comint in the Korean War: From the Approach of War to the Chinese Intervention," in *The Clandestine Cold War in Asia, 1945–1965: Western Intelligence, Propaganda and Special Operations,* ed. Richard J. Aldrich et al. (London: Frank Cass, 2000), 17–22; Maochun Yu, *OSS in China: Prelude to Cold War* (New Haven, Conn.: Yale University Press, 1996), 248–62; Richard J. Aldrich, *Intelligence and the War against Japan: Britain, America and the Politics of Secret Service* (Cambridge: Cambridge University Press, 2000), 314, 373. "Hidden hand" is Richard J Aldrich's qualification of the American and British intelligence establishments for the Cold War in his ground-breaking study, *The Hidden Hand: Britain, America and Cold War Secret Intelligence* (Woodstock, N.Y.: Overlook Press, 2001).

8. Charles C. Stelle to Everett Drumright, 5 September 1946, Records of the Division of China Affairs, box 8.

After the initial contact with eastern Mongols, the American intelligence network made an effort to follow up. Because Manibadara forewarned his American interviewers that U.S. personnel could probably not enter the Wangyemiao area without the permission of the Soviet military authorities, Mongol agents had to be deployed. The endeavor was, however, delayed. Not until the winter of 1946 did a Mr. Richardson (known to the Mongols by his Chinese name, Li Jiasheng), a member of the U.S. Naval intelligence staff in China, contact Prince De in Beiping. Although at the time Prince De was deemed by the State Department to be a spent force, American intelligence operatives obviously still valued his intelligence assets. Richardson asked the prince to recommend some Mongol radio operators who could proceed to the Wangyemiao area to collect information. Prince De recommended two young Tumed Mongols, through whom Richardson was later able to recruit more Mongols into his organization. The Wangyemiao operation, however, was unsuccessful because the two Tumed agents stayed in Wangyemiao only briefly and were unwilling to do things "harmful to the [Mongolian] nation."[9]

Despite Washington's increasing interest in knowing about the postwar conditions of China's borderlands, its intelligence inquiry in the Inner Mongolian frontier proved slow in informing policymakers. As of mid-1946, the State Department still could not get some basic facts right. For instance, in the summer of 1946, Dean Acheson, the acting secretary of state, advised the U.S. embassy in Moscow that, according to the State Department's "best information," Yun Ze had founded an "Inner Mongolian Autonomous Association" in June 1945. The date should have been November 1945. As for the movement centered in Wangyemiao, Acheson dismissed it as a temporary autonomous regime staffed by a few "undisarmed ex-puppet Mongols."[10]

A few days after Acheson sent his message to Moscow, the U.S. Embassy in Nanjing completed its first detailed, though flawed, analysis of the Inner Mongolian situation. The embassy was critical of the GMD regime's Mongolian policy, pointing out that the regime's by no means "savory" record in dealing with the Mongols actually tended to make the latter's autonomous

9. Edward Rice to the Secretary of State, 14 August 1945, GRDS, 893.00/8-1445; Sechin Jagchid, *The Last Mongol Prince: The Life and Times of Demchugdongrob, 1902–1966* (Bellingham: Center for East Asian Studies, Western Washington University, 1999), 373; Demchugdongrob, "Demuchukedonglupu Zishu" (Autobiography of Demchugdonrob), *Neimenggu Wenshi Ziliao* (Literary and Historical Materials of Inner Mongolia; hereafter *NWZ*), 13: 150.

10. Dean Acheson to U.S. Embassy in Moscow, 30 July 1946, GRDS, 893.00 Mongolia/7-3046.

demands "legitimate." Although admitting the Soviet and Outer Mongolian presence in Inner Mongolia, the embassy stated that it believed the autonomous trend in the region was fundamentally caused by conditions internal to China. In view of the GMD regime's recent rejection of the Manibadara mission, the embassy deplored that the GMD had missed an opportunity to strengthen the anti-CCP and anti-Soviet elements in Wangyemiao.

Although the embassy's observations of the GMD–Mongolian relationship were basically sound, its understanding of the Inner Mongolian autonomous movement and the CCP–Mongolian relationship was seriously confused. According to the embassy, there existed two "distinct movements" in Inner Mongolia, one under Yun Ze in Chahar that was "inspired and directed [by the CCP], and with definite separatist tendencies," and another in Wangyemiao that was "an indigenous and milder movement for limited autonomy." The embassy was convinced that the CCP's dynamic and radical approach to the Mongolia question would "meet with sincere autochthonous support [from the Inner Mongols] wholly aside from the question of any artificial outside stimulus," and that the GMD regime's lack of "active and energetic steps to undercut the Communist appeal" would soon allow Yun Ze's group to "absorb the latter [the Wangyemiao group]." Thus, the State Department was told to anticipate an Inner Mongolia–wide separatist movement manipulated by the CCP.[11]

This assessment was erroneous because, although the GMD's negative Mongolian policy did have the effect of driving the Inner Mongols to secessionism, the CCP's positive engagements with the Inner Mongols during the civil war years worked to end any separatist tendency among them. The U.S. embassy's impression on the moderation of the Wangyemiao movement may have been derived from Manibadara's presentation in Beiping. In its report to the State Department, the embassy even followed Manibadara's suggestion and quoted Lattimore's writings several times. The embassy's qualification of Yun Ze's organization as "separatist," however, was a result of confusing partisan politics with ethnopolitics, a mistake typical among U.S. officials in postwar China. Although no longer regarding the GMD regime as the "representative of American ideals" in China, these officials still identified the regime with the Chinese national state.[12] In this perception,

11. Walton Butterworth to the Secretary of State, 9 August 1946, GRDS, 893.00 Mongolia/8-946.

12. John King Fairbank and Merle Goldman, *China: A New History* (Cambridge: Harvard University Press, 1998), 327.

any political force opposing the GMD regime was by definition "separatist" in its relationship with the Chinese state.

Only after American officials in China lost any direct contact with the eastern Mongolian movement did they begin to receive information from some third party sources that helped correct their misconceptions. Between late 1946 and 1948, certain documents issued by the "Eastern Mongolian Autonomous Government" reached the Americans and changed their earlier opinion about Wangyemiao's moderation. Now the State Department realized that the movement "savors more of independence than of local autonomy." New information also revealed factional struggles within the eastern Mongolian leadership and the Inner Mongols' by no means harmonious relationship with the CCP and the Soviet–Mongolian Army, which had earlier been described by the U.S. embassy as upbeat and almost flawless.[13] But the "new" information actually lagged behind relevant events by months or even years. To officials of the State Department, dispatches of this kind from China were interesting occasional readings but served no purpose of updating their knowledge about the rapidly changing situation in China.

This is not to suggest that more accurate and timely intelligence information would have propelled the State Department to act differently on the Inner Mongolian situation. Throughout the duration of the eastern Mongolian autonomous movement (August 1945–May 1947), U.S. officials in China did not receive any instruction from the State Department on how America's China policy should take the Inner Mongolia question into account. Neither were such instructions solicited by the U.S. Embassy in Nanjing. During this period, American diplomats in China and the Soviet Union formed a consensus that although the Inner Mongols might have legitimate *ethnic* claims against the GMD authorities, under the postwar circumstances the Mongolia question had to be evaluated in terms of the *partisan* struggle in China and the *interbloc* competition in East Asia. It was agreed that, currently, Moscow had adopted a "policy of aloofness" toward Inner Mongolia while reining in any pan-Mongol tendency of its Outer Mongolian ally and allowing the CCP to take the driver's seat in Inner Mongolian politics. Moscow could afford aloofness because, in the words of an American diplomat

13. Walton Butterworth to the Secretary of State, 17 September 1946, GRDS, 893.00 Mongolia/9-1746; Clubb to the Secretary of State, 11 July 1947, and enclosures, GRDS, 893.00 Manchuria/7-1147; Joseph Touchette to the Secretary of State, 24 June 1948, GRDS, 893.00 Mongolia/6-2448; Joseph Touchette to Leighton Stuart, 8 October 1948, GRDS, 893.00 Mongolia/10-848.

in Moscow, the GMD's "modern mandarins . . . have learned nothing and forgotten nothing" with respect to Inner Mongolia, and the GMD regime's influence in both Inner Mongolia and Manchuria could not reach "much beyond the range of rifle shot."

Consequently, the CCP, Moscow's close ally, became the only vigorous force to engage the Inner Mongols. In this line of analysis, the ethnopolitical character of the Inner Mongols' movements only assumed a secondary significance, for, according to a generally shared opinion among American military and diplomatic officers in China and the USSR, no matter whether the Inner Mongols would come under Yan'an's influence, be absorbed into the MPR, or form an autonomous government of their own, "the end result was likely to be the same—subservience to Moscow."[14] American officials in the anticommunist front of East Asia thereby relegated the Inner Mongols to the other side of the Cold War. The State Department back in Washington had no reason to think otherwise.

In retrospect, Inner Mongolia was a frontier of U.S. foreign policy that did not attract much pioneer effort. When the Inner Mongols were making their most drastic political move in the twentieth century, the Americans chose to remain "sedentary." Aside from overrating the CCP's ability to manipulate the Inner Mongols, the Americans also held a conviction that the GMD's counterproductive policies toward China's non-Han peoples were immutable. It is remarkable that although criticizing in one voice the GMD's ethnopolitics, between 1945 and 1947 American officials in China and the USSR did not produce a single piece of advice for Washington about applying pressure on that regime for policy improvement. During these years, when the U.S. government's mediation between the GMD and the CCP was frustrated, it indeed did not seem advisable for America to meddle in the relationship between the Inner Mongols and the Chinese authorities, another "internal" problem of China. Yet from the onset, a tendency among American officials was to classify the Inner Mongolia question as part of the communist problem in China. Accordingly, the Inner Mongolia question had to be dealt with through the GMD's anti-CCP struggle. During the first

14. Butterworth to the Secretary of State,17 September 1946, GRDS, 893.00 Mongolia/9-1746; John Davies to the State Department, 18 October 1946, GRDS, 893.00 Mongolia/10-1846; Clubb to the Secretary of State, 11 July 1947, and enclosures, GRDS, 893.00 Manchuria/7-1147; Philip D. Sprouse to Wedemeyer, 30 July 1947, *FRUS,* 1947, 7: 689–90; "Intelligence Report" no. 36-S-47, from U.S. Naval Attaché, Nanjing, China, 12 September 1947, Truman Papers: PSF/Subject Files, box 173.

two years of the Chinese Civil War, even the GMD's severest American critics did not expect the GMD regime to collapse soon. Thus, while envisioning the inexorable fall of the Inner Mongolian autonomous movement into the CCP's arms, American intelligence and diplomatic officials in China also anticipated that once the GMD overcame the CCP, the usually vengeful regime would deal severely with the CCP's Inner Mongol collaborators and thus end the Mongolia question altogether.[15] History, of course, did not give the GMD such an opportunity.

"Racial Mongols"

Despite its initial military superiority over the CCP, by mid-1947 the GMD regime began to lose the initiative in the war. After a series of operations in the summer and fall of 1947, the CCP forced the GMD to adopt a defense posture in Manchuria. Afterward, the strategic initiative in the nationwide power struggle began to shift to the CCP's side.[16] It was in this context that U.S. officials in China began to have frequent contacts with a group of Inner Mongols in GMD-controlled regions. These people identified themselves as "Racial Mongols," meaning that they were affiliated with neither of the two warring Chinese parties and worked purely for Mongolian interests. In reality, this group included mostly people who in the war years had followed Prince De in his collaboration with Japan and in the postwar years wandered and conspired at the brink of GMD power. Because these people were anxious to gain potency in China's political stage with assistance from the United States, officials at the U.S. Embassy in Nanjing and the State Department slowly developed some interest in them. In other words, only when the GMD's anticommunist effort was thrown into disarray did the Americans begin to cultivate a relationship with a group of uprooted Inner Mongols. It remained to be seen whether or not U.S. foreign policy could or would rebuild an Inner Mongolian frontier away from Inner Mongolia.

During the Chinese Civil War, the Inner Mongols on the GMD side did not have one voice. They were plagued by the same kind of factional disease that infected the GMD itself. At the time, there were two established

15. Butterworth to the Secretary of State,17 September 1946, GRDS, 893.00 Mongolia/9-1746.

16. Jiang Kefu, *Minguo Junshishi Luegao* (Military History of the Republic) (Beijing: Zhonghua Shuju, 1987–95. 4 books and 6 vols.), 4 (1): 316–29; 4 (2): 421–22.

Mongolian groups within the GMD. One group, headed by Bai Yunti, belonged to the faction of Zhu Jiahua, who was a leading figure of the GMD Central Committee and in different times was in charge of the GMD Organization Department and the Ministry of Education. The other group was headed by Li Yongxin, a member of the CC clique.[17] These men's connections with the GMD went back to the 1920s. As far as their ideas about Inner Mongolia's political future were concerned, these "GMD Mongols" limited their effort to persuading the GMD leadership to honor its recent promise, which was made in 1946, to restore the prewar Council of Mongolian Local Autonomous Political Affairs.[18]

Along with these two, a third group included people of assorted backgrounds. Some were Prince De's wartime followers and some were disgruntled local Mongol elites or officials who wanted to push the GMD regime to do more to change its rigid policies in Inner Mongolia. Finding the CCP abhorrent and lingering on the verge of the similarly detestable GMD power, these people, including Prince De himself, actually regarded the eastern Mongolian movement as the pace setter for the Inner Mongols' struggle. The most vigorous in this group hoped that one day they would be able to hold the Mongol mass's attention and snatch the political initiative from the hands of the CCP-influenced eastern Mongols. For this purpose, at the beginning of 1947, some twenty people, including former members of Prince De's wartime regime and Mongol delegates to the GMD's "national assembly," formed a Mongolian Youth Alliance (MYA).

Sechin Jagchid, one of the organizers of the MYA, does not explain clearly in his memoir-study of postwar Inner Mongolian politics why Prince De was not included in the organization, except to say that its founders did not want the prince to have "too extensive" influence on the organization. The reason is, however, not difficult to deduce: Prince De's failed prewar association with the GMD and wartime collaboration with the Japanese could have been detrimental to the MYA's image as a "new and progressive" movement.[19] The group was most active in Nanjing and Beiping and utilized the press and the GMD "national assembly" as its forums. As intended, it soon caught American officials' attention. In the summer of

17. The CC clique was under the Chen (Lifu and Guofu) brothers. For a concise discussion of the GMD factions, see Lloyd E. Eastman et al., *The Nationalist Era in China, 1927–1949* (Cambridge: Cambridge University Press, 1991), 26–32.

18. Sechin Jagchid, *Last Mongol Prince,* 322–23, 347–48.

19. Sechin Jagchid, *Last Mongol Prince,* 353, 368–70, 374.

1947, through Frank Bessac, the MYA established contact with the American embassy.[20]

The MYA was not the only group that sought American attention. After the summer of 1947, all Inner Mongolian groups in the GMD areas began to intensify their efforts to get Western powers' support. These included Prince De's followers in Beiping, Mongol officials in the GMD "central government," Mongol delegates to the GMD's "national assembly," Mongol petitioners from Inner Mongolian banners, and local Mongol officials who visited or sojourned in Beiping or Nanjing at the time. By then, the CCP had already tightened its grip on the eastern Mongolian movement. In western Inner Mongolia, the GMD and the CCP were caught on a military seesaw. Unable to influence the situation directly, Inner Mongol activists in the GMD areas sought to persuade or pressure the GMD regime to change its rigid Inner Mongolian orientation in order to drive a wedge between the CCP and its Mongol followers. In July 1947, U.S. president Harry Truman sent General Albert Wedemeyer to China to make "an appraisal of the political, economic, psychological and military situations" there.[21] The event raised hope among these Inner Mongols that the Inner Mongolia question could be added to Wedemeyer's agenda and that American pressure could thus be put on the GMD regime.

When communicating with U.S. officials, these Mongols shared some common themes. They were generally in despair about the GMD regime's devious and repressive policies toward the Inner Mongols and held these policies responsible for the Inner Mongols' sufferings during the Republican period and for the current spread of CCP influence in Inner Mongolia. They contended that neither the GMD nor the CCP would bring about meaningful improvement to the Inner Mongols' conditions and that, therefore, international, preferably American, interference on behalf of the Mongols would be needed. Because some of these disgruntled Mongols held high positions in the GMD government, their American interlocutors were often amazed by the intensity of their attack on the regime.[22]

20. Sechin Jagchid, *Last Mongol Prince,* 376; Demuchugdonrob, *Demuchukedonglupu Zishu,* 150.

21. William Stueck, *The Wedemeyer Mission: American Politics and Foreign Policy during the Cold War* (Athens: University of Georgia Press, 1984), 1.

22. Assistant Director of Central Intelligence Group to Arthur Ringwalt, Chief of Far Eastern Affairs of the Department of State, 14 July 1947, GRDS, 893.00/7-1447; Philip D. Sprouse to Wedemeyer, 30 July 1947, *FRUS,* 1947, 7: 689–90; Lewis Clark to

The Wedemeyer mission was in China for about a month and then proceeded to Korea in late August. After visiting some locations in northern China, General Wedemeyer openly criticized the GMD regime's political and military performance in the war with the CCP. In hoping to shock GMD officials into undertaking serious reforms, the general appeared brutally frank in making his remarks. Yet he only managed to arouse strong anti-American emotions among GMD officials, which in turn were used by conservative party ideologues to advance their own interests.[23] Wedemeyer's critique, however, overlooked the Inner Mongolia question, then a sore spot of GMD officials' Han-centric psychology and also a key issue in the GMD–CCP rivalry for Manchuria. Actually, neither in his addresses to GMD officials in China nor in his final report to President Truman did Wedemeyer make a single reference to the question. Consequently, many years later, when Wedemeyer wrote his memoirs and historians wrote their accounts of his mission, the issue of Inner Mongolian autonomy was completely ignored.[24]

The fact is that Wedemeyer did meet with Inner Mongols when he visited Beiping and Shenyang (Mukden), though the meetings were arranged by Ma Hansan, the head of the GMD secret service in North China, and Xiong Shihui, the chief of the GMD's military headquarters for Manchuria. These GMD officials wanted the Inner Mongols to tell Wedemeyer that they were completely satisfied with the GMD government's rule and that the troubles in Inner Mongolia were nothing but part of a Soviet–CCP conspiracy. Afterward, these Inner Mongols had to write a letter to Wedemeyer to inform him of their real feelings about the GMD's Mongolian policy.[25] State Department official Philip D. Sprouse, who was detailed to the Wedemeyer mission, was briefed by the staff of the U.S. embassy about Inner Mongolia. While in Nanjing in early August, he also personally received a number of "Mongol representatives," who outlined for him Inner Mongols' desire for "racial

---

the Secretary of State, 2 April 1948, GRDS, 893.00 Mongolia/4-248; Edmund Clubb to the Secretary of State, 25 May 1948, and enclosure, GRDS, 893.00/5-2548.

23. Stuek, *Wedemeyer Mission,* 44-50.

24. See Albert C. Wedemeyer, *Wedemeyer Reports!* (New York: Henry Holt, 1958), 381–91, 461–79, "Appendix VI: 'Report to the President, 1947, Parts I–V'"; Stueck, *Wedemeyer Mission,* 29–53.

25. Division of China Affairs Memorandum by K. C. Dougall, 5 November 1947, Records of the Division of Chinese Affairs (hereafter RDCA), box 11; American Embassy in Nanjing to the State Department, 13 October 1947, enclosure: Ruth F. Bean to Mr. Perkins and Mr. Ludden, 3 October 1947, GRDS, 893.00/10-1347.

autonomy" and disputed the GMD authorities' misrepresentation of the Mongolian people's will. Thus, aside from his personal encounter with Inner Mongols, Wedemeyer also learned about the Inner Mongolia question from memoranda by Sprouse and other American officials.[26]

Therefore, the GMD authorities and the "Nanjing Mongols," to borrow Sprouse's term, did succeed in inserting the Inner Mongolia question into the itinerary of the Wedemeyer mission. But, obviously, Wedemeyer did not want to be distracted by the GMD–Mongolian friction that seemed irrelevant to the central task of his mission. Nevertheless, a different strain of the GMD authorities' disinformation, which concerned interbloc politics, did register in the general's mind. That was a GMD claim that the Inner Mongols had been used by the Soviet Union. Before he left China, in a message to Secretary of State George C. Marshall, Wedemeyer made the sole reference to Inner Mongolia during his entire mission. He stated as a fact that the Soviet government was creating "conditions that strongly contribute to the establishment ultimately of a satellite or puppet state in Inner Mongolia, Sinkiang [Xinjiang], Manchuria and throughout Korea."[27]

Wedemeyer's observation contributed nothing new to U.S. policymakers' understanding of the Inner Mongolia question. The impact of his mission, therefore, was limited to intensifying Inner Mongols' efforts to contact the Americans. Meanwhile, the dialogue between the U.S. embassy and the MYA, which developed simultaneously with the Wedemeyer mission, began to change the perspective on the American side. The Inner Mongols' interlocutor in the embassy was Ruth F. Bean (known as Ruo Sibing to the Mongols), an SSU officer in the embassy's political section. Some time in the first half of 1947, Ruth Bean was a member of the ESD 44 unit, and in Beiping she established a connection with Inner Mongols with Frank Bessac's help. Bean's Mongolian connection would continue after she was reassigned to the embassy in Nanjing.[28]

26. Philip D. Sprouse to Wedemeyer, 30 July 1947, *FRUS,* 1947, 7: 689–90; Philip D. Sprouse to Wedemeyer, 18 August 1947, ibid., 730–32; W. T. Kenny (Naval Attache of U.S. Embassy) to Wedemeyer, 28 July 1947, Wedemeyer Papers, box 95; memo (no author), "Sino-Soviet Relations," n.d. (1947), Wedermeyer Papers, box 95.

27. General Wedemeyer to the Secretary of State, 8 August 1947, *FRUS,* 1947, 7: 713; Marshall to Truman, n.d., enclosure, Wedemeyer to Marshall, 8 August 1947, Truman papers, PSF/Subject File, box 173.

28. Sechin Jagchid, *Last Mongol Prince,* 376; John Robinson Beal, *Marshall in China,* 273; U.S. Embassy in Nanking to the State Department, 13 October 1947, enclosure: Ruth F. Bean to Mr. Perkins and Mr. Ludden, 3 October 1947, GRDS, 893.00/10-1347.

Unlike Philip Sprouse, who inclusively classified all the Inner Mongols in Nanjing as "Nanjing Mongols" or "Government Mongols," Bean accepted the MYA's self identification as "Racial Mongols." As Bean reported to the State Department, the group claimed to be open or secret participants in a "Mongolian 'racial' movement in opposition to Communism, 'Sun Yat-senism', and all other political theories which . . . conflict with the problems of the Mongolian people." The most active members of the group, as identified by Bean, were "Rashidondok" (Rashidondog, a.k.a. Xi Zhenduo), "Janhungju" (Jakhunju, a.k.a. Ji Zhenfu), "Gombochab" (Gombojab, a.k.a. Hangin), "Urrgunge" (Urgungge Onon), and "Jacchid-Sechin" (Sechin Jagchid).

All these people were founding members of the MYA, though at the time they did not reveal the organization to Bean lest it create an impression that they represented only a small partisan group. Without a standard "party line" in communicating with the Americans, the intensity of these people's criticisms of the GMD varied.[29] Although claiming that only they were "true Mongols" differing from those who had lost their Mongolian identity to the GMD's and the CCP's ideologies, the people in this group could not deny that they themselves were affiliated with the GMD regime in one way or another. To impress the Americans, the group produced two lists of forty names in total, identified separately as "Mongols actively participating in the 'racial' movement" and "Mongols who support the racial movement." Yet some of the people listed were at the time in CCP-controlled areas, and some were actually working against the so-called Racial Mongols. Later, Bean's interlocutors admitted that a number of the people in these lists were actually "potential supporters" of their movement.[30]

The listing practice showed a dilemma of the "Racial Mongols"—how to claim a unique political stance without appearing isolated. Their solution was to argue that, even among the "GMD Mongols" and the "CCP Mongols," there were potential allies of the "racial movement" and "true heroes"

29. Assistant Director of Central Intelligence Group to Arthur Ringwalt, Chief of Far Eastern Affairs of the Department of State, 14 July 1947, GRDS, 893.00/7-1447; U.S. Embassy in Nanking to the State Department, 13 October 1947, enclosure: Ruth F. Bean to Mr. Perkins and Mr. Ludden, 3 October 1947, GRDS, 893.00/10-1347.

30. U.S. Embassy in Nanking to the State Department, 13 October 1947, enclosure: Ruth F. Bean to Mr. Perkins and Mr. Ludden, 3 October 1947, GRDS, 893.00/10-1347; U.S. Embassy in Nanjing to the State Department, 11 February 1948, Enclosure 1: Ruth Bean to Mr. Clough and Mr. Ludden, 17 December 1947, and Enclosure 2: Ruth Bean to Mr. Clough and Mr. Ludden, 31 January 1948, GRDS, 893.00 Mongolia/2-1148.

working for Mongolian interests. The MYA group also suffered from the lack of a prominent leader. In their presentations to the Americans, the "Racial Mongols" had no other choice but to introduce Prince De as their leader, though the prince was in fact excluded from MYA activities. Given the group's experience in the war years, it was not surprising that they regarded the Japanese occupation period as "something of a 'golden age'" to the Inner Mongols, because, they contended, no matter how hateful the occupation was, it allowed a "resurgence of Mongolian nationalism" and a degree of modern progress in Mongolian society.[31]

Thus, the Americans were presented with a "Mongolian racism" (Bean's term) that denied association with any side of the principal struggles in postwar China and East Asia and sought political roots retrogressively in a period under the Japanese shadow. Such a stand could hardly befit Washington's postwar agenda in China. To the Americans, this "racial" stand seemed to favor the principle of "self-determination" while maintaining an ambivalent and puzzling attitude toward other political criteria. After her initial conversations with members of the group, Bean wrote in her report that, beyond an "abstract" aim of self-determination,

> it is impossible to tell whether or not they aim ultimately at a reinstitution of the status quo which existed in the Ch'ing [Qing] dynasty, whether they aspire to the creation of a new Mongol state, or whether they simply seek personal power as a goal in itself. Similarly, it is impossible to tell whether they are proposing "democracy," "fascism," a new brand of "racial-Communism," or a reversion to and a consolidation of feudalism.[32]

From the American perspective, the "Racial Mongols" adopted a rather awkward position in the postwar struggles in China and Asia: They endeavored to discredit the GMD regime but in the meantime were unwilling to sever their connections with that regime; they professed anticommunism on the one hand but warned the Americans on the other that if U.S. aid was not forthcoming, more and more Mongols would embrace the communist cause.

---

31. U.S. Embassy in Nanking to the State Department, 13 October 1947, enclosure: Ruth F. Bean to Mr. Perkins and Mr. Ludden, 3 October 1947, GRDS, 893.00/10-1347; Lewis Clark to the Secretary of State, 16 April 1948, enclosure: R. F. Bean to F. D. Schultheis, 14 April 1948, GRDS, 893.00 Mongolia/4-1648.

32. U.S. Embassy in Nanking to the State Department, 13 October 1947, enclosure: Ruth F. Bean to Mr. Perkins and Mr. Ludden, 3 October 1947, GRDS, 893.00/10-1347.

The ambiguity of the alleged "racial movement" toward those political creeds of the postwar years was not the only problem that perturbed U.S. officials. The American embassy also had to evaluate the "Racial Mongols" as a political force. In this regard, the "Racial Mongols" bewailed Americans' general ignorance about the Mongolian people and avowed that the Inner Mongols, "though small in number, could offer more substantial aid [to the United States] than the Chinese Government in opposing Communism in China."[33] Nevertheless, the group could not claim any tangible connection to the autonomous movements in Inner Mongolia and western Manchuria. To impress the American embassy that participants in the eastern Mongolian movement could be easily persuaded to defect from the CCP camp, the MYA promised to deliver a letter to the Americans written by some eastern Mongol autonomists. Such a letter was never delivered.

The "Racial Mongols" approached the Americans with two assumptions. First, because President Woodrow Wilson had advocated national self-determination at the end of World War I, the U.S. government would naturally be sympathetic to the Inner Mongols' struggle for the same goal after World War II. Second, because the United States wanted to stop communist expansion in the world, it "would back any strong movement which could counteract Communism."[34] At the time, however, neither did the American authorities act according to the Wilsonian principle nor were they moved by the "Racial Mongols'" theory that a strong, anticommunist Mongolian movement would emerge in Inner Mongolia and Manchuria at the moment when Washington extended its support to the Mongolian cause.

Among the Mongolian petitions for support received by the Americans in 1947, the most forthright called for an American solution to the whole Mongolia problem, including Outer Mongolia, and for the establishment of a direct relationship between the United States and Inner Mongolia. The more prudent only asked the Americans to pressure the GMD government to change its Mongolian policy. These petitions presented a troubling question to American policy in China. That was, when the delicate U.S.–GMD partnership in containing Communism was tested by the fierce GMD–CCP war, should U.S. policy be further burdened by the quarrel between the GMD authorities and the Inner Mongols? Through their contacts with the Mongols

---

33. Assistant Director of Central Intelligence Group to Arthur Ringwalt, Chief of Far Eastern Affairs of the Department of State, 14 July 1947, GRDS, 893.00/7-1447.

34. U.S. Embassy in Nanjing to the State Department, 13 October 1947, enclosure: Ruth F. Bean to Mr. Perkins and Mr. Ludden, 3 October 1947, GRDS, 893.00/10-1347.

in the summer of 1947, U.S. officials recognized that, unlike their earlier assumptions, Inner Mongolian nationalism had not been completely commandeered or monopolized by international communists and did seem to have an anticommunist wing. Yet the new insight did not appear to have any immediate value to America's China policy. Instead, an American response to these Mongols' urgent request for assistance might seriously compromise Washington's foreign policy efforts in China.

The Mongols' animosity against Fu Zuoyi was an example to the point. In their presentations, the "Racial Mongols" made Fu the "epitome of all that the Mongols hate in the Chinese people." He was blamed for Inner Mongolia's ongoing sinicization and for blocking even minor concessions to the Mongols that the GMD "central government" was willing to make. However, these complaints could not gain American sympathy. As Bean noted in her report, "Fu Tso-yi [Zuoyi] is looked upon by the Chinese and by American military personnel as one of the most honest and capable of Chinese militarists. It has been reported that his policies regarding the administration of Inner Mongolian provinces are more liberal and more concerned with the living condition of the people than are the policies of most Chinese military-political figures."[35] In these years, Fu was a central figure in the multilateral and multidimensional contest in Inner Mongolia. To the Americans, Fu's proven effectiveness in fighting the CCP dwarfed any of his defects in other matters.

During the second half of 1948, when the GMD's military and political power was disintegrating in northern China, the U.S. embassy recommended that Washington allocate adequate aid materials to Fu, vouching for his "energy and proven ability in utilizing the forces and resources at his command."[36] In terms of both ideology and power, therefore, the "Racial Mongols" could not match the GMD in a contest for American partnership in the anticommunist enterprise in China. Although in 1947 the "Racial Mongols" announced their existence to both the U.S. and the British governments, policymakers in Washington saw no reason to alter their attitude toward the Inner Mongolia question.[37]

35. U.S. Embassy in Nanjing to the State Department, 13 October 1947, enclosure: Ruth F. Bean to Mr. Perkins and Mr. Ludden, 3 October 1947, GRDS, 893.00/10-1347.
36. Butterworth to the Secretary of State, 11 August 1948, GRDS, 893.00/8-1148.
37. Division of China Affairs memorandum by K. C. Dougall, 5 November 1947, RDCA, box 11; Lord Ammon to the Secretary of State, 7 November 1947, and enclosure: S. Jagchid et al. to Lord Ammon and members of the British Parliamentary Good Will

In 1948, the "Racial Mongols" continued to feed the U.S. embassy information about their activities. The Americans were told that, through political competitions, the "racial movement" would be able to take over certain local GMD headquarters and to increase the movement's voice in the center. The electioneering by the "Racial Mongols" in the period did manage to increase their influence among the Mongols residing in Nanjing. By the late spring of 1948, one-fourth of the Mongol delegates in the National Assembly and other government branches had become supporters of the "racial movement." In addition, because of the GMD authorities' continued intransigence regarding Inner Mongolia, a possibility emerged that the "GMD Mongols" and the "Racial Mongols" might work together for a basic agenda.[38]

These progresses seem to have enhanced the self confidence of the "Racial Mongols" and prompted them to take a bolder step. In the late spring of 1948, they prepared a plan for American–Inner Mongolian cooperation and soon petitioned U.S. ambassador John Leighton Stuart for their case. Afterward, the U.S. embassy suggested to the State Department that a more positive approach toward the Inner Mongols be adopted.[39] This change of attitude on the Americans' part, however, had nothing to do with the Inner Mongols' persuasiveness. If earlier the Americans' preoccupation with Soviet projection into northeastern China led them to omit the Inner Mongolian frontier from policy consideration, now the disintegration of the GMD barrier against communist expansion caused the Americans to reevaluate the usefulness of the Inner Mongols.

"Change of Climate"

Hu Zhengzhi, the general manager of *Da Gong Bao* (Grand Public News), remarked in late 1945 that during World War II the United States valued the

---

Mission to China, 15 September 1947, Foreign Office, Registry Files (hereafter FO), 371/ 63420.

38. U.S. Embassy in Nanjing to the State Department, 11 February 1948, enclosures 1 and 2: Ruth F. Bean to Mr. Clough and Mr. Ludden, 17 December 1947 and 31 January 1948, GRDS, 893.00 Mongolia/2-1148; Lewis Clark to the Secretary of State, 16 April 1948, and enclosure: R. F. Bean to F. D. Schultheis, 14 April 1948, GRDS, 893.00 Mongolia/4-1648.

39. Lewis Clark to the Secretary of State, 16 April 1948, and enclosure: R. F. Bean to F. D. Schultheis, 14 April 1948, GRDS, 893.00 Mongolia/4-1648.

CCP because it wanted to enlist all anti-Japanese forces, and after the war the United States spared no effort to promote China's political unity because it wanted stability. Zhou Enlai quoted this remark in a report to the CCP Central Committee, observing that "this is the most accurate interpretation of the American policy."[40] Yet, during the second half of the Chinese Civil War, because construction of "stability" around the GMD regime seemed no longer feasible, the goal of U.S. foreign policy in China began to shift. In a memorandum drafted in July 1949, George F. Kennan, then director of the State Department's Policy Planning Staff, called for a "change of climate" in America's Asia policy in response to the disintegration of the GMD government in China. It was during this general context that the U.S. government readjusted its approach to the Mongolia question. But before the readjustment can be discussed, the developments in U.S. foreign policy leading to the "change of climate" need to be clarified.[41]

It is probably not farfetched to suggest that in the postwar years the U.S. government would not have become entangled in China's domestic politics had it not been obsessed with the question of Soviet expansion. Even before Japan surrendered, U.S. officials already became concerned that a "Soviet-Communist belt extending from Siberia almost to Peiping" would soon emerge in the Far East. In the postwar years, as the GMD–CCP power struggle was unfolding in China, American officials sensed a danger that "slowly and circumspectly," the Soviets might achieve eventual domination of China.[42] Thus, as in Europe, containment must be applied in China to stop Soviet expansion.

The difference was that whereas the line of containment in Europe was well demarcated by the Western Allies' and the Soviet Union's respective military positions at the war's end, such a line did not exist in China. Here, the U.S.–Soviet contest first had to start on China's northern frontiers, which were characterized by complex historical-cultural contentions, contradictory

40. "On the GMD–CCP Negotiations," 5 December 1945, Zhou Enlai, *Zhou Enlai Junshi Wenxuan* (Selected Military Writings of Zhou Enlai) (Beijing: Renmin Chubanshe, 1997), 3: 23.

41. Memorandum for the Secretary of State, n.d. (July 1949), Records of the Office of Chinese Affairs (hereafter ROCA), 1945–1950 / Top Secret Subject Files, 1945–1950, box 13.

42. Edward E. Rice to the Secretary of State, 21 May 1945, and the Assistant Chief of the Division of Chinese Affairs Chase's comment, 26 June 1945, *FRUS*, 1945, 7: 390–91, and n. 51 on p. 390; W. T. Kenny to Wedemeyer, 28 July 1947, Wedemeyer papers, box 95.

and ambiguous legal claims, and circuitous intrigues that cut across ethnic, national, and interstate divides. On the basis of China's own war experience against Japan, American officials had learned to appreciate China as a gigantic arena where "space can be traded for time" in a time of war. But, after two years into the struggle for China, U.S. officials were prepared to write off vast areas like Xinjiang and Inner Mongolia. In these regions, Soviet influence was deemed to be well established, and, presumably, the "loss" of these regions would not "damage the structure of China's stability."[43]

To U.S. policymakers, Manchuria was *the* area in China that really mattered. They were convinced that no government of China would regard the country as unified without Manchuria, and that the region was also the "last missing segment" of Moscow's "Asian defense corridor" and should therefore be denied to the Soviets.[44] More important, the control of Manchuria could tip the balance of power in the Far East. The region's strategic significance was spelled out in a 1947 CIA report, in which the State, War, and Navy Departments concurred. According to the report, Manchuria was the "natural crossroads of land communications linking Siberia, China, and Japan-Korea [*sic*]"; its extensive railroad network, abundant food supplies, and favorable location meant that there was great potential for the development of heavy industries. These features made Manchuria a region of the "greatest significance in international disputes of the past 50 years." After Japan's defeat, the Soviet Union advanced in Manchuria and achieved a "position of unmatched power among Far Eastern nations." Consequently, the CIA pointed out, the responsibility for restoring the "balance in Far Eastern power relationship" fell "directly upon the United States."[45]

But the superpower competition for China's borderlands was phenomenally asymmetric. According to analyses originating in the U.S. embassy in China, the conditions that favored the Soviet scheme included "geographical

43. Office of China Affairs, "U.S. Assistance to China," n.d. (1947), Record of the Office of China Affairs, 1945–50 / Top Secret Subject File, 1945–50, box 12; Charles Stelle to Walton Butterworth, 3 October 1947, enclosure, OIR Report 4517, "The Strategic Importance of China Proper and Manchuria to the Security of the U.S," 18 September 1947, GRDS, 893.00/10-347.
44. O. Edmund Clubb to the Secretary of State, 6 December 1945, GRDS, 893.00/12-645; Clubb, "Soviet Policies, Attitudes and Actions in Respect to Manchuria," n.d., Wedemeyer Papers, box 89; Charles Stelle to Walton Butterworth, 3 October 1947, enclosure, OIR Report 4517, "The Strategic Importance of China Proper and Manchuria to the Security of the U.S," 18 September 1947, GRDS, 893.00/10-347.
45. SR-8: "China," November 1947, Truman Papers, PSF / Intelligence Files, box 259.

propinquity, ethnic similarities, anti-Chinese minority groups, the corruption and ineptitude of the [Chinese] Central Government, the poverty and ignorance of the masses, a strong Chinese Communist Party, and 55,000 Soviet citizens in Greater China." CIA analysts especially identified the CCP and "frontier separatist movements" as Moscow's two strong arms in Manchuria and other border regions.[46] Thus, despite American policymakers' conviction about America's "direct" responsibility for redressing the balance of power in East Asia, they also understood that the China game had to be played with proxies. In this contest, although assorted conditions seemed to line up to facilitate Soviet expansion, Washington's China policy appeared amazingly complacent in pursuing a one-legged countermeasure tied solely to the GMD regime.

The long process of the Chinese revolution and the chronic feud between the GMD and the CCP may easily lead to an oversight of the fact that to both Washington and Moscow the Chinese Civil War of 1945–49 was their first proxy war in Asia. In such a competition, the two superpowers' direct involvement would be inappropriate. Soon after Japan's surrender, despite the GMD regime's complaint about Soviet military activities beyond Manchuria, the U.S. State and War Departments did not want to interpret these as part of a Soviet strategic move or as violation of the wartime agreements among the Allies. Their principal concern was to speedily ship GMD troops northward to prevent a CCP state from emerging in northern China, Inner Mongolia, and Manchuria.[47] This became the mission of the U.S. Army Command in the China Theater right after Japan's defeat. As of the beginning of September 1945, 63,000 American troops, including 50,000 newly arrived Marines, were deployed in the mission. The effort of transporting GMD troops northward also involved the U.S. Seventh Fleet and Air Force.

46. W. T. Kenny to Wedemeyer, 28 July 1947, Wedemeyer Papers, box 95; memo (no author), "Sino-Soviet Relations," n.d. (1947), ibid., box 95; SR-8: "China," November 1947, Truman Papers, PSF / Intelligence Files, box 259; ORE-45, "Implementation of Soviet Objectives in China," 15 September 1947, Records of the CIA: "Estimates of the Office of Research Evaluation, 1946–50," box 1.

47. Joint Chiefs of Staff to Wedemeyer, 10 August 1945, Wedemeyer Papers, box 89; "Minutes of Combined Staff Meeting, Number 111," 20 August 1945, Records of the China Theater of Operations, U.S. Army (CT), Records of the Office of the Commanding General (Wedemeyer), box 1550; WARX 50703, from War Department to Chongqing and Manila, n.d. (August 1945), Wedemeyer Papers (Hoover), box 89; John Vincent to Dean Acheson, 17 November 1945, enclosure: memo by E. F. Drumright, "The Situation in China," 16 November 1945, RDCA / Subject Files, 1944–47, box 10.

The latter, in General Wedemeyer's words, "succeeded in handling the largest air movement of troops in history with a minimum of delay or accident."[48]

The American forces in China, however, were never intended as a direct policy instrument either to contain Soviet expansion or to control the CCP. America's postwar military strategy in East Asia designated Korea and Japan as high-priority zones, and therefore America could only have a limited military presence in China and play a role of assistance and advice.[49] At the beginning, leaders in Washington assumed that American troops could aid the GMD regime without becoming entangled in the "fratricidal war" between the GMD and the CCP. When the GMD–CCP rivalry in Manchuria intensified, however, it became clear that America's military association with the GMD would inevitably cause some "incidental effects" between American personnel and the CCP. Actually, in Inner Mongolia the U.S. Air Force had already become involved in Fu Zouyi's maneuvering against the CCP. Even more troubling to Washington was the GMD regime's explicit intention of dragging the U.S. government into its own dealings with the Russians in Manchuria. These developments combined to speed up the U.S. government's decision to withdraw the Marines and to terminate the China Theater on May 1, 1946.[50]

Not all the principals in Washington agreed with amputating the military arm of America's China policy. In a Cabinet meeting in August 1946, Dean Acheson, then acting secretary of state, voiced a strong objection: "This withdrawal of the Marines would be foolhardy. . . . We are not interfering Chinese affairs but we will prevent by our very presence and by the presence of our marines some other country from interfering in China to our own regret."[51] Yet U.S. forces' direct involvement in postwar China would not only extend the American–Soviet military confrontation from Europe to East Asia but would also constitute a serious departure from the legal and actual balance of power between the two superpowers created by World

---

48. Wedemeyer, "Report of the China Theater to the Chief of Staff of the Army, 24 October 1944 to 15 February 1946," Wedemeyer Papers, box 86.

49. Marshall to Wedemeyer, 14 August 1945, Wedemeyer Papers, box 89.

50. "China Theater Directives": b. WARX47513 (11 August 1945), d. WARX88636, and e. WARX82100 (26 March 1946), Wedemeyer Papers / "Black Book, Volume 7, Book 3," box 86; Wang Shuming to Jiang Jieshi, 5 November 1945, Jiang Zhongzheng Zongtong Dang'an: Geming Wenxian (Kanluan Shiqi) (Archives of President Jiang Zhongzheng: Revolutionary Documents [Period of Suppressing Rebellion]), 3: 361; Marshall to Truman, 9 February 1946, Truman Papers / PSF, box 183.

51. "Cabinet Meeting, Friday, August 2, 1946," Connelly Papers, box 1.

War II. In the war against Japan, the American military forces had bypassed China and left the GMD government and the Soviet Red Army facing each other in Manchuria. Without a legitimate occupation task in China, the best justification for the American military presence in postwar China was to assist the GMD regime's takeover of Japan-occupied territories. By definition, such a presence had both political and time limitations. As a fluctuating civil war became the dominant theme in China's political scene, the American military presence became less and less tenable. Despite Acheson's assertion meaning to implicate the Soviet Union, the same conditions also restricted the Soviet Red Army, which completed its withdrawal from Manchuria about the same time as America's China Theater was terminated.[52]

Postwar China, therefore, did not become a place for direct superpower confrontation but remained a land of international intrigues. In the immediate postwar years, two master plans for China emerged on the American side. One was Wedemeyer's trusteeship plan for Manchuria, which was never implemented. The other was General George Marshall's mediation effort between the GMD and the CCP, which did not succeed. There is no need to belabor these well-studied cases here. However, the connections between these schemes and the ethnopolitical front in postwar China should be highlighted.

Wedemeyer's policy proposition was based on a fundamentally pessimistic view of China's situation, whereas Marshall's reflected a cautious optimism. Together, they reflected a deep chasm in the perception of China by the American foreign policy community. In the spring of 1946, in one of his despairing moments as commanding officer of the Chinese Theater, Wedemeyer wrote in private correspondence that the real solution to China was "to quarantine all of China insofar as the remainder of the world is concerned and let the Chinese fight it out, determining for themselves how and by whom they would be governed."[53] By contrast, the confidence behind the Marshall mission was best expressed by President Harry Truman at a Cabinet meeting in early August 1946: "For the first time we now have a voice in China and for the first time we will be in a position to carry out the policy of 1898."[54] By the "policy of 1898," Truman did not mean the old-fashioned

---

52. The Soviet Red Army's withdrawal from Manchuria began in March 1946 and was completed on May 3.

53. Wedemeyer to Ray Maddocks, 12 April 1946, Wedemeyer Papers, box 82.

54. Minutes of Cabinet Meetings," 2 August 1946, Connelly Papers, box 1.

Open Door orientation but a policy of America's "own," free from other foreign governments' interference.

Given such a stark contrast between the two sentiments about China, two formulas emerged that were far apart in their proposed approaches for dealing with the China question. The Wedemeyer approach, first broached in November 1945 and then repeated in September 1947, prescribed a "surgical" procedure for China. In recognizing the Soviets' advantages in exploiting the CCP's strong position in northern China and the frontier ethnic groups' grievances against the GMD regime, the Wedemeyer plan was premised on the notion that for a considerable time the GMD regime would not be able to establish itself in all Chinese territories, especially in northern and northeastern China. Accordingly, Wedemeyer proposed that the geopolitical meaning of "China" be modified by putting Manchuria under international trusteeship, even though this would postpone for an unstated period the Chinese government's exercising of what Wedemeyer termed its "legal and ethnological rights" in the region.[55]

In contrast, the Marshall mission pursued a "holistic" treatment of the China predicament, in honoring America's wartime pledge to support a unified, strong, and democratic China—which, because of the rise of Soviet power in Northeast Asia, had assumed a new meaning. Thus the United States must not endorse any remedy to the Chinese Civil War crisis at the expense of China's nationhood, in either a political or territorial sense. According to this line of thinking, any emphasis on China's internal ethnic conflicts would cause more damage than benefit to the Chinese government. The Marshall mission therefore attempted to redress the "core," not "peripheral," problem of the Chinese state, and it put General Marshall's as well as the U.S. government's prestige on the line in an effort to broker a GMD–CCP truce.

The mission was propelled by a military estimate and a political judgment. At the beginning of his mission, Marshall assumed that neither of the two Chinese parties would be able to militarily dictate the events in China, and, if they chose to fight, they would become deadlocked and break China into pieces. Such a military prospect could only benefit Moscow and there-

---

55. COMGENCHINA to WAR, 20 November 1945, Wedemeyer Papers, box 86; memorandum by P. D. Sprouse to the Secretary of State through Butterworth, "Implementation of the Recommendations of the Wedemeyer Report," 19 February 1948, ROCA, 1945–1950 / Top Secret Subject Files, 1945–50, box 13; Wedemeyer, *Wedemeyer Reports!*, 461–79, "Appendix VI: 'Report to the President, 1947, Parts I–V.'"

fore must be prevented.[56] Marshall's political formula for averting a civil war in China was to include the two rivals in a coalition government. It was believed that somehow a valid and broadly based central government would emerge in China if the GMD regime was cleaned of its "reactionary and corrupt" elements and the CCP was deprived of its partisan army.[57] In other words, the GMD and the CCP could together organize a government to meet the American standard after they shed their own undesirable qualities. History, however, invalidated both the military and political premises underlining the Marshall mission.

This does not mean that the Wedemeyer plan, if adopted by the U.S. government, would have had a better chance to succeed than the Marshall mission. Wedemeyer's "incomplete China" approach would have conflicted directly with both the GMD government's political-military strategy and the strong national emotion in China favoring unification.[58] The Marshall mission's coalition-government formula was an "incomplete power" solution in the eyes of suspicious GMD officials but represented political pluralism that was then welcomed by other political groups, including the CCP. The goal of America's China policy in the postwar years was, however, to contain Soviet influence, not to promote political pluralism. After the Marshall mission failed, the Truman administration could not see any alternative to continuous aid to the GMD regime, even though President Truman admitted that under the circumstances an American effort in China was like "pouring sand in a rat hole."[59]

A lot of "sand" indeed. As of February 1948, according to an assessment by the State Department, the Soviet Union had assisted the CCP's scramble for Manchuria with captured Japanese weapons that were sufficient to arm 250,000 to 300,000 troops.[60] The U.S. government did much better than Moscow in aiding its own ally in China, which between 1945 and 1949

56. Memo for President Truman by James Shepley, Attaché to General Marshall, 28 February 1946, Truman Papers / PSF, box 173.

57. Memo of the Office of China Affairs, "U.S. Assistance to China," n.d. (1947), ROCA, 1945–1950 / Top Secret Subject Files, 1945–1950, box 12.

58. Wedemeyer to Jiang Jieshi, 10 November 1945 and 5 December 1945, Wedemeyer Papers, box 85.

59. Minutes of Cabinet Meetings, 7 March 1947, Connelly Papers, box 1.

60. Charles Stelle to Philip Sprouse, 10 February 1948, GRDS, 893.00/2-1048. For a discussion of the subject based on Russian archival information, see Yang Kuisong, *Mao Zedong yu Muosike de Enen Yuanyuan* (The Gratuities and Misgivings between Mao Zedong and Moscow) (Nanchang: Jiangxi Remin Chubanshe, 1999), 223, 250 n. 1.

received $1 billion in military aid plus another $1 billion in economic aid.[61] But the quantitative picture could not reveal the essence of the China question. The "rat hole" was the problem.

American policymakers had always known that the GMD regime was a defective instrument for containing communism in China, but an alternative was hard to find. When a solution for the China question could not be found, U.S. foreign policy opted out of the dilemma by lowering the importance of the question itself. At the beginning of his mission in China, Marshall told President Truman that in the next eighteen months nothing in international politics would be more important to the United States than the development in China.[62] In September 1947, or nineteen months later, the CIA ranked the Far East as the least significant area, behind Europe, the Near East, and the Middle East, where containment of the Soviet Union ought to be conducted. According to the CIA's rationalization, the Far East got the lowest ranking because (1) the region's remoteness and the weakness of the GMD regime would make the contest there an unequal one for the United States, (2) the region's vastness and underdevelopment would prevent the Soviets from effectively controlling strategically important objectives, and (3) the region was too remote from Moscow to permit the Soviets to exert effective influence. The conclusion was that American control of the Pacific and Japan should be sufficient to counterbalance any Soviet influence in the Far East.[63]

Yet, the demolition of the American partnership with the GMD regime, which had existed for about a decade, was easier said than done. Not until the second half of 1948 did many in the U.S. government begin to realize that America's involvement with the GMD regime had to be terminated. George Kennan pointed out in a memorandum to the State Department's Office of Chinese Affairs that the GMD could not be saved by continuous American assistance because "there is a vital 'something'" missing in that regime—a "quality of political health and vigor without which no great cause can be advanced." This view was also shared by the American military advisory group in China.[64]

---

61. *The China White Paper, August 1949* (Stanford, Calif.: Stanford University Press, 1967); Originally issued as *United States Relations with China with Special Reference to the Period 1944–1949,* Department of State Publication 3573, 354.

62. Memo for President Truman by James Shepley, Attaché to General Marshall, 28 February 1946, Truman Papers / PSF, box 173.

63. CIA 1, "Review of the World Situation as It Relates to the Security of the United States," 26 September 1947, doc. no. 32 of *CIA Cold War Records.*

64. Memorandum by Geroge F. Kennan, 2 December 1948, ROCA, 1945–1950 / Top Secret Subject Files, 1945–1950, box 13; jusmagchina (Barr) to the Department of

Because American policymakers were accustomed to identifying the GMD with China, however, they tended to read more into its disintegration than a regime's failure. In February 1949, Dean Acheson, who had been appointed secretary of state just a month before, told members of the National Security Council:

> Historically, a nationalist government had been merely a facade in China, with a rough equilibrium maintained among feudal barons. It is only a fiction that China is called a nation today. Consequently, when the [GMD] Government collapses now China would be back where it had been many times before. Before the communists could do anything, they would have to create something."[65]

Thus, as China seemed to disintegrate along with the GMD regime, Kennan and his policy planning staff in the State Department called for a "change of climate" in America's foreign policy in this part of the world. Ever since Japan's surrender, the U.S. government had tormented itself with the China question and could not find a solution. Now the question seemed to have dissolved itself. But the battle against communist expansion must continue. In Washington's policy language, this was to "broaden the present China problem into the larger problem of Asia."[66] As "China" was fading out, new policy options became necessary to carry on the fight against Communism.

Princely Connection

The "change of climate" in U.S. foreign policy in East Asia between 1948 and 1949 had an immediate effect on the U.S. government's attitude toward

---

the Army (Maddocks), 18 December 1948, ibid.; jusmagchina (Barr) to the Department of the Army (Wedemeyer), 2 December 1948, ibid.

65. Memorandum for the President, 4 February 1949, Truman Papers, PSF/NSC Files, box 220. Dean Acheson would get stuck with this view in years to come. In a 1955 interview, he said that it was "completely erroneous" to consider China "as a nation, a state, a geographic area." Borrowing something Napoleon had said about Italy, Acheson suggested that "China was a geographic expression" only, and that if China were divided into a communist and a noncommunist one, the two "would have canceled one another out" and the "world would have been better off." See interview with Dean Acheson by Hillman and Noyes, Kansas City, 17 February 1955, Truman Papers / Post-Presidential Memoirs: Interviews with Associates of President Truman, box 641.

66. Memorandum for the Secretary of State, n.d. (July 1949), ROCA, 1945–1950 / Top Secret Subject Files, 1945–1950, box 13.

Inner Mongolia. Until this time, Washington's sensitivity toward the GMD regime's jealously guarded "internal sovereignty" had impeded any open American criticism or advice regarding the GMD's ethnopolitics.[67] After 1948, the GMD's rapid collapse seemed to give U.S. policymakers an opportunity to act with less concern about "diplomatic correctness." As suggested by Edmund Clubb, the American consul general in Beiping, the new situation in China would allow the American government to end its hitherto "simple, direct," and "legitimist" approach tied to the GMD regime. A new policy, according to Clubb, should be in close contact with the popular currents in China and should "more readily advance into racial strata in more direct contact with the Soviet Union—the Moslems (Sinkiang), Mongols, and Japanese."[68]

Even if the Americans now cared less about the departing GMD regime's objection to foreign involvement in China's ethnic-frontier affairs, there was still the question about the Inner Mongols' usefulness to U.S. foreign policy. As mentioned above, at the time an established view among American diplomats in China and the Soviet Union had identified Mongolian nationalism as a force commandeered by Moscow and the CCP.[69] The feeling of helplessness in this regard was best expressed by W. Walton Butterworth, minister-counselor of the American embassy in China. In June 1947, Butterworth wrote to the State Department that "as far as the United States and American interests are concerned, the Mongolian People's Republic, except in one sense, is about as important and pertinent as Atlantis. To all intents and purposes it is a closed case." The MPR, however, remained relevant to U.S. foreign policy because it could serve Moscow's purpose in China by influencing the Inner Mongols. In Butterworth's opinion, "the relatively favorable conditions of the Outer Mongolians as a result of Soviet tutelage is more persuasive to the Chinese Mongols than any amount of fine words and arguments." But, he observed, "there seems to be little that can be done about it from an American standpoint except through the over-all solution of the Chinese Communist problem."[70]

67. John Davies memo to the State Department, 18 October 1946, GRDS, 893.00 Mongolia/10-1846; memorandum by the Second Secretary of Embassy in China (Melby), n.d., *FRUS,* 1947, 7: 678–82.

68. Edmund Clubb to George (Atcheson?), 28 November 1948, ROCA, 1945–50 / Top Secret Subject Files, 1945-50, box 13.

69. U.S. Embassy in Moscow to the State Department, 18 October 1946, GRDS, 893.00 Mongolia/10-1846; Ambassador in China (Stuart) to the Secretary of State, 6 January 1947, *FRUS,* 1947, 7: 6–12.

70. Walton Butterworth to the Secretary of State, June 1947, Melby Papers, box 2.

There were indeed others in the embassy who urged the State Department to pay more attention to Inner Mongolia. But, in the words of an officer in the embassy, any notion along this line "has been treated by Washington with the silent scorn it doubtlessly so justly deserves."[71] In 1947, Ruth Bean's reports on the Inner Mongols were treated merely as informational materials in the Office of Chinese Affairs of the State Department.[72] The Joint Chiefs of Staff seemed more interested than the State Department in ethnic groups caught between China and the Soviet Union. In the summer of 1947, in a memorandum addressed to the State-War-Navy Coordinating Committee, the Joint Chiefs argued that to thwart Soviet domination in China, the American military interest would need "the nations of Eurasia" in opposing Soviet expansion, and that an overall plan should be made to provide American assistance to "those nations on the periphery of Soviet controlled areas in Eurasia."[73]

The Inner Mongols were one such nation. Yet the practical question at the time was who would receive American assistance. The eastern Inner Mongols represented the largest Mongolian population in China, but by that time the group had already been "lost" to the communist side. This left the Mongolian population in Chahar, Suiyuan, and regions further west as potential recipients of American assistance. In 1948, the U.S. Consulate General in Beiping informed the State Department of the conditions in these provinces. Through its various contacts, the consulate learned that more than 300,000 Mongols, or 8 percent of the total population of Chahar and Suiyuan, resided in three "leagues" and thirteen "banners" in the two provinces. According to the sources, to avoid driving the Mongols to the CCP's side, the local GMD authorities taxed the Mongols slightly lighter than they taxed the Han peasants. Still, the Mongols' position was "extremely depressed," and their main complaints were about the local GMD authorities' arbitrary taxation system and suppression. Some local Mongol princes asserted that the Mongols were perfectly capable of defending themselves against the CCP if they could be given weapons *and* autonomy from the tyrannical control of the GMD provincial governments. The consulate's informants, however, could not provide any evidence that an organized Mongolian force existed in these areas.[74] To those in the American embassy who wanted to do

---

71. Diary entry on 1 September 1947, in John F. Melby, *The Mandate of Heaven: Record of a Civil War, China 1945–49* (New York: Doubleday, 1971), 290.

72. Memorandum by K. C. Dougall, 5 November 1947, RDCA, box 11.

73. Memorandum by the Joint Chiefs of Staff to the State-War-Navy Coordinating Committee, 9 June 1947, *FRUS,* 1947, 7: 844–45.

74. Edmund Clubb to the Secretary of State, 13 May 1948, GRDS, 893.00/5-1348; Clubb to the Secretary of States, 11 June 1948, GRDS, 893.00 Mongolia / 6-1148; Joseph

something about the Inner Mongolia situation, therefore, the "Racial Mongols" in Nanjing and Beiping became the most important potential collaborators, even though there were warnings from Mongols outside the group that some leading members of the "racial" group were self-serving opportunists who were using the name of Prince De and Mongolian nationalism to advance their personal ambitions.[75]

Nevertheless, in early 1948, the U.S. embassy under Leighton Stuart began to make recommendations to the State Department for actively responding to the Mongolia question. At first, the embassy suggested that the U.S. Information Service use its programs to expose the Soviet Union as the real imperialist power in China. Cases like Manchuria, Mongolia, Xinjiang, Dalian (Dairen), and Korea might be cited to make the point. The State Department demurred on the ground that these areas and their connections to the Soviet Union had rarely been subjects in the American press or the U.S. government's official commentaries, and that these territories involved too many legal and international political complications to be used beneficially by an American propaganda operation. The State Department was especially mindful of America's own involvement in the Yalta diplomacy of 1945, which loomed large behind these territorial issues. The obvious contrast between the GMD's conservative and the CCP's reformist approaches to China's ethnic problems would also likely put the American government in a difficult position.[76]

Ambassador Stuart persevered. In May 1948, after an interview with members of the "Racial Mongols," he wrote to the State Department again, recommending this time that the U.S. government sponsor Mongolian nationalism. As a rare American official document that bluntly supported Mongolian nationalism, Stuart's communication deserves a full quotation here:

> I have the honor to report on problems centering around Inner and Outer Mongolia. The latter has been attached to the Soviet Union as a more or less unwilling and helpless satellite. The Chinese are trying to use similar tactics in coercing the Mongols in Inner Mongolia to become an integral part of the Republic. But there seems to be a very strong yearning

---

Touchette to Leighton Stuart, 30 July 1948, GRDS, 893.00 Mongolia / 7-3048; Touchette to Stuart, 20 August 1948, GRDS, 893.00 Mongolia / 8-2048.

75. Joseph Touchette to Leighton Stuart, 6 October 1948, GRDS, 893.00 Mongolia/ 10-648.

76. Secretary of State to Stuart, 4 March 1948, Melby Papers, box 3.

in both regions for a unified and independent Mongol State. We Americans instinctively sympathize with such aspirations. For other practical reasons an autonomous Mongolia would serve to contain Soviet expansion southward, whereas the present methods of the Chinese agents tend to drive the Mongols toward Chinese or even Russian Communism. As with all such suppressive policies the Chinese employ more pliant Mongols as their own puppets against those described as "racial Mongols." In effect it is the usual pattern of the police-state directed in this instance by the [Central Committee] clique.

Mongol delegates to the National Assembly have called on me and others of the Embassy staff and we are brought into contact with these "racial Mongols" through these and other circumstances. My own impression is that their case is a worthy one and that their presentation of it is both reasonable and with dignified restraint. From all accounts the economic plight of all those at least in Inner Mongolia is very bad which of course aggravates the dangers.

It would be hopeless perhaps to point out to the present Chinese leadership what a noble course they could adopt in conferring on the Mongol race the same independence they have been demanding for themselves and how immensely more effective this would be in holding their spontaneous loyalty to the National Government in some form of alliance. It might be possible to urge this with a more progressive group. Or it may even seem advisable to our Government, after considering the matter in all its aspects, to give the Chinese authorities some friendly, if unsolicited, advice. Left to themselves they will certainly allow things to go from bad to worse until it becomes too late to stop the trend.[77]

The Stuart communication is interesting for several reasons. First, although expressing his sympathy toward the Mongols, confidence about their potential contribution to the anti-Soviet struggle, and misgivings about the GMD regime's Mongolian policy, Stuart only made a rather meager policy recommendation. He proposed that Washington give "friendly advice" to the GMD government, a course of action that he himself knew would probably not work. Then, Stuart explained the Mongolian cause only in connection to the "Racial Mongols" and left out other Mongolian groups that were struggling not in Nanjing but in Inner Mongolia. Last, the ambassador

77. Stuart to the Secretary of State, 18 May 1948, GRDS, 893.00 Mongolia/5-1848.

seemed convinced that between the Soviets' detachment of Outer Mongolia from China and the GMD's integration of Inner Mongolia with China, a third option—a unified, independent Mongolian state—was possible and worth struggling for. Thus, after the Yalta diplomacy and the Sino-Soviet negotiations in Moscow had underwritten the Soviets' and China's respective relationships with the "outer" and "inner" halves of Mongolia, Stuart now proposed to deliver a coup de grace to the Yalta–Moscow structure without indicating a clear course of action.

It was generally agreed among American officials in China that in 1946 Stuart, because of his liberal reputation and connections to different sides of Chinese politics, was appointed ambassador to facilitate a peace settlement in China. After the Marshall mission failed, however, Stuart's liberal idealism became extraneous to both the China situation and Washington's China policy. In addition, as a missionary-educator turned diplomat, Stuart called himself a "tyro in diplomacy," proud of his independent-mindedness and indifference to instructions from the "august Department of State."[78] With these elements considered, the political naiveté of the Stuart communication was not surprising. Neither was the way in which the State Department treated this remarkable document. The State Department never bothered to respond to Stuart's suggestion, and the Far Eastern Division simply filed the Stuart communication with a note of "no action" in the margin.

Some internal discussions in the State Department did occur, however. An internal memo from the Office of European Affairs to the Office of Chinese Affairs made a brief comment on the suggestion of encouraging an independent Mongolia, saying that it was difficult to see the emergence of a truly independent Mongolia "even in the relatively long future," and that the Soviet Union had been prevented from controlling entire Mongolia only because it still recognized China's legal sovereignty in Inner Mongolia.[79] Accordingly, despite evidence from China that the GMD government was alienating even those anticommunist Inner Mongols, U.S. policy in China must not show sympathy toward the Mongols lest such a gesture undermine China's legal authority in Inner Mongolia.[80]

The embassy, however, continued its Mongolian initiative. In August, it

78. John Leighton Stuart, *Fifty Years in China* (New York: Random House, 1954), introduction by Hu Shih, xix; Melby, *Mandate of Heaven,* 168–69.

79. Robert G. Hooker to Walton Butterworth, 8 July 1948, GRDS, 893.00 / 7-848.

80. Lewis Clark to the Secretary of State, 2 April 1948, GRDS, 893.00 Mongolia / 4-248; Edmund Clubb to the Secretary of State, 25 May 1948, GRDS, 893.00 / 5-2548.

transmitted to the State Department a statement by the "Mongolian Youth League," that is, the MYA, with its own comments. This statement was by far the most comprehensive and articulate discussion of the programs supported by the "Racial Mongols." Shedding all previous modesties, the MYA now announced that its ultimate goal was to establish a great Mongolian state unifying "all Mongol units included in the area east from the Putchha [?] Tribe in the valley of the Su [Sungari or Songhua?] River, west to include all the Mongolian Leagues and Banners of Chinghai [Qinghai] and Hsinkiang [Xinjiang], south from the Great Wall, and north to the northern boundary of the Buriats." To stress the progressive character of the new state, the document promised to eliminate the influence of "reactionary feudal princes" and "rotten Lamaism," to adopt democracy, to practice a mixed economy consisting of private enterprises and state-controlled sectors, and to follow an ethnic policy of "complete equality for all." Its discussion of the origins of modern Mongolian nationalism and progressivism would have disturbed American eyes a few years before, but it did not seem to matter now:

> Japanese control [in the war years] fostered the Mongolians' self consciousness and their feeling for independence. At the same time it tended to prevent further development of the Mongolians' feudalistic system, and Lamaism at this time also declined. Education also became widespread. Except for the very small section of western Inner Mongolia which remained under the control of the Chinese Government, . . . the face of Mongolia was completely changed. She threw off corrupt antiquity and looked toward a new era.

Whereas the document's condemnation of the "Chinese super-patriots" of the nationalist and communist persuasions was not new, the MYA for the first time declared its stand in the Cold War. While naming the Soviet Union a "red imperialist country" from whose grip the Mongolian nation must escape, the document praised the United States lavishly for its spirit of "curbing the strong and supporting the weak" and recommended direct contacts between the two peoples. In urging the U.S. government to pressure the GMD regime to change its Mongolian policies, the MYA promised to reward the United States with a "pro-American, democratic, peaceful, independent Mongolian nation in central Asia" that could balance anti-American Russia, militarist Japan, and unreliable China.

Commenting on these ideas, the U.S. embassy gave a wholehearted endorsement to the MYA: "Given the growing influence of nationalistic ideas among the Mongols, and the declining authority of the Chinese in border areas, the [Mongolian Youth] League has considerable potential influence. Since it is pro-American in its orientation, and opposed to the Soviet Union, and since the Mongols occupy areas of strategic significance, its activities are of considerable interests to the United States."[81]

The State Department, however, remained unimpressed and unresponsive. By contrast, the State Department reacted swiftly to the embassy's other suggestion that U.S. policy in China shift focus from Jiang Jieshi's "central government" to effective local forces. Just a few weeks after he urged the State Department to take up the Mongolian cause, Ambassador Stuart sent another report to Washington. Aside from making a complaint about the Beiping students' anti-American sentiment and their indifference toward China's "immediate danger as dramatized by the loss of Outer Mongolia and the imminent loss of Inner Mongolia, the Northeast (Manchuria), etc.," Stuart recalled his recent conversation with Fu Zuoyi, which, in the ambassador's words, "strengthened my belief in his [Fu's] military abilities and in his concern over the welfare of his men." At the time, Fu was in charge of the GMD government's defense in five northern provinces; but according to Stuart, Fu had so far received very little equipment from Jiang Jieshi. Stuart suggested that the American government provide the general with what he needed.[82]

It is unlikely that Stuart was unaware of the Inner Mongols' deep resentment against Fu as the worst adversary to their cause. Yet he obviously shared a popular opinion among U.S. officials in China that Fu, especially now, was the only military commander who could stop the CCP along the Great Wall, and that the American government should either pressure Jiang Jieshi to allocate more materials to Fu or put Jiang's "central government" aside and send American aid directly to the general.[83] The State Department concurred and, in mid-August, asked the Department of Defense to consider the "desirability of ensuring that General Fu Zuoyi obtain an appropriate share" of American matériel to the Chinese government.[84]

81. Lewis Clark (for the Ambassador) to the Secretary of State, 20 August 1948, and enclosure, "The Significance and Hopes of the Establishment of the Mongolian Youth League," GRDS, 893.00 Mongolia / 9-2048.

82. Stuart to the Secretary of State, 30 June 1948, *FRUS,* 1948, 7: 328–29.

83. British Embassy in Nanjing to the Foreign Office, 19 July 1948, FO 371 / 69537; Walton Butterworth to the Secretary of State, 11 August 1948, GRDS, 893.00 / 8-1148.

84. Walton Butterworth to the Secretary of State, 27 July 1948, GRDS, 893.00 / 7-2748; George F. Kennan to the Secretary of State, 12 August 1948, GRDS, 893.00 /

The Americans' high expectations for Fu would not be met. In the fall and winter of 1948, the U.S. embassy, American military advisory group in China, and the U.S. Western Pacific Fleet all became involved in political and logistical maneuvers aimed at getting American aid to Fu's troops. All these came to nil. In December, Fu lost half his best troops in a battle with the CCP between Zhangjiakou and Beiping.[85] On December 31, 1948, the U.S. Consulate General in Beiping reported to the State Department that Fu was seeking peace with the CCP. The consulate general's analysis deplored Fu's "hedgehog strategy," which involved barricading his troops in a few northern cities, and it concluded that the earlier high hopes for Fu had been misplaced. Fu was now described as a "good disciplinarian and tactician in small-scale operations in backwoods of Suiyuan" who was easily "out-generaled and out-smarted by the Communists." America's belated arms and equipment for Fu were wasted because he would probably not put up a "good fight" before retreating. Actually, in the consulate's opinion, Fu had already missed the opportunity to retreat either to the far west or to the south.[86] Exactly one month after this report, Fu joined the CCP in declaring Beiping's "peaceful liberation."

When contemplating direct assistance to Fu, the State Department was perfectly conscious of the possibility that as a local force Fu could use American matériel in a power competition against Jiang Jieshi's "central government." In 1948, when U.S. policymakers were convinced that the "trend [in China] is toward regionalism and fragmentation," they became less hesitant about entanglement with centrifugal forces in China as long as doing so could facilitate the anticommunist struggle.[87] The anticommunist

---

8-1248; P. D. Sprouse to the Officer in Charge of the American Mission, Nanjing, 23 August 1948, enclosure: Letter from the Secretary of State to Secretary of Defense, 13 August 1948, GRDS, 893.00 / 6-3048.

85. Walton Butterworth to the Secretary of State, 11 August 1948, GRDS, 893.00 / 8-1148; Fang Zhengzhi, "Brief Record of the Peiping–Tianjin Campaign," *Ping Jin Zhanyi Qinli Ji (Yuan Guomindang Jiangling de Huiyi)* (Personal Experiences in the Peiping–Tianjin Campaign: Recollections by Former GMD generals), compiled by the Committee on Literary and Historical Materials of the National Committee of the Chinese People's Political Consultative Council (Beijing: Zhongguo Wenshi Chubanshe, 1996), 11–18; Du Jianshi, "The Extinction of GMD Troops in the Battle of Tianjin," ibid., 207–19; Zhou Beifeng, "Record of the Peiping Peace Talk," ibid., 292–93.

86. Edmund Clubb to the Secretary of State, 31 December 1948, GRDS, 893.00 / 12-3148.

87. Walton Butterworth to the Secretary of State, 27 July 1948, GRDS, 893.00 / 7-2748; Butterworth to the Secretary of State, 11 August 1948, GRDS, 893.00 / 8-1148.

priority of America's postwar China policy therefore remained unchanged. But the tilt toward local forces did indicate a clear divorce between America's Cold War efforts and a long-established principle in U.S. foreign policy, which was to help China maintain its territorial and sovereign integrity. Ironically, Washington's willingness to collaborate with local Chinese military leaders like Fu also meant the removal of previous restrictions against American cooperation with Fu's ethnopolitical adversaries, the Inner Mongols. In 1949, American officials in China began to contact Prince De with a new enthusiasm, and, this time, with the State Department's cautious endorsement.

The Fu interval between Ambassador Stuart's Mongolian initiative in May 1948 and the State Department's interest in cultivating some kind of relationship with the Inner Mongols in 1949 was significant. It indicated that the U.S. government had prioritized its instrumental options in the anticommunist struggle in China. Only after its successive disappointments with the GMD "central government" and Fu's regional force could Washington consider collaboration with the Inner Mongols as an option at the bottom of the barrel. It was a policy readjustment that had little to do with the Americans' moral sympathy toward the Inner Mongols or with the merit of Stuart's "principled" argument in May 1948.

But in 1949, the opportunity to organize a Mongolian resistance against the CCP in Inner Mongolia was dimmer than ever. A good indicator of the political trend in Inner Mongolia was the conditions of Shilingol League of northern Chahar. Shilingol—strategically located in the middle of Inner Mongolia and between Zhangjiakou and Outer Mongolia—was one of the richest pastoral lands and also the least sinicized regions of Inner Mongolia. Between 1946 and 1947, when the military balance between the GMD and the CCP was seesawing, the CCP's Mongolian work in the region could not hold its ground. Then, before 1948 ended, the situation turned completely in favor of the CCP. In November 1948, the State Department got an intelligence report based on stories told by a Mongol lama who had recently fled Beizimiao (today's Shilinhot), the political and religious center of Shilingol. According to the informant, the CCP was in solid control of the region and was conducting "liquidation struggles" against the rich and the lamas. Even the wealthy classes gave up any attempt to flee the region and accepted their fate, for they realized that the GMD regime was finished.[88]

88. Edmund Clubb to the Secretary of State, 26 November 1948, GRDS, 893.00 Mongolia / 11-2648.

When the GMD regime and Fu Zuoyi's force in northern China were doomed, opportunities seemed to emerge for Prince De, whose involuntary seclusion in Beiping finally came to an end. He was suddenly remembered by everyone. During the fall and winter of 1948, before Beiping changed hands, GMD and CCP agents, Fu Zuoyi, the Americans, and the Soviets took turns approaching Prince De and trying to secure his affiliation.[89] Regardless, the prince wanted to return to the political arena under nobody's aegis other than the United States'. The mutual interest between the Americans and Prince De, however, did not automatically lead to an agreement on how they could benefit from each other.

The GMD's retreat from northern China released Prince De physically from secret police surveillance. The development of the Chinese Civil War convinced the prince that western Inner Mongolia was becoming a political vacuum and, therefore, a promising location for launching a Mongolian autonomous government. It was to be hoped that such a government could rally those Inner Mongols who were not yet controlled by the CCP. It could also serve as a fait accompli to deal with any political contingency of China.[90] In April 1949, Prince De, members of the "Racial" group, and some local Mongol officials arrived in Dingyuanying (today's Bayanhot) of Alashan Banner, the westernmost banner of Inner Mongolia.[91] In August, a "Conference of Mongolian People's Delegates" was held in this desolate location, and a "Mongolian Autonomous Government" was launched under Prince De. This "government," however, stayed in Dingyuanying for less than two months before Prince De had to start his journey into exile in the MPR.[92]

In contrast to the resilient eastern Mongolian movement, Prince De's "government" in Alashan was just a fleeting phenomenon during the GMD–CCP power transition in 1949. Without a territory and a substantive force of his own, Prince De plunged into China's ethnopolitics—again with two expectations. First, he hoped that in its last and desperate moment as China's "central government," the GMD regime could finally be persuaded to endorse a Mongolian autonomous government. After making Dingyuanying his new base, Prince De immediately headed south to lobby the GMD

89. Sechin Jagchid, *Last Mongol Prince,* 389; Demchugdonrob, *Demuchukedonglupu Zishu,* 151–52.

90. Sechin Jagchid, *Last Mongol Prince,* 388, 395.

91. At the time, Alashan was a Mongolian banner of Ningxia province bordering Gansu in the west.

92. Demchugdongrob, "Demuchukedonglupu Zishu," 173.

government, which had just retreated from Nanjing to Guangzhou. Second, he thought that the American government was morally sympathetic toward the cause of Mongolian unification and would be willing to support his autonomous effort now and to endorse a greater Mongolian state when World War III began.[93] Thus, after his futile collaboration with the Japanese in the war years, Prince De again let wishful thinking guide his actions. In Nanjing and Guangzhou, the prince was cold-shouldered repeatedly by GMD officials, and in the end he had to accept the reality of intransigent GMD ethnopolitics.

Between late 1948 and mid-1949, the Americans did give Prince De some encouraging signals. These helped foster the prince's illusion about American assistance but did not bring about any tangible result in the end. During this period, American officials met with Prince De or his lieutenants at least six times.[94] On these occasions, Prince De urged the Americans to pay closer attention to the Mongolia question and sought direct assistance from the American government. Also on these occasions, the Americans appeared interested in the prince's northwestern plan and encouraged him to create a situation in that direction. In his meeting with Ambassador Stuart in Nanjing in January 1949, Prince De was quite heartened by the ambassador's citing of an old Chinese adage, "success goes to the determined" (*you zhi zhe shi jing cheng*).[95]

The most interesting of these encounters happened in Guangzhou in late May 1949, when Prince De was there to lobby the GMD government for the last time. According to a report prepared by the U.S. Consulate in Guangzhou, on May 30 the prince visited the consulate and informed the Americans of his effort in the northwest. Prince De told the Americans that his current objective was to launch an "autonomous Mongol democratic government" within the constitutional confinement of the Chinese Republic.

---

93. Demchugdongrob, "Demuchukedonglupu Zishu," 149, 153–54, 159–62, 178–79; Sechin Jagchid, *Last Mongol Prince,* 398–404.

94. These officials were Ruth Bean, Raymond Meitz, F. D. Schultheis, and Ambassador Stuart. In *The Last Mongol Prince,* 388, Sechin Jagchid identifies Raymond Meitz as the head of the U.S. Naval intelligence group in China. In his autobiography, Prince De identifies Meitz as an undercover agent working for the U.S. Information Service. His name has never surfaced from the State Department's documents on Mongolia. Schultheis was a political officer in the U.S. Embassy and one of the embassy's contact persons with the "Racial Mongols" over the years.

95. Sechin Jagchid, *Last Mongol Prince,* 388–89, 403; Demchugdongrob, "Demuchukedonglupu Zishu," 150–51, 153, 179–80.

As far as his ultimate goal, Mongolian independence, was concerned, the prince hoped that it would be able to materialize after a third world war or "until [the] US [was] able [to] make its influence felt in Central Asian affairs." For now, his effort in the northwest was to "at least keep alive [a] spark of Mongol nationalism in [the] dark days to come." The "spark" would, however, need some American fuel. Prince De's formula for a Mongolian–American partnership, as recorded in the consulate report, included these elements:

1. the United States provide "all economic aid feasible" to the Dingyuanying movement;
2. a "small amount of military help" from the Americans to arm a symbolic "Independent Mongol People's Army" as the Inner Mongols' "rallying point";
3. the Americans "caution" the Muslim forces in northwestern China not to harm the Mongolian movement in their neighborhood;
4. American journalists visit the northwest and report the aims and achievements of the Mongolian movement;
5. the United States duplicate Japan's wartime programs for training Mongol youths; and
6. the U.S. government send a "competent observer" immediately to the northwest who should report back on "what might be done [to] aid at least some Mongols of his [Prince De's] political persuasion [to] survive until time comes when Mongol independence [becomes] practical and possible."

Lewis Clark, the U.S. minister representing the Embassy in Guangzhou, characterized the prince's presentation as "restrained and dignified by determination and sincerity." American officials present at the interview "expressed admiration [of] Te Wang's devotion to [the] cause of Mongol peoples [*sic*]" and promised to transmit the prince's views and demands to the State Department.[96]

According to Prince De's recollection, at the meeting his American interlocutors gave him more than just perfunctory admiration. F. D. Schultheis was present at the interview and told the prince that although Ambassador

96. Clark to the Secretary of State, 1 June 1949, GRDS, 893.00 Mongolia / 6-149. In April 1949, the CCP took over Nanjing. The American Embassy, as did many other Western countries' embassies, decided not to follow the GMD government to Guangzhou.

Stuart was currently not in Nanjing, he had sent a message for Prince De. Allegedly, the ambassador had received a State Department reply to his earlier report about Prince De's movement, which "recognizes you [Prince De] as the representative of Mongolia and the counterpart of [America's] Mongolian work in the future." Prince De was also told that the U.S. embassy was actually considering sending a representative to his government in Dingyuanying.[97] Similarly encouraging was Prince De's separate meeting with Raymond Meitz in Guangzhou. Meitz provided Prince De with some equipment for radio communication and a number of trained Mongol operators. He also promised that arrangements would be made for the United Nations Relief and Rehabilitation Administration (UNRRA), which was ending its operations in the northwest, to hand over its remaining materials to the Dingyuanying movement.[98]

After all these promises from the Americans, an American–Mongolian partnership would not be burgeoning. Evidence of the alleged communication between the State Department and Ambassador Stuart cannot be found in the department's archives. The communication probably never took place. As a matter of fact, the State Department's reply to the Guangzhou consulate's report was ambiguous and noncommittal. The reply came in late June under the name of Secretary of State Dean Acheson. The State Department instructed U.S. diplomats in China that in any future discussions with Prince De they "should continue [to] evince sympathetic interest [in] his plans and efforts." Meanwhile, the State Department was either evasive or negative toward the prince's six demands. It pointed out that military aid to Prince De was unlikely because the $125 million allocated to China for military assistance by Congress' China Aid Act had already been exhausted. As for the prince's request for economic help, the State Department instructed the Guangzhou consulate, "without any indication [of] support or lack [of] support," to direct Prince De to officials of the U.S. Economic Cooperation Administration's (ECA) China Mission and the China–United States Joint Commission for Rural Reconstruction (JCRR) for further discussions. This

97. Demchugdongrob, "Demuchukedonglupu Zishu," 153. Sechin Jagchid, *Last Mongol Prince,* 403, offers a slightly different version of Schultheis' words, who set a precondition, or a "breakthrough" by Prince De's movement, for the embassy to send an agent to the northwest. Sechin Jagchid did not accompany the prince at this meeting, but when writing his book he consulted Rashidondog, who was at the prince's side during the meeting.

98. Demchugdongrob, "Demuchukedonglupu Zishu," 180; Sechin Jagchid, *Last Mongol Prince,* 403.

course of action would subject any American assistance to the Inner Mongols to the regulation of relevant Sino-American agreements governing ECA and JCRR operations. Given the GMD government's continued animosity toward Prince De and Inner Mongolian autonomy, this course could hardly lead to any result.

The State Department also refused to be seen as openly siding with Prince De, lest any such gesture be misinterpreted "as constituting U.S. intervention in Chinese internal affairs" or "provoke Communist pressure against Prince Te's faction." Therefore, the U.S. government must neither serve as a good office between the Mongols and the northwestern Muslims nor send any observer to Dingyuanying. The State Department was nevertheless willing to authorize its representatives in China to "mention informally" to American journalists Prince De's desire to have them visit the northwest. Notification might also be given to ECA agents already in the area "who to some degree [will be] able to report situation there."[99] Consequently, none of Prince De's demands were met by the State Department. Nor did Meitz's arrangements materialize: instead of transporting their materials to Dingyuanying, for some unknown reason, the UNRRA officials in the northwest turned over the materials to the Chinese authorities in Lanzhou.[100]

The inconsequential American connection, especially the failure to receive the promised UNRRA materials, severely demoralized Prince De and his collaborators in Dingyuanying. In August, when the group formally launched an "autonomous government," the occasion was decorated with a meager foreign presence. Probably in pursuance of the State Department's instruction, Frank Bessac, then an ECA agent in western Inner Mongolia, was there to observe the process, along with a British journalist and a local foreign missionary. Bessac had only a trivial role to play in the last episode of Prince De's political career. For the young American himself, Dingyuanying was just the beginning of an extremely dangerous, near-death journey out of China.[101]

99. Dean Acheson to U.S. Consulate, Canton, 27 June 1949, GRDS: 893.00 Mongolia / 6-149.

100. Sechin Jagchid, *Last Mongol Prince,* 410.

101. According to Sechin Jagchid, *Last Mongol Prince,* 410, Bessac was in Dingyuanying to see that Prince De's group receive the UNRRA materials. In his recollection, 181, Prince De mentions a conversation between himself and Bessac in which Bessac advised the prince to conduct a military operation against the GMD troops in Suiyuan and contact the MPR. At the time, Prince De could not figure out what motivated Bessac's "odd" suggestions. None of these are mentioned in Bessac's own recollection

The U.S. government's languid response to Prince De contrasted sharply with its swift action to aid Fu Zuoyi. If earlier American officials had entertained wishful thinking about Fu's ability to stop the CCP along the Great Wall, they now cherished no illusions about Prince De's chance to make even some sustainable troubles for the incoming Communist power in China's far west. In July 1949, the CIA did a head count of America's potential anticommunist assets in China. It was decided that the GMD was completely hopeless. Some regional warlords might be able to last for a couple of years, but none of them could gain popular support. Those lesser political parties between the GMD and the CCP were pro-Western, but none had military strength of its own and most of them had already become attached to the CCP. In comparison, "the prospects for long-term political resistance are somewhat better among the Mongols of Western Manchuria and Inner Mongolia, the Moslems of the Northwest, and the Tibetans of the far western provinces, but these peoples total only a few millions, and none of their leaders is of sufficient stature to attract widespread Chinese support."[102] Obviously, such an estimate could not lend credibility to any American plan to assist Prince De's group.

It is interesting that, having found non-Han leaders in frontier China wanting, the CIA's appraisal still juxtaposed them with desirable "widespread Chinese support" in China. The combination of these two elements had been rare in China's ethnopolitical past and was highly unlikely in the 1940s, when the tide of nationalism was high among the Chinese populace. The CIA's focus on "*Chinese,*" actually *Han,* support even when discussing non-Han groups' resistance was evidence that the U.S. government was hesitant about the Dinyuanying movement only partially because of the latter's

---

of his postwar experience in northwestern China. In "This Was the Perilous Trek to Tragedy," *Life* (November 1950), 131–41, Bessac identified himself as a State Department grain distributor in the Mongolian Ordos region after the war and a Fulbright scholar to study Mongolian anthropology in Alashan. The article is mainly about the second lap of his journey from Xinjiang to India via Tibet, in which he was detained by the Tibetan authorities and Douglas Mackiernan, his travel companion and the American vice consul in Urumqi, was killed by Tibetan troops. According to Thomas Laird, *Into Tibet: The CIA's First Atomic Spy and His Secret Expedition to Lhasa* (New York: Grove Press, 2002), 102–3, Bessac has denied to this day his connection with U.S. intelligence after 1947, even though at least one former CIA agent has insisted that after 1947 Bessac remained a "contract CIA agent" disguised as a Fulbright scholar.

102. CIA Intelligence Memorandum No. 197, 25 July 1949, Records of the National Security Council (hereafter RNSC) / Policy Papers, box 6.

material weakness. During the first half of the twentieth century, whether maneuvering against other foreign powers within the framework of China's "unequal treaty system," fighting the Japanese in World War II, or rivaling Soviet power in the Cold War, America's China policy tended to identify forces of Chinese nationalism as virtual or actual allies. Although American foreign policy rarely took an unequivocal stand on China's ethnopolitical issues for their own sake, Washington's larger policy needs often resulted in an American stance in these matters that was essentially pro-Han Chinese. In 1949, this rule was not changed by the State Department. Thus, at a time when Secretary of State Dean Acheson decided that the Chinese nation was just a "fiction," when the "China problem" in American foreign policy was "broadened" into a "larger general problem of Asia," and when American policymakers became inclined to fragment the allegedly non-existent Chinese state for the sake of anticommunism, the U.S. government still avoided committing itself openly to a position contradictory to Chinese nationalism.[103]

Therefore, any American operation against the "Chinese nation" that appeared destined to go under the CCP's control had to be carried out in a circuitous way. This approach is most clearly documented in the State Department's deliberations on the Taiwan question in early 1949. In a secret statement circulated among members of the National Security Council, the State Department favored an American effort to foster separatism in Taiwan. But it cautioned that the U.S. government must "carefully conceal our wish to separate the island from mainland control" because there was a "potential threat of irredentism spreading throughout the great expanse of continental China." The point was that while the United States was seeking to exploit the "Soviet-created irredentist issues" in China's northern borderlands, it must avoid "raising the specter of an American-created irredentist issue" in Taiwan.[104] In a word, America's sponsorship of any separatism in China had to be a "sensitive" operation and differ drastically from the Soviet approach, which affronted Chinese nationalism. Obviously, in 1949 Prince

---

103. "Memorandum for the President" (on the discussion at the 33rd meeting of the National Security Council), 4 February 1949, Truman Papers, PSF / NSC Files, box 220; memorandum for the Secretary of State, n.d. (July 1949), ROCA, 1945–1950 / Top Secret Subject Files, 1945–1950, box 13.

104. "Memorandum for the National Security Council" (on the circulation of a statement made by the Secretary of State at the 35th meeting of the NSC), 3 March 1949, Truman Papers, PSF / NSC Files, box 205.

De's movement in Dingyuanying was an unlikely candidate for such operations. Unable to stay alive on its own, Prince De's "spark of Mongolian nationalism" could not possibly serve as a sustainable front for any covert American operation. Thus, having encouraged Prince De to start the "spark" in western Inner Mongolia, the Americans refused to add any fuel and let it die out.

The undramatic ending of the brief American–Prince De flirtation did not end the Inner Mongolia question in Washington's policy deliberations about China. In 1949, as the CCP's military success in China exceeded many earlier predictions, U.S. policymakers, true to their determination to contain Soviet expansion in East Asia, began to regard Inner Mongolia as one of the "natural points of conflict" between the CCP and Moscow that would sooner or later cause a crack in the Eurasian communist monolith.[105]

U.S. foreign policy's postwar involvement in the Mongolia question in China reflected the ethnographic reach and political depth of America's entanglement in China's internal affairs. This was a multidimensional entanglement bearing on the interbloc, interstate, and interethnic politics of postwar East Asia. If, in the long history of Sino-American relations, Washington's anticommunist effort in postwar China constituted a new venture, Inner Mongolia was a tantalizing frontier for the effort that did not generate any bonanza for America's diplomatic pioneers. Nor did the Americans explore the frontier in earnest. Americans' halfhearted venture evolved in three phases. In 1945 and 1946, U.S. officials were worried about an alleged Inner Mongolian arm of Soviet expansion in northeastern China; in 1947 and 1948, they studied meticulously yet guardedly the "Racial Mongols" in Nanjing; in 1949, they courted Prince De lukewarmly. In all these times, a Mongolian stratagem hovered in the air like a ghost but never appeared with flesh and blood. In a word, America's foreign policy operations in postwar China saw the question of Inner Mongolia as marginal if not entirely immaterial.

Yet, the real significance of America's postwar involvement in Inner Mongolia lies elsewhere. While the USSR adopted a policy of separating

---

105. Note by the Executive Secretary of the National Security Council (Souers) to the Council, 28 February 1949, *FRUS,* 1949, 9: 493–94; NSC34/2, "United States Policy toward China," 28 February 1949, RNSC / Policy Papers, box 4. David Allan Mayers, *Cracking the Monolith: U.S. Policy against the Sino-Soviet Alliance, 1949–1955* (Baton Rouge: Louisiana State University Press, 1986), 39, 49, 68, 71, 104, 122, offers some interesting observations of the Inner Mongolia question in Washington's policy toward the People's Republic of China.

permanently the "outer" and "inner" halves of Mongolia, America's shifting attitude toward Inner Mongolian nationalism, ranging from complete avoidance to evasive engagement, helped consummate an international environment in the postwar period that stifled the Inner Mongols' struggle for autonomy. The true beneficiary of this environment was the Chinese national state, which would soon rise in the form of the People's Republic of China.

9

The Range of "Wild Wind": Moscow's Inner Mongolia Stratagem

In 1945, Bayanbulag was an ordinary teenager living in West Sunid Banner of Shilingol League. In mid-August, he witnessed an event that would remain vivid in his memory for the rest of his life. This is how he remembered it four decades later:

> July 7th, 1945 of the lunar calendar [August 14], around noon, a wild wind blew the sky away, and under the noises of trucks, tanks, and motorcycles the earth was trembling. . . . In this way the [Soviet–Mongolian] joint army passed through our area for seven days."[1]

Largely ignored by Comintern and Mongol revolutionaries in the 1920s, the pasture land of Shilingol in the summer of 1945 was cratered by Soviet mortars and ditched by Soviet tanks. To Bayanbulag's impressionable young mind, the Soviet–Mongolian troops' seven-day march through his home area was shockingly spectacular. He and most people in the area, however, did not know that these troops were just a small fraction of a massive invasion that involved 1.5 million troops, 5,500 tanks and self-propelled guns, and about 4,000 airplanes. To the east of Bayanbulag's home, according to a detailed study, Soviet tanks were pushing ahead in formation of a "belt of armor fifteen to twenty kilometers wide."[2]

---

1. Bayanbulag, "Soviet–Mongolian Red Army Passed through Sunid Right Banner," *Sunite Youqi Wenshi Ziliao* (Historical and Literary Materials of Sunid Right Banner) 1–2 (1982): 33–34.
2. C. M. Shtemenko, *Zhanzheng Niandai de Zong Canmoubu* (General Staff in the War Years), trans. Hong Ke (Beijing: Sanlian Shudian, 1972), 2: 537; David M. Glantz,

Contemporary Soviet writers gave the massive invasion a righteous name, "short purifying storm."[3] The Soviet military would afterward praise the Mongolian People's Republic (MPR) for contributing to the final strike against Japan. Quantitatively, the Mongolian contribution was trivial. The MPR's four cavalry divisions of 21,000 troops, as part of the "Soviet–Mongolian Cavalry-Mechanized Group" under Soviet general I. A. Pliyev's command, accounted for merely 1.4 percent of the total Soviet ground forces against Japan. The direction of these troops' operation was to cross the vast desert and grassland in western Inner Mongolia and advance toward Zhangjiakou and Duolun. Because this area had only some small and scattered Japanese units, it was not even included in the Soviet Red Army's three-pronged offensive against Japan's main force, the Kwantung Army in Manchuria. In military terms, therefore, the MPR troops participated in an auxiliary of the Soviet Red Army operation in clearing its right flank.[4]

The significance of the MPR's participation in World War II, however, rested more on the political side. As early as 1943, the Chinese government anticipated the MPR's declaration of war on Japan. Chinese officials believed that once the Soviet Union decided to enter the war against Japan, the MPR, as a Soviet satellite, would inevitably join the foray as well. At the time, the Chinese government was prepared to greet such a development with a low-key statement on China's responsibility for defending Outer Mongolia, a "national territory," from plundering by Japan.[5] In August 1945, however, the MPR entered the war under different circumstances. At midnight on August 14, or about twelve hours after Bayanbulag saw a Soviet tank for the first time in his life, the Soviet and Chinese governments concluded a "Treaty of Friendship and Alliance" in Moscow. As part of the diplomacy, a set of notes exchanged between the two sides established a procedure for China to recognize the MPR's independence.

August Storm: The Soviet 1945 Strategic Offensive in Manchuria (Fort Leavenworth, Kans.: Combat Studies Institute of U.S. Army Command and General Staff College, 1983), 83.

3. John Stephan, *The Russian Far East: A History* (Stanford, Calif.: Stanford University Press, 1994), 241–42.

4. Shtemenko, *Zhanzheng Niandai,* 517, 524–26; M. B. Zaharov, *Jieju* (Finale), trans. Jun Qing (Shanghai: Shanghai Yiwen Chubanshe, 1978), 185, 188; Baabar, *Twentieth Century Mongolia* (Cambridge: White Horse Press, 1999), 409.

5. Meeting Minutes of the International Questions Study Group of the Supreme Council of National Defense, 3 July 1943, Guofang Zuigao Weiyuanhui Dang'an (Archives of the Supreme Council of National Defense; hereafter GZWD), 005/0002.5.

Soviet military planners did not wait for Soviet diplomacy to succeed in Moscow.[6] It has been speculated that before his diplomatic dealings with the Chinese, Joseph Stalin had already decided that the MPR should assert its independence from China by partaking in the war. During the Moscow negotiations, Stalin did try to thwart his Chinese counterparts' argument about Chinese sovereignty over Outer Mongolia, saying that "Outer Mongolia was lost [to China] anyway—declared war on Japan." In addition, the MPR's fighting at the side of the Soviet Union would also provide Choibalsan with a chance to show MPR superiority to the Inner Mongols. That was why the main task of the MPR cavalries was to destroy Prince De's puppet troops in western Inner Mongolia.[7]

Whereas these motives seem plausible, the MPR's entry into the war, as an ethnopolitical showcase, might actually have contradictory connotations to the Chinese authorities and to the Inner Mongols. To the former, Soviet-sponsored MPR belligerency on the Allied side could mean one more step taken by Moscow in the direction of formal MPR independence from China. To the latter, the event could mean Soviet-endorsed MPR enticement of the Inner Mongols' political loyalty. If this was an intended effect, Moscow's two-Mongolia orientation would have to be reversed and the specter of pan-Mongolism awakened. The historical question, therefore, is which between the two effects was sought by Stalin.

A Sense of Limits

At first glance, an advance policy in Inner Mongolia would seem in accord with Stalin's general international strategy at the end of World War II. As he told some Yugoslav Communist leaders in early 1945, at the end of this war, "whoever occupies a territory also imposes on it his own social system. Everyone imposes his own system as far as his army can reach. It cannot be otherwise."[8] Having learned a lesson from their 1939 mistake of

6. According to Shtemenko, *Zhanzheng Niandai*, 501, 526–27, Soviet military planning for entry into the war against Japan began in late September 1944 and were completed in June 1945.

7. Baabar, *Twentieth Century Mongolia*, 409; "Notes taken at Sino–Soviet Conferences, Moscow, 1945": Stalin's conversation with the Chinese delegation on 10 August 1945, Victor Hoo Papers, box 2.

8. Cited in Marc Trachtenberg, *A Constructed Peace: The Making of the European Settlement, 1945–1963* (Princeton, N.J.: Princeton University Press, 1999), 36.

replacing a buffer with a direct border with Nazi Germany in Poland, which proved indefensible under Hitler's blitzkrieg in June 1941, during and after World War II Stalin and his associates worked hard to establish a string of buffer states that could separate the Soviet Union from the West. In East Europe, Stalin reversed Lenin's approach of providing military assistance to native revolutions and instead used the Soviet Red Army directly to spearhead his "system imposition." In East Asia, Soviet leaders retrogressed to the tsar's times, "restored" Russian sphere of influence in Manchuria, seized the Kuriles and South Sakhalin from Japan, and pushed Russia's security frontier in the east from the Amur River to the 38th parallel in the Korean Peninsular. Without the American government's firm objection, Stalin would have landed the Red Army on Hokkaido of Japan, where, in Stalin's mind, a Soviet "line of optimum conquest" should lie at least for now.[9]

Indeed, to Moscow's Cold War adversaries, Soviet foreign policy fitted well with a dictum articulated by Henry Kissinger years later—"torn between obsessive insecurity and the proselytizing zeal, Russia on the march rarely showed a sense of limits."[10] In 1945, the seemingly boundless Soviet expansion could easily engulf Inner Mongolia. It was so at least in the eyes of Guomindang (GMD, Nationalist Party) officials. A 1946 report by Dai Li's Juntong (Mililtary Statistics Bureau) asserted that "no matter how the political situation in China changes, the Soviet Union will pursue the established policy of luring Inner Mongolia to gain independence," and that "if necessary, [Moscow] will direct Outer Mongolia to start border conflicts with Inner Mongolia . . . in order that Outer Mongolia can annex Inner Mongolia through a territory-nibbling policy." Inevitably, similar "intelligence" was also fed into the American intelligence system.[11] Reports of this kind

9. Dmitri Trenin, *The End of Eurasia: Russia on the Border between Geopolitics and Globalization* (Washington, D.C.: Carnegie Endowment for International Peace, 2002), 49–50; Dmitri Volkogonov, *Stalin: Triumph and Tragedy,* trans., Harold Shukman (New York: Grove Weidenfeld, 1991), 502; John P. LeDonne, *The Russian Empire and the World, 1700–1917: The Geopolitics of Expansion and Containment* (Oxford: Oxford University Press, 1997), 181; Boris Slavinsky, "Soviet Amphibious Landing on Hokkaido and the Southern Kurile Islands: Facts and Fiction," *Far Eastern Affairs* (hereafter *FEA*) 3 (1992): 51–53.

10. Henry Kissinger, *Diplomacy* (New York: Simon & Schuster, 1994), 25.

11. Combined Central Secretariat [of the GMD government], "Report on Recent Collusion between the CCP and the Soviet Army, first issue, 10 February 1946," *Zhonghua Minguo Zhongyao Shiliao Chubian* (Preliminary Compilation of Important Historical Documents of the Republic of China; hereafter *ZZSC*) 7(1): 580, 582; "Military Information: Russian Activities in Manchuria," 21 July 1946, Central Intelligence Agency

were, however, intelligence noises that would die down as events unfolded. The case of Inner Mongolia would eventually appear atypical of Soviet foreign policy.

According to Vyacheslav Molotov's recollections, shortly after Japan's surrender, Stalin expressed to his colleagues a general satisfaction with the emerging geostrategic landscape of East Asia:

> The Kurils now belong to us. All of Sakhalin belongs to us, . . . and Port Arthur, and Dalny [Dalian] and the Chinese Eastern Railroad—all belong to us. China, Mongolia—everything seems in order.[12]

It is easy to overlook the fact even today that in this expansionist assertion Mongolia was *not* a new territorial advance made by the Soviets. Rather, Stalin's satisfaction was derived from his success in freezing Mongolia's status quo through the Yalta–Moscow diplomacy between February and August of 1945. As Stalin made abundantly clear to Western and Chinese leaders in the process, Mongolia's status quo meant the continuation of MPR independence from China and Mongolia's division into two political entities.

In other words, in the case of Inner Mongolia, Stalin showed a rare "sense of limits." Unlike Soviet occupation in Manchuria, which was governed by a Sino-Soviet agreement concluded in Moscow in August 1945, the issue of Soviet–Mongolian military presence in Inner Mongolia was completely ignored by the Chinese–Soviet negotiations. Furthermore, in Moscow Chinese and Soviet diplomats failed to agree on a clearly demarcated *international* border between Inner and Outer Mongolia. Last, negotiators in Moscow scheduled a plebiscite in the MPR to decide on its independence from China, but they did not establish any mechanism to prevent the occasion from becoming a pan-Mongol rally or an opportunity for the MPR to project its influence into Inner Mongolia.[13] Under these circumstances,

---

Freedom of Information Act (CIA FOIA) release case EO-1997-00002; "Military Information: Soviet–Mongolian Military Mission to Kalgan," 17 August 1946, CIA FOIA release case EO-1997-00002.

12. Valentin M. Berezhkov, *At Stalin's Side: His Interpreter's Memoirs from the October Revolution to the Fall of the Dictator's Empire,* trans. Sergei V. Mikheyev (New York: Carol Publishing Group, 1994), 31–32.

13. "Agreement on Chinese–Soviet Joint War Effort against Japan and the Relationship between the Soviet Army Headquarters and the Chinese Administrative Authorities

Moscow had considerable room for maneuvering to augment its gain of territories or influence Inner Mongolia at the expense of China. Yet the joint Soviet–Mongolian force entered Inner Mongolia and then left a few months later without adding any new territory to Moscow's security cordon.

Despite the declassification of Soviet archival materials in recent years, Stalin's intentions toward Inner Mongolia during the few crucial postwar months remain shrouded in mystery. An undocumented assertion suggests that as late as 1947 Stalin "very nearly added" Inner Mongolia to the territory of the MPR.[14] A more cautious view holds that only during the first two weeks after Japan's surrender did Stalin direct his "opportunistic expansionism" toward Inner Mongolia by encouraging MPR leaders' ambition for national unification. Accordingly, pan-Mongolism could have been Stalin's leverage against the Chinese government if the latter had refused to support MPR independence according to the new Sino-Soviet treaty.[15]

During the Moscow negotiations, the question of Mongolia was indeed one of the principal obstacles debated heatedly by the two sides. A few months later, Stalin told Choibalsan how during the negotiations the Chinese side was forced to concede over the subject: "Our side said to the Chinese: 'If China fails to recognize the independence of Mongolia, we shall not fight Japan.'" Stalin's cuddling of Choibalsan has misled several historical studies.[16] In reality, during the Moscow negotiations Soviet belligerency against Japan was *not* something desired by the GMD regime over which vital Chinese interests could be bargained away. Both Soviet and

---

after Soviet Troops' Entry into the Three Eastern Provinces of China," 14 August 1945, *ZZSC* 3(2): 666–67; notes exchanged between Soviet and Chinese foreign ministers on Outer Mongolia, 14 August 1945, ibid., 656–58; Song Ziwen and Wang Shijie to Jiang Jieshi, 12 August 1945, ibid., 648.

14. Marko Milivojevic, "The Mongolian People's Army: Military Auxiliary and Political Guardian," in *Mongolia Today,* ed. Shirin Akiner (London: Kegan Paul International, 1991), 139.

15. Christopher Atwood, "Sino-Soviet Diplomacy and the Second Partition of Mongolia, 1945–1946," in *Mongolia in the Twentieth Century: Landlocked Cosmopolitan,* ed. Stephen Kotkin and Bruce Elleman (Armonk, N.Y.: M. E. Sharpe, 1999), 137–58.

16. Togoochiyn Lkhagva, "What Was Stalin's Real Attitude to [*sic*] the Mongols," *FEA* 4 (1991): 120; Atwood, "Sino-Soviet Diplomacy," 137; Sergei Luzianin, *Rossiia–Mongoliia–Kitaii v pervoii polovine XX v: Politicheskie vzaimootnosheniia v 1911–1946 g.* (Russia, Mongolia, and China in the first half of the twentieth century: Political relations, 1911–1946) (Moscow: Far Eastern Institute of Russian Academy of Sciences, 2000), 215; and Luzianin, "The Yalta Conference and Mongolia in International Law before and during the Second World War," *FEA* 6 (1995): 39.

Chinese participants were constantly aware that a settlement of their bilateral difficulties was less about the two governments' alliance in the final stage of war against Japan than about a power balance in postwar East Asia, where the United States was already a salient party. To Stalin, Mongolia was part of the Yalta–Moscow system; its settlement had to be accomplished according to the "status quo" formula hammered out at Yalta.[17] Therefore, if Moscow's self-restraint regarding Inner Mongolia appeared to be an aberration in the general pattern of Soviet expansion after World War II, the policy was not an opportunistic improvisation on Stalin's part. It was a scripted act that had origins in both the recent Yalta diplomacy and Moscow's two-Mongolia orientation adopted in the late 1920s.

To put Stalin's postwar Mongolian stratagem in perspective, it is helpful to retrieve briefly the relevant historical background. In the 1920s, it was not totally by coincidence that Mongolia, Asia's first ethnopolitical rebel tearing itself away from the traditional Chinese empire, teamed up with the Soviet Union, the world's first ideological insurgent defying the prevalent international system. At their inceptions, both states faced overwhelming hostile forces and their mutual needs were obvious. Yet their needs were asymmetric. The partnership was unfavorable to the Mongols in the sense that their collaboration with Moscow made their country an accomplice to an international outlaw, which was thematically contradictory to their ethnonationalist revolution. For unless Mongolia was accepted by the international community, its so-called independence was illegitimate and, in the shadow of Moscow, illusory. To escape Moscow's smothering patronage, many nationalistic Mongol leaders offended the Kremlin in trying to foster normal foreign relations for their country.

In the meantime, Moscow's disposal of Mongolia followed the rules of some of the most rigid bloc politics in the twentieth century. While tabling its world revolution agenda and gradually reestablishing diplomatic relations with Western countries in the 1920s and 1930s, Moscow nevertheless kept Mongolia insulated from any foreign contact. In the prewar years, Mongolia's isolation was a mirror image of Soviet leaders' own sense of

---

17. For two discussions of Sino-Soviet diplomacy in the summer of 1945, see John W. Garver, *Chinese–Soviet Relaltions, 1937–1945: The Diplomacy of Chinese Nationalism* (New York: Oxford University Press, 1988), 214–30, and Xiaoyuan Liu, *A Partnership for Disorder: China, the United States, and Their Policies for the Postwar Disposition of the Japanese Empire, 1941–1945* (New York: Cambridge University Press, 1996), 258–86.

insecurity. Thus, when the interwar international system was shattered by World War II, the extent to which the MPR could enter the international community hinged entirely on the degree of the Soviet Union's own reconciliation with or repositioning in a new world order emerging from the war.

Japan's 1931 aggression against Manchuria felled the first domino of interwar peace. The impact on the Soviet Union was immediate. In 1937, when Japan's continuous aggression in China finally flared into a full-scale Sino-Japanese war, Moscow sent an infantry army and a motorized division into the MPR. Given Japan's long-standing plan for developing a pro-Japanese "Man-Meng" (Manchurian-Mongolian) region as a launching base against both China and the Soviet Union, Moscow's military reinforcement in the MPR was justified. The measure paid off in August 1939, when Soviet and Japanese troops fought a costly battle along a disputed portion of the MPR–Manchurian border. The event, known differently to the two sides as the Nomonhan or the Halhyn River incident, attested to Moscow the effectiveness of its Mongolian buffer. After the incident, Japan and the Soviet Union would remain nonbelligerent toward each other until August 1945.[18] In the meantime, Moscow purged "unreliable elements" from the Russian Far East as a cautionary measure against the Japanese-controlled Manchuria. The process included the relocation of about 175,000 Korean residents from the region to Kazakhstan and Uzbekistan in Central Asia.[19]

While holding the line in the east, Moscow saw an opportunity in the west, where World War II tore the "capitalist world" apart. On the eve of

18. Japanese Cabinet decision, "Principal Orientations in Dealing with the Man-Meng Question," 12 March 1932, Japanese History Group of Department of History, Fudan University, comp. and trans., *Riben Diguozhuyi Duiwai Qinlue Shiliao Xuanbian* (Selected Historical Documents on Japanese Imperialist Aggression against Other Countries) (Shanghai: Renmin Chubanshe, 1975), 63–64; Staff Department of the Kwantung Army, "Essential Measures toward Inner Mongolia," 25 July 1935, ibid., 168–75; Staff Department of the Kwantung Army, "Course of the Mongolian Work and the Kwantung Army's Future Orientation," ibid., 208–9; Lin Sanlang, *Guandongjun he Sulian Yuandongjun* (Kwangtung Army and the Soviet Far Eastern Army) (Changchun: Jilin Renmin Chubanshe, 1979), 100–29; Baabar, *Twentieth Century Mongolia*, 382–90.

19. Document 02321: Resolution by the People's Commissariat and Soviet Communist Party Central Committee on Moving Korean Residents Away from Border Regions, 21 August 1937, *Sulian Lishi Dang'an Xuanbian* (Selected Historical Archives of the Soviet Union; hereafter *SLDX*) 12: 364–65; Document 02325: Resolution by the People's Commissariat on the Budget for Moving the Koreans, 11 September 1937, ibid., 12: 370–72; Document 02331: Resolution by the People's Commissariat on the Budget for Moving the Second Group of Korean Residents in the Far Eastern Border Region, 7 October 1937, ibid., 12: 377–78.

Hitler's invasion of Poland in September 1939, fearing a Western conspiracy to turn Hitler's war machine against the Soviet Union, Stalin gambled by entrusting Soviet security to secret agreements with the Nazis. It has been aptly pointed out that by doing so, although receiving a big chunk of Central Europe and "a 1,500 km long common border with Germany and its satellites, Stalin placed the USSR in danger of a potentially massive, surprise German attack."[20] Stalin did not foresee what was in store in Hitler's foreign policy. In November 1940, after Germany, Italy, and Japan signed a tripartite pact to endorse one another's spheres of influence in the world, Stalin sent Molotov to Berlin to explore the possibility of the Soviet Union's taking part in the Axis powers' world order. Hitler appeared accommodative. As far as Asia was concerned, Hitler proposed dividing the continent into a Japanese eastern and a Soviet central sphere. He also suggested that in the next 50 to 100 years the Soviets push their sphere southward to the Indian Ocean.[21]

Several months later, when a German blitzkrieg blew the Soviet Union's "1941 borders" away, Stalin's gambling with Hitler proved a total fiasco. To the Soviet leadership, the disastrous advance of Soviet borders in the west after 1939 made the stationary Mongolian buffer in the east especially successful. Thus, after 1941, when Soviet leaders began to consider postwar strategy again in the context of their alliance with the Western powers, the tendency was to apply the Asian model of the Mongolian satellite to the European borders of the Soviet Union, not the other way around.

Less than three weeks after Japan attacked Pearl Harbor, Solomon Lozovsky, the Soviet deputy foreign minister, suggested to Stalin that it was time to make preparations for postwar arrangements. According to Lozovsky, in a postwar world minus four big powers (Germany, Italy, Japan, and France), the Soviet Union would still likely face a united front among capitalist powers headed by the United States and the United Kingdom. He proposed

20. Trenin, *End of Eurasia,* 49. For documents on the Soviet–German relationship in this period, see "Treaty of Non-Aggression between the USSR and Germany and Secret Additional Protocol," 23 August 1939, in *Soviet Documents on Foreign Policy,* ed. Jane Degras (New York: Octagon Books, 1978), 3: 359–61; Document 05761: Secret Supplementary Agreement between USSR and Germany on Division of Sphere of Interests, 28 September 1939, *SLDX* 4: 537; Document 05762: Secret Agreement between USSR and Germany on Border Demarcation, 4 October 1939, ibid., 4: 538–42.

21. Document 10787: Stalin's Directive on Molotov's Trip to Berlin, 9 November 1940, *SLDX* 16: 107–9; Documents 01660 and 01662: Minutes of Two Conversations between Molotov and Hitler, 12 and 13 November 1940, ibid., 16: 119–26, 130–42.

setting up committees to assess the questions of war damages, postwar Soviet boundaries from the "angle of security and transportation freedom," and the Soviet position and interests in East Asia in the event of a Soviet–Japanese war. In the next two years, the Politburo established three committees for these purposes, separately headed by Molotov, Maxim Litvinov, and Klim Voroshilov.[22]

A complete knowledge about the activities of these committees has to wait for further studies and declassification of Soviet archives, but the general direction of Soviet strategists' thinking can be discerned from what has transpired so far. In recent years, several wartime planning position papers written by Maxim Litvinov, Ivan Maisky, and Andrei Gromyko—leading Soviet diplomats of the war years and participants in Moscow's postwar foreign policy planning—have come under historians' scrutiny. Their analyses and policy recommendations did not necessarily agree on every point, but they share some common features.

These policymakers' documents, which have been characterized as "truly representative of more advanced and sophisticated Soviet thinking" about great power relationships in the postwar years, reflected a significant change of self-identity of the Soviet Union in world affairs.[23] Contemplating Soviet foreign policy during the heyday of Moscow's wartime alliance with the United States and the United Kingdom, Soviet strategists were no longer scheming for revolutionary and subversive conspiracies befitting their country's prewar identity as the world's largest outcast. Rather, they were preparing for the Soviet Union's reentry onto the world stage as a responsible leading power. Indeed, the old habit lingered on and some (e.g., Maisky) still talked about an unlikely scenario of "proletarian revolution in Europe." But in the main, the predicted political trend in the postwar world was not this type of revolution but "wide-range democracy."

These documents also shared another common feature: They all predicted postwar cooperation between the Soviet Union and the Anglo-Saxon powers based on democratic principles. In categorizing the United States

22. Document 03197: Lozovsky to Stalin, 26 December 1941, *SLDX* 16: 665–67; Document 03198: Excerpts from Soviet Communist Party Politburo Meeting Minutes no. 36, 28 January 1942, ibid., 16: 668–71; Document 03199: Excerpts from Soviet Communist Party Politburo Meeting Minutes no. 41, 4 September 1943, ibid., 16: 672–3.

23. Vladimir O. Pechatnov, *The Big Three after World War II: New Documents on Soviet Thinking about Postwar Relations with the United States and Great Britain,* Cold War International History Project Working Paper 13 (Washington, D. C.: Woodrow Wilson International Center for Scholars, 1995).

and the United Kingdom separately as "new" and "conservative" imperialist powers, Soviet strategists believed that the danger of interest conflicts between these two would be greater than that between the Soviet Union and either one. This view constituted an important departure from Lozovsky's 1941 cliché about capitalist countries' united front against the Soviet Union. Last, in supporting "restoration" of the so-called 1941 borders plus further territorial readjustments in Europe and Asia, these documents landed firmly in the conventional camp of international practices in their recommended approach to achieving postwar security for the Soviet Union. In other words, the Soviet Union must maximize its "sphere of security" through big power arrangements but not by unilateral territorial expansion.[24]

In the postwar years, the degeneration of the Grand Alliance into the Cold War indicated that both the Soviets and the Western allies in the war years inflated the commonality between them. As reflected in their planning documents, Soviet strategists obviously failed to anticipated a potential conflict between the Soviet Union's geopolitical quest for security and what they termed America's economic, financial, and technological expansion. Although wartime optimism evaporated quickly, the new legalism of Soviet foreign policy remained real, and Moscow's struggle for international legitimacy would actually become part of the superpowers' rivalry in the Cold War period. Here lay the opportunity for the MPR to enter the international community.

Like the Tibet question between the British and the Chinese governments, the Mongolia question was one of the taboos in the wartime inter-Allied diplomacy, discussion of which was deemed disconcerting to the unity of the Grand Alliance. Nevertheless, both the Chinese and Soviet governments made efforts to court the Western allies' sympathy to their respective stands. The British government held a sympathetic attitude toward independent Outer Mongolia because of British India's connection to Tibet. In the war years, annoyed by the Chinese government's manifested sympathy toward the Indian independence movement, British officials believed that the Chinese were not in position to denounce Western colonialism when they "themselves busying asserting imperialist claims to dominate their non-

---

24. Document 03200: Litvinov's Letter to Stalin and Molotov on the Issues to be Studied by the Committee on Peace Treaties and Postwar Arrangements, 9 September 1943, *SLDX* 16: 674–83; Document 03201: Maisky's Report to Molotov on "the Best Fundamental Principles for Peace in the Future," 11 January 1944, ibid., 16: 684–713.

Chinese neighbors such as Mongolia and Tibet."[25] The Franklin Roosevelt administration of the United States, in promoting China as a great power to balance British and Soviet influence in Asia, did not want its policy to be confused by the subject of "Chinese imperialism." Rather, U.S. officials defined the issue of Outer Mongolia as one of interest adjustment between the Chinese and the Soviets. As long as the matter could be settled between the two sides, the Americans did not really care one way or another. Meanwhile, they did think that after so many years of Soviet control in Outer Mongolia, the Chinese assertion about regaining the territory appeared quixotic.[26]

Washington's power politics with respect to the Mongolia question may have been one of the reasons for Moscow's success in its diplomatic contest with China for American support. In addition, the Soviets were apparently more accomplished players than the Chinese in obscure international games. In the summer of 1944, Moscow finally opened Mongolia, the forbidden land, to a prominent American visitor, Vice President Henry Wallace. Accompanied by Owen Lattimore and others, Wallace traveled from Alaska to Chongqing to meet with Jiang Jieshi. The Americans' stop at Ulaanbaatar had no particular political significance to Washington, even though they were greeted by Choibalsan himself. For Stalin, it was good enough that the American visitors traveled to the MPR from the Soviet side, not the Chinese side. He would certainly have been pleased if he had learned about the content of Wallace's report to Roosevelt after the trip. In the report, while indicating the unmistakable existence of strong Soviet influence in the MPR, Wallace suggested that China's sovereignty there could not be realistically renewed.[27]

Stalin's progress with the Americans was further consolidated at the Yalta Conference in February 1945. Characteristically, he managed to persuade Roosevelt and Winston Churchill to join his game of ambiguity and accept a clause on maintaining the "status quo of Outer Mongolia" in a secret

25. British Foreign Office (FO) commentary, "Chinese Policy Regarding Outer Mongolia," 24 April 1942, FO 371/31702.

26. PG [Political Agenda Group] document-34, 4 October 1943, Notter Records, box 119; memorandum of conversation between T. V. Soong and Cordell Hull, 31 March 1943, T. V. Soong Papers, box 30; John P. Davies, *Dragon by the Tail: American, British, Japanese and Russian Encounters with China and One Another* (New York: W. W. Norton, 1972), 278.

27. Baabar, *Twentieth Century Mongolia,* 399–402.

agreement. In the same agreement, as a price for the Soviet promise to enter the war against Japan, the Western leaders also conceded to Stalin's
demands for restoring tsarist privileges in Manchuria and gaining two northern territories (the Kuriles and Southern Sakhalin) from Japan. Thus, after
Yalta, the Western allies appeared inclined to support the Soviet solution of
the Mongolia conundrum. The Soviet tactic proved rather effective a few
months later, when the Chinese and Soviet governments entered a bilateral
negotiation in Moscow.

In contrast, despite his success at the Cairo conference of November
1943 in winning the Western allies' commitment to restore to China territories seized by Japan, Jiang Jieshi missed the opportunity to obtain Roosevelt's and Churchill's explicit support to China's stand on Mongolia. Nor
did the Chinese government visibly react to Wallace's visit to the MPR in
1944. After the Yalta conference, the Chinese government became extremely
worried that the Big Three nations made some secret deals at China's expenses. But Outer Mongolia was not a cause of Chongqing's concern. For,
shortly after Yalta, President Roosevelt, ingenuously or not, told the Chinese
ambassador to the United States that Stalin's demand for maintaining Outer
Mongolia's status quo did not contradict Chinese sovereignty. But, in July
and August, when Stalin was using the Yalta agreement to press Chinese
diplomats to give up Outer Mongolia, Roosevelt was no longer alive to
insist on his interpretation of Yalta.[28]

Stalin's bargaining with the Western allies over Asian interests at Yalta
was not merely for a revanchist reversal of the consequences of the Russo-
Japanese War of 1904–5. It was part of an advance policy to secure the Soviet
"sphere of security" in East Asia, which would include a legitimate Mongolian buffer and internationally endorsed Soviet influence in Manchuria,
and, if possible, Xinjiang. To convince the Western allies to accept such
an arrangement, in post-Yalta conversations with American officials Stalin
promised that Soviet influence in Manchuria would not be contradictory to
America's "open door" principle, and that the MPR was "not a part of the
USSR and was open to all."[29] Stalin's rhetoric was deceitful, because he
had no intention of opening Manchuria and Outer Mongolia to Western

28. Liu, *Partnership for Disorder,* 126–47, 242–47.
29. Bohlen notes of Truman–Stalin meeting, 12 July 1945, *Foreign Relations of the
United States: Diplomatic Papers: Berlin* 1: 43–47; "Hopkins–Stalin Conversation
Record, Moscow, May 1945," Harry Hopkins Papers, box 338.

infiltration. Especially, he would not allow a return of Chinese influence to the MPR. This is, however, not to say that Stalin's depiction of the geographic limits of the Soviet sphere was untruthful. As far as Mongolia was concerned, Moscow's foreign policy in the last stage of World War II and the initial postwar months was to finalize the long-standing two-Mongolia formula by supplementing Outer Mongolia's actual separation from China with the Chinese and other governments' formal recognition.

Containing Nationalism

Considering that in World War II Soviet diplomacy began to pursue legitimate MPR independence as a key building block in the Soviet Union's postwar security structure, it is highly unlikely that Stalin contemplated a strategic reversal on that policy during his negotiations with the Chinese in the summer of 1945 and afterward. Although Soviet foreign policy can be defined as opportunistic, the seemingly unprincipled and unpredictable Soviet behavior in international affairs must not be mistaken for a lack of stable foreign policy objectives. Ever since the Tsarist government became involved in the Mongolian revolution in the early twentieth century, Russian–Soviet policymakers had generally regarded any form of Mongolian unification as a threat to their country's security. In 1945, this stand was further fortified by Stalin's incorporating of the MPR into his grand arrangements with the Western allies.

The Yalta understanding could still have been overturned if, during the 1945 Sino-Soviet negotiations in Moscow, Stalin had failed to browbeat the Chinese into accepting his interpretation of the Yalta clause on the Outer Mongolian "status quo." During the negotiations, the Chinese indeed put up resistance to the Soviets' demand for Mongolian independence, but they were alone in this fight. The Harry Truman administration—much less optimistic than the Roosevelt administration about the prospect of American–Soviet cooperation in the postwar world and alarmed by the Soviets' high-handed approach in negotiating with the Chinese—nevertheless did not want to nullify the Yalta agreement or to inject itself into the Chinese–Soviet talks. Soviet entry into the war against Japan was still deemed necessary in Washington. Besides, it was still believed that the Chinese government might well let Outer Mongolia go if in return Moscow would respect Chinese sovereignty in Inner Mongolia and Manchuria. During the Potsdam conference, which temporarily interrupted the Sino-Soviet negotiations, President Truman was satisfied that his conversations with Stalin "clinched the Open Door in Manchuria."[30]

Having effectively prevented the Americans from taking the Chinese side over the Mongolia question and positioned the Red Army to invade Manchuria, Stalin knew that Chinese quibbling about Mongolia did not pose any real threat to his plan. Stalin was so confident that on July 4, just two days after his first heated debate with the Chinese delegation over Outer Mongolia, he brought Choibalsan to Moscow and, on the next day, showed him a "joint Soviet–Chinese draft agreement" on recognizing MPR independence. Although admitting that the Chinese were still stalling on the issue, Stalin told Choibalsan unabashedly that they would eventually give in.[31] Expressing his gratitude to Stalin for making the arrangement, Choibalsan did not know that in presenting his argument about MPR independence to the Chinese, Stalin had mainly demanded the Soviet Union's "juridical right to defend ourselves in Outer Mongolia." Stalin had told the Chinese: "Port Arthur, Chinese Eastern Railway, Southern Sakhalin, Outer Mongolia, all is guided by consideration of our strategic position against Japan." Stalin did use the Outer Mongols to strengthen his case, but in a way unspeakable to Choibalsan:

> Outer Mongolia people do not want to join either China or [the] Soviet Union. They want to be independent. [It will be] More advantageous for China to sever Outer Mongolia. If this does not happen, Outer Mongolia will be [a] rallying point for all Mongolians. It's to the detriment of China and us, the unifying of Mongolians, from Inner and Northern Mongolia.[32]

Here Stalin was either stating what he believed would happen or trying to use pan-Mongolism to scare the Chinese. If the latter was his intention, he was pushing the wrong button.

Unlike the Russians, who always seemed to dread a unified Mongolia, Chinese nationalists never lacked confidence that Mongolian nationalism, without Soviet meddling, could be handled within the framework of the

30. Liu, *Partnership for Disorder,* 267–73.

31. Document 10833: Entry on 5 July 1945 of Visitors' Registration for Stalin's Office in the Kremlin, *SLDX* 20: 510; Luzianin, "Yalta Conference and Mongolia," 39; Atwood, "Sino-Soviet Diplomacy," 141.

32. "Notes Taken at Sino-Soviet Conferences, Moscow, 1945": Stalin–Soong conversation on 2 July 1945, Victor Hoo Papers, box 2.

Chinese state. As a matter of fact, after receiving the Chinese delegation's report on Stalin's intransigence on Mongolian independence, Jiang Jieshi and his principal aides were surprised. In their urgent discussions of the diplomatic impasse in Moscow, the specter of pan-Mongolism was not mentioned at all. These leaders' real fear was that without a treaty with Moscow before the Soviet Red Army entered the war against Japan, they would risk losing Manchuria to the Soviets and giving Stalin a free hand in assisting the Chinese Communist Party (CCP). These considerations persuaded Jiang Jieshi that a concession on Outer Mongolia should be made in exchange for Stalin's promises about Manchuria and the CCP.[33]

Inner Mongolia never entered the Chinese government's quid pro quo formula. Rather, it was Stalin who repeatedly used Inner Mongolia to induce the Chinese concession on Outer Mongolia. In early August, when the Moscow negotiations again stalled over the issue of the Chinese–Mongolian border, Stalin expressed one more time his negative attitude toward Mongolian unification:

> To prevent [the] Mongols to have dreams, recognition [of MPR independence] should be given, and if they [Outer Mongols] want Inner Mongolia, threaten them with war. Russia will by no means help them to extend their frontier. They can't do alone and we'll keep quiet.[34]

As opportunistic and cynical as Stalin was in conducting international affairs, he did not deceive the Chinese diplomats on this occasion. During his July visit to Moscow, Choibalsan vented his indignation at continued Chinese oppression of the Inner Mongols, pledging that now, "as a sovereign state, we shall call them to account." If Stalin really wanted to encourage Outer Mongolia's drive for unification with Inner Mongolia, he only needed to utter a word of approval to Choibalsan. But according to Russian and Mongolian scholars who have access to Soviet and Mongolian archival materials, Stalin "kept quiet" on Choibalsan's appeal, as he promised the Chinese. During Choibalsan's July 1945 visit and two other visits in 1946 and 1947, neither Stalin nor other Soviet leaders said anything to encourage Choibalsan's ambitions about Inner Mongolia.[35]

33. Liu, *Partnership for Disorder,* 261–62.

34. "Notes Taken at Sino–Soviet Conferences, Moscow, 1945": Stalin's conversation with the Chinese delegation on 10 August 1945, Victor Hoo Papers, box 2.

35. Luzianin, "Yalta Conference and Mongolia," 42; Lkhagva, "What Was Stalin's Real Attitude to the Mongols," 126.

In September 1945, during a foreign ministers' conference in London, U.S. secretary of state James Byrnes questioned Chinese ambassador Wellington Koo (Gu Weijun) on why the Chinese government had made an "unnecessary concession" over Outer Mongolia.[36] In view of American leaders' action at Yalta and inaction during the Sino-Soviet negotiations, Byrnes's question was disingenuous. At the time, the diplomatic battle over Outer Mongolian independence was already over, but the ethnopolitical war over Mongolian unification had just begun. Obviously Byrnes laid the responsibility for "losing" Outer Mongolia at the doorstep of the Chinese government, though the territory was never important to America's Asian strategy. Inner Mongolia was different. Because of the territory's close geographic connection to Manchuria, American strategists had to consider it in their postwar strategy for containing Soviet influence in China. For the Mongols and the Chinese, after the Sino-Soviet treaty the battleground for Mongolia shifted to the Chinese side of the border. What was unforeseen in Washington, Nanjing, and Ulaanbaatar alike was that in the Inner Mongolian round of the struggle, Moscow's stand was more conducive to China's purposes than to Mongolia's.

Constantly practicing double or even triple dealings in international affairs, Stalin's foreign policy received complaints from all directions. Many years after the CCP took power in China, Ulanhu criticized the Soviets for allegedly supporting the three Inner Mongolian regimes in West Sunid, Wangyemiao, and Hulunbuir in the mid-1940s. According to Ulanhu's analysis, the Soviets did so because, having no confidence in the CCP's ability to control Manchuria and Inner Mongolia, they wanted to create a series of independent and semi-independent regimes as buffers. Ulanhu was right in making a connection between Moscow's policy in Inner Mongolia with the Chinese Civil War. But his speculation about Soviet intentions of creating independent Mongol regimes in Inner Mongolia and Manchuria was groundless.[37]

It is a conventional wisdom in the field that Stalin "wanted to keep the Chinese [Communist] revolution in check."[38] This judgment has to be

---

36. Gu Weijun, *Gu Weijun Huiyilu* (Memoirs of Gu Weijun) (Beijing: Zhonghua Shuju, 1987), 5: 566.

37. Liu Jieyu, "Restore Truth to the History of Inner Mongolia," *Neimenggu Wenshi Ziliao* (Literary and Historical Materials of Inner Mongolia; hereafter *NWZ*) 50: 261.

38. Sergei N. Goncharov, John W. Lewis, and Xue Litai, *Uncertain Partners: Stalin, Mao, and the Korean War.* (Stanford, Calif.: Stanford University Press, 1993), 7–8.

qualified in terms of time and geography. In comparison with the American geopolitical scientist Nicholas Spykman's ominous warning that a "modern, vitalized, and militarized China" would likely dominate Asia, Moscow's perception of China had a distinct ideological tincture.[39] To Moscow, the really scary prospect of postwar China, as Maisky spelled it out in his wartime memo, was China in an anti-Soviet alliance with the United States that would combine American technology with Chinese manpower.[40] Believing that the CCP-inspired rising of "millions of starving peasants had nothing in common with a socialist or democratic movement" and fearing that this peasants rebellion might provoke the Americans to take drastic measures in China, Stalin nevertheless regarded the CCP as a most important asset in consolidating the Yalta–Moscow arrangements.[41] The policy issue for Moscow was therefore not how to contain the CCP revolution but how to contort it to fit the silhouette of Soviet geostrategy in China. As far as Soviet interests in Manchuria and Inner Mongolia were concerned, Moscow's intention was not to shut the CCP out but to use it to promote these interests.

GMD officials involved in dealing with the Soviets understood Moscow's concerns in Manchuria. In November 1945, Jiang Jingguo and Zhang Jia'ao, who negotiated with the Soviets in Manchuria, informed Jiang Jieshi that in the region the Soviets principally feared American infiltration, and that, because the Soviets themselves could not violate the open door principle in Manchuria without overthrowing the recent Sino-Soviet treaty and related agreements, they decided to use the CCP to create chaos and block the door to the region.[42] The GMD government's dilemma was that, relying on American assistance in reasserting its authority in postwar China, it could not convince the Soviet leaders that American influence would not follow GMD power into Manchuria and Inner Mongolia.

In late December, Jiang Jieshi sent his son Jingguo to Moscow on a mission for "linking up good feelings" between himself and Stalin. Yet, not authorized to conduct any concrete negotiations with Stalin, in Moscow Jiang Jingguo's oral pledge of goodwill did not get any tangible return from Soviet

39. Nicholas J. Spykman, *America's Strategy in World Politics* (New York: Harcourt, Brace, 1942), 469–70.

40. Document 03201: Maisky to Molotov, 11 January 1944, *SLDX* 16: 712–13.

41. Volkogonov, *Stalin,* 538, 540.

42. Jiang Jingguo to Jiang Jieshi, 6 November 1945, Jiang Zhongzheng Zongtong Dang'an: Geming Wenxian (Kanluan Shiqi) (Archives of President Jiang Zhongzheng: Revolutionary Documents [Period of Suppressing Rebellion]; hereafter JZZD/GW (KLS) 1: 176; Zhang Jia'ao to Jiang Jieshi, 9 November 1945, ibid., 1: 189.

leaders. Jiang Jingguo did his best to imply a linkage between Moscow's policy and the CCP's aggressiveness in North and Northeast China. He also tried to dissuade the Soviets from setting up separatist regimes in China's borderlands. Stalin countered Jiang's insinuations with outright denials or his own complaints about the CCP. Hearing Jiang Jingguo's remark that the CCP wanted Inner Mongolia to follow the example of Outer Mongolia and become independent, Stalin retorted: "That is stupid. The Soviet government cannot be responsible for the CCP's actions."[43]

The exchange on Inner Mongolia between Stalin and Jiang Jingguo exemplifies how complex political relationships can be distorted in perfunctory diplomacy. Stalin was perfectly aware that Jiang Jingguo was either misinformed of or was intentionally misstating the CCP's stand on the Inner Mongols' *ethnic* separatism. But Stalin chose not to dispute Jiang on this point. His focus was on a much larger question possibly implied in Jiang's falsified accusation of the CCP. That was whether or not Moscow was behind the relationship between the CCP and the Inner Mongols, no matter how that relationship might be characterized. Stalin adamantly and deceptively denied any Soviet connection with CCP activities in Inner Mongolia. This was a deception because, at least in the initial postwar months, the Soviets played a key role in assisting the CCP's efforts to incorporate Inner Mongolian autonomous movements.

Without further archival evidence from China and Russia, it is difficult to ascertain how Soviet military planners considered CCP forces in northern China in relation to their strategy against Japan. Yet it should be obvious that geographically Inner Mongolia, not Manchuria, was the direction where the Soviet Red Army could most easily establish contacts with the CCP. Therefore, whereas leaders in Ulaanbaatar wanted to send troops into Inner Mongolia to liberate their ethnic brethren, Stalin's concern was to direct the Soviet–Mongolia column toward Zhangjiakou in order to reach the CCP. Moscow probably informed the CCP of this intention even before the Yalta conference. In early February 1945, Yan'an secretly ordered its Jin-Sui (Shanxi-Suiyuan) military district to make preparations for receiving the Soviet Red Army in Suiyuan. A few days after the Soviet Union entered the war against Japan, on August 19, the Soviet–Mongolian column in west-

43. "Chairman Jiang's [Jieshi] Directive to the Envoy to the Soviet Union, 24 December 1945," Waijiaobu Yaxisi (West Asian Division of the Ministry of Foreign Affairs; hereafter WJB/YXS), 112; "Minutes of Stalin–Jiang Jingguo Conversations, December 1945–January 1946," *Zhonggong Dangshi Ziliao* 61 (1997): 193–218.

ern Inner Mongolia established contact with CCP representatives near Zhang-jiakou.[44] Just hours after meeting with CCP representatives, the Soviet–Mongolian army received liaison officers from the GMD government, Moscow's formal ally in the war.[45] Thus, in injecting the Soviet–Mongolian army into Inner Mongolia, Moscow helped complicate further the already highly volatile situation in the area. The original goal of the Soviet–Mongolian invasion against Japan was achieved easily and forgotten swiftly. During the months to come, it was the political ramifications of the Soviet–Mongolian military presence in Inner Mongolia that held the attentions in different quarters within and without China.

When the Soviet–Mongolian army entered Inner Mongolia, there was a widely shared hope among Inner Mongol elites that their powerful brethren from the north would help them realize their political aspirations. Prince De and his associates were the first group that was disappointed. The Soviet–Mongolian military authorities identified the prince as Japan's "running dog" and drove back Prince De's envoys.[46] The act was, however, based more on wartime animosity against Japan than on class-struggle orientation against "feudal" princes. In western Inner Mongolia as well as in the east, it was commonplace for the Soviet–Mongolian army to use old Mongolian banner and league officials to maintain local order and to provide services to the invading troops. The MPR also opened its border to Inner Mongol princes and banner officials who were willing to emigrate and could bring their subjects along with them.[47] Yet the key question at this juncture of history was whether or not the Soviet–Mongolian entry into the political fray of Inner Mongolia opened any real opportunity for national unification between Inner and Outer Mongolia.

44. Lu Zhengcao and Lin Feng to Zhang Jiafu et al., 6 February 1945, in *Daqingshan Kang Ri Youji Genjudi Ziliao Xuanbian* (Selected Materials on the Anti-Japanese Base in the Daqing Mountains) (Hohhot: Neimenggu Renmin Chubanshe, 1987), 1: 56–57; Zhan Da'nan, "Recollection of Making Contact with the Soviet–Mongolian Army," *Zhangjiakou Wenshi Ziliao* 4–5: 20–21; Yang Kuisong, *Zhonggong yu Mosike de En En Yuan Yuan* (Gratitude and Grievances between Mao Zedong and Moscow) (Nanchang: Jiangxi Renmin Chubanshe, 1999), 523.

45. Bai Zhen, "Recollection of Making Contact with the Soviet–Mongolian Army," *Zhangbei Wenshi Ziliao* 1: 47–49.

46. Sechin Jagchid, *The Last Mongol Prince: The Life and Times of Demchugdongrob, 1902–1966* (Bellingham: Center for East Asian Studies, Western Washington University, 1999), 329–31; Demchugdongrob, "Demuchukedonglupu Zishu" (Autobiography of Demchugdonrob), *NWZ*, 135–36.

47. Jagchid, *Last Mongol Prince*, 330–31.

In western Inner Mongolia, the test case was the independence movement in West Sunid Banner. According to Ulanhu's recollection, the "provisional government of Inner Mongolian republic" in Sunid was established with the support of the Soviet–Mongolian military authorities. Therefore Ulanhu's alleged three-day debate with a Soviet political commissar over the matter and his eventual victory seem to have constituted a remarkable achievement in his career as a CCP operative. Yet, as far as Soviet policy was concerned, Ulanhu's trip to Sunid in October 1945 did not make any difference. What faced Ulanhu in Sunid was not an Inner Mongolian operation directed by Moscow. Rather, he encountered a "frontier" phenomenon in which few, maybe just one, overzealous Soviet military officers on the spot acted out of ignorance of Moscow's delicate political orientation.

The distinction between Moscow and these officers, however, could not be known to Ulanhu at the beginning. The challenge to him therefore appeared formidable. In his report to the Jin-Cha-Ji Bureau, he identified a Soviet officer named Ivanov and an MPR officer named Lubsang as the ones who had incited the people of Sunid to start their own government. Because the "government" was established in September and Ulanhu did not arrive in Sunid until mid-October, his allegation was based on second-hand information obtained by talking to participants in the Sunid movement. When recalling the event many years later, Ulanhu would not change his story.[48]

Nevertheless, to the Sunid group anxiously seeking Soviet–Mongolian endorsement, the situation was rather different. Delgerchogtu and Sechin Jagchid, both involved in organizing an "Inner Mongolian liberation committee (western Mongolia)" in Sunid that preceded the "provisional government," attested in their reminiscences that the Soviet–Mongolian military authorities at best acquiesced in Inner Mongols' political initiative in Sunid but did not provide any concrete advice about organizing a government. They identified Ivanov and Lubsang as two intelligence officers acting as Inner Mongols' contact persons on behalf of the Soviet–Mongolian army. These officers, however, declined to give their approval to the Sunid movement on

---

48. "Recent Conditions in the Leagues and Banners of Chahar and the Work in Chahar and Shilingol Leagues, 27 October 1945," *Minzu Wenti Wenxian Huibian* (Collected Documents on the Nationality Question; hereafter *MWWH*), 966; Liu Jieyu, "The Role and Contribution of the Inner Mongolian People during the War of Liberation in the Northeast: A Record of Recollections by the Ex-Vice-President Ulanhu," *NWZ* 50 (1997): 239; Hao Yufeng, *Wulanfu Zhuan* (Biography of Ulanfu) (Hohhot: Neimenggu Renmin Chubanshe, 1990), 366–67; Oljeinaren, "In the Mighty Torrent of Inner Mongolian National Liberation," *NWZ* 50 (1997): 199–200.

the ground that as military officers they were not in position to prove or disapprove developments in Inner Mongols' internal affairs. They did, however, suggest that the Inner Mongols seek guidance in Ulaanbaatar or Moscow.

Ulaanbaatar did not wait for the Inner Mongols to come. In mid-September, an MPR delegation, headed by deputy premier Lhamujab, arrived in Sunid. All reminiscent materials agree that in some way Lhamujab was connected to the change of the Sunid "Inner Mongolian liberation committee" into a "provisional government." But he also brought a disappointing news to Sunid that as a result of the recent Sino-Soviet treaty, the MPR obtained independence but had to refrain from interfering in Inner Mongolia. From their contacts in the Soviet–Mongolian army, members of the "provisional government" also learned that under the circumstances they must work with the CCP. Soon, two CCP representatives came to Sunid, which was followed by a Sunid delegation's visit in the Zhangjiakou area and meeting with the CCP authorities there. All these took place before Ulanhu's trip to Sunid.[49]

When Ulanhu had his three-day quarrel with the nameless Soviet political commissar, officers Ivanov and Lubsang did not seem to be around. Very likely, after helping the Sunid group make connection with the CCP authorities in Zhangjiakou, they proceeded with their other intelligence responsibilities. So the job of receiving Ulanhu fell upon the unfortunate political commissar who, obviously, could recite Leninist dogmas on national self-determination but had no clue about Stalin's stratagem on Inner Mongolia. After his encounter with Ulanhu, the political commissar was quickly removed from his position in Sunid not only because he offended CCP comrades but also because the rumor about a Soviet-backed "Inner Mongolian republic" in Sunid already caused international attention. Marshal Rodion Ia. Malinovsky, supreme commander of the Soviet Far Eastern Army, became concerned about the situation and ordered the Soviet Red Army unit in Zhangbei to investigate. About the same time, a Soviet adviser to the MPR government named Nicholayev traveled from Ulaanbaatar to Zhangjiakou

49. Jagchid, *Last Mongol Prince,* 333–35, 337; Delgerchogtu, "The 'Inner Mongolian Youth Party' as I Knew It," *Wulanchabu Wenshi Ziliao* (Historical and Literary Materials of Ulachab) 2 (1984): 110–11; Oljeinaren, "In the Might Torrent," 197–98; Liu Jieyu, "Role and Contribution of the Inner Mongolian People," 239. The names of these CCP agents are not known. The Sunid delegation to Zhangjiakou was headed by Tegshibuyan (a.k.a. Wang Zongluo), who was a member of Prince De's wartime government under Japan and "minister of the propaganda department" of the Sunid "provisional government."

and confirmed for CCP officials that Moscow completely agreed with the CCP's approach to the situation in Inner Mongolia.[50]

Although Ulanhu felt perturbed during his initial encounter with the Soviet–Mongolian authorities in Sunid, his experience should be regarded as a royal reception if compared with the treatment received by GMD liaison officers. When the Soviet–Mongolian troops entered Shilingol, their "mission of liberation" targeted both Japanese and GMD troops. As a nominal ally of the Soviet–Mongolian army, local Chinese forces affiliated with the GMD government only got a choice between leaving the area and being destroyed. To prevent unpleasant incidents, in late August, General Fu Zuoyi sent nine of his officers to the MPR to establish contact with the Soviet–Mongolian command. But, after crossing the border, seven of these officers were shot by MPR troops and the remaining two were detained. Fu had to dispatch a second team in early September. The second team encountered no outright hostility in the MPR territory but could not avoid humiliation. They were lectured by MPR officials that the MPR armed forces had the duty to maintain security in "Mongolian areas" on the Chinese side of the border and to encourage the Mongols to administer their own affairs. As to the fate of the first liaison team, MPR officials stated that they had been executed as bandits sneaking across the border. Then, these officials asked, "arrogantly" according to Fu's liaisons, "How does the Chinese side think about this?" In mid-September, when the Soviet–Mongolian units in Sunid held mass meetings and encouraged autonomous activities, Fu again dispatched his representatives to the region in an attempt to establish some control. But, as Fu later reported to Jiang Jieshi, the Soviet–Mongolian military authorities "refused to turn over [the local affairs] and questioned instead why the [GMD] government attacked the Eight Route Army."[51]

Thus, to the extent that MPR troops were allowed by their Soviet advisers to vent their anti-Chinese animosities, the exercise was selectively directed toward the GMD authorities. Ulanhu was able to accomplish his task in Sunid

---

50. "Request for the [CCP] Center's Directive on the Question of the 'Provisional Government of the Inner Mongolian People's Republic, 27 October 1945," *MWWH,* 972–73; Liu Chun, "Recollections of Inner Mongolia Work," *NWZ* 50 (1997): 39; Liu Jieyu, "Role and Contribution of the Inner Mongolian People," 240–41. Hao Yufeng, *Wulanfu Zhuan,* 367; and Atwood, "Sino-Soviet Diplomacy," 155; indicate that in this period Ulanhu made a trip to the MPR to appeal to the high command of the Soviet–Mongolian army.

51. Kong Xiangduo to Pu Daoming, 18 October 1945, WJB/YXS, 112; Jiang Jieshi to Xu Shichang and Wang Shijie,13 September 1945, ibid.

relatively easily, not because he was a Mongol but because Yan'an was in the same ideological bloc with Moscow and Ulaanbaatar, which, during the first few postwar months, was rapidly materializing into a political-military alliance. The Sunid situation's swift solution after Ulanhu's arrival was indicative of a fundamental policy agreement between Yan'an and Moscow as far as the ethnopolitics of Inner Mongolia was concerned. Ulanhu's cancellation of the Sunid "government" also marked the beginning of the end of the MPR's "mission of liberation" in Inner Mongolia. Ethnopolitically, this meant that the Chinese authorities would stay in the region, though they would be newly represented by the CCP, for the time being personified by a Tumed Mongol (Ulanhu).

In essence, Ulanhu's ability to rollback MPR influence in Shilingol reflected Moscow's effectiveness in reining in Ulaanbaatar. Until this time, Moscow had been using the MPR to do its dirty job in China. But the chosen location of operations was Xinjiang. Starting in the spring of 1944, the MPR provided weapons to antigovernment Kazaks in Xinjiang. Shortly after an "Eastern Turkestan" uprising broke out in November 1944, Moscow adopted a secret policy of sending Soviet military personnel and Kazak units of the MPR Army into Xinjiang to join Uygur and Kazak insurgents in fighting Chinese government troops. As late as July 1945, Soviet leaders regarded the ethnic conflict in Xinjiang as a "real opportunity to topple the [Chinese] provincial government and bring into power representatives of the indigenous population loyal to the Soviet Union." The subversive policy in Xinjiang was, however, interrupted after the Sino-Soviet treaty was concluded in August 1945. To the dismay of MPR leaders, in World War II Moscow never considered a similar policy for Inner Mongolia. Having served as Moscow's revolutionary mercenary in exploring opportunities in Xinjiang, Ulaanbaatar was not rewarded with an opportunity of its own in Inner Mongolia.[52]

In Inner Mongolia, as in Manchuria, Moscow's chosen ally was the CCP, while the Inner Mongols, many of whom had collaborated with the Japanese in the war, were treated by the Soviets with suspicions. An illustrative case was the Soviet military authorities' treatment of the ninth division of Prince De's Mongolian army. On August 10, 1945, while stationed near

---

52. Zhu Peimin, "Changes in the Soviet Policy in Xinjiang from 1943 to 1949," *Zhonggong Dangshi Yanjiu* (Studies of the CCP's History), supplementary issue (December 1990): 87–92; Luzianin, *Rossia–Mongolia–Kitaii,* 210–11; Valery Barmin, "Xinjiang in the History of Soviet–Chinese Relations from 1937 to 1946," *FEA* 1 (2000): 73–75.

Guisui (Hohhot), the division held an uprising against its Japanese superiors. The leader was Oljeiochir, a secret Comintern agent who had infiltrated Prince De's government in the 1930s. As a force of 2,000 troops equipped with heavy guns and automobiles, the ninth division could have become the backbone of a new Inner Mongolian army serving either under the CCP or under an autonomous Inner Mongolian regime. Oljeiochir first contacted the CCP authorities in Suiyuan, and the latter welcomed him to take the troops into the CCP's "Sui-Meng Army." But, after the Soviet–Mongolian army arrived in the area, the ninth division was disarmed by the Soviet military authorities and ordered to travel to the MPR to go through a process of "verification." Allegedly, this procedure was ordered by Stalin himself and was applied to all troops controlled by Comintern agents who had lost contact with Moscow in the past decade. Eventually, in early 1946, only 128 "verified" troops were allowed to return to China to join Ulanhu's group.[53]

All these signs indicated that in anticipating the Soviet–Mongolian army's departure from Inner Mongolia, Stalin had no intention of using the Inner Mongols for the purpose of creating a pro-Soviet regime in the vacuum. Nor did he want to turn the area over to the GMD. Unlike Manchuria—where, according to the Sino-Soviet treaty of August 1945, the Soviet military authorities had an obligation to turn over Soviet-controlled regions to the GMD government—Inner Mongolia was an open arena for ambiguous and evasive games. Thus, to CCP personnel, Soviet–Mongolian troops in Inner Mongolia acted more like comrades-in-arms than Soviet troops in Manchuria. To the GMD, of course, this meant repeated frustrations caused by deceptive and evasive Soviet behaviors. Initially, the Soviets promised to return Rehe, Chahar, and Suiyuan to the GMD government. But in the field, Soviet troops used excuses such as military security and noninterference in China's internal affairs to delay the advance of GMD personnel. The Soviet military authorities warned that any force causing troubles in Soviet-controlled areas would be destroyed. In the meantime, CCP troops could maneuver uninhibited. Under the circumstances, the GMD regime found it extremely difficult to implement its "restoration" and "pacification" plans for Inner Mongolia.[54]

53. Wang Duo, *Wushi Chuqiu* (Fifty Eventful Years) (Hohhot: Neimenggu Renmin Chubanshe, 1992), 168–69; Qian Linbao, *Jiefang Zhanzheng Shiqi Neimenggu Qibing* (Inner Mongolian Cavalries during the War of Liberation) (Hohhot: Neimenggu Daxue Chubanshe, 1989), 23–24; *Daqingshan Kang Ri Youji Genjudi Ziliao Xuanbian,* 1: 59.
    54. Jiang Jieshi to Wang Shijie, 17 August 1945, WJB/YXS, 112; Ministry of Foreign Affairs memorandum to the Soviet Embassy, 29 August 1945, ibid.; Jiang Jieshi

Moscow's camouflaged assistance to the CCP in Inner Mongolia was nevertheless not a simple act of helping its ideological ally against the GMD. There was also an ethnopolitical dimension. In mid-September 1945, the CCP Central Committee received urgent advice from the Soviet side that because the GMD government was using the recent Sino-Soviet treaty to pressure Soviet–Mongolian troops to leave Inner Mongolia, the CCP should dispatch a main force immediately to take over the region to keep open the line of communications between the CCP and the Soviet Union. It was pointed out by the Soviets that with Inner Mongolia under control, the CCP would be able to receive secret assistance from the Soviet Union and the MPR. And, should the military situation turn unfavorable to the CCP, it could retreat into the MPR via Inner Mongolia.[55]

The emergency was, however, not just caused by GMD–Soviet diplomacy. In a September 17, 1945, telegram to Mao Zedong, who was then in Chongqing negotiating with Jiang Jieshi, Liu Shaoqi indicated that the Soviet–Mongolian army was ready to withdraw and had lately asked the CCP three times to take over a specified area from Prince De's palace to Bailingmiao (Bat-khaalag).[56] The request was particularly interesting because it did not make any sense to the CCP's military strategy. At the time, the CCP's military force was positioned to enter a resolute competition with the GMD in Manchuria. Efforts were made to establish a barrier from Zhangjiakou in the west to Shanhaiguan in the east. The intention was to block the GMD's way into Manchuria from both the southern and western directions and thus secure Manchuria as the CCP's new power base.[57] The area specified by the Soviet–Mongolian army for the CCP to take over, however, was far away from the Zhangjiakou–Shanhaiguan line and lay in a northwestern desert between West Sunid Banner of Shilingol and Darhanmingan Banner of Ulanchab. This remote area was not a potential front line of any great importance to the GMD–CCP military contest, though it was a

---

to Gan Jiehou, 7 September 1945, ibid.; Jiang Jieshi to Xu Shichang and Wang Shijie, 13 September 1945, ibid.; Gan Naiguang to Soviet Embassy, 15 September 1945, ibid.

55. Yang, *Zhonggong yu Mosike,* 533.

56. The CCPCC to the CCP delegation in Chongqing, 17 September 1945, *Liu Shaoqi Nianpu* 1: 493. According to GMD intelligence, about 3,000 Outer Mongolian troops left Chahar in mid-September, but before the end of the month some 2,400 Mongolian troops retreated to Bailingmiao from Suiyuan. See Kong Xiangduo to Pu Daoming, 18 October 1945, WJB/YXS, 112.

57. CCPCC to the CCP delegation in Chongqing, 18 September 1945, *Liu Shaoqi Nianpu* 1: 494.

current ethnopolitical battleground because of the recent Sunid episode. Therefore, the Soviet–Mongolian army's urgent request for a CCP takeover of the area, just a few days after the Sunid "government" had surfaced, could only be motivated by a consideration of ethnopolitical responsibility. Obviously, the request would not have been made if the Soviets had intended to assume that responsibility themselves or to allow the MPR to implement its own pan-Mongol plans.

The Soviet request was typical of Moscow's coordinated international, partisan, and ethnopolitical orientation in Inner Mongolia at the time: Only a CCP takeover could satisfy all Moscow's policy needs, which included its treaty obligation to the GMD regime about China's sovereignty in Inner Mongolia, a desire to keep the region in friendly hands, and a long-established policy of preventing Ulaanbaatar's undue influence among the Inner Mongols. The Soviets were probably surprised by the way the CCP responded to their request. The CCP, unwilling to divert any force of a significant size to the Sunid area, instead sent Ulanhu there to bring the "provisional government" back to Zhangjiakou.

While the CCP persevered with its own strategic course, the Soviet–Mongolia army in Inner Mongolia agreed to delay its departure. In late September, the Soviet military command in Rehe asked for the CCP's help in collecting food and winter clothing that could last for three months, promising to turn over to the CCP a string of cities east of Zhangjiakou when the Soviet–Mongolian army pulled out.[58] This secret promise would be honored. At the beginning of 1946, the GMD government announced that the Soviet Red Army would withdraw in a few days from Rehe and the entire province would be taken over by government forces. The actual Soviet withdrawal took longer than just a few days. By the end of January, the CCP organ *Jiefang Ribao* (Liberation Daily) declared that Soviet troops had left Chifeng, one of the largest cities of Rehe, and that local order was now maintained by a "democratically elected government" and "local security forces," meaning the CCP's political and military apparatuses.[59] Contradictory announcements like these by the GMD and the CCP set the tone for

58. CCPCC to the CCP delegation in Chongqing, 26 September 1945, *Zhonggong Zhongyang Wenjian Xuanji* (Selected Documents of the CCP Central Committee; hereafter *ZZWX*) 15: 295.

59. *Zhongyang Ribao* (Central Daily), 3 January 1946, *Zhong Su Guojia Guanxi Shi Ziliao Huibian* (Selected Materials on the History of Sino-Soviet Relations), 3: 57; *Jiefang Ribao* (Liberation Daily), 22 and 25 January 1946, ibid., 45–49, 60.

the political contest in western Inner Mongolia following Soviet–Mongolian military departure. Meanwhile, the Inner Mongols' struggle for autonomy in the area no longer played an audible note.

The autonomous movement in eastern Mongolia was not silenced so easily, however. Like their counterparts in Sunid, the leaders in Wangyemiao were pressured to fold their nationalist banner not so much by the GMD government as by their supposed allies. Taking place in a region beyond the range of MPR troops' operations, the eastern Mongolian movement was not a fleeting response to Ulaanbaatar's pan-Mongol propaganda but a true popular upheaval with solid local support and real vitality. Nevertheless, rushing onto the political stage of Manchuria where the Soviets replaced the Japanese as predominant influence, the eastern Mongolian movement could not have taken its initial steps without being issued a birth certificate by the Soviet military authorities.

The initial encounter between the two sides was awkward. Entering the Wangyemiao area on August 13, the Soviet army units were cautious in dealing with the eastern Mongol mutineers who had just declared war on their Japanese superiors. At first, the Soviets disarmed the Mongols and destroyed their weapons but then rearmed them after mutual trust was established. The historical ties of Temurbagana, Khafengga, and Buyanmandukhu to the Comintern were helpful in establishing a working relationship between the eastern Mongols and the Soviet military authorities. The Soviets, however, fell short of the eastern Mongols' expectations. On August 16, Marshal Rodion Malinovsky received Buyanmandukhu and Khafengga in Wangyemiao. Malinovsky told the two that although they had served under the Japanese during the war, they had not been arrested because the Red Army knew about their secret history with the Comintern. The marshal, however, showed only the slightest interest in the "Inner Mongolian People's Liberation Committee (eastern Mongolia)" that the eastern Mongols had organized in Wanyemiao. He just ordered Buyanmandukhu and Khafengga to restore the provincial government of Xing'an under the Red Army's direction. At the time, the Soviet military authorities were assigning responsibilities to various ex-Manchukuo officials in different places to maintain local order and provide services to the Red Army. Malinovsky's treatment of the eastern Mongol leaders did not appear to show much special favor.[60]

60. Buyantu, "Awakening before Dawn: August 11 Uprising Remembered," *Xing'an Geming Shihua* 3: 195–98; Butegechi, *Fengyu Jiancheng Wushinian* (Advance in Trials and Hardships for Fifty Years) (Hohhot: Neimenggu Renmin Chubanshe, 1997), 14–16;

Soon enough, the Red Army had to differentiate the Wangyemiao group from other ex-Mongol officials of Manchukuo, for the group started a potent autonomous struggle. On August 17, the same day when they restored the Xing'an provincial government as ordered, they also revived the Inner Mongolian People's Revolutionary Party (IMPRP). To the Soviets, the eastern Mongolian situation was almost a déja vu of the 1920s. Again, they found themselves in the middle of Chinese and Mongolian revolutions and capable of having an impact on both. Although the Red Army's presence put Moscow in a much stronger position than in the 1920s to influence events directly in Manchuria, at this time Moscow's policies toward revolutionary movements in China were more conservative. In the second half of the 1940s, Soviet foreign policy no longer suffered from ideological vacillation between world revolution and national security, and it was decisively in favor of the latter. The bureaucratic competition between the Comintern and the Soviet Foreign Ministry was also history. Now, with a long-established two-Mongolia orientation and a "legitimate" grand strategy for the postwar years, the Soviets responded cautiously to the eastern Mongolian movement, which, as put by Christopher Atwood, seemed "a strange echo of their old rhetoric of Inner Mongolian self-determination and Mongolian unity."[61]

The Soviets' calculated interaction with the eastern Mongols constituted a sharp contrast to their erratic handling of the Sunid group. At the front of Soviet contact with the eastern Mongols was a Buryat Mongol, Major Delikov Sangjai. Sangjai's official position in Marshal Malinovsky's headquarters was as editor of a "Mongolian News of the Soviet Red Army" published in Changchun twice a week. The Sino-Soviet treaty of August 1945 featured prominently in the first issue of the newspaper. In early September, when Wangyemiao's envoy Sangjaijab went to Changchun for the second time to make contact with local Mongols, he learned from Major Sangjai that after the Chinese government recognized the MPR's independence, it was no longer realistic for the Mongols to pursue unification between Outer and Inner Mongolia. Consequently, the movement in Wangyemiao should struggle for high-degree self-government within China. In

---

Bukhe, "The Struggle of Suppressing Bandits and Opposing Local Tyrants in West Khorchin Central Banner," *Xing'an Dangshi Wenji* 2: 280; Bukhe and Sayan, *Boyanmandu Shengping Shilue* (A Brief Biography of Buyanmandukhu) (Hohhot: Neimenggu Daxue Tushuguan, 1999), 73–74.

61. Christopher Atwood, "The East Mongolian Revolution and Chinese Communism," *Mongolian Studies* 15 (1992): 23–24.

early December, having returned from Ulaanbaatar, Khafengga himself went to Changchun to consult with Major Sangjai. At the time, the eastern Mongols already shelved their original goal of accession to the MPR. Major Sangjai suggested to Khafengga that after the eastern Mongolian autonomous government was established, Wangyemiao should send a delegation to Chongqing to gain the GMD regime's recognition. No matter what would be the GMD regime's attitude, Sangjai insisted, it was imperative for the eastern Mongols to conduct a "legal struggle." As mentioned in chapter 4, the eastern Mongols heeded the advice and dispatched the Manibadara mission southward.[62]

The Soviet definition of the "legality" of the eastern Mongols' activities had nothing to do with the GMD government's view or procedures. The "legal struggle" by Inner Mongols was measured by the "correctness" of the Soviets' own behavior in China. As long as the eastern Mongols acted within China's "internal" political arena and did not implicate Moscow and Ulaanbaatar, their struggle would be deemed "legitimate" under the framework of the Sino-Soviet treaty of August 1945. In other words, the eastern Mongols' struggle was "legal" if it appeared a "Chinese," but neither a "Soviet" nor an "MPR," trouble to the GMD regime. Aside from advising leaders in Wangyemiao, the Soviets took steps with the GMD and the CCP to ensure the "Chinese" character of the Wangyemiao movement. Shortly after Major Sangjai imparted to Khafengga tactics of a "legal struggle," information about the meeting reached the GMD authorities in Manchuria. This was probably a controlled leakage from Marshal Malinovsky's headquarters. GMD officials learned that Major Sangjai had recently told the eastern Mongols to rely on themselves because, mindful of international criticism, the Soviets had decided to stop giving assistance to the Inner Mongolian independence movement.[63]

After giving an innocent nod to the GMD authorities, the Soviets took a more important step to ensure both the "Chinese" appearance of the eastern Mongolian movement and the vigor of the "problem" to the GMD regime. That was to help the CCP rein in this spontaneous mass struggle. In Ulaanbaatar, the eastern Mongols learned from the MPR's leaders that the center for them to rally should be Yan'an. In China, the Soviet military authorities

62. Dawa-ochir, "My Life and Experiences," *NWZ* 31 (1988): 157–59, 161–65; Bukhe and Sayan, *Boyanmandu*, 83.

63. Xiong Shihui to Wang Shijie, 25 December 1945, Quanzonghao (general record number; hereafter QZH) 18 / 1094.

acted to bring the CCP and the Wangyemiao group together. In late January 1946, the CCP's Ji-Re-Liao (Hebei-Rehe-Liaobei) Branch Bureau received a Matynov, political commissar of the Soviet Red Army unit stationed in Chifeng, who came to discuss with CCP officials the conditions of eastern Mongolia. According to Matynov, the movement in Wangyemiao decided to establish an "autonomous republic" under the Chinese government. Currently, the Wangyemiao regime had a military force of four "armies" and refused to allow any Chinese troops to enter its territories. Because the GMD government was trying to enlist the Inner Mongols in its anticommunist effort, Matynov suggested that the CCP frustrate the GMD by recognizing the Wangyemiao regime and supporting its struggle to establish a "Mongolian autonomous republic."[64] Obviously, Commissar Matynov tried to be helpful to the CCP. Yet, like his more contentious colleague in Sunid, Matynov was able to envision a Chinese federation of red republics after the Soviet model but was unfamiliar with the CCP's ethnopolitical stance.

In mid-February, a CCP Central Committee directive cautioned its apparatuses in Manchuria not to support Inner Mongolian independence or self-determination lest this provide evidence to "rumors" spread by the GMD government. At about this time, Ulanhu discussed the question of the Wangyemiao movement with Nie Rongzhen, the secretary of the CCP Jin-Cha-Ji Bureau, and a Nicholayev, Soviet adviser to the MPR. Nicholayev supported the CCP's orientation of solving the eastern Mongolian question through negotiations. He informed Ulanhu and Nie that Moscow had an established Inner Mongolia policy and had conveyed it to Choibalsan through Marshal Malinovsky: "The question of Inner Mongolia has to be solved first and foremost according to the CCP's opinion. No matter which side has whatever demands, the decision must be made by the CCP, not Outer Mongolia." In early March, the Soviet military authorities in Wangyemiao delivered to eastern Mongol leaders a telegram from the CCP's Western Manchurian Bureau, which invited these leaders to meet with Ulanhu in Chifeng.[65]

For all practical purposes, this act completed the Soviets' delivery of the

64. Ji-Re-Liao Branch Bureau's Report on the Mongolian Question in Northern Rehe, 26 January 1946, *MWWH*, 995.

65. CCPCC's Telegraph on Cautious Treatment of the National Question of Inner Mongolia, 18 February 1946, *MWWH*, 1000; Liu Jieyu, "The Necessary Path for the Inner Mongolian Autonomous Movement," *NWZ* 50 (1997), 221–22; Bukhe and Bayan, *Boyanmandu*, 86.

eastern Mongolian movement to the CCP. This significant development was best captured in a conversation between Ulanhu and Temurbagana during the ensuing meeting between CCP and Wangyemiao representatives in Chengde in April. Trying to persuade Temurbagana to give up the idea of having a separate Inner Mongolian party and government, Ulanhu said: "Both of us were sent back [to China] by the Comintern. But what have you accomplished by organizing the IMPRP? Nothing. You do not understand the conditions of the Chinese revolution and do not know that the fate of the Inner Mongolian revolution is tied to that of the Chinese revolution."[66] In other words, the time had come for the eastern Mongol leaders to accept the CCP's leadership and ditch the old idea of developing an independent movement with Moscow's or Ulaanbaatar's help. Indeed, during the Chengde conference both Temurbagana and Khafengga were inducted into the CCP, an act that tied the eastern Mongolian movement organizationally to China's domestic revolution and further stifled any chance for Wangyemiao's international reach.

Hierarchy of Patronage

In late 1945, Jiang Jieshi lamented to his foreign minister Wang Shijie that "for a while the area north of the Yellow River cannot be rectified as a pure land for national reconstruction."[67] Strangely, Jiang's sense of loss about the specified region might well have been shared by Choibalsan in Ulaanbaatar. But, if Jiang deplored the situation from a stand of Chinese "state-building nationalism," Choibalsan did so from that of Mongolian "irredentist nationalism."[68] To leaders in Ulaanbaatar, the defeat of Japan constituted a golden opportunity for the Mongols. They were convinced, according to I. A. Ivanov, the Soviet ambassador to the MPR, that "their country's participation in the war against Japan would lead to the unification of the MPR, Inner Mongolia, and Barga [the Hulunbuir region]."[69] The MPR's leaders—

66. Liu Chun, "Recollections of Inner Mongolia Work," 57.
67. Wang Shijie, *Wang Shijie Riji* (Wang Shijie's Diaries) (Taipei: Zhongyang Yanjiuyuan Jidaishi Yanjiusuo, 1990), 5: 207.
68. Michael Hechter, *Containing Nationalism* (Oxford: Oxford University Press, 2000), 15–17, differentiates these and other types of nationalism in terms of their respective relationships with territoriality.
69. Luzianin, "Yalta Conference and Mongolia," 41.

extremely disappointed by Stalin's diplomacy with China, which followed strictly the Yalta script on Mongolia's "status quo"—strove during the initial postwar months to gain a status-quo-plus result. Sure enough, the MPR's satellite status did not leave Choibalsan and his colleagues much room for maneuvering. Still, in respect to Inner Mongolia, Ulaanbaatar had its own distinct goals and managed to remain relevant in Inner Mongolian politics longer than did the Soviets.

From the MPR leaders' point of view, the military and international political developments at the end of World War II created two favorable conditions of which they must take full advantage. First, the Sino-Soviet formula for MPR independence introduced the factor of popular will into the Mongolia question, which could be applied to Inner Mongolia as well. Second, MPR troops entered Inner Mongolia as a "liberating force," and their political deployment could open many possibilities. It is ironic that while refusing even to identify the non-Han ethnic groups in China as *minzu* or minority nationalities, the GMD government should have chosen the plebiscite as the form for the Outer Mongols to express their will of self-determination. Apparently, to rationalize its diplomatic failure over Outer Mongolia in Moscow, the GMD regime felt that the Outer Mongols' will for self-determination was its own best political defense at home. This defense would be an arduous task for, after all, in Moscow the GMD regime "signed off" more than 14 percent of the officially claimed territory of the Republic of China (ROC).[70]

To salvage as much face as possible from the disaster, the GMD government, through diplomatic channels in Moscow, invited Ulaanbaatar to send a delegation to Chongqing on October 10, 1945, the national day of the ROC, to present the result of the MPR plebiscite to the Chinese government. The MPR leaders did not fall into this trap of protocol. In his reply to the Chinese government, also through Moscow, Choibalsan indicated that it was really redundant and unnecessary to ask the Mongolian people to express their will of independence, for they had been defending their independence for twenty-five years. The MPR agreed to conduct the plebiscite only as a gesture of granting Chongqing its wish. The plebiscite, however, would be held according to Ulaanbaatar's own schedule, which was October 20. After that, if the Chinese government still wanted to learn

70. The area of the MPR was 1,621,200 square kilometers, or 14.2 percent of the 11,418,000-square-kilometer territory claimed by the Republic of China as of August 1945.

about the result directly from the MPR government, then a delegation could be sent.[71]

Ulaanbaatar easily won this ceremonial contest, because Chongqing had no means to impose its own timetable on the MPR government. Yet, on the MPR side, the timing of the plebiscite did not just carry a ceremonial significance. In August, after receiving the Sino-Soviet notes exchanged on MPR independence, the leaders in Ulaanbaatar detected what they thought was a pregnant wording discrepancy between the Chinese and the Soviet texts. Though the Chinese note used "current borders" to define MPR independence, the Soviet note expressed respect to the MPR's political independence and "territorial integrity." As far as Sino-Soviet diplomacy was concerned, the discrepancy carried two meanings: First, the two sides reached no agreement on the boundaries of the MPR; and second, Moscow vouched not to incorporate the MPR into the Soviet Union at a future date. Yet, wishfully, the MPR leaders believed that the Soviet note left the door open for them to push national unification in Inner Mongolia.[72]

During the initial postwar months, the plebiscite in Outer Mongolia and MPR-encouraged autonomous activities in Inner Mongolia constituted Ulaanbaatar's two-pronged drive for unification. Whereas the Inner Mongolian operations were largely unknown to the outside world, the plebiscite was an internationally reported event. As recalled by Bazaryn Shirendev, to guarantee a smooth plebiscite operation, the MPR government organized more than 13,000 meetings and study sessions in all districts of the country. These occasions were used not only to instruct ordinary workers and herdsmen about the voting procedure but also to discuss topics and government pamphlets on MPR independence. On October 20, the first votes were cast at six o'clock in the morning and, by midnight, "the plebiscite was one hundred percent complete."[73]

In contrast, in Inner Mongolia an undeclared "plebiscite" began two months earlier. The Chinese government got wind of the operation but could not ascertain its scope. Unlike in the 1920s and 1930s, when Outer Mongol

---

71. Memorandum on a conversation between Lozovsky and Ambassador Fu Bingchang, 17 September 1945, unpublished documents on Sino-Soviet relations from Russian State Archives, provided by Shen Zhihua, document 12120.

72. Luzianin, *Rossiia–Mongoliia–Kitaii,* 216–17; notes exchanged between Chinese and Soviet foreign ministers, 14 August 1945, *ZZSC* 3(2): 656–58.

73. Bazaryn Shirendev, *Through the Ocean Waves: The Autobiography of Bazaryn Shirendev* (Bellingham: Western Washington University Press, 1997), 116–17.

and Comintern agents traveled to Inner Mongolia to set up secret revolutionary cells and to organize armed uprisings, in late 1945 Ulaanbaatar followed the "legal" approach established by the Sino-Soviet treaty. When MPR troops entered Inner Mongolia, Ulaanbaatar conducted a propaganda campaign calling upon the Inner Mongols, after their liberation from Japanese occupation, to "choose which country to lean on for support, what kind of government to create, and where to go for help." Not to leave the matter completely to Inner Mongols' spontaneity, Choibalsan also dispatched special units into MPR troops' operational areas to weed out "pro-Japanese" elements and to "restore order."[74]

The handiwork of MPR military-political operatives can be classified into two categories, "recall" and "referendum." "Recall" was a formula advocated by the MPR leadership in the late 1920s, when the chance for territorial unification of all Mongolian sectors seemed slim. At the time MPR leaders, with only limited success, called upon all Mongols to migrate to the new Mongolian state as a second best option.[75] In 1945, the approach was tried again. According to a Chinese intelligence report, Ulaanbaatar made preparations along its border with China to accommodate 300,000 emigrants from Inner Mongolia. Although this is yet to be verified by sources from the Mongolian side, information of different backgrounds proves that thousands of Inner Mongols and their livestock, voluntarily or unwillingly, moved across the border when the Soviet–Mongolian army was still in Inner Mongolia. To leaders in Ulaanbaatar, these people "voted" with their feet in favor of unification with the MPR. To those Chinese officials, GMD and CCP alike, who were oblivious to the ethnopolitical significance of these migrations, the Soviet–Mongolian army committed crimes of "robbery" and "coercion."[76] A massive Mongolian exodus from China did not happen

74. Luzianin, "Yalta Conference and Mongolia," 42; Atwood, "Sino-Soviet Diplomacy," 144.

75. Baabar, *Twentieth Century Mongolia,* 278.

76. Ministry of Military Ordinance to Ministry of Foreign Affairs, 18 November 1945, Waijiaobu Yataisi (Asian–Pacific Division of the Ministry of Foreign Affairs), 097.1; Mongolian and Tibetan Affairs Commission to Jiang Jieshi, "The Organizations and Military Forces of the Outer Mongolian Government and the Situation of its Invasion," 19 April 1948, Zongtongfu Dang'an (Archives of the Presidential Palace), 055/1659; "Recent Conditions in Leagues and Banners of Chahar and the Work in Chahar and Shilingol Leagues, 27 October 1945," *MWWH,* 967; Budebara, "Recollections and Memories," *Xilinguole Shi Wenshi Ziliao* (Literary and Historical Materials of the Shilingol Municipality) 1 (1985): 46–72 (the citations here are on 53–54, 67); Jagchid, *Last Mongol Prince,* 330–31.

and was probably not planned by Ulaanbaatar in 1945. Yet, in retrospect, those Inner Mongols relocated to the MPR constituted the only irreversible achievement of Ulaanbaatar's drive for national unification.

A more ambitious operation of Ulaanbaatar's was to replace the Japanese military authorities as the new political center for the Inner Mongols within their own territories. For this purpose, MPR officials, often accompanied by their Soviet advisers, held mass meetings in Shilingol and Hulunbuir. To achieve a "referendum" effect, signatures were collected on these occasions to support Inner Mongolia's accession to the MPR. The operation in Hulunbuir, the home base of the Merse uprising in 1928, was typical. On August 19, 1945, some MPR military units entered the capital city, Hailar, and they were followed by an "MPR consolation delegation" headed by N. Lhamsuren, the MPR's deputy propaganda chief. Three days later, the delegation held a mass meeting at Solon Banner (today's Ewenk Autonomous Banner). Mass signatures were collected during the meeting, and a resolution on Hulunbuir's accession to the MPR was passed. On August 23, buttressed by evidence of the people's will garnered in such manner, a Hulunbuir delegation traveled with Lhamsuren to the MPR to petition for Hulunbuir's annexation.[77]

Aside from organizing local "referendums" at the grassroots level, MPR officials also tried to accomplish an authority switch at the top level of Inner Mongolian communities. This was carried out by MPR deputy prime minister Lhamujab when he toured Chahar during the second half of August and before he came to Sunid to give advice to the organizers of the "provisional government" there. In most cases, he just reappointed old banner and league officials to their positions.[78] In view of the fact that the Soviet–Mongolian troops were still implementing their war tasks, Lhamujab's distribution of offices could be interpreted as part of the Soviet–Mongolian civil operations for stabilizing local conditions and obtaining local services. Nevertheless, because Ulaanbaatar was clearly pursuing its nationalist agenda in Inner Mongolia, Lhamujab's activities were not simply prompted by wartime necessities.

Choibalsan did not miss the chance to visit Inner Mongolia personally. Perhaps in late August 1945, he first visited places in Rehe and Chahar to

77. Bei Xiaoyan, "The Birth of the Inner Mongolian Autonomous Government," *NWZ* 50 (1997): 294; Atwood, "Sino-Soviet Diplomacy," 151–52.

78. Budebara, "Recollections and Memories," 67; Atwood, "Sino-Soviet Diplomacy," 149.

congratulate Soviet–Mongolian troops. Then, in mid-September, he stayed in West Sunid for a couple of days. The records do not agree on what attitude he displayed to members of the "provisional government" there.[79] More than any other leader in the MPR government, he was conscious of Stalin's objection to pan-Mongolism. It is therefore unlikely that he went to Sunid to openly promote Inner Mongolian separatism at the risk of offending his patron in Moscow. Yet, he might have believed that a silent tour to Sunid by himself would be symbolic enough to encourage the Inner Mongols.

Eventually, the actions of organizing referendums and appointing offices proved inconsequential. After receiving many petitions from Inner Mongols, Ulaanbaatar had to turn them down summarily. As recalled by Delgerchogtu, a member of the Sunid delegation to Ulaanbaatar, on October 17, 1945, Choibalsan held a banquet to entertain Inner Mongol representatives from different areas. He told those present: "As a Mongol I can only take you in and should not push you away. But international conditions do not allow me to do so." When some Inner Mongols confronted him with a question about why Outer Mongolian troops had to disarm Inner Mongolian military forces, the dinner had to end unpleasantly.[80] Three days later, when the plebiscite was held in the MPR, it could not be turned into a "whole-Mongolia" event without effective referendums from Inner Mongolia. Those political appointments made by the MPR authorities in Inner Mongolia were also soon rendered irrelevant as the GMD–CCP military struggle swept the region.

Among all the efforts made by MPR personnel in Inner Mongolia during the initial postwar months, Hulunbuir's autonomy survived longer than the others. After their accession petition was rejected by Ulaanbaatar, Hulunbuir elites organized an autonomous government in early October. The region's remote location from the GMD–CCP struggle in Manchuria and Soviet authorities' endorsement helped sustain its relative autonomy between 1945 and 1947. Then, after the Inner Mongolian Autonomous Government was launched in April 1947 with the CCP's blessing, the Hulunbuir regime could no longer continue. After consulting with the Soviet consulate general in Harbin, the CCP downgraded the regime to an ordinary league government.[81]

79. According to Jagchid, *Last Mongol Prince,* 338, in Sunid, Choibalsan "expressed no opinion regarding the new political regime established there." But Atwood, "Sino-Soviet Diplomacy," 155, suggests that he "honored the new government with a personal tour of inspection." Chinese studies of this period mention nothing about Choibalsan's trip.

80. Delgerchogtu, "Mongolian Youth Party," 112.

81. Bei Xiaoyan, "Birth of the Inner Mongolian Autonomous Government," 295; Layi, "Recollection of the Political Situation in Hailar after September 3," *Hulunbei'er*

In these events, there was nothing remarkable about MPR officials' skill of mass mobilization. In many areas, propelled by spontaneous "nationalist fever," the Inner Mongols needed minimal agitation from the outside to start their movements. What was remarkable was the fact that, having existed for more than two decades as a state entity, the MPR in 1945 was so restrained by Moscow's policy intentions that it could not independently implement a policy even in a neighboring Mongolian land. The local referendums and office appointments produced by MPR officials depended completely on the Soviet–Mongolian military presence in Inner Mongolia. They were doomed from the outset in the contexts of Moscow's policy orientation and the extant Soviet–MPR relationship. In mid-November 1945, Choibalsan made an effort to salvage any chance in the future. When the MPR government was preparing its official notification to China about the result of the plebiscite, Choibalsan tried to include in the text a phrase about respecting the MPR's territorial integrity. He intended to convey to the Chinese a message that "the issue of the MPR's present borders is a moot point as these borders do not encompass the whole of actual Mongolian territory." To him, this would be a way to leave the door open for settling the Inner Mongolia question in a later date. The notion, however, was rejected by the Soviet ambassador.[82] Hence, the end of Ulaanbaatar's "legal" effort for Inner Mongolia.

An interesting question is that without restrictions from Moscow, could Ulaanbaatar have succeeded in incorporating into the MPR at least some Inner Mongolian communities along the border? The GMD government was actually poorly prepared for such a scenario. Because the Sino-Soviet diplomacy in the summer of 1945 did not produce an agreement on where the "current borders" between the ROC and the MPR lay, Chinese officials feared that the MPR plebiscite would likely be extended into Inner Mongolia. But, as pointed out by the Mongolian and Tibetan Affairs Commission, the chaotic conditions of Inner Mongolia would frustrate any attempt to ascertain the Chinese–Mongolian border at this time. Thus, the GMD government, with Jiang Jieshi's personal approval, prepared only two counter-measures in case a MPR incursion by plebiscite took place: The local Chinese authorities concerned would issue a statement to point out the irregularities, and the Chinese government would present to the Soviet and

---

Wenshi Ziliao (Historical and Literary Materials of Hulunbuir), 3: 1–6; Liu Chun, "Recollections of Inner Mongolia work," 88–89.

82. Luzianin, "Yalta Conference and Mongolia," 43.

MPR governments "memoranda of reservation" on China's right to redress the disputed borders.[83]

At the time, GMD officials were more troubled by the prospect of the MPR army's collaboration with the CCP in Inner Mongolia or its being used by the Soviet Union as a tool of aggression. An expanding plebiscite, in comparison, posed only a lesser threat. Two years after the MPR plebiscite, U.S. ambassador John Leighton Stuart learned from the Chinese Ministry of Foreign Affairs that in 1945, in the event of the MPR's conducting a plebiscite on the Chinese side of the border, Jiang Jieshi decided neither to object nor to endorse. For Jiang did not want to cause an international incident over "an additional few thousand square miles of relatively useless territory" after the entire Outer Mongolia had been signed away.[84] Given the GMD regime's passivity, the MPR's inroads into Inner Mongolia were prevented mainly because of Moscow's orientation at the international level.

At the regional level, however, an opportunity really missed by Ulaanbaatar was to use its moral authority and ethnic intimacy with the Inner Mongols to foster a sustainable and coherent Inner Mongolian movement. During the MPR's military presence in Inner Mongolia, Ulaanbaatar did nothing in this direction but busied itself with "lawful" political procedures intended to draw Inner Mongolian communities toward the MPR in a piecemeal manner. Indeed, because the Mongolian population in Inner Mongolia was twice as large as that in the MPR, the emergence of a powerful political center in Inner Mongolia could have outshone or weakened Ulaanbaatar as the center of gravity for all Mongols.[85] It cannot be proven whether or

83. Mongolian and Tibetan Affairs Commission to the Ministry of Foreign Affairs, no date, QZH 141/1223; Jiang Jieshi to Wang Chonghui, 6 October 1945, and appendix: "Matters in Respect to the Delegation of Inspection of Outer Mongolia's Plebiscite and Preparations for Receiving the Outer Mongolian Delegation," ibid.

84. Executive Yuan Directive on Recognition of Outer Mongolia Independence, 6 January 1946, Q141/1223; memo by West Asia Division of the Ministry of Foreign Affairs, "Outer Mongolian–Soviet Relations," [later than February] 1946, QZH 18 / 3359; Tang Enbo to Jiang Jieshi, 28 February 1946, Jiang Zhongzheng Zongtong Dang'an: Tejiao Wendian (Edi Yinmou Bufen) (Archives of President Jiang Zhongzheng: Specially Submitted Telegrams [Part on Russian Imperialist Conspiracy]), 6/35032173; Xiong Shihui to Jiang Jieshi, 26 December 1946, JZZD/GW (KLS), 39: 409–10; Stuart to the Secretary of State, 20 November 1947, General Records of the United States Department of State Central Files: China, 893.00 Mongolia / 11-2047.

85. In this period, old tribalism continued to function to pit different Mongolian sectors against one another. But the MPR, which was mainly a state of the Khalkha Mongols, held a general appealing power over the others. As late as 1947, according to a re-

not this thought ever entered Choibalsan's or any other MPR leader's mind. The fact remains that, when a promising political party, the IMPRP, was revived outside the operational range of MPR troops, Choibalsan ordered its dissolution or reorganization.

The crux of the IMPRP issue, as Christopher Atwood points out astutely, was whether or not the Inner Mongols could have an "alternative to the Chinese parties" after the option of accession to the MPR was denied.[86] When leaders in Wangyemiao organized their delegation to Ulaanbaatar, they not only wanted to petition for unification but also hoped to legitimize the IMPRP. That was why, originally, the delegation was headed by Khafengga, the secretary general of the revived IMPRP. But when the delegation was already on its way to Ulaanbaatar, a request from the MPR added Buyan-mandukhu to the delegation and made him the new head of the mission. Hereby the "party" character of the delegation was immediately diluted. The delegates arrived in Ulaanbaatar in early November, but they had to wait for more than two weeks before they got any answer from Choibalsan about their petitions. During this period, the MPR Ministry of Internal Affairs interrogated each of the delegates carefully.

On November 20, Choibalsan finally received the delegates and told his visitors that, as part of China, Inner Mongolia could not unify with the MPR, though he did promise to provide secret support to the Inner Mongols' cause of liberation. An eastern Mongolian autonomous government, he proposed, could be established first. Choibalsan's emphasis on the unity of the Inner Mongols seemed to be on target, but his advice for the eastern Mongols to follow the CCP leadership actually rejected the prospect of an independent Inner Mongolian movement. On this day, Choibalsan did not explicitly express his attitude toward the IMPRP. A week later, as the eastern Mongols were ready to return to Wangyemiao, Choibalsan's secretary Lhamsuren conveyed his boss's opinion that the IMPRP should be dissolved because the party included elements of complicated backgrounds and therefore could not lead the movement in Inner Mongolia. One more suggestion from

---

port within the CCP-led Inner Mongolian Autonomous Movement Association, people in Shilingol mistrusted cadres from eastern Mongolia, Tumed, and Kharachin while being attracted to the MPR. See "Wang Zongluo's Report at an Enlarged Meeting of the Executive Committee of the Alliance on Work in Shilingol, 16 April 1947," *Neimenggu Zizhi Yundong Lianhehui Dang'an Shiliao Xuanbian* (Selected Archival Materials on the Inner Mongolian Autonomous Movement Association), 210–11.

86. Atwood, "East Mongolian Revolution," 29.

Choibalsan was that class struggles should not be conducted in Inner Mongolia, lest such an orientation impair unity among the Inner Mongols.[87]

A revelation of Choibalsan's true motives in negating the IMPRP has to wait for further research into the historical archives. The IMPRP did not appear contradictory to Moscow's China policy or the MPR's compliance with it. No evidence indicates that Moscow, which had its own ally, the CCP, in China, would have objected if Ulaanbaatar had wished to copy the tactic and keep the IMPRP intact. Nor at the time did the CCP know enough about the restored IMPRP to make a representation to the MPR authorities. If the MPR leadership did indeed make the decision on the IMPRP's dissolution independently and if further speculations are allowed here, Ulaanbaatar might have two considerations. First, the IMPRP's revolutionary mode was outdated, given the MPR's current need to absorb Inner Mongolian communities through "legal" means. Choibalsan's warning against class struggles could be an indirect indicator of such a notion. Second, in the eyes of MPR leaders, the Inner Mongols had wrongly affiliated themselves with the Japanese since the 1930s and had proved themselves politically impotent. A party made up of these people would therefore be a futile exercise.

The eastern Mongol leaders proved more resourceful and spontaneous than Choibalsan and his associates thought. Having returned to Wangyemiao, they dissolved the IMPRP in public but started a new party in secret.[88] Nonetheless, the damage had been done. The IMPRP was dissolved at a time when it was experiencing a "frantic increase in the rate of party expansion," and, although Khafengga and others in Wangyemiao would try again, a legitimate Inner Mongolian party with its own revolutionary tradition was terminated by Choibalsan in November 1945.[89]

When the initial confusion and excitement caused by Japan's surrender passed, it became clear that politically the Inner Mongols were suffering from a dual deprivation: Mongolia's division according to the Sino-Soviet agreement of August 1945 deprived them of the opportunity of accession to the MPR, and Ulaanbaatar's own "legal" approach deprived them of a sustainable Inner Mongolian ethnopolitical revolution. At the time, however, the Ulaanbaatar-cum-Moscow advice to Inner Mongolian partisans on limit-

---

87. Bukho and Sayan, *Boyanmandu,* 76–79; Dawa-ochih, "My Life and Experiences," 161–62.

88. CCP Northeast Bureau's Report to the CCPCC on the Mongolia Question, 20 February 1946, *MWWH,* 1002–3.

89. Atwood, "East Mongolian Revolution," 36.

ing their activities within the realm of China and cooperating with the CCP did not appear to be a total abandonment. Unlike in the 1920s and 1930s, in the postwar years for the first time China appeared to offer two political centers to ethnic minorities. The CCP emerged from the margin of China's political life and, as a viable contender for national power, provided the Inner Mongols with a revolutionary alternative against the old choice of submission to the Chinese status quo. Ulaanbaatar and Moscow did not ask the eastern Mongols to abolish their struggle but suggested that they converge their politics of ethnic grouping with the CCP politics of class struggle. These two entities with obviously antithetical politics at least shared a common ground in their enmity against the official ROC.

In the informal hierarchy of the communist world, adjustment of patronage was not unusual. In the case of the eastern Mongolian movement, however, its ethnopolitical characteristic prevented a complete and clean transition of responsibilities between Ulaanbaatar and Yan'an. As a matter of fact, when Choibalsan told the eastern Mongol leaders to cooperate with the CCP, Ulaanbaatar also made preparations to keep itself in the game. In late November 1945, an intelligence officer of the MPR Ministry of Internal Affairs named Bansalgechi accompanied the eastern Mongolian delegation back to Wangyemiao. For the next one and a half years, Bansalgechi was stationed in Wangyemiao, disguised as a journalist for the MPR version of *Pravda*. Then, in mid-1946, when Ulaanbaatar finally decided to return Pungsug, who had been in the MPR since the mid-1930s, back to Wangyemiao, two more intelligence officers were sent. Although, in general, the CCP cooperated with the MPR's widely spread intelligence activities in Inner Mongolia, MPR agents' activities in the Wangyemiao area were often regarded by CCP officials as "incorrect" and bordering on the subversive.[90]

In Wangyemiao, Bansalgechi lived in the same quarter with Khafengga. The close contact between the two aroused the attention of the CCP's Social Department (Shehuibu), which was in charge of internal security. Soon, Bansalgechi was accused by the CCP of encouraging the eastern Mongol leaders to continue their effort to restore the IMPRP and unify Inner Mongolia with the MPR. In the late spring of 1947, Bansalgechi's presence especially annoyed CCP officials when some eastern Mongolian leaders,

90. Bukho and Sayan, *Boyanmandu,* 79, 91–92. "Special Issue on Historical Materials about Darijahyaga and Wife Jin Yuncheng," *Bayanno'er Wenshi Ziliao* 9 (1988): 115, 130, shows that MPR intelligence activities reached as far as Alashan Banner in the west.

including Khafengga, Temurbagana, Oljeiochir, and Pungsug, tried to organize an election contest against Ulanhu's group during the preparations for the Inner Mongolian Autonomous Government (IMAG). Allegedly, in trying to gain support to a selected group of candidates, Khafengga spread the word that his list of candidates had been approved by the MPR agent in Wangyemiao. This tactic was troubling enough for Ulanhu to send a request Ulaanbaatar that the MPR authorities not interfere in Inner Mongolian affairs. Afterward, Ulanhu was able to turn many young Mongol activists against Khafengga by showing them a telegram, allegedly from Choibalsan himself, that supported the CCP's stand against the restoration of the IMPRP.[91]

Bansalgechi's contacts were not limited to top leaders in Wangyemiao. After Khafengga and his associates reluctantly accepted the CCP's arrangements for the IMAG in May 1947, Bansagechi shifted his focus to a group within the autonomous government's public security system. The group's leader was Nima (a.k.a. Zhang Nima), a native of Khorchin Left Central Banner who in the war years received military training in Japanese-occupied Xing'an Province. Nima joined the Wangyemiao movement from the very beginning and then held several responsible positions for the movement's "internal defense." After May 1947, he was a branch chief of the Public Security Department of the IMAG but secretly organized an underground "Advance Society for Inner Mongolian Farmers and Herdsmen."

By interrogating some of the society's members, CCP officials found out that this group harbored a deep suspicion of people with Yan'an connections. Nima and his associates asserted that the CCP wanted to assimilate the Mongols, just as all previous Chinese authorities had. The group also resented the CCP's class-struggle orientation. In the spring of 1947, Nima openly backed his father-in-law Shumingga, the former chief of the Manchukuo's Southern Xing'an Province and a target of the CCP's "liquidation" struggle, in staging a confrontation with local peasant association cadres. The society justified its activities with a message allegedly sent by Choi-

---

91. Northeast Bureau to the CCPCC, 18 April 1947, *MWWH*, 1100–1; Wang Zaitian, "Recollections of My Work in the Social Department before and after the Establishment of the Inner Mongolian Autonomous Government," *NWZ* 50 (1997): 118–42 (the citation here is on 136); Liu Chun, "Recollections of Inner Mongolia Work," 79–81; Hu Shaoheng, "Excerpts from Hu Shaoheng's diary," entry on 30 March 1947, *Xing'an Geming Shihua*, 3: 234–35; Tegus, "The May First Conference as I Knew," *Xing'an Dangshi Wenji*, 1: 15–16.

balsan through Oljeiochir, which instructed the Inner Mongols not to follow the CCP blindly, or they would be punished as criminals against the Mongolian nation when unification between Inner Mongolia and the MPR was achieved. At the moment, the society would sustain the IMPRP as a follower of the MPR and maintain cooperation with the CCP in the struggle against the GMD. But in the long run, its goal was to wrest the Inner Mongolian movement from the CCP by penetrating the military and governmental organizations of the IMAG.

Although unable to ascertain the degree of Ulaanbaatar's involvement with the organization, CCP officials believed that they had uncovered a conspiracy and feared that a military coup was in preparation. They acted swiftly in Wangyemiao and purged the public security personnel, 80 percent of whom were allegedly sympathetic to the Nima group. Yet the CCP's effort to force Nima to confess was unsuccessful. In July, he fled to the MPR and took with him an unknown number of CCP documents. After the incident, the MPR authorities refused the CCP's request for Nima's repatriation on the ground that he was an MPR intelligence officer and therefore must be punished by the MPR for "violating disciplines." Ulaanbaatar, however, recalled Bansalgechi after the CCP fingered him as an influence in the Nima affair.[92]

Thus, like the alliance between the CCP and Moscow in the early postwar years, the "class brotherhood" between the CCP and Ulaanbaatar was choppy as well. Without sufficient documentation about Ulaanbaatar's operations in China after the withdrawal of the Soviet–Mongolian army, it can nevertheless be deduced from the available information that, in following Moscow's practices, Ulaanbaatar played its own double games in postwar China. In its relations with the GMD government, Ulaanbaatar strictly observed diplomatic protocols and respected the GMD regime's legal authority over Inner Mongolia. For instance, in late June 1946, on the ground of diplomatic considerations, the MPR authorities declined to receive a Wangyemiao delegation that hoped to come to Ulaanbaatar to celebrate the MPR's national day.[93] At the same time, the MPR leaders helped the CCP

92. Hu Shaoheng, "Excerpts from Hu Shaoheng's diary," entry on 6 July 1947, *Xing'an Geming Shihua,* 3: 258–60; Wang Zaitian, "Recollections," 136, 140–42; Butegechi, *Fengyu Jiancheng Wushinian,* 70–75. The MPR authorities gave Nima a twenty-five-year sentence but in 1954 repatriated him to the People's Republic of China, where he died in prison in the 1970s.

93. Bukhe and Sayan, *Boyanmandu,* 91.

to establish its revolutionary authority over Inner Mongolian autonomists. Yet, as the CCP's revolutionary strategies and Inner Mongol autonomists' ethnopolitical objectives diverged over certain basic issues, Ulaanbaatar found room to reassert, even though obliquely and tentatively, its ethnic authority in Inner Mongolia affairs.

This was well understood and expected by the CCP side. That was why, soon after the Japanese surrender, top CCP officials in Inner Mongolia and western Manchuria suggested to the CCP Central Committee that the CCP must have a unified leadership over Inner Mongolian affairs and unified contact with the MPR authorities. During the first few postwar months, because Ulaanbaatar was rapidly retreating from its legal claim on and "liberation" responsibility for the Inner Mongols, the MPR never constituted a real obstacle to the CCP's effort of incorporating the Inner Mongolian autonomous movement. During the last two years of the Chinese Civil War, the only remaining basis for Ulaanbaatar to voice any opinion about the CCP's policies in Inner Mongolia was its ethnic bond with the Inner Mongols. Ethnicity alone, however, never carried much weight in the international communist hierarchy. Depending on circumstances, the CCP could value or devaluate the ethnic tie between Inner and Outer Mongols. For instance, in a difficult moment in the summer of 1946, Nei Rongzhen instructed Ulanhu to get help in the MPR because Inner Mongolia and the MPR "belonged to the same nation." But in April 1947, Ulanhu asked the MPR authorities not to mess with Wangyemiao politics because this was the CCP's realm. Then, in early 1948, after Ulaanbaatar telegraphed the CCP leadership to express its concerns about the "leftist" tendencies in the CCP's "democratic reforms" in Shilingol and Chahar, Ulanhu sent a message to Ulaanbaatar to explain how the CCP had already redressed the mistakes, as if acknowledging the MPR's complaints as legitimate.[94]

Ultimately, friction between the CCP and Inner Mongol autonomists with MPR connections, to borrow a CCP participant's comment, "did not affect the overall situation."[95] After Stalin decided to keep Mongolia divided, with Inner Mongolia under Chinese sovereignty, a correlated outcome was inevitable. The Inner Mongolian autonomous movement had to come under the CCP's revolutionary jurisdiction. Between 1945 and 1949, China went

---

94. Nei Rongzhen, Yun Ze, and Lu Zhengcao to the CCPCC, 29 September 1945, *ZZWX,* 15: 378–79; Wang Zaitian, "Recollections," 121; Liu Chun, "Recollections of Inner Mongolian Work," 94.

95. Liu Chun, "Recollections of Inner Mongolian Work," 87.

through profound sociopolitical upheavals, including a regime change. Under the circumstances, Inner Mongolia's internalization into China could not have been decisively settled without the CCP's successful incorporation of the Inner Mongolian autonomous movement into its own revolution. By reluctantly handing the Inner Mongols' fate over to the CCP, Ulaanbaatar relinquished a most powerful justification for its irredentism: the necessity for the MPR to play a liberator's role in the Inner Mongols' emancipation from Chinese rule.

Yet pan-Mongol dreams lingered. On the eve of the CCP's victory in China, the MPR leaders became uncertain about their own country's future. Tsedenbal, the first secretary of the MPRP, was inclined to believe that the MPR should follow Tannu Tuva's path and become a member republic of the Soviet Union. Choibalsan was against the idea because, as reported by Soviet ambassador Y. K. Prikhodov, he was still "obsessed with the dream" of reunification between Inner Mongolia and the MPR.[96] Yet, when Ulaanbaatar's Chinese comrades-in-arms were about to take power in China, Choibalsan's dream not only became more illusory than ever but was also overshadowed by the CCP's own dream of restoring China's "grand unity," including the MPR's return to China.

96. Cited in Tsedendamba Batbayar's unpublished "Introduction" to two Soviet documents to be published by the Cold War International History Project, provided to the author by Christian Ostermann.

10

The Structure of Bloc Politics:
Mao, Stalin, and Mongolian Independence

In August 1945, China emerged the victor from its eight-year war with Japan. The triumph came with horrendous costs to millions of individual Chinese citizens. Collectively, in the last moment of the war, the Chinese people also had to accept a heavy price tag fixed by the Yalta–Moscow diplomacy. China's losses in the Yalta–Moscow scheme, however, carried rather different meanings to those political forces that were acting in the name of the Chinese nation. Outer Mongolia's final, legal independence from China would forever be in the historical record of the Guomindang (GMD, Nationalist Party), either as a credit or a blemish, depending on the observer's own stand. The GMD regime's submission in its 1945 treaty with Moscow to Soviet demands for special privileges in Manchuria was reminiscent of China's old "unequal treaties." Yet to GMD leaders these diplomatic concessions were part of a necessary trade-off to guarantee a favorable international environment for their "party-state" in postwar years. Indeed, Moscow's promise in the 1945 treaty of giving moral and material support only to the GMD government was unsettling to the Chinese Communist Party (CCP), the GMD's archenemy. It has been suggested that the GMD–Soviet treaty of 1945 "collided with some of the most cherished tenets of the Chinese Communist Party" and, because of the agreement on Outer Mongolia, the treaty even discredited Mao Zedong himself, who had predicted the reunion of the Mongolian People's Republic (MPR) with China in a 1936 interview with Edgar Snow.[1]

---

1. Sergei N. Goncharov, John W. Lewis, and Xue Litai, *Uncertain Partners: Stalin, Mao, and the Korean War* (Stanford, Calif.: Stanford University Press, 1993), 6.

This interpretation of the GMD–Soviet treaty overvalues the CCP leaders' nationalist sentiment against their confidence, misplaced or not, in Moscow at the time. As far as the top CCP leaders were concerned, years of self-reliant struggle for survival and observation of the Soviet Union's capricious international behavior had taught them to interpret Moscow's diplomatic deals "dialectically." They believed, rightly or wrongly, that they were able to reconcile Moscow's long-term strategy with its short-term tricks: Whereas the former was definitely in concert with the goals of the Chinese revolution, the latter might just appear irregular but actually served the long-term strategy. The time would come for the two largest communist parties of the world to jettison their "internationalism" and to deal with each other like two ordinary national ruling parties. But 1945 was not such a moment.

After Japan's surrender, the CCP did not simply return to its prewar, narrowly construed class-struggle orientation. Instead, while resorting to radical land programs in the countryside as a means to maintain Chinese peasants' support, the CCP did not abandon Chinese nationalism as a most effective ideology to woo anxious, patriotic groups in the cities. The momentum of China's arduous victory over Japan pushed China's political organizations and the general public alike to strive more urgently for such goals as national unification, peaceful reconstruction, and achieving the country's deserved place in the international community. Although tailoring its public policy statements to this sentiment, the CCP nevertheless found the "national losses" in recent GMD diplomacy a partisan gain for itself. While the GMD regime's concession over Outer Mongolia in Moscow disgraced its foreign policy among patriotic Chinese and even embittered many GMD members, the CCP sought to capitalize on the postwar expansion of Soviet–Mongolian influence in northeastern China.

Namely, when bloc politics became increasingly dominant in the form of the Cold War in the postwar years, the CCP's "class brotherhood" with the MPR again took precedence over its nationalist considerations of Chinese sovereignty in Outer Mongolia. From the CCP's perspective in 1945, Moscow's success in annulling the GMD's hollow claim of sovereignty over the MPR would strengthen the revolutionary bloc. In the long run, the development also would not contradict the CCP's goal of renewing China's national tie with Outer Mongolia after the GMD was defeated. In 1936, Mao told Snow that Outer Mongolia would return to a "new" China. The prediction remained valid to CCP leaders during the Chinese Civil War because the GMD–Soviet treaty was an undertaking by an "old regime" in China, and therefore it could not be final.

The same trust in the Soviet ally would both sustain CCP leaders' confidence in their final victory and lead them to bitter disillusionment when the victory was finally won in 1949. The simple fact was that the CCP's ascendance to power in 1949 transformed it from a revolutionary movement into a national government. Meanwhile, its attempt to transform revolutionary ties with the MPR into a national combination was blocked. Thus, Outer Mongolia, not Inner Mongolia as predicted by some American officials in 1949, changed from a corridor connecting the CCP revolution and Moscow to one of the first "natural points of conflict" between the two communist giants.

A Fractured Revolutionary Alliance

Years after the Chinese Civil War ended, a senior CCP cadre likened the GMD–CCP struggle with "two people fighting in the street": "We had the Soviet giant standing behind us and our morale was immensely enhanced."[2] What this official failed to mention is that beside the Soviet Union, standing behind the CCP in the civil war period were also the MPR and a new member of the communist bloc, North Korea. In the last month of the war against Japan, the CCP already feared that the United States might replace Japan in Inner Mongolia and block the CCP's connection with the MPR. In August, after the MPR issued its declaration of war on Japan along with the Soviet Union, the CCP organ, *Jiefang Ribao* (Liberation Daily), carried the entire document, and the Eighth Route Army Headquarters ordered its troops in Inner Mongolia to "coordinate with the Outer Mongolian People's Republic's army's entry" into the region.[3]

The benefit for the CCP in identifying the MPR force separately from the

2. Bo Yibo, *Ruogan Zhongda Juce yu Shijian Huigu* (Recollections of Certain Important Policies and Events), 2 vols. (Beijing: Zhongyang Dangxiao Chubanshe, 1991, 1993), 1: 36.

3. "Saibei Military District Report on the Conditions of the Japanese, the Puppets, and the GMD in the Suiyuan Mongolian Area, 22 July 1945," in *Daqingshan Kang Ri Youji Genjudi Ziliao Xuanbian* (Selected Materials on the Anti-Japanese Base in the Daqing Mountains) (Hohhot: Neimenggu Renmin Chubanshe, 1987), 2: 269; "Outer Mongolia's Declaration of War on Japan," *Jiefang Ribao* (Liberation Daily), 12 August 1945, *Zhong Su Guojia Guanxi Shi Ziliao Huibian* (Selected Materials on the History of Sino-Soviet Relations), 2: 665; "Order No. 3, 11 August 1945," *Minzu Wenti Wenxian Huibian* (Collected Documents on the Nationality Question; hereafter *MWWH*), 750–51.

Soviet Red Army was threefold. First, the CCP could thus indicate to the Inner Mongols that while the GMD government kept an awkward silence about the MPR's entry into the war against Japan, the CCP and the MPR were close allies fighting together. During the next two years, the CCP–MPR alliance indeed facilitated the CCP's ethnopolitical operations among the Inner Mongols. While CCP operatives urged the Inner Mongols to learn from the MPR's revolutionary spirit, the MPR leaders advised the Inner Mongol autonomists to follow the CCP's leadership. The CCP operatives in Inner Mongolia also used the MPR as a sanctuary when their work suffered setbacks in late 1946.[4]

Second, the separate identity of MPR forces would allow the CCP to ignore the GMD–Soviet understanding that territories liberated by the Soviets would be turned over to the GMD authorities. In the initial months of the GMD–CCP competition for territories in northern and northeastern China, the CCP took over territories from the joint Soviet–Mongolian force in Inner Mongolia but claimed that Soviet troops were not involved. This approach proved especially useful during the American mediation between the GMD and the CCP in 1946.[5]

Third, after the CCP and MPR forces finally made direct contact within China, the territory of the MPR, together with those of the Soviet Union and North Korea, for the first time became a practical rear area for the CCP's military operations in northern and northeastern China. As a matter of fact, during the rest of 1945, the CCP's military strategy in these areas included an important component: The connection with Outer Mongolia must be kept open, and any strategic move must be planned with the MPR–USSR–North Korea crescent as the backup area. Thus, the CCP's declared coordination with the MPR in the final offensive against Japan actually legitimized the CCP–MPR "class brotherhood" in the renewed Chinese Civil War.[6]

4. Wang Shusheng and Hao Yufeng, *Wulanfu Nianpu* (Chronicle of Ulanhu's Life) (Beijing: Zhonggong Dangshi Ziliao Chubanshe, 1989), 149, 152; Wang Duo, *Wushi Chunqiu* (Fifty Eventful Years) (Hohhot: Neimenggu Renmin Chubanshe, 1992), 214–16.

5. Yang Kuisong, *Mao Zedong yu Mosike de En En Yuan Yuan* (Gratitude and Grievances between Mao Zedong and Moscow) (Nanchang: Jiangxi Renmin Chubanshe, 1999), 231; "We cannot consider the plan that wants us to give up Chifeng and Duolun, 8 January 1946," *Zhou Enlai Yi Jiu Si Liu Nian Tanpan Wenxuan* (A Selection of Zhou Enlai's Writings and Documents during the 1946 Negotiations), comp. Central Documentary Research Office and the CCP Committee of the Nanjing Municipality (Beijing: Zhongyang Wenxian Chubanshe, 1996), 41–42.

6. "[CCP] Military Committee's Directive to He Long and Others on Making a Full-Scale Effort to Control All Suiyuan, Chanar and Jehol, 30 August 1945," *Zhonggong*

Despite the fanfare at the beginning, the CCP–MPR relationship during the Chinese Civil War did not add as much to the CCP's war effort as CCP leaders expected or as GMD officials feared. At the beginning, one of the GMD government's worst nightmares was that countless Mongol cavalries equipped with Soviet weapons would rush across the border and fight abreast CCP troops. Warnings repeatedly came through the GMD intelligence network that an increasingly large number of Mongolian brigades were gathering along the MPR's southern border and would soon join with the CCP in the neighborhood of Zhangjiakou. This never happened. During the entire civil war period, the forces of the GMD government and the MPR engaged each other only once along the MPR–Xinjiang border. That was during the so-called Beitashan incident in early June 1947. In this incident, the MPR used a battalion-size force and had support from the Soviet air force. The incident was caused neither by the CCP nor by boundary disputes. It was part of an ethnic conflict in Xinjiang, in which the GMD authorities and its local allies were on one side and an "eastern Turkestan" regime supported by the Soviets on the other.[7]

In China, in closely following the script of Moscow's foreign policy, MPR troops basically avoided any direct entanglement with the GMD–CCP fighting. According to GMD information, in November 1945, the MPR Army turned over some military equipment to the CCP in Inner Mongolia. If this indeed happened, the MPR Army probably just "abandoned" some captured Japanese weapons to the CCP, a behavior that would be repeated by the Soviet Red Army in Manchuria before its withdrawal in March 1946.

Zhongyang Wenjian Xuanji (Selected Documents of the CCP Central Committee; hereafter *ZZWX*), 15: 260; "Military Committee's Directive on Strategy and Operations with Regard to the Struggle for the Northeast, 28 September 1945," ibid., 15: 300; "[CCP] Center's Directive to Liu Bocheng and Deng Xiaoping on the Basic Orientation in Shanxi, 17 October 1945," ibid., 15: 361; "Liu Shaoqi's Telegram to Peng Zhen on Using the Main Force to Establish bases in Eastern, Western and Northern Manchuria, 24 December 1945," ibid., 15: 513; "Military Committee's Plan for Protecting Zhangjiakuo and Chengde, 29 December 1945," ibid., 15: 526.

7. Central Joint Secretariat of the Party, Government, and Military, "Report on Recent Developments of the Collusion between the CCP and the Soviet Armies, 10 February 1946," *Zhonghua Minguo Zhongyao Shiliao Chubian* (Preliminary Compilation of Important Historical Documents of the Republic of China), 7(1): 580; Central Joint Secretariat of the Party, Government, and Military, "Report on Recent Developments of the Collusion between the CCP and the Soviet Army, March 1946," ibid., 7(1): 585; Sun Fushen, "The Cause and Course of the Soviet Aggression in Beitashan," 1952, ibid., 7(1): 774–79; Jiang Jieshi's diary entries on 10, 11, and 15 June 1947, ibid., 7(1): 780–81.

After the Soviet–MPR forces left China, the MPR actually refused to provide military assistance even to Ulanhu's group, lest such assistance cause complications with the GMD government. Ulaanbaatar's concern with discreetness was even extended to the field of commerce. After 1947, a trade relationship began between the MPR and CCP-controlled regions in Manchuria and Inner Mongolia. To address the MPR's diplomatic concerns, the CCP conducted the trade under the cover of a "Western Mongolian Trading Company."[8]

As it turned out, during the Chinese Civil War, the CCP's revolutionary brotherhood with the North Koreans was much more rewarding than that with the MPR. The North Korean communist leader Kim Il Song not only allowed the CCP to use Korean territories as recuperating bases and gave material aid to CCP troops in Manchuria but also provided labor power to the CCP's "war of liberation." Between 1950 and 1953, Mao would reciprocate the favor with China's intervention in the Korean War on Kim's side. In contrast, despite the direct and indirect benefits that the friendly MPR bestowed on the CCP before 1949, it would in later years not be counted by the CCP as a big help. When the MPR leader Choibalsan died in 1952, Mao's telegram of condolence to the MPR government stated that Marshall Choibalsan would be remembered forever in China for giving "assistance to the Chinese people during the war against Japanese imperialism," omitting noticeably China's "war of liberation" between 1945 and 1949.[9] Having always defined the Chinese revolution as an ethnically inclusive journey and regarded the Mongolian struggle as part of it, the CCP leadership finally decided that the MPR had played no part in China's "war of liberation."

The MPR's connection with the Chinese Civil War would, however, be remembered by the CCP leadership in a different context. Wang Jiaxiang,

---

8. Department of Military Ordinance to the Ministry of Foreign Affairs, 18 November 1945, Waijiaobu Yataisi (Asian–Pacific Division of the Ministry of Foreign Affairs), 097.1; Wang Duo, *Wushi Chunqiu,* 214–16, 267–68.

9. "Recollections of the Liaison Office of the Northeastern Bureau in North Korea during the War for Liberating the Northeast," *Zonggong Dangshi Ziliao* (Materials on the CCP's History) 17 (1986): 197–210; Bruce Cumings, *The Origins of the Korean War, Volume II: The Roaring of the Cataract, 1947–1950* (Princeton, N.J.: Princeton University Press, 1990), 358; Goncharov, Lewis, and Xue, *Uncertain Partners,* 140–41, 329 n. 56; "[Mao's] Telegram to Bumtsend Condoling the Death of Choibalsan, 27 January 1952," Mao Zedong, *Jiangguo Yilai Mao Zedong Wengao* (Mao Zedong's Manuscripts since the Establishment of the State) (Beijing: Zhongyang Wenxian Chubanshe, 1987–), 3: 110.

the first chief of the CCP Central Committee's Liaison Department in charge of China's relations with foreign communist organizations, once made a deceivingly simple remark on these relations. He said that China and other communist entities in the world were "simultaneously members of the same family and members of different families."[10] Wang, a returnee from Moscow during the Comintern period, believed in the duality of China's interests, which thus could overlap and differ from the interests of other members of the "great socialist family" at the same time. During the Chinese Civil War, on their way to replacing the GMD as the power holder in China, the CCP leaders learned their first grave lesson from the MPR case about the brawling "family division" of the communist world.

When China's postwar period began, CCP cadres operating in northern China encountered the issue of the MPR no longer as an abstract idea but as a concrete policy matter. The political significance of the MPR's military presence in China caused confusion among CCP officials. Some believed that the political mobilization of the Inner Mongols could be done in "close association with Outer Mongolia," but others saw a downside of the MPR connection: "Some [Inner Mongolian] youths cherish hope about Outer Mongolia but do not know much about us."[11] The question to these CCP cadres was whether or not the MPR was really part of "us" and had an identical interest with the CCP's in postwar Inner Mongolian ethnopolitics. A few years later, when the Chinese Civil War entered its final phase and the CCP was poised triumphantly to ascend to power, the question about "part of us" transformed into one concerning the MPR's status in relation to the incoming People's Republic of China (PRC).

At a party conference in the fall of 1948, when making a report on international conditions, Zhou Enlai listed the recent achievements of the Soviet Union, the emergence of new "democratic countries" in East Europe, and national liberation movements in Asia as favorable conditions for China's "war of liberation." The MPR was missing from Zhou's political landscape.[12]

10. Xu Zehao, *Wang Jiaxiang Zhuan* (Biography of Wang Jiaxiang) (Beijing: Dangdai Zhongguo Chubanshe, 1996), 515.

11. "Minutes of the Sui-Meng government's discussion of the Mongolian work, 11 August 1945," in *Daqingshan Kang Ri Youji Genjudi Ziliao Xuanbian,* 2: 294; "Nie Rongzhen et al.'s Request for the [CCP] Center's Directive on the Policy in Inner Mongolia, 29 September 1945," *ZZWX,* 15: 378.

12. Zhou Enlai, "Three-Point Estimation of the Development of the War of Liberation, 30 September 1948," *Zhou Enlai Junshi Wenxuan* (Selected Military Works of Zhou Enlai) (Beijing: Renmin Chubanshe, 1997), 3: 470.

This omission might have just been accidental. But, in view of the MPR's constant presence in the CCP's military and political strategies in the past and the CCP's first *diplomatic* encounter with Moscow that would soon take place, it is more likely that at the time CCP leaders deliberately avoided reference to the MPR to keep the territoriality of Outer Mongolia an open question.

The diplomatic encounter happened between December 1949 and February 1950, when Mao made his first trip to Moscow as head of the PRC. This interstate diplomacy was, however, preceded by two secret interparty missions in 1949. Whereas these encounters have been closely scrutinized in some recent studies based on newly declassified CCP and Soviet archival materials, the meaning of these encounters to the evolving Mongolia question has not been a focal point in any of these studies.[13] It is therefore worth inquiring, as the CCP was on its way to power in China, how the question of the MPR's inclusion in or exclusion from the forthcoming communist state weighed in CCP leaders' dealing with the Soviets.

From January to February 1949, Anastas I. Mikoyan, a member of the Politburo of the Soviet Communist Party, came to Xibaipo, northern Shaanxi, to meet with the CCP leadership. The Mikoyan mission was a stopgap for Mao's proposed trip to Moscow, which Mao had pressed in the past few months but was regarded as premature by Moscow.[14] In this first meeting between a senior Soviet official and the Mao-centered CCP leadership, the two sides had much to find out about each other and many views to exchange.

This was also the first occasion when the CCP and Moscow found themselves on opposing sides over the Mongolia question. In 1960, as the Sino-Soviet polemics were flaring up, at a senior party officials meeting Zhou recalled several events in the Joseph Stalin period that allegedly affected CCP–Soviet relations negatively. Mikoyan's 1949 mission was one of these. According to Zhou, Mikoyan revealed Moscow's reluctance to give aid to

---

13. Chinese scholar Yang Kuisong's two major studies—*Zhonggong yu Mosike de Guanxi, 1920–1960* (The Chinese Communist Party's Relationship with Moscow, 1920–1960) (Taipei: Dongda Tushu Gongsi, 1997), and *Mao Zedong ye Mosike de En En Yuan Yuan;* and Russian scholar A. M. Ledovsky's *SSSR i Stalin v Sudbax Kitaya* (The Soviet Union and Stalin in China's Destiny; a Chinese version was published in 2001 by Xinhua Chubanshe in Beijing)—bring some important historical documents to light. Goncharov, Lewis, and Xue's *Uncertain Partners* and Chen Jian's *Mao's China and the Cold War* (Chapel Hill: University of North Carolina Press, 2001) offer important insights on these events.

14. Yang Kuisong, *Mao Zedong yu Mosike,* 258–70.

the CCP and lack of confidence in the CCP's ability to liberate China. In addition, "he was very afraid that we mention the issue of Outer Mongolia, but in reality we had no intention to do so at all."[15] In other words, it was Soviet leaders' unfounded suspicion of the CCP's reservation about MPR independence, not any real disagreement on the issue between the two sides, that cast a shadow on their relationship. Zhou's spin on the matter is no longer maintained unanimously in recent historical literature in China. Although studies in China now admit that the issue of Outer Mongolia was a test to the CCP–Moscow relationship during the Mikoyan mission, they cannot agree which side was administering the test.[16]

Not by accident, in 1960 Mikoyan did a similar exercise as Zhou's in Moscow. But his story was rather different. In a report to the Presidium of the Soviet Communist Party Central Committee, dated September 22, 1960, Mikoyan described the Mongolia question during his 1949 trip to China as an outright disagreement between the CCP and Moscow. According to Mikoyan, during his three-day discussion with Mao, Mao raised three issues pertinent to Sino-Soviet relations.[17] The first concerned the continuation,

15. Wu Lengxi, *Shinian Lunzhan, 1956–1966: Zhongsu Guanxi Huiyilu* (Ten Years of Debates, 1956–1966: A Memoir of Sino-Soviet Relations) (Beijing: Zhongyang Wenxian Chubanshe, 1999), 1: 315–33, summarizes a three-day report (July 14–16, 1960) made by Zhou on the history of the CCP–Comintern–Soviet relationship to an enlarged CCP politburo conference at Beidaihe.

16. Qiu Jing, "Meeting between the Two Red Giants: The First Mutual Visitation by Chinese and Soviet Senior Leaders," in *Waijiao Fengyun: Waijiaoguan Haiwai Miwen* (Diplomatic Storms: Overseas Experiences by Diplomats), ed. Fu Hao and Li Tongcheng (Beijing: Zhongguo Huaqiao Chubanshe, 1995), 206; Yu Zhan and Zhang Guangyou, "An Inquiry into Whether or Not Stalin Tried to Dissuade Us from Crossing the Yangtze River," in *Xin Zhongguo Waijiao Fengyun* (New China's Diplomatic Storms), Office of Diplomatic History of the Ministry of Foreign Affairs (Beijing: Shijie Zhishi Chubanshe, 1990), 16.

17. Mikoyan's report summarizes his several conversations with CCP leaders but does not date the contents of these conversations. The Chinese version of the report is published separately as A. M. Ledovsky, "Secret Negotiations between Mikoyan and Mao Zedong, January–February 1949, Part Two," trans. Li Yuzhen, *Dang de Wenxian* (Party Documents) 1 (1996): 90–96, and A. M. Ledovsky, *Sidalin yu Zhongguo* (Stalin and China), trans. Chen Chunhua, Liu Cunkuan, et al. (Beijing: Xinhua Chubanshe, 2001), 58–72. For an English version, see Andrei Ledovsky, "Mikoyan's Secret Mission to China in January and February 1949," *Far Eastern Affairs* (hereafter *FEA*) 2 (1995): 78–94. Shi Zhe, *Zai Lishi Juren Shenbian: Shi Zhe Huiyilu* (At the Side of Historical Giants: Memoirs of Shi Zhe) (Beijing: Zhongyang Wenxian Chubanshe, 1995), 374–88, mentions six conversations, four with Mao and one each with Zhou Enlai and Ren Bishi. The most important, according to Shi, was a three-day monologue by Mao from Febru-

after the CCP's victory, of the Soviet military base in Lüshun (Port Arthur), which had been obtained under the GMD–Soviet treaty of 1945. In refuting an opinion allegedly voiced by a certain female nationalist politician who was in favor of abolishing the Soviet base after the CCP victory, Mao supported a continued Soviet military presence in Manchuria on the ground that the CCP and Moscow shared common strategic goals against the United States and Japan. On this issue, the Mikoyan report includes a response from Stalin himself that termed the GMD–Soviet treaty of 1945 an "unequal treaty" and proposed a Soviet military departure from Lüshun sooner rather than later. The second question was Soviet involvement with the separatist movement centered in Yili (Ili), Xinjiang. Again, Mao used information allegedly from a GMD source to form his question. In sensing Mao's suspicion of Soviet motives, Mikoyan pledged that Moscow neither supported any ethnic independence movement in Xinjiang nor harbored any territorial ambitions in the region.

But the most troublesome was the third question, Outer Mongolia. The relevant paragraphs of the Mikoyan report are worth quoting here:

> On Mongolia. Mao Zedong himself raised the question of our attitude toward the unification of Outer and Inner Mongolia. I replied that we did not support such a unification since it would lead to the loss of considerable Chinese territory. Mao Zedong said that he was of the opinion that Outer and Inner Mongolia could unite and become part of the Chinese Republic. To this I replied that was impossible, since the Mongolian People's Republic had long since won independence. Following the victory over Japan, the Chinese state had also recognized the independence of Outer Mongolia. The MPR had its own army, its own culture, and was moving rapidly along the path of cultural and economic development. It had long since grown accustomed to the taste of freedom, and was unlikely ever to surrender that independence voluntarily. If it ever did unite with Inner Mongolia, then a united and independent Mongolia would no doubt form as a result. Ren Bishi, who was present during the conversation, replied to this that there were three million people in Inner

---

ary 1 to 3 with Mikoyan's occasional comments and questions. Not only the Mongolia question but also the entire Sino-Soviet relationship are missing in Shi Zhe's narrative. Mikoyan's report disputes the "monologue" impression and indicates that serious exchanges of opinions between the two sides took place.

Mongolia, and one million in Outer Mongolia. In connection with this information, Stalin sent me a telegram to give to Mao Zedong, which said:

"The leaders of Outer Mongolia support the unification of all the Mongolian regions of China with Outer Mongolia to form an independent and united Mongolian state. The Soviet government does not agree with this plan, since it means taking a number of regions from China, although this plan does not threaten the interests of the Soviet Union. We do not think that Outer Mongolia would agree to surrender its independence in favor of autonomy within the Chinese state, even if all the Mongolian regions are united in one autonomous entity. Clearly the final word on this issue belongs to Outer Mongolia itself."

On hearing the contents of this telegram, Mao Zedong said that he would take note of it and that, of course, "they did not defend the Great China chauvinist policy and would not raise the question of the unification of Mongolia."[18]

This Mao–Mikoyan exchange, if it indeed happened as Mikoyan alleged, is interesting for two reasons. First, it started the process through which the CCP–Moscow relationship would be transformed from an alliance between two revolutionary parties into dealings between two national governments. As if Mao's unorthodox revolution was not suspicious enough to Moscow, the process was compounded by the communist bloc's concurrent denunciation of Yugoslavian Communist leader Josip Tito for his independent international orientation. To show its loyalty to international communism as defined by Moscow, in late 1948 the CCP joined the chorus by issuing a long article titled "On Internationalism and Nationalism" under Liu Shaoqi's name. But the CCP leadership could still sense Moscow's suspicion that Maoism was Titoism of Asia.[19] Therefore, conversing with Mikoyan, Mao consciously avoided taking an outright national position vis-à-vis the Soviet Union. That was why, in raising the issues of Lüshun and Xinjiang, he resorted to a tactic of making oblique references and used nationalist person-

18. Andrei Ledovsky, "Mikoyan's Secret Mission to China in January and February 1949," *FEA* 2 (1995): 88–89. The female nationalist leader was probably Song Qingling, widow of Sun Yat-sen.

19. Goncharov, Lewis, and Xue, *Uncertain Partners,* 33. According to Yang, *Mao Zedong yu Mosike,* 260, when a CCP delegation visited Moscow and other eastern bloc countries in the summer of 1948, its members were surprised that in these quarters Mao and Tito were regarded as the same.

alities as his surrogates. This approach could shield Mao against likely criticism from the Soviets for, if necessary, he could easily take the Soviet side in these matters and repudiate his nationalist sources.

In contrast, the Soviets appeared businesslike and fully prepared to deal with their Chinese comrades as counterparts in interstate negotiations. The fact that Yan'an and Moscow were in different gears in their relationship transition is best revealed by their different attitudes toward the GMD–Soviet treaty of 1945. In the spirit of camaraderie, Mao told Mikoyan that the CCP regarded the treaty as a "patriotic" one because it helped China in the war against Japan. This statement caused a telegram from Stalin the following day, saying: "When the Chinese Communists come to power, the situation will change radically. The Soviet government has decided to annul this unequal agreement. . . . "[20] This could be read optimistically by CCP leaders as a promise of a new, post-GMD, Sino-Soviet relationship. But, in the meantime, Stalin's readiness in confessing that the Soviet Union, just like any other imperial power, could impose inequality on China also served a cautionary note to the CCP leaders. The question for Mao and his associates was whether or not they could count on Stalin not to do the same to their communist state.

Second, the Mikoyan mission not only dashed the CCP's hope for Outer Mongolia's "return" to China but also its illusion about Lenin's formula on socialist federation based on national groups' free will. Mikoyan and other members of the mission had different recollections about whether or not Mao also used nationalist surrogates to bring up the topic of Outer Mongolia.[21] Whatever was the case in Xibaipo, the CCP's Mongolia complex was never a secret. To Mikoyan, Mao just repeated what he had told Edgar Snow thirteen years before. However, now facing the Soviets in the Mongolia question, the CCP leadership seemed to lose its self-righteous confidence, which had hitherto been demonstrated in its criticism of the GMD's ethnopolitics.

---

20. Ledovsky, *Sidalin yu Zhongguo,* 141; Ledovsky, "Mikoyan's Secret Mission," 87.

21. Ivan Kovalev, who was a member of the Mikoyan mission, recalled that Mao used the "female Nationalist politician" to bring up both the issue of Lüshun and that of Outer Mongolia. See Sergei Goncharov, "The Stalin–Mao Dialogue; Ivan Kovalev, Stalin's Personal Envoy to Mao Zedong, Interviewed by Historian and Sinologist Sergei Goncharov," *FEA* 1 (1992): 100–16; the citation here is on 104–5. Shi Zhe, in an interview to comment on Kovalev's reminiscences, insisted that Mao did not raise the *issue* of Outer Mongolia at all during Mikoyan's visit. See Li Haiwen, "The Inaccuracies in Kovalev's Reminiscences: An Interview with Shi Zhe," *Guoshi Yanjiu Cankao Ziliao* (Reference Materials for the Study of State History) 1 (1993): 92.

As reflected in the Soviet sources, the CCP leaders only used two meager arguments to defend their stand on Mongolia's reunion with China: (1) Inner Mongolia had more Mongolian population than Outer Mongolia, and (2) Mongolia's reunion could help the CCP win over the left wing of the GMD.[22]

Surprisingly, on this occasion the CCP leaders did not cite a word from Marxist dogmas in defending their position on Mongolia. By this time, the CCP leadership had already mustered enough knowledge about the Marxist-Leninist theoretic formula on the "national question" and should have been able to use it and even the Soviet model itself in defending a multinational Chinese federation. Earlier, in 1945, Mao and his comrades appeared so confident about their "theoretical correctness" on this matter that when the CCP adopted a new charter at its seventh national congress, a "new democratic federal republic" based on "all revolutionary classes' alliance and all nationalities' free union" was officially established as the party's goal.[23] But in Xibaipo, this confidence seemed to dissipate completely in Mao's encounter with the Soviets. If, on the Mongolia question, the GMD regime had always felt frustrated by its weakness vis-à-vis Soviet power, power confrontation was not the question between the CCP and Moscow in 1949. At the time, Mao probably suffered from a pupil's inadequacy in challenging the CCP's ideological mentor.

It should be noted that during the Moscow negotiations of 1945, Stalin used arguments about Soviet security interests to force the GMD to accept Mongolian independence. In contrast, in 1949 Mikoyan and Stalin persuaded Mao to back down with authoritative statements about the Mongols' right to self-determination, balanced by a seemingly magnanimous concern about China's territorial integrity. This tactic induced Mao to reaffirm the CCP's rejection of "Great China chauvinism" and to continue the pretension that there was neither interest conflict nor ideological contradiction between the Soviet Union and the forthcoming Communist China over the issue of the MPR.

It has been suggested that "for all its international pretensions, communism has turned out to be one of the most nationalistic of all modern ideologies . . . [and] red nationalism is even more intense, more xeno-

---

22. Ledovsky, "Mikoyan's Secret Mission," 88–89; Goncharov, "Stalin–Mao Dialogue," 104–5.

23. "Charter of the Chinese Communist Party, Adopted Unanimously by the CCP's Seventh National Congress, 11 June 1945," *MWWH*, 748.

phobic than the common garden varieties of nationalism found every-where."[24] The intensity of usually disingenuous "communist" nationalism granted, the late 1940s was not yet a time for "brotherly" falling-out in the communist world. At the time, communist countries other than the Soviet Union just obtained material possession of their national states and began to differentiate their respective national political inheritances and the so-called international communist cause. As shown in the Mikoyan mission, the conflict between Chinese and Soviet national interests in the Mongolia question did not flare up, because the two sides' momentary common ground was still highlighted by their long partisan cooperation in the past and their imperative bloc partnership in the future. Yet even though the CCP–Moscow disagreements on Mongolia were for the moment managed and wrapped within a consensus about an ideologically "correct" course, the encounter already set off one of the first sparks that would eventually lead to the Sino-Soviet conflict of the 1960s. It is not by accident that when the CCP–Moscow dispute began in 1960, both Zhou and Mikoyan immediately revisited the Mongolia question in their respective reviews of the two parties' historical relationship.

Resetting the Interstate Relationship

The Mikoyan mission decisively ended the CCP's earlier misconceptions about Moscow's intentions for Outer Mongolia. The CCP leaders were never so naive to believe that the Outer Mongols would voluntarily abolish their independence and rejoin China. They nevertheless never accepted the notion that the Mongolia question was purely about the Mongolian people's *self*-determination. In casting his questions to Mikoyan, Mao expected to get Moscow on the CCP's side with respect to Mongolia's inclusion in a Chinese federation, which the CCP had been advocating for the past three decades. The anticipated Soviet blessing did not come. Stalin's attitude not only shattered the CCP's hopes for outdoing the GMD regime in recovering Outer Mongolia but also deprived the CCP of an opportunity to restore China's "grand unity." Although Mao did not feel adequate or appropriate to engage Stalin in a debate about China's or Mongolia's territoriality in

---

24. Donald S. Zagoria, "The Strategic Environment in East Asia," in *Soviet Policy in East Asia,* ed. Donald S. Zagoria (New Haven, Conn.: Yale University Press, 1982), 6.

terms of Marxist dogmas, the Soviets' emphasis on the Mongols' exclusive right to determine their own status did not sound convincing and entirely sincere to the CCP leaders. That was why Mao repeatedly returned to the subject in talking with the members of the Mikoyan mission in 1949.[25] But the CCP leaders would not express their misgivings until Stalin's death. In April 1956, in a conversation with Mikoyan, Zhou wanted the new Soviet leadership to admit that during Mikoyan's 1949 mission Stalin had made a mistake in handling the Mongolia question in an "evasive" way not befitting "party principles" and the "conversation between communists."[26]

During his 1949 visit in Xibaipo, Mikoyan also conveyed advice from Moscow that, after taking power, the CCP should not be "excessively broad-minded" toward China's ethnic minorities, which should be given only autonomy but not independence.[27] The advice proved unnecessary. Mao told Mikoyan that all the nationalities in China were "Chinese" (Zhongguoren), just as all those in the Soviet Union were "Soviets."[28] The obvious inconsistency between this unsolicited advice and Moscow's insistence on Outer Mongols' right to self-determination must have left a big question mark in CCP leaders' minds. As a matter of fact, not long before Stalin had promoted a plan for regrouping Eastern European countries into three federations (Polish–Czechoslovak, Romanian–Hungarian, and Yugoslav–Bulgarian–Albanian).[29] Had CCP leaders known about this, they could have asked Mikoyan: Why not a Chinese–Mongolian federation in Asia?

At the time, the real reasons for Moscow's unwillingness to see the emergence of a greater communist China were either too hard for CCP leaders to fathom or too dark for them to believe. Several years later, Zhou made an effort to understand Stalin's hesitation about the CCP during the Chinese Civil War. In recalling the Mikoyan mission with some senior CCP officials, Zhou asserted that at the time Stalin wanted the CCP to stop its southward offensive and preferred to have China divided along the Yangtze River in order to preserve the Soviet–American understanding at Yalta about their

25. Goncharov, "Stalin–Mao Dialogue," 107.

26. Information memorandum by I. Kalabukhov, first secretary of the Far Eastern Department of the USSR, "About the Claims of the Chinese Leaders With Regard to the Mongolian People's Republic," 30 January 1964, Cold War International History Project (CWIHP) Virtue Archive, http://wwics.si.edu.

27. Ledovsky, "Mikoyan's Secret Mission," *FEA* 3 (1995): 87.

28. Shi Zhe, *Zai Lishi Juren Shenbian,* 384.

29. "Report of Milovan Djilas about a secret Soviet–Bulgarian–Yugoslav meeting 10 February 1948," CWIHP, *Bulletin, Issue 10,* (March 1998): 131.

spheres of influence in China. Zhou reasoned that Stalin probably feared a third world war with the United States.[30] There is, however, no evidence that the CCP leadership applied the same analysis to Stalin's prevention of the CCP from moving northward into Outer Mongolia, which might have been motivated by a fear of Communist China itself.

Such fear was once voiced by N. V. Roshchin, the Soviet ambassador to the GMD government before the CCP's takeover. At the end of 1948, in a conversation with Peng Zhaoxian, the interior minister in the GMD government, Roshchin admitted that Moscow suspected a Titoist tendency in the CCP. Therefore, he explained, it would be ideal to end the Chinese Civil War with foreign mediation because, if a big communist country emerged along the Soviet Union's eastern border, it would create a series of serious problems for the Soviet government.[31]

Mutual suspicions, second guessing, and misunderstandings between the CCP and Moscow would neither slow down the CCP's sweeping triumph in China nor hinder the formation of a formal PRC–Soviet alliance. The Mongolia question, however, continued to bedevil the emerging partnership between the two communist states. Although the Mikoyan mission dashed the CCP leaders' hope for incorporating the MPR into the PRC, it did not solve the question of how Outer Mongolian independence arranged Moscow and the CCP's domestic enemy, the GMD regime, should be inherited by the incoming CCP government. Obviously, after the CCP took power, the fate of the 1945 GMD–Soviet treaty had to be decided, and Mongolia would be affected.

In June 1949, when the CCP sent its own secret mission to Moscow headed by Liu Shaoqi, the future of the 1945 treaty was on the mission's agenda. Liu—accompanied by two senior CCP officials, Gao Gang and Wang Jiaxiang—had several meetings with Stalin. In a "report" hurriedly prepared in Moscow, the CCP envoys presented to Stalin a series of issues that they wished to discuss.[32] Conspicuously, despite Stalin's known qualification of the 1945 treaty as an "unequal" one, the Chinese still informed Stalin that

30. Liu Xiao, *Chushi Sulian Banian* (Eight-Year Ambassadorship in the Soviet Union) (Beijing: Zhonggong Dangshi Ziliao Chubanshe, 1986), 4. After Stalin's death, this point was made repeatedly by the CCP leadership as one of his mistakes. Recent scholarship in China disputes the assertion and categorizes it as a misunderstanding of the Soviet policy on the CCP's part. See Yang Kuisong, *Mao Zedong yu Mosike*, 266–70.

31. Zhou Qiliang and Chu Liangru, *Teshu er Fuza de Keti* (A Peculiar and Complex Subject) (Wuhan: Hubei Renmin Chubanshe, 1993), 456–57.

32. Xu Zehao, *Wang Jiaxiang Zhuan*, 456, 458–60.

the CCP was "completely willing to inherit the treaty" because it had helped the Chinese people in the past and would continue to do so in the future. The "report" also proposed some alternative "procedures" to deal with the technical aspects of the treaty's continuation.

Then, interestingly, the "report" raised the Mongolia question not in relation to the 1945 treaty but as one of the grievances against the Soviet Union among some allegedly misinformed Chinese people ("democratic parties, students, and workers"). The CCP envoys also let the Soviets know that the Chinese people had complaints about the continued Soviet occupation of Lüshun and about the Soviet Red Army's removal of machinery from Manchuria after Japan's surrender. The "report" explained how the CCP defended the Soviet policies in these matters and had made efforts to correct the Chinese people's "wrong" ideas. About Outer Mongolia, the "report" stated:

> As for the question of the Mongolian People's Republic, our explanation is that the Mongolian people wanted independence, and we should recognize Mongolian independence according to the principle of national self-determination. But if the MPR is willing to join China, we of course welcome it. This matter should be decided solely by the Mongolian people.

The Chinese wanted to know "whether or not these explanations are correct" in Stalin's opinion.[33]

To Stalin, the CCP's reiteration of its willingness to continue the 1945 treaty must have been both perplexing and satisfying. In considering the matter in conjunction with a statement made by Liu's "report" that the CCP would obey decisions made by the Soviet Communist Party, Stalin could only take these as evidence that the CCP leadership lacked national consciousness. When making his response to the "report," Stalin repeated his view to the CCP envoys that the 1945 treaty was "unequal" but had to be so at the time because the Soviet government was dealing with the GMD regime. He was quite willing to settle the treaty question with Mao, who was scheduled to come to Moscow in December.

Sincerely or not, Stalin also rejected the notion that the CCP should obey Moscow's decisions, asserting that "both parties have to be accountable to

33. "Report to the Soviet Communist Party Central Committee and Stalin on Behalf of the CCP Central Committee, 4 July 1949," Liu Shaoqi, *Jianguo yilai Liu Shaoqi Wengao* (Liu Shaoqi's Manuscripts after the Establishment of the State; hereafter *JYLW*) (Beijing: Zhongyang Wenxian Chubanshe, 1998), 1: 15–16.

their own people." This subject led him to lecture the CCP envoys: "One must protect his own state and national interests. You do not understand this because during a century of colonial and semicolonial conditions [Chinese] people's interests were violated by others wantonly."[34] Stalin's admonition seemed to be on target when Gao Gang in one of the conversations proposed that Manchuria be turned into the seventeenth republic of the Soviet Union. Whereas Liu was upset by Gao's proposition, Stalin appeared lighthearted and addressed Gao mockingly as "comrade Zhang Zuolin," the warlord who had ruled Manchuria in the 1920s and collaborated with the Japanese.[35]

Yet, while appearing generous and accommodating in general, Stalin remained adamant in dealing with the Mongolia question raised circuitously in Liu's "report." In the "report," Stalin highlighted the sentence on the Mongolian people's right to decide their status and wrote "yes" in the margin. He told Liu in effect that as far as the Soviet government was concerned, the question of Outer Mongolia was settled, and that the Chinese and Mongolian comrades would have to talk to each other directly if any change should be made.[36]

Liu's mission was another bizarre episode in the CCP's interparty diplomacy with Moscow on the eve of its transformation into China's government. If Liu and his co-envoys appeared overly respectful to Stalin, it was partially because of Stalin's stature in the minds of CCP leaders and partially because of the CCP leadership's anxiety to dispel any suspicion in Moscow about its reliability. Liu's "report" was an exemplary document that mixed Chinese Communists' explicit homage to Moscow's revolutionary hegemony with incoming PRC leaders' implicit exploration of Soviet foreign policy parameters. Liu overdid the first part. After learning of the envoys' suggestion about CCP obedience to Moscow, Mao said he thought such a notion was inappropriate even for internal discussions in the CCP. He immediately cabled Liu and asked him to get Stalin's agreement to delete the content from the "report."[37]

34. Liu Shaoqi, Gao Gang, and Wang Jiaxiang to the CCP Center, 18 July 1949, *JYLW,* 1: 22–28 n. 16; Shi Zhe, *Wo de Yisheng: Shi Zhe Zishu* (My Life: In Shi Zhe's Own Words) (Beijing: Renmin Chubanshe, 2001), 306.

35. Goncharov, "Stalin–Mao Dialogue," 109–10; Xu Zehao, *Wang Jiaxiang Zhuan,* 460–61.

36. Andrei Ledovsky, "The Moscow Visit of a Delegation of the Communist Party of China in June to August 1949," *FEA* 4 (1996): 70, 83; Qiu Jing, "Meeting between the Two Red Giants," 211.

37. Mao Zedong to Liu Shaoqi, 14 July 1949, *JYLW,* 1: 21 n. 15.

The Gao Gang episode was similarly revealing. According to any national standard, his behavior was overtly treacherous to China's interests. It is nevertheless remarkable that in 1949 neither did Gao feel any restraint in openly making his suggestion nor was his behavior disciplined within the CCP afterward.[38] At the time, among senior CCP leaders, Gao's subordination of China's national interests to the CCP's international loyalty might appear extreme, but it was by no means unique. Thus, the overall undertone of the Liu mission appeared to have a placating effect on Stalin's psyche; otherwise, he would not have given a lecture on national consciousness to the CCP's envoys and forgotten temporarily that this very party was suspected in Moscow as a traveler with Tito.

After the two rounds of interparty diplomacy conducted with the Mikoyan and Liu missions, the CCP and the Soviets had to stop testing the waters when Mao himself made a trip to Moscow in December 1949. During the early years of the Cold War, this communist summit was one of the most mysterious events to policymakers on the other side of the "Iron Curtain." Today, despite intermittent declassifications of archival materials in both China and Russia, certain important aspects of the summit remain in obscurity.[39] Among these the most baffling to historians is the reason for Stalin's "change of mind" about the fate of the 1945 Sino-Soviet treaty.

Having learned from the Mikoyan and Liu missions about the Soviet government's view that the 1945 treaty was an "unequal" one, Mao came to Moscow fully prepared to negotiate a new treaty with Stalin. Yet there is

38. Goncharov, "Stalin–Mao Dialogue," 111–13.

39. Shuguang Zhang and Jian Chen, eds., *Chinese Communist Foreign Policy and the Cold War in Asia: New Documentary Evidence, 1944–1950* (Chicago: Imprint Publications, 1996), collects and translates into English a good selection of CCP documents on foreign policy that surfaced in China in recent years. Mao's trip to Moscow is reflected in documents 2.39-2.69, pp. 127–48. These, however, must be compared with Soviet documents made available by "Stalin's Conversations with Chinese Leaders," *Cold War International History Project Bulletin* (hereafter *CWIHP Bulletin*), issues 6–7 (Winter 1995–96): 3–29; "Mao on Sino-Soviet Relations: Two Conversations with the Soviet Ambassador, Introduction by Odd Arne Westad," ibid., 157–69; and "Translated Russian and Chinese Documents on Mao Zedong's Visit to Moscow, December 1949–February 1950," *CWIHP Bulletin,* issues 8–9 (Winter 1996–97): 226–36. The recent English edition of Dieter Heinzig's *The Soviet Union and Communist China, 1945–1950: The Arduous Road to the Alliance* (Armonk, N.Y.: M. E. Sharpe, 2004) is perhaps the most exhaustive effort of using available information to sort out the CCP–Moscow relationship of the period.

evidence that after the Mikoyan and Liu encounters, the Soviet side became less certain. In November, the Chinese side twice indicated to the Soviets that if Mao's visit would lead to the conclusion of a new treaty, Zhou would travel with Mao and participate in treaty negotiations. Moscow's reaction to Zhou's visit was ambiguous, seemingly implying a hesitation about the treaty question.[40] Still, Mao was dumbfounded at his first meeting with Stalin on December 16. Completely departing from his earlier rhetoric about how the CCP victory would recast the Sino-Soviet relationship, at the meeting Stalin told Mao that because the 1945 treaty had been concluded "with the consent of America and England," the Soviet government "[has] decided not to modify any of the points of this treaty for now," lest any change give the Western powers an excuse to raise other questions, such as Southern Sakhalin and the Kurils. Stalin offered instead to adjust certain aspects of the treaty "in reality" while maintaining all the old treaty provisions "in form." Then, during the next month, the treaty question was suspended in the air while the two sides only had exchanges of secondary significance. Mao, between his good and bad moods, used the time to visit several places in his host country.[41]

When Mao and Stalin met again on January 22, 1950, however, Stalin appeared a different person. Now he suggested that all the existing agreements between China and the Soviet Union, including the 1945 treaty, should be changed. He explained to Mao that in 1945 the war against Japan was "at the very heart of the treaty," but since Japan's defeat the treaty had become an "anachronism." When Mao reminded Stalin that changing the old treaty would contradict the Yalta decisions, Stalin said:

> True, it does—and to hell with it! Once we have taken up the position that the treaties must be changed, we must go all the way. It is true that

40. Shen Zhihua, *Mao Zedong, Sidalin yu Chaoxian Zhanzheng* (Mao Zedong, Stalin and the Korean War) (Guangzhou: Guangdong Renmin Chubanshe, 2003), 132. Shen's interpretation of the 1949 encounters between the two sides differs from the argument presented here in contending that before meeting with Mao, Stalin never "sincerely" expressed willingness to change the old 1945 treaty. Stalin's sincerity is not the question here. The issue is how the Soviets' qualification of the 1945 treaty as an "unequal" one may have impressed CCP leaders.

41. "Conversation between Stalin and Mao, Moscow, 16 December 1949," *CWIHP Bulletin,* issues 6–7 (Winter 1995–96): 5; Pei Jianzhang, ed., *Zhonghua Renmin Gongheguo Waijiaoshi, 1949–1956* (Diplomatic History of the People's Republic of China, 1949–1956) (Beijing: Shijie Zhishi Chubanshe, 1994), 18–19.

for us this entails certain inconveniences, and we will have to struggle against the Americans. But we are already reconciled to that.[42]

A number of historical studies have made judicious analyses of Stalin's vacillation. Scholars in China tend to attribute Stalin's change of mind on January 22 to the PRC's diplomatic progress with noncommunist countries and Mao's firm demand for a new treaty, whereas Cold War studies in the West ascribe Stalin's volt-face mainly to certain developments in the U.S. government's Asia policy.[43] The Chinese scholar Shen Zhihua's meticulous study points out that actually in early January the Soviet side had already decided to grant Mao's demand for a new treaty and that, by January 22, the Central Committee of the Soviet Communist Party approved a series of draft agreements to be used for negotiations with the Chinese. These draft agreements indicated, however, that Moscow's so-called new démarche merely reversed Stalin's earlier formula about "form" and "reality." Now a new treaty of alliance would be concluded with the PRC "in form" while the old treaty privileges would be preserved "in reality."[44] In Shen's account, therefore, Stalin's "to hell with it" statement was more rhetorical than substantial and did not represent a drastic policy reversion.

The old treaty restraints were nevertheless overstepped on that day. Ascending to power in China, the CCP was making conscientious efforts to start China's interstate relations anew. On different occasions in the spring and summer of 1949, including those conversations with Mikoyan in Xibaipo, Mao defined a two-pronged foreign policy orientation with his characteristic lingo: "Set up a new kitchen," meaning nonrecognition of treaties and diplomatic arrangements made by the GMD regime in the past and replacement of these with the PRC's own; and "cleaning the house before inviting

42. "Conversation between Stalin and Mao, Moscow, 22 January 1950," *CWIHP Bulletin,* issues 6–7 (Winter 1995–96): 7–8.

43. For different views, see Pei Jianzhang, *Zhonghua Renmin Gongheguo Waijiaoshi,* 19–20; Yang Kuisong, *Zhonggong yu Mosike de Guanxi,* 617–18, and *Mao Zedong yu Mosike,* 297–98; Vladislav Zubok, "'To Hell with Yalta!' Stalin Opts for a New Status Quo," *CWIHP Bulletin,* issues 6–7 (Winter 1995–96): 24–27; Odd Arne Westad, "Unwrapping the Stalin–Mao Talks: Setting the Record Straight," ibid., 23–24, and "Fighting for Friendship: Mao, Stalin, and the Sino-Soviet Treaty of 1950," *CWIHP Bulletin,* issues 8–9 (Winter 1996–97): 224–26; Heinzig, *The Soviet Union and Communist China,* 298.

44. Shen Zhihua, "Clashes of Interests and Their Settlement during Negotiations on the Chinese–Soviet Treaty of 1950," *FEA* 3 (2002): 101–3.

guests in," meaning the postponement of establishing diplomatic relationship with "imperialist" countries until the new CCP government had purged China of vestiges of internal hostile forces and foreign imperialist influence.[45]

In practice, these processes involved not only a series of complex policy decisions regarding individual foreign countries but also a strenuous and slow grooming of the CCP's own diplomatic personnel that could carry out these policies. Although Mao chose to single out "imperialist" countries as the targets of the orientation, the policy had a general impact on China's foreign relations, and even the Soviet Union was not completely exempted.[46] Without question, though never admitted by the CCP's official history, a new treaty with the Soviet Union at the beginning of the PRC would be the most important building block for the "new kitchen." Yet, after Mao's arrival in Moscow, Stalin appeared tenaciously nostalgic about the old Chinese "kitchen" until January 22. Stalin's behavior not only upset the CCP leaders' historical memory of the spirit of the 1919 Karakhan Declaration but also contradicted their recent positive impression derived from the Mikoyan and Liu missions.

Between National and Bloc Interests

With respect to Stalin's shifting preference of "kitchens," a couple of questions remain untouched by previous studies. One is why Stalin, not once but twice, changed his mind on the treaty question between the Mikoyan mission in February 1949 and his talk with Mao on January 22, 1950. Another is what policy adjustments or change of attitude happened on the Chinese side during the same period that may have affected Stalin's stand on the treaty question. An attempt to answer these questions is made here, in what has to be a hypothetical analysis waiting for further information from Chinese,

45. Shi Zhe, *Zai Lishi Juren Shenbian,* 379; Pei Jianzhang, *Zhonghua Renmin Gongheguo Waijiao Shi,* 2–3.

46. For the generational evolution of the PRC's diplomatic personnel, see Xiaohong Liu, *Chinese Ambassadors: The Rise of Diplomatic Professionalism since 1949* (Seattle: University of Washington Press, 2001). Xiaodong Wang's "China Learning to Stand Up: Nationalism in the Formative Years of the People's Republic of China," in *Exploring Nationalisms of China: Themes and Conflicts,* ed. C. X. George Wei and Xiaoyuan Liu (Westport, Conn.: Greenwood Press, 2002), 77–100, uses Russian and regional Chinese archival materials to reveal how the PRC and USSR annoyed and adapted to each other when the CCP was stepping into the role of national state government.

Mongolian, and Russian archives. This analysis goes beyond the Cold War paradigm and finds that Stalin's vacillation had more to do with the Mongolian buffer between China and Russia than with the Cold War contest between the Eastern and Western blocs.

In the East Asian international politics of the late 1940s and early 1950s, a fundamental question was what force challenged the postwar status quo. In this period, despite their global competition dubbed the "Cold War," both the Soviet Union and the United States followed the rules in a power-balancing game and were interested in maintaining their power relationship based on the military realities and diplomatic dealings wrought during World War II. In Asia, the Soviet–U.S. balance was mainly reflected in the geopolitical consequences of the Yalta diplomacy and the Sino-Soviet negotiations in Moscow in the summer of 1945. It was the CCP, already a quasi-state force at the end of World War II, that posed the most serious challenge to this Yalta–Moscow system. This was so not only because the CCP was not a party in the system's making but also because the specter of the CCP's victory in China threatened to insert a reunified China as a third force into East Asian affairs, which had hitherto been dominated by the two superpowers.

As of 1949, much of the American share of the Yalta–Moscow system had been demolished when the CCP drove the GMD regime onto the island of Taiwan. The development was not interpreted in the Kremlin as a pure gain for the Soviet Union because now the Soviet share of the system became problematic as well. Though appearing incongruous with its ideological alliance with Moscow, Communist China, not the United States, posed a power-political question about the Soviet gains in the Yalta–Moscow system. Therefore, although previous studies are right about Stalin's obsession with the spoils from the Yalta–Moscow system and about his attention to the Americans' reaction to the collapse of that system, they tend to exaggerate U.S. foreign policy as *the* compelling reason that Stalin adjusted his stand on the postwar status quo in East Asia in general and on the 1945 treaty in particular.

Because a significant portion of the Yalta–Moscow spoils was underwritten by the 1945 treaty, in dealing with the CCP challenge, the Soviet leaders had to find out what was the CCP's attitude toward the treaty. They also had to decide what should be the premise for the relationship between the Soviet Union and a Communist China. Hence the trial balloons during the Mikoyan and Liu missions. As shown above, on both occasions the Soviet strategy was to signal to the CCP that a new beginning of the Sino-Soviet relationship would be initiated upon the CCP victory in China. The Soviets hoped to discover the extent to which the CCP would want to cancel or modify the legacies of the GMD policy toward the Soviet Union. To Moscow's surprise, although operating in China's postwar political environment of upsurging nationalism, CCP leaders appeared quite satisfied with the benefits from the "friendly" existence of Soviet influence in Manchuria. Before Mao's visit in Moscow, therefore, it was the Soviet side that repeatedly made negative references to the "unequal treaty" of 1945, while the CCP appeared flexible with regard to this "patriotic" instrument.

Over only one concrete issue with the 1945 treaty, MPR independence, did the two sides completely lack such reciprocal accommodations. The tenacity of the CCP's Mongolian complex was sustained by the CCP leaders' commitment to the traditional Chinese ideal of "grand unity," an ideological adaptation of the Soviet federal state model, and a political urge to outdo the GMD in defending the integrity of China's "national territory." To Stalin and his associates, the Mongolian buffer was not just a result of the 1945 treaty but also the culmination of more than three decades' Soviet security policy. After two rounds of encounters with the CCP leaders in 1949, Moscow was compelled to make two strategic readjustments in dealing with the CCP challenge. One was to shelve the notion that the CCP victory in China should be treated as an overriding factor in the next stage of the Sino-Soviet relationship. Especially, the CCP should be discouraged from believing so. Another was to stop posing the 1945 treaty as an open-ended question to the CCP and instead to prepare to avail the Soviet government of all the necessary legal and political grounds provided by the treaty to fend off the CCP's overture on Mongolia.

In other words, although Moscow's postwar strategic focus in Asia was on the United States and Washington indeed had every reason to regret President Franklin Roosevelt's concessions to Stalin at Yalta, these did not blunt the Soviet leaders' sense of the geopolitical challenge coming with the rise of Communist China. Actually, during the months between the CCP's victory in China and the beginning of the Korean War, Communist China was the only geopolitical challenge to Moscow's security arrangements along its southeastern borders. To the Soviet leaders, in 1949 as in 1945, their advance position in Manchuria was negotiable, but the Mongolian buffer was untouchable.

This was the main reason that Stalin surprised Mao at their December 16 meeting. Although the name of Mongolia was not uttered even once during the meeting, the issue must have loomed large in Stalin's mind. In contending that *every* point of the 1945 treaty should be maintained, Stalin of course included the 1945 decision on Mongolia. To preempt any of Mao's arguments for treaty revision based on the CCP victory, Stalin now used the Yalta system, or the superpower relationship, as his premise for discussing the 1945 treaty. This tactic clearly indicated that insofar as Soviet treaty rights were concerned, Stalin would deal with Mao in the same manner as he had dealt with Jiang Jieshi's diplomats in 1945. Power relations, not revolutionary camaraderie, would underline the Stalin–Mao negotiations.

In his seemingly pliable response, Mao said that the American–British angle had not been considered by the CCP leadership. The CCP leadership certainly understood how a CCP–Moscow alliance would affect the American–British angle. Mao was only surprised that Stalin would use the Western powers to delimit the new Sino-Soviet relationship. Or, his words might also be a circuitous way to tell Stalin that the CCP regarded the treaty as a bilateral issue between the PRC and the USSR in which both sides' interests, not just Russian interests in Sakhalin and the Kurils, mattered equally. According to Mao's telegram to Liu Shaoqi after the meeting, he also told Stalin what he believed should be the premise for the treaty question: "The public opinion in China believes that as the old treaty was signed by the GMD, it has lost its standing with the GMD's downfall." This was in effect what Stalin had conveyed to the CCP leadership via the Mikoyan mission. After listening to Mao, Stalin conceded that the old treaty should be revised, but this had to wait for two more years.[47]

In retrospect, Stalin's tactic erred in unnecessarily alienating Mao, who in the years to come would repeatedly grumble about Stalin's initial reluctance to sign a new treaty with him. On the basis of the available evidence, it can be concluded that in coming to Moscow, Mao was already convinced of Soviet leaders' intransigence in maintaining Mongolian independence

---

47. "Conversation between Stalin and Mao, Moscow, 16 December 1949," *CWIHP Bulletin,* issues 6–7 (Winter 1995–96): 5. Mao's telegram is cited in Pei Jianzhang, *Zhonghua Renmin Gongheguo Waijiao Shi,* 17–18, and for an English version see "Telegram, Mao Zedong to Liu Shaoqi, 18 December 1949," in *Chinese Communist Foreign Policy and the Cold War in Asia,* ed. Zhang and Chen, 128. Heinzig, *The Soviet Union and Communist China,* 281, hypothesizes Stalin's first "change of mind" by accepting Stalin's words at their face value; i.e., Stalin "was telling the truth" in expressing a fear that the Western powers use a new Sino-Soviet treaty as the pretext to alter the Yalta arrangements about southern Sakhalin and the Kurils. This is not convincing and fails to explain why such a fear did not exist during the Mikoyan and Liu Shaoqi missions just a few months before.

and was therefore ready to comply. The problem was that Stalin was just as convinced of the CCP leaders' determination to reincorporate the MPR into China.

In this regard, the first few diplomatic steps made by the new Beijing government in 1949 did not mollify Moscow's concern. On October 3, 1949, the Soviet Union became the first country to establish diplomatic relations with the PRC. In the next four days, seven other communist bloc countries, including the MPR, extended diplomatic recognition to the PRC and offered to establish diplomatic relations with Beijing. Each of these governments, except the MPR, received a positive reply from Zhou the same day of its own telegram to Beijing. Choibalsan alone had to wait for ten embarrassing days before hearing from Zhou.[48] This was a time when no event in Beijing's relationship with other communist bloc countries, especially with Ulaanbaatar, could escape the Kremlin's scrutiny. Beijing's positive response to Choibalsan was a good sign to Moscow, but the CCP leadership's hesitation was suspicious enough to give Stalin pause for thought about the sincerity of the CCP leaders' diplomatic gesture toward the MPR.

Stalin did not wait idly for the CCP's next move, and he took an unusual step in preparing the MPR leadership to fend off Beijing's Mongolian overture. In August 1949, Choibalsan visited Moscow for a medical examination. At the time, some MPR leaders wished to discuss with Moscow the MPR's entry into the Soviet Union. What featured in Stalin's conversation with Choibalsan in late September was, however, the issue of unification between Inner and Outer Mongolia. Stalin informed Choibalsan of a recent exchange with Mao on the subject and of Mao's favorable attitude. Choibalsan agreed that that would be "the right thing to do" but insisted that Inner Mongolia join the MPR and an independent Mongolia not become part of China. Then Stalin made these comments:

> So you are in favor of independence rather than autonomous privileges? I feel the same way. This is something you must decide for yourselves. But there is probably no need to hurry and decide under what conditions

---

48. O. Chuluun, "The Two Phases in Mongolian–Chinese Relations, 1949–1972," *FEA* 1 (1974): 24; Ma Yong, comp., *Guoshi Quanshu* (Complete Manual of Country Affairs), 4 vols. (Beijing: Tuanjie Chubanshe, 1997), 3: 3077–79. The other six countries were Bulgaria, Rumania, Hungary, North Korea, Czechoslovakia, and Poland. Interestingly, in an official diplomatic history compiled by the PRC Foreign Ministry, Pei Jianzhang, *Zhonghua Renmin Gongheguo Waijiaoshi,* 83, postdates the MPR telegram for ten days and thus renders Zhou's reply an "immediate" one.

unification will take place. You need to adopt a clever policy that is not going to cause any dispute with China. Since Mao Zedong and his government are directing all their attention right now toward capturing Guangdong and completely liberating their own nation, they do not have time to consider domestic nationalities, nor do they have the experience. However, after the occupation of Guangdong, they will probably be willing to discuss this matter. There is something else you should also take into consideration. If you propose to Mao Zedong that Inner Mongolia should be unified with Outer Mongolia, he will probably object; he has his own problems. When Jiang Jieshi took power he broke his nation into pieces and gave them to foreign imperialists. He even accepted the independence of Outer Mongolia. Mao Zedong, however, intends to put together what the Guomindang dismembered, and make the country unified. Therefore, for Mao Zedong, it would even more difficult to allow Inner Mongolia to unite with another nation. After the October Revolution, nations such as Finland and Poland separated from Russia and made into independent states. Only Lenin was able to do this. Mao Zedong is not Lenin, and cannot do this.

At that point, Choibalsan asked whether or not a unified Mongolia could become part of the USSR. Stalin responded:

You would not need to become a part of the Soviet Union. In supporting the unification of Outer and Inner Mongolia, we wish for it to be a unified, independent state that does not fall under the jurisdiction of Russia or China. In the same mind-set, we have always stood for the unification of a single Bolshevik nation, and accordingly, have united Western Ukraine with Western Belarus, for example."[49]

In the light of Stalin's rejection of Mao's overture over Outer Mongolia during the Mikoyan mission, this conversation was typical of the satellite relationship between Moscow and Ulaanbaatar, which was less equal but closer than the CCP–Soviet partnership. Surely Stalin did not need to sound

49. Ookhnoin Batsaikhan, "Issues Concerning Mongolian Independence from the Soviet Union and China: The Attempt to Incorporate Mongolia within the USSR and the Positions of Soviet Leaders, Stalin, Molotov, and Mikoyan," 3–5, paper presented at the "International Workshop on Mongolia and the Cold War," Ulaanbaatar, March 19–20, 2004.

out Mongolian leaders' thinking for the sake of getting back to the Chinese, which he had already done in accord with Moscow's established two-Mongolia policy. The session took place only because Stalin wanted to prepare Choibalsan mentally for a new round of Sino-Soviet diplomacy that might affect the MPR. To Choibalsan, it was crystal clear that in greeting the ascending CCP power in China, the only "clever policy" for him to follow was to obey Stalin's order: to resist any possible CCP démarche for abolishing Outer Mongolian independence but not to scheme in Inner Mongolia, lest it disturb the Sino-Soviet alliance in the making. In making the distinction between Lenin and Mao, Stalin demonstrated his grasp of the nationalist, unifying drive of the emerging Communist China. Although still belittling the CCP's experience in dealing with "domestic nationalities," Stalin did not underestimate the CCP's determination to reverse the disintegrating process of the Chinese state. He was fully prepared for a maneuvering with the CCP leadership premised on an "international," not "internationalist," basis.

Yet Stalin overprepared himself with regard to Mongolia. Arriving in Moscow, Mao was ready to put the Mongolia question aside for now and concentrate on another goal as the inaugural feat of the new China's diplomacy. This was a new treaty of alliance with the Soviet Union, a goal for which the Soviets had so far appeared more willing to cooperate. In Moscow, Mao told Ivan Kovalev, Stalin's personal envoy to the CCP who accompanied Mao on his trip, that "relying on agreements with the Soviet Union, we would be able to immediately revise and annul the unequal treaties concluded by Chiang Kai-shek [Jiang Jieshi] government with imperialist countries."[50] To the CCP leadership, a new treaty with the Soviet Union would not just accomplish its revolutionary goal of bringing China into the socialist camp headed by the Soviet Union but would also, just as important, facilitate its nationalist aspiration of equalizing China's standing with the international community in general. Now Mao appeared completely receptive of Stalin's own earlier rhetoric on the 1945 "unequal" treaty and was prepared to start with Moscow in setting up China's "new kitchen."

On January 2, 1950, Mao's intention of discussing the 1945 treaty with the Soviet government was publicized by the Soviet press in the form of Mao's press interview. On the same day, Stalin sent Molotov and Mikoyan to Mao to probe his thinking about how the summit should proceed next.

---

50. Goncharov, "Stalin–Mao Dialogue," 103–4.

According to Mao's ensuing telegram to the CCP Central Committee, his visitors wanted to know Mao's opinion about the "Sino-Soviet treaty and other matters." Mao took the opportunity to propose three options for dealing with the treaty question. Both options two and three would not lead to a new treaty, and clearly option one was Mao's preference:

(A) To conclude a new Sino-Soviet treaty of friendship and alliance. This approach will bring about immense benefit. If the Sino-Soviet relationship is solidified on the basis of a new treaty, China's workers, peasants, intellectuals and the left wing of the national bourgeoisie will be thrilled, and the right wing of the national bourgeoisie will be isolated; in the international scene, we will be able to augment enormously our political capital to deal with imperialist countries, and to reexamine all the treaties concluded between China and these countries in the past.[51]

By "new treaty," Mao did not mean that *every point* of the 1945 treaty had to be scuttled. The next day, he sent a telegram to his colleagues in Beijing spelling out the connections between the prospective new treaty and the old one:

In comparison to the old treaty, [the new treaty] may perhaps make some changes regarding the question of Lüshun and Dalian, but the concrete content is yet to be negotiated. Meanwhile the objective of defense against possible aggressions from Japan and allies and recognition of Outer Mongolia's independence will remain the fundamental spirit of the new treaty.[52]

Thus a negotiation strategy of quid pro quos emerged from the CCP side: Communist China would join the Soviet camp and recognize MPR independence, and in return Moscow would agree to conclude a new treaty and modify its old treaty privileges in Manchuria.

The tricky part of this strategy was that Mao had no intention of using

---

51. "Telegrams to the CCPCC on Zhou Enlai's trip to the Soviet Union to Participate in the Negotiations" (1), 2 January 1950, in *Jianguo Yilai Mao Zedong Wengao,* by Mao Zedong,(Mao Zedong's Manuscripts since the Foundation of the State) (Beijing: Zhongyang Wenxian Chubanshe, 1987), 1: 211 (hereafter cited as *JYMW*).

52. "Telegrams to the Center on Zhou Enlai's Trip to the Soviet Union to Participate in the Negotiations" (2), 3 January 1950, *JYMW,* 1: 213.

the Mongolia question as an explicit bargaining chip for other concrete issues. Mao might have two reasons for not doing so. For one thing, given Mao's reluctance in acquiescing in MPR independence, it would go against his nature to profess the CCP's concession on Mongolia before Stalin unequivocally supported a new treaty with China. For another, the GMD regime's disgraced diplomatic formula of 1945 was still fresh in the collective memory of the Chinese people, which had used Mongolia as a bargaining chip with the Soviet government. Mao certainly did not want to create even a slim impression that he was following Jiang Jieshi's footsteps. He would rather leave the credit for "losing" Mongolia entirely to his nationalist predecessor. Yet Mao understood his task perfectly: To wrest a new treaty from Stalin, he must firmly side with the Soviet Union against Japan *and allies,* meaning the United States, and he must leave Outer Mongolia alone.

Thus, the contemporary issue of the Cold War and the historical question of Mongolia became intertwined in the making of a new Sino-Soviet alliance. This signified the duality of an emerging, post-Yalta geopolitical status quo in East Asia: A Sino-Soviet bloc was being forged to counterbalance the Unites States in East Asia, but this bloc would be sustained by an internal balance of power between the two communist giants in Inner Asia, with Mongolia and China's other northern regions serving as buffer zones. This structure would become even clearer after the new treaty was signed.

To Stalin and his associates, Mao's vigorous push since his arrival for a new treaty and his perfect silence on the Mongolia question constituted a sharp contrast to the CCP leadership's mindset on these matters reflected during the Mikoyan and the Liu missions. For a while, they did not know how to proceed. Only after Mao sent impatient signals to the Kremlin through "cursing and complaining" did Soviet leaders realize that a new approach for dealing with Mao had to be adopted soon to avoid a disastrous failure of the first PRC–USSR summit.[53] Hence the Molotov–Mikoyan visit to Mao was staged on January 2 before Stalin himself could formalize a new démarche. On that day, Mao's continued silence on Mongolia must have been reassuring to the Soviets. As a matter of fact, when conversing with Mao on January 2, Molotov agreed on the spot, necessarily on behalf of Stalin, that Zhou should come to Moscow to participate in the negotiations

53. Wu Lengxi, *Shinian Lunzhan,* 1: 14, 146, quotes Mao's two speeches in 1956 and 1957 that include two slightly different versions of how Mao made his intention about a new treaty known to Stalin.

for a new treaty. To Mao, the prospect of his visit in Moscow immediately brightened.

Yet Soviet leaders still could not completely trust Mao—the clever "Chinese Pugachev," in Molotov's words.[54] Nor did Mao take the treaty issue for granted after reaching his understanding with Molotov. On January 6, in a meeting with Soviet foreign minister Andrei Vyshinsky, Mao applied further pressure in adopting a persuasive tone that he was "increasingly coming to the conclusion" about the necessity of concluding a new treaty between the PRC and the USSR. Vyshinsky, despite Molotov's concurrence with Mao four days before, repeated Stalin's December 16 argument that a new treaty or even "reviewing of the existing treaty" might provide the Americans and the British with an excuse to alter existing treaty arrangements and "cause damage to Soviet and Chinese interests." The Molotov–Vyshinsky contradiction necessarily reflected Stalin's own hesitation.[55] To the Soviets, a further test of Mao had to be administered. Here U.S. secretary of state Dean Acheson entered the picture.

On January 12, in a speech to the National Press Club in Washington, Acheson clarified the current American policy on Asia. Whereas Acheson's statement on Washington's hands-off approach to the Taiwan situation might sound suspicious to Beijing, his accusation of the Soviet Union for turning Chinese northern territories, including Outer Mongolia, into Soviet colonies "struck a raw nerve" in the Mao–Stalin talks and especially agitated the Soviets.[56] The Acheson speech was seen in the Kremlin as part of a malicious

54. "Telegrams to the Center on Zhou Enlai's Trip to the Soviet Union to Participate in the Negotiations" (1), 2 January 1950, *JYMW,* 1: 211–12; Felix Chuev, *Molotov Remembers: Inside Kremlin Politics; Conversations with Felix Chuev* (Chicago: Ivan R. Dee, 1993), 81.

55. "From the Diary of A. Y. Vyshinsky: Memorandum of Conversation with the Chairman of the People's Central Government of the People's Republic of China, Mao Zedong, 6 January 1950," *CWIHP Bulletin,* issues 8–9 (Winter 1996–97): 230–31. Heinzig, *The Soviet Union and Communist China,* 293, suggests that the Molotov–Mikoyan visit on January 2 was a decisive breakthrough on the treaty question, and attributes "Vyshinskii's strange behavior" on January 6 to his not being a member of the Politburo and therefore not privy to Stalin's change of mind about the treaty (p. 311). Heinzig, however, fails to explain an important fact revealed in his own study that after January 2, Vyshinsky, Molotov, and Mikoyan were in a three-member commission in charge of preparations for treaty negotiations with the Chinese. On January 5, under Vyshinsky's supervision, the Foreign Ministry completed the first draft treaty (p. 312). Hence Vyshinsky had to be aware of the possible forthcoming treaty negotiations with the Chinese. Together, these facts indicate at most an indecisive "breakthrough" on January 2.

56. Goncharov, Lewis, and Xue, *Uncertain Partners,* 101–2.

American wedge strategy against the Sino-Soviet alliance in the making. Yet, conversely, Acheson provided the Soviets with an opportunity to test Mao on two key issues in their emerging partnership: Communist China's side taking in the Cold War, and its acceptance of the Yalta–Moscow endorsement of the Soviet sphere in northeastern Asia. On January 17, Molotov and Vyshinsky visited Mao and invited him to act in coordination with the Soviet government in refuting Acheson.

According to Molotov's diary, on that day he and Mao understood each other perfectly on how the two governments should respond to the Acheson speech. In referring to the speech, Molotov called Mao's attention to Washington's "clear slander against the Soviet Union" and pointed out that Acheson's accusation of alleged Soviet inroads in China's northern territories was an "example of the extent of Acheson's fabrications." Mao appeared more sarcastic than angry. He said jokingly that "the Americans are making progress" as their secretary of state adopted the "kinds of scoundrels" usually made only by American journalists. Mao had a different concern about the Acheson speech, however. He asked Molotov whether or not the speech might be a "smoke screen" for an American occupation of Taiwan. Molotov did not deny the possibility, but he emphatically suggested that the Chinese government issue a statement to refute Acheson's fabrications, because they also insulted China by implying that the Chinese people had no control over their territories.

Mao agreed to do so but asked whether or not a statement by the Xinhua New Agency would be better. Molotov again stressed that a matter of this magnitude should be handled by the Ministry of Foreign Affairs of the PRC. According to Molotov's record, Mao agreed to take steps as suggested, but he pointed out that the statement would be issued by the deputy minister of foreign affairs because Foreign Minister Zhou Enlai was then on his way to Moscow. Then Mao launched himself into a presentation on how lately the Americans used different channels to test the ground for negotiations with the PRC and how, "to win time to put the country in order," the CCP devised tactics to "postpone the hour of recognition by the USA."[57]

If Stalin intended to use Acheson's "fabrications" about Soviet aggression in China's northern frontiers to pressure Mao to take a clear stand between Moscow and Washington, Mao's attention toward Taiwan showed to the

57. "Document 17: Conversation, V. M. Molotov and A. V. Vyshinsky with Mao Zedong, Moscow, 17 January 1950," *CWIHP Bulletin,* issues 8–9 (Winter 1996–97): 232–34.

Soviet leaders that China's anti-American struggle pointed to a different geographic direction. Mao's claimed success in delaying Washington's recognition of the PRC, regardless the facts, also informed the Soviets of what leverage the CCP might in theory or in practice possess in its bargaining with Moscow. Nevertheless, Mao treated the matter of refuting the Acheson speech seriously. He personally prepared a statement and sent it back to Liu Shaoqi in Beijing on January 19. But instead of publicizing the statement through the Ministry of Foreign Affairs as he had promised Molotov, Mao ordered its publication under the name of Hu Qiaomu, chief of the PRC's News Agency. When the statement appeared in the *People's Daily* of January 21, it was decorated with a cartoon by the caricaturist Hua Junwu. Thus, the form of the statement's publication made it more like a piece of sarcastic polemic than a solemn government protestation.[58]

Furthermore, the content of Mao's refutation of Acheson diverged remarkably from the Soviet government's statement issued under the name of Soviet foreign minister Vyshinsky on January 21. The Soviet piece targeted Acheson's remark on Outer Mongolia directly, stating that Mongolia had been an independent country for more than thirty years and that this fact had been accepted by both the Yalta Conference and the Chinese government in 1945. It also pointed out that a "normal diplomatic relationship" now existed between the MPR and the PRC.[59] In contrast, Mao's rejoinder not only did not utter a word to justify MPR independence but also avoided any reference to the MPR as a separate state. After accusing Acheson of making the "most shameless lie" in suggesting Soviet aggressions in "*China's* four northern areas [Outer Mongolia, Inner Mongolia, Xinjiang, and Manchuria; emphasis added]," Mao just pointed out that in the past two years the American government had made a series of self-contradictory statements about the relationship between the CCP and the Soviet Union.[60]

This peculiar difference between Mao's and Moscow's statements

58. "Telegram on the Publication of a Talk to Repudiate Rumors Made by Acheson, 19 January 1950," *JYMW*, 1: 245; "Central People's Government News Agency Director Hu Qiaomu Refutes the Shameless Rumor Made by U.S. Secretary of State Acheson," *Renmin Ribao*, 21 February 1950.

59. "Soviet Foreign Minister Vyshisky's statement of Refuting Acheson's Absurd Accusations," *Renmin Ribao*, 22 February 1950; Shi Zhe, *Wo de Yisheng*, 349–50.

60. Mao Zedong, "Refutation of Acheson's Shameless Lies," in *Mao Zedong Waijiao Wenxuan* (Selected Works of Mao Zedong on Diplomacy) (Beijing: Zhongyang Wenxian Chubanshe and Shijie Zhishi Chubanshe, 1994), 126–28.

puzzled a Chinese participant in the Moscow negotiations for five decades. Shi Zhe was Mao's interpreter during the Moscow negotiations. When his memoir was first published in 1991, he did not or could not say anything about the Mao/Soviet divergence in refuting Acheson. But, in a more personal recollection told to his daughter, which was completed in April 1998, four months before his death, Shi could not resist adding one pregnant comment to his story: "How did Mao think about Acheson's lies? It cannot be known." On Mao's side in Moscow, Shi felt mystified by a certain attitude of Mao's that was at least incompatible with his open statement on the Acheson speech.[61]

Now it is no longer a mystery how Mao and other CCP leaders thought about the Soviet responsibility for separating Outer Mongolia from China. In a conversation with some Japanese socialists in July 1964, Mao blamed the Yalta diplomacy for allowing Moscow to place Outer Mongolia under its domination "under the pretext of assuring the independence of Mongolia". Obviously, Mao wanted to treat the matter as a case of China's victimization by deals among great powers rather than a result of the 1945 GMD–Moscow agreement on MPR independence. Afterward, Mao's remarks were published by the Japanese and Western press. When confronted by an inquiry from an official MPR delegation, Chinese foreign minister Chen Yi was evasive. Chen contended that the Japanese and Western press made a scandal out of the matter, whereas their own "publications are very confused." Yet he declined to offer a written clarification to the Mongols.[62] A recent memoir of Wang Dongxing, another Chinese participant in the Moscow negotiations, reveals that in his last few years, Mao still fumed over Stalin's Yalta diplomacy along the same line: "They wanted to divide the world, to cut away China's Mongolia, to incorporate Xinjiang and the Northeast into the Soviet sphere of influence where no other countries would be allowed, and to include Japan in America's sphere of influence." The most recent

61. Shi Zhe's first memoir, *Zai Lishi Juren Shenbian,* which covers the years from 1924 to 1954, was published in two editions in 1991 and 1995. His second memoir, *Wo de Yisheng,* covers his life from 1904 to 1998. It was recorded by his daughter Shi Qiulang and was published in 2001. The quotation is from p. 349.

62. John Gittings, *Survey of the Sino-Soviet Dispute* (London: Oxford University Press, 1968), 166–67; "Record of Conversation between the Mongolia People's Republic Government Delegation and the Deputy Chairman of the People's Republic of China State Council, Foreign Minister Chen Yi, 30 September 1964," CWIHP Virtual Archive, http://wwics.si.edu.

accusation by a top CCP leader of the Soviet Union for separating Outer Mongolia from China was made by Deng Xiaoping during his 1989 conversation with Mikhail Gorbachev.[63]

Several previous studies have suggested that in the Acheson episode Mao coordinated with the Soviets well. Despite his misstep in the *form* of the Chinese statement, Mao took Moscow's side in attacking the Americans and thus satisfied Stalin's prerequisites for a new treaty with the PRC. Such interpretations discount the significance of an unpleasant encounter between Stalin and Mao after the publication of the Chinese statement.[64] As a matter of fact, if Mao's refutation was puzzling to Shi Zhe, it was outright alarming to the Soviets in turning on the red light on Mongolia. Mao's silence about Mongolia since his arrival made the Soviets nervous. To ready themselves for dealing with a possible Chinese move of inserting the Mongolia question into the negotiations, a Soviet expert of international law was assigned to search the Foreign Ministry files for documentation on the MPR's 1945 plebiscite. The result was delivered to Vyshinsky on January 16, one day before he and Molotov requested Mao to make a rebuttal of Acheson.[65] Although Mao's rebuttal did not directly raise the Mongolia question for the Sino-Soviet talks, its ambiguous reference to Mongolia along with other three regions as "China's" and lack of a clear justification of MPR independence did seem to confirm the Soviets' suspicion about Mao's continued ambition toward Mongolia.

Now they wanted to talk this over with Mao. Shi Zhe's memoir offers the only information available about the resultant encounter between Stalin and Mao. According to Shi, on a late January day, Stalin and Molotov had a brief meeting with Mao and Zhou in which Shi served as interpreter. In the conversation, Stalin and Molotov took turns castigating Mao for breaching his earlier promise to issue an "official" rebuttal of the Acheson speech. Stalin

63. Wang Dongxing, *Wang Dongxing Huiyi Mao Zedong yu Lin Biao Fangeming Jiduan de Douzheng* (Mao Zedong's Struggle with the Lin Biao Counterrevolutionary Clique as Remembered by Wang Dongxing) (Beijing: Dangdai Zhongguo Chubanshe, 2004), 141–42; "Information Note of Romanian Embassy from Beijing to Ministry of Foreign Affairs, 23 May 1989," CWIHP Virtual Archive, http://wwics.si.edu.

64. Goncharov, Lewis, and Xue, *Uncertain Partners,* 103, 104–5; Odd Arne Westad, "Fight for Friendship," *CWIHP Bulletin,* issues 8–9 (Winter 1996–97): 225; Yang Kuisong, *Mao Zedong yu Mosike,* 300–1.

65. Heinzig, *The Soviet Union and Communist China,* 362, documents this development with a letter to Vyshinsky from the legal expert, Vsevolod D. Durdenevsky, found in the Archives of Foreign Policy of the Russian Federation, Moscow.

referred to the Chinese statement as a "worthless" remark issued under an individual's name, and Molotov accused Mao of "violating our agreement" and preventing the two sides' actions from "achieving our expected effect." Molotov's vehement language is understandable, because Mao's willfulness made him appear incompetent in Stalin's eyes. To Stalin, as long as he knew that the statement represented Mao's view, its form, in his words, "is no big deal." He nevertheless admonished Mao that "because we did not act as originally planned and fell out of steps with each other, a crack may have been created for the enemy to exploit."[66] If the *form* was no big deal, the only matter worth this condescending censuring, which was apparently out of sync with the two sides' generally equal dialogues in Moscow, was the *content* of Mao's statement. But, because in Moscow Mao did not explicitly make the northern territories an issue between Beijing and Moscow, understandably Stalin could only resort to ambiguity as well.

In his memoir, Shi attributes this episode to a misunderstanding between the two sides about what constituted an "official" statement and to Stalin's lack of patience as an "elder brother" in helping a "younger brother" understand the protocols of international affairs.[67] In the light of the Molotov record, such a misunderstanding did not exist. Neither, throughout the affair, did Mao appear an innocent novice in international affairs. The two sides' behaviors reflected a more serious dissonance than what was recognized by Shi Zhe's inference about Mao and Stalin. Shi, who claimed familiarity with both Mao's and Stalin's mindset and whose recollections have influenced many studies of the Mao–Stalin summit, apparently lacked a necessary degree of cynicism to understand either Mao or Stalin and tended to assume the best of the two leaders' intentions.[68] In this case, even though Shi suspected that Mao had concealed his real feelings about the MPR and about Soviet inroads into northern Chinese territories, he failed to make a connection between the *content* of Mao's statement and the Soviet leaders' reprimand of Mao.

A question should be asked as to when and for what reason Stalin wanted to stage such an encounter with Mao. It seems unlikely that the meeting took place before January 25. On that day, Mao sent an upbeat telegram to Liu Shaoqi informing him of progress in the negotiations since Zhou's arrival on January 20. By now, the two sides had basically agreed on a draft treaty

---

66. Shi Zhe, *Wo de Yisheng,* 351.
67. Shi Zhe, *Wo de Yisheng,* 350–51.
68. Shi Zhe, *Wo de Yisheng,* 353.

and, on the Chinese side, the preparations for other agreements had also advanced nicely. In Mao's words, "in general the work has proceeded rather smoothly."[69]

The smoothness, however, was interrupted by the Americans. The U.S. State Department did a follow-up on Acheson's accusation of Soviet territorial expansion in northern China by providing "proofs" to the press. These "proofs" were published by American newspapers on January 26. Therefore, only as a reaction to this new development can Soviet leaders' abrasive behavior in their meeting with Mao and Zhou be understood. With the American action as evidence, the Soviets now had serious questions about the meaning and effect of Mao's rebuttal of Acheson. They felt it necessary to tell Mao face to face how he had ruined the "original plan" and "expected effect."[70]

What was the Kremlin's original plan? If the plan was to frustrate Washington's wedge strategy against the Sino-Soviet alliance and silence official American propaganda on Soviet expansion at China's expenses, these goals could be achieved only if Mao openly and unequivocally committed himself to the Soviet position on the MPR and defended Soviet policies toward other northern Chinese territories as well. As a matter of fact, for the Soviets, in this case the means was really the goal. The Soviet leaders were so irritated by Washington's propaganda only because they were not sure whether or not the Chinese might actually agree with what the Americans were saying. In the whole Acheson episode, therefore, the PRC–USSR unity vis-à-vis the United States was just part of the issue. Another crucial aspect was the internal balance between the two communist powers.

Having decided to forgo the formality if not the substance of the Yalta–Moscow system, Stalin was anxious to know how far Mao would want to go in rolling back the Soviet Union's geostrategic position in Northeast Asia endorsed by Yalta. In Moscow, Mao said a lot but constantly refrained from

69. "Telegram to Liu Shaoqi on the Sino-Soviet Negotiations and the Status of Document Preparations, 25 January 1950," *JYMW,* 1: 251.

70. According to the Molotov–Mao understanding on January 17, Mao would prepare the Acheson rebuttal the next day and give the statement to the Soviets for "suggestions and corrections." Mao may have or have not done so before he cabled the statement to Liu Shaoqi on January 19. Goncharov, Lewis, and Xue, *Uncertain Partners,* 321 n. 154, indicates that the Soviet newspaper *Pravda* did not carry the Chinese statement until January 24. The point is that in the whole week, until the new development in the United States on January 26, Soviet leaders might be displeased by Mao's willful action but did not have any ground for accusing him for giving the enemy an opportunity.

supporting Mongolian independence in a positive way. Thus, Stalin, just like Shi Zhe, could not fathom Mao's real thinking about Soviet expansion in Northeast Asia, even after reading Mao's rebuttal of the Acheson speech. If the Acheson episode was intended by the Soviet leaders as a test for Mao, then it appeared that Mao the examinee outsmarted the examiners—Stalin and Molotov—and cheated on the test with skill and style.

According to Shi, during the (later than January 26?) meeting, Mao appeared to be controlling his anger as Molotov and Stalin took turns reproving him, "not saying a word and keeping an emotionless face." Mao's indignation may, however, have been feigned. A few years later, when Mao recalled the occasion to a Polish Communist delegation, he said that "I just laughed in my nose and did not defend myself a bit."[71] Mao had a good reason to laugh because his handiwork neither budged on the Mongolia question nor gave the Soviets a reason to question his revolutionary spirit against the United States. Hence, Stalin and Molotov could ventilate their displeasure about Mao's mischief only by pounding on a secondary issue—the *form* of his statement.

Mongolian Independence, Again

It is rather revealing that the Acheson episode, which could have been a good opportunity for Beijing and Moscow to show their solidarity to the world, caused such strong mutual grievances between the two sides. In qualifying his unpleasant meeting with Mao as an "exchange of opinions within a small group," Stalin obviously had no intention of creating new difficulties for the first communist summit, though the session inevitably became an occasion that sowed new seeds of distrust between Beijing and Moscow. The situation occurred mainly because Mao continued to hold his Mongolia card under the table and because the patience of his Soviet hosts was running thin. Mao was nevertheless determined that the Chinese side should decide when and how to lay the Mongolia card on the table.

On January 25, the Chinese delegation, under Zhou's direction, completed its draft agreement on the issues of the Lüshun and Dalian ports and the Chinese Changchun Railroad. The draft agreement was presented to the Soviets as a one-package counteroffer to their earlier separate proposals on

---

71. Shi Zhe, *Wo de Yisheng,* 351; Yang Kuisong, *Mao Zedong yu Mosike,* 301.

these matters. The Chinese draft agreement basically wanted to cancel all Soviet treaty privileges related to these establishments and thus make Moscow's intention of using a new treaty to preserve the old gains unattainable.[72] After listening to Zhou's report on the Chinese draft agreement, Mao expressed his opinion on how the Soviets should be rewarded, provided that they agreed to give up their rights and interests in Manchuria:

> We need to make one more statement. When the People's Republic of China was established, we declared nullification of all international agreements and treaties concluded between the old China and foreign countries. But Outer Mongolia was an exception. Although the independence of Outer Mongolia was processed by the GMD government, we respect the 1945 plebiscite by the Mongolian people in which they unanimously supported independence. Now, through negotiations the two governments [of the PRC and the USSR] should confirm the independent status of the Mongolian People's Republic. The Soviet Union ought to support China's stand on this matter and in the meantime to hope that Mongolia will respond by making a statement as well.

Zhou understood Mao's intention perfectly and said that "such an approach would be better."[73]

By now, Mao had laid out his stratagem for playing the Mongolia card: (1) Because the PRC had renounced all China's foreign treaties concluded by the GMD regime, *legally* the PRC had not accepted the independence of the MPR; (2) but the Chinese delegation could make an *additional* statement to *reconfirm* MPR independence only *after* the Soviets made concessions on other matters in the 1945 treaty; and therefore (3) MPR independence would appear to have been settled *through negotiations* just like other issues, though in reality there were no negotiations about the MPR at all.

Thus, after the interparty Mikoyan–Liu diplomacies in 1949 made it clear to the CCP leadership that the issue of Mongolia was nonnegotiable with Moscow, Mao finally found a way to insert the issue into the interstate diplomacy between the himself and Stalin. The cleverness of Mao's tactic was twofold. First, in the actual negotiations in Moscow, the Chinese side would use the Mongolia question as a silent inducement for the Soviets to

72. Shen Zhihua, "Clashes of Interests," 104.
73. Diary entry on 25 January 1950, in *Wang Dongxing Riji* (Wang Dongxing's Diaries) by Wang Dongxing (Beijing: Zhongguo Shehui Kexue Chubanshe, 1993), 195.

concede on other issues. In this regard, the Acheson episode proved an unsolicited help to Mao: It highlighted the suspense between Beijing and Moscow with respect to China's northern territories and gave Mao an opportunity to show his calculated ambiguity about Mongolia. Second, once Moscow agreed to a deal on other issues to the CCP's satisfaction, MPR independence would be declared as part of the package to impress the world and the Chinese public back home that the CCP had made an effort about Outer Mongolia but had to endorse its independence as a matter of principle and in exchange for Soviet concessions in Manchuria. This way, even though the CCP could not redress the GMD's loss of Mongolia, its diplomacy in Moscow would still appear superior to the GMD's in recovering other rights in Manchuria.

Consistent with Mao's effort in Moscow of building up the Mongolia suspense, Zhou did not raise the topic at all during his negotiations with the Soviets. The silence on the Chinese side thus rendered the Soviet preparations for defending the 1945 arrangements about Mongolia a futile exercise.[74] Mao's tactic seemed to have worked. According to Shen Zhihua, who has examined Soviet archival materials on the Moscow negotiations, Stalin's "ire and irritation are quite evident" in his marginal notes in a copy of the Chinese counterproposal about Soviet interests in Manchuria. Yet somehow the Soviets managed to suppress their anger and accepted the essence of the Chinese document on January 28.[75] Although Stalin's need for a successful summit with Mao was overwhelming, his desire for Mao's acceptance of the Mongolian buffer also underlay his bitter concessions in Manchuria.

Consequently, only after reaching a basic agreement with the Soviets on the content of the new treaty did Zhou, at a meeting before January 31, inform Stalin of Mao's notion about issuing a statement on the MPR. Having endured the Mongolia suspense administered by Mao during the past two months, Stalin did not foresee this sudden end. His initial reaction was defensive:

---

74. Zhou Enlai's telegram to Liu Shaoqi and the Central Politburo, 8 February 1950, cited in Jin Chongji, *Zhou Enlai Zhuan, 1949–1976* (Biography of Zhou Enlai, 1949–1976) (Beijing: Zhongyang Wenxian Chubanshe, 1998), 1: 35–39. The telegram summarized in nine items the Sino-Soviet negotiations over various questions since Zhou Enlai's arrival in Moscow. These did not mention the Mongolia question in any form. According to Shen Zhihua, "Clashes of Interests," 106, as of January 16, 1950, the Soviet Foreign Ministry dug out all the documents relating to the 1945 Sino-Soviet agreement about MPR independence to be used in negotiating with the PRC delegation.

75. Shen Zhihua, "Clashes of Interests," 104.

Was not the Mongolia question settled long time ago? If there is no problem at all, why is a statement needed? Besides, since the Mongolian comrades are not here, for what purpose should we discuss the Mongolia
question? What right do we have to discuss other peoples' fate?[76]

It has been suggested that on the occasion Stalin was "at his demagogical
best," as if he had not interfered with other peoples' fate before.[77] This may
be so, but the Chinese initiative did make Stalin nervous. The worst scenario for Stalin was that Mao would raise the Mongolia question *after* the
Soviet government agreed to sign a new treaty with the PRC *and* to retreat
from its privileged position in Manchuria. Zhou immediately put Stalin at
ease, explaining to him what the Chinese side intended to do. Stalin relaxed
and supported the idea. Hence came the end of the underplayed Mongolia
drama in Moscow.

The PRC–USSR Treaty of Friendship, Alliance, and Mutual Assistance
was signed on February 14. A Chinese–Soviet joint communiqué of the
same date clarified the relationship between the new treaty and the 1945
treaty:

> In connection with the signing of the Treaty of Friendship, Alliance, and
> Mutual Assistance, and the Agreement on the Chinese Changchun Rail-
> road, Lüshun, and Dalian, Zhou Enlai, Premier and the Minister of For-
> eign Affairs, and A. Ia. Vyshinskii, Minister of Foreign Affairs, exchanged
> notes to the effect that the respective treaty and agreements concluded

76. Shi Zhe, *Wo de Yisheng,* 346–47.
77. Goncharov, Lewis, and Xue, *Uncertain Partners,* 120. These authors, relying
on the recollections of Wu Xiuquan, a member of Zhou Enlai's negotiation team, mistakenly date the exchange on January 22. Because Zhou and his team arrived in Moscow
just two days before, it was highly unlikely that he brought up this matter to Stalin at
this date. The date also contradicts Wang Dongxing's diary entry on January 25 about
the Mao–Zhou conversation on Mongolia (see n. 73 above). Heinzig, *The Soviet Union
and Communist China,* 362–63, proves that on January 31 Zhou handed the Chinese draft
of exchange notes to Vyshinsky, the second point of which addressed MPR independence. Heinzig's source is Vyshinsky's letter to Stalin dated February 1, 1950, located
in Archives of the President of the Russian Federation, Moscow. Therefore, most likely
the Zhou–Stalin conversation on Mongolia took place between January 28 and 30. Apparently, the Soviet side accepted Zhou's draft of notes without raising many questions.
According to Zhou Enlai's February 8 telegram to Liu Shaoqi, cited in Jin Chongji, *Zhou
Enlai Zhuan,* 1: 38, the two sides agreed that the nullification of the 1945 treaty would
be achieved through exchanging notes between foreign ministers.

on August 14, 1945, between China and the Soviet Union are now null and void, and also that both governments affirm that the independent status of the Mongolian People's Republic is fully guaranteed as a result of the plebiscite of 1945 and the establishment with it of diplomatic relationship by the People's Republic of China.[78]

Also at Mao's insistence, the Agreement on the Chinese Changchun Railroad, Lüshun, and Dalian explicitly stated that the old agreements on these issues were overturned because "since 1945 the situation in the Far East has changed fundamentally, e.g.: Imperialist Japan has been defeated, reactionary GMD government has been overthrown, and China has become a people's democratic republic and has established a new, people's government."[79] In this way, Stalin finally conceded to Mao's notion that the new treaty should not just be a negative instrument in dealing with the Western powers and Japan but should mainly be a positive response to the successful Chinese revolution.

Thus, as far as the Soviet Union was concerned, China's "old kitchen" was closed and the "new kitchen" was in business. Yet the CCP still had to invite the Soviets into China as privileged "guests." Although relinquishing their old treaty rights in Manchuria, the Soviets managed to get new rights from Mao, including joint-stock companies in Xinjiang, a monopoly over China's export of surplus industrial sources during the period of Soviet loans to China, and China's agreement to close Xinjiang and Manchuria to any third foreign interests. After Stalin's death, Mao would openly make many complaints about these arrangements, accusing Stalin of turning Xinjiang and Manchuria into Soviet "spheres of influence" or "half-colonies." At last, Mao belatedly revealed his concurrence with Dean Acheson's 1950 incrimination of Moscow's design for colonizing northern Chinese territories.[80]

---

78. "Chinese–Soviet Communiqué on the Conclusion of Treaty of Friendship, Alliance, and Mutual Assistance Agreements, Moscow, 14 February 1950," in *Jianguo Yilai Zhongyao Wenxian Xuanbian* (Selection of Important Documents since the Establishment of the State), comp. Documentary Research Office of the CCP Central Committee (Beijing: Zhongyang Wenxian Chubanshe, 1992), 1: 118.

79. "PRC–USSR agreement on the Chinese Changchun Railroad, Lüshun, and Dalian," *Jianguo Yilai Zhongyao Wenxian Xuanbian,* 1: 121; Zhou Enlai to Liu Shaoqi and the Central Politburo, 8 February 1950, cited in Jin Chongji, *Zhou Enlai Zhuan,* 1: 37.

80. "Mao's Conversation with Yudin, 31 March 1956," *CWIHP Bulletin,* issues 6–7 (Winter 1995–96): 166; "First Conversation of N. S. Khrushchev with Mao Zedong, Hall of Huaizhentan [*Huairentang?*] [Beijing], 31 July 1958," *CWIHP Bulletin,* issues 12–13 (Fall–Winter 2001): 251.

Yet, in 1950, these concessions were concealed from the outside world and the Chinese public. The CCP leaders' bitterness was then painted over with Beijing's glowing words in publicly praising the new treaty. To Beijing, the secretiveness was necessary because these concessions had nothing to do with the old GMD treaty and were the price that the CCP leadership had agreed to pay for its junior partnership with the Soviet Union in an anti-Western bloc.[81] The new Sino-Soviet partnership forged in this manner was by no means an anomaly to intrabloc relationships in the Cold War years, which often tolerated exceptions to the rule of equality among nation-states.

In general, Mao and his associates were satisfied with their success in Moscow in overcoming Stalin's resistance to a new treaty. Zhou was quite proud of the result of the Moscow diplomacy and asserted afterward that "this time we achieved a general solution of some unsettled cases from history, and such a result could be reached with the Soviet Union only by a people's China under the CCP leadership." This estimate has been restated in Chinese historical studies ever since. It has been suggested in a recent work that the 1950 treaty in effect nullified "all those unequal agreements that had satisfied Stalin and humiliated the Chinese."[82] In 1950, the general public in China seemed to get the same impression. It learned about Mao's success in Moscow in abolishing the GMD regime's concessions to the Soviets but knew nothing about the CCP's new price tag for its alliance with Moscow.

In reality, not all agreements in the 1945 package were nullified in 1950. Clearly, the 1950 treaty inherited the 1945 agreement on the MPR. With one exception, all previous studies of the Mao–Stalin talks have overlooked the significance of the Mongolia question in the making of the new Sino-Soviet alliance.[83] Surely, the shadow boxing between Mao and Stalin over Mon-

81. According to Zhou Enlai, cited in Pei Jianzhang, *Zhonghua Renmin Gongheguo Waijiaoshi,* 25, the Chinese delegation reluctantly accepted these Soviet conditions to maintain unity with Moscow in opposition to the Anglo-American bloc. To sweeten these concessions for the Chinese, Stalin promised Mao that the Soviet air force would provide protection to Shanghai and some captured Japanese properties in Manchuria would be turned over to Beijing. This picture is, however, incomplete. Heinzig, *The Soviet Union and Communist China,* 373 and 503 n. 670, finds evidence from Russian archives that in early January the Chinese side took the initiative in inviting the Soviets for joint efforts in exploring Xinjiang's mineral resources, though the resultant agreements embittered the Chinese.

82. Jin Chongji, *Zhou Enlai Zhuan,* 1: 41; Yang Kuisong, *Mao Zedong yu Mosike,* 307.

83. Shen Zhihua, "Clashes of Interests," 106–7, contends that Stalin made concessions in Manchuria to the Chinese side *after* Zhou Enlai tied the PRC's recognition of

golia did not decide the success or failure of the entire realm of Sino-Soviet diplomacy between December 1949 and February 1950. Neither Stalin nor Mao could afford to fail in their first summit when their common strategy against the United States was at stake. This overall common concern was a powerful enough inducement to both sides and made the Moscow negotiations a "time when Mao's revolutionary ambitions and Stalin's power interests converged the most closely."[84] After the negotiations, a Eurasian communist monolith emerged in Western governments' eyes.

Nevertheless, during the better part of the Moscow negotiations, the Mongolia question hovered silently in the air; its settlement, or resettlement, was necessary for painting over, if not patching up, one of the major cracks in the PRC–USSR "monolith." A question for Mao and Stalin to answer was that, after the CCP added China to the Soviet side of the global power equation, how should Moscow's geopolitical arrangements in Northeastern and Central Asia, which were first set up when China was still on the "other" side, be readjusted. In this question resided all the nationalistic poisons of a proclaimed internationalist brotherhood between Beijing and Moscow. The hypothesis presented here suggests that Mao's silent, suspenseful tactics induced Stalin to accept a Mongolia-for-Manchuria formula. The overall significance of this development was that a double-layered geopolitical balance of power finally materialized to replace the Yalta–Moscow system, which had only one fault line in Northeast Asia. In other words, whereas the Mongolian buffer and the 1950 formulas for Manchuria and Xinjiang served to stabilize the internal balance of the USSR–PRC bloc, the bloc was ready to counter America's security system Asia-wide.

The Moscow diplomacy of 1950 left a lasting bitter taste in the mouths of both sides. According to an insider's account, shortly after Mao's departure from Moscow in February 1950, a Politburo meeting took place at Stalin's dacha in Kuntsevo. Stalin surprised those present by saying that "the battle for China isn't over yet. It has only just begun." He complained that during the negotiations Mao had sought more aid than Russia could afford,

---

MPR independence to Soviet relinquishment of rights in Manchuria, suggesting that the Chinese side did use the Mongolia question as an explicit bargaining chip. Shen cannot document the date of Zhou's raising of the Mongolia question except relying on Shi Zhe's recollection. Yet Shi Zhe's memoirs put Zhou's presentation on Mongolia in a time *after* the Soviet side accepted the Chinese proposals concerning Manchuria.

84. Vojtech Mastny, *The Cold War and Soviet Insecurity: The Stalin Years* (New York: Oxford University Press, 1996), 88.

and that the Soviet Union could not be safe from the PRC as long as Mao coveted its resources. One way to block Mao, Stalin suggested, was to convert Xinjiang, Inner Mongolia, and especially Manchuria into independent states so that they could serve as buffers between the two great Asian powers. Allegedly Stalin instructed the Soviet Communist Party Central Committee and the Ministry of State Security (known as the MGB) to set up clandestine, pro-Soviet party cells in all three regions.[85]

The authenticity of this story is yet to be verified by evidence from the Russian archives, but the apprehension of China seemed commonly shared among Soviet leaders. At the time, former Soviet foreign minister Maxim Litvinov was already out of Stalin's favor but could still hear things from government circles. After the 1950 treaty was concluded, Litvinov put these words in a note: "China has been promised a big loan as well as technical and military aid . . . it's a dangerous venture . . . we are speeding up the emergence of a powerful and dangerous competitor—China. We are also bringing nearer a new conflict for the reallocation of raw materials and markets . . . if Stalin imagines that he can force Mao to pull the chestnuts out of the fire . . . and China is not Yugoslavia [original omissions]."[86]

Surely the CCP leaders' collective feeling about the Mongolia question was more complicated than that of humiliation. Mao's public acceptance of MPR independence in Moscow was not a simple matter of continuing a national disgrace bequeathed from the GMD regime. The event reflected the CCP's own failure to translate its "class brotherhood" with the MPR into a national one. In reaffirming MPR independence in Moscow, the CCP leadership not only forfeited an assumed right of the Chinese nation to collect a historical debt from the Russians but also suspended a dream cherished for a long time by the party, which was to establish a great Chinese federation according to the Leninist formula.

This, of course, was not what Beijing's propaganda machine told the Chinese people after Mao's return. During the first two weeks after the Sino-Soviet treaty was concluded, the *People's Daily* published an editorial and a series of articles to educate its readers about the significance of the development. The Soviet Union's agreement to return the ports and railways in Manchuria to China was lavishly praised as evidence of the socialist neighbor's "great morality" and "generosity," and the reaffirmation of MPR

85. Peter S. Deriabin, *Inside Stalin's Kremlin: An Eyewitness Account of Brutality, Duplicity, and Intrigue* (Washington: Brassey's, 1998), 108–10.
86. Maxim Litvinov, *Notes for a Journal* (New York: William Morrow, 1955), 314–15.

independence was defined as the PRC's own action in implementing historical justice and revolutionary principles.[87]

The cracks in the "monolith" were thereby painted over. This, however, cannot change a historical fact that along with other mutual misgivings, the CCP–Soviet discord over Mongolia, which surfaced in 1949–50 and would continue in the years to come, marred the intimacy between the two communist allies from the outset. After Stalin's death, the new Soviet leadership under Nikita Khrushchev took steps to redress the CCP leaders' grievances about the lingering Soviet privileges in Manchuria and Xinjiang. The Mongolian buffer was not abolished, though the de-Stalinization of the Sino-Soviet relationship did initially lead to a significant downsizing of the Mongolian military force.[88] Yet, as Khrushchev recalled, during one of his visits to the PRC, Mao gestured to him with a little finger and said: "There is still one unsettled question—Mongolia." This Soviet recollection has been challenged by a Chinese one. Shi Zhe contended that when Khrushchev led a Soviet delegation to China in 1954, Nikolai Bulganin, not any Chinese official, proposed that Outer Mongolia be reincorporated into China. Either way, the Mongolia question was identified as a legacy of the 1950 diplomacy that continued to torment the PRC–USSR relationship after Stalin's death.[89]

87. "A New Era of Sino-Soviet Friendly Cooperation," *Renmin Ribao,* 15 February 1950; Hu Hua, "Sino-Soviet Treaty of Friendship and Alliance and the Sino-Soviet Treaty of Friendship, Alliance and Mutual Assistance," *Renmin Ribao,* 20 February 1950; "Transference of the Chinese Changchun Railroad," *Renmin Ribao,* 21 February 1950; "New Agreement on Lüshun and Dalian," *Renmin Ribao,* 22 February 1950; "Soviet Loans to China," *Renmin Ribao,* 23 February 1950; and "Recognition and Guarantee the Independence of the Mongolian People's Republic," *Renmin Ribao,* 24 February 1950.

88. Wu Lengxi, *Shinian Lunzhan,* 1: 160–61; "Khrushchev's Speech at the Eleventh Meeting of the Soviet Union Communist Party Congress, 28 June 1957," in *Sulian Gongchandang Zuihou Yige Fandang Jituan* (The Last Anti-Party Faction in the Soviet Communist Party) (Beijing: Zhongguo Shehui Chubanshe, 1997. This contains the complete minutes of the June 1957 conference and the October 1964 conference of the Soviet Union Communist Party Congress originally published in Russia and translated into Chinese by Zhao Yongmu et al.), 2: 894–95; Marko Milivojevi, "The Mongolian People's Army: Military Auxiliary and Political Guardian," in *Mongolia Today,* ed. Shirin Akiner (London: Kegan Paul International, 1991), 142–43.

89. Chuev, *Molotov Remembers,* 71; Li Haiwen, "Inaccuracies in Kovalev's Recollections," 92. For an insightful discussion of the Mongolia question in the Sino-Soviet relationship of the 1960s, see Sergey S. Radchenko, *The Soviets' Best Friends in Asia: The Mongolian Dimension of the Sino-Soviet Split,* CWIHP Working Paper 42 (Washington, D.C.: Woodrow Wilson International Center for Scholars, 2003).

11

Epilogue: Territoriality, Power, and Legitimacy

In late May 1949, after Chinese Communist Party (CCP) troops entered Shanghai, Mansfield Addis, then first secretary of the British Embassy in Nanjing, wrote to his mother back home: "Shanghai liberated! We rejoice that it was not more difficult! It brings the end nearer." About a year later, impressed by the efficiency and idealism brought into the Chinese government and society by the CCP, in another letter Addis recounted to his mother an episode he had recently experienced in the western suburbs of Beijing. When he and a Chinese friend toured the famous Eight Great Temples (*Badachu*), they were blocked by a guard at the entrance. An argument ensued between his friend and the guard, with the former saying: "Have we been liberated or haven't we? All China's beauty spots belong to the people now!" About the scene Addis observed: "There was the greatest good humor on both sides. . . . There is no trace of the terrified whispering which I knew in Hitler's Germany." Then he added: "I do wish all the English papers which I now see weren't so blindly prejudiced against the new China."[1]

The sentiment expressed in Addis's letters must neither have been merely private nor unique among British diplomats in China, for the British Foreign Office felt the matter serious enough to warrant a special telegram to its Nanjing embassy in July 1949:

We notice a growing tendency in telegrams from China to refer to the Communist occupation of an area as "liberation." In the case of a Consular officer reporting to you *en clair* and *post facto* the expression may

---

1. Addis to Lady Addis, 27 May 1949 and 20 June 1950, Mansfield Addis Collection.

possibly be unavoidable, but we feel bound to point out that China telegrams get a wide distribution here with the consequent danger that ex-
pressions such as this, oft repeated, may serve to strengthen beliefs all too
prevalent that Chinese Communism is different from the Soviet brand.
We hope therefore that posts will in future refrain from using this word
in a sense so far divorced from its true meaning.[2]

Given the obvious disagreement between Addis and his superior in London, it was even less likely to establish a roundly accepted "true meaning"
of "liberation" in a larger realm of political communications. For instance,
to the vast population of China, what mattered in 1949 was not how similar Chinese Communism was to its Soviet predecessor but how different
the CCP government was from the Guomindang (GMD, Nationalist Party)
regime. The new government in Beijing, which had been created by what
has been defined as the "greatest and most popular of modern revolutions,"
could justifiably assert that its own ascendancy had changed the direction
of Chinese history.[3] The CCP's unprecedented sociopolitical engineering in
China after 1949 easily made the two terms "preliberation" (*jiefangqian*)
and "postliberation" (*jiefanghou*) part of the ordinary people's daily vocab-
ulary. Yet, depending on the historian's chosen lens, the landmark significance
of 1949 may either tower to the skies like the Himalayas or stretch like one
of those nameless rolling hills in the Mongolian Plateau.

In February 1950, when the Treaty of Friendship, Alliance, and Mutual
Assistance between the People's Republic of China and the Soviet Union
was signed, the "liberated" China accomplished its first international act. The
treaty also ended any lingering doubt about the status of the Mongolian
People's Republic (MPR), and it thus finalized Outer Mongolia's liberation
from China, though both countries now belonged to the same emerging
"socialist camp." Until then, the Mongolia question had been closely associated with the revolutions in China, Mongolia, and Russia. But its 1950
settlement was a far cry from the principle of national self-determination
that all these revolutions claimed to support. Mongolia's ethnonationalist
revolution never managed to break its international and interethnic restraints.
During the twentieth century, the more powerful forces on the two sides of
Mongolia were alternately hostile and conciliatory toward each other, and,

2. Foreign Office to Nanjing, 25 July 1949, FO 371/75764.
3. Maurice Meisner, "Mao Zedong," in *The Oxford Companion to Politics of the
World,* ed. Joel Krieger (New York: Oxford University Press, 1993), 561.

in the meantime, they constantly kept Mongolia divided against the Mongols' will. This was the case even when Mao and Stalin forged their "communist monolith" over the Eurasian land mass. Under the circumstances, the independent Mongolian state could be easily viewed as a geopolitical creation of others' schemes but not as a dynamic national entity of its own devices.

In reality, although Outer Mongolia's separation from China was successively supported and protected by the Tsarist and the Soviet governments, Mongolian separatism was never a Russian creation. Except for a deep, southward suspicion, Mongolian nationalism, in seeking absolute national independence and unification, shared little common interest with Tsarist or Soviet hegemony, which played games for the relative nicety of balance of power. Even the southerly adversary was construed differently in Ulaanbaatar and in Moscow. To Ulaanbaatar, it was always the Mongols' ethnic nemesis, the "Chinese." So in August 1945, the MPR marked the oppressive "Chinese" as the intended enemy even when declaring war on Japan. To Moscow, the southern threat could come from a variety of antagonists, ranging from great power competitors such as Japan and the United States to those onetime revolutionary collaborators like the GMD and the CCP regimes.

Despite those repeated "settlements" of the Mongolia question between the Chinese and the Russian governments, as of 1950 MPR independence essentially marked a compromise between centralizing Chinese nationalism and secessionist Mongolian nationalism. After a half-century contest, neither the Chinese nor the Mongolian geopolitical visions prevailed completely. If MPR independence constituted the single irreversible loss to Chinese nationalism in the twentieth century, Inner Mongolia's incorporation into the People's Republic of China (PRC) left Mongolian nationalists regretting bitterly for the rest of their lives.

Although Inner Mongolia never left Chinese control—except during Japan's occupation in World War II—the region's successive inclusion in the GMD's Republic of China and in the CCP's People's Republic insinuated rather different meanings to the Mongols. In subscribing to the Moscow-inspired "national-liberation" mode of ethnopolitical movement, most Mongol partisans regarded the GMD phase of Inner Mongolia as a "preliberation" period in which ethnic resistance was sanctioned by revolutionary forces in China and the Soviet Union. During the Chinese Civil War and the early Cold War years, however, leftist Inner Mongol autonomists were so deeply engulfed by Moscow–Yan'an–Ulaanbaatar bloc politics that they could not prevent the CCP's class-based "national liberation" from overtaking their ethnonationalist movement. No matter how reluctant they might be, the MPR leaders and most Inner Mongol autonomists had to accept the establishment of the PRC as the consummation of the Inner Mongols' "national liberation" as well. Consequently, October 1, 1949, marked the end of "national-liberation" history for both the Chinese and the Mongols.

The PRC, in capping a century of rebellions, revolutions, and civil and foreign wars, assumed an epochal role in redefining China's territoriality. Although the GMD regime's relocation to Taiwan complicated the task, the founders of the PRC would proceed to establish effective control over the late Qing's imperial domain minus independent Mongolia. In the process, they made a most important alteration of China's administrative system to accommodate the Inner Mongols' aspirations. Earlier, in 1935, the CCP rhetoric on the abolition of the Chinese provincial system in Inner Mongolia and on the return of all Inner Mongolian territories to the Inner Mongols was closely associated with the party's agitation for the Inner Mongols to gain "independence" from the GMD's anticommunist state. The rhetoric was a short-lived attempt on the CCP's part to use the Leninist strategy to win Inner Mongols' sympathy at present, not a far-reaching proposition for the Inner Mongols to maintain "regional autonomy" within a CCP-dominated China in the future. There is no evidence that when the CCP resumed its military struggle with the GMD in late 1945, its leadership had any ready formula for rearranging China's ethnic frontiers. Therefore, it was the Inner Mongols', especially the eastern Mongols', struggle for territorial autonomy—a toned-down demand from their original goal of accession to the MPR—that pressured the CCP to accept the arrangement in exchange for the Inner Mongols' cooperation in its war against the GMD. In this sense, as of 1949 the Inner Mongols made a decisive impact on Chinese territoriality as we know it today.

Although the provincial system was first introduced into China by the Mongol rulers of the Yuan Dynasty in the late thirteenth century, by the twentieth century the power relationship between the Chinese and the Mongols had developed in such a way that the Inner Mongols felt it necessary to reject the system as a Chinese means of ethnic oppression. After 1949, the model of Inner Mongolian territorial autonomy not only rolled back, at least symbolically, the provincial system in Inner Mongolia but also on most of China's ethnic frontiers. Therefore, although the CCP government used the formula of "regional autonomy of (minority) nationalities" (*minzu quyu zizhi*) to administer the PRC's multiethnic territoriality, it would distort history to suggest that on its own initiative the CCP adopted the "national autonomous region system" in lieu of the federation model of the Soviet Union. If the vigorous eastern Mongolian autonomous movement taught the CCP leaders any lesson, they learned that the unpredictable principle of national self-determination, embodied theoretically in the Soviet model, must be avoided. Instead, they embraced "regional autonomy" as a safer concession to frontier ethic groups that would cause minimal uncertainty and facilitate the central government's unitary control of China's territoriality.

From the 1950 settlement of the Mongolia question, Moscow emerged as the only party with no regrets. The 1950 treaty did not alter the MPR's orbiting around the Soviet Union, though, now internal to the newly forged Beijing–Moscow alliance, the Mongolian buffer functioned significantly more subtly than before. In the meantime, Moscow's retreat from its Yalta privileges in Manchuria proved worthwhile in exchange for Communist China's allegiance. Just a few months after the Stalin–Mao talks, the Korean War broke out. It would soon attest to Soviet leaders the value of Mao's friendship. In the immediate post–World War II years, Soviet and American influence in Asia was only separated by a human-made thin line, the 38th parallel in Korea. This perilous situation was changed in 1949 and 1950. Korea was no longer a direct buffer between the two superpowers after Moscow decided to take its troops out of the Korean Peninsula in 1949 and to return its sphere of influence in Manchuria to the CCP government in 1950. In the fall of 1950, when Mao and his associates decided to intervene in the Korean War, Stalin's "layered buffer" strategy was officially in business. Thus, as a geostrategic instrument, the Sino-Soviet treaty of 1950 significantly reduced the danger of the Soviet Union becoming involved in a direct confrontation with the United States in East Asia. Communist China, however, after losing national sovereignty over Mongolia, got a "revolutionary responsibility" to fight American troops in Korea.

The American share in the 1950 settlement was indirect yet significant. Ever since the first American merchantman, *Empress of China,* arrived in Guangzhou (Canton) in 1784, the United States had maintained an exceptional position among great powers in not infringing on China's peripheral territories. Yet, during China's twentieth-century transformation into a national state, U.S. foreign policy became increasingly involved in the question of Chinese territoriality. From the Chinese perspective, the American involvement was a mixed blessing. After 1931, Washington's moralistic and legalistic stand against the Japanese occupation of Manchuria was certainly helpful in buttressing Chinese morale. During World War II, President

Franklin D. Roosevelt and his administration adopted a policy of assisting China in restoring its great power status, which not only led to the end of the "unequal treaties" between China and Western powers but also promised China to recover its "lost territories" from Japan. President Roosevelt's stumbling on the Mongolia question and concession to Stalin's Manchurian ambitions at Yalta, however, were not appreciated by Chinese of any political persuasion. After Yalta, Moscow's Mongolian satellite and Manchurian sphere seemed to bear an American stamp.

During the period under study, U.S. foreign policy was neither propelled by a primary Inner Asian interest nor pushed by a principled concern about Asian "minorities." Having always approached China from the eastern direction of the Pacific Ocean and constantly focused on their "Chinese" counterpart, American policymakers were handicapped in developing an Inner Asian equation in their China interests. Washington's geostrategic bias in favor of the eastern coast of Asia was most clearly reflected in how it was involved in China's territoriality question during and after World War II: Whereas President Roosevelt accepted Stalin's claim for Mongolia rather casually, his successors would be continuously preoccupied with the conditions and statuses of Manchuria, Korea, and Taiwan. Even today, it cannot be said that U.S. foreign policy has overcome its Inner Asian blind spot. Since the collapse of the Soviet Union, in the words of Zbigniew Brzezinski, Central Asia between China and Europe has remained a "geopolitical black hole" to which "America is too distant to be dominant . . . but too powerful not to be engaged."[4] So the Inner Asian predicament continues.

In addition to the geopolitical puzzle, there was also an ideocultural bewilderment. Apparently, during World War II and the early Cold War years, Washington had not yet been embedded in China's politics long and deeply enough to develop a publicly defensible policy for an entanglement in China's ethnopolitics. The State Department remained cautious in these years, and its deliberations on the subject differed distinctly from British Foreign Office officials' stereotypical and condescending remarks about the Mongols. In the meantime, American foreign policy officials did not consider China's ethnopolitics in the same manner as they did the "minorities question" of Europe. During the early stage of the Chinese Civil War, amazed by the simultaneous processes of the GMD–CCP talks in Nanjing and their fighting in Manchuria, Walton Butterworth of the U.S. Embassy in China

---

4. Zbigniew Brzezinski, *The Grand Chessboard: American Primacy and Its Geostrategic Imperatives* (New York: Basic Books, 1997), 148, 195.

remarked to a colleague that "we have been schooled and trained in a European type of politics, a politics so highly developed and sophisticated. . . . Chinese politics, however, are still in a relatively primitive stage, and events do not take on the same meaning in relation to the whole."[5] This observation was also reflective of American officials' views on the "underdeveloped" stage of China's ethnopolitics, which rarely gave agency to the frontier ethnic groups.

In Washington's postwar Asian policy, Japan constituted an exception that connected the country's democratization directly with American security. In the rest of East Asia, U.S. foreign policy was more concerned with Asian governments' external alignments than with their internal orientations. Even when General George Marshall was promoting a "democratic solution" of the Chinese Civil War, his immediate objective was to bring two authoritarian Chinese parties together under American patronage. During these pre–"democratization" and pre–"human rights" years of Washington's Asian policy, the ethnopolitical connotations of the Mongolia question could hardly fit into American policymakers' agenda for China. It should be added, however, that the reasons for the incompatibility between the Mongols' and the Americans' interests in China affairs were not one-sided. Between the powerful yet pro-CCP eastern Mongolian movement and the pro-American yet extremely weak "Racial Mongols" and Prince De's group, American policymakers did not have a viable choice even if they had intended to translate their "genuine sympathy" with the Inner Mongols into policy measures.

In the postwar years, Washington's Asian policy would eventually get an Inner Asian foothold only in a place where legacies of the receding British Empire existed. Whereas the Inner Mongols failed to catch the attention of Washington, the Tibetans made their American connections. But, again, Washington's Tibetan enterprise did not begin with a premise of "democratization" or with the public support of ethnic minorities' resistance against the Chinese. Rather, as rationalized by the U.S. Embassy in India in the late 1940s, isolated from its radicalized surroundings and having a conservative and religious populace, Tibet could serve as a "bulwark against the spread of Communism throughout Asia, or at least as an island of conservatism in a sea of political turmoil."[6] Just like Washington's surreptitious dealings with Prince De in the late 1940s, American support of the Tibetan "island

5. John F. Melby to Lillian Hellman, 9 November 1946, Melby Papers, box 36.
6. George R. Merrell to the Secretary of State, 13 January 1947, General Records of the U.S. Department of State Central Files: China, 711.93 Tibet / 1-1347.

of conservatism" began quietly and evasively in the 1950s. In this sense, Inner Mongolia set a precedent for America's clandestine and lukewarm interference in China's interethnic affairs during the Cold War period.

The 1950 settlement of the Mongolia question did not end China's modern bewilderment about territoriality. The event just marked the conclusion of a historical period in which the issue of Chinese territoriality was intertwined with large-scale wars and violent revolutions. It can also serve as a point of reference for our understanding of many current problems along China's peripheries. In less than a decade after Stalin and Mao cemented their Eurasian alliance along the Mongolian frontier, the geopolitical landscape of East Asia created by the early Cold War events began to erode amid the Moscow–Beijing polemics over a range of ideological and geopolitical issues. As the two sides' "anti-imperialist" struggles increasingly turned toward each other in the 1960s, the Mongolian buffer again became an explicit geopolitical fact in Asia. While the MPR continued to orbit around Moscow in the new confrontation, tens of thousands of Inner Mongols, including Ulanfu and former eastern Mongol leaders, became the targets of Mao's "Cultural Revolution." Challenged by the new orthodoxy of Maoism, Moscow's "revolutionary hegemony" since the Comintern's time could no longer hold its ground. In the meantime, the CCP's "revolutionary sovereignty" over China's ethnic frontiers was exhausted. Soon, international and interethnic conflicts between and within these communist powers were laid bare in the rubble of Stalinist and Maoist brands of communist ideologies.

The disintegration of the Soviet Union ushered in an era of arduous democratization in Russia and other former member republics of the Stalinist Empire. A logical corollary was Mongolia's "de-satellitization." Today, finally freed from Soviet domination, Mongolia is striving to stabilize its newly gained multiparty system, redefine its geopolitical identity between China and Russia, and find its position in a rapidly globalizing world economy. The impact of these developments has been felt in China. Whereas there are cyberspace noises in some Chinese Web sites calling for Mongolia's "return to the (Chinese) motherland," government geostrategists in China have noticed a "burgeoning pan-Mongolism" in Mongolia and have cautioned against a "Mongolian independence" (*meng du*) tendency in Inner Mongolia, along with separatist activities in Xinjiang and Tibet.[7] Will,

7. Shen Weilie and Lu Junyuan, *Zhongguo Guojia Anquan Dili* (State Security Geography of China) (Beijing, Shishi Chubanshe, 2001), 403–4; Lou Yangliang, *Diyuan Zhengzhi yu Zhongguo Guofang Zhanlue* (Geopolitics and China's National Defense

as many commentators have already predicted, the PRC's multiethnic system follow the path of the former Soviet Union and disintegrate before democratization? Or will events in China follow a different sequence, as independent Chinese writer-scholar Wang Lixiong warned recently: When China goes through a "democratic transformation" in the future, will its "nationality question" "become the first and foremost challenge"?[8] These questions point to a possibility that the Central Asian "geopolitical black hole" may expand. In the circumstances, the Mongolia question will likely be revived. Speculation, however, cannot go very far here. The German philosopher Friedrich von Schlegel is believed to have said: "The historian is a prophet in reverse." This seems to mean that historians, even when doing their best, can only have hindsight. Or, put in a Chinese proverb, history can show the "warning taken from the overturned cart ahead" (*qian che zhi jian*).

History does seem to indicate that the multinational republic system of the former Soviet Union and the multiethnic system of the PRC evolved from different historical processes. In contrast to the Soviet Empire, which conveniently succeeded its Tsarist predecessor, the Republic of China relayed to the People's Republic an arduous "transition from empire to nation" that, as Prasenjit Duara deftly puts it, is "one of the most problematic and enduring manifestations of the imperialism–nationalism continuum for the anti-imperialist nation."[9] Even though the Soviet Union's disintegration served the PRC a warning of "an overturned cart ahead," the PRC system, buttressed with a unitary "Chinese nation" ideology, will probably follow a different path from the Soviet system, which was structured by a federal constitution.

In the final analysis, China's modern territoriality crisis has been about domestic and international legitimacy more than about power. Although power is the key to territorial control, legitimacy, which has to be measured with generally accepted standards and principles, is the foundation of the effective, stable, and civil management of territoriality. In the early twentieth

Strategy) (Tianjin: Renmin Chubanshe, 2002), 156–57. Some of the flagrant remarks on Mongolia's "reunion" with China can be found in the pages of *Qiangguo Luntan* (Strong Power Forum) of the *People's Daily*'s official site, http://www.people.com.cn.

8. Wang Lixiong, "Xifang Minzuzhi Jihua Zhongguo Minzu Chongtu" ("Western Democratic System Will Intensify China's Ethnic Conflict"), *Duowei Youbao* (Duowei Electronic News) 115, 6 September 2003.

9. Prasenjit Duara, *Sovereignty and Authenticity: Manchukuo and the East Asian Modern* (Lanham, Md.: Rowman & Littlefield, 2003), 18.

century, the Manchu court took a series of reform measures in attempting to relegitimize both its imperial ranking in international society and its ethnic sovereignty within the Qing Empire. These only expedited the demise of the Qing Dynasty. After 1911, China's Republican and Nationalist Revolutions aimed to substitute the ageless, dynastic premises of the Chinese state with a set of nationalist values so that China could "become socialized into the international system."[10] Although the GMD and other "central governments" of the Republican period managed to gain international acceptance of their legal claims over most of the Qing Empire's territorial legacies, their domestic legitimacy was constantly challenged in Chinese provinces and was never accepted in China's ethnic frontiers.

These regimes' weakness was only part of the reason for their frustrations on the frontiers. More than anything else, their explicit Sinocentric nationalism was accountable for a bankrupt approach in dealing with ethnonationalisms evolving in China's borderlands. In contrast, the Chinese Communist Revolution repackaged Chinese nationalism with a supranational ideology and joined the Soviet Union in an effort to refashion the existing Chinese political culture and international system. As of 1950, with the support of the Soviet bloc, the Chinese Communist state was able to establish its "revolutionary" legitimacy with Chinese society and with China's northern and western ethnic frontiers.[11] For its "socialization" with the Soviet bloc, Beijing paid a price in accepting the MPR as a "brotherly socialist country" in a short-lived "socialist camp." Meanwhile, China became segregated from the capitalist West.

The frenzied revolutionary age in China ended with Mao in 1976. The end of the Cold War some fifteen years later also concluded an era when state legitimacy was sanctioned by the political and ideological particularism of segregated international blocs. Since then, post–Cold War ethnic and regional conflicts, transnational terrorist attacks, and "counterterrorist" wars have proved that there is no "end of history." Although China's convergence with the Western type of democracy is yet to be determined by the history of the future, the unstoppable trend of globalization and its harbinger, international

10. Mlada Bukovansky, *Legitimacy and Power Politics: The American and French Revolutions in International Political Culture* (Princeton, N.J.: Princeton University Press, 2002), vii.

11. By this time, Inner Mongolian autonomists and leaders of the "Eastern Turkestan" movement in Xinjiang had agreed to cooperate with the CCP. The issue of Tibet would, however, remain unsettled until an agreement was reached between Beijing and Lhasa in May 1951.

trade, have already pressured Beijing to relegitimize its state system at home and in the world. Just as Stalin used an antifascist "popular front" approach in World War II to reconnect the Soviet Union with Western powers, after 1978 Deng Xiaoping's "reform and openness" démarche also aimed to reintegrate China into the general international community. In this context, Chinese territoriality, which was stabilized after 1949 in the revolutionary mode, becomes problematic again, even though now the Chinese state is immensely more powerful than at any previous time in its modern history.

China's current perilous transition defies any simple qualification, and its end result cannot be predicted. It is a clichéd theme that if there is any certainty verifiable from China's modern experience, it is unpredictability compounded by paradoxicalness. Today, when China is being predicted to become the next economic dynamo of the world, it is also the only great power that cannot even ascertain its territoriality, one of the fundamentals of a national state. The future of the Taiwan question; "one country, two systems" in Hong Kong; and ethnic discord in Xinjiang, Tibet, and Inner Mongolia—all indicate the awkward territoriality predicament facing the PRC. Surely China is not an immature state. As Warren Cohen has pointed out, when the Chinese were practicing realpolitik in their own "international system" some three millenniums ago, Central Europe, statecraft's modern birthplace, "was still populated with neolithic scavengers."[12] China is overly mature on its own terms. But its search for a modern identity is far from over. So China's territoriality today and for the foreseeable future will be affected by the same questions as in 1840, 1911, 1949, and 1978: In what direction will China strike out, and in what international system will China fit in?

12. Warren I. Cohen, *East Asia at the Center: Four Thousand Years of Engagement with the World* (New York: Columbia University Press, 2000), 2.

A Note on Transliteration

Most Chinese names are transliterated with pinyin. Familiar Wade-Giles forms such as "Chiang Kai-shek," "Kuomintang," and "Canton" are replaced with "Jiang Jieshi," "Guomindang," "Guangzhou." These pinyin forms are already widely in use in today's historical writings. The exceptions are Wade-Giles spellings that have not been replaced with pinyin forms in historical writings, such as "Sun Yat-sen" and "Manchukuo." Transliterations of Mongolian names follow the practices in the field of Mongolian studies whenever possible. In cases where the proper rendering of Mongolian pronunciations cannot be ascertained, pinyin is used. Titles of all Chinese books and journals are transliterated and translated, but titles of Chinese articles are translated without transliteration. The usages of the two adjectives, "Mongolian" and "Mongol," are confusing even among specialists in Mongolian studies. This study follows a practice of using "Mongolian" when matters, institutions, and locations are in question but "Mongol" when people are referred to.

433

Acronyms and Abbreviations

CCP	Chinese Communist Party
CWIHP	Cold War International History Project
DFZZ	*Zhongguo Gongnong Hongjun Disi Fangfianjun Zhanshi Ziliao Xuanbian, Changzheng Shiqi* (Selected Materials on the Combat History of the Fourth Front Army of the Chinese Workers' and Peasants' Red Army, the Long March Period).
EMPAA	Eastern Mongolian People's Autonomous Army
EMPAG	Eastern Mongolian People's Autonomous Government
FEA	*Far Eastern Affairs*
FRUS	*Foreign Relations of the United States: Diplomatic Papers*
GDW	Guomindang Dangshi Weiyuanhui (Historical Council of the Guomindang)
GLZD	*Gongchan Guoji, Liangong (Bu) yu Zhongguo Geming Dang'an Ziliao Congshu* (Selected Archival Materials on the Comintern, Soviet Communist Party (Bolshevik) and the Chinese Revolution)
GMD	Guomindang (Nationalist Party)
GRDS	General Records of the United States Department of State Central Files: China
GSGD	Guoshiguan Dang'anguan (Archives of Academia Historica)
GZD	Guomin Zhengfu Dang'an (Archives of the National Government)

GZWD	Guofang Zuigao Weiyuanhui Dang'an (Archives of the Supreme Council of National Defense)
IMAG	Inner Mongolian Autonomous Government
IMAMA	Inner Mongolian Autonomous Movement Association
IMPRP	Inner Mongolian People's Revolutionary Party
JW	Junshi Weiyuanhui (Council of Military Affairs)
JYLW	*Jianguo Yilai Liu Shaoqi Wengao* (Liu Shaoqi's Manuscripts since the Foundation of the State)
JYMW	*Jianguo Yilai Mao Zedong Wengao* (Mao Zedong's Manuscripts since the Foundation of the State)
JZZD/GW (KLS)	Jiang Zhongzheng Zongtong Dang'an: Geming Wenxian (Kanluan Shiqi) (Archives of President Jiang Zhongzheng: Revolutionary Documents [Period of Suppressing Rebellion])
JZZD/GW (KZS)	Jiang Zhongzheng Zongtong Dang'an: Geming Wenxian (Kangzhan Shiqi) (Archives of President Jiang Zhongzheng: Revolutionary Documents [Period of the War of Resistance])
JZZD/TD (FG)	Jiang Zhongzheng Zongtong Dang'an: Tejiao Dang'an (Fang Gong) (Archives of President Jiang Zhongzheng: Specially Submitted Documents [Defense against the Communists])
JZZD/TD (JF)	Jiang Zhongzheng Zongtong Dang'an: Tejiao Dang'an (Jiao Fei) (Archives of President Jiang Zhongzheng: Specially Submitted Documents [Banditry Suppression])
JZZD/TD (ZZ)	Jiang Zhongzheng Zongtong Dang'an: Tejiao Dang'an (Zhengzhi) (Archives of President Jiang Zhongzheng: Specially Submitted Documents [Political])
JZZD/TW (EY)	Jiang Zhongzheng Zongtong Dang'an: Tejiao Wendian (Edi Yinmou Bufen) (Archives of President Jiang Zhongzheng: Specially Submitted Telegrams [Part on Russian Imperialist Conspiracy])
MPP	Mongolian People's Party
MPR	Mongolian People's Republic
MPRP	Mongolian People's Revolutionary Party
MTAC	Mongolian and Tibetan Affairs Commission

MWWH	*Minzu Wenti Wenxian Huibian* (Collected Documents on the Nationality Question)
MYA	Mongolian Youth Alliance
NWZ	*Neimenggu Wenshi Ziliao* (Literary and Historical Materials of Inner Mongolia)
NZYL	*Neimenggu Zizhi Yundong Lianhehui Dang'an Shiliao Xuanbian* (Selected Archival Materials on the Inner Mongolian Autonomous Movement Association)
PRC	People's Republic of China
QZH	Quanzonghao (general record number)
RCPCC	Russian Communist Party Central Committee
RCTO	Records of the China Theater of Operations, United States Army (CT): Records of the Office of the Commanding General (Wedemeyer)
RDCA	Records of the Division of Chinese Affairs
RNSC	Records of the National Security Council
ROCA	Records of the Office of Chinese Affairs
ROC	Republic of China
SLDX	*Sulian Lishi Dang'an Xuanbian* (Selected Historical Archives of the Soviet Union)
WJB/YTS	Waijiaobu Yataisi (Asian–Pacific Division of the Ministry of Foreign Affairs)
WJB/YXS	Waijiaobu Yaxisi (West Asian Division of the Ministry of Foreign Affairs)
XZY	Xingzhengyuan (Executive Yuan [chamber])
ZD	Zongtongfu Dang'an (Archives of the Presidential Palace)
ZSGG	*Zhong Su Guojia Guanxi Shi Ziliao Huibian* (Selected Materials on the History of Sino-Soviet Relations)
ZZSC	*Zhonghua Minguo Zhongyao Shiliao Chubian* (Preliminary Compilation of Important Historical Documents of the Republic of China)
ZZWX	*Zhonggong Zhongyang Wenjian Xuanji* (Selected Documents of the CCP Central Committee)

Bibliography

Manuscript Collections

Mansfield Addis Collection, Public Record Office, Kew Gardens, Surrey, England.

Chen Kuang-fu. "Reminiscences of Chen Kuang-fu." Oral History Project of Columbia University (1961), Butler Library, Columbia University, New York City.

Clark M. Clifford Papers, Truman Library, Independence, Missouri.

Matthew J. Connelly Papers, Truman Library.

Victor Ch'i-ts'a Hoo (Hu Shize) Papers, Archives of the Hoover Institution, Stanford, Calif.

Stanley K. Hornbeck Papers, Hoover Institution.

Harry L. Hopkins Papers, Franklin D. Roosevelt Library, Hyde Park, New York.

Harry N. Howard Papers, Truman Library.

Hsiung Shihui (Xiong Shihui) Collections, Butler Library.

Philip C. Jessup Papers, Library of Congress, Washington.

Jiang Zhongzheng Zongtong Dang'an (Archives of President Jiang Zhongzheng [Jiang Jieshi]), Academia Historica, Taiwan: Geming Wenxian (revolutionary documents), Tejiao Dang'an (specially submitted documents), Tejiao Wendian (specially submitted telegrams).

Owen Lattimore Papers, Library of Congress.

John F. Melby Papers, Truman Library.

Franklin D. Roosevelt Papers, Roosevelt Library: Mam Room Files, President's Secretary's Files.

T. V. Soong (Song Ziwen) Papers, Hoover Institution.

Harry S. Truman Papers, Truman Library: Intelligence Files, Post-Presidential Memoirs, President's Secretary's Files.

Albert C. Wedemeyer Papers, Hoover Institution

Unpublished Government Documents
People's Republic of China

Archives of the Inner Mongolian Autonomous Region, Hohhot: Quanzonghao 4: Dongmeng Zhengfu (General record number 4 [Eastern Mongolian Government]);

Quanzonghao 6: Neimenggu Zizhi Yundong Lianhehui (Alliance of the Inner Mongolian Autonomous Movements).

Second Historical Archives of China, Nanjing: Quanzonghao 1: Guominzhengfu (Na-
tionalist Government); Quanzonghao 18: Waijaobu (Ministry of Foreign Affairs);
Quanzonghao 141: Meng Zang Shiwu Weiyuanhui (Mongolian and Tibetan Affairs
Commission); Quanzonghao 761: Junshi Weiyuanhui (Military Council).

Russia

Russian Center for Preservation and Study of Documents of Contemporary History,
Moscow: Juntiaochu Zhixingbu Huiyi Jilu, 1946 (Meeting Minutes of the Executive
Committee of the Military Mediation Group) (in Chinese); Yiju Zuozhanshi, "Wuge
Yue Lai Tingzhan Gongzuo Zongjie Cailiao," 1946. 6. ([CCP] Operation Office of
the First Bureau, "Materials that Summarize the Cease-Fire Work in the Past Five
Months," June 1946) (in Chinese).

Taiwan

Guoshiguan (Academia Historica): Guomin Zhengfu Dang'an (Records of the National
Government); Xingzhengyuan Dang'an (Records of the Executive Yuan); Zongtonfu
Dang'an (Records of the Presidential Palace).

Guomindang Dangshi Weiyuanhui (Historical Council of the GMD): Guofang Zuigao
Weiyuanhui Dang'an (Records of the Supreme Council of National Defense).

Waijiaobu Dang'an Zixunchu (Desk of Archives of the Ministry of Foreign Affairs):
Waijiaobu Yataisi Dang'an (Records of the Asia-Pacific Division of the Ministry of
Foreign Affairs); Waijiaobu Yaxisi Dang'an (Records of the Western Asian Division
of the Ministry of Foreign Affairs).

United Kingdom

India Office, London: L/P&S/12, Political Department, Annual Files.

Public Record Office, Kew Gardens, Surrey, England: FO 371, Foreign Office, Registry
Files.

United States

Cold War International History Project Virtual Archive, http://wilsoncenter.org.

National Archives and Federal Records Center, Suitland, Md.: Records of the China Theater of Operations, United States Army (CT): Records of the Office of the Commanding General (Albert C. Wedemeyer); Top Secret General Records of Chungking
Embassy, China, 1943–45.

National Archives II, College Park, Md.: General Records of the United State Department
of State Central Files: China (RG 59); Records of the Division of Chinese Affairs
(RG 59).

Records of Harley A. Notter (Postwar Planning) (RG 59); Records of the Joint Chiefs
of Staff (RG 165, microfilm); Records of the National Security Council (RG 273);
Records of the Office of Chinese Affairs (RG 59); Records of the Office of Strategic
Services (RG 226).

Published Documentary and Manuscript Collections

In English

Chinese Ministry of Information (Taiwan). *The Collected Wartime Messages of Generalissimo Chiang Kai-shek, 1937–1945.* New York: Kraus Reprint Co., 1969.

Cold War International History Project. *Bulletin, Issues 6–7: The Cold War in Asia.* Washington, D.C.: Woodrow Wilson International Center for Scholars, 1995–96.

———. *Bulletin, Issues 8–9: New East-Bloc Evidence on the Cold War in the Third World and the Collapse of Détente in the 1970s.* Washington, D.C.: Woodrow Wilson International Center for Scholars, 1996–97.

———. *Bulletin, Issue 10: Leadership Transition in a Fractured Bloc.* Washington, D.C.: Woodrow Wilson International Center for Scholars, 1998.

———. *Bulletin, Issues 11–12: The End of the Cold War.* Washington, D.C.: Woodrow Wilson International Center for Scholars, 2001.

Degras, Jane, ed. *Soviet Documents on Foreign Policy.* 4 vols. New York: Octagon Books, 1978.

U.S. Department of State. *Foreign Relations of the United States: Diplomatic Papers, 1944: China.* Washington, D.C.: Government Printing Office, 1967.

Zhang Shuguang and Chen Jian, eds. *Chinese Communist Foreign Policy and the Cold War in Asia: New Documentary Evidence, 1944–1950.* Chicago: Imprint Publications, 1996.

In Chinese

Chaoxian Zhanzheng: Eguo Dang'anguan de Jiemi Wenjian (The Korean War: Declassified Documents from the Russian Archives). Compiled by Shen Zhihua. 3 vols. Taipei: Zhongyang Yanjiuyuan Jindaishi Yanjiusuo, 2003.

Daqingshan Kang Ri Youji Genjudi Ziliao Xuanbian (Selected Materials on the Anti-Japanese Guerrilla Base in the Daqingshan Mountain). Compiled by the Committee on the Collection of Party History Materials of the CCP Committee of the Inner Mongolian Autonomous Region and the Archives of the Inner Mongolian Autonomous Region. Hohhot: Neimenggu Renmin Chubanshe, 1987.

Geming Wenxian (Revolutionary Documents). Compiled by Historical Council of the Guomindang. Multivolume. Taipei: Guomindang Dangshi Weiyuanhui, 1976–.

Gongchan Guoji, Liangong (Bu) yu Zhongguo Guomin Keming Dang'an Ziliao Congshu (Series of Archival Materials on the Comintern, the Soviet Communist Party [Bolshevik], and the Chinese Revolution). Translated and compiled by First Research Department of the Research Office on the Party History of the CCP Central Committee. 12 vols. Beijing: Beijing Tushuguan Chubanshe, 1997 (vols. 1–6); Beijing: Zhongyang Wenxian Chubanshe, 2002 (vols. 7–12).

Jianguo yilai Liu Shaoqi Wengao (Liu Shaoqi's Manuscripts after the Establishment of the State). Beijing: Zhongyang Wenxian Chubanshe, 1998.

Jianguo Yilai Mao Zedong Wengao (Mao Zedong's Manuscripts since the Foundation of the State). Beijing: Zhongyang Wenxian Chubanshe, 1987.

Jianguo Yilai Zhongyao Wenxian Xuanbian (Selection of Important Documents since the Establishment of the State). Compiled by the Documentary Research Office of the CCP Central Committee. Multivolume. Beijing: Zhongyang Wenxian Chubanshe, 1992.

Mao Zedong Junshi Huodong Jishi (Records of Mao Zedong's Military Activities). Compiled by Chinese Military Museum. Beijing: Jiefangjun Chubanshe, 1994.

Mao Zedong Shuxin Xuanji (Selected Correspondence of Mao Zedong). Beijing: Renmin Chubanshe, 1983.

Mao Zedong Waijiao Wenxuan (Selected Diplomatic Works of Mao Zedong). Beijing: Zhongyang Wenxian Chubanshe, 1994.

Mao Zedong Wenji (Manuscripts of Mao Zedong). 5 vols. Beijing: Renmin Chubanshe, 1993–96.

Mao Zedong Zaoqi Wengao (Early Writings of Mao Zedong). Changsha: Hunan Chubanshe, 1995.

Minzu Wenti Wenxian Huibian (Collected Documents on the Nationality Question). Compiled by United Front Department of the Central Committee of the Chinese Communist Party. Beijing: Zhonggong Zhongyang Dangxiao Chubanshe, 1991 (internal circulation).

Neimenggu Dang'an Shiliao (Archival Materials on Inner Mongolian History). Quarterly. Hohhot: Neimenggu Dang'anguan, 1992–.

Neimenggu Tongzhan Shi: Dang'an Shiliao Xuanbian (History of the United Front in Inner Mongolia: Selected Archival Materials). Compiled by United-Front Department of CCP Committee of Inner Mongolia and Archives of Inner Mongolian Autonomous Region, 1987 (internal circulation).

Neimenggu Zizhi Yundong Lianhehui Dang'an Shiliao Xuanbian (Selected Archival Materials on the Inner Mongolian Autonomous Movement Association). Beijing: Dang'an Chubanshe, 1989.

Riben Diguozhuyi Duiwai Qinlue Shiliao Xuanbian (Selected Historical Documents on Japanese Imperialist Foreign Aggression). Compiled and translated by Japanese History Group of the History Department of Fudan University. Shanghai: Renmin Chubanshe, 1975.

Suiyuan "Jiu Yi Jiu" Heping Qiyi Dang'an Shiliao Xuanbian (Selected Archival and Historical Materials on the 19 September Peaceful Uprising in Suiyuan). Compiled by Inner Mongolian Archives. Hohhot: Neimonggu Renmin Chubanshe, 1986.

Sulian Gongchandang Zuihou Yige Fandang Jituan (The Last Antiparty Clique in the Soviet Communist Party). Complete minutes of June 1957 conference and October 1964 conference of Soviet Union Communist Party Congress, translated by Zhao Yongmu et al. Beijing: Zhongguo Shehui Chubanshe, 1997.

Sulian Lishi Dang'an Xuanbian (Selected Historical Archives of the Soviet Union). Translated and compiled by Shen Zhihua et al. 34 vols. Bejing: Shehui Kexue Wenxian Chubanshe, 2002.

Woguo Minzu Quyu Zizhi Wenxian Ziliao Huibian (Collected Documents on the Nationality Regional Autonomy of Our Country). Compiled by Nationalities Institute of Chinese Academy of Social Sciences (no pub., n.d.).

Xian Zongtong Jiang Gong Sixiang Yanlun Zongji (Complete Works of the Late President Jiang [Jieshi]). Compiled by Historical Council of the Guomindang. 40 vols. Taipei: Guomindang Dangshi Weiyuanhui, 1984.

Zhan Dong Zonghui Wenxian Ziliao Huiyilu (Materials and Recollections on the General Society for Wartime Mobilization). Compiled and published by Party History Research Office of the Chinese Communist Party Shanxi Committee, 1987.

Zhonggong Zhongyang Wenjian Xuanji (Selected Documents of the Chinese Communist Party Central Committee). Compiled by the Central Archives. 18 vols. Beijing: Zhonggong Zhongyang Dangxiao Chubanshe, 1992.

Zhongguo Gongnong Hongjun Disi Fangfianjun Zhanshi Ziliao Xuanbian, Changzheng

Shiqi (Selected Materials on the Combat History of the Fourth Front Army of the Chinese Workers' and Peasants' Red Army, the Long March Period). Beijing: Jiefangjun Chubanshe, 1992.

Zhonghua Minguo Zhongyao Shiliao Chubian: Dui Ri Kangzhan Shiqi (Preliminary Compilation of Important Historical Records of the Republic of China: The Period of the War of Resistance against Japan). Historical Council of the Guomindang. 7 vols. Taipei: Guomindang Dangshi Weiyuanhui, 1981.

Zhong Su Guojia Guanxi Ziliao Huibian (Collected Documents on the History of Sino-Soviet Interstate Relations). Compiled by Xue Xiantian et al. Multivolume. Beijing: Zhongguo Shehui Kexue Chubanshe, 1993–.

Zhou Enlai Junshi Wenxuan (Selected Military Works of Zhou Enlai). Beijing: Renmin Chubanshe, 1997.

Zhou Enlai Yijiusiliu Nian Tanpan Wenxuan (Selected Documents on Zhou Enlai's Negotiations in 1946). Compiled by Documentary Research Office of Chinese Communist Party Central Committee and Chinese Communist Party Committee of Nanjing. Beijing: Zhongyang Wenxian Chubanshe, 1996.

Selected Reminiscent and Scholarly Works

In English

Adas, Michael. "Imperialism and Colonialism in Comparative Perspective," *International Historical Review* 20(2) (June 1998): 371–88.

Akiner, Shirin, ed. *Mongolia Today.* London: Kegan Paul International, 1991.

Aldrich, Richard J., et al., eds. *The Clandestine Cold War in Asia, 1945–1965: Western Intelligence, Propaganda and Special Operations.* London: Frank Cass, 2000.

Anderson, Benedict. *Imagined Communities: Reflections on the Origin and Spread of Nationalism.* London: Verso, 1991.

Anderson, Malcolm. *Frontiers: Territory and State Formation in the Modern World.* Cambridge: Polity Press, 1996.

Atwood, Christopher. "A. I. Oshirov (c. 1901–1931): A Buriat Agent in Inner Mongolia." In *Opuscula Altaica: Essays Presented in Honor of Henry Schwarz,* ed. Edward H. Kaplan and Donald W. Whisenhunt. Bellingham: Center for East Asian Studies of Western Washington University, 1994.

———. "East Mongolian Revolution and Chinese Communism," *Mongolian Studies* 15 (1992): 7–82.

———. *Encyclopedia of Mongolia and the Mongol Empire.* New York: Facts on File, 2004.

———. "National Party and Local Politics in Ordos, Inner Mongolia (1926–1935)." *Journal of Asian History* 26(1) (1992): 2–10.

———. *Young Mongols and Vigilantes in Inner Mongolia's Interregnum Decades, 1911–1931.* Leiden: Brill Academic Publishers, 2002.

Baabar. *Twentieth Century Mongolia.* Cambridge: White Horse Press, 1999.

Banac, Ivo, ed. *The Diary of Georgi Dimitrov, 1933–1949.* New Haven, Conn.: Yale University Press, 2003.

Barany, Zotan. "Soviet Takeovers: The Role of Advisers in Mongolia in the 1920s and in Eastern Europe after World War II." *Eastern European Quarterly* 28(4) (January 1995): 409–33.

Barfield, Thomas. *The Perilous Frontier: Nomadic Empires and China.* Cambridge: Basil Blackwell, 1989.

Barmin, Valery. "Xinjiang in the History of Soviet–Chinese Relations from 1937 to 1946." *Far Eastern Affairs* 1 (2000): 63–77.

Batbayar, Tsedenbambyn. "Stalin's Strategy in Mongolia, 1932–1936," *Mongolian Studies* 22 (1999): 1–17.

Batsaikhan, Ookhnoin. "Issues Concerning Mongolian Independence from the Soviet Union and China: The Attempt to Incorporate Mongolia within the USSR and the Positions of Soviet Leaders, Stalin, Molotov, and Mikoyan." Unpub. paper presented at International Workshop on Mongolia and the Cold War, Ulaanbaatar, March 19–20, 2004.

Bawden, C. R. "A Joint Petition of Grievances Submitted to the Ministry of Justice of Autonomous Mongolia in 1919." *Bulletin of the School of Oriental and African Studies* 30(3) (1967): 548–63.

———. *The Modern History of Mongolia.* London: Kegan Paul International, 1989.

Berezhkov, Valentin M. *At Stalin's Side: His Interpreter's Memoirs from the October Revolution to the Fall of the Dictator's Empire.* Trans. Sergei V. Mikheyev. New York: Carol Publishing Group, 1994.

Bobrick, Benson. *East of the Sun: The Epic Conquest and Tragic History of Siberia.* New York: Poseidon Press, 1992.

Brown, William, and Urgunge Onon, trans. *History of the Mongolian People's Republic.* Cambridge: East Asian Research Center of Harvard University, 1976.

Brzezinski, Zbigniew. *The Grand Chessboard: American Primacy and Its Geostrategic Imperatives.* New York: BasicBooks, 1997.

Bukovansky, Mlada. *Legitimacy and Power Politics: The American and French Revolutions in International Political Culture.* Princeton, N.J.: Princeton University Press, 2002.

Bulag, Uradyn E. *The Mongols at China's Edge: History and the Politics of National Unity.* Lanham, Md.: Rowman & Littlefield, 2002.

———. *Nationalism and Hybridity in Mongolia.* Oxford: Oxford University Press, 1998.

Campi, Alicia J. "Perceptions of the Outer Mongols by the United States Government as Reflected in Kalgan (Inner Mongolia) U.S. Consular Records 1920–1927." *Mongolian Studies* 14 (1991): 81–109.

Chen Jian. *Mao's China and the Cold War.* Chapel Hill: University of North Carolina Press, 2001.

Chuev, Felix. *Molotov Remembers: Inside Kremlin Politics, Conversations with Felix Chuev.* Chicago: Ivan R. Dee, 1993.

Chuluun, O. "The Two Phases in Mongolian–Chinese Relations, 1949–1972." *Far Eastern Affairs* 1 (1974): 24–32.

Clubb, O. Edmund. *China & Russia: The "Great Game."* New York: Columbia University Press, 1971.

Cohen, Warren I. *East Asia at the Center: Four Thousand Years of Engagement with the World.* New York: Columbia University Press, 2000.

Connor, Walker. *Ethnonationalism: The Quest for Understanding.* Princeton, N.J.: Princeton University Press, 1994.

Crossley, Pamela Kyle. *A Translucent Mirror: History and Identity in Qing Imperial Ideology.* Berkeley: University of California Press, 1999.

Davies, John Paton Jr. *Dragon by the Tail: American, British, Japanese, and Russian Encounters with China and One Another.* New York: W. W. Norton, 1972.

Deriabin, Peter S. *Inside Stalin's Kremlin: An Eyewitness Account of Brutality, Duplicity, and Intrigue.* Washington, D.C.: Brassey's, 1998.

Di Cosmo, Nicola. "Mongolian Topics in the U.S. Military Intelligence Reports." *Mongolian Studies* 10 (1986–87): 97–106.

———. "Qing Colonial Administration in Inner Asia." *International History Review* 20(2) (June 1998): 287–309.

Dijkink, Gertjan. *National Identity and Geographical Visions: Maps of Pride and Pain.* New York: Routledge, 1996.

Dikotter, Frank. *The Discourse of Race in Modern China* (Stanford, Calif.: Stanford University Press, 1992.

Duara, Prasenjit. *Sovereignty and Authenticity: Manchukuo and the East Asian Modern.* Lanham, Md.: Rowman & Littlefield, 2003.

Elleman, Bruce A. *Diplomacy and Deception: The Secret History of Sino-Soviet Diplomatic Relations, 1917–1927.* Armonk, N.Y.: M. E. Sharpe, 1997.

———. "Secret Sino-Soviet Negotiations on Outer Mongolia, 1918–1925." *Pacific Affairs* 66 (Winter 1993–94): 554–58.

———. "Soviet Policy on Outer Mongolia and the Chinese Communist Party." *Journal of Asian History* 28(2) (1994): 108–23.

Elliott, Mark C. *The Manchu Way: The Eight Banners and Ethnic Identity in Late Imperial China.* Stanford, Calif.: Stanford University Press, 2001.

Esherick, Joseph W., ed. *Lost Chance in China: The World War II Dispatches of John S. Service.* New York: Random House, 1974.

Ewing, Thomas E. *Between the Hammer and the Anvil? Chinese and Russian Policies in Outer Mongolia, 1911–1921.* Bloomington: Research Institute for Inner Asian Studies of Indiana University, 1980.

———. "Ch'ing Policies in Outer Mongolia 1900–1911." *Modern Asian Studies* 14(1) (1980): 145–57.

Fitzgerald, John. *Awakening China: Politics, Culture, and Class in the Nationalist Revolution.* Stanford, Calif.: Stanford University Press, 1996.

Fletcher, Joseph. "Ch'ing Inner Asia c. 1800." In *The Cambridge History of China, Volume 10: Late Ch'ing, 1800–1911, Part I.* Cambridge: Cambridge University Press, 1978.

———. "The Heyday of The Ch'ing Order in Mongolia, Sinkiang and Tibet." In *The Cambridge History of China, Volume 10: Late Ch'ing, 1800–1911, Part I.* Cambridge: Cambridge University Press, 1978.

———. "Sino-Russian Relations, 1800–62." In *The Cambridge History of China, Volume 10: Late Ch'ing, 1800–1911, Part I.* Cambridge: Cambridge University Press, 1978.

Friters, Gerard M. *Outer Mongolia and Its International Position.* Baltimore: Johns Hopkins University Press, 1949.

———. "The Prelude to Outer Mongolian Independence." *Pacific Affairs* 10 (2) (June 1937): 168–89.

Futaki, Hiroshi. "A Re-Examination of the Establishment of the Mongolian People's Party, Centering on Dogsom's Memoir." *Inner Asia* 2 (2000): 37–61.

Garver, John W. *Chinese–Soviet Relations, 1939–1945: The Diplomacy of Chinese Nationalism.* New York: Oxford University Press, 1988.

Gelber, Harry G. *Nations Out of Empires: European Nationalism and the Transformation of Asia.* New York: Palgrave, 2001.

Gellner, Ernest. *Nations and Nationalism.* Ithaca, N.Y.: Cornell University Press, 1983.

Glantz, David M. *August Storm: The Soviet 1945 Strategic Offensive in Manchuria.* Fort Leavenworth, Kan.: Combat Studies Institute of U.S. Army Command and General Staff College, 1983.

Goncharov, Sergei. "The Stalin–Mao Dialogue; Ivan Kovalev, Stalin's Personal Envoy to Mao Zedong, interviewed by historian and sinologist Sergei Goncherov." *Far Eastern Affairs* 1 (1992): 100–16.

Goncharov, Sergei N., John W. Lewis, and Xue Litai. *Uncertain Partners: Stalin, Mao, and the Korean War.* Stanford, Calif.: Stanford University Press, 1993.

Grousset, Rene. *Empire of the Steppes: A History of Central Asia.* New Brunswick, N.J.: Rutgers University Press, 1970.

Guo Tao-fu (Merse). "Modern Mongolia." *Pacific Affairs* 3(8) (August 1930): 754–62.

Hammond, Thomas T. "The Communist Takeover of Outer Mongolia: Model for Eastern Europe?" *Studies on the Soviet Union* 11(4) (1971): 107–44.

Hechter, Michael. *Containing Nationalism.* Oxford: Oxford University Press, 2000.

Heinzig, Dieter. *The Soviet Union and Communist China, 1945–1950: The Arduous Road to the Alliance.* Armonk, N.Y.: M. E. Sharpe, 2004.

Heuschert, Dorothea. "Legal Pluralism in the Qing Empire: Manchu Legislation for the Mongols." *International History Review* 20(2) (June 1998): 310–24.

Ho, Ping-ti. "In Defense of Sinicization: A Rebuttal of Evelyn Rawski's 'Reenvisioning the Qing.'" *Journal of Asian Studies* 57(1) (February 1998): 123–55.

Hobsbawn, E. J. *Nations and Nationalism since 1780.* Cambridge: Cambridge University Press, 1990.

Hopkirk, Peter. *Setting the East Ablaze: Lenin's Dream of an Empire in Asia.* New York: Kodansha International, 1995.

Hostetler, Laura. *Qing Colonial Enterprise: Ethnography and Cartography in Early Modern China.* Chicago: University of Chicago Press, 2001.

Huang, Ray. *China: A Macro History.* Armonk, N.Y.: M. E. Sharpe, 1990.

Hunt, Michael H. *The Genesis of Chinese Communist Foreign Policy.* New York: Columbia University Press, 1996.

Isono, Fujiko. "Soviet Russia and the Mongolian Revolution of 1921." *Past and Present* 83 (March 1979): 116–40.

Jagchid, Sechin. *The Last Mongol Prince: The Life and Times of Demchugdongrob, 1902–1966.* Bellingham: Center for East Asian Studies, Western Washington University, 1999.

Johnson, Chalmers A. *Peasant Nationalism and Communist Power.* Stanford, Calif.: Stanford University Press, 1962.

Kaplonski, Christopher. "Creating National Identity in Socialist Mongolia." *Central Asian Survey* 17(1) (1998): 35–49.

Kennan, George F. *Memoirs, 1925–1950.* New York: Pantheon Books, 1967.

Kotkin, Stephen, and Bruce Elleman, eds. *Mongolia in the Twentieth Century: Landlocked Cosmopolitan.* Armonk, N.Y.: M. E. Sharpe, 1999.

Krasner, Stephen D. *Sovereignty: Organized Hypocrisy.* Princeton, N.J.: Princeton University Press, 1999.

Kriukov, Mikhail. "Once Again about Sun Yatsen's Northwest Plan." *Far Eastern Affairs* 5 (2000): 69–84.

Kuznetsov, I. I. "The Soviet Military Advisors in Mongolia, 1921–1939." *Journal of Slavic Military Studies* 12(4) (December 1999): 118–37.

LaFeber, Walter. *The Clash: U.S.–Japanese Relations throughout History.* New York: W. W. Norton, 1997.

Laird, Thomas. *Into Tibet: The CIA's First Atomic Spy and His Secret Expedition to Lhasa.* New York: Grove Press, 2002.

Lattimore, Owen. *China Memoirs: Chiang Kai-shek and the War against Japan.* Compiled by Fujiko Isono. Tokyo: University of Tokyo Press, 1990.

———. "Mongolia Enters World Affairs." *Pacific Affairs* 7(1) (March 1934): 15–28.

———. *Nationalism and Revolution in Mongolia.* New York: Oxford University Press, 1955.

———. *Nomads and Commissars: Mongolia Revisited.* New York: Oxford University Press, 1962.

———. "Prince, Priest and Herdsman in Mongolia." *Pacific Affairs* 8(1) (March 1935): 35–47.

———. *Studies in Frontier History: Collected Papers 1929–58.* London: Oxford University Press, 1962.

LeDonne, John P. *The Russian Empire and the World, 1700–1917: The Geopolitics of Expansion and Containment.* Oxford: Oxford University Press, 1997.

Ledovsky, Andrei. "Mikoyan's Secret Mission to China in January and February 1949." *Far Eastern Affairs* 2 (1995): 72–94.

———. "The Moscow Visit of a Delegation of the Communist Party of China in June to August 1949." *Far Eastern Affairs* 4; 5 (1996): 64–86; 84–97.

Levine, Steven I. *Anvil of Victory: The Communist Revolution in Manchuria, 1945–1948.* New York: Columbia University Press, 1987.

Lieven, Dominic. *Empire: The Russian Empire and Its Rivals.* New Haven, Conn.: Yale University Press, 2000.

Litvinov, Maxim. *Notes for a Journal.* New York: William Morrow, 1955.

Liu Xiaohong. *Chinese Ambassadors: The Rise of Professionalism since 1949.* Seattle: University of Washington Press, 2001.

Liu Xiaoyuan. *Frontier Passages: Ethnopolitics and the Rise of Chinese Communism, 1921–1945.* Washington, D.C., and Stanford, Calif.: Woodrow Wilson Center Press and Stanford University Press, 2004.

———. *A Partnership for Disorder: China, the United States, and Their Policies for the Postwar Disposition of the Japanese Empire, 1941–1945.* Cambridge: Cambridge University Press, 1996.

Lkhagva, Togoochiyn. "What Was Stalin's Real Attitude to [sic] the Mongols." *FER* 4 (1991): 117–6.

Luzianin, Sergei. "Mongolia: Between China and Soviet Russia. *Far Eastern Affairs* 2 (1995): 53–70.

———. *Rossiia–Mongoliia–Kitaii v pervoii polovine XX v: Politicheskie vzaimootnosheniia v 1911–1946 g.* (Russia, Mongolia, and China in the first half of the twentieth century: Political relations, 1911–1946). Moscow: Far Eastern Institute of Russian Academy of Sciences, 2000.

———. "The Yalta Conference and Mongolia in International Law before and during the Second World War." *Far Eastern Affairs* 6 (1995): 34–45.

Maier, Charles S. "Consigning the Twentieth Century to History: Alternative Narratives for the Modern Era." *American Historical Review* 105(3) (June 2000): 807–31.

March, G. Patrick. *Eastern Destiny: Russia in Asia and the North Pacific.* Westport, Conn.: Praeger, 1996.

Mastny, Vojtech. *The Cold War and Soviet Insecurity: The Stalin Years.* New York: Oxford University Press, 1996.

Mayers, David Allan. *Crack the Monolith: U.S. Policy against the Sino-Soviet Alliance, 1949–1955.* Baton Rouge: Louisiana State University Press, 1986.

Melby, John F. *The Mandate of Heaven: Record of a Civil War, China 1945–49.* New York: Doubleday, 1971.

Memmi, Albert. *The Colonizer and the Colonized.* Boston: Beacon Press, 1991.

Morley, James W., ed. *The China Quagmire: Japan's Expansion on the Asian Continent, 1933–1941.* New York: Columbia University Press, 1983.

Morozova, Irina Y. *The Comintern and Revolution in Mongolia.* Cambridge: White Horse Press, 2002.

Murphy, George G. S. *Soviet Mongolia: A Study of The Oldest Political Satellite.* Berkeley: University of California Press, 1966.

Newman, Robert P. *Owen Lattimore and the "Loss" of China.* Berkeley: University of California Press, 1992.

O'Connor, Timothy Edward. *Diplomacy and Revolution: G. V. Chicherin and Soviet Foreign Affairs, 1918–1930.* Ames: Iowa State University Press, 1988.

Onon, Urgunge, and Derrick Pritchatt. *Asia's First Modern Revolution: Mongolia Proclaims Its Independence in 1911.* Leiden: E. J. Brill, 1989.

Paine, S. C. M. *Imperial Rivals: China, Russia, and Their Disputed Frontier.* Armonk, N.Y.: M. E. Sharpe, 1996.

Pechatnov, Vladimir O. *The Big Three after World War II: New Documents on Soviet Thinking about Postwar Relations with the United States and Great Britain.* Cold War International History Project Working Paper 13. Washington, D.C.: Cold War International History Project, Woodrow Wilson International Center for Scholars, 1995.

Perdue, Peter C. "Boundaries, Maps, and Movement: Chinese, Russian, and Mongolian Empires in Early Modern Central Eurasia." *International History Review* 20(2) (June 1998): 263–86.

———. "Comparing Empires: Manchu Colonialism." *International History Review* 20(2) (June 1998): 255–61.

———. "Military Mobilization in Seventeenth and Eighteenth-Century China, Russia, and Mongolia." *Modern Asian Studies* 30(4) (1996): 757–93.

Persits, Moisei. "A New Collection of Documents on Soviet Policy in the Far East in 1920–1922." *Far Eastern Affairs* 5 (1997): 79–93.

Pipes, Richard, ed. *The Unknown Lenin: From the Secret Archive.* New Haven, Conn.: Yale University Press, 1996.

Purenvdorzh, Ch. "Soviet–Mongolian Cooperation during the Second World War." *Far Eastern Affairs* 4 (1985): 35–43.

Radchenko, Sergey S. *The Soviets' Best Friends in Asia: The Mongolian Dimension of the Sino-Soviet Split.* Cold War International History Project Working Paper 42. Washington, D.C.: Woodrow Wilson International Center for Scholars, 2003.

Rawski, Evelyn S. "Presidential Address: Reenvisioning the Qing: The Significance of the Qing Period in Chinese History." *Journal of Asian Studies* 55(4) (November 1996): 829–50.

Rossabi, Morris. *Khubilai Khan: His Life and Times.* Berkeley: University of California Press, 1988.

Rupen, Robert. *How Mongolia Is Really Ruled: A Political History of the Mongolian People's Republic.* Stanford, Calif.: Stanford University Press, 1979.

Sandag, Shagdariin, and Harry H. Kendall. *Poisoned Arrows: The Stalin–Choibalsan Mongolian Massacres, 1921–1941.* Boulder, Colo.: Westview Press, 2000.

Serruys, Henry. "Documents from Ordos on the 'Revolutionary Circles,' Part I." *Journal of the American Oriental Society* 97(4) (October–December 1977): 482–507.

Service, Robert. *Lenin: A Biography.* Cambridge, Mass.: Harvard University Press, 2000.

Shen Zhihua. "Clashes of Interests and Their Settlement during Negotiations on the Chinese–Soviet Treaty of 1950." *Far Eastern Affairs* 3 (2002): 97–112.

Shirendev, Bazaryn. *Through the Ocean Waves: The Autobiography of Bazaryn Shirendev.* Bellingham: Western Washington University Press, 1997.

Shlapentokh, Vladimir. "The World Revolution as a Geographic Instrument of the Soviet Leadership." *Russian History / Historire Russe* 26(3) (Fall 1999): 315–34.

Smith, Anthony D. *The Ethnic Origins of Nations.* Oxford: Basil Blackwell, 1988.

Sneath, David. *Changing Inner Mongolia: Pastoral Mongolian Society and the Chinese State.* Oxford: Oxford University Press, 2000.

Stephan, John. *The Russian Far East: A History.* Stanford, Calif.: Stanford University Press, 1994.

Stueck, William. *The Wedemeyer Mission: American Politics and Foreign Policy during the Cold War.* Athens: University of Georgia Press, 1984.

Tang, Peter S. H. *Russian and Soviet Policy in Manchuria and Outer Mongolia, 1911–1931.* Durham, N.C.: Duke University Press, 1959.

Thaxton, Ralph A. *Salt of the Earth: The Political Origins of Peasant Protest and Communist Revolution in China.* Berkeley: University of California Press, 1997.

Tikhvinsky, S. "China in My Life." *Far Eastern Affairs* 4 (1989): 88–105.

Totrov, Yuri. "American Intelligence in China." *Far Eastern Affairs* 2 (2002): 100–16.

Trachtenberg, Marc. *A Constructed Peace: The Making of the European Settlement, 1945–1963.* Princeton, N.J.: Princeton University Press, 1999.

Trenin, Dmitri. *The End of Eurasia: Russia on the Border between Geopolitics and Globalization.* Washington, D.C.: Carnegie Endowment for International Peace, 2002.

Volkogonov, Dmitri. *Stalin: Triumph and Tragedy.* Trans. Harold Shukman. New York: Grove Weidenfeld, 1991.

Wakeman, Frederic, Jr. *The Great Enterprise: The Manchu Reconstruction of Imperial Order in Seventeenth-Century China.* Berkeley: University of California Press, 1985.

Wang, David D. *Under the Soviet Shadow: The Yining Incident: Ethnic Conflicts and International Rivalry in Xinjiang, 1944–1949.* Hong Kong: Chinese University Press, 1999.

Wedemeyer, Albert C. *Wedemeyer Reports!* New York: Henry Holt, 1958.

Westad, Odd Arne. *Cold War and Revolution: Soviet–American Rivalry and the Origins of the Chinese Civil War, 1944–1946.* New York: Columbia University Press, 1993.

———. *Decisive Encounters: The Chinese Civil War, 1946–1950.* Stanford, Calif.: Stanford University Press, 2003.

Xiang Lanxin. *Recasting the Imperial Far East: Britain and America in China, 1945–1950.* Armonk, N.Y.: M. E. Sharpe, 1995.

Yakhontoff, Victor A. "Mongolia: Target or Screen?" *Pacific Affairs* 9(1) (March 1936): 13–23.

Yu Maochun. *OSS in China: Prelude to Cold War.* New Haven, Conn.: Yale University Press, 1996.

Zubok, Vladislav, and Constantine Pleshakov. *Inside the Kremlin's Cold War: From Stalin to Khrushchev.* Cambridge, Mass.: Harvard University Press, 1996.

In Chinese

Bai Zhen. "Recollection of Making Contact with the Soviet–Mongolian Army." *Zhangbei Wenshi Ziliao* (Literary and Historical Materials of Zhangbei) 1 (n.d.): 47–49.

Balgud. "The Rebellions in the Zasagtu and Zhenguogong Banners." *Neimenggu Wenshi Ziliao* (Literary and Historical Materials of Inner Mongolia) 1 (1962): 63–82.

Bayanbulag. "Soviet–Mongolian Red Army Passed through Sunid Right Banner." *Sunite Youqi Wenshi Ziliao* (Historical and Literary Materials of Sunid Right Banner) 1–2 (1985): 33–34.

Bayantu. "Awakening before Dawn: August 11 Uprising Remembered." *Xing'an Geming Shihua* (Historical Record of the Revolution in Xing'an) 3 (1990): 192–201.

Bei Xiaoyan. "The Birth of the Inner Mongolian Autonomous Government." *NWZ* 50 (1997): 278–311.

Budebara. "Recollections and Memories." *Xilinguole Shi Wenshi Ziliao* (Literary and Historical Materials of the Shilingol Municipality) 1 (1985): 46–72.

Bukhe. "The Struggle of Suppressing Bandits and Opposing Local Tyrants in West Khorchin Central Banner." *Xing'an Dangshi Wenji* (Collected Essays on the Party History of Xing'an) 2 (1993): 278–302.

Bukhe and Sayin. *Boyanmandu Shengping Shilue* (Buyanmandukhu's Life and Time). Hohhot: Neimenggu Daxue Tushuguan, 1999 (internal circulation).

Butegechi. *Fengyu Jiancheng Wushinian* (Advance in Trials and Hardships for Fifty Years). Hohhot: Neimenggu Renmin Chubanshe, 1997.

Buyanmandukh. "The Incident of Prince Wutai's Rebellion." *NWZ* 1 (1962): 83–94.

———. "Recollections of My Participation in the Mongol Conference in Nanjing." *NWZ* 16 (1985): 150–61.

Buyantu. "Awakening before Dawn: August 11 Uprising Remembered." *Xing'an Geming Shihua* 3 (1990): 185–202.

———. "Brief Chronicle of Wandannima's Career." *NWZ* 19 (1985): 36–43.

Chang Ch'i-hsiung. *Shoufu Waimeng Zhuquan, 1917–1920* (Restoration of Sovereignty in Outer Mongolia, 1917–1920). Taipei: Meng Zang Weiyuanhui, 1998.

———. *Waimeng Zhuquan Jiaoshe* (Negotiations over Sovereignty in Outer Mongolia). Taipei: Zhongyang Yanjiuyuan Jindaishi Yanjiusuo, 1995.

Dalizhaya ji Furen Jin Yuncheng Shiliao Zhuanji (Special Issue on Historical Materials about Darijahyaga and Wife Jin Yuncheng). *Bayanno'er Wenshi Ziliao* (Literary and Historical Materials of Buyannuur) 9 (1988).

Dangdai Zhongguo de Neimenggu (Inner Mongolia of Contemporary China). Beijing: Dangdai Zhongguo Chubanshe, 1992.

Dawa-ochir. "My Experiences." *NWZ* 31 (1988): 104–85.

Delgerchogtu. "The 'Inner Mongolian Youth Party' as I Knew It." *Wulanchabu Wenshi Ziliao* (Historical and Literary Materials of Ulachab) 2 (1984): 89–115.

Demchugdongrob. "Demuchukedonglupu Zishu" (Autobiography of Demchugdongrob).

Neimenggu Wenshi Ziliao (Literary and Historical Materials of Inner Mongolia) 13, 1984.

Documentary Research Office of the Chinese Communist Party Central Committee. *Liu Shaoqi Nianpu* (Chronicle of Liu Shaoqi's Life). Beijing: Zhongyang Wenxian Chubanshe, 1996.

———. *Mao Zedong Nianpu* (The Chronicle of Mao Zedong's Life). Beijing: Zhongyang Wenxian Chubanshe, 1993.

———. *Zhou Enlai Nianpu* (The Chronicle of Zhou Enlai's Life). Beijing: Zhongyang Wenxian Chubanshe, 1989.

Dugurjab. "Recollections of the Days and Nights of the First Division of the Inner Mongolian Cavalry." *Xing'an Dangshi Wenji* (Collected Essays on the Party History of Xing'an) 2 (1993): 209–17.

Gan Fengling. "Brief Biography of the Eleven Members of the Political Council of Inner Mongolia." *NWZ* 50 (1997): 335–45.

Geng Binying, ed. *Shuguang Zhaoyao Zhelimu* (Dawn upon Jerim). Beijing: Minzu Chubanshe, 1988.

Gu Jigang and Shi Nianhai. *Zhongguo Jiangyu Yange Shi* (History of China's Changing Territories). Beijing: Shangwu Yanshuguan, 2000.

Gu Weijun (Wellington Koo). *Gu Weijun Huiyilu* (Memoirs of Gu Weijun). 12 vols. Beijing: Zhonghua Shuju, 1983–93.

Hao Yufeng. *Wulanfu Zhuan* (Biography of Ulanfu). Hohhot: Neimenggu Renmin Chubanshe, 1990.

Hu Shaoheng. "Excerpts from Hu Shaoheng's Diary." *Xing'an Geming Shihua* 3 (1990): 213–94.

Huang Xiurong, ed. *Sulian, Gongchan Guoji yu Zhongguo Geming de Guanxi Xintan* (New Studies of the Relationship between the Soviet Union, Comintern, and Chinese Revolution). Beijing: Zhonggong Dangshi Chubanshe, 1995.

Jiang Kefu. *Minguo Junshishi Luegao* (Brief Military History of the Chinese Republic). 4 vols. Beijing: Zhonghua Shuju, 1991.

Jiang Mingsheng. "Brief biography of Temurbagana." *Xing'an Dangshi Wenji* (Collected Essays on the Party History of Xing'an) 1 (1993): 226–36.

Jiang Shuchen. *Fu Zuoyi Zhuanlue* (Biography of Fu Zuoyi). Beining: Zhongguo Qingnian Chubanshe, 1990.

Jin Chongji. *Zhou Enlai Zhuan, 1949–1976* (Biography of Zhou Enlai, 1949–1976). Beijing: Zhongyang Wenxian Chubanshe, 1998.

Kho'erge. "Recollections of the Unification of Inner Mongolian Autonomous Movement." *NWZ* 50 (1997): 143–55.

Layi. "Recollection of the Political Situation in Hailar after September 3." *Hulunbei'er Wenshi Ziliao* (Historical and Literary Materials of Hulunbuir) 3 (1985): 1–6.

Ledovsky, Andrei. *Sidalin yu Zhongguo* (Stalin and China). Trans. Chen Chunhua and Liu Cunkuan. Beijing: Xinhua Chubanshe, 2001.

Li Haiwen. "The Inaccuracies in Kovalev's Reminiscences: An Interview with Shi Zhe." *Guoshi Yanjiu Cankao Ziliao* (Reference Materials for the Study of State History) 1 (1993): 91–94.

Li Shouxin. *Li Shouxin Zishu* (Autobiography of Li Shouxin). *NWZ* 20 (1985).

Literature and History Committee of the Political Consultative Council of the Yekejuu League. "Sini Lama and the *Duguilan* Movement under His Leadership." *NWZ* 19 (1985): 4–17.

Liu Chun. "Remembrance of Work in Inner Mongolia." *NWZ* 50 (1997): 33–98.

Liu Xiao. *Chushi Sulian Banian* (Eight-Year Ambassadorship in the Soviet Union). Beijing: Zhonggong Dangshi Ziliao Chubanshe, 1986.

Lowangjab. "Night attack on Tuquan." *Xing'an Dangshi Wenji* (Collected Essays on the Party History of Xing'an) 2 (1993): 218–24.

Lu Minghui. *Menggu "Zizhi Yundong" Shimo* (The Beginning and End of the Mongolian "Autonomous Movement"). Beijing: Zhonghua Shuju, 1980.

Mongolian History Compiling Group. *Mengguzu Jianshi* (Brief History of the Mongolian Nationality). Hohhot: Neimenggu Renmin Chubanshe, 1985.

Office of Diplomatic History of the Ministry of Foreign Affairs. *Xin Zhongguo Waijiao Fengyun* (New China's Diplomatic Storms). Beijing: Shijie Zhishi Chubanshe, 1990.

Office for Party History Research of the Chinese Communist Party Committee of Inner Mongolia. *Neimenggu Dang de Lishi he Dang de Gongzuo* (The Party's History and Works in Inner Mongolia). Hohhot: Neimenggu Renmin Chubanshe, 1994.

Oljeinaren. "In the Mighty Torrent of Inner Mongolia's Liberation Movement." *NWZ* 50 (1997): 193–206.

Oljeiochir. "Muohai Hongtao" ("Tidal Waves in the Sea of Deserts"). *Keqi Wenshi Ziliao* (Historical and Literary Materials of Khorchin Banner) 1 (1985): 21–26.

Pei Jianzhang. *Zhonghua Renmin Gongheguo Waijiao Shi, 1949–1956* (Diplomatic History of the People's Republic of China, 1949–1956). Beijing: Shijie Zhishi Chubanshe, 1994.

Qian Linbao. *Jiefang Zhanzheng Shiqi Neimenggu Qibing* (Inner Mongolian Cavalries during the War of Liberation). Hohhot: Neimenggu Daxue Chubanshe, 1989.

Second Historical Archives of China. *Jiang Jieshi Nianpu Chugao* (Preliminary Draft of the Chronicle of Jiang Jieshi's Life). Beijing: Dang'an Chubanshe, 1992.

Shen Zhihua. *Mao Zedong, Sidalin yu Chaoxian Zhanzheng* (Mao Zedong, Stalin and the Korean War). Guangzhou: Guangdong Renmin Chubanshe, 2003.

Shi Bo. *Waimenggu Duli Neimu* (Inside Story of Outer Mongolian Independence). Beijing: Renmin Zhongguo Chubanshe, 1993.

Shi Zhe. *Feng yu Gu: Shi Zhe Huiyilu* (Peaks and Valleys: Memoirs of Shi Zhe). Beijing: Hongqi Chubanshe, 1997.

———. *Wo de Yisheng: Shi Zhe Zishu* (My Life: In Shi Zhe's Own Words). Beijing: Renmin Chubanshe, 2001.

———. *Zai Lishi Juren Shenbian: Shi Zhe Huiyilu* (At the Side of Historical Giants: Memoirs of Shi Zhe). Beijing: Zhongyang Wenxian Chubanshe, 1995.

Tegus. "The May First Conference as I Knew." *Xing'an Dangshi Wenji* (Collected Essays on the Party History of Xing'an) 1 (1993): 10–19.

Temle. *Jianguo qian Neimenggu Difang Baokan Kaolu* (Investigation and Classifications of Newspapers and Journals in the Area of Inner Mongolia before the Foundation of the State). Hohhot: Neimenggu Tushuguan, 1987.

Tumen and Zhu Dongli. *Kang Sheng yu Neirendang Yuan'an* (Kang Sheng and the Unjust Case of the IMPRP). Beijing: Zhongyang Dangxiao Chubanshe, 1995.

Ulanfu. *Wulanfu Huiyilu* (Memoirs of Ulanfu). Beijing: Zhonggong Dangshi Ziliao Chubanshe, 1989.

Wang Dongxing. *Wang Dongxing Huiyi Mao Zedong yu Lin Biao Fangeming Jituan de Douzheng* (Mao Zedong's Struggle with the Lin Biao Counterrevolutionary Clique as Remembered by Wang Dongxing). Beijing: Dangdai Zhongguo Chubanshe, 2004.

————. *Wang Dongxing Riji* (Wang Dongxing's Diaries) (Beijing: Zhongguo Shehui Kexue Chubanshe, 1993.

Wang Duo. *Wushi Chunqiu* (Fifty Eventful Years). Hohhot: Neimenggu Renmin Chubanshe, 1992.

Wang Haishan. "Recollections of the Bandits' Suppression Operations of the First Division of the Inner Mongolian Cavalry." *Xing'an Dangshi Wenji* (Collected Essays on the Party History of Xing'an) 1 (1993): 50–63.

Wang Shijie. *Wang Shijie Riji* (Wang Shijie's Diaries). Taipei: Zhongyang Yanjiuyuan Jidaishi Yanjiusuo, 1990.

Wang Shusheng and Hao Yufeng. *Wulanfu Nianpu* (Chronicle of Ulanfu's Life). Beijing: Zhonggong Dangshi Ziliao Chubanshe, 1989.

Wang Zaitian. "Recollections of My Work in the Social Department before and after the Establishment of the Autonomous Government of Inner Mongolia." *NWZ* 50 (1997): 118–42.

Wulanfu Jinian Wenji (Memorial Essays on Ulanfu). Hohhot: Neimenggu Renmin Chubanshe, 1990.

Wulanfu Yanjiu Lunwenji (Essays on Ulanfu Studies). Compiled by Inner Mongolia Society of Ulanfu Studies. Hohhot: Neimenggu Wenhua Chubanshe, 1994.

Wu Lengxi. *Shinian Lunzhan, 1956–1966: Zhongsu Guanxi Huiyilu* (Ten Years of Debates, 1956–1966: A Memoir of Sino-Soviet Relations). Beijing: Zhongyang Wenxian Chubanshe, 1999.

Wu Xiuquan. *Wo de Jingli* (My Experience). Beijing: Jiefangjun Chubanshe, 1984.

Xu Zehao. *Wang Jiaxiang Zhuan* (Biography of Wang Jiaxiang). Beijing: Dangdai Zhongguo Chubanshe, 1996.

Yang Kuisong. *Mao Zedong yu Mosike de En En Yuan Yuan* (Gratitude and Grievances between Mao Zedong and Moscow). Nanchang: Jiangxi Renmin Chubanshe, 1999.

————. *Xi'an Shibian Xintan* (New Study of the Xi'an Incident). Taipei: Dongda Tushu, 1995.

————. *Zhonggong yu Mosike de Guanxi, 1920–1960* (The Chinese Communist Party's Relationship with Moscow, 1920–1960). Taipei: Dongda Tushu Gongsi, 1997.

Yun Shiying and Chao Luomeng. "Recollections of Works of the Shilingol League." *NWZ* 50 (1997): 156–75.

Zai Jiang Jieshi Shenbian Ba Nian: Shicongshi Gaoji MuliaoTang Zong Riji (With Jiang Jieshi for Eight Years: Senior Member of the Aides' Office Tang Zong's Diary). Compiled by the Ministry of Public Security Archives. Beijing: Qunzhong Chubanshe, 1992.

Zhahalofu (M. B. Zakharov). *Jieju: 1945 Nian Dabai Riben Diguozhuyi Lishi Huiyilu* (The Finale: A Historical Memoir of the Defeat of Japanese Imperialism in 1945). Translated from Russian by Jun Qing. Shanghai: Shanghai Yiwen Chubanshe, 1978.

Zhang Ce. "My Onerous Lifetime." *Xing'an Geming Shihua* 3 (1990): 1–184.

Zhang Ce, Hu Shaoheng, and Fang Zhida. "Some Events from the Time of the Eastern Mongolian Autonomous Government to the Establishment of the Inner Mongolian Autonomous Government." *Xing'an Dangshi Wenji* (Collected Essays on the Party History of Xing'an) 1 (1993): 1–9.

Zhang Qigao. "General Information about the Sino-American Cooperation Organization in Shanba." *Bayannuo'er Wenshi Ziliao* 3 (1984): 124–30.

Zhonghua Minguo Shi Neizheng Zhi (Chugao) (History of the Republic of China: A Chronicle of Domestic Administration). Compiled by Academia Historica. Taipei: Guoshiguan, 1992.

Zhou Qingshu. *Neimenggu Lishi Dili* (Historical Geography of Inner Mongolia). Hohhot: Neimengu Daxue Chubanshe, 1993.

Zhou Wending and Chu Liangru. *Teshu er Fuzai de Keti: Gongchan Guoji, Sulian he Zhongguo Gongchandang Guanxi Biannianshi, 1919–1991* (A Unique and Complex Subject: The Chronicle of the Relationship between the Comintern, the Soviet Union and the Chinese Communist Party). Wuhan: Hubei Renmin Chubanshe, 1993.

Zhu Peimin. "Changes in the Soviet Policy in Xinjiang from 1943 to 1949." *Zhonggong Dangshi Yanjiu* (Studies in the Chinese Communist Party's History), supplementary issue (December 1990): 87–92.

Index

243; MPR relationship, 78–111, 245, 378–83; as a national government, 378; as a nation-building force, 79; New Fourth Army and, 141, 142; Ningxia campaign, 96, 97, 97–98n41; organization of (1921), 59, 80; Outer Mongolia national liberation, 88; postwar political power struggles, 235; "preliberation" (*jiefangqian*) vs. "postliberation" (*jiefanghou*), xvii, 423; as a revolutionary movement, 79–83, 378; Soviet-Mongolian army in, 251, 330–31, 348–49; Soviet relations, 79, 79n4, 86, 98, 150, 238, 240n11, 347, 348; Tibet national liberation, 88; Titoist tendency in, 391; war of resistance against Japan, 31–32, 34, 37–38, 84, 96, 100–104, 106, 118, 198, 237. *See also* CCP-GMD conflict and power struggle

Chinese Communist Party (CCP) bases: Daqingshan Mountain area guerrilla base, 104–6, 104n49, 240; Shaanxi base, 94, 95, 96, 237, 240

Chinese Communist Party (CCP) bureaus: Jin-Cha-Ji (Shanxi-Chahar-Hebei) Central Bureau, 153, 162, 215, 242, 244, 251, 254–55, 257, 286, 350, 360; Jin-Sui Bureau, 244; Ji-Re-Liao (Hebei-Rehe-Liaobei) Branch Bureau, 259; Ji-Re-Liao (Hebei-Rehe-Liaoning) Branch Bureau, 156, 157, 360; Liao-Ji (Liaoning and Jilin) Provincial Committee, 169. *See also* Northeast Bureau; West Manchurian Branch Bureau

Chinese Communist Party (CCP) in eastern Mongolia: CCP cautionary policy, 256–61; Chengde conference concessions, 155–61; ethnic strategy, 151–94; and relationship with EMPAG, 143–50

Chinese Communist Party (CCP) in Inner Mongolia: members of IMPRP and, 64, 137; "national fever" and, 125; partnership and "revolutionary independence" from GMD, 219;

postwar work, 117, 371–75; regional autonomy formula, 243, 244, 246, 261, 262, 425–26; Soviet-Mongolian army as ally to, 251, 330–31, 348–49, 353–57; U.S. policy, 292–93

Chinese Communist Party (CCP) in Manchuria: CCP "exclusive control" (*duzhan*) to "a certain position" (*yiding diwei*), 241, 242; military strategy, 239–43; "regularization" of, 242–43; Soviet military assistance and, 240n11, 241, 242, 309–10

Chinese Communist Party Central Committee (CCPCC): IMPRP, restoration or dissolution of, 190; Inner Mongolia autonomy, six-point directive on, 179, 188–89; Inner Mongolia autonomy, Yun Ze report on, 176; Manchuria, Rehe, and Chahar invasion, 238; Suiyuan military strategy, 244

Chinese Empire: imperial system, 4; Inner Asia territorial claims, 9, 10–11, 18; intervention in Mongolia (1919), 19; Manchu conquest of, 9; Mongolian boundaries and, 3; Mongolian rule under Genghis Khan in, 5; territories as "part of China" question, 11–12; tributary states, 11; Western influence and "opening" of, 7, 8, 13. *See also* Qing Empire

Chinese federation or federal republic (proposed), 59, 82, 84, 88, 91, 99–100, 137; multinational federation vs. unitary state system, 266

"Chinese imperialism," 51, 340, 341

Chinese-Japanese conflict. *See* Sino-Japanese war (1937–45)

Chinese-Mongolian federation proposal, 390

Chinese nation. *See zhonghua minzu* (Chinese nation)

Chinese nationalism: CCP balance with non-Han ethnonationalisms, 263; CCP ideology and, 377; "five-race republic" creed, 24–25, 42, 198; formation of a "Chinese nation," 14, 63; from